MICHAEL RHETA MARTIN has written THE GRAPHIC GUIDE TO WORLD HISTORY and THE ARTS: A Graphic Guide to Painting, Sculpture, Architecture, Music, and Theater Through the Ages; co-authored THE NEW DICTIONARY OF AMERICAN HISTORY, AN ENCYCLOPEDIA OF LATIN-AMERICAN HISTORY, and PICTURE HISTORY OF THE MODERN WORLD; and edited THE WORLD'S LOVE POETRY. She lives in La Jolla, California.

BOOK is formerly Chairman, ...partment, New York ...and is now Professor of English at the University. He has contributed articles to such publications as *Shakespeare Quarterly*, *Modern Language Quarterly*, and *Seventeenth-Century News*. He is also the editor of the two-volume ANTHOLOGY OF JACOBEAN DRAMA and STUDIES IN THE RENAISSANCE.

THE CONCISE ENCYCLOPEDIC GUIDE TO SHAKESPEARE

MICHAEL RHETA MARTIN
and
RICHARD C. HARRIER

 DISCUS BOOKS/PUBLISHED BY AVON

To my son, Geoffrey Warren Martin

Good night, sweet Prince,
And flights of angels sing thee to thy rest.

—THE HAMLET

We are such stuff
As dreams are made on, and our little life
Is rounded with a sleep.

—THE TEMPEST

AVON BOOKS
A division of
The Hearst Corporation
959 Eighth Avenue
New York, New York 10019

ISBN 0-380-00238-8

First Discus Printing, February, 1975.

DISCUS TRADEMARK REG. U.S. PAT. OFF. AND
FOREIGN COUNTRIES, REGISTERED TRADEMARK—
MARCA REGISTRADA, HECHO EN CHICAGO, U.S.A.

Printed in the U.S.A.

CONTENTS

*See page preceding the Guide for abbreviations of titles.

PREFACE

Our knowledge of the man Shakespeare and of his work has grown over nearly four centuries; it is growing still. In our day, with the proliferating millions of copies of the plays and poems in paperback editions, with new productions flourishing in theaters, films and television, with new characterizations by actors and adventurous experiments by directors, our interest in Shakespeare is greater than ever. The enduring fascination of his work has become less and less the exclusive province of a few scholars and theater professionals, and more and more magnetic to readers, theater-goers and television viewers, to students and teachers, to amateur as well as professional actors, directors, designers and producers.

This encyclopedic guide has been designed to present—in a single comprehensive and easily usable volume—the information about the subject that the modern reader may need in order to bring the world of Shakespeare closer and enhance his pleasure in it. Thus it can be used not only as a ready companion to the plays and poems but also as a guide both to the times in which they were written and to their interpretations and performances up to the present day.

The plan of this guide is comprehensive, and simple to use. The main encyclopedic section is of course alphabetically arranged. It covers:

THE PLAYS: with synopses of all the plots, the times and places in which they occur, details of the characters, the original sources of the plays, the known dates on which the plays were written, and published; and summarizing comments by major critics and scholars are quoted.

THE CHARACTERS: These appear as separate entries (in addition to their inclusion under the title-entries of the plays in which they appear) and are cross-referenced to the plays. The background and significance of each character is given concisely; the lines characterizing him in the play he appears in are quoted; and critical comments by scholars are frequently included.

MEANINGS OF WORDS, PHRASES, ALLUSIONS: For the phrases, entries are under their key words. The definition is followed by the name of the character who speaks it, cross-referenced to the title of the play, the act number, scene number, and line number in which it is spoken.

QUOTATIONS: There is a large selection of lesser known as well as the most significant quotations, given as separate entries, either under key words (example: the soliloquy beginning "to be or not to be" is found under *to be*) or under subject headings (example: if a passage is *about* love, even if the actual word does not appear in it, the passage is found under the entry *love*); followed by the source: poem or play title, with act, scene, line numbers, and character who speaks it.

CRITICS AND SCHOLARS: The important figures in Shakespearean scholarship from the 17th century to the present, given by dates, titles of books and articles, nature of contribution. Contemporaries of Shakespeare, and those who influenced his work, will be found in the main encyclopedia section. Those who are of later periods, and most apt to be consulted by the general reader, are listed under the separate section CRITICS AND SCHOLARS OF SHAKESPEARE.

Additional separate sections include:

SHAKESPEARE'S LIFE AND THEATER: a concise biographical account giving the major facts known to recent scholarship and the known origins and nature of the theater in his time.

PEOPLE OF THE THEATER: sections listing members of the Shakespearean contemporary theater, with dates of joining; important dramatists contemporary with Shakespeare; actors, actresses, directors and producers; with life dates of the significant figures, backgrounds, plays and theaters in which they appeared, characters they played, dates and places of productions, etc., both in the United States and abroad.

MODERN PRODUCTIONS OF PLAYS: entries for stage productions and major films are under play titles, giving dates, names and roles of starring actors and actresses; lists of the Stratford Shakespeare Festivals and the New York Shakespeare Festival, with dates, plays and names of cast members.

MUSIC: a selected list of composers of music based on the works of Shakespeare, including life dates, biographical references, dates and titles of songs, incidental music, operas, ballets, etc., a selected list of the best recordings by composer's name, with titles, names of performers, record labels and numbers; plays on records, with similar details; and readings on records, by names of actors and albums.

AN INTRODUCTORY READING LIST: a recommended selection representative of the vast library of Shakespearean material, under these categories: general reference works, dictionaries and language guides, biography, dramatic and theatrical background, general background, critical works and collections, sources, and texts: editions of Shakespeare's works.

Finally, there are genealogies of the historical characters and sections of illustrations from the time of Shakespeare up to the present day.

We want to express our appreciation to copy-editors Virginia and Jim Hawkins, to Peter Mayer, Ben Raeburn, Henry Edwards, Frederick S. Leber, Francis J. Hughes, Ralph Sandler and Eggo J. Tempel for their assistance in the preparation of this book, and to Sheila Lalwani, Mary Traina, Laura Vajda and Susan Waldron for their labors in its production.

Michael Rheta Martin
Richard C. Harrier

ABBREVIATIONS OF TITLES OF PLAYS AND POEMS

ADO: Much Ado About Nothing

ALL'SW: All's Well that Ends Well

A&C: Antony and Cleopatra

AYL: As You Like It

CofE: The Comedy of Errors

COR: Coriolanus

CYM: Cymbeline

HAM: Hamlet, Prince of Denmark

1H4: First Part of Henry IV

2H4: Second Part of Henry IV

HEN5: Henry the Fifth

1H6: First Part of Henry VI

2H6: Second Part of Henry VI

3H6: Third Part of Henry VI

HEN8: Henry the Eighth

JOHN: King John

JC: Julius Caesar

LLL: Love's Labour's Lost

LEAR: King Lear

LUCRECE: The Rape of Lucrece

MACB: Macbeth

MEAS: Measure for Measure

MERV: The Merchant of Venice

MND: A Midsummer Night's Dream

MWW: The Merry Wives of Windsor

OTH: Othello, the Moor of Venice

PASSPIL: The Passionate Pilgrim

PER: Pericles, Prince of Tyre

PHOENIX: The Phoenix and Turtle

RICH2: Richard the Second

RICH3: Richard the Third

R&J: Romeo and Juliet

SHREW: The Taming of the Shrew

SONNET: The Sonnets

TEMP: The Tempest

TIMON: Timon of Athens

TITUS: Titus Andronicus

T&C: Troilus and Cressida

TwN: Twelfth Night; or, What You Will

2GENT: The Two Gentlemen of Verona

2NK: The Two Noble Kinsmen

VENUS: Venus and Adonis

WINT: The Winter's Tale

Act, Scene and Line numbers follow *The Complete Works of Shakespeare* edited by George Lyman Kittredge, and published by Ginn and Company (1936).

The Appendix which follows the Dictionary Guide contains additional material on many of the persons mentioned in the text.

Aaron, villainous, sadistic Moor; lover of Queen Tamora; responsible for the murder of Bassianus, execution of Quintus and Martius and the mutilation of Titus and Lavinia; tortured to death.
TITUS: II, 1.

abandoned, banished from.
SHREW: Lady Page, Induction, 2, 117.

abate, shorten, lessen, cut down.
MND: Helena, III, 2, 432.

abate throw at novum, except for a throw of the dice at novum (novem quinque); game played by five persons; best throws were nine and five.
LLL: Berowne, V, 2, 547.

a-batfowling, night hunting for birds with the aid of torches (or the light of the moon) and bats or sticks.
TEMP: Sebastian, II, 1, 185.

ABC. See ABSEY-BOOK.

abed
. . . Not to be abed after midnight is to be up betimes; and *"diluculo surgere,"* thou know'st—
TwN: Toby, II, 3, 1. See BE-TIME, *diluculo surgere.*

Abergavenny, Lord, arrested with Buckingham, his father-in-law, and sent to the tower. [George Neville, 3rd Baron (d. 1535); married Mary Stafford, daughter of the 3rd Duke of Buckingham.]
HEN8: I, 1.

Abhorson, executioner; with Pom-

pey, prepares Barnardine for execution.
MEAS: IV, 2.

abide, wait for; dare to face or meet in a fight.
MND: Demetrius, III, 2, 422.
2H4: Lady Percy, II, 3, 36.

abide
A rotten case abides no handling.
2H4: Westmoreland, IV, 1, 161. See HANDLING.

about a round, devious path, roundabout, around in a circle or circuit.
MND: Puck, III, 1, 109.

Abraham, Montague's servant.
R&J: I, 1.

abram, auburn.
COR: 3Citizen, II, 3, 21.

abridgment, cutting short; entertainment.
HAM: Hamlet, II, 2, 439.
MND: Theseus, V, 1, 39.

abroach, let loose, set on foot; metaphor comes from opening tap of barrel of liquid.
RICH3: Richard, I, 3, 325.
2H4: John, IV, 2, 14.
R&J: Montague, I, 1, 3.

absence. See WINTER.

absent time, time when the king is not present.
RICH2: Berkeley, II, 3, 79.

Absey-book, ABC book, primer, hornbook.
JOHN: Bastard, I, 1, 196.
2GENT: Speed, II, 1, 23.

absolute, perfect, free from imperfection, complete.
COR: Aufidius, IV, 5, 141.

absolute Milan, the actual Duke of Milan, rather than merely the person designated to act for him.
TEMP: Prospero, I, 2, 109.

absque hoc nihil est, Latin, without this there is nothing.
2H4: Pistol, V, 5, 30.

abstinence
. . . abstinence engenders maladies.
LLL: Berowne, IV, 3, 295.

abstract, summary.
HAM: Hamlet, II, 2, 548—*abstract and brief chronicles of the time.*

abstract, epitome, highest degree.
A&C: Caesar, I, 4, 8—*A man who is the abstract of all faults / That all men follow,* refers to Antony.

Absyrtus, brother of Medea, whom she cut to pieces while fleeing with Jason, to delay pursuit by her father.
2H6: Clifford, V, 2, 59.

abundance. See FAMINE.

abuse, mislead, deceive, cheat.
HAM: Hamlet, II, 2, 631.
TEMP: Alonso, V, 1, 112.
OTH: Brabantio, I, 1, 174.

abuse of greatness
Th' abuse of greatness is, when it disjoins
Remorse from power.
JC: Brutus, II, 1, 18.

aby, pay the price, pay for, abide.
MND: Demetrius, III, 2, 175.

accidence, Latin grammar, primer.
MWW: Mrs. Page, IV, 1, 16.

accident, event, circumstance, experience.
TEMP: Prospero, V, 1, 305.
MND: Oberon, IV, 1, 71.
OTH: Othello, I, 3, 135.

accite, summon.
TITUS: Marcus, I, 1, 27.
2H4: Prince, V, 2, 141.

accompt. See ACCOUNT.

account, reckoning.
RICH2: Mowbray, I, 1, 130.
LLL: Berowne, V, 2, 200.

accountant, accountable, liable, responsible.
OTH: Iago, II, 1, 302.

accoutred, equipped, fully armed.
JC: Cassius, I, 2, 105.

accuse my zeal, condemn me for being zealous.
RICH2: Mowbray, I, 1, 47.

ace, throw of one in dice (one dot on the die).
MND: Demetrius, V, 1, 312.

Acheron, hell or one of the rivers of Hades, the underworld in classical mythology.
MND: Oberon, III, 2, 357.
MACB: Hecate, III, 5, 15.
TITUS: Titus, IV, 3, 44.

Achilles, handsomest, bravest of the Greeks; hero of HOMER's *Iliad;* according to legend, his mother, Thetis, tried to make him immortal by dipping him into the Styx, and succeeded, except for the heel by which she held him; killed by Paris, with an arrow guided by Apollo into his vulnerable heel, in the battle at the Scaean Gate during the Trojan War.
T&C: II, 1.

Achilles' spear, made by Vulcan, the blacksmith god, it had the power to cure; Telephus was cured with the rust from the spear that had wounded him.
2H6: York, V, 1, 100.

Achitophel, traitor; refers to the adviser to David's son Absalom (II Samuel, 15-17).
2H4: Falstaff, I, 2, 41.

aconitum, poisonous herbs of the buttercup (crowfoot) family; monkshood, wolfsbane.
2H4: King, IV, 4, 48.

Actaeon, famed huntsman; when he saw Diana (Artemis) and her nymphs bathing, she turned him into a stag; killed by his dogs on Mt. Cithaeron.
MWW: Pistol, II, 1, 122—suggests horns of a stag become horns of a cuckold.
TITUS: Tamora, II, 3, 63.

action

Action is eloquence, and the eyes of th' ignorant
More learned than the ears.
COR: Volumnia, III, 2, 76.

With this regard their currents turn awry
And lose the name of action.
HAM: Hamlet, III, 1, 87.

To be the same in thine own act and valour,
As thou art in desire? Would'st thou have that
Which thou esteem'st the ornament of life,
And live a coward in thine own esteem,
Letting "I dare not" wait upon "I would,"
Like the poor cat i' the adage?
MACB: Lady Macbeth, I, 7, 39
—refers to the cat who wanted to catch a fish, but didn't want to get her feet wet.

action. See SUIT, VIRTUE.

actions

. . . When our actions do not,
Our fears do make us traitors.
MACB: Lady Macduff, IV, 2, 3.

Actium, promontory and town in southwestern Greece; site of a temple to Apollo (5th century BC); Octavius Caesar won an important offshore naval victory over the fleets of Antony and Cleopatra (31 BC).
A&C: III, 7.

actors

. . . These our actors,
As I foretold you, were all spirits and
Are melted into air, into thin air.
TEMP: Prospero, IV, 1, 148.
See VISION.

acts

. . . Each your doing
So singular in each particular,
Crowns what you are doing in the present deed,
That all your acts are queens.
WINT: Florizel, IV, 4, 143.

Adam, Orlando's faithful old servant who follows him into exile.
AYL: I, 1.

Adam, probably refers to Adam Bell, famous archer and outlaw, celebrated in ballads.
ADO: Benedick, I, 1, 261.

Adam, according to Genesis, 2:15, the first man, and gardener, in the Garden of Eden.
RICH2: Queen, III, 4, 73.

adamant, lodestone, magnetic stone that is very hard.
MND: Helena, II, 1, 195.

addiction, predilection, inclination, impulse or bent toward.
OTH: Herald, II, 2, 6.

addition, title added to a man's name as an honor or means of distinction.
HAM: Hamlet, I, 4, 20.
MACB: Ross, I, 3, 106.
OTH: Cassio, IV, 1, 105.

addle, rotten, bad, spoiled.
T&C: Pandarus, I, 2, 145.

address, apply, direct.
MND: Lysander, II, 2, 143.

addressed, ready, prepared.
MND: Philostrate, V, 1, 106.
HEN5: King, III, 3, 58—addrest.
JC: Brutus, III, 1, 29.

ad manes fratrum, Latin, to the shades, ghosts or departed spirits of our brothers.
TITUS: Lucius, I, 1, 98.

admiral, flagship of the fleet.
A&C: Enobarbus, III, 10, 2.
1H4: Falstaff, III, 3, 28.

Admiral's Men, players' company; second to the Chamberlain's as the most important one of the period; patron was Charles Howard, 1st Earl of Nottingham (1536-1624); Lord High Admiral (1585), commander of the fleet that destroyed the Armada (1588); details of company's activities found in Philip Henslowe's *Diary*, successful manager of the company (with Edward Alleyn).

admiration, astonishment, bewilderment, wonder.
HAM: Rosencrantz, III, 2, 339.
TEMP: Prospero, V, 1, 154.

admir'd Miranda, play on name, Latin meaning of miranda being "she who should be wondered at."
TEMP: Ferdinand, III, 1, 38.

Adrian, lord attending Alonso, King of Naples.
TEMP: II, 1.

Adriana, jealous wife of Antipholus of Ephesus; while entertaining Antipholus of Syracuse, thinking he is her husband, she locks his twin out of the house.
CofE: II, 1.

adsum, Latin, I am here.
2H6: Asmath (spirit), I, 4, 26.

advance, lift up, raise, bring forth, open, display.
TEMP: Prospero, I, 2, 408.
COR: Marcius, I, 6, 61.
MND: Helena, III, 2, 128.

advantage, moment, chance, opportunity.
OTH: Othello, I, 3, 298.
COR: Cominius, IV, 1, 43.
TEMP: Sebastian, III, 3, 13.

advantage
Advantage feeds him fat while men delay.
1H4: King, III, 2, 180.

adventure my discretion, jeopardize my reputation for intelligence or good sense.
TEMP: Gonzalo, II, 1, 187.

adversity
Sweet are the uses of adversity,
Which, like the toad, ugly and venomous,
Wears yet a precious jewel in his head;
And this our life, exempt from public haunt,
Finds tongues in trees, books in the running brooks,
Sermons in stones, and good in everything.
AYL: Duke Senior, II, 1, 12.

advertise, inform, teach, counsel.
1H4: King, III, 2, 172.

MEAS: Duke, I, 1, 42.
ADO: Leonato, V, 1, 32.

aediles, magistrates of Rome in charge of police, public buildings, etc.; in this period, plebeians.
COR: Brutus, III, 1, 173.

Aegeon, merchant of Syracuse; husband of Aemilia, father of twin sons, Antipholus of Ephesus and Antipholus of Syracuse; condemned to death by Solinus, Duke of Ephesus, for landing in an unfriendly city.
CofE: I, 1.

Aemilia, Abbess of Ephesus; wife of above, mother of the twins; believes family lost; gives sanctuary to Antipholus of Syracuse and refuses to relinquish him into the custody of his wife, Adriana; reconciled with family.
CofE: V, 1.

Aemilius, noble Roman; acknowledges Lucius as emperor.
TITUS: V, 1.

Aeneas, Trojan hero of classical legend and VERGIL's *Aeneid;* one of the few Trojans to escape the sack of the city; rescued his old father, Anchises, and carried him off to Italy, stopping at Carthage; his descendants founded the city of Rome and, according to British folklore, London.
TEMP: Sebastian II, 1, 99. See DIDO.
JC: Cassius, I, 2, 112.
TITUS: Titus, III, 2, 27.

Aeneas, Trojan commander; tells Troilus that he has to give up Cressida.
T&C: I, 1. See above.

Aeneas' tale to Dido, story told by Aeneas to Dido, Queen of Carthage, of the sack of Troy; in VERGIL's *Aeneid,* and used by MARLOWE in play *Dido, Queen of Carthage;* use of this passage as satire is disputed and improbable.
HAM: Hamlet, II, 2, 469.

Aeolus, god of the winds.
2H6: Queen, III, 2, 92.

aëry (aerie, eyrie), eagle's nest
and brood; also that of a hawk
or other bird of prey.
RICH3: Richard, I, 3, 264.
JOHN: Bastard, V, 2, 149.
HAM: Rosencrantz, II, 2, 354
—*eyrie of children,* refers to
young choristers (actors) of the
CHAPEL ROYAL and St. Paul's.

Aesculapius, Greek god of healing and medicine; son of Apollo
and Coronis (or Arsinoë),
brought up by Chiron; not a
divine character in HOMER.
MWW: Host, II, 3, 29.
PER: Cerimon, III, 2, 112.

Aesop, Greek (6th century); noted
for famous fables or tales with
a moral; said to have been deformed; represented as a slave;
possibly not an historical person.
3H6: Prince, V, 5, 25.

Aetna, volcano in northeastern
Sicily, Italy, near the coast.
MWW: Falstaff, III, 5, 129.

affection
Affection is a coal that must be
cool'd;
Else, suffer'd, it will set the heart
on fire.
VENUS: 387.

affects, affections, passions, in-
clinations, dispositions toward.
HAM: King, III, 1, 170.
RICH2: Richard, I, 4, 30.
COR: Menenius, I, 1, 107.

affeer, legal term meaning to
certify or assure.
MACB: Macduff, IV, 3, 34—
affeer'd, pun meaning afraid
might be intended.

affiance, trust, confidence, loyalty.
HEN5: King, II, 2, 127.
CYM: Iachimo, I, 6, 163.

affin'd, bound by feeling for,
obliged.
OTH: Iago, I, 1, 39.

affront, come across, meet face
to face, encounter.
HAM: King, III, 1, 31.

affy, betrothed, affianced.
SHREW: Tranio, IV, 4, 49—
affied.
2H6: Lieutenant, IV, 1, 80.

affy, trust, have faith in.
TITUS: Bassianus, I, 1, 47.

after fleet, second or reserve fleet.
OTH: Messenger, I, 3, 35.

against, in anticipation or expec-
tation of, in preparation for.
HAM: Player, II, 2, 505.
MND: Theseus, I, 1, 125.

against that time
Against that time when thou
shalt strangely pass
And scarcely greet me with that
sun, thine eye,
When love, converted from the
thing it was,
Shall reasons find of settled
gravity—
SONNET: XLIX, 5.

Agamemnon, King of Mycenae,
brother of Menelaus; commander-in-chief of the Greek forces
against Troy. (In Greek legend,
murdered by his wife, Clytemnestra, when he returned victorious from the war.)
T&C: I, 3.
2H4: Doll, II, 4, 238.
HEN5: Fluellen, III, 6, 7.

agate, small figure cut in agate
seal ring.
ADO: Hero, III, 1, 65.
2H4: Falstaff, I, 2, 19.

age
Age cannot wither her nor cus-
tom stale
Her infinite variety. Other wom-
en cloy
The appetites they feed, but she
makes hungry
Where most she satisfies; for
vilest things
Become themselves in her, that
the holy priests
Bless her when she is riggish.
A&C: Enobarbus, II, 2, 240.
See RIGGISH.
A man loves the meat in his
youth that he cannot endure in
his age.
ADO: Benedick, II, 3, 247.

But age with his stealing steps
Hath clawed me in his clutch,
And hath shipped me intil the
   land,
As if I had never been such.
  HAM: Clown, V, 1, 79.

A man can no more separate
age and covetousness than 'a
can part young limbs and
lechery; but the gout galls the
one, and the pox pinches the
other; and so both degrees prevent my curses.
  2H4: Falstaff, I, 2, 256. See
  PREVENT.

To me, fair friend, you never
  can be old,
For as you were when first your
  eye I ey'd,
Such seems your beauty still.
  SONNET: CIV, 1.

age. See VALE OF YEARS.

Agenor, father of Europa. See
EUROPA.
  SHREW: I, 1, 173.

ages of man. See WORLD'S A STAGE.

aglet-baby, ornamental carved figure on aglet, the point of a lace,
or fastened to the ends of the
points.
  SHREW: Grumio, I, 2, 79.

agnize, admit to, own up to, confess.
  OTH: Othello, I, 3, 232.

Agrippa, friend of Octavius;
suggests Antony marry Octavia.
[M. Vipsanius Agrippa (63-12
BC) advised Octavius to go to
Rome immediately after Cae-
sar's assassination; commander
of the fleet at Actium (31); mar-
ried Julia, daughter of Augustus
(Octavius).]
  A&C: II, 2.

ague, fever, usually malarial,
which causes one to shiver.
  TEMP: Stephano, II, 2, 68.
  1H4: Hotspur, III, 1, 69.
  MERV: Salerio, I, 1, 23.

Aguecheek, Sir Andrew, foppish,
foolish old knight; delightful as
well as absurd in his childlike
capacity for enjoyment; sponged

on by Sir Toby, who persuades
him he can win Olivia.
  TWN: I, 2.

ahold, in navigation, to hold close
to the wind; thought by some
to be a possible variation of
a-hull, that is without any sail.
  TEMP: Boatswain, I, 1, 52.

aim, guess, surmise, conjecture.
  HAM: Gentleman, IV, 5, 9.
  SHREW: Katherina, II, 1, 234.
  OTH: 2Senator, I, 3, 6.

**"Aio te, Aeacida, Romanos vin-
cere posse,"** ambiguous answer
the Pythian Apollo gave Pyrrhus, meaning either I affirm that
thou, descendant of Aeacus,
canst conquer the Romans, or I
affirm that the Romans can vanquish thee, descendant of Aeacus.
  2H6: York, I, 4, 65.

air, melody, tune, as opposed to
an intricate madrigal.
  TEMP: Prospero, V, 1, 58.

Ajax, one of Greek heroes in
HOMER's *Iliad;* son of Telamon;
strong, second to Achilles in
heroic deeds; disappointed when
shield of the dead Achilles was
not given to him, went mad and
slew flock of sheep, blaming
them for the gods granting the
shield to Ulysses; in frustration,
he killed himself.
  LLL: Berowne, IV, 3, 7.
  CYM: Guiderius, IV, 2, 252.
  LEAR: Kent, II, 2, 132.

Ajax, Grecian commander; Alexander's description of him possibly a reference to Ben JONSON.
  T&C: I, 2. See above.

Alarbus, eldest son of Tamora;
sacrificed by the sons of Titus.
  TITUS: I, 1.

alarum, call to arms, summons.
  OTH: Iago, II, 3, 26.
  RICH3: Richard, I, 1, 7.

a laughter, the winner has the
chance to laugh at the loser, to
make fun of him.
  TEMP: Antonio, II, 1, 33.

Albany, Duke of, gentle, rela-

tively ineffectual husband of Goneril; comes to hate his wife, but forced to repel the French forces brought to Lear's aid by Cordelia; King of Britain after Lear's death.
LEAR: I, 1.

Albion, ancient name for England or Britain.
LEAR: Fool, III, 2, 91.
2H6: Queen, I, 3, 48.
3H6: Margaret, III, 3, 7.

Alcibiades, Athenian captain; asks Senate to pardon a friend, refused, he gets angry and is banished; Timon gives him gold to support his attack on Athens to avenge them against their ungrateful friends. [c450-404 BC; general; brilliant, charming, capable, but his temper got him into trouble; fled to Sparta, from there to the Persians; recalled to Athens, defeated Spartan fleet; murdered on order of Lysander of Sparta in Phrygia.]
TIMON: I, 1.

Alcides. See HERCULES.
A&C: Antony, IV, 12, 44.
SHREW: Gremio, I, 2, 258.
MERV: Morocco, II, 1, 35.

alderliefest, dearest of all.
2H6: Queen, I, 1, 28.

ale
I would give all my fame for a pot of ale and safety.
HEN5: Boy, III, 2, 13.

Alecto, one of the Furies.
2H4: Pistol, V, 5, 39.

Alençon, Duke of, supporter of the Dauphin; admirer of Joan of Arc. [Jean, 2nd Duke of Alençon; supported the Dauphin against his father, Charles VII; condemned to death (1456); sentence changed to life imprisonment; pardoned.]
1H6: I, 2.

Aleppo, flourishing trading center in northwestern Syria for Levant company; important in Elizabethan period; also Alep, Haleb (Arabic), ancient Beroea.

Alexander, reference to Alexander the Great, who ruled as king of Macedon (336-323 BC); conqueror of a large part of Asia and one of the great leaders of all time.
HAM: Hamlet, V, 1, 218—it has been suggested that Hamlet uses the names of great men either to stress his own inferiority or the power of death over greatness.

Alexander, Cressida's servant.
T&C: I, 2. See AJAX.

Alexas, Cleopatra's attendant; treachery and death told by Enobarbus.
A&C: I, 2.

Alice, lady-in-waiting to Princess Katherine of France; teaches her English (after a fashion).
HEN5: III, 4.

Aliena, name assumed by Celia when she runs away with Rosalind into the Forest of Arden.
AYL: Celia, I, 3, 130.

Alla nostra casa ben venuto, molto honorato signor mio Petrucio, Italian, welcome to our house, my much honored Signor Petruchio.
SHREW: Hortensio, I, 2, 25.

alla stoccata, Italian, with a thrust, fencing term.
R&J: Mercutio, III, 1, 77.

allaying Tiber, diluting water of the Tiber river.
COR: Menenius, II, 1, 53.

allayment, antidote, mitigation.
CYM: Queen, I, 5, 22.

All-hallond eve, Halloween, Oct. 31; eve of All Saints' Day.
MEAS: Froth, II, 1, 130.

Allhallowmas, All Saints' Day, Nov. 1.
MWW: Simple, I, 1, 211.

All-hallown summer, Indian summer.
1H4: Prince, I, 2, 178—refers to youthful old age.

allowance, approval, acknowledgment of a claim or assertion, agreement.
OTH: Roderigo, I, 1, 128.

All Souls' Day, November 2.

RICH3: Buckingham, V, 1, 10.

All's Well that Ends Well, usually dated about 1602; possibly *Love's Labour's Won,* mentioned by Meres (1598), in an earlier version, but this is not certain; derived from novellas *Betramo de Rossiglione* and *Giglietta di Nerbone,* in BOCCACCIO's *Decameron* (III, 9), translated in William PAINTER's *Palace of Pleasure* (1566); however, there were plot changes and characters added; first recorded performance at Goodman's Fields 1741; published 1623.

PLOT: The King of France is cured by Helena with a drug her father, a famous physician, willed to her; as a reward, she asks the King to arrange her marriage to Bertram, Count of Rossillion; the unwilling groom leaves immediately for the Tuscan war, sending her a message that he will come back when she can get the ring off his finger and prove she is pregnant with his child; Helena follows him to Florence, where she discovers he is attempting to seduce Diana, the daughter of her hostess; she succeeds in taking Diana's place in bed with Bertram, managing to exchange his ring for one given her by the King; when she is able, with the help of Diana, to prove this to the King, Bertram repents and returns to her; the subplot revolves about the cowardly braggart, Parolles.

all the world

For you, in my respect, are all the world.

Then how can it be said I am alone

When all the world is here to look on me?

MND: Helena, II, 1, 224. See RESPECT.

allycholly, mistaken form of old word for melancholy.

2GENT: Host, IV, 2, 27.

Almain, a German.

OTH: Iago, II, 3, 86.

alms-drink, the leavings or dregs for the poor; more than the drinker can handle.

A&C: 1Servant, II, 7, 6.

almsman, needy man dependent on alms or charity; usually prayed for his benefactor.

RICH2: Richard, III, 3, 149.

along, prone, at full length, dead.

COR: 3Conspirator, V, 6, 56.

Alonso, King of Naples; aided Antonio in expelling the latter's brother, Prospero, from the Duchy of Milan; shipwrecked on Prospero's magic island on his return from Tunis; subjected to many trials by Prospero and Ariel, repents his misdeeds; consents to the marriage of his son Ferdinand to Miranda, daughter of Prospero.

TEMP: I, 1.

alteration. See LOVE.

Althaea, told by the Fates that her son Meleager would die when a firebrand (piece of wood) burning in the fire was consumed, she snatched the brand from the fire and hid it; years later, Meleager (then Prince of Calydon) killed her brothers and, after much soul searching and hesitation, she threw the firebrand into a fire and Meleager died; grieving, she hung herself.

2H6: York, I, 1, 234.

2H4: Page, II, 2, 94—*Althaea's dream,* actually her was Hecuba who dreamed of giving birth to a firebrand.

Amaimon, notorious devil or fiend, one of four demons ruling the universe—imaginary king of the East.

MWW: Ford, II, 2, 308.

1H4: Falstaff, II, 4, 370—*Amamon.*

amain, speedily, swiftly, forcefully.

TEMP: Iris, IV, 1, 74.

Amazons, heroic women in Greek mythology; name comes from the cutting off of their right breasts (*a*, without; *mazos*, breast), which made it easier to draw their bows.

> COR: Cominius, II, 2, 95.
> JOHN: Bastard, V, 2, 155.
> 1H6: Dauphin, I, 2, 104.

ambassadors. See also ENGLISH AMBASSADORS.

> HAM: V, 2; 1H6: V, 1; HEN5: I, 2.

ambition

Who doth ambition shun
And loves to live i' th' sun . . .

> AYL: All, II, 5, 40—beginning of song.

. . . and I hold ambition of so airy and light a quality that it is but a shadow's shadow.

> HAM: Rosenkrantz, II, 2, 267.

Then are our beggars bodies, and our monarchs and out-stretched heroes the beggars' shadows.

> HAM: II, 2, 269. See DREAM.

. . . the noble Brutus
Hath told you Caesar was ambitious.
If it were so, it was a grievous fault,
And grievously hath Caesar answered it.

> JC: Antony, III, 2, 83.

As Caesar loved me, I weep for him; as he was fortunate, I rejoice at it; as he was valiant, I honour him; but as he was ambitious, I slew him. There is tears for his love; joy for his fortune; honour for his valour; and death for his ambition.

> JC: Brutus, III, 2, 26.

. . . But 'tis a common proof
That lowliness is young ambition's ladder,
Whereto the climber-upward turn his face;
But when he once attains the upmost round,
He then unto the ladder turns his back,

Looks in the clouds, scorning the base degrees
By which he did ascend.

> JC: Brutus, II, 1, 21.

Thriftless ambition, that wilt raven up
Thine own life's means!

> MACB: Ross, II, 4, 28—*raven up*, devour greedily as the raven eats his prey.

. . . I have no spur
To prick the sides of my intent, but only
Vaulting ambition, which o'er-leaps itself
And falls on the other—

> MACB: Macbeth, I, 7, 25.

amerce, punish, usually by payment of a fine.

> R&J: Prince, III, 1, 195.

ames-ace, two aces, the lowest throw at dice.

> ALL'sW: Lafew, II, 3, 85.

Amiens, Lord, singer for the banished Duke; sings "Under the greenwood tree," and other songs.

> AYL: II, 1.

amity

The amity that wisdom knits not, folly may easily untie.

> T&C: Ulysses, II, 3, 110.

amort, dejected, dispirited, melancholy.

> SHREW: Petruchio, IV, 3, 36.

Amurath, Turkish sultan; had his brothers strangled, when he succeeded to the throne (1574).

> 2H4: Prince, V, 2, 48.

Amyot, Jacques (1513-93). French prelate, classical scholar, writer, and translator of PLUTARCH's *Lives* (*Vies des hommes illustres de Plutarque*, 1559-65); English translation of Amyot's work by Sir Thomas NORTH (1579) used by Shakespeare as the source of material for his Roman plays.

an, if, even if, though.

> TEMP: Sebastian, II, 1, 181.

anatomize, dissect, analyze.

> 2H4: Rumour, Induction, 21.

LEAR: Lear, III, 6, 80.
AYL: Oliver, I, 1, 163.

an auspicious, and a dropping eye, one cheerful or gay eye and one tearful or sad.
HAM: King, I, 2, 11.

Anchises. See AENEAS.
JC: Cassius, I, 2, 114.
T&C: Aeneas, IV, 1, 21.

anchor, recluse, hermit, anchorite.
HAM: Player Queen, III, 2, 229.

ancient, misspelling of ensign, third officer in company; standard bearer.
OTH: Iago, I, 1, 32.
1H4: Falstaff, IV, 2, 26.
HEN5: Bardolph, II, 1, 3.

Andrew, name of a ship; possibly named after the carrack *St. Andrew* captured off Cadiz (1596).
MERV: Salerio, I, 1, 27.

Andromache, devoted wife of Hector; tries to stop him from fighting against the Greeks; heroine of several important tragedies.
T&C: V, 3.

Andronicus. See MARCUS ANDRONICUS and TITUS ANDRONICUS.

angel, gold coin having the archangel Michael stamped on it; valued at approximately half a pound.
1H4: Bardolph, IV, 2, 6.
SHREW: Bionello, IV, 2, 61.
JOHN: Bastard, II, 1, 590.

Angelo, goldsmith; makes chain for Antipholus of Ephesus, gives it to Antipholus of Syracuse by mistake, then demands payment from the former.
COFE: III, 1.

Angelo, villainous lord deputy; "a man whose blood is very snow-broth;" infatuated with Isabella; forced by the Duke to marry Mariana.
MEAS: I, 1.

angle, hook and line used in fishing; tackle, fishhook.
HAM: Hamlet, V, 2, 66.
A&C: Cleopatra, II, 5, 10.
WINT: Polixenes, IV, 2, 52.

angry woman
A woman moved is like a fountain troubled,
Muddy, ill-seeming, thick, bereft of beauty;
And while it is so, none so dry or thirsty
Will deign to sip or touch one drop of it.
SHREW: Katherina, V, 2, 142— *moved,* angry, irritated.

Angus, Scottish nobleman; supports Malcolm against Macbeth.
MACB: I, 2.

Anna, sister and confidante of Dido, Queen of Carthage; VERGIL'S *Aeneid* (Book 4).
SHREW: Lucentio, I, 1, 159.

Anne, Lady, curses Richard, but marries him; crowned; dies mysteriously; her ghost appears to Richard before Bosworth. [Anne Neville (1456-85), daughter of Warwick, the kingmaker.]
RICH3: I, 2.

Anne Boleyn, Queen. See BULLEN, Anne.

anointed king
Not all the water in the rough rude sea
Can wash the balm off from an anointed king.
The breath of worldly men cannot depose
The deputy elected by the Lord.
RICH2: Richard, III, 2, 54. See BALM.

Antenor, capable Trojan commander; captured by the Greeks; exchanged for Cressida.
T&C: I, 2.

anter, cave, cavern.
OTH: Othello, I, 3, 140.

Anthropophagi, cannibals.
MWW: Host, IV, 5, 10.

antic, clown, buffoon, odd person.
RICH2: Richard, III, 2, 162.

See SCOFFING HIS STATE.
A&C: Caesar, II, 7, 130.
ADO: Hero, III, 1, 63.

antic round, fantastic or grotesque dance performed in a circle.
MACB: 1Witch, IV, 1, 130.

antidote. See MIND.

Antigonus, Sicilian lord; Paulina's husband; Leontes orders him to leave Perdita in some desert place to perish; eaten by a bear.
WINT: II, 1.

Antiochus, evil king of Antioch; when Pericles discovers the king's incestuous relationship with his daughter, Antiochus attempts to have him killed; shriveled by fire from heaven.
PER: I, 1.

Antipholus of Ephesus, son of Aegon and Aemilia, Abbess of Ephesus; twin brother of Antipholus of Syracuse, husband of Adriana; victim of mistaken identity, locked out of his house and arrested for debt and theft.
CofE: III, 1.

Antipholus of Syracuse, twin brother of above; mistaken for him, he receives money, jewelry and the attentions of his wife; falls in love with Luciana.
CofE: I, 2.

antipodes, inhabitants of the other half of the world.
RICH2: Richard, III, 2, 49.
ADO: Benedick, II, 1, 273.
3H6: York, I, 4, 135.

antique Roman, ancient Roman; often took their own lives or followed their leaders into death rather than continue life under dishonorable conditions.
HAM: Horatio, V, 2, 352.

Antonio, the Merchant of Venice, although not the hero of the play; wealthy, generous, melancholy; lends money to Bassanio so that he can woo Portia; unaware that his morality is no better than his adversary's, he is ably defended by Portia at the trial and wins out against Shylock.
MERV: I, 1.

Antonio, Leonato's brother, Hero's uncle; challenges Claudio.
ADO: I, 2.

Antonio, Prospero's crafty brother who usurped the dukedom of Milan; shipwrecked on Prospero's island, he is forced to return it to him.
TEMP: I, 1.

Antonio, Proteus' father.
2GENT: I, 3.

Antonio, sea-captain; Sebastian's friend; mistakes Viola for her twin and demands his purse.
TWN: II, 1.

Antony (Mark Antony), great Roman leader, member of triumvirate that ruled the empire following Caesar's assassination (see CAESAR, Julius); noble, magnanimous, yet an impulsive, decadent middle-aged lover torn between honor as a military hero and Cleopatra, he gives his life for the woman he loves.

His face was as the heavens, and
   therein stuck
A sun and moon, which kept
   their course and lighted
The little O, the earth. . . .
His legs bestrid the ocean; his
   reared arm
Crested the world; his voice was
   propertied
As all the tuned spheres, and
   that to friends;
But when he meant to quail and
   shake the orb,
He was as rattling thunder. For
   his bounty,
There was no winter in't; an
   autumn 'twas
That grew the more by reaping.
   His delights
Were dolphin-like, they showed
   his back above
The element they lived in. In his
   livery
Walked crowns and crownets.
   Realms and island were

As plates dropped from his
pocket.
A&C: Cleopatra, V, 2, 82. See
PLATE.

I must not think there are
Evils enow to darken all his
goodness.
His faults, in him, seem as the
spots of heaven,
More fiery by night's blackness;
hereditary
Rather than purchas'd; what he
cannot change
Than what he chooses.
A&C: Lepidus, I, 4, 10. See
DEATH OF ANTONY.

*Antony and Cleopatra, The Trag-
edy of,* written 1607-08; registered May 20, 1608; published
1623; source of material, Sir
Thomas NORTH's translation
from the French version made
by Jacques AMYOT of PLU-
TARCH's *Life of Antonius* (published, 1579); historically the
period covered is 40 BC (date of
Fulvia's death) to August 29,
30 BC (date of Cleopatra's
death).

PLOT: Antony, one of the
triumvirs ruling the Roman
empire, tired of responsibility,
ignores the messages from Octavius Caesar asking him to
return to Rome, preferring to
remain in Alexandria with Cleopatra, the sensuous, desirable,
clever Queen of Egypt. However, when the young Pompey
threatens revolt and news of
his wife's death reaches Antony,
he prepares to return. Making
peace with Caesar and Lepidus,
Antony agrees to marry Octavia,
Caesar's widowed sister, as a
means of further strengthening
the alliance. But, as Enobarbus,
Antony's officer and trusted
friend predicts, Octavia cannot
make him forget Cleopatra.

The triumvirs meet with Pompey at a drunken feast and agree
to terms of peace. The truce
doesn't last very long and Caesar
is at odds with Antony, who has

returned to Egypt following
Ventidius' successful campaign
in Parthia. Caesar defeats Pompey, arrests Lepidus on charges
of conspiracy and, after Antony
neglects his sister and proclaims
Cleopatra's sons kings, war between the two becomes inevi-
table. Antony, defeated by Caesar at sea near Actium when
Cleopatra and the Egyptian fleet
flee, is, nevertheless, persuaded
by her to fight again on land.
The troops opposing Antony
are made up largely of his former soldiers. When Antony
blames himself for Enobarbus'
desertion and sends him his
abandoned treasure, his former
friend dies of a broken heart.

Antony, defeated when the
Egyptian fleet again takes flight,
charges Cleopatra with treachery. Hoping to win him back,
she escapes to her burial monument and sends word to him
that she is dead. Antony, in
grief, stabs himself and, learning that she still lives, requests
that they take him to Cleopatra,
where, reconciled with her, he
dies in her arms. Meanwhile,
Dercetas, who had witnessed
Antony's action, takes the sword
with which he had stabbed himself to Caesar with the news of
his enemy's death. Octavius
sends Proculeius to bring Cleopatra, unharmed, to Rome.
When she is captured, Cleopatra, realizing that she will
become a spectacle of shame in
Rome, attempts to kill herself
with a dagger, but Caesar, anticipating this action has her closely
watched and she is quickly dis-
armed. However, she finally succeeds in having asps, smuggled
into a basket of figs, brought to
her and kills herself with them.
Coleridge considered "of all
Shakespeare's historical plays,
Antony and Cleopatra is by far
the most wonderful."

ap (Welsh), son of.

RICH3: Urswick, IV, 5, 15.

Apemantus, churlish, cynical philosopher; warns Timon of the falseness of his friends.
TIMON: I, 1.

Apollo, important Olympian god of youth and the arts; in earliest time, he was guardian of both youth and the flocks and herds.
LLL: Berowne, IV, 3, 343.
SHREW: Lord, Induction, 2, 37.
WINT: Florizel, IV, 4, 30—exiled from heaven by Jupiter, Apollo, disguised as a shepherd and serving Admetus, won Alcestis.

Apollodorus, a Sicilian who, according to PLUTARCH, carried Cleopatra, rolled in a mattress tied with a great leather thong, on his back through the castle gate and into the presence of Caesar.
A&C: Pompey, II, 6, 68.

apoplexed, completely unable to function, paralyzed, incapacitated, crippled.
HAM: Hamlet, III, 4, 73.

Apothecary, seller of poisons.
R&J: V, 1.

appeach, indict, accuse openly.
RICH2: York, V, 2, 79.

appeal, accuse, impeach, charge with; the accuser was prepared to prove his claim by fighting the defender to the death.
RICH2: Richard, I, 1, 4.

appellant, the accuser; one who accuses another of treason.
RICH2: Bolingbroke, I, 1, 34.
2H6: York, II, 3, 49.

appendix, addition, appendage (wife).
SHREW: Biondello, IV, 4, 106.

apple John, apple picked on St. John's Day (June 24), kept until shriveled, and still flavorful.
1H4: Falstaff, III, 3, 5.
2H4: Francis, II, 4, 2.

appointment, equipment.
HAM: Horatio, IV, 6, 16.
1H4: Prince, I, 2, 197.
T&C: Agamemnon, IV, 5, 1.

apprehension, idea, conception, thought.
OTH: Iago, III, 3, 139.
RICH2: Bolingbroke, I, 3, 300.
HAM: Queen, IV, 1, 2. See
BRAINISH APPREHENSION.

approbation, support, confirmation, proof.
HEN5: King, I, 2, 19.
WINT: Leontes, II, 1, 177.
MEAS: Claudio, I, 2, 183—novitiate

approve, prove, confirm.
RICH2: 2Herald, I, 3, 112.
MACB: Banquo, I, 6, 4.
WINT: Polixenes, IV, 2, 32.

approve, convict, prove guilty.
OTH: Othello, II, 3, 211.

appurtenance, fitting accessory or accompanying action; belonging to something usually more important.
HAM: Hamlet, II, 2, 388.

apron-men, mechanics, artisans.
COR: Menenius, IV, 6, 96.

apron stage, that part of the stage which extends into the pit or "yard"; in the FORTUNE theater, the apron stage which projected "to the middle of the yarde" was 27½ feet deep and 43 feet wide.

aqua-vitae, liquor; spirits especially favored by old women; whiskey, brandy.
TwN: Toby, II, 5, 215.
MWW: Ford, II, 2, 316.
R&J: Nurse, III, 2, 88.

Aquilon, the north wind.
T&C: Ajax, IV, 5, 9.

Arabia, refers to desert where there is no hiding place.
COR: Volumnia, IV, 2, 24.

Arabian bird. See PHOENIX.
A&C: Agrippa, III, 2, 12.
CYM: Iachimo, I, 6, 17.

Arabian tree, date-palm; occupied by the phoenix.
TEMP: Sebastian, III, 3, 22.
PHOENIX: 2.

arbitrement, judgment, judicial decision, assessment.
1H4: Worcester, IV, 1, 70.
CYM: Frenchman, I, 4, 52.

arch. See SPACE.

Archidamus, Bohemian lord; opens play and then is heard no more.
WINT: I, 1.

Arcite, a hero of the play; nephew of Creon, King of Thebes; imprisoned with cousin Palamon; released; ordered by Theseus to fight in tournament against Palamon for love of Emilia, wins, but is thrown from his horse; dying, he gives her to his rival.
2NK: I, 2.

Arde. See GUYNES AND ARDE.

Ardea, wealthy, ancient city of Latium, about 24 miles south of Rome.
LUCRECE: Argument, 8.

Arden, Forest of, refers to Arden in Warwickshire; Shakespeare's mother was an Arden of Wilmcote.
AYL: Charles, I, 1, 121—scene actually set in Ardennes forest of France (Flanders).

argal, corruption of Latin word *ergo,* meaning therefore, and often used in logical or formal reasoning or debate.
HAM: Clown, V, 1, 13.

argentine, from French, *argent;* silvery.
PER: Pericles, V, 1, 251.

Argier, old name for Algiers; Algher was a town in Sardinia whose ancient name was Corax.
TEMP: Ariel, I, 2, 261. See SYCORAX.

argosy, large merchant vessel; name derives from Ragusa, port in Sicily, known at that time as "Arragosa"; vessel sometimes called a carrack.
SHREW: Gremio, II, 1, 376.
MERV: Salerio, I, 1, 9.
3H6: Edward, II, 6, 36.

argument, summary of the plot; at court performances it was often the custom to provide the audience with a written or printed synopsis or summary of the plot of the play or performance.
HAM: Rosencrantz, II, 2, 372.
1H4: Prince, II, 4, 310.

argument, cause, reason, subject, topic.
HAM: Hamlet, IV, 4, 54.
LEAR: France, I, 1, 218.
MACB: Malcolm, II, 3, 126.

Argus, watchman of the gods; monster with a hundred eyes all over his body; sent by Juno to guard Io and to keep Jove away.
T&C: Man, I, 2, 31.
MERV: Portia, V, 1, 230.
LLL: Berowne, III, 1, 201.

Ariachne, probably Arachne, who was challenged to a weaving contest by Athene (Minerva); when Athene tore Ariachne's fine-spun web, she hung herself, and the goddess changed her into a spider.
T&C: Troilus, V, 2, 152.

Ariadne, daughter of Minos, King of Crete; left by Theseus on the island of Naxos.
2GENT: Julia, IV, 4, 172. See THESEUS.

Ariel, "airy spirit" imprisoned by the witch, Sycorax, in a cloven pine tree; Prospero frees Ariel through his magic and in return the spirit becomes his servant; Ariel, whose sex is never stated in the play, has the capacity to take any form and carry out almost any magical task; Prospero frees Ariel at the play's end.
TEMP: I, 2.

Arion, Greek poet and musician of Lesbos who so charmed the dolphins with his music that they carried him safely to land after he had jumped overboard to escape some murderous pirates.
TWN: Captain, I, 2, 15.

Ariosto, Lodovico (1474-1533). Italian poet; noted for *Orlando Furioso,* epic work on Roland; subplot in *The Taming of the Shrew* probably derived from his comedy *I Suppositi* (performed, 1566; pub., 1573), translated by George GASCOIGNE.

Aristotle, Greek philosopher, (384–322 BC); one of the world's greatest thinkers; pupil of Plato, teacher of Alexander the Great; combined speculation with empirical analysis for study of both physical world and metaphysics; profound influence on subsequent thought; lived long after the siege of Troy.
T&C: Hector, II, 2, 166.

Armado, Don Adriano de, fantastical Spaniard (a caricature); rival of Costard for love of Jaquenetta; plays Hector in the interlude.
LLL: I, 2.

armed head, apparition; symbolic of Macbeth's coming fight against Macduff.
MACB: S.D., IV, 1, following line 68.

armigero, Latin, literally, bearer of arms; esquire, entitled to bear heraldic arms.
MWW: Slender, I, 1, 10.

arms crossed, Elizabethan gesture of melancholy or sadness.
LLL: Moth, III, 1, 19.

Arragon, Prince of, one of Portia's suitors; chooses the silver casket and finds "the portrait of a blinking idiot."
MERV: II, 6.

arrant, through - and - through, downright, absolute, thoroughly.
HAM: Hamlet, I, 5, 124.
1H4: Falstaff, II, 2, 106.
2H4: Hostess, II, 1, 42.

arras, draped tapestry hanging on or at enough distance from the wall to conceal a person.
HAM: Polonius, II, 2, 163.
CYM: Iachimo, II, 2, 26.
ADO: Borachio, I, 3, 63.

arrest, accept as a guarantee, take for security.
LLL: Princess, II, 1, 160.

arrose, besprinkle, strew.
2NK: Theseus, V, 4, 104.

Artemidorus of Cnidos, teacher of rhetoric; sends Caesar a note warning him of the conspiracy, but Caesar refuses to read it.
JC: II, 3.

Arthur, Duke of Bretagne, son of Constance and Geoffrey Plantagenet, John's older brother; the King orders him blinded, then killed; dies trying to escape. [1187-1203, considered by many in French dominions the lawful ruler, but the Great Council of England chose John.]
JOHN: II, 1.

Arthur's show, each year a group of London archers gave an exhibition at Mile-End Green; they took the names of the knights of the round table.
2H4: Shallow, III, 2, 300.

articulate, come to terms.
COR: Cominius, I, 9, 76.

artificial, artistically creative, skilled in constructive art.
MND: Helena, III, 2, 203.

Art to Love, refers to OVID's *Ars Amandi, The Art of Love.*
SHREW: Lucentio, IV, 2, 8.

Arviragus, younger son of Cymbeline, brother of Imogen and Guiderius; brought up by Belarius, who names him Cadwal; discovers Imogen apparently dead; helps to repel the Roman invasion; reunited with his father.
CYM: III, 3.

Ascanius, son of Aeneas. See DIDO.
2H6: Queen, III, 2, 116.

asinico, little ass.
T&C: Thersites, II, 1, 49.

Asmath, prophetic spirit, conjured up by Bolingbroke for the Duchess of Gloucester.
2H6: I, 4.

aspersion, blessing; literally, sprinkling of dew or rain.
TEMP: Prospero, IV, 1, 18.

aspic, asp, small poisonous snake.
OTH: Othello, III, 3, 450. See BOSOM.
A&C: Cleopatra, V, 2, 296.

assassination

  . . . If th' assassination
Could trammel up the conse-
  quence, and catch,
With his surcease, success, that
  but this blow
Might be the be-all and the end-
  all here,
But here, upon this bank and
  shoal of time,
We'd jump the life to come.
  MACB: Macbeth, I, 7, 2. See
  TRAMMEL, SUCCESS.

assay, provoke an interest in,
tempt, try to win over.
  HAM: Queen, III, 1, 15.

assay, attack, assault, try, test,
attempt, challenge.
  OTH: Othello, II, 3, 207.
  1H4: King, V, 4, 34.
  HAM: Voltimand, II, 2, 71.

assays of bias, indirect course,
devious approaches; bowling
term for judging the effect of a
weight in the bowling ball which
causes it to curve.
  HAM: Polonius, II, 1, 65.

assigns, adjuncts, appurtenances;
added to or goes with.
  HAM: Osric, V, 2, 157.

ass's or "Ases," pun on the many
times an "as" is used in official
papers and ass, beast of burden.
  HAM: Hamlet, V, 2, 43.

astonish, stun; flog or beat into
submission.
  HEN5: Gower, V, 1, 40.

Astraea, goddess of justice; in
mythology she lived among men
in the Golden Age; when evil
increased, she was forced to
leave the earth and live among
the stars as the constellation
Virgo; daughter of Jupiter.
  1H6: Dauphin, I, 6, 4.
  TITUS: Titus, IV, 3, 4.

As You Like It, written 1598-
1600; registered Aug. 4, 1600;
published 1623; probably first
performed at the GLOBE Theater
1599; source, Thomas LODGE's
*Rosalynde, or Euphues' Golden
Legacie* (1590), a version of a
14th-century story, *Tale of Gam-*

lyn; Shakespeare added the
comic characters.

PLOT: Although Duke Fred-
erick has usurped the dukedom
of his older brother, he has permitted the latter's daughter
Rosalind to live at court with
his own daughter, Celia. When,
however, he later banishes her,
she disguises herself as a boy
and, with Celia and Touchstone,
seeks refuge in the Forest of
Arden. While the sons of Sir
Roland de Boys are at court,
Oliver, the elder, keeps his
younger brother, Orlando, "under his thumb." When Orlando
threatens to rebel, Oliver plans
to kill him. Orlando, who has
fallen in love with Rosalind,
accompanied by his faithful old
servant, Adam, flees to Arden.

Rosalind and Celia purchase
a flock of sheep and a pasture
and decide to live like shepherds,
calling themselves Ganymede
and Aliena. Orlando meets
Ganymede (Rosalind) and she
persuades him to pretend that
she is Rosalind and to "practice" making love to her. Meanwhile Duke Frederick sends
Oliver after Orlando, threatening to take away his lands if he
returns without him. Orlando
saves his brother's life and they
are reconciled. Oliver and Celia
are paired off, as Rosalind, revealing her true identity, is reunited with her father and
married to Orlando. Touchstone
(the Clown) has fallen in love
with Audrey, and Phebe is returned to Silvius. A repentant
Duke Frederick restores the
dukedom to his brother.

Atalanta, in Greek mythology,
daughter of Iasus and Clymene;
remarkable huntress; would only
marry a suitor who could outrun her; finally outwitted by
Melanion (Hippomenes) with
the help of Aphrodite.
  AYL: Celia, III, 2, 155.

Ate, daughter of Greek goddess

Eris; created mischief or discord; incited men to impetuous actions.
ADO: Benedick, II, 1, 264.
JOHN: Chatillon, II, 1, 63.
LLL: Berowne, II, 1, 264—*Ates.*

at foot, close at his heels, directly behind.
HAM: King, IV, 3, 56.

athwart, cutting across; thwarting.
1H4: Westmoreland, I, 1, 36.

Atlas, Titan in Greek mythology; condemned by Zeus to stand at the western end of the earth and carry the heavens on his head and hands; stories of Atlas not consistent; father of Calypso, the Pleiades and the Hyades.
3H6: Warwick, V, 1, 36.

atone, bring together, reconcile, harmonize.
RICH2: Richard, I, 1, 202.
2H4: Archbishop, IV, 1, 221.
A&C: Maecenas, II, 2, 102.

Atropos, one of the three Fates; cut the thread of life.
2H4: Pistol, II, 4, 213. See SISTERS THREE.

attach, arrest, seize.
RICH2: York, II, 3, 156.
OTH: Brabantio, I, 2, 77.
TEMP: Alonso, III, 3, 5.

attainder, humiliating, dishonorable accusation, condemnation; such a charge threatened loss of title.
RICH2: Aumerle, IV, 1, 24.

at the flight, long-range shooting in an archery duel with "flight" arrows.
ADO: Beatrice, I, 1, 39.

attorneyed, performed by proxy or through assistants or deputies.
WINT: Camillo, I, 1, 30.
1H6: Suffolk, V, 5, 56.

attribute, reputation, eminence, honor, merit.
HAM: Hamlet, I, 4, 22.
1H4: Hotspur, IV, 1, 3.

audit, account, probably referring to the accumulated evaluation in the book of judgment.
HAM: Hamlet, III, 3, 82.

Audrey, an "ill-favour'd thing," goat-girl; Touchstone meets her in the Forest of Arden; marries her.
AYL: III, 3.

Aufidius, Tullus, General of the Volscians; opponent of Coriolanus, whom he both hates and admires; when Coriolanus fails in his resolve to attack Rome, Aufidius kills him.
COR: I, 2.

auger, carpenter's tool for boring small holes.
Cor: Cominius, IV, 6, 87.
MACB: Donalbain, II, 3, 128—*auger's hole,* harm may befall us from the least obvious source.

augury, prophecy by omens, fortune-telling, soothsaying.
HAM: Hamlet, V, 2, 230.
A&C: Scarus, IV, 12, 4.
JC: Cassius, II, 1, 200.

Aumerle, Edward, Duke of, Earl of Rutland, son of Duke of York, becomes 2nd Duke of York; cousin of Richard II and Bolingbroke; one of the most faithful of Richard's followers; accused during the session of Parliament of participating in the murder of his uncle, the Duke of Gloucester; with Carlisle and the Abbot of Westminster, plots to kill Bolingbroke; his father discovers the plot and reports it to King Henry IV; through the intercession of his mother (see YORK, Duchess of), pardoned, but deprived of dukedom.
RICH2: I, 3. See YORK, Duke of.

aunt, old woman, dame or crone, gossip.
MND: Puck, II, 1, 51.
WINT: Autolycus, IV, 3, 11. See DOXY.

Aurora, Roman goddess of the

dawn, morning; in Greek mythology, Eos.

R&J: Montague, I, 1, 143.

Aurora's harbinger, morning star, which portends or is the forerunner of dawn.

MND: Puck, III, 2, 380.

Austria, Duke of, supports Arthur and France against John; killed by Philip Falconbridge (the Bastard). [Leopold V, 1st Archduke of Austria; captured and imprisoned Richard I; killed at siege of the castle of the Vicomte de Limoges; confused by Shakespeare with the Vicomte.]

JOHN: II, 1.

Autolycus, rogue, peddler, balladmonger; a "snapper-up of unconsidered trifles" (pickpocket); changes clothes with Florizel to aid in the prince's escape; extorts money from the shepherd and his son; in Greek mythology, the son of Mercury and the cleverest of thieves.

WINT: IV, 3.

Auvergne, Countess, fails in an attempt to trap Talbot in her castle.

1H6: II, 3.

avarice

This avarice
Sticks deeper, grows with more
   pernicious root
Than summer-seeming lust; and
   it hath been
The sword of our slain kings.

MACB: Macduff, IV, 3, 84.

avaunt, be gone! order to leave; be off!

OTH: Othello, III, 3, 335.
A&C: Antony, IV, 12, 30.

avoid, be gone, depart, leave.

TEMP: Prospero, IV, 1, 142.
COR: 3Servingman, IV, 5, 25.
WINT: Polixenes, I, 2, 462.

avouch, assurance, certainty, guarantee.

HAM: Horatio, I, 1, 57.
MND: Lysander, I, 1, 106—
avouch it to his head, tell it to
his face.

awful, full of respect and awe, reverential.

RICH2: Richard, III, 3, 76.

aye, ever.

HAM: King, III, 2, 210—*This
world is not for aye.*

azured vault, blue sky, dome of blue.

TEMP: Prospero, V, 1, 43.

babbled of green fields. See DEATH OF FALSTAFF.

baboon
Cool it with a baboon's blood, Then the charm is firm and good.
MACB: 2Witch, IV, 1, 37. See WITCHES' CURSE.

bacare, stand back, take it easy, down boy!
SHREW: Gremio, II, 1, 73.

bacchanals, dances in honor of Bacchus, god of wine and revelry.
A&C: Enobarbus, II, 7, 109.

bachelor
. . . Because I will not do them the wrong to mistrust any, I will do myself the right to trust none; and the fine is (for the which I may go the finer), I will live a bachelor.
ADO: Benedick, I, 1, 245.

backsword man, singlestick fencer or expert; singlestick is a sword with basketwork protection for the hand, or a guard near the handle.
2H4: Shallow, III, 2, 70.

badges, metal plates displaying the coat of arms of the master; the badge designated to which household the servant belonged.
TEMP: Prospero, V, 1, 267.
LUCRECE: 1054.

baffle, disgrace, degrade from knighthood, hold up to scorn; to subject a knight, who had broken his oath and been convicted of perjury, to public scorn by stripping him of his armor

and showing a picture of him hanging by his heels.
RICH2: Mowbray, I, 1, 170.

bag and baggage
. . . let us make an honourable retreat; though not with bag and baggage, yet with scrip and scrippage.
AYL: Touchstone, III, 2, 169. See SCRIP.

Bagot, Sir William, of Baginton near Coventry; court favorite of Richard II; imprisoned by Bolingbroke; appears in parliament scene to accuse Aumerle of complicity in the murder of the Duke of Gloucester. [d. c1400.]
RICH2: I, 3.

bags, money, moneybags.
SHREW: Grumio, I, 2, 178.

baille, fetch.
MWW: Caius, I, 4, 92.

Bajazet's mule, not entirely explained; some authorities suggest it might be Balaam's ass, others that it refers to a mistreated character in MARLOWE'S *Tamburlaine*.
ALL'sW: Parolles, IV, 1, 46.

baked meats, foods, pies, pasties, feast.
HAM: Hamlet, I, 2, 180.

bald
There's no time for a man to recover his hair that grows bald by nature.
COFE: Dromio S., II, 2, 73.

baldrick, belt for carrying hunting horn.
ADO: Benedick, I, 1, 244.

bale, harm, poison, injure; get the worst of it.
COR: Menenius, I, 1, 167.

balk, bandy, practice, use.
SHREW: Tranio, I, 1, 34.

balked, piled up in ridges, stopped in their tracks; balk is a mound or ridge.
1H4: King, I, 1, 69.

ballet, ballad, simple song.
MND: Bottom, IV, 1, 215.

balm, the oil with which kings are anointed at their coronations.
RICH2: Richard, III, 2, 55.

Balthasar, squire in Don Pedro's service; sings "Sigh no more, ladies."
ADO: II, 3.

Balthasar, Portia's servant; she adopts his name when in disguise.
MERV: III, 4.

Balthasar, Romeo's servant; brings news to Mantua of Juliet's death; hides outside the Capulet monument; captured by the Watch.
R&J: I, 1.

Balthazar, a merchant; friend of Antipholus of Ephesus; persuades him not to use force when his wife locks him out of his house.
COFE: III, 1.

ban, curse.
LEAR: Edgar, II, 3, 19.

Banbury cheese, very thin cream cheese, made at Banbury, near Stratford.
MWW: Bardolph, I, 1, 130—refers to Slender.

band, bond, pledge, obligation.
RICH2: Richard I, 1, 2.

Bandello, Matteo (1480-1565). Italian novelist; became Bishop of Agen (1550); famous for novellas (1554-73), translated into French by BELLEFOREST (1565), into English by Sir Geoffrey FENTON (1567); Shakespeare indirectly indebted to him for elements of *Romeo and Juliet, Much Ado, Twelfth Night* and *Rape of Lucrece.*

bandogs, band-dogs, watchdogs, mastiffs; tied securely because they were vicious.
2H6: Bolingbroke, I, 4, 21.

bands, bonds, fetters, chains; troops, companies, armies.
TEMP: Prospero, Epilogue, 9.
RICH2: Queen, II, 2, 70.
A&C: Caesar, III, 12, 25.

bands of law, binding according to the law; legal assurance or guarantee.
HAM: King, I, 2, 24.

bane, poison; ruin.
MERV: Shylock, IV, 1, 46.
MEAS: Claudio, I, 2, 133.
CYM: Posthumus, V, 3, 58.

bankrout, bankrupt, from French, *banqueroute.*
RICH2: York, II, 1, 151.
HEN5: Grandpré, IV, 2, 43.
LLL: Longaville, I, 1, 27.

Bankside, district of Southwark, London; on south bank of the Thames, east of Charing Cross, extending for about half a mile west of London Bridge; old amphitheaters for bear and bull baiting once stood there; site of the Clink (prison), palace of the Bishop of Winchester and White Hart Inn; famous Bankside theaters, from west to east, were The SWAN (c1594), The HOPE (1614), The ROSE (c1587) and The GLOBE (1599).

banquet, light meal or supper ("snack") which usually included fruits, wines, sweets, etc.
TEMP: S.D., III, 3.

Banquo, Scottish nobleman, general; the witches prophesy that he shall be the ancestor of kings (traditionally, the Stuarts); suspects Macbeth of Duncan's murder; Macbeth has him killed; his ghost appears at the banquet and frightens the king into creating suspicion in the minds of the other thanes.
MACB: I, 3.

Baptista Minola, rich gentleman of Padua; father of Katherina and Bianca; determined to find a husband for his eldest daughter before consenting to Bianca's marriage.
SHREW: I, 1.

Barbary, area, not including Egypt, lying along the northern coast of Africa; short for a breed of horses known for their speed and endurance.
HAM: Osric, V, 2, 155.
RICH2: Richard, V, 5, 78.
2H4: Falstaff, II, 4, 107—
Barbary hen, Guinea hen.

Barbason, fiend, demon.
HEN5: Nym, II, 1, 57.
MWW: Ford, II, 2, 309.

barbed, armored, caparisoned with barbs (covering for the breast of a warhorse) or other protective metal coverings.
RICH2: North, III, 3, 117.
RICH3: Richard, I, 1, 10.

Bardolph, "arrant Malmsey-nose knave," Falstaff's dissolute drinking companion; works as a tapster at the Garter Inn (MWW); hanged with Nym for looting churches (HEN5).
1H4: II, 2; 2H4: II, 1; MWW, I, 1; HEN5: II, 1.

Bardolph, Lord, a leader of the northern rebellion; brings false report of Hotspur's victory at Shrewsbury; with Northumberland, defeated by Sheriff of Yorkshire. [Thomas, 5th Baron (1368-1408).]
2H4: I, 1.

barge
The barge she sat in, like a burnish'd throne,
Burn'd on the water. The poop was beaten gold;
Purple the sails, and so perfumed that
The winds were lovesick with them; the oars were silver
Which to the tune of flutes kept stroke, and made
The water which they beat to follow faster,
As amorous of their strokes.
A&C: Enobarbus, II, 2, 196.

Barkloughly, probably Harlech, a castle in Wales; point of arrival of Richard II after his Irish campaigns.
RICH2: Richard, III, 2, 1.

barm, head or froth on the ale that comes from the yeast and gives the drink life.
MND: Fairy, II, 1, 38.

barnacle, bernicle wild goose, bred in far northern Europe; old belief that creatures (tree geese) were either hatched from seashells which grew on submerged rotten wood, or developed from the fruit of the tree.
TEMP: Caliban, IV, 1, 249.

Barnardine, Bohemian, "dissolute prisoner"; Duke orders the Provost to have Barnardine executed instead of Claudio, but Barnardine refuses to die; eventually pardoned.
MEAS: IV, 3.

barne, child, bairn; northern dialect.
WINT: Shepherd, III, 3, 72.
ADO: Beatrice, III, 4, 49—pun.
ALL'sW: Clown, I, 3, 28.

Barrabas, thief freed by Pontius Pilate (Luke 23:18-19) or character in MARLOWE'S *The Jew of Malta.*
MERV: Shylock, IV, 1, 296.

barred your better wisdoms, excluded your opinions, advice or wishes; the Danes elected their king, he was not granted sovereignty by divine right or birth.
HAM: King, I, 2, 14.

barren sort, stupid, empty-headed group.
MND: Puck, III, 2, 13.

barricado, defense to repel an enemy; barricade.
WINT: Leontes, I, 2, 204.
ALL'sW: Helena, I, 1, 124.

Bartholomew boar-pig, roast pig was the favorite dish served at Bartholomew Fair in London, held on St. Bartholomew's Day (August 24).

2H4: Doll, II, 4, 250.

Basan (Bashan), reference to biblical bulls of the hills of Bashan (Psalms 68:15, 22:12-13, in Prayer Book version).

A&C: Antony, III, 13, 127.

base court, lower or exterior courtyard of a castle.

RICH2: Northumberland, III, 3, 176.

bases, pleated skirt attached to the doublet; mantle worn while on horseback, probably in two parts and hanging from the waist to the knee.

PER: Pericles, II, 1, 167.

Basilisco-like, Basilisco was the braggart, cowardly knight of *Soliman and Perseda,* a play of the period, probably by Thomas Kyd.

JOHN: Bastard, I, 1, 244.

basilisk, large, heavy brass cannon.

1H4: Lady, II, 3, 56.

HEN5: Queen, V, 2, 17.

basilisk. See COCKATRICE.

WINT: Polixenes, I, 2, 388.

RICH3: Anne, I, 2, 150.

2H6: King, III, 2, 52.

Basimecu, pun on *baise mon cul,* kiss my bottom; contemptuous term for a fawning Frenchman.

2H6: Cade, IV, 7, 31—refers to the Dauphin.

Basingstoke, town in Hampshire.

2H4: Gower, II, 1, 182.

Bassanio, attractive, clever, though irresponsible and self-centered, young friend of Antonio; borrows money from him to go to Belmont to woo Portia; chooses the leaden casket and wins her.

MERV: I, 1.

Basset, Lancastrian; quarrels with Vernon, the Yorkist.

1H6: III, 4.

Bassianus, Emperor Saturninus' brother; marries Lavinia; murdered by Tamora's sons.

TITUS: I, 1.

bass my trespass, in the deep tones of a bass voice, my sin was announced or proclaimed.

TEMP: Alonso, III, 3, 99.

basta, Italian, enough.

SHREW: Lucentio, I, 1, 203.

bastard, sweet Spanish wine, similar to muscatel.

1H4: Prince, II, 4, 31.

MEAS: Elbow, III, 2, 4.

Bastard. See FAULCONBRIDGE.

Bastard of Orleans. See ORLEANS.

bastard to the time

For he is but a bastard to the time

That doth not smack of observation—

JOHN: Bastard, I, 1, 207.

bastardy of Edward's children, the Bishop of Bath and Wells told Richard that Edward had contracted to wed Lady Eleanor Butler before he married Elizabeth Woodville and, as this was binding, his marriage to Elizabeth was not legal and the children were, therefore, bastards.

RICH3: Richard, III, 5, 75.

bastinado, beating; usually on the feet with a stock or cudgel; thrashing.

1H4: Falstaff, II, 4, 371.

JOHN: Bastard, II, 1, 463.

AYL: Touchstone, V, 1, 60.

bate, shorten, lessen; dispute, to flap the wings; permit, allow.

TEMP: Ariel, I, 2, 249.

LLL: King, I, 1, 6.

HAM: Hamlet, V, 2, 23.

Bates, English soldier at Agincourt.

HEN5: IV, 1.

batlet, wooden paddle, club or bat used in washing clothes.

AYL: Touchstone, II, 4, 47.

batten, become a glutton, grow fat upon, greedily consume.

HAM: Hamlet, III, 4, 67.

COR: Coriolanus, IV, 5, 35.

battery, legal right to sue for attack upon a person; modern assault and battery charge.

HAM: Hamlet, V, 1, 112.
COR: Menenius, V, 4, 22—assault.

bauble, plaything, toy; foolish, childish person.
OTH: Cassio, IV, 1, 139.

bauble, stick carried by a fool, with a doll's head as an ornament on the top.
TITUS: Aaron, V, 1, 79.
R&J: Mercutio, II, 4, 97.
ALL'SW: Clown, IV, 5, 32.

bavin, kindling, brushwood, faggots.
1H4: King, III, 2, 61.

bawcock, fine fellow, term of affection and friendship; from French *beau coq*.
TWN: Toby, III, 4, 125.
WINT: Leontes, I, 2, 121.
HEN5: Pistol, III, 2, 26.

Bawd, wife of Pandar, brothelkeeper of Mytilene; takes charge of Marina.
PER: IV, 2.

bawd, madam, brothel-keeper, procurer, go-between.
HEN5: Pistol, V, 1, 90.
TIMON: Apemantus, II, 1, 62.
HAM: Polonius, I, 3, 130.

Baynard's Castle, London home of the Duchess of York, Richard's mother.
RICH3: Richard, III, 5, 98.

bay trees, trees of ill omen.
RICH2: Welsh Captain, II, 4, 8 —HOLINSHED recounts that in 1399 all the bay trees withered; this was considered a sign of ill omen.

beadle, parish officer of low rank who punishes petty crimes.
LEAR: Lear, IV, 6, 164.
LLL: Berowne, III, 1, 177.
HEN5: King, IV, 1, 179.

beadsmen, aged pensioners who prayed for their benefactors, from the Middle English word bede.
RICH2: Scroop, III, 2, 116.
2GENT: Proteus, I, 1, 18.

beak, prow of a ship.
TEMP: Ariel, I, 2, 196.

beam, bar of a balance.
HAM: Laertes, IV, 5, 157—*turn the beam*, tip the scales.
T&C: Agamemnon, V, 5, 9.

bear, manipulate, engineer, manage, conduct, handle, make, execute.
HAM: King, IV, 3, 7.
TEMP: Ferdinand, I, 2, 425.

bears, nautical term, lies; stands.
SHREW: Petruchio, V, 1, 10.

bears up, nautical term, to put up more sail, to helm into the direction of the wind.
OTH: Senator, I, 3, 8.
TEMP: Stephano, III, 2, 3— here used to mean drink up.

beast
. . . The beast
With many heads butts me away.
COR: Coriolanus IV, 1, 1—the mob, or common herd seen as HYDRA (see).

(O God! a beast that wants discourse of reason
Would have mourned longer.)
HAM: Hamlet, I, 2, 150.

Let a beast be lord of beasts, and his crib shall stand at the king's mess.
HAM: Hamlet, V, 2, 88. See CRIB, MESS.

A very gentle beast, and of a good conscience.
MND: Theseus, V, 1, 231—refers to LION.

Beatrice, high-spirited, witty, sharp-tongued niece of Antonio, cousin of Hero; tricked into confessing her love for Benedick.
ADO: I, 1.

Beaufort, Edmund, continues feud of brother John with the Duke of York; made Regent of France, but loses it; killed by York at St. Albans. [1404-55; Earl of Dorset (1442); 2nd Duke of Somerset, appointed lord high constable of England (1450); supported Margaret.]
2H6: I, 1.

Beaufort, Edmund, 4th Duke of

Somerset; joins Warwick against Edward IV; sends Richmond (Henry IV) to Brittany for safety; captured at Tewkesbury; executed. [c1438-71, younger son of 2nd Duke; succeeded to title (1464) when Edward IV executed his brother.]

  3H6: IV, 1.

Beaufort, Henry, great-uncle of the King, Bishop of Winchester, Cardinal; Gloucester accuses him of having murdered Henry V; crowns Henry VI in Paris; partly responsible for disgrace of the Duchess of Gloucester, her husband's arrest on a false charge of treason and his murder. [c1377-1447, illegitimate son of John of Gaunt and Catherine Swynford, who later became John's third wife (legitimatized by their marriage, 1396); half brother of Henry IV; created Bishop of Winchester (1404), Chancellor (1403-05, 1413-17, 1424-26), Cardinal (1427).]

  1H6: I, 1.

Beaufort, John, 1st Duke of Somerset; tries to keep peace between Gloucester and Bishop; quarrels with Duke of York throughout the play. [1404-44, nephew of Cardinal and Thomas, grandfather of Henry VII; created 1st Duke (1443), Shakespeare sometimes confused him with his brother Edmund, 2nd Duke (see above).]

  1H6: II, 4.

Beaufort, Sir Thomas, Duke of Exeter; plays peacemaker, but foresees outbreak of the Wars of the Roses. [c1375-1427, younger brother of the Cardinal; admiral of the fleet (1403); commanded royal forces in Scroop rebellion (1405); created Duke of Exeter (1416) after death of Henry V; with Henry V in France, 1412-27.]

  HEN5: I, 2; 1H6: I, 1.

Beaumont, Francis (1584-1616). English poet, dramatist; friend of Ben JONSON; wrote The *Woman Hater* for the Children of Paul's (c1606); *The Knight of the Burning Pestle* (1607); with John FLETCHER, approximately 50 plays, including *Philaster* (printed, 1620), *The Coxcomb* (printed 1647).

beauty

. . . for beauty is a witch
Against whose charms faith melteth into blood.

  ADO: Claudio, II, 1, 186.

Beauty provoketh thieves sooner than gold.

  AYL: Rosalind, I, 3, 112.

Beauty is bought by judgment of the eye,
Not uttered by base sale of chapmen's tongues.
I am less proud to hear you tell my worth
Than you much willing to be counted wise
In spending your wit in praise of mine.

  LLL: Princess, II, 1, 15. See CHAPMEN.

Beauty itself doth of itself persuade
The eyes of men without an orator.

  LUCRECE: 29.

Beauty is but a vain and doubtful good

  PASSPIL: XIII, 1.

O, she doth teach the torches to burn bright!
It seems she hangs upon the cheek of night
Like a rich jewel in an Ethiop's ear—
Beauty too rich for use, for earth too dear!

  R&J: Romeo, I, 5, 46.

O, how much more doth beauty beauteous seem
By that sweet ornament which truth doth give!
The rose looks fair, but fairer we it deem
For that sweet odour which doth in it live.

  SONNET: LIV, 1.

. . . let her beauty be her wedding dower
SONNET: Duke, III, 1, 78.

beauty's legacy. See UNTHRIFTY
LOVELINESS.

beauty's rose, often a symbol of
the perfect beauty of youth.
SONNET: I, 2.
1H4: Northumberland, I, 3,
175.
HAM: Ophelia, III, 1, 160.

beauty's treasure
. . . treasure thou some place
With beauty's treasure ere it be
self-killed.
SONNET: VI, 3, 4. See TREAS-
URE.

beauty's use
How much more praise deserved
thy beauty's use.
SONNET: II, 9—use as short
form of "usury" or increase.

beauty's waste
But beauty's waste hath in the
world an end,
And kept unus'd, the user so de-
stroys it.
SONNET: IX, 11.

Beauty within itself should not
be wasted.
Fair flowers that are not gath'red
in their prime
Rot and consume themselves in
little time.
VENUS: 130.

beaver, face-guard or front part
of the helmet; visor that moves
and can be raised.
HAM: Horatio, I, 2, 230.
1H4: Vernon, IV, 1, 104.
HEN5: Grandpré, IV, 2, 44.

bedded, lying flat or prone.
HAM: Queen, III, 4, 121.

bedfellows. See MISERY.

Bedford, Duke of. See JOHN OF
LANCASTER.

Bedlam, Hospital of St. Mary of
Bethlehem in London for the
mentally ill.
LEAR: Edmund, I, 2, 148—
Tom o'Bedlam—mad lunatic
discharged from the hospital—
used throughout the play as

Edgar disguises himself as Tom
o'Bedlam.
HEN5: Pistol, V, 1, 19—used
as an adjective meaning mad,
lunatic.
JOHN: King John, II, 1, 183.

bed of Ware, very large (eleven
feet square) four-poster bed fa-
mous in the period, now in the
Victoria and Albert Museum in
London.
TWN: Toby, III, 2, 51.

bed-swerver, unfaithful to the
marriage bed; adulteress.
WINT: Leontes, II, 1, 93.

bedwork, armchair strategy, work
so easy it can be done from bed.
T&C: Ulysses, I, 3, 205.

bee
Where the bee sucks, there
suck I
In a cowslip's bell I lie;
There I couch when owls do
cry.
On the bat's back I do fly
After summer merrily.
Merrily, merrily shall I live now
Under the blossom that hangs
on the bough.
TEMP: Ariel's song, V, 1, 88.
See COUCH.

bee. See HUMBLEBEE.

been put on, given an opportunity
to prove himself, put to the test
or tried.
HAM: Fortinbras, V, 2, 408.

beetle, mallet used in ramming
paving stones; pile-driver.
2H4: Falstaff, I, 2, 255—*three-
man beetle,* rammer requiring
three men to lift it. See FILLOP.
SHREW: Petruchio, IV, 1, 160
—*beetle-headed,* stupid.

beetles over, overhangs, juts out
over.
HAM: Horatio, I, 4, 71.

beggar
Well, whiles I am a beggar, I
will rail
And say there is no sin but to be
rich;
And being rich, my virtue then
shall be

To say there is no vice but
beggary.
JOHN: Bastard, II, 1, 593.

beggar-fear, cringing, beggar-like,
groveling fear.
RICH2: Bolingbroke, I, 1, 189.

beggars
. . . Our basest beggars
Are in the poorest thing super-
fluous.
Allow not nature more than na-
ture needs,
Man's life is cheap as beast's.
LEAR: Lear, II, 4, 267.

beggars. See AMBITION.

beggar's dog, dogs were trained
to lead the blind as far back as
the 17th century.
TIMON: Senator, II, 1, 5.

begging but a beggar, Feste, a
beggar himself, has asked for a
Cressida and that lady became
a leper in Robert HENRYSON's
Testament of Cressid.
TwN: Clown, III, 1, 61.

beguile, delude, fool, deceive.
MACB: Lady Macbeth, I, 5, 64.
See TIME.

beg us, claim guardianship over
us as fools; Court of Wards (established by Henry VIII, discon-
tinued under Charles II) could
be petitioned to for the right of
custody of a minor or mentally
retarded individuals.
LLL: Costard, V, 2, 490.

behaviour
So, when this loose behaviour I
throw off
And pay the debt I never promised,
By how much better than my
word I am,
By so much shall I falsify men's
hopes
1H4: Prince, I, 2, 232. See
HOLIDAYS, REFORMATION.

behove, benefit, advantage, profit.
HAM: Clown, V, 1, 71.

Belarius, banished lord, who, under the assumed name of Morgan, brings up the two sons of
Cymbeline as his own; helps to

repel the Roman invasion; restores the princes to their father.
CYM: III, 3.

Belch, Sir Toby, Olivia's reckless,
riotous uncle; "in his own
coarse, swashbuckling manner
is witty, but he is not the cause
of wit in other men" (J. B.
Priestley); helps to trick Malvolio; marries Maria.
TwN: I, 3.

beldame, grandmother, hag, old
woman.
1H4: Hotspur, III, 1, 32.
JOHN: Hubert, IV, 2, 185.
MACB: Hecate, III, 5, 2.

belee'd, nautical metaphor meaning placed on the lee or to the
leeward side which was unfavorable; "take the wind out of his
sails."
OTH: Iago, I, 1, 30.

belike, no doubt, probably.
RICH2: Northumberland, III,
3, 30.
COFE: Courtesan, IV, 3, 91.
2H4: Prince, II, 2, 11.

bell
. . . The bell invites me.
Hear it not, Duncan, for it is a
knell
That summons thee to heaven,
or to hell.
MACB: Macbeth, II, 1, 62.

Silence that dreadful bell! It
frights the isle
From her propriety.
OTH: Othello, II, 3, 175. See
PROPRIETY.

bell, book, and candle
Bell, book, and candle shall not
drive me back
When gold and silver becks me
to come on.
JOHN: Bastard, III, 3, 12—used
in ceremonial of excommunication.

Belleforest, François de (1530-
83). French author, favorite of
Margaret of Navarre; *Histoires
Tragiques Extraites des Oeuvres
Italiennes de Bandello* (pub-
lished, 1580, in 7 vols.); Shake-

speare used either the French or English translations (of first four volumes) as source of *Hamlet, Rape of Lucrece, Romeo and Juliet, Much Ado* and *Twelfth Night.*

Bellenden (Ballantyne), John (c1533-1587). Scottish poet, scholar; at the suggestion of King James VI, he translated Hector BOECE's *Scotorum Historiae* (1527) from the Latin; probably used by HOLINSHED and in turn by Shakespeare for *Macbeth.*

bellman, town crier; also rang bell to toll condemned prisoner the night before his execution; watchman.
MACB: Lady Macbeth, II, 2, 3.

Bellona, Roman goddess of war; often represented as the wife or sister of Mars.
MACB: Ross, I, 2, 54.

Bel's priests, from tale of *Bel and the Dragon* in the Apocrypha; priests of Baal; refers to three-score and ten priests in Apocryphal book of Daniel overcome by Daniel.
ADO: Borachio, III, 3, 144.

Belzebub, prince of devils; able to possess "mad" people.
TwN: Clown, V, 1, 291.

bemoil, muddy, befoul, besmear with mud.
SHREW: Grumio, IV, 1, 78.

be naught awhile, North Country expression meaning "a mischief or evil befall you"; scram, clear out, beat it, make yourself scarce.
AYL: Oliver, I, 1, 39.

bench, raise to higher position or place in authority.
WINT: Leontes, I, 2, 314.

bend, direct one's thought or action, incline.
HAM: King, I, 2, 115.
TEMP: Ariel, IV, 1, 174.

bending, humble, submissive, bowing (under weight of theme); overhanging.

HEN5: Epilogue, 2.
LEAR: Gloucester, IV, 1, 74.

Benedick, gay young lord of Padua; confirmed bachelor who falls in love with Beatrice.
ADO: I, 1.

bent, prepared or ready; an archery term referring to a bent bow ready for shooting.
HAM: King, IV, 3, 47.
TwN: Duke, II, 4, 38—*hold the bent,* keep the tension, maintain the ardor or pitch.

ben venuto, Italian, welcome.
LLL: Holofernes, IV, 2, 164.
SHREW: Hortensio, I, 2, 282.

Benvolio, nephew of Montague, friend of Romeo and Mercutio; persuades Romeo to go to the Capulets' ball where he meets Juliet.
R&J: I, 1.

berattle, revile, malign, abuse, decry.
HAM: Rosencrantz, II, 2, 358.

Bergomask, wild rustic dance, named after the crude peasants of Bergame, a district of Venice, Italy, whose manners and speech were rough and coarse.
MND: Bottom, V, 1, 360.

Berkeley, Thomas, member of Richard's party; one of group sent to notify him of his deposition. [5th Baron of Berkeley Castle, Gloucestershire.]
RICH2: II, 3.

Bermoothes, the Bermudas, islands in the Atlantic Ocean; in Shakespeare's time the Bermudas were supposedly a place of storms and enchantments, inhabited by witches and devils; it is thought that he was probably familiar with several contemporary works describing a shipwreck there (1609) of Sir George Somers and a fleet of nine vessels carrying colonists.
TEMP: Ariel, I, 2, 229.

Bernardo, officer of the guard; with Marcellus, sees Ghost of Hamlet's father; they persuade

Horatio to witness what they have seen.
HAM: I, 1.

Berowne (Biron), gay, young, fun-loving lord attending the King of Navarre; takes an oath to study and avoid the company of women for three years; falls in love with Rosaline. [Armand (c1524-92) and Charles de Gontaut (1562-1602), Ducs de Biron, supported Henry of Navarre in his fight for the French throne (1589-93); Armand was marshal of France (1577), killed at Épernay; Charles was admiral of France (1592), marshal (1594), governor of Burgundy (1595); executed for plotting against France.]
LLL: I, 1.

berries. See GREW TOGETHER.

berard, (berrord), bearward, keeper of bears and monkeys; often kept trained apes.
ADO: Beatrice, II, 1, 43.
2H4: Falstaff, I, 2, 192—*berod*.
SHREW: Beggar (Sly), Induction, 2, 21.

Bertram, Count of Rossillion, handsome, self-centered son of the Countess; forced (by the King) to marry Helena, who has fallen in love with him; deserts her; in attempting to seduce Diana, he is tricked into accepting his wife; repents and returns.
ALL'sW: I, 1.

beseeming, appearance, disguise.
CYM: Posthumus, V, 4, 409.

beshrew, curse, damn, plague, wish ill luck to; beshrew me and beshrew my heart were common expletives or oaths of a mild nature.
HAM: Polonius, II, 1, 113.
OTH: Desdemona, III, 4, 150.
LLL: Katherine, V, 2, 46—*beshrow*.

besom, brush or broom made of twigs, from Isaiah, 14:23.
2H6: Cade, IV, 7, 34.

Besonian, base rascal; possibly

from Italian *bisogno* meaning needy man.
2H4: Pistol, V, 3, 117.
2H6: Suffolk, IV, 1, 134—*bezonians*.

besort, proper attendants, suitable servants or retinue.
OTH: Othello, I, 3, 239.

best arrow, Cupid's arrow with the golden head caused its victim to fall in love, the arrow with the leaden head caused hatred or aversion; the former is sharp, the latter blunt.
MND: Hermia, I, 1, 170.

bestow, shelter, house, lodge; employ, use; dispense with, dispose of.
HAM: Hamlet, II, 2, 547.
LEAR: Regan, II, 4, 292.

bestraught, distracted, distraught, mad.
SHREW: Beggar (Sly), Induction, 2, 27.

beteem, allow, permit.
HAM: Hamlet, I, 2, 141.
MND: Hermia, I, 1, 131.

betid, happened, occurred, befallen.
RICH2: Richard, V, 1, 41.
TEMP: Prospero, I, 2, 31.

betime, early; quickly, soon.
HAM: Ophelia, IV, 5, 49.
RICH2: Gaunt, II, 1, 36.
A&C: Antony, IV, 4, 20.

betrim, decorate or trim with wild flowers; perhaps kingcups, a kind of buttercup that grows by streams.
TEMP: Iris, IV, 1, 65.

better
Striving to better, oft we mar what's well.
LEAR: Albany, I, 4, 369.

better not to have had
. . . Better not to have had thee than thus to want thee.
WINT: Polixenes, IV, 2, 14.

Bevis, a legendary hero of a popular medieval romance (printed, 1500); Bevis of Hampton (Southampton) was known for his feats of daring.

HEN8: Norfolk, I, 1, 38.

Bevis, George, throws in his lot with Cade. [Bevis and John Holland were actors in Shakespeare's company.]
2H6: IV, 2.

bevy, circle, company, group; usually refers to ladies.
HAM: Hamlet, V, 2, 196.
HEN8: Guildford, I, 4, 4.

bewray, betray, reveal, expose, bare.
LEAR: Gloucester, II, 1, 109.
3H6: Exeter, I, 1, 211.
COR: Volumnia, V, 3, 95.

Bianca, Cassio's mistress; used by Iago in his plot to make Othello jealous.
OTH: III, 4.

Bianca, gentle younger sister of Kate (the Shrew); daughter of Baptista; marries Lucentio.
SHREW: I, 1.

bias, in bowling, the bowl was made with one side sticking out and this protrusion was called the bias; not being a perfect sphere the bowl took a curving or indirect course. See BOWLS.
RICH2: Queen, III, 4, 5.
TwN: Sebastian, V, 1, 267.
JOHN: Bastard, II, 1, 574.

bide the touch, put to, undergo or endure the test.
1H4: Archbishop, IV, 4, 10.

big, threatening, defiant, angry.
SHREW: Petruchio, III, 2, 230.

biggen, nightcap.
2H4: Prince, IV, 5, 27.

Bigot, Lord, one of the noblemen who switch allegiance and go over to the French side upon discovering the dead Arthur; later returned to join the English forces. [Robert (actually Roger), 3rd Earl of Norfolk d. 1220.]
JOHN: IV, 3.

bilberry, common name of whortleberry; blueberry.
MWW: Pistol, V, 3, 49.

bilbo, expertly tempered blade of a sword or rapier of Bilbao, Spain, that could be bent into a circle and would straighten out perfectly.
MWW: Falstaff, III, 5, 113.

bilboes. See MUTINES IN THE BILBOES.

bill, halberd; long pole with combination axe and spear head; carried as a badge of office by a constable; watchman's weapon.
ADO: Dogberry, III, 3, 44.
RICH2: Scroop, III, 2, 118.
R&J: Officer, I, 1, 80.

bill, written order.
JC: Brutus, V, 2, 1.

billet, cudgel, log of wood or heavy stick used as a weapon.
MEAS: Barnardine, IV, 3, 58.

Biondello, Lucentio's servant; aids in plot to win Bianca.
SHREW: I, 1.

birdbolt, relatively harmless blunt-headed arrow used for shooting small birds, which were usually eaten.
LLL: Berowne, IV, 3, 25.
TwN: Olivia, I, 5, 100.
ADO: Beatrice, I, 1, 41—*burbolt.*

birding, hawking with a sparrow hawk, used for small birds in the bush.
MWW: Page, III, 3, 247—*a-birding.*

birdlime, sticky substance used to ensnare birds; good for people who drop things and thieves (thus the expression "sticky fingers").
TEMP: Trinculo, IV, 1, 246.
OTH: Iago, II, 1, 127.

birds. See SINGING BIRDS.

Birnam, high hill near Dunkeld, 12 miles from Dunsinane.
MACB: Third Apparition, IV, 1, 93. See LION-METTLED, DUNSINANE.

Biron. See BEROWNE.

bisson rheum, blinding tears or mois---
---Player, II, 2, 529.

bite my thumb, insulting gesture of defiance.
R&J: Sampson, I, 1, 48.

Blackfriars, Dominican priory (built 1275) in the center of London, near St. Paul's; estate split (1538) into a number of holdings, one assigned to the Master of the Revels, Sir Thomas Cawarden; at his death (1559), given to Sir William More, who leased it to Richard Farrant (1576) for performances by Children of the Chapel; second Blackfriars Theater bought by James Burbage (1596); Richard Burbage formed a company (including Shakespeare) who performed there (1608); demolished (1655).
HEN8: King, II, 2, 139.

black hangings
Hung be the heaven with black, yield day to night!
1H6: Bedford, I, 1, 1—black curtains were used on stage when a tragedy was being played; here the set is draped in black in mourning for the death of Henry V.

Black Monday, Easter Monday; name given in remembrance of the day (1360) when Edward III stormed Paris and many soldiers died of the cold.
MERV: Launcelot, II, 5, 25.

Black Prince, son of Edward III; spent a good deal of time at war against the French.
ALL'SW: Clown, III, 5, 44.

blains, swellings, blisters, pustules, sores.
TIMON: Timon, IV, 1, 28.

Blanch of Spain, beautiful daughter of Alphonso IX, niece of King John; marriage to Dauphin brings about alliance between John and the French; truce broken when Pandulph excommunicates John. [Blanche of Castile (c1187-1252), daughter of Alphonso IX of Castile and Eleanor of England; acted as regent during minority of Louis IX.]
JOHN: II, 1.

blank, mark, white bull's-eye of target; to blanch or grow pale.
LEAR: Kent, I, 1, 161.
OTH: Desdemona, III, 4, 128.
HAM: Player Queen, III, 2, 230.

blank charters, carte blanche, a form of check payable to the king; i.e. the rich were often called upon to submit promissory notes to the king's treasury; the crown reserved the right to fill in the amount.
RICH2: Richard, I, 4, 48.

blasted, withered, blighted, destroyed.
A&C: Antony, III, 13, 105.
HAM: Ophelia, III, 1, 168—*blasted with ecstasy,* destroyed by madness.

blast in proof, explode or burst when tested, like a cannon which is found faulty during trial shooting.
HAM: King, IV, 7, 155.

blaze of riot
His rash fierce blaze of riot cannot last,
For violent fires soon burn out themselves;
Small showers last long, but sudden storms are short . . .
RICH2: Gaunt, II, 1, 33.

blazon, shield or coat of arms in heraldry; armorial bearings.
TWN: Olivia, I, 5, 312.
MWW: Quickly, V, 5, 68.
ADO: Pedro, II, 1, 307—heraldic term used to mean description.

blazoning pens, describe or write with a flourish; praises extolled in words, usually by a poet.
OTH: Cassio, II, 1, 63. See BEAUTY.

blench, wince, flinch; hunting term for the deer's dodging from nets.
HAM: Hamlet, II, 2, 625.
T&C: Troilus, I, 1, 28.

WINT: Leontes, I, 2, 333—
swerve from reason, deceive
himself.

blind
'Tis the times' plague when mad-
men lead the blind.
LEAR: Gloucester, IV, 1, 46.

blind boy, Cupid, son of Venus,
usually seen with a blindfold
over his eyes.
TEMP: Ceres, IV, 1, 90.

blind Cupid, sign hung in front
of a brothel.
LEAR: IV, 6, 141.

blindfold death, common image
of death as an eyeless skull;
made blind by death.
RICH2: Gaunt, I, 3, 224.

blind fool
Thou blind fool, Love, what
dost thou to mine eyes
That they behold, and see not
what they see?
They know what beauty is,
see where it lies,
Yet what the best is take the
worst to be.
SONNET: CXXXVII, 1.

blind love
Because Love is blind.
2GENT: Speed, II, 1, 76.

blindworm, small snakelike slow-
worm, believed to be venomous
but actually harmless, common
in the English countryside; leg-
less lizard, formerly called an
adder.
MND: 1Fairy, II, 2, 11.
MACB: 2Witch, IV, 1, 16. See
WITCHES' CURSE.

block, wooden mold used to
shape felt hats; design, style,
fashion.
ADO: Beatrice, I, 1, 77.
LEAR: Lear, IV, 6, 187.

blood, emotions, passions; con-
dition; natural reactions or im-
pulses; vigor.
COR: Menenius, I, 1, 163.
OTH: Brabantio, I, 3, 104.
MND: Theseus, I, 1, 68.

The veins unfilled, our blood is
cold, and then

We pout upon the morning, are
unapt
To give or to forgive; but when
we have stuffed
These pipes and these convey-
ances of our blood
With wine and feeding, we have
suppler souls
Than in our priest-like fasts.
COR: Menenius, V, 1, 51.

There is no sure foundation set
on blood,
No certain life achieved by
others' death.—
JOHN: King, IV, 2, 104.

It will have blood, they say;
blood will have blood.
Stones have been known to
move and trees to speak;
Augures and understood rela-
tions have
By maggot-pies and choughs
and rooks brought forth
The secret'st man of blood.
What is the night?
MACB: Macbeth, III, 4, 122.
See AUGURY, CHOUGH, ROOK.

But now the blood of twenty
thousand men
Did triumph in my face, and
they are fled,
And, till so much blood thither
come again,
Have I not reason to look pale
and dead?
All souls that will be safe, fly
from my side;
For time hath set a blot upon
my pride.
RICH2: Richard, III, 2, 76.

blood-boltered, hair matted, tangled with blood.
MACB: Macbeth, IV, 1, 123.

bloody child, apparition; symbolic of premature birth of
Macduff.
MACB: S.D., IV, 1, following
line 76.

bloody thought
. . . my bloody thoughs, with
violent pace,
Shall ne'er look back, ne'er ebb
to humble love,

Till that a capable and wide revenge
Swallow them up.
OTH: Othello, III, 3, 457.

blow, make foul, taint; swell, inflate or fill to bursting.
A&C: Enobarbus, IV, 6, 34.
TEMP: Ferdinand, III, 1, 63—
fly which laid its eggs on dead flesh and putrefied or decayed it.
TwN: Fabian, II, 5, 48.

blow. See ROOM.

blown, completely bloomed, blossomed, full-blown; rosy-cheeked like a fully opened, brilliant flower.
HAM: Ophelia, III, 1, 167.
RICH3: Queen, IV, 4, 10.
A&C: Cleopatra, III, 13, 39.

blowse, ruddy, fat-faced slut.
TITUS: Aaron, IV, 2, 72.

bluecaps, Scots; wore blue woolen bonnets or caps.
1H4: Falstaff, II, 4, 392.

blue-eyed, with bluish-black, dark rings or circles under or around the eyes.
TEMP: Prospero, I, 2, 269.

Blunt, Sir James, supporter of Richmond.
RICH3: V, 2.

Blunt, Sir John, put in charge of the rebel Colevile by Prince John. [d. 1418, son of Sir Walter, see below.]
2H4: IV, 3.

Blunt, Sir Walter, soldier, faithful supporter of the King; attempts to reconcile King and Hotspur; mistaken for the King, killed by Douglas at Shrewsbury. [d. 1403, with Edward (Black Prince) and John of Gaunt to Spain (1367); killed by Archibald, 4th Earl of Douglas.]
1H4: I, 3.

blushing, discontented sun, a reddish morning sun was believed to indicate an approaching storm.
RICH2: Bolingbroke, III, 3, 63.

Boaisteau, Pierre (d. 1566). French translator; associated with BELLEFOREST; his version of BANDELLO'S novella (pub., 1559) was the source of Arthur BROOKE'S poem from which Shakespeare took the story for *Romeo and Juliet.*

board, address, accost, greet; nautical term, close in on, attack, capture.
HAM: Polonius, II, 2, 170.
SHREW: Petruchio, I, 2, 94.
ADO: Beatrice, II, 1, 149.

boar of Thessaly, wild, ferocious boar unleased by Diana (Artemis) in revenge for neglecting to worship her; killed by Meleager, son of the king of Calydon.
A&C: Cleopatra, IV, 13, 2.
MND: Theseus, IV, 1, 129.

boats
Light boats sail swift, though greater hulks draw deep.
T&C: Agamemnon, II, 3, 277.

Boatswain, served on the vessel wrecked on the island where Prospero is living in exile.
TEMP: I, 1.

bob, taunt, bitter jest; beat, thrash; cheat, trick, swindle.
AYL: Jaques, II, 7, 55.
T&C: Helen, III, 1, 74.
OTH: Iago, V, 1, 16.

Boccaccio, Giovanni (1313-75). Italian poet, novelist, humanist; famous author of the *Decameron* (100 tales, 1348-53); Shakespeare indirectly indebted to him for themes or plots for *Merchant of Venice, All's Well, Cymbeline, Troilus and Cressida, Two Noble Kinsmen.*

bodies. See OURSELVES.

bodkin, dagger, stiletto; lady's jeweled hairpin; pin.
HAM: Hamlet, III, 1, 76.
LLL: Dumain, V, 2, 615.
WINT: Clown, III, 3, 87.

Boece (Boyce, Boethius, Bois), Hector (c1465-c1536). Scottish humanist and historian; first principal of the University of

Aberdeen (c1498); his *Scotorum Historiae* (17 vols., 1527), history of Scotland (in Latin), put into prose and translated by John BELLENDEN, used by HOLINSHED (and Shakespeare).

boggle, shy, waver, shift, change, equivocate.
ALL'sW: King, V, 3, 233.

boggler, shifty dissembler, waverer, opportunist.
A&C: Antony, III, 13, 110.

boisterous, violent, painfully rough.
AYL: Orlando, II, 3, 32.
JOHN: Arthur, IV, 1, 95.

Boleyn, Anne. See BULLEN, Anne.

bolin, early form of bowline, rope from weather-side of square sail to bow.
PER: 1Sailor, III, 1, 43.

Bolingbroke, Henry, became King Henry IV (1399-1413), first of the Lancastrian kings; nephew of York, cousin of Richard II and Aumerle; mistrusted by Richard, banished from England; returns with the support of all of Richard's enemies; frightens the king into acquiescing to his seemingly simple demands; by clever diplomatic maneuvers, causes Richard to abdicate in his favor; throughout the tragedy, Bolingbroke masks his ambition to be crowned king. [1367-1413, son of Gaunt, Duke of Lancaster; took name of Bolingbroke from castle or town in Lincolnshire where he was born; Earl of Derby, Duke of Hereford (1397) following marriage to Mary de Bohun, daughter of the Earl.]
RICH2: I, 1.

Bolingbroke, Roger, conjurer; calls up the spirit, Asmath, for the Duchess of Gloucester; discovered and hung.
2H6: I, 4.

bolster, lie down, sleep together.
OTH: Iago, III, 3, 399.

bolt, select carefully, sift, refine.

COR: Menenius, III, 1, 322.
WINT: Florizel, IV, 4, 375.
HEN5: King, II, 2, 137.

bolter, sieve; box, chest, or hutch in which flour is sifted.
1H4: Falstaff, III, 3, 81.
1H4: Prince, II, 4, 496—*bolting hutch.*

bolt of Cupid
Yet marked I where the bolt of Cupid fell.
It fell upon a little Western flower,
Before milk-white, now purple with love's wound,
And maidens call it love-in-idleness.
MND: Oberon, II, 1, 165. See LOVE-IN-IDLENESS.

bombard, big black leather jug, tankard or bottle for wine or liquor.
TEMP: Trinculo, II, 2, 23.
1H4: Prince, II, 4, 497.
HEN8: Chamberlain, V, 4, 85.

bombast, inexpensive cotton wadding or batting used for padding garments.
LLL: Princess, V, 2, 790.
1H4: Prince, II, 4, 359.

bombast circumstance, grandiloquent, bombastic tirade or diatribe.
OTH: Iago, I, 1, 13.

Bona, at Warwick's suggestion, she agrees to marry Edward IV; when she learns he has already married Lady Grey, she urges her brother-in-law, the King of France, to support Queen Margaret in her struggle against him.
3H6: III, 3.

bona roba, flashy whore, harlot.
2H4: Shallow, III, 2, 26.

bona terra, mala gens, Latin, good land, evil or bad people.
2H6: Say, IV, 7, 61.

bones, clappers of bone were held between the fingers and "music" was produced by shaking the hand; something like castanets.
MND: Bottom, IV, 1, 31.

bones, bobbins, used to make bone lace.
TwN: Duke, II, 4, 46.

book, manuscript volume of incantation and magic spells; his book of "tricks."
TEMP: Prospero, V, 1, 57.

book, agreement, written document, deed.
1H4: Mortimer, III, 1, 223.
2H4: Westmoreland, IV, 1, 91.

Book of Songs and Sonnets, famous collection of love poetry; *Tottel's Miscellany* (published, 1557).
MWW: Slender, I, 1, 206.

boor, peasant.
WINT: Clown, V, 2, 173.

boot, enrich, give in addition; profit, gain; help, aid.
RICH2: Richard, I, 1, 164.
A&C: Cleopatra, II, 5, 71.
WINT: Camillo, IV, 4, 651.

bootless, futile, in vain, to no avail.
TEMP: Miranda, I, 2, 35.
MND: Fairy, II, 1, 37.
LEAR: Edgar, V, 3, 294.

boots, booty, profit, plunder, spoils.
1H4: Gadshill, II, 1, 91.
HEN5: Exeter, I, 2, 194.

Borachio, follower of Don John; suggests to him the plot to discredit Hero; arrested by the Watch, cross-examined by Dogberry, confesses.
ADO: I, 3.

Bordeaux, Richard of, one of Richard II's titles.
RICH2: Exton, V, 6, 33.

bore, cheat, deceive, gull.
HEN8: Buckingham, I, 1, 128.

bore, caliber, gunnery term.
HAM: Horatio, IV, 6, 26.

bore arms, had a coat of arms, the symbol of a gentleman.
HAM: Clown, V, 1, 37.

Boreas, the north wind.
T&C: Nestor, I, 3, 38.

boresprit, bowsprit, large spar projecting out and forward from the stem of a ship or vessel.
TEMP: Ariel, I, 2, 200.

born
Be bloody, bold, and resolute; laugh to scorn
The power of man, for none of woman born
Shall harm Macbeth.
MACB: Second Apparition, IV, 1, 79.

borne in hand, victimized, deceived, deluded, imposed upon.
HAM: Voltimand, II, 2, 67.
MACB: Macbeth, III, 1, 81.

borrower
Neither a borrower nor a lender be.
HAM: Polonius, I, 3, 75.

bosky, with shrubs, wooded, bushy.
TEMP: Ceres, IV, 1, 81.

bosom of good old Abraham, heaven, eternal rest, paradise.
RICH2: Bolingbroke, IV, 1, 103—from Luke, 16:22.

bossed, embroidered, embossed.
SHREW: Gremio, II, 1, 355.

botch, contrive to fit together, patch, badly mended.
HAM: Gentleman, IV, 5, 10.
TwN: Clown, I, 5, 51—tailor.
COR: Menenius, II, 1, 98—bungler.

botchy core, inflamed, hard matter of a boil.
T&C: Thersites, II, 1, 7.

bots, intestinal worms, maggots or parasites that cause disease in horses.
1H4: 2Carrier, II, 1, 11.
SHREW: Biondello, III, 2, 56.

bottle, bundle, truss of hay.
MND: Bottom, IV, 1, 35.

bottle, wicker basket.
ADO: Benedick, I, 1, 259—probably means basket which held cat used as a mark in archery.

bottled, swollen, shaped like a bottle, big-bellied, unwholesomely fat.

RICH3: Queen Margaret, I, 3, 242.

bottom, skein or ball of thread; to bottom is to wind.
2GENT: Thurio, III, 2, 53.

Bottom, Nick, weaver of Athens; plays part of Pyramus and manages the show; "a realist who doesn't understand reality"— (Sen Gupta); at rehearsal, Puck gives him an ass's head and, using magic on Titania, gets her to fall in love with him.
MND: I, 2.

Bottom's dream
It shall be called "Bottom's dream," because it hath no bottom.
MND: Bottom, IV, 1, 215.

boughs. See BRANCHES.

Boult, Pandar's servant; takes Marina to a brothel in Mytilene; told by the Bawd to "crack the glass of her virginity."
PER: IV, 2.

bounce, Elizabethan equivalent of bang; sound of cannon.
JOHN: Bastard, II, 1, 462.
2H4: Shallow, III, 2, 304.

bound, limits of an area; circumscribed, confined.
TEMP: Gonzalo, II, 1, 152.
JC: Brutus, IV, 3, 221.

bound, leap, bounce, rebound.
RICH2: Duchess of Gloucester, I, 2, 58.
HEN5: King, V, 2, 146.

bounty
My bounty is as boundless as the sea,
My love as deep; the more I give to thee,
The more I have, for both are infinite.
R&J: Juliet, II, 2, 133.

Bourbon, Duke of, a leader of French forces; urges attack on the English ("bastard Normans"); captured. [John, uncle of Charles VI; died in England (1433).]
HEN5: III, 5.

Bourchier, Cardinal, weakly agrees to having the Duke of York and the queen mother brought out of sanctuary. [Thomas (c1404-86), Lancastrian; created Archbishop of Canterbury (1454), Cardinal (1473); arbiter at the peace of Amiens (1475).]
RICH3: III, 1.

bourn, border, boundary, domain, region, confine.
HAM: Hamlet, III, 1, 79.
TEMP: Gonzalo, II, 1, 152.
A&C: Cleopatra, I, 1, 16.

bourn, brook.
LEAR: Edgar, III, 6, 27.

bow
The bow is bent and drawn; make from the shaft.
LEAR: Lear, I, 1, 145.

bowls, popular Elizabethan game similar to modern bowling on the green.
RICH2: Lady, III, 4, 3.
SHREW: Petruchio, IV, 5, 24.
COR: Menenius, V, 2, 20— bowl, a wooden ball.

boy, refers to young boys who played all of the female parts; no women appeared on the English stage until after the Restoration (1660).
A&C: Cleopatra, V, 2, 220.
When that I was and a little tiny boy . . .
TwN: Clown, V, 1, 398—beginning of a song.

Boyet, lord, court usher attending the Princess; "pins the wenches on his sleeve"; tells the ladies that the Muscovite masquers are the King and his companions.
LLL: II, 1.

Brabantio, Venetian senator; heartbroken father of Desdemona; charges Othello with having stolen his daughter by magic; predicts she will deceive her husband as she has her father.
OTH: I, 1.

brabble, brawl, quarrel.
TwN: 1Officer, V, 1, 68.
JOHN: Dauphin, V, 2, 162.
TITUS: Aaron, II, 1, 62.

brace, defensive position or condition; ready for attack; armor.
OTH: 1Senator, I, 3, 24.

brach, bitch; hunting hound.
1H4: Hotspur, III, 1, 238.
LEAR: Fool, I, 4, 125.
SHREW: Lord, Induction, 1, 18.

braggart
. . . Who knows himself a braggart,
Let him fear this; for it will come to pass
That every braggart shall be found an ass.
ALL'sW: Parolles, IV, 3, 370.

braid, twisted in and out, probably deceitful, cunning.
ALL'sW: Diana, IV, 2, 73.

brain. See THOUGHTS.

brains
Whereon his brains still beating puts him thus
From fashion of himself.
HAM: King, III, 1, 182.

brake, thicket, thorn bush, underbrush.
MEAS: Escalus, II, 1, 39. See SIN.
VENUS: 237.
3H6: Sinklo, III, 1, 1.

Brakenbury, Sir Robert, lieutenant of the Tower; on a warrant from Richard, he surrenders the sleeping Clarence to the murderers.
RICH3: I, 1.

branches
. . . Superfluous branches
We lop away, that bearing boughs may live.
RICH2: Gardener, III, 4, 63

branchless, unadorned, "pruned" of honor, destitute, unprotected.
A&C: Antony, III, 4, 24.

Brandon. See SUFFOLK, Duke of.

brands, logs in the fireplace, burning wood, firebrands.

RICH2: Richard, V, 1, 46.
MND: Puck, V, 1, 382.

brave, admirable, fine, handsome, splendid.
TEMP: Miranda, I, 2, 6.
1H4: Hotspur, IV, 1, 7.
LEAR: Fool, III, 2, 80.

brave, defy, challenge, provoke, dare, insult, defiant threat.
OTH: Cassio, V, 2, 326.
JOHN: King, IV, 2, 243.
SHREW: Hortensio, III, 1, 15.

brave new world. See WORLD.

bravery, pretentious, ostentatious, overdramatic display, bravado.
HAM: Hamlet, V, 2, 79.
T&C: Troilus, IV, 4, 139.
OTH: Brabantio, I, 1, 100.

brawl, French dance (*branle*) popular in England during second half of the 16th century; resembled cotillion (quadrille).
LLL: Moth, III, 1, 10—probably refers to civil wars in France.

brawn, fat pig, boar, mass of flesh.
1H4: Prince, II, 4, 123.
2H4: Lord Bardolph, I, 1, 19.

brazed, hardened or plated with brass; made bold or impenetrable.
HAM: Hamlet, III, 4, 37.
RICH2: Bolingbroke, III, 3, 33
—*brazen*, made of bronze.

breach, breaking waves; surf.
TwN: Sebastian, II, 1, 24.

breach, break in the wall or fortification of a city during an assault by the enemy.
OTH: Othello, I, 3, 136.

breathing time, part of the day set aside for mild exercise.
HAM: Hamlet, V, 2, 181.

Brecknock, Brecon, South Wales.
RICH3: Buckingham, IV, 2, 124.

breeching, liable to be whipped or flogged.
SHREW: Bianca, III, 1, 18.

breed-bate, mischief-maker.
MWW: Quickly, I, 4, 12.

breeding
> . . . Much is breeding
> Which, like the courser's hair,
>   hath yet but life
> And not a serpent's poison.

A&C: Antony, I, 2, 199—refers to superstition that a horsehair put into water will change into a snake or worm.

breed of men
> This happy breed of men, this
>   little world,
> This precious stone set in the
>   silver sea,
> Which serves it in the office of
>   a wall,
> Or as a moat defensive to a
>   house,
> Against the envy of less happier
>   lands; . . .

Rich2: Gaunt, II, 1, 45. See SCEPTERED ISLE.

breese (brize), gadfly.
A&C: Scarus, III, 10, 14.
T&C: Nestor, I, 3, 48.

brevity
> . . . brevity is the soul of wit.

Ham: Polonius, II, 2, 89. See WIT.

Briareus, in Greek mythology, hundred-handed giant.
T&C: Man, I, 2, 30.

brief, memo, list, letter, short written account.
MND: Philostrate, V, 1, 42.
A&C: Cleopatra, V, 2, 138.

brief authority
> . . . But man, proud man,
> Drest in a little brief authority,
> Most ignorant of what he's most
>   assured
> (His glassy essence), like an
>   angry ape,
> Plays such fantastic tricks be-
>   fore high heaven
> As make the angels weep . . .

Meas: Isabella, II, 2, 117.

briers
> O, how full of briers is this
> working-day world!

AYL: Rosalind, I, 3, 12.

Bristow, Bristol (Bristol Castle) in Gloucestershire.

Rich2: Bolingbroke, II, 3, 164.

Britain, Breton.
Rich3: Richard, IV, 3, 40.

broach, break open, set going, let loose; to tap (a keg or cask of liquor); put on a spit, usually a sword's point.
Timon: Timon, II, 2, 186.
1H4: King, V, 1, 21.
Hen5: Chorus, V, 32.

broad, unfettered, free, unrestrained.
Ham: Polonius, III, 4, 2.

brock, badger; used with contempt in referring to a filthy person.
TwN: Toby, II, 5, 114.

broken, lacking teeth.
All'sW: Lafew, II, 3, 66.

broken his staff, white staff, symbol of court officials, was broken upon the resignation or death of their sovereign.
Rich2: Green, II, 2, 59.

broken music, part-music; music played by various instruments; concerted.
Hen5: King, V, 2, 265.
T&C: Pandarus, III, 1, 52.

broken with, communicated or traded information with; disclosed opinions to; originally to break one's mind with.
Hen8: Gardiner, V, 1, 47.

broker, middleman, agent, gobetween.
Ham: Polonius, I, 3, 127.
All'sW: Widow, III, 5, 74.
John: Bastard, II, 1, 568.

broking pawn, pawnbroker, who lent the king money.
Rich2: Northumberland, II, 1, 293.

brooch, a "jewel"; ornament, usually worn about the neck; gem; adorn.
Ham: Laertes, IV, 7, 94.
Rich: Richard, V, 5, 66.

brook, endure, tolerate, permit.
Rich2: Aumerle, III, 2, 2.
JC: Cassius, I, 2, 159.
Rich3: Richard, I, 1, 125.

brook

Smooth runs the water where the brook is deep . . .

TEMP: Iris, IV, 1, 66. See BROWN FURZE.

2H6: Suffolk, III, 1, 53.

Brooke (Broke), Arthur (d. 1563). English poet, translator; his version of BANDELLO'S story, from the French translation of BOAISTEAU and BELLEFOREST, *The Tragicall Historye of Romeus and Iulieit* (1562), probably the main source of Shakespeare's play, *Romeo and Juliet.*

broom, flowering shrub with yellow flowers.

TEMP: Iris, IV, 1, 66. See BROWN FURZE.

brothers

We few, we happy few, we band of brothers;

For he to-day that sheds his blood with me

Shall be my brother.

HEN5: King, IV, 3, 60.

brow

. . . this man's brow, like to a title leaf,

Foretells the nature of a tragic volume.

So looks the strond whereon the imperious flood

Hath left a witnessed usurpation.

2H4: Northumberland, I, 1, 60. See STROND.

brow of Egypt

One sees more devils than vast hell can hold:

That is the madman. The lover, all as frantic,

Sees Helen's beauty in a brow of Egypt.

MND: Theseus, V, 1, 9—gypsies were believed to be Egyptians; to a lover a gypsy was as beautiful as blond Helen of Troy.

brown furze, hardy, prickly, bushy shrub that grows in wastelands.

TEMP: Gonzalo, I, 1, 69. See LONG HEATH.

Brownist, adherent of the puritanical sect founded (c1580) by Robert Browne (c1550-c1633); early Congregationalist.

TwN: Andrew, III, 2, 34.

bruit, report, rumor.

3H6: Richard, IV, 7, 64.

TIMON: Timon, V, 1, 196.

1H6: Countess, III, 3, 68.

bruit, echo, reverberate, repeat.

HAM: King, I, 2, 127.

MACB: Macduff, V, 7, 22.

2H4: Morton, I, 1, 114.

Brutus, Decius, Roman general; one of the conspirators; brings Caesar to the Capitol by misinterpreting Calpurnia's dream. [Really Decimus Junius Brutus, surnamed Albinus (c84-43 BC), named by Caesar as one of his heirs; captured and put to death by Antony.]

JC: II, 1.

Brutus, Junius, tribune of the people; with Sicinius, incenses people against Coriolanus and succeeds in getting him banished on a charge of being a tyrant; when Coriolanus returns with the Volscians to attack Rome, they deny responsibility and plead with Menenius to stop him.

COR: I, 1.

Brutus, Marcus Junius, noble idealist; hero of the play; joins conspiracy against Caesar, not out of envy, but in the honest belief that it is for the good of the people. [Also Quintus Calpio Brutus (c85-42 BC); joined Pompey against Caesar (49); pardoned by Caesar after Pharsalia and made governor of Cisalpine Gaul; married to Portia, Cato's daughter; killed himself after his defeat at Philippi.] "He is not the hero-villain whose fall inspires awe, nor the eager hero who fully commands our sympathy."—(Spencer.) "Brutus has precisely the qualities which in every age have rendered the conscientious liberal ineffectual in public life."—(J. Palmer.)

JC: I, 1.

bubukles, carbuncles, large red swellings or pimples.
HEN5: Fluellen, III, 6, 108.

buck, dirty clothes.
2H6: Smith, the Weaver, IV, 2, 51.

buck-basket, basket for dirty clothes or soiled linen, which was soaked in alkaline lye, beaten and washed clean in running water, bleached and laid out or stretched in the sun to dry.
MWW: Mrs. Ford, III, 3, 4.

Buckingham, Edward Stafford, 3rd Duke of, "mirror of all courtesy," greatly admired by Commons; enemy of Wolsey who has him arrested; accused of threatening to murder Henry; found guilty and taken to be executed.
HEN8: I, 1.

Buckingham, Henry Stafford, 2nd Duke of, professed friend of Edward IV, but really supporter of Gloucester whom he succeeds in making king; when he hesitates at killing the Princes, Richard decides to get rid of him; attempting to join Richmond, he is captured and executed; his Ghost appears to Richard the night before the battle of Bosworth Field.
RICH3: I, 3.

Buckingham, Humphrey Stafford, 1st Duke of, uncovers Duchess of Gloucester's interest in magic and helps bring about disgrace and death of her husband; persuades the followers of Cade to disperse. [1402-60, in Paris at coronation of Henry VI (1431); lord high constable of England; created Duke (1444); killed at Northampton (1460) not at St. Albans (1455) as mentioned in 3H6: I, 1.]
2H6: I, 1.

buckler, to shield, defend; small shield with spikes protruding from the center.
SHREW: Petruchio, III, 2, 241.
ADO: Benedick, V, 2, 17.

1H6: Dauphin, I, 2, 95—fight in close combat.

Bucklersbury, street or district in London, off Cheapside, where herbs (simples) and perfumes were sold.
MWW: Falstaff, III, 3, 79.

buckram, coarse linen material stiffened with glue or gum.
1H4: Poins, I, 2, 201.
2H6: Cade, IV, 7, 28.

budget, bag, sack or pouch, usually of leather.
WINT: Autolycus, IV, 3, 20—tinkers were known by the pigskin bag they carried.

buffet, box, come to blows, strike, beat.
1H4: Hotspur, II, 3, 31.
HEN5: King, V, 2, 146.

buffets

I am one, my liege,
Whom the vile blows and buffets of the world
Have so incensed that I am reckless what
I do to spite the world.
MACB: 2Murderer, III, 1, 108.

bug, bugbear, imaginary bogey of fear or terror.
HAM: Hamlet, V, 2, 22.
WINT: Hermione, III, 2, 93.
SHREW: Petruchio, I, 2, 211.

bugle, tube-shaped, long, glass bead, usually black.
WINT: Autolycus, IV, 4, 224.
AYL: Rosalind, III, 5, 47.

bulk, projection from building; stall of shop; buttress of a church.
OTH: Iago, V, 1, 1.
COR: Brutus, II, 1, 226.

Bullcalf, one of men provided by Shallow for the King's service; although he protests he is a sick man, Falstaff presses him into service; bribes Bardolph and escapes.
2H4: III, 2.

Bullen, Anne, attracts attention of the King at Cardinal Wolsey's masque (GLOBE caught fire during this scene, June 16, 1613);

created Marchioness of Pembroke; beheaded for adultery;
attention concentrated on birth
of her daughter, Elizabeth.
[c1507-36, daughter of Sir
Thomas Bullen; married Henry
(1533), although not guilty of
all the crimes with which she
was charged, her complete innocence (or her involvement)
has never been clearly established.]
    HEN8: I, 4.

Bullingbrook, alternate spelling of
Bolingbroke giving, perhaps, an
indication of pronunciation.
    RICH2: See BOLINGBROKE.

bully rook, fine, gay fellow; 17th
century term "bully rock";
bully; term of endearment,
friendly attitude.
    MWW: Host, I, 3, 2.

bum-baily, bailiff; sheriff's officer
who made arrests (usually for
debt).
    TwN: Toby, III, 4, 194.

bums, posteriors, backsides.
    TIMON: Apemantus, I, 2, 237.

bung, pickpocket; synonymous
with cutpurse.
    2H4: Doll, II, 4, 138.

bunghole, the hole in a beer barrel.
    HAM: Hamlet, V, 1, 226.

burgonet, helmet, light casque or
steel cap.
    A&C: Cleopatra, I, 5, 24.
    2H6: Clifford, V, 1, 200.

Burgundy, Duke of, brings Henry
of England and Charles VI of
France together (HEN5); arranges the marriage of Henry
and Katherine; persuades the
French king to acknowledge
Henry as heir to the French
throne; ally (1H6) of the English (Duke of Bedford married
his sister), but, persuaded by
Joan that the English are only
"using" him, he switches his allegiance. [1396-1467, Philip the
Good, ruled 1419-67.]
    HEN5: V, 2: 1H6: II, 1.

Burgundy, Duke of, rival for
Cordelia's love until she is disinherited.
    LEAR: I, 1.

burnet, weed with a brown flower; fodder.
    HEN5: Burgundy, V, 2, 49.

burthen (burden), refrain of a
song.
    TEMP: Ariel, I, 2, 380.
    2GENT: Julia, I, 2, 85.
    AYL: Celia, III, 2, 261.

Burton Heath, identified as Bar-
ton-on-the-Heath, village 16
miles from Stratford; Joan Lambert, Shakespeare's aunt, lived
there.
    SHREW: Beggar (Sly): Induc-
    tion, 2, 19.

bush of thorns, believed that the
man in the moon carried a
bundle of sticks or faggots and
a lantern; he had been trans-
planted to the moon as punishment for gathering firewood on
a holy day.
    MND: Quince, III, 1, 60.

Bushy, Sir John, court favorite;
speaker of House of Commons
(1394); beheaded by Bolingbroke (1399).
    RICH2: I, 3.

buskin, high-heeled leather hunting boots; possibly a kind of
leather legging.
    MND: Titania, II, 1, 71.

busky, wooded, bushy, bulky.
    1H4: King, V, 1, 2.

butt, cask used for wine or ale;
contained 2 hogsheads.
    TEMP: Stephano, II, 2, 125.

buttery, storage room for liquors.
    SHREW: Lord, Induction, 1,
    102.
    TwN: Maria, I, 3, 74—buttery
    bar, ledge on half-door or hatch
    of buttery where tankards were
    set down; "bring your hand to
    the buttery bar" was a "come
    on," an invitation to flirt.

Butts, Doctor, Physician to the
King; discovers Cranmer kept
waiting outside the Council

Chamber by order of Bishop Gardiner and reports this to the King. [Sir William (d. 1545), favorite physician in ordinary to the King.]
HEN8: V, 2.

butt-shaft, blunt arrow used in target practice; often refers to Cupid's arrow.
R&J: Mercutio, II, 4, 16.
LLL: Armado, I, 2, 181.

"but yet"
I do not like "but yet." It does allay
The good precedence. Fie upon "but yet"!
"But yet" is as a jailer to bring forth
Some monstrous malefactor.
A&C: Cleopatra, II, 5, 50.

buxom, lively, brisk, sturdy.
HEN5: Pistol, III, 6, 28.

buzz buzz, expression of derision used when information or news announced is "old hat."
HAM: Hamlet, II, 2, 412.

buzzer, gossip, scandalmonger, one who whispers rumors.
HAM: King, IV, 5, 90.
RICH2: York, II, 1, 26.

by-and-by, immediately, soon, right away.
TEMP: Stephano, III, 2, 156.

by'r lakin, by Our Lady; lakin, short for ladykin or Blessed Virgin.
TEMP: Gonzalo, III, 3, 1.
MND: Snout, III, 1, 14.

by the card, exactly, precisely, to the point; from card marked by the thirty-two points of the mariner's compass.
HAM: Hamlet, V, 1, 149.

by the heels, imprisoned; put in the stocks.
2H4: Justice, I, 2, 141.

cabileros, cavaliers, gay gentlemen, gallants.
2H4: Shallow, V, 3, 62.
MWW: Host, II, 1, 201—*Cavaleiro Justice,* Sir Knight.

cacodemon, evil spirit, devil.
RICH3: Queen Margaret, I, 3, 144.

caddisses, short for caddis-ribbons, worsted tape or ribbons used for garters.
WINT: Servant, IV, 4, 208.
1H4: Prince, II, 4, 79—*caddis-garter.*

cade, barrel of 720 herrings.
2H6: Butcher, IV, 2, 35.

Cade, Jack, reckless rebel leader; claims to be Lord John Mortimer (a cousin of the Duke of York); marches with his mob, comprised mostly of Kentishmen, to London, after defeating the royal force at Seven Oaks; Buckingham and Clifford persuade his followers to desert him in Southwark; escapes, but is killed by Alexander Iden in his garden. [Probably an Irishman, living in Kent (d. 1450)]
2H6: IV, 2.

caduceus, wand of Mercury (Hermes); rod having serpents twined around it.
T&C: Thersites, II, 3, 14.

Cadwallader, last of the Welsh kings; ancestor of Queen Elizabeth.
HEN5: Pistol, V, 1, 29.

Caesar, Julius, dictator of the Roman Empire; conspiracy formed against him; murdered in the Senate (March 15, 44 BC); portrayed as a weak character. [Gaius Julius Caesar (100-44 BC), famous general, statesman and writer; formed first triumvirate with Pompey and Crassus (60), made consul (59) invaded Britain (55), crossed the Rubicon (49), became dictator (49), defeated Pompey (48), reformed the calendar (46), refused the crown (Feb. 15, 44); author of *Commentaries,* history of first seven years of the Gallic Wars.]
JC: I, 2.

Caesar, Octavius (Emperor Augustus), became one of the triumvirs (second triumvirate, 43 BC) after murder of his greatuncle; with Antony (JC) defeats Brutus and Cassius at Philippi; cold-blooded ambitious man (A&C) who will sacrifice his sister to Antony to gain what he wants; gets rid of Lepidus and Antony (other triumvirs); defeats Antony at Actium (31), invades Egypt, left sole master of the Roman Empire. [Gaius Octavius (63 BC-AD 14), son of Julius Caesar's niece; first Emperor of Rome (Augustus, 27).]
JC: IV, 1; A&C: I, 4.

Caesar
Imperious Caesar, dead and turned to clay,
Might stop a hole to keep the wind away.
O, that that earth which kept the world in awe
Should patch a wall t' expel the winter's flaw!

HAM: Hamlet, V, 1, 236. See FLAW.

Caesarion, son of Cleopatra and Julius Caesar; Octavius was Caesar's adopted son.
A&C: Caesar, III, 6, 6.

Caesar's ambition
He hath brought many captives home to Rome,
Whose ransoms did the general coffers fill.
Did this in Caesar seem ambitious?
When that the poor have cried, Caesar hath wept;
Ambition should be made of sterner stuff.
JC: Antony, III, 2, 94.

cage, local or parish lock-up or jail.
2H6: Butcher, IV, 2, 56.

Cain-coloured, yellowish-red; Cain was usually depicted in tapestries as having had a light yellow or yellowish-red beard.
MWW: Simple, I, 4, 23.

Caithness, Scottish nobleman; supports Malcolm against Macbeth.
MACB: V, 2.

caitiff, wretch, miserable or wicked person, coward, slave.
LEAR: Lear, III, 2, 55.
RICH2: Duchess of Gloucester, I, 2, 53.
OTH: Cassio, IV, 1, 109.

Caius, Doctor, French physician in love with Anne Page; supported by her mother in his suit; thwarted by Fenton and the Host.
MWW: I, 4.

Caius Lucius, ambassador, general of the Roman army invading Britain; takes Imogen, disguised as a boy, into his service; Romans are defeated by the British; captured, later released by Cymbeline.
CYM: III, 1.

cake is dough, plans fall flat, fail.
SHREW: Gremio, I, 1, 110.

cakes and ale
Dost thou think, because thou art virtuous, there shall be no more cakes and ale?
TwN: Toby, II, 3, 123.

Calais (Callice), town in northeastern France; an English outpost.
RICH2: Mowbray, I, 1, 126.

calamity
. . . there is no true cuckold but calamity . . .
TwN: Clown, I, 5, 56—calamity here is a personification of misfortune. See CUCKOLD.

Calchas, Trojan priest, seer who joined the Greeks; Cressida's father; attempts to exchange the Trojan prisoner Antenor for his daughter, who is still in Troy; does not object to Diomedes' seduction of Cressida.
T&C: III, 3.

calendar
A calendar, a calendar! Look in the almanac. Find out moonshine, find out moonshine!
MND: Bottom, III, 1, 54.

Caliban, deformed, semihuman slave; son of the witch, Sycorax; found by Prospero on the lonely island to which he drifts after expulsion from Milan; Prospero teaches him to speak but cannot civilize him; Caliban (with Stephano and Trinculo) fails in his plot to kill Prospero and make Stephano ruler of the island.
TEMP: I, 2.

Calipolis, wife in George Peele's *Battle of Alcazar.*
2H4: Pistol, II, 4, 193.

caliver, light musket or harquebus; infantry weapon.
1H4: Falstaff, IV, 2, 21.
2H4: Falstaff, III, 2, 290.

call, decoy; birds were used as traps.
JOHN: Pandulph, III, 4, 174.

callet, whore, lewd woman, female vagabond, slut.
OTH: Emilia, IV, 2, 121.

WINT: Leontes, II, 3, 90—*cal-lat.*

2H6: Queen, I, 3, 86—*callot.*

Calphurnia (Calpurnia), wife of Julius Caesar; frightened by dreams, she begs him not to go to the senate, but is defeated in argument by Decius. [Married, 59 BC.]

JC: I, 2.

calumny, scandal, vilification, slander.

HAM: Hamlet, III, 1, 140—*be thou as chaste as ice, as pure as snow, thou shalt not escape calumny.*

No might nor greatness in mortality
Can censure scape. Back-wounding calumny
The whitest virtue strikes. What king so strong
Can tie the gall up in the slanderous tongue?

MEAS: Duke, III, 2, 196.

calves' guts, violin strings.

CYM: Cloten, II, 3, 34.

Cambridge, Richard, Earl of, traitor; with Scroop and Grey, plans murder of Henry at Southampton; discovered by King and executed. [c1374-1415, 2nd son of 1st Duke of York (Edmund of Langley in *Richard II*); married Anne Mortimer, whose brother Edmund he attempts to make king; son is York (HEN6); grandsons, Edward IV and Richard III.]

HEN5: II, 2.

camel
. . . "as hard to come as for a camel
To thread the postern of a small needle's eye."

RICH2: Richard, V, 5, 16 (Matthew, 19:24). See POSTERN(

Camillo, Lord of Sicilia, trusted adviser of Leontes, who asks him to poison Polixenes; with his intended victim, escapes to Bohemia; 16 years later, Polixenes, with the help of Camillo, discovers that his son Florizel is in love with Perdita, a shepherd's daughter; ordered to renounce them, Camillo helps the lovers escape to Sicilia.

WINT: I, 1.

camomile, small creeper with flower resembling the daisy; heavily scented; medicinal properties used as antispasmodic.

1H4: Falstaff, II, 4, 441.

Campeius, Cardinal, legate commissioned (with Wolsey) by the Pope to consider the divorce of Katherine of Aragon from the King. [1472-1539; made Bishop of Salisbury (1524-34).]

HEN8: II, 2.

canakin, little can or mug.

OTH: Iago, II, 3, 71.

canary, sweet, rather light, wine from the Canary Islands.

TwN: Toby, I, 3, 85.

2H4: Hostess, II, 4, 29.

MWW: Host, III, 2, 89.

canary, lively dance believed to have been originated in the Spanish Canary Islands (Fortunate Isles).

LLL: Moth, III, 1, 12.

ALL'sW: Lafew, II, 1, 77.

MWW: Quickly, II, 2, 61—quandary, state of excitement.

Cancer, fourth sign of the Zodiac; the sun enters the summer solstice on June 21st and the hot weather begins.

T&C: Ulysses, II, 3, 206.

candied, honeyed with hypocrisy, smooth-tongued, wheedling words from sugared lips; "soft-soap."

HAM: Hamlet, III, 2, 65.

candied, sugared, hardened sweet.

TEMP: Antonio, II, 1, 279. See CONSCIENCE.

TIMON: Apemantus, IV, 3, 226—frozen.

candle
How far that little candle throws his beams!

So shines a good deed in a naughty world.
MerV: Portia, V, 1, 90.

candle-waster, one who stays up late, either to study (bookworm) or to enjoy life (reveler); moral philosopher.
ADO: Leonato, V, 1, 18.

Candy, Candia, now known as Crete.
TwN: 1Officer, V, 1, 64.

Canidius, lieutenant-general to Antony; agrees with Enobarbus that Antony should fight on the land instead of on the sea at Actium; when Antony's defeat seems certain, switches his allegiance to Caesar.
A&C: III, 7.

canker, maggot, worm, caterpillar; ulcer, destructive spreading cancer. See BEAUTY'S ROSE.
TEMP: Prospero, I, 2, 415.
HAM: Laertes, I, 3, 39.
MND: Titania, II, 2, 3.

canker, wild rose or dog rose; contrasted with the beautiful, cultivated flower; destructive weed.
MND: Hermia, III, 2, 282—canker-blossom.
ADO: John, I, 3, 28.
1H4: Hotspur, I, 3, 176.

canon, law, rule, usually divine or church law.
HAM: Hamlet, I, 2, 132. See FLESH.

canopy, covering, blanket; first used by Shakespeare in relation to air, firmament or sky; an actual roof over the stage was painted with stars, planets and the signs of the Zodiac.
HAM: Hamlet, II, 2, 312.
COR: Coriolanus, IV, 5, 41.

Canterbury, Archbishop of, sets the scene for the appearance of a "new" reformed Henry; urges the King to assert his claim to the French crown, providing the arguments to support the claim, and promising the assistance of the Church in the campaign. [Henry Chichele (Chicheley), c1362-1443; created Archbishop (1414); founded All Souls', Oxford (1437).]
HEN5: I, 1.

cantle, part, segment, section, slice.
A&C: Scarus, III, 10, 6.
1H4: Hotspur, III, 1, 100.

canzonet, from the Italian, *canzonetta,* short song, vocal piece, usually light and gay.
LLL: Holofernes, II, 2, 124.

capable, responsive to feeling and emotion, impressionable, susceptible.
HAM: Hamlet, III, 4, 127.

cap-a-pe, head to toe, head to foot.
HAM: Horatio, I, 2, 200.
WINT: Autolycus, IV, 4, 762.

caparison, dress, outfit, deck out.
AYL: Rosalind, III, 2, 205.
RICH3: Richard, V, 3, 290.

caparison, trapping of a horse; long saddlecloth used for special occasions.
COR: Lartius, I, 9, 12.

caper, leap or jump into the air; low prickly shrub whose greenish flower buds are pickled and used in sauces and as a condiment for mutton.
TwN: Andrew, I, 3, 128.

Caphis, servant; sent by his master, a senator, to ask Timon for settlement of a debt, which, of course, he cannot pay.
TIMON: II, 1.

capital, punishable by death; fatal, deadly.
HAM: Laertes, IV, 7, 7.
COR: Volumnia, V, 3, 104.

Capitol, Temple of Jupiter on Capitoline Hill, Rome.
COR: 1Citizen, I, 1, 49.

capon, love letter; probably from French *poulet* which means both chicken and *billet-doux.*
LLL: Princess, IV, 1, 56.

caprichio (capriccio), caprice, whim, notion.
ALL'sW: Parolles, II, 3, 310.

cap'ring, capering, dancing or skipping about with joy.
TEMP: Boatswain, V, 1, 238.

Capucius, ambassador from the Emperor Charles V to the Queen; delivers message to dying Katherine from Henry and one from her to the king.
HEN8: IV, 2.

Capulet, head of the family; father of Juliet; ignorant of his daughter's secret marriage to Romeo, he insists she marry Paris immediately, thereby hastening the ensuing tragedy.
R&J: I, 1.

Capulet, Lady, supports her husband (above) in the proposed marriage of Juliet to Paris.
R&J: I, 1.

car, chariot, usually of Helios, the Greek sun god.
SONNET: VII, 9.
MND: Bottom, I, 2, 37.

carack, very large merchant ship, used by Portuguese and Spanish to carry valuable cargo; also used in war as a galleon; also spelled careck, carrack, carrect.
OTH: Iago, I, 2, 50.

carbonado, slice, slash; referring to meat scored for broiling or cooking.
LEAR: Kent, II, 2, 41.
COR: 1Servingman, IV, 5, 198.
WINT: Autolycus, IV, 4, 268.

carbuncles, brilliant, shining red stones, possibly rubies.
HAM: Hamlet, II, 2, 485.
A&C: Antony, IV, 8, 28.
COR: Lartius, I, 4, 55.

carcanet, collar or necklace made of gold, sometimes set with jewels.
COFE: Antipholus E., III, 1, 4.
SONNET: LII, 8.

card, compass; card on which 32 points of compass were marked; geographical chart used in navigation.
MACB: 1Witch, I, 3, 17. See BY THE CARD.

cardecue, small French coin, *quart d'écu,* worth about 25 cents.
ALL'SW: Parolles, IV, 3, 311.

carded, diluted, debased, adulterated; usually used by Elizabethans in referring to mixing drinks.
1H4: King, III, 2, 62.

card-maker, producer of cards for combing wool.
SHREW: Beggar (Sly), Induction, 2, 20.

card or calendar of gentry, the very model of the perfect gentleman; guide to courtly manners.
HAM: Osric, V, 2, 114.

carduus benedictus, Latin, blessed thistle, medicinal herb, used as a cure for everything.
ADO: Margaret, III, 4, 73.

care
Care is no cure, but rather corrosive,
For things that are not to be remedied.
1H6: Pucelle, III, 3, 3.
I am sure care's an enemy to life.
TWN: Toby, I, 3, 2.

career, charge, headlong gallop, course of action, bout.
RICH2: Duchess of Gloucester, I, 2, 49.
WINT: Leontes, I, 2, 286.
LLL: Boyet, V, 2, 482. See MANAGE.

cares
Your cares set up do not pluck my cares down.
My care is loss of care, by old care done;
Your care is gain of care, by new care won.
The cares I give I have, though given away;
They tend the crown, yet still with me they stay.
RICH2: Richard, IV, 1, 195.

caret, Latin for wanting, lacking, missing.
LLL: Holofernes, II, 2, 127.
MWW: Evans, IV, 1, 55.

care-tuned, tuned in a sad or minor key; sorrow-telling.
RICH2: Scroop, III, 2, 92.

carl, churl, peasant.
CYM: Iachimo, V, 2, 4.
AYL: Silvius, III, 5, 108—
carlot.

Carlisle, Bishop of, loyal supporter of the King; lands in Wales after the King's disastrous Irish expedition to offer assistance; announces death of Mowbray; with the King when he surrenders to Bolingbroke at Flint Castle; arrested for treason when he protests Bolingbroke's ascendancy; foretells Wars of the Roses; involved in plot to overthrow Henry IV; forced to retire to a monastery. [Thomas Merke (d. 1409), Bishop of Carlisle (1397).]
RICH2: III, 2.

carpet, Oriental rugs or carpets were used as tablecloths or covers, not on the floor.
SHREW: Grumio, IV, 1, 52.

carpet-monger, carpet-knight, one who fought at home instead of on the field of battle; armchair general.
ADO: Benedick, V, 2, 33.

carriage, significance or meaning of, import; gun carrier, the wheeled frame that held the cannon.
HAM: Horatio, I, 1, 94.
HAM: Osric, V, 2, 158.
JOHN: Salisbury, V, 7, 90.

carrion, contemptuous expression for a living person being like a piece of rotten flesh; bawd or prostitute.
MWW: Mrs. Ford, III, 3, 205.
R&J: Capulet, III, 5, 157.

carry coals, do anything base or degrading; capable of thievery and cowardice.
HEN5: Boy, III, 2, 50.

cart, driven in an open cart through the streets and subjected to public ridicule; common punishment for "difficult" or loose women.
SHREW: Gremio, I, 1, 55.

carve, cut one's food; select, choose; make amorous or affected gestures with the hand.
HAM: Laertes, I, 3, 20.
RICH2: York, II, 3, 144.
MWW: Falstaff, I, 3, 49.

Casca, conspirator; first to stab Caesar, then disappears from the play. [Publius Servilius Casca, tribune, fought at Philippi.]
JC: I, 2.

case, condition, state; mask, cover, encase; skin, flay; set of pistols.
TEMP: Trinculo, III, 2, 29.
1H4: Gadshill, II, 2, 55.
HEN5: Nym, III, 2, 5.

cashier, dismiss, fire, turn out; rob, clean out (pickpocket).
OTH: Iago, I, 1, 48.
MWW: Bardolph, I, 1, 183.

casque, helmet, headpiece.
RICH2: Gaunt, I, 3, 81.
COR: Aufidius, IV, 7, 43.
HEN5: Prologue, 13.

Cassandra, prophetess; daughter of King Priam and Queen Hecuba of Troy; in Greek legend, given gift of prophecy by Apollo, but when she rejected him, he cursed her and warned that though her prophecies be true, she would not be believed; foretells the destruction of Troy, and death of her brother Hector; after the Trojan War, made a slave by Agamemnon; killed by Clytemnestra.
T&C: II, 2.

Cassibelan, Cassivellaunus, leader of Britain's resistance to Julius Caesar's second invasion (54 BC).
CYM: Lucius, III, 1, 5.

Cassio, Florentine; handsome, young lieutenant; used by Iago in his plot to make Othello jealous.
OTH: I, 2.

Cassius, Roman general and politician involved in Caesar's assassination; defeated by Antony at Philippi (42 BC), kills himself. [Gaius Cassius Longinus supported Pompey against Caesar in Civil War; pardoned after Pharsalia (48); made Praetor (44); sent to Syria, which he plundered before joining Brutus at Sardis.] See ENVY.
  JC: I, 2.

cast, thrown up or back, spewed forth; discharged, dismissed, ousted; reckoned, totaled; tint, tinge.
  TEMP: Antonio, II, 1, 251.
  OTH: Iago, I, 1, 150.
  2H4: Shallow, V, 1, 21.
  HAM: Hamlet, III, 1, 85.

cast
  . . . I have set my life upon a cast
  And I will stand the hazard of the die.
  RICH3: Richard, V, 4, 9. See HAZARD.

Castiliano vulgo, of doubtful Spanish origin; perhaps Castilians were noted for politeness; possibly keep a straight face.
  TwN: Toby, I, 3, 45—Sir Toby was probably trying to be impressive in being vague.

cat, domesticated animal; allusion is to the expression that a drink of good liquor will make a person talk or will even loosen the tongue of a cat.
  TEMP: Stephano, II, 2, 87.

cataplasm, poultice or plaster.
  HAM: Laertes, IV, 7, 144.

catastrophe, bottom, posterior, rump; conclusion, end, denouement.
  2H4: Falstaff, II, 1, 66.
  LLL: Armado, IV, 1, 78.

Catayan (Cataian) native of Cathay (China); reputedly shrewd and cunning, therefore, trickster or sharp dealer.
  TwN: Toby, II, 3, 80.
  MWW: Page, II, 1, 148.

catch, song for three or more unaccompanied voices, with continuous melody taken up by each voice in turn; a round.
  TEMP: Caliban, III, 2, 126.
  TwN: Toby, II, 3, 18.

catch a wrench, accidentally twist out of joint or shape; slip up.
  TIMON: Steward, II, 2, 218.

cater-cousins, close friends.
  MERV: Gobbo, II, 2, 139.

caterpillars, parasites (from "pillage"); flatterers of the king for their own profit.
  RICH2: Bolingbroke, II, 3, 166.
  1H4: Falstaff, II, 2, 88.
  2H6: Messenger, IV, 4, 37.

cates, delicacies, dainty tidbits.
  1H4: Hotspur, III, 1, 163.
  COFE: Antipholus E., III, 1, 28.
  SHREW: Petruchio, II, 1, 190.

Catesby, Sir William, loyal follower of Richard (and Buckingham); discovers Hastings is loyal to the young Prince of Wales. [Made Chancellor of the Exchequer for life by Richard, d. 1485.]
  RICH3: I, 3.

Catherine of Aragon. See KATHERINE.

Catherine of Valois. See KATHERINE.

catling, catgut, string of an instrument.
  T&C: Thersites, III, 3, 306.

cat-o'-mountain, mountain lion, lynx, catamount; wild man.
  TEMP: Prospero, I, 1, 262.
  MWW: Falstaff, II, 2, 27.

Cato, the Censor, noted for views on ethics and austerity.
  COR: Lartius, I, 4, 57.

Cato, the Younger, son of Marcus Cato, friend of Brutus and Cassius; killed at Philippi. [Marcus Porcius Cato (95-46 BC), Roman patriot, stoic philosopher; actually great grandson of Cato the Elder (234-149 BC); supported Cicero against Catiline and Pompey against Caesar

(49); killed himself when he heard that Caesar had been victorious at Thapsus.]
JC: V, 3.

Caucasus, mountain range of Russia.
RICH2: Bolingbroke, I, 3, 295.

caudle, warm, thin drink, usually with spiced, sweetened gruel and ale or wine; used for heartburn and as comfort to children and invalids.
LLL: Berowne, IV, 3, 174.
TIMON: Apemantus, IV, 3, 226.
2H6: Cade, IV, 7, 95—*hempen caudle,* halter of hangman's rope.

cautel, treachery, deceit, trickery.
HAM: Laertes, I, 3, 15.
COR: Coriolanus, IV, 1, 33.
JC: Brutus, II, 1, 129.

cavalery, gallant, gentleman, cavalier.
MND: Bottom, IV, 1, 24—misuse of *cavaleiro* or *caballero.*

caveto, from Latin, *caveo,* meaning caution, beware, take care.
HEN5: Pistol, II, 3, 55.

caviary, caviar; roe of the sturgeon; Russian delicacy enjoyed by the gourmet of the period.
HAM: Hamlet, II, 2, 458.

Caxton, William (c1422-91). First English printer; first book he printed was his own translation from the French of *The Recuyell of the Historyes of Troye* (1475), used by Shakespeare for the Grecian camp-scenes in *Troilus and Cressida.*

Celia, cousin, close friend of Rosalind; daughter of Duke Frederick; flees with Rosalind to the Forest of Arden; paired off with a repentant Oliver.
AYL: I, 2.

censer, container for burning incense; perfuming pan having an ornamental lid.
2H4: Doll, V, 3, 21.
SHREW: Petruchio, IV, 2, 91.

censure, opinion, judgment, belief; evaluate, judge, in terms of judicial sentence.
HAM: Polonius, I, 3, 69.
OTH: Iago, IV, 1, 281.
JOHN: Citizen, II, 1, 328.

Centaurs' feast, wedding party of Hippodamia and Pirithous; Centaurs, creatures who were half-man, half-horse, attempted to carry off the bride and a battle ensued between the Centaurs and the Lapithae; from OVID's *Metamorphoses.*
MND: Theseus, V, 1, 44.
TITUS: V, 2, 204.

centre, the earth, center of the universe in Ptolemaic terms; also, soul as innermost part of the body or earth.
HAM: Polonius, II, 2, 159.
WINT: Leontes, II, 1, 102.

century, Roman company or division of 100 men.
COR: Lartius, I, 7, 3.
LEAR: Cordelia, IV, 4, 6.

Cerberus, in Greek mythology, watchdog of Hades; described by Hesiod as fifty-headed and by later writers as three-headed; Hercules brought Cerberus up from the gates of hell as his eleventh feat.
LLL: Holofernes, V, 2, 593.
2H4: Pistol, II, 4, 182 (mistaken use).
T&C: Thersites, II, 1, 37.

cere, shroud; grave-cloth dipped in wax used in embalming; shrivel.
CYM: Posthumus, I, 1, 116.
HAM: Hamlet, I, 4, 48—*cerements.*
MERV: Morocco, II, 7, 51—*cerecloth.*

ceremony
. . . What infinite heart's-ease
Must kings neglect that private men enjoy!
And what have kings that privates have not too,
Save ceremony, save general ceremony?
HEN5: King, IV, 1, 253.

Ceres, spirit invited by Prospero to the masque celebrating the engagement of his daughter, Miranda, to Ferdinand; sings blessings on the forthcoming marriage; Roman goddess of corn, grain, harvests and fertility, associated with Demeter (Greek); scene possibly written in celebration of the marriage of Princess Elizabeth (daughter of James I) and the Elector Palatine, before whom the play was performed at court (Feb. 1613).
TEMP: IV, 1.
2H6: Duchess of Gloucester, I, 2, 2.

Cerimon, lord of Ephesus, skilled physician; restores Thaisa to life; helps her become a priestess at the temple of Diana.
PER: III, 2.

certes, unquestionably, certainly.
TEMP: Gonzalo, III, 3, 30.
CofE: Dromio E., IV, 4, 78.
OTH: Iago, I, 1, 16.

Cesario, name used by Viola when she becomes Duke Orsino's page.
TwN: I, 4.

cess, proportion, reason, measure.
1H4: Carrier, II, 1, 8.

cesse (cease), death, decease.
HAM: Rosencrantz, III, 3, 15.

chairs of order, stalls for Knights of the Garter in Royal Chapel of Windsor, each with individual insignia.
MWW: Quickly, V, 5, 65.

challenge, claim, deserve, demand as a right.
OTH: Othello, II, 1, 213.
RICH2: Bolingbroke, II, 3, 134.

Cham, khan; ruler of the Tartars.
ADO: Benedick, II, 1, 277.

chamber, London was known as "The King's Chamber" (*camera regis*) soon after the Norman conquest, according to William Camden in *Britannia.*
RICH3: Buckingham, III, 1, 1.

chamberers, fun-loving gallants; profligate courtiers found in ladies' chambers.
OTH: Othello, III, 3, 265.

chamberlain, officer in charge of a king's or lord's personal apartments or needs; valet.
TIMON: Apemantus, IV, 3, 222.

Chamberlain, steward of inn at Rochester; tells Gadshill when guests are about to leave, in return for a share of the booty when they are robbed.
1H4: II, 1.

Chamberlain's-King's Men. See Appendix.

chamber-lye, urine.
1H4: 2Carrier, II, 1, 23.

chamblet, camlet, rich, light cloth made of silk and angora goat's hair.
HEN8: Man, V, 4, 93.

chameleon Love
. . . Though the chameleon Love can feed on the air, I am one that am nourished by my victuals, and would fain have meat.
2GENT: Speed, II, 1, 178.

chameleon's dish, air was supposed to be what the lizard lived on.
HAM: Hamlet, III, 2, 98.

champain (champian), fertile, flat plain; open country.
LEAR: I, 1, 65.
TwN: Malvolio, II, 5, 174.
LUCRECE: 1247.

chance
. . . In the reproof of chance
Lies the true proof of men. The sea being smooth,
How many shallow bauble boats dare sail
Upon her patient breast, making their way
With those of nobler bulk!
T&C: Nestor, I, 3, 33. See BAUBLE.

change, exchange, trade; political uprising, rebellion, revolution.
HAM: Hamlet, I, 2, 163.
RICH2: Welsh Capt., II, 4, 11.

change
It is the lesser blot, modesty finds,
Women to change their shapes than men their minds.
2GENT: Julia, V, 4, 108.

change a mind
With every minute you do change a mind
And call him noble that was now your hate,
Him vile that was your garland.
COR: Marcius, I, 1, 186.

changed eyes, love at first sight; exchange of looks of love.
TEMP: Prospero, I, 2, 441.

changeling, substitution of one thing for another; refers to beautiful baby or child stolen by the fairies who leave an ugly one in its place.
MND: Puck, II, 1, 23.
HAM: Hamlet, V, 2, 53.
COR: Aufidius, IV, 7, 11.

chantry, small chapel with only one or two priests to serve the founders and others.
TWN: Olivia, IV, 3, 24.

chaos
Excellent wretch, perdition, catch my soul
But I do love thee, and when I love thee not,
Chaos is come again.
OTH: Othello, III, 3, 90—wretch here is a term of affection.

chap, jaw, cheek.
TEMP: Stephano, II, 2, 90.
MACB: Sergeant, I, 2, 22.
JOHN: Bastard, II, 1, 352.

chape, metal tip of a scabbard or sheath.
SHREW: Biondello, III, 2, 48.
ALL'SW: 1Lord, IV, 3, 164.

Chapel Royal, members of the royal household including Gentlemen of the Chapel, clergy, musicians, choir boys or Children of the Chapel; important in the development of English music and drama.

chapfallen, crestfallen, dejected, downcast, "down in the mouth."
HAM: Hamlet, V, 1, 212—with pun on CHAPLESS.

chapless, without the lower jaw, jawless, lacking the lower CHAP.
HAM: Hamlet, V, 1, 97.

chapmen, dickering merchants, haggling customers or buyers; peddlers, hucksters.
T&C: Paris, IV, 1, 75.
LLL: Princess, II, 1, 16.

character, inscribe, engrave, mark; handwriting.
HAM: Polonius, I, 3, 59.
TWN: Olivia, V, 1, 354.
WINT: Antigonus, III, 3, 47.

charge house, probably a boarding school where children were taught at the charge or expense of the parish; allusion to satirical passage in Erasmus' *Colloquies*, known to contemporary schoolboys.
LLL: Armado, V, 1, 87.

chariness, scrupulous honesty or integrity; careful preservation.
MWW: Mrs. Ford, II, 1, 103.

Charing Cross, village between the City and Westminster; today in the heart of London.
1H4: 2Carrier, II, 1, 27.

Charles, wrestler in the employ of Duke Frederick; thrown by Orlando.
AYL: I, 1.

Charles VI, King of France; signed Treaty of Troyes with Henry V; agreed to the marriage of his daughter Katherine to the King. [1368-1422; reigned (1380-1422); first evidence of insanity (1392) retired him from active rule; the Dukes of Burgundy and Orléans struggled for power, and the former ruled until 1404; Henry V defeated the French at Agincourt (1415); succeeded by his son, Charles VII.]
HEN5: II, 4.

Charles VII, incorrectly called the Dauphin in the play; falls in love with Joan of Arc and credits her with the French successes; after her capture, humbly accepts the position of viceroy of his dominions, subject to Henry VI of England. [1403-61; succeeded to the throne (1422); started to win France back from the English (1429).]

1H6: I, 2.

Charles' wain, wagon or chariot of Charlemagne; old name for the Great Bear or the Big Dipper.

1H4: 1Carrier, II, 1, 2.

charm, magic spell.

OTH: Brabantio, I, 1, 172.

. . . The charm dissolves apace;
And as the morning steals upon
      the night,
Melting the darkness, so their
      rising senses
Begin to chase the ignorant
      fumes that mantle
Their clearer reason.

TEMP: Prospero, V, 1, 64.

Charmian, one of the loyal attendants of Cleopatra; dies from the bite of an asp a few minutes after her mistress.

A&C: I, 2.

charneco, sweet wine, possibly from Portugal.

2H6: 2Neighbor, II, 3, 62.

Charon, boatman who ferried the souls of the departed across the river Styx.

T&C: Troilus, III, 2, 11. See STYGIAN.

charter, publicly conceded privilege or right; authoritative sanction.

HEN5: Canterbury, I, 1, 48.
OTH: Desdemona, I, 3, 246.
RICH2: York, II, 1, 195—Richard was breaking the law of legal succession by which he himself was king.

Chartreux, Charterhouse or Carthusian monastery in Smithfield, London.

HEN8: Brandon, I, 1, 221.

Charybdis. See SCYLLA.

Chatillon, French ambassador; opens the play threatening war in the name of Philip of France, if John will not renounce the throne in favor of Arthur; announces the invasion of France to the King at Angiers.

JOHN: I, 1.

Chaucer, Geoffrey (c1344-1400). Famed author of *The Canterbury Tales* (c1387-1400); served with the English army invading France (1359-60); believed to have studied at the Inner Temple; served as a diplomat; justice of the peace for Kent (1385); member of Parliament (1386); buried in the Poets' Corner of Westminster Abbey; Shakespeare was indebted to him as a source for *The Rape of Lucrece*, and parts of *A Midsummer Night's Dream, Troilus and Cressida* and *The Two Noble Kinsmen.*

chaudrons, entrails.

MACB: 3Witch, IV, 1, 34.

che, I, in the dialect of southwestern England.

LEAR: Edgar, IV, 6, 247.

cheat, swindle, fraud; from petty thievery or in thieves' language, the "sucker" or "easy mark."

WINT: Autolycus, IV, 3, 28.

cheaters, escheaters, officers of the King's Exchequer; collected fines and could easily cheat or pocket money.

MWW: Falstaff, I, 3, 77.

check, term from falconry; a hawk that leaves its quarry and flies off after the wrong prey; pursuit of a false quarry; reprimand, rebuke.

TwN: Toby, II, 5, 124.
OTH: Iago, I, 1, 149.
JC: Cassius, IV, 3, 97.

checkin, sequin, Italian *zecchini,* a gold coin worth about $2.25.

PER: Pander, IV, 2, 28.

checking at, diverge or swerve from; stopping short; refers to a hawk or falcon that midway in flight turns from one prey to another.

HAM: King, IV, 7, 63.

cheek

See how she leans her cheek upon her hand!
O that I were a glove upon that hand,
That I might touch that cheek!
R&J: Romeo, II, 2, 23.

cherry-pit, children's game of throwing cherry stones (pits) into a hole.
TwN: Toby, III, 4, 129.

Chertsey, town in Surrey, 15 miles from London; Henry VI buried in the monastery or abbey there, according to HOLIN-SHED.
RICH3: Anne, I, 2, 29.

cherub, an angel which was believed able to see and know all.
HAM: Hamlet, IV, 3, 50.

cheveril, kidskin; allusion to flexibility.
TwN: Clown, III, 1, 13.
R&J: Mercutio, II, 4, 87.
HEN8: Old Lady, II, 3, 32—*chiverel*.

chewet, jackdaw; small fried mince pie; fat fellow.
1H4: Prince, V, 1, 29.

chide, chaff or beat against; roar at; scold.
1H4: Glendower, III, 1, 45.
OTH: 2Gentleman, II, 1, 12.
MND: Helena, III, 2, 312.

chief head, basic aim, important source.
HAM: Horatio, I, 1, 106.

childing, productive, fruitful, fertile; child, a baby girl.
MND: Titania, II, 1, 112.

chine, saddle, roast.
2H6: Cade, IV, 10, 61.

chink, coin, money.
R&J: Nurse, I, 5, 119.

chipochia, Italian *capocchia,* simpleton; knob of a stick (bawdy).
T&C: Pandarus, IV, 2, 32.

Chiron, youngest son of Tamora; with his brother Demetrius, rapes and mutilates Lavinia, Titus' daughter; arranges the deaths of two of his sons by making them appear guilty of the murder of Bassianus; Titus cuts their throats (as Lavinia catches their blood in a basin) and serves them baked in a pie to their mother.
TITUS: I, 1.

chirurgeonly, as an able surgeon would.
TEMP: Antonio, II, 1, 140.

choice

. . . there's small choice in rotten apples.
SHREW: Hortensio, I, 1, 138.

choler, anger; bile; incensed, irritated.
HAM: Guildenstern, III, 2, 315.
OTH: Iago, II, 1, 280.
1H4: Northumberland, I, 3, 129.

chopine, thick, cork-soled shoe worn by women in Spain and Venice, Italy.
HAM: Hamlet, II, 2, 447.

choplogic, hair-splitter, sophist, one who uses subtle logic in an argument.
R&J: Capulet, III, 5, 150.

chopping, changing, altering, exchanging.
RICH2: Duchess of York, V, 3, 124.

chops, fat-face, fat-jawed or jowly.
1H4: Poins, I, 2, 151.
2H4: Doll, II, 4, 235.

chopt, chapped, cracked.
AYL: Touchstone, II, 4, 48.
MACB: Banquo, I, 3, 44—*choppy*.
SONNET: LXII, 10.

chough, fluttering, chattering, foolish creature; jackdaw and other members of the crow family.
HAM: Hamlet, V, 2, 89.
TEMP: Antonio, II, 1, 266.
LEAR: Edgar, IV, 6, 13.

christendom, first or Christian name.
ALL'sW: Helena, I, 1, 188—*adoptious christendoms,* nicknames.

Christian burial, interment in consecrated ground.

HAM: Clown, V, 1, 1—suicides were buried at crossroads, but because Ophelia was a lady of the court, she was allowed a Christian burial, which scandalized the gravediggers.

christom, newly christened, in christening robe; innocent.

HEN5: Hostess, II, 3, 12.

chronicle small beer, keep account of trifles or petty household expenditures.

OTH: Iago, II, 1, 161.

chud, I would, in Somerset dialect.

LEAR: Edgar, IV, 6, 243.

chuff, miser, avaricious rich man; boor.

1H4: Falstaff, II, 2, 94.

churl, boor, one with bad manners, usually a peasant; miser.

MND: Puck, II, 2, 78.
TIMON: Timon, I, 2, 26.
COfE: Balthazar, III, 1, 24.

cicatrice, scar.

HAM: King, IV, 3, 62.

Cicero. See TULLY.

Ciceter, Cirencester, very old town in Gloucestershire.

RICH2: Bolingbroke, V, 6, 3.

Cilicia, country on seacoast of southeastern Asia Minor, north of Cyprus.

A&C: Caesar, III, 6, 16.

Cimber. See METELLUS CIMBER.

Cimmerian, dwellers in a land of darkness; in HOMER'S *Odyssey* (XI:14) described as dwelling on the confines of the earth "shrouded in mist and darkness"; Milton refers to the "dark Cimmerian desert" in *L'Allegro* (10).

TITUS: Bassianus, II, 3, 72—refers to Aaron, the Moor.

cincture (ceinture), girdle, belt.

JOHN: Bastard, IV, 3, 155.

Cinna (Gaius Helvius), Roman tribune, poet; friend of Catullus; mistaken for Cinna, the conspirator, and murdered by the frenzied mob at the funeral of Caesar.

JC: III, 3.

Cinna, one of the conspirators; part of plot to win Brutus' support; doesn't appear after the assassination. [Lucius Cornelius, Roman politician, brother-in-law of Julius Caesar; praetor.]

JC: I, 3.

Cinthio (Giovanni Battista Giraldi) (1504-73). Italian scholar, poet, novelist; professor of medicine, philosophy and letters at the University of Ferrara (1525-60); published *Gli Hecatommithi* (A Hundred Tales, 1565), a series of prose romances, the source of the plot of Shakespeare's *Othello;* indirectly the source of the plot of *Measure for Measure.*

Circe, enchantress who transformed men into swine; subdued by Ulysses in HOMER's *Odyssey* (10).

1H6: York, V, 3, 35.
COfE: Duke, V, 1, 270.

circle, crown.

A&C: Ambassador (Euphronius), III, 12, 18—specifically the crown of Egypt.

circum circa, Latin, round and round; roundabout.

LLL: Moth, V, 1, 72.

circummured, walled in or round; enclosed by a wall.

MEAS: Isabella, IV, 1, 28.

circumstance, detailed or elaborate talk or argument; formality, ceremony, rite.

COfE: Angelo, V, 1, 16.
HAM: Hamlet, I, 5, 127.

cital, account, mention, recital.

1H4: Vernon, V, 2, 62.

citizen, delicate, feminine, spoiled, city-bred.

CYM: Imogen, IV, 2, 8.

cittern-head, head of a cittern (cither), a lute-like instrument; often carved with a grotesque face.

LLL: Boyet, V, 2, 614.

civet, popular perfume with young men of the period; extract from glandular secretion of civet cat.
  ADO: Pedro, III, 2, 50.
  AYL: Corin, III, 2, 66.
  LEAR: Lear, IV, 6, 134.

clack-dish, wooden dish or bowl; carried by beggars who clacked (hit) the lid to attract attention.
  MEAS: Lucio, III, 2, 135.

clap, when concluding a bargain, people clapped and clasped hands; pledge.
  WINT: Leontes, I, 2, 104.
  SHREW: Gremio, II, 1, 327.
  JOHN: King Philip, III, 1, 235.

clap, break or enter briskly into; strike up (as a song).
  ADO: Margaret, III, 4, 44.

clap, closed or shut in; secured.
  TEMP: Boatswain, V, 1, 231.

clap, pet, stroke.
  RICH2: Richard, II, 5, 86.

clapperclaw, maul, thrash, scratch and claw.
  MWW: Host, II, 3, 67.
  T&C: Thersites, V, 4, 1.

Clare, St. See SAINT CLARE.

Clarence, George, Duke of, "simple, plain Clarence"; created Duke by his elder brother, Edward IV, after Yorkist victory at Towton; when Edward marries Lady Grey, Clarence joins Warwick in opposition (3H6); deserts Warwick and rejoins Edward before Barnet; Edward IV imprisons him in the Tower (RICH3) and orders his death; Richard intercepts his reprieve and he is murdered. [George Plantagenet (1449-78), brother of Edward and Richard; married Isabel, daughter of Richard, Earl of Warwick (1469); a legend persists that has him "drowned in a butt of Malmsey wine."]
  3H6: II, 1; RICH3: I, 1.

Clarence's dream. See DROWNING.

Clarence, Thomas, Duke of, second son of the King, who requests him to advise Prince Henry upon his succession to the throne. [1388-1421, killed at Beaugé.]
  2H4: IV, 4; HEN5: V, 2.

Claribel. See ALONSO.

Claudio, young Florentine lord in love with Hero; fooled into believing her unfaithful and of easy virtue; proven wrong, repents and marries her.
  ADO: I, 1.

Claudio, young gentleman of Vienna, lover of Juliet; paraded in disgrace through the streets and imprisoned; eventually released and married to Juliet.
  MEAS: I, 2.

Claudius, King of Denmark, brother-in-law and husband of Gertrude, uncle and stepfather of Hamlet; having murdered his brother and married his widow, he became King of Denmark; though touched with remorse, he cannot undo the action and must plot to retain his position; though guilty, and the unscrupulous villain of the play, he is also a clever diplomat, careful intriguer and strong opponent who shows courage and dignity; ruthless, he arranges to have Hamlet killed in England, and when that fails, contrives the fencing match between Laertes and the prince in which Hamlet is to be killed with a poisoned sword; killed instead with the murder weapon by Hamlet.
  HAM: I, 2.

Claudius, faithful servant to Brutus; sleeps in his master's tent the night before Philippi.
  JC: IV, 3.

claw, flatter, fondle, cajole.
  LLL: Dull, II, 2, 66.
  ADO: John, I, 3, 19.

clear, innocent, pure; serene, unclouded countenance; blameless.
  TEMP: Ariel, III, 3, 82.
  MACB: Lady Macbeth, I, 5, 72.
  A&C: Cleopatra, V, 2, 122.

cleave, favor, honor, ally.
  MACB: Macbeth, II, 1, 25.

Cleomenes, lord of Sicilia; sent by Leontes to the Isle of Delphos to ask the Oracle of Apollo the truth about Hermione's chastity.
  WINT: III, 1.

Cleon, governor of Tarsus, strongly influenced by his wife Dionyza; welcomes the arrival of Pericles primarily because the provisions from his ships will feed the starving people of Tarsus; placed in charge of Marina; to avenge her attempted murder, he is burned to death.
  PER: I, 4.

Cleopatra, queen of Egypt, "she has never learnt to compromise with life, nor had to reconcile her own nature's extremes" (Granville-Barker); "the character of Cleopatra is a masterpiece" (Hazlitt); "a creature who makes defect perfection, and, when breathless, power breathes forth" (Enobarbus); met Antony (41 BC) and became his mistress; after their defeat at Actium (31), when she realizes she will be carried a captive to Rome, she kills herself. [Cleopatra VII, last Macedonian Queen of Egypt (60-30 BC); with her brother, Ptolemy XII, succeeded her father, Ptolemy Auletes, on the throne of Egypt (51); deposed (49), restored to power by Julius Caesar (48), with whom she lived in Rome (46-44); bore him a son, Caesarion, who was later killed by Augustus; supported the Triumvirate after his murder; met Antony, bore him three children; committed suicide.]
  A&C: I, 1.

clepe (clip), to call, name.
  HAM: Hamlet, I, 4, 19.
  MACB: Macbeth, III, 1, 94.
  LLL: Holofernes, V, 1, 24.

clerk, old word for scholar, man of learning; took part in Church of England services.
  MND: Theseus, V, 1, 93.
  RICH2: Richard, IV, 1, 173.
  SONNET: LXXXV, 6.

Clerk of Chatham, "can write and read and cast accompt"; Cade has him hung "with his pen and inkhorn."
  2H6: IV, 2.

Clifford, Lord, supporter of the King; with Buckingham, persuades the mob to desert Cade; supports the King in the Wars of the Roses; killed by York at St. Albans. [Thomas Clifford (1414-55), 12th Baron.]
  2H6: IV, 8.

Clifford, Lord, the younger; sees his father (above) killed, escapes; follows Queen Margaret in war against York (in 3H6); stabs York's son, the Earl of Rutland, kills the captured York after the battle at Wakefield; killed on the eve of the battle of Towton. [John, 13th Baron Clifford, 9th Baron of Westmoreland (c1435-61); known as "the Butcher" for his bloodthirsty beheading of the dead Edmund, Duke of York (1460), and his presentation of the head, with a crown on it, to Queen Margaret.]
  2H6: V, 1; 3H6, I, 1.

clinquant, glittering, shining (with gold).
  HEN8: Norfolk, I, 1, 19.

clip (cleep), embrace, kiss; enclose, encompass, surround.
  LLL: Dumain, V, 2, 603.
  A&C: Antony, IV, 8, 8.
  COR: Marcius, I, 6, 29.

clipper, cut, chip, trim or otherwise mutilate a coin (gold or silver); considered a crime under English law.
  HEN5: King, IV, 1, 246.

Clitus, faithful servant to Brutus, refuses his master's request to kill him at Philippi; escapes

when Octavius and Antony advance.
JC: V, 5.

clock. See WOMAN.

clog, weight tied to an animal to keep it from straying; burden, weight; ball and chain.
ALL'sW: Bertram, II, 5, 58.
ADO: John, I, 3, 35.
RICH2: Percy, V, 6, 20.

close, secret, private, concealed.
MND: Puck, III, 2, 7.
HAM: King, III, 1, 29—*closely.*
TEMP: Prospero, I, 2, 90—*closeness.*

close, grapple, hand-to-hand combat.
1H4: King, I, 1, 13.

close, enclosure, garden.
TIMON: Timon, V, 1, 208.

closestool, box containing a chamber pot.
LLL: Costard, V, 2, 580.

closes with you in this consequence, agrees or follows through with you in this answer.
HAM: Polonius, II, 1, 45.

closet, personal or private sitting room.
HAM: Ophelia, II, 1, 77.
MWW: Quickly, I, 4, 39.
HEN5: King, V, 2, 211.

Cloten, arrogant son of the queen by a former marriage; stepbrother of Imogen; anxious to win her from the banished Posthumus, Cloten puts on his clothes and follows Imogen to Milford Haven, planning to kill Posthumus and take her by force; killed by Guiderius.
CYM: I, 2.

Clotharius (Clothair). See PEPIN.
HEN8: Lord Chamberlain, I, 3, 10.
HEN5: Canterbury, I, 2, 67.

clotpoll, blockhead, sod or bonehead, dolt, nincompoop.
LEAR: I, 4, 51.
TWN: Toby, III, 4, 208—*clodpoll.*
CYM: Guiderius, IV, 2, 184.

clout, center of canvas target used in archery; pieces of cloth, clothes, bandages.
LEAR: Lear, IV, 6, 92.
2H4: Shallow, III, 2, 52.
HAM: Hamlet, II, 2, 401.

clouted, patched, hobnailed, studded with heavy nails.
2H6: Cade, IV, 2, 195.

clown, peasant, rustic, boor, countryman, clod; Elizabethans sometimes used "clown" and "fool" interchangeably; however, the clown, a stock character in several of Shakespeare's plays, uses broad comedy as contrasted to the intelligent, subtle, thoughtful fools such as Touchstone and Feste. See LANCE, STEPHANO, COSTARD, PETER etc.
HAM: Hamlet, III, 2, 43—*Let those that play your clowns speak no more than is set down for them . . . that's villainous, and shows a most pitiful ambition in the fool that uses it.*

cloy, to satiate; to claw.
RICH2: Bolingbroke, I, 3, 296.
CYM: Sicilius Leonatus, V, 4, 118.

clyster, pipe, tube, syringe used for injection.
OTH: Iago, II, 1, 179.

coat, armor, coat of mail.
RICH2: Bolingbroke, I, 4, 61.
OTH: Cassio, V, 1, 25.

cobbler, bungler, botcher.
JC: Cobbler, I, 1, 11.

Cobbler, a "surgeon to old shoes" who has joined the others in a holiday to "see Caesar and to rejoice in his triumph."
JC: I, 1.

cobloaf, small, crusty, uneven loaf of bread with a round head; bun.
T&C: Ajax, II, 1, 41.

Cobweb, one of Titania's fairies chosen to "do courtesies" to Bottom, who promises to make use of Master Cobweb if he cuts his finger. (A cobweb was

an old wives' remedy for cuts.)
MND: III, 1.

Cock, contemporary popular form of God; similar to modern "Gee."
HAM: Ophelia, IV, 5, 61—part of song.

cock, weathervane in form of a cock, usually on top of steeples or roofs.
LEAR: Lear, III, 2, 3.

cock, wine spout.
TIMON: Steward, II, 2, 171—weeping.

cock, small ship's boat (cock-boat).
LEAR: Edgar, IV, 6, 19.

cockatrice, fabulous creature, said to be hatched by a snake or toad from a cock's egg, whose glance could kill; basilisk; serpent.
TWN: Toby, III, 4, 215.
CYM: Posthumus, II, 4, 107.
R&J: Juliet, III, 2, 47.

cockered, pampered, spoiled.
JOHN: Bastard, V, 1, 70.

cockle, weed that grows in wheat; possibly "tares" of Matthew 13:25.
COR: Coriolanus, III, 1, 70.
LLL: Berowne, IV, 3, 383.

cockle hat, hat with a scallop or cockle shell stuck into it; worn by pilgrim to show that he had been to the shrine of St. James of Compostela in Spanish Galicia.
HAM: Ophelia, IV, 5, 25—see TRUE-LOVE.

cockney, affected, effeminate person; fop; stupid milksop; spoiled child; city bred.
TWN: Clown, IV, 1, 15.

cockpit, enclosed arena where they staged cockfights.
HEN5: Prologue, 11.

Cockpit-at-Court, small theater at Whitehall Palace; performances of *Henry IV, Julius Caesar* and *The Merry Wives* were given there (1639); plan and elevation for the new Cockpit-at-Court (c1632) by Inigo Jones is at Worcester College, Oxford.

Cockpit Theatre, called the PHOENIX; a cockpit in Drury Lane was converted into a private theater (1616); owned by Christopher Beeston; headquarters for the Worcester's-Queen Anne's company (1617-19); taken over by Prince Charles' company; following the Restoration, when the theaters were re-opened (1660), *Pericles* was the first of Shakespeare's plays to be produced there.

cockshut time, twilight, sunset, evening.
RICH3: Ratcliff, V, 3, 70.

Cocytus, river of sorrow (or lamentation) in Hades.
TITUS: Martius, II, 3, 236.

codding, lewd, lustful, lecherous.
TITUS: Aaron, V, 1, 99.

codling, unripened or green apple.
TWN: Malvolio, I, 5, 167.

codpiece, part of male hose or attire which conspicuously covered the phallus; often stuffed and decorated.
LEAR: Fool, III, 2, 27.
LLL: Berowne, III, 1, 186.
ADO: Borachio, III, 3, 146.

Coeur-de-lion (Cordelion) Richard I, the lion-hearted.
JOHN: Bastard, I, 1, 54.
1H6: Talbot, III, 2, 83.

coffin, pastry mold; pie-crust shaped like a box or coffin.
TITUS: Titus, V, 2, 189.

cog, cheat, fraud, swindle; deceit.
LLL: Princess, V, 2, 235.
ADO: Antonio, V, 1, 95.
MWW: Falstaff, III, 3, 50—flatter, beguile.

cognizance, heraldic badge, sign or token; worn by retainers or servants of a noble or great man's house.
JC: Decius, II, 2, 89.
CYM: Posthumus, II, 4, 127.
1H6: Richard, II, 4, 108.

coign, cornerstone, projection; advantageous corner from which to observe activity.

MACB: Banquo, I, 6, 7.
COR: Menenius, V, 4, 1.

coil, turbulence, turmoil, tumult, fuss.

HAM: Hamlet, III, 1, 67. See TO BE.
TEMP: Prospero, I, 2, 207.
JOHN: Arthur, II, 1, 165.

Colbrand, Danish giant slain by Guy of Warwick; last defeated opponent of Warwick in old romances.

JOHN: Bastard, I, 1, 225.
HEN8: Man, V, 4, 22—*Colebrand*.

Colchos, actually Colchis, home of Medea, to which Jason sailed in the *Argo* to capture the Golden Fleece.

MERV: Bassanio, I, 1, 171.

coldly set, without regard for, indifferent toward.

HAM: King, IV, 3, 64.

Colevile (Colville), Sir John, one of the leaders of the northern rebellion; yields to Falstaff without a blow when they meet in Gaultree Forest.

2H4: IV, 3.

collateral, indirectly or as an accessory to or part of.

HAM: King, IV, 5, 266.

Collatium, Collatia, city of Latium, 10 miles east of Rome.

LUCRECE: 4.

collection, conclusion, inference; to deduce from implied meaning.

HAM: Gentleman, IV, 5, 9.

collied, blackened, darkened; to colly means to blacken with coal.

MND: Lysander, I, 1, 145.
OTH: Othello, II, 3, 206.

collier, coal peddler or dealer; carriers of coal were known for their "black" ways; reference to Satan (the devil), who was depicted as black.

TWN: Toby, III, 4, 130.
R&J: Gregory, I, 1, 2.
LLL: Longaville, IV, 3, 267.

collop, slice of meat; small portion; piece of flesh.

1H6: Shepherd, V, 4, 18.
WINT: Leontes, I, 2, 137—my own flesh and blood.

Colmekill, modern island of Iona; former site of Saint Columba's monasteries; ancient burying place of the kings of Scotland.

MACB: Macduff, II, 4, 33.

coloquintida, very bitter cathartic medicine, made from the fruit of the colocynth vine, grown in the Mediterranean area and Africa; known as bitter apple and bitter cucumber.

OTH: Iago, I, 3, 355. See FOOD.

Colossus, man of monstrous size; allusion to the Colossus of Rhodes, gigantic statue of Apollo, the sun god, that guarded the harbor of Rhodes; considered one of the Seven Wonders of the ancient world; destroyed 3rd century BC.

1H4: Prince, V, 1, 123.
JC: Cassius, I, 2, 136.

. . . he doth bestride the narrow world
Like a Colossus, and we petty men
Walk under his huge legs and peep about
To find ourselves dishonourable graves.

JC: Cassius, I, 2, 135—refers to Julius Caesar.

colour, camouflage, conceal, disguise; excuses, pretexts.

HAM: Hamlet, II, 2, 290.
CYM: Cymbeline, III, 1, 51.
WINT: Florizel, IV, 4, 566.

colour

Green indeed is the colour of lovers; but to have a love of that colour, methinks Samson had small reason for it. He surely affected her for her wit.

LLL: Armado, I, 2, 90—green was also the color of hope and rejoicing.

colt, mount; fool, trick.

> CYM: Posthumus, II, 4, 133.
> 1H4: Falstaff, II, 2, 40.

columbine, plant, usually wild, with beautifully shaped flowers; symbol of faithlessness or thanklessness.

> HAM: Ophelia, IV, 5, 180.

combinate, affianced, betrothed.

> MEAS: Duke, III, 1, 232.

Comedy of Errors, The, written 1592-3, possibly 1591; published in First Folio (1623); first performance (Dec. 28, 1594) at Gray's Inn; adapted from PLAUTUS' *Menaechmi* (one scene of *Amphitryon*), using six of nine characters, adding second slave (Dromio), substituting Luciana for stock character Senex, and adding Aegeon and Aemilia (now an Abbess) from plot in *Apollonius of Tyre* by Lydgate (later also used in *Pericles*), making the play a romantic farce. "The play is on a lower plane than any of his other works. It is the only Shakespearean play without a deep philosophical idea. . . . It is also the first play that shows a fine sustained power of dramatic construction." — (Masefield.) Others suggest that the play, with its excessive and elaborate wit, is inventive rather than creative and evidence of Shakespeare's recognition of what makes popular rather than good theater.

PLOT: Aegeon, merchant of Syracuse, risks a visit to Ephesus, a rival city, after five years of fruitless searching for a lost twin son and twin slave, and is condemned to death by Solinus, Duke of Ephesus. However, after telling the Duke the story of how, following a shipwreck, he had been separated from his wife, twin son and slave who had been tied to the other end of the mast, Aegeon is allowed one day to raise 1,000 marks ransom. Antipholus of Syracuse, warned not to tell where he has come from, sends his servant Dromio to the Centaur (Inn) with 1,000 marks.

When he meets Dromio of Ephesus, he mistakes him for his own servant and beats him for denying he gave him the money. Adriana, the jealous wife of Antipholus of Ephesus, sends Dromio back to bring his master home, ignoring the business of the money. When Antipholus of Syracuse is taken to Adriana's house, he is welcomed as her husband and invited to dinner. When Antipholus of Ephesus arrives home, he is refused admittance, and in anger goes to visit a courtesan and decides to give her a chain he had intended for his wife. Meanwhile, Antipholus of Syracuse tells Luciana he has no wife and attempts to make love to her. The confusion is too much for the two from Syracuse and they decide to pack and leave the city.

In the street Antipholus is met by a goldsmith and given the chain intended for his twin, who subsequently is charged for the chain which he denies having received. He is then arrested and sends a bewildered Dromio of Syracuse to Adriana to send the necessary money to bail him out, which, of course, she does. Dromio returns to his master with the money, who, needless to say, knows nothing about it and, instead, is accosted by the courtesan who demands the chain he is carrying in exchange for the ring she gave Antipholus of Ephesus. As he hasn't the ring, she feels she has been cheated and goes to Adriana. Dromio of Ephesus is beaten when he hasn't the money for his master, who, in a rage, beats Pinch, the schoolmaster brought by Adriana to cure her husband's madness.

When Adriana arrives, she is accused by her husband of having locked him out of their home, which she denies, "proving" his insanity. Meanwhile the merchant and goldsmith fight over the chain and are joined by the women. Antipholus and Dromio of Syracuse are given refuge in the abbey. The Duke, who happens to pass with the condemned Aegeon, manages to untangle the identities and confusion and all pairs are happily matched, including Aegeon and the Abbess, who is revealed as his lost wife, Aemilia.

comet, heavenly body having a long nebulous tail; a superstition prevailed in that period that comets flashing across the sky portended evil or disaster.
1H4: Bedford, I, 1, 2.
JC: Calphurnia, II, 2, 30.

comets
When beggars die there are no comets seen;
The heavens themselves blaze forth the death of princes.
JC: Calphurnia, II, 2, 30.

comfect, comfit, confection, sweetmeat, candy.
ADO: Beatrice, IV, 1, 319.
1H4: Hotspur, III, 1, 251—*comfit-maker.*

Cominius, Consul and commander-in-chief of the Roman army against the Volsces; pleads Coriolanus' cause to the Tribunes; tries to prevent his banishment; unsuccessful in his attempt to persuade Coriolanus not to attack Rome.
COR: I, 1.

command, order help or support.
OTH: Brabantio, I, 1, 182.

command
We were not born to sue, but to command.
RICH2: Richard, I, 1, 196. See SHAME.

Those he commands move only in command,

Nothing in love. Now does he feel his title
Hang loose about him, like a giant's robe
Upon a dwarfish thief.
MACB: Angus, V, 2, 19.

commend, give over to, entrust with; recommend, commendation, wish.
RICH2: Northumberland, III, 3, 116.

commodity, self-interest, expediency, gain; consignment, lot.
JOHN: Bastard, II, 1, 572.
TWN: Clown, III, 1, 50.
1H4: Falstaff, IV, 2, 19.

common
. . . but it was always yet the trick of our English nation, if they have a good thing, to make it too common.
2H4: Falstaff, I, 2, 240.

commons' suit, request for publication of deposition.
RICH2: Northumberland, IV, 1, 154—from HOLINSHED; the House of Commons had asked that after Richard II was lawfully deposed, the information regarding the deposition be made public.

common stages, professional theaters with adult performers or acting companies were considered lower in class than the private houses occupied by the children's or boys' companies.
HAM: Rosencrantz, II, 2, 358.

compact, composed or made of; created by.
MND: Theseus, V, 1, 8. See IMAGINATION.
AYL: Duke Senior, II, 7, 5.
COFE: Luciana, III, 2, 22.

compass, circle, size or circumference, round.
RICH2: Gaunt, II, 1, 101.
T&C: Pandarus, I, 2, 120—bay.

compass, accomplish, effect, manage.
TEMP: Stephano, III, 2, 66.
OTH: Iago, I, 3, 367.
TWN: Captain, I, 2, 44.

competitor, associate, partner.
A&C: Caesar, I, 4, 3.
TwN: Clown, IV, 2, 12.
RICH3: Messenger, IV, 4, 504.

complexion, personal appearance
as an index of character; tem-
perament, disposition.
TEMP: Gonzalo, I, 1, 32.
LLL: Armado, I, 2, 82.
COR: Brutus, II, 1, 228.

compliment, formality, formal
ceremony.
LEAR: Goneril, I, 1, 306.

composition, uniformity, consist-
ency; agreement, terms of peace,
treaty.
OTH: Duke, I, 3, 1.
A&C: Pompey, II, 6, 59.
COR: Lartius, III, 1, 3.

compound, settle, agree, come to
terms.
COR: Coriolanus, V, 6, 83.
LEAR: Edmund, I, 2, 140.
SHREW: Hortensio, I, 2, 27.

compound mass, the earth, considered as compounded or composed of the four elements.
HAM: Hamlet, III, 4, 49.

compt, in trust, accountable.
MACB: Lady Macbeth, I, 6, 26.
OTH: Othello, V, 2, 273—final
judgment.

comptible, sensitive, susceptible.
TwN: Viola, I, 5, 168.

con, memorize, learn by heart.
MND: Quince, I, 2, 103.
TwN: Viola, I, 5, 186.
COR: Coriolanus, IV, 1, 11.

conceit conceive, comprehend,
understand; mental capacity,
judgment.
WINT: Leontes, I, 2, 224.
COFE: Adriana, IV, 2, 65.
JC: Cassius, I, 3, 162.

conceit, idea, conception, thought,
imagination, notion; witticism,
fancy.
HAM: Hamlet, II, 2, 579.
OTH: Othello, III, 3, 115.
SHREW: Petruchio, IV, 3, 102.

conceits, artfully, cleverly con-
trived compliments or tokens of
love.

MND: Egeus, I, 1, 33.

conclave, college of cardinals.
HEN8: King, II, 2, 100.

conclusions, experiments.
HAM: Hamlet, III, 4, 195.
A&C: Caesar, V, 2, 358.

Concolinel, probably title of unknown song.
LLL: Moth, III, 1, 3.

concupiscible, lecherous, sensuous.
MEAS: Isabella, V, 1, 98.

condign, justly deserved, worthy
of.
LLL: Armado, I, 2, 27.
2H6: Gloucester, III, 1, 130.

condition, rank, position; temperament, character, quality, nature.
2H4: Falstaff, IV, 3, 1.
LLL: Katherine, V, 2, 20.
COR: Sicinius, V, 4, 10.

condition, pact, contract, terms
of a bargain.
TEMP: Prospero, I, 2, 117.

condole, lament, mourn, show
sorrow or grief.
MND: Bottom, I, 2, 28.

condolement. See OBSTINATE CON-
DOLEMENT.

confection, compounded drug,
preparation.
CYM: Queen, I, 5, 15.

confederate, ally, co-conspirator;
working or synchronized with.
HAM: Lucianus, III, 2, 267.
TEMP: Prospero, I, 2, 3.
RICH2: Aumerle, V, 3, 53.

confess
. . . Confess yourself to heaven;
Repent what's past; avoid what
is to come;
And do not spread the compost
on the weeds
To make them ranker.
HAM: Hamlet, III, 4, 149.

confidence, private conference.
ADO: Dogberry, III, 5, 3.

confiner, dweller, inhabitant.
CYM: Captain, IV, 2, 337.

confound, ruin, destroy, waste.
RICH2: Carlisle, IV, 1, 141.

SONNET: V, 6. See WINTER.
MACB: Lady Macbeth, II, 2,
11.

confusion, destruction, ruin.
LEAR: Lear, II, 4, 96.
A&C: Antony, III, 13, 115.
TIMON: Timon, IV, 3, 327.

And ere a man hath power to
say 'Behold!'
The jaws of darkness do devour
it up:
So quick bright things come to
confusion.
MND: Lysander, I, 1, 147.

congee, form of curtsy or bow.
HEN8: Vision, IV, 2, 87.

conger, eel; term of contempt
or derision.
2H4: Hostess, II, 4, 58.

congied with, taken formal leave
of.
ALL'sW: Bertram, IV, 3, 100.

congreeing. See GOVERNMENT.

congrue, acquiesce, agree, consent.
HAM: King, IV, 3, 66.

conjoin, unite, join.
HAM: Hamlet, III, 4, 126.

conjunctive, joined or united
closely together; intimate.
HAM: King, IV, 7, 14.
OTH: Iago, I, 3, 375.
HEN8: Lord Surrey, III, 2, 45
—conjunction.

conjure, plead with, entreat.
HAM: Hamlet, II, 2, 294.
WINT: Polixenes, I, 2, 400.
JOHN: King, IV, 2, 269.

Conrade, one of the followers of
Don John; unable to help in the
scheme to deceive Claudio, having been arrested (with Borachio) by the Watch.
ADO: I, 3.

conscience, capacity for understanding, serious thought, honest opinion.
HAM: Hamlet, III, 1, 83.

conscience
What stronger breastplate than
a heart untainted?

Thrice is he armed that hath his
quarrel just,
And he but naked, though
locked up in steel,
Whose conscience with injustice
is corrupted.
2H6: King, III, 2, 232.

. . . Make thick my blood;
Stop up th' access and passage
to remorse,
That no compunctious visitings
of nature
Shake my fell purpose nor keep
peace between
Th' effect and it!
MACB: Lady Macbeth, I, 5, 44.

For conscience is a word that
cowards use,
Devised at first to keep the
strong in awe.
RICH3: Richard, V, 3, 310.

I'll not meddle with it; it
makes a man a coward. A man
cannot steal, but it accuseth
him; a man cannot swear, but it
checks him; a man cannot lie
with his neighbour's wife, but
it detects him. 'Tis a blushing
shamefaced spirit that mutinies
in a man's bosom. It fills a man
full of obstacles. It made me
once restore a purse of gold
that (by chance) I found. It
beggars any man that keeps it.
It is turned out of towns and
cities for a dangerous thing, and
every man that means to live
well endeavours to trust to himself and live without it.
RICH3: 2Murderer, I, 4, 137.

Love is too young to know what
conscience is;
Yet who knows not conscience
is born of love?
SONNET: CLI, 1.

. . . Twenty consciences
That stand 'twixt me and Milan,
candied be they
And melt, ere they molest!
TEMP: Antonio, II, 1, 278. See
CANDIED.

Men must learn now with pity
to dispense;

For policy sits above conscience.
TIMON: 1Stranger, III, 2, 93.

conserve, preserved, marinated, salted food.
SHREW: Sly, Induction, 2, 7.

consistory, papal court; college of cardinals presided over by the pope.
HEN8: Wolsey, II, 4, 92.

consonant, nonentity.
LLL: Holofernes, V, 1, 55.

consort, company of musicians, harmonious music.
2GENT: Proteus, III, 2, 84.

consorted crew, group of secret plotters, conspirators or connivers.
RICH2: Bolingbroke, V, 3, 138.

conspectuities, sight, vision.
COR: Menenius, II, 1, 72.

constable. See DULL.

Constable of France, called by the French king, "Charles Delabreth"; High Constable of France; confident of victory against the English at Agincourt; killed in battle.
HEN5: II, 4.

Constance, mother of Arthur; her strong claim to the English throne on behalf of her son is supported by France and Austria; when Arthur is captured after the defeat of her allies by John, she goes mad. [d.1201; daughter of Duke of Bretagne (Brittany); married twice after the death of Geoffrey Plantagenet, John's older brother and Arthur's father.]
JOHN: II, 1.

constant, settled, calm, steady; rational, logical, consistent, certain.
TEMP: Stephano, II, 2, 119.
MND: Hippolyta, V, 1, 26—*constancy.*

But I am constant as the northern star,

whose true-fixed and resting uality

s no fellow in the firmat.

JC: Caesar, III, 1, 60.

Constantine the Great (274-337 AD), powerful Roman Emperor (Constantine I); made Christianity the official religion of the empire (323).
1H6: Dauphin, I, 2, 142.

conster, construe, interpret.
OTH: Iago, IV, 1, 102.

construe. See OBJECTIVITY.

consul, councilor or senator.
OTH: Iago, I, 1, 25.
COR: Sicinius, II, 1, 238—one of Rome's two chief magistrates.

contempts
What our contempts doth often hurl from us,
We wish it ours again.
A&C: Antony, I, 2, 127.

content, embodiment; wish, desire; reward, remunerate.
SONNET: I, 11.
RICH2: York, V, 2, 38.
OTH: Cassio, III, 1, 1.

He that commends me to mine own content
Commends me to the things I cannot get.
COFE: Antipholus S., I, 2, 33.

contented. See MARRIAGE.

contention
. . . Contention, like a horse
Full of high feeding madly hath broke loose
And bears down all before him.
2H4: Northumberland, I, 1, 9.

continent, sum total; all-embracing; large container, receptacle.
HAM: Osric, V, 2, 115.
LLL: Boyet, IV, 1, 112.
A&C: Antony, IV, 14, 40.

contracted, contraction, betrothed, married; marriage contract.
HAM: Hamlet, III, 4, 46.
SONNET: I, 5—pun on "limited to"; allusion to Narcissus.

contrive, pass, spend time; wear away.
SHREW: Tranio, I, 2, 276.

control, disprove, refute, rebuke.
TEMP: Prospero, I, 2, 439.

controller, critic, detractor.
2H6: Queen, III, 2, 205.

contumely, sneers, verbal abuse, disdain.
HAM: Hamlet, III, 1, 71.

Con tutto il core (cuore) ben trovato, Italian, with all my heart, welcome.
SHREW: Petruchio, I, 2, 24.

convent, summon, convene.
TwN: Duke, V, 1, 391—convenient.
MEAS: Peter, V, 1, 158.
COR: Sicinius, II, 2, 58.

conventicles, secret or clandestine meetings, usually for an evil purpose.
2H6: Gloucester, III, 1, 166.

conversation, behavior, manner or way of life.
A&C: Enobarbus, II, 6, 131.
2H4: John, V, 5, 106.
MWW: Mrs. Page, II, 1, 25.

convert, turn aside; change, alter.
SONNET: VII, 11.
RICH2: Richard, V, 1, 66.

conveyance, convoy, escort which accompanies the march; transport of an army.
HAM: Fortinbras, IV, 4, 3.

conveyance, adroitness, dexterity, cunning, trickery, fraud.
ADO: Benedick, II, 1, 253.
1H6: Gloucester, I, 3, 2.
3H6: Margaret, III, 3, 160.

conveyer, escort; robber, trickster.
RICH2: Richard, IV, 1, 317.

convince, overcome, overpower; prove.
MAC2: Lady Macbeth, I, 7, 64.
LLL: King, V, 2, 755.

cony, rabbit.
AYL: Rosalind, III, 2, 357.
COR: 3Servingman, IV, 5, 226.

cony-catch, cheat; card-sharp.
SHREW: Curtis, IV, 1, 45.
MWW: Slender, I, 1, 128.

cooling card, having one's hopes "trumped"; common Elizabethan

expression meaning to "dampen one's courage or spirit."
1H6: Suffolk, V, 3, 84.

copatain, high-crowned; high sugar-loaf or cone-shaped hat.
SHREW: Vincentio, V, 1, 70.

cope, encounter, meet; fight; repay.
HAM: Hamlet, III, 2, 60.
WINT: Polixenes, IV, 4, 435.
AYL: Duke Senior, II, 1, 67.

copesmate, companion.
LUCRECE: 925. See MISSHAPEN TIME.

Cophetua. See "KING AND THE BEGGAR."
2H4: Falstaff, V, 3, 106.
R&J: Mercutio, II, 1, 14.

coragio, Italian, courage.
TEMP: Stephano, V, 1, 258.

coram, corruption of quorum; justice; justices necessary to constitute a full bench; word begins the official clause in appointment of justices of the peace or magistrates.
MWW: Slender, I, 1, 6.

Corambis. See POLONIUS.

coranto, dance with running steps, something like Victorian Gallop.
TwN: Toby, I, 3, 137.
HEN5: Bourbon (Britaine), III, 5, 33.
ALL'sW: Lafew, II, 3, 49.

Cordelia, youngest daughter of the King; refusing to make a public declaration of her love for him, she is disinherited and banished; marries the King of France; lands with French forces to help her father, when he has been turned out by his other daughters; reconciled with him; captured following the defeat of the French forces; hanged by order of Edmund.
LEAR: I, 1.

cordial, remedial, restorative.
CYM: Queen, I, 5, 64.
WINT: Leontes, I, 3, 318.

Corin, old shepherd.
AYL: II, 4.

Corinth, brothel, house of ill-repute; cant term; ancient Corinth was noted for licentiousness.
TIMON: Fool, II, 2, 73.

Corinth, part of ancient Greece, occupying most of Isthmus of Corinth and part of Northeast Peloponnesus; believed to have been founded by Dorian invaders (9th century BC); leading commercial center.
CofE: Aegeon, I, 1, 87.

Corinthian, playboy, gay blade, one who enjoys a life of pleasure.
1H4: Prince, II, 4, 13.

Coriolanus, The Tragedy of, written 1607-8; registered and published 1623; no record of an early performance; source, NORTH's translation of PLUTARCH's *Life of Coriolanus.*

PLOT: Caius Marcius, Roman general who has captured the Volscian town of Corioli, is rewarded with the surname Coriolanus and granted a consulship. Contemptuous of the people who revolt during a famine in Rome, he incurs their wrath and is banished. In revenge he joins his former enemies and leads the Volscian army against Rome. Comenius and Menenius, his former friends and supporters, try to persuade him to spare the city, but he refuses. He relents when his mother, Volumnia, his wife, Virgilia, and his son, come to his tent and, kneeling before him, plead with him. When he returns in triumph to Corioli, he is murdered by conspirators under orders from the jealous Aufidius. "It is from first to last, for all its turmoil of battle and clamor of contentious factions, rather a private and domestic than a public or historical tragedy. . . . The subject of the whole play is not the exile's revolt, the rebel's repentance, or the traitor's reward, but above all it is the son's tragedy."—(Swinburne.)

Coriolanus, Roman general and consul; "essentially the splendid oaf who has never come to maturity" (Palmer); completely dominated by his mother; his patriotism is expressed in purely selfish, personal terms, and he is, therefore, a traitor to himself and to Rome. [Gaius Marcius, fl. first half of the 5th century BC; legendary hero; conqueror of Volscian city of Corioli.]
COR: I, 1.

cormorant, glutton, greedy, rapacious; sea bird with pouch under beak for captured fish; voracious eater.
RICH2: Gaunt, II, 1, 38.
COR: 1Citizen, I, 1, 125.
LLL: King, I, 1, 4.

corn, wheat, oats, rye or any grain other than maize.
MND: Titania, II, 1, 94.
2H6: Duchess, I, 2, 1.
HEN8: Cranmer, V, 1, 111.

Cornelia, mother of the Gracchi, two famous Roman political leaders; greatly admired.
TITUS: IV, 1, 12.

Cornelius, Queen's honest doctor, who gives her a drug that makes a "show of death" instead of the requested poison, and thus saves Imogen's life.
CYM: I, 5.

Cornelius, courtier; with Voltimand, sent by Claudius to ask aid in stopping an invasion attempt by Fortinbras.
HAM: I, 2.

corner-cap, biretta, cap with three or four corners, worn by scholars, divines, judges.
LLL: Berowne, IV, 3, 53.

cornet, squadron of cavalry; name derived from standard, originally a horn-shaped pennon, attached to a lance.
1H6: York, IV, 3, 25.

cornet, leather-covered wooden

instrument with finger-holes; blown like a horn or trumpet; often used in theaters.

cornuto, cuckold.
MWW: Falstaff, III, 5, 71.

Cornwall, Duke of, ambitious, treacherous husband of Regan; puts Kent, Lear's messenger, in the stocks and orders Gloucester to shut the doors on the wretched king; when Gloucester goes to Lear's aid, Cornwall puts out his eyes; killed by one of his own servants.
LEAR: I, 1.

corollary, more than enough, excess.
TEMP: Prospero, IV, 1, 57.

coronet weeds, garland or wreath of wild flowers woven or strung together into a crown for the head.
HAM: Queen, IV, 7, 174.

correspondent, obedient, compliant, submissive.
TEMP: Ariel, I, 2, 297.

corrival, partner, associate.
1H4: Hotspur, I, 3, 207. See
HONOUR.

corrupted currents. See OFFENSE.

corse, corpse.
HAM: King, I, 2, 105.
COR: 1Lord, V, 6, 144.
WINT: Florizel, IV, 4, 129.

corslet, embrace, clasp; breast-plate.
2NK: 1Queen, I, 1, 177.
COR: Menenius, V, 4, 21.

costard, large apple; slang reference to head.
LLL: Moth, III, 1, 71.
MWW: Evans, III, 1, 14.
LEAR: Edgar, IV, 6, 247.

Costard, clown; illiterate peasant acting the educated wit; placed in jail by Don Armado, his rival for the love of Jaquenetta; serving as a messenger he gets the letters mixed; plays "Pompion the Great" in "The NINE WORTHIES."
LLL: I, 1.

costermonger, street hawker; from costard monger, seller of apples.
2H4: Falstaff, I, 2, 191.

cote, outdistance, pass; cottage.
HAM: Rosencrantz, II, 2, 329.
AYL: Corin, II, 4, 83.

cot-queen, "old woman"; man who meddles in woman's affairs.
R&J: Nurse, IV, 4, 6.

Cotshall, the Cotswold hills in Gloucestershire, famous for athletic events; the spelling gives an indication of Tudor pronunciation.
RICH2: Northumberland, II, 3, 9.
MWW: Slender, I, 1, 92—Cots-all.

couch, lie hidden, hide, lie in ambush.
HAM: Hamlet, V, 1, 245.
MWW: Page, V, 2, 1.
TEMP: Ariel's song, V, 1, 90.
See BEE.

coulter, blade or knife of the plowshare.
HEN5: Burgundy, V, 2, 46.

count, trial, legal indictment, judgment.
HAM: King, IV, 7, 17.

countenance, special favor, approval; authority, honor; show respect for.
HAM: Hamlet, IV, 2, 17.
1H4: Falstaff, I, 2, 175.
SHREW: Curtis, IV, 1, 101.

counter, debased coin; valueless token or bone disc used in counting.
AYL: Jaques, II, 7, 63.
JC: Brutus, IV, 3, 80.
OTH: Iago, I, 1, 31—counter-caster, bookkeeper, used derisively as one who used counters to add up accounts or make change.

counter, hunting term which refers to the hound that follows the scent backward, in the wrong direction, or opposite to the one the prey has taken.
HAM: Queen, IV, 5, 110.

Counter, name for debtors' prisons in London, Southwark and other places.

MWW: Falstaff, III, 3, 85.

counterfeit, portrait, likeness; "fake."

HAM: Hamlet, III, 4, 54.

TIMON: Timon, V, 1, 83.

MACB: Macduff, II, 3, 81.

To die is to be a counterfeit; for he is but the counterfeit of a man who hath not the life of a man; but to counterfeit dying when a man thereby liveth, is to be no counterfeit, but the true and perfect image of life indeed.

1H4: Falstaff, V, 4, 116.

Countess Richmond, Margaret Beaufort, widow of Edmund Tudor, Earl of Richmond, son of Katherine Valois and Owen Tudor; great-granddaughter of John of Gaunt, mother of Henry VII, who claimed his kingdom from both sides, although through illegitimacy it was a weak claim; married the Earl of Derby.

RICH3: Queen, I, 3, 20.

country-dialect, speech of Devonshire, and other western counties, used by rustics in plays of the period.

LEAR: Edgar, IV, 6, 240-51.

country-matters, probably a pun on sexual activities of barnyard animals; uncouth or indecent action or behavior.

HAM: Hamlet, III, 2, 123.

couple a gorge, mispronunciation of French *couper la gorge,* cut the throat.

HEN5: Pistol, II, 1, 75.

couplet, twin, pair; dove or pigeon lays two eggs at a time.

HAM: Queen, V, 1, 310.

courage

But screw your courage to the sticking-place,

And we'll not fail.

MACB: Lady Macbeth, I, 7, 60.

course, chase, pursue.

A&C: Enobarbus, III, 13, 11.

LLL: Berowne, IV, 3, 2.

course, in bear-baiting, one attack.

MACB: Macbeth, V, 7, 2.

LEAR: Gloucester, III, 7, 54.

courser's hair. See BREEDING.

Court, Alexander, soldier; speaks to the King on the night before the battle at Agincourt.

HEN5: IV, 1.

Courtesan, "pretty and witty, wild"; demands a gold chain from Antipholus of Syracuse in exchange for a ring she claims she gave him.

COFE: IV, 3.

court of guard, guard room, headquarters or post of the guard.

OTH: Iago, II, 1, 220.

A&C: Sentry, IV, 9, 2.

courtship, manners of the courtier, courtliness of behavior.

OTH: Iago, II, 1, 172. See GYVE.

cousin, used to refer to kinsmen in general or any near relative other than the immediate family; often referred to nephew, niece or cousin in modern usage.

HAM: King, I, 2, 64.

RICH2: Duchess of Gloucester, I, 2, 46.

TWN: Maria, I, 3, 5.

OTH: Iago, I, 1, 114—legally, next of kin.

Covent Garden Theatre, London, opened by John Rich (1732) with Congreve's comedy, *The Way of the World;* first performance of Goldsmith's *She Stoops to Conquer* (1773); John Philip Kemble became manager (1803); burned down (September, 1808), rebuilt (1809); Charles Kemble took over as manager (1817); became the Royal Italian Opera House (1847); burned down (March, 1856); present theater designed by E. M. Barry and opened (May, 1858).

cover, lay or set the table.

AYL: Amiens, II, 5, 32.

2H4: 1Drawer, II, 4, 11.

coward dogs
. . . coward dogs
Most spend their mouths when
  what they seem to threaten
Runs far before them.
HEN5: Dauphin, II, 4, 69.

cowards
Plenty and peace breeds
  cowards; hardness ever
Of hardiness is mother.
CYM: Imogen, III, 6, 21.

Cowards die many times before
  their deaths;
The valiant never taste of death
  but once.
JC: Caesar, II, 2, 32.

cowl-staff, pole used by two people to carry a "cowl" or basket
between them.
MWW: Mrs. Ford, III, 3, 155.

cowslip, wild primrose having
clusters of small yellow-orange
flowers (Great Britain); marsh-
marigold (United States).
MND: Fairy, II, 1, 10.

Cox, God's or for God's.
ALL'SW: Lafew, V, 2, 42.

coxcomb, cap worn by clown or
professional fool shaped like a
cock's comb; fool.
LEAR: Fool, I, 4, 114.
LLL: Berowne, IV, 3, 84.
ADO: Conrade, IV, 2, 71.

coxcomb, head.
TWN: Andrew, V, 1, 179.
HEN5: Fluellen, V, 1, 57.

coy, disdain, scorn; caress, pat or
stroke gently.
COR: Menenius, V, 1, 6.
SHREW: Petruchio, II, 1, 245.
MND: Titania, IV, 1, 2.

coystrill (coistrel, custrel), knave,
base, low-born, contemptible
fellow.
TWN: Toby, I, 3, 43.
PER: Marina, IV, 6, 176.

cozen, deceive, dupe, trick, cheat.
HAM: Hamlet, III, 4, 77.
OTH: Emilia, IV, 2, 132.
LEAR: Lear, IV, 6, 167—*The
usurer hangs the cozener.*

cozier, cobbler.
TWN: Malvolio, II, 3, 97.

crab, crabapple; roasted apples
were put into drinks (usually
ale) which gave it added flavor
or made a thicker drink called
a "posset."
MND: Puck, II, 1, 48.
LLL: Winter, V, 2, 935.
TEMP: Caliban, II, 2, 171.

crabbed age and youth
Crabbed age and youth cannot
live together:
Youth is full of pleasance, age
  is full of care . . .
PASSPIL: XII, 1—beginning of
lengthy comparison.

crack, boast, brag.
LLL: King, IV, 3, 268.
JOHN: Austria, II, 1, 147.

crack, rogue, impish little boy.
COR: Virgilia, I, 3, 74.
2H4: Shallow, III, 2, 34.

crack, flaw, defect.
WINT: Camillo, I, 2, 322.
OTH: Iago, II, 3, 332.
HAM: Hamlet, II, 2, 448—
cracked within the ring, when
milled the rim or edge encircling a coin protected it from
"cracking within the ring"; before this was done the designed
coin would often crack, and
become worthless; Hamlet here
refers to the crack in a young
boy's voice whose tone quality
is changing; also a play on
"ring" meaning sound.

crackhemp, gallows bird; one to
be hanged by a hemp rope.
SHREW: Vincentio, V, 1, 46.

craft, cunning, trickery; sly op-
ponent.
HAM: Hamlet, II, 2, 290.
TWN: Duke, V, 1, 169.
HAM: Hamlet, III, 4, 210.

crank, winding path or passage.
COR: Menenius, I, 1, 141.
1H4: Hotspur, III, 1, 98.

Cranmer, Thomas, honest church-
man, secures the King's divorce
from Katherine; made Archbishop of Canterbury; crowns
Anne queen; when charged with
heresy, he is backed by the King
and honored by being made

godfather to Elizabeth. [1489-1556, reformer, outstanding archbishop; leading figure in newly founded Anglican Church; charged with treason for attempting to help Lady Jane Grey, but pardoned; when charged with heresy, at first recanted and signed belief in Catholic doctrine, but reversed himself prior to being burned at the stake.]
HEN8: V, 1.

crant, garland, wreath.
HAM: Priest, V, 1, 255.

crare, small trading vessel.
CYM: Belarius, IV, 2, 205.

craven, cowardly cock; one that will not fight, is not "game."
SHREW: Katherina, II, 1, 228.
CYM: Imogen, III, 4, 80.

crazed, flawed, unsound; illegal.
MND: Demetrius, I, 1, 92.
1H6: Talbot, III, 2, 89—*crazy.*

credent, credulous, trusting; believable.
HAM: Laertes, I, 3, 30.
TEMP: Gonzalo, II, 1, 59.
OTH: Iago, II, 1, 296—*credit.*

crescive, growing, increasing, developing.
HEN5: Ely, I, 1, 66.
A&C: Pompey, II, 1, 10.
HAM: Laertes, I, 3, 11—*crescent.*

cresset, beacon; fire-basket or other vessel holding combustible material as a torch and either mounted on a tall stand or attached to a pole and swung from a high point.
1H4: Glendower, III, 1, 15.

Cressida, heroine of tragedy; daughter of Calchas, beloved of Troilus, who finds her making love to Diomedes; yet, "She is a more helpless being than CHAUCER'S *Criseyde,* a flower growing in Trojan slime."—(Tucker Brooke.)
T&C: I, 2.

crib, manger, stall for cattle; hovel, hut, cabin.

HAM: Hamlet, V, 2, 89. See BEAST.
2H4: King, III, 1, 9.

crickets, chattering, chirping ladies-in-waiting.
WINT: Mamillius, II, 1, 31.

cried I aim?, cried game, term in bear-baiting.
MWW: Host, II, 3, 93.

Crier, announces Queen Katherine.
HEN8: II, 4.

crime
. . . Crimes, like lands,
Are not inherited.
TIMON: 1Senator, V, 4, 37.

cringe, distort, shrink, grimace.
A&C: Antony, III, 13, 100.

crisp, rippling, curled.
TEMP: Iris, IV, 1, 130.
1H4: Hotspur, I, 3, 106.

Crispin Crispian, October 25, day sacred to Saints Crispinus and Crispianus.
HEN5: King, IV, 3, 57.

critical
For I am nothing if not critical.
OTH: Iago, II, 1, 120—here critical means captious, censorious or bitter.

crocodile, myth credits the crocodile with mournful cries that attracted people to him; then he snatched and ate them; thus, crocodile tears.
2H6: Queen, III, 1, 226.

It is shaped, sir, like itself, and it is as broad as it hath breadth. It is just so high as it is, and moves with its own organs. It lives by that which nourisheth it, and the elements once out of it, it transmigrates.
A&C: Antony, II, 7, 47.

If that the earth could teem with woman's tears,
Each drop she falls would prove a crocodile.
OTH: Othello, IV, 1, 256.

Cromwell, Thomas, servant to Wolsey; defends Cranmer against Gardiner. [c1485-1540;

chancellor of the exchequer (1533); as vicar-general to the king (1536) suppressed the monasteries and confiscated their property; lord high chamberlain of England (1539); arranged marriage of Henry and Anne of Cleves; created Earl of Essex (1540); executed for high treason.]

HEN8: III, 2.

Crosby House, Richard's town house in London; originally in Bishopsgate Street, it was moved to Chelsea, where it is today.

RICH3: Richard, I, 2, 212.

cross, coin with cross stamped on reverse side.

LLL: Moth, I, 2, 36.

cross, stubborn, perverse; thwart, frustrate, hinder; trouble, annoy.

MND: Hermia, I, 1, 136.
CYM: Pisanio, III, 5, 168.
RICH2: York, II, 2, 78.

cross-gartered, wearing ribbon garters that cross behind the knee and are tied in a large bow in front.

TwN: Malvolio, II, 5, 167.

cross-row, alphabet; letters were placed in narrow rows in children's hornbooks; first sign on the page was a cross; sometimes called Christ or criss-cross-row.

RICH3: Clarence, I, 1, 55. See HORNBOOK.

crossways, crossroads where suicides were buried.

MND: Puck, III, 2, 383.

crotchets, very small musical notes (half the value of minim); whims, fancy.

ADO: Pedro, II, 3, 58.
MWW: Mrs. Ford, II, 1, 159.
MEAS: Lucio, III, 2, 135.

crow, crowbar.

R&J: Friar, V, 2, 21.

crow, quarrel, pick a fight.

COFE: Dromio E., III, 1, 83.

crow

. . . and the crow
Makes wing to th' rooky wood.

MACB: Macbeth, III, 2, 50. See ROOK.

crowflowers, buttercups or marsh marigolds; old name, wild hyacinth; also called "fair maid of France."

HAM: Queen, IV, 7, 171.

crown, gold coin, "dollar."

SHREW: Gremio, II, 1, 352.
ALL'SW: Clown, II, 2, 23— *French crown.*

crown

Uneasy lies the head that wears a crown.

2H4: King, III, 1, 31.

My crown is in my heart, not on my head;
Not decked with diamonds and Indian stones,
Nor to be seen. My crown is called content;
A crown it is that seldom kings enjoy.

3H6: King, III, 1, 62—*Indian stones,* pearls.

crowned child, apparition; symbolic of Duncan's son, Malcolm; carries a tree in his hand which foretells his strategy of camouflaging his men as trees and surprising Macbeth in battle.

MACB: S.D., IV, 1, following line 86.

crowner, coroner.

HAM: Other (Clown), V, 1, 4.

cruel

I must be cruel only to be kind.

HAM: Hamlet, III, 4, 198.

cruel act

If thou didst but consent
To this most cruel act, do but despair;
And if thou want'st a cord, the smallest thread
That ever spider twisted from her womb
Will serve to strangle thee; a rush will be a beam
To hang thee on. Or wouldst thou drown thyself,
Put but a little water in a spoon,
And it shall be as all the ocean,
Enough to stifle such a villain up,

I do suspect thee very grievously.
  JOHN: Bastard, IV, 3, 125.

crusado (cruzado), Portuguese
gold coins, with design of a
cross.
  OTH: Desdemona, III, 4, 26.

cry, pack (hounds); group.
  HAM: Hamlet, III, 2, 289.
  MND: Theseus, IV, 1, 127.
  OTH: Roderigo, II, 3, 370.

cry aim, archery term, encourage,
applaud.
  JOHN: France (Philip), II, 1,
196.
  MWW: Ford, III, 2, 46.

cry havoc, call for mass or merci-
less slaughter; cry of "no quar-
ter."
  COR: Menenius, III, 1, 275.
  JOHN: Bastard, II, 1, 357.
Cry 'Havoc!' and let slip the
  dogs of war,
That this foul deed shall smell
  above the earth
With carrion men, groaning for
  burial.
  JC: Antony, III, 1, 273.

crystals, eyes.
  HEN5: Pistol, II, 3, 56.

cry woe
Cry woe, destruction, ruin, and
  decay:
The worst is death, and death
  will have his day.
  RICH2: Richard, III, 2, 102.

cub-drawn, sucked or nursed dry
and therefore, hungry and ferocious.
  LEAR: Gentleman, III, 1, 12.

cubiculo, bedroom, private bedchamber.
  TWN: Toby, III, 2, 56.

cuckold, husband whose wife
has deceived or been unfaithful
to him; horns were the symbol
of the cuckold.
  HAM: Laertes, IV, 5, 118.
  COR: 2Servingman, IV, 5, 244.
  1H4: Falstaff, II, 4, 371.

cuckoo, bird that lays its eggs in
other birds' nests instead of
building one for itself.

  A&C: Pompey, II, 6, 28.
  LLL: Spring, V, 2, 917.
The hedge-sparrow fed the
  cuckoo so long
That it had it head bit off by it
  young.
  LEAR: Fool, I, 4, 235.

cuckoo-buds, probably buttercups.
  LLL: Spring, V, 2, 906.

cucullus non facit monachum,
proverbial Latin expression
meaning a cowl does not make
a monk.
  MEAS: Lucio, V, 1, 263.
  TWN: Clown, I, 5, 62—nor a
fool's costume a fool.

cullion, scoundrel, base fellow,
rascal.
  HEN5: Fluellen, III, 2, 22.
  SHREW: Hortensio, IV, 2, 20.
  2H6: Queen, I, 3, 43.

culverin, small cannon; very long
in proportion to bore; 5½-inch
caliber, 17-lb. shot.
  1H4: Lady, II, 3, 56.

*cum privilegio ad imprimendum
solum,* Latin, with exclusive
printing rights.
  SHREW: Biondello, IV, 4, 93.
  HEN8: Lovell, I, 3, 34—*cum
privilegio,* with the king's special grant or immunity.

cunning, well-made, carefully
constructed or wrought; know-
ing; skill.
  RICH2: Mowbray, I, 3, 163.
  OTH: Desdemona, III, 3, 49.
  A&C: Antony, II, 3, 34.
She is cunning past man's
thought.
  A&C: Antony, I, 2, 150—ref-
erence to Cleopatra.

Cupid
This wimpled, whining, pur-
  blind, wayward boy;
This senior junior, giant dwarf,
  Dan Cupid.
  LLL: Berowne, III, 1, 181. See
WIMPLED.
  TIMON: I, 2—masker plays
part of Cupid.

Cupid's flower. See PANSIES.

Curan, courtier; tells Edmund that Cornwall and Regan are coming to Gloucester's castle; reports discord between Cornwall and Albany.
LEAR: II, 1.

curb, "kowtow" or bow to.
HAM: Hamlet, III, 4, 155.

curfew, nine o'clock ringing of the bells was a signal for people to go indoors and leave the night to the fairies and the elves.
TEMP: Prospero, V, 1, 40.

Curio, gentleman attending Orsino, Duke of Illyria.
TWN: I, 1.

curious, meticulous, precise, exact, fastidious, particular; anxious, concerned; elaborately decorated or embroidered; delicately made.
HAM: Horatio, V, 1, 227.
SHREW: Pedant, IV, 4, 36.
WINT: Camillo, IV, 4, 525.
CYM: Belarius, V, 5, 361.

current, valid, genuine, sound; credited.
RICH2: Gaunt, I, 3, 231.
1H4: Hotspur, I, 3, 68.

curse in love
O, 'tis the curse in love, and still approved,
When women cannot love where they're beloved!
2GENT: Proteus, V, 4, 43.

curst, savage, vicious, bad-tempered, shrewish, "fishwife."
MND: Helena, III, 2, 300
WINT: Clown, III, 3, 135.
ADO: Antonio, II, 1, 22.

Curtain Theatre, probably built by Henry Laneman soon after Burbage's theater; north of Bishopsgate and south of THE THEATRE; reopened by the Chamberlain's company (1597); used by the Worcester's-Queen's Men (1603-09); not mentioned after 1627.

curtal, shortened tail (of dog); docked, clipped tail.
COFE: Dromio S., III, 2, 151.

MWW: Pistol, II, 1, 114.
ALL'SW: Lafew, II, 3, 65.

curtleaxe, cutlass, used after lance has been broken.
HEN5: Constable, IV, 2, 21.
AYL: Rosalind, I, 3, 119.

Curtis, servant in Petruchio's country house; prepares for arrival of Petruchio and Katherina; originally played as a man, now usually cast as older woman or housekeeper.
SHREW: IV, 1.

curvet, prancing or leaping of a high-spirited horse.
ALL'SW: Parolles, II, 3, 299.

cushes, cuisses, armor for the thighs.
1H4: Vernon, IV, 1, 105.

cushion, senator's seat; symbol of peace and ease; place in government.
COR: Aufidius, IV, 7, 43.

custalorum, blunder or corruption of Latin *custos rotulorum,* keeper of the rolls; most important of magistrates in county, or principal justice of the peace.
MWW: Shallow, I, 1, 7.

custard coffin. See COFFIN.

customer, prostitute, harlot.
OTH: Cassio, IV, 1, 121.

cut, ornamental cutting of fabric to display underbody; embroidered squares inserted into cut material; satin, silk lining, slip.
ADO: Margaret, III, 4, 19.

cut, gelded or dock-tailed horse; term of contempt.
TWN: Toby, II, 3, 203.
1H4: 1Carrier, II, 1, 6.

cutpurse, thief, usually one who stole money by cutting the purse worn as a belt or girdle; pickpocket.
HAM: Hamlet, III, 4, 99.

cuttle, knife used by cutpurse; cutthroat, bully.
2H4: Doll, II, 4, 140.

cycle
Things at the worst will cease, or else climb upward

To what they were before.
MACB: Ross, IV, 2, 24.

Cyclops, Titans, one-eyed giants; helped Vulcan, the blacksmith god, forge armor for Mars, god of war; made thunderbolts for Zeus.
HAM: Player, II, 2, 511.
TITUS: Titus, IV, 3, 46.

Cydnus, ancient river in Cilicia, Asia Minor, now Tarsus River; flows southeast from Tarsus Mountains into the Mediterranean.
CYM: Iachimo, II, 4, 71.
A&C: Enobarbus, II, 2, 192.

cygnet. See SWAN.

Cymbeline, written c1609-10, probably performed at the GLOBE April, 1611, published 1623; HOLINSHED source of historical parts of the play; wager theme from BOCCACCIO's *Bernabo of Genoa* (II, 9), popular folk tale; Belarius theme possibly from *The Rare Triumphs of Love and Fortune,* an old play (printed, 1589); claims of relationship to BEAUMONT and FLETCHER's *Philaster* are vague.

PLOT: Cymbeline, King of Britain, banishes Posthumus from the kingdom, when told of his secret marriage to his daughter, Imogen. Upon his departure, Posthumus exchanges gifts with his wife, giving her a bracelet while she presents him with a diamond ring. In Rome, Posthumus is induced by Iachimo to wager ten thousand ducats that his wife is incorruptible. Iachimo, by unscrupulous means, gains access to her bedroom and steals the bracelet, which he later uses to prove to Posthumus that Imogen has been unfaithful.

Meanwhile the Queen, who had wished to arrange a marriage between her son Cloten and Imogen, has obtained some poison from her physician, Cornelius, and plans to kill Posthumus. The doctor, however, distrusting the Queen, gives the messenger a drug which is not poison but a heavy sedative. Posthumus writes to Imogen telling her to meet him at Milford Haven and orders his servant Pisanio to kill her on the way. Instead he persuades Imogen to disguise herself as a man and to join the Roman general, Lucius, who has declared war on Britain.

Meanwhile, Cloten attempts to force his attentions on Imogen who rejects him. The princess meets Belarius, a banished lord, and his two sons in their mountain cave, unaware that she has been followed by Cloten, who, disguised as Posthumus, plans to ravish her and kill her husband. However, before he can find her, he is killed by her two brothers. Alone in the cave, Imogen feels ill, takes the Queen's restorative and falls into a dead faint. When her brothers find her, they carry her apparently lifeless body into the forest and place it beside the body of the headless Cloten.

When she awakens, she mistakes the corpse for Posthumus and goes to join Lucius, whom she serves as a page. Posthumus, disguised as a British peasant, Belarius and the two princes fight valiantly in a battle against the Roman armies, one led by Iachimo, and the Romans are defeated. The Queen goes mad when she learns of the death of her son. At a meeting before the King, all relationships are revealed, lovers united, villains exposed and peace is made with Rome.

Cymbeline, King of Britain, character based on legendary ruler, Cunobeline; dominated by his queen, he is an unimpressive figure in a fairytale play.
CYM: I, 1.

Cynthia, moon goddess.
  R&J: Romeo, III, 5, 20.
  VENUS: 728.

cypress, sheer, transparent black
silk fabric used for veils and
scarves; imported from Cyprus.
  TwN: Olivia, III, 1, 132.
  WINT: Autolycus, IV, 4, 221.

Cytherea, surname of Venus
(Aphrodite); believed born
(arose) from the waves near
the island of Cythera (painted
by Botticelli).
  WINT: Perdita, IV, 4, 122.
  CYM: Iachimo, II, 2, 14.
  SHREW: 2Manservant, Induction, 2, 53.

dace, small fish used as bait for pike.

2H4: Falstaff, III, 2, 356.

daff, doff; push or thrust aside.

ADO: Pedro, II, 3, 176.
1H4: Hotspur, IV, 1, 96.
A&C: Antony, IV, 4, 13.

daffodils

When daffodils begin to peer . . .
WINT: Autolycus IV, 3, 1—opening line of song.

dagger

Is this a dagger which I see before me,
The handle toward my hand?
Come, let me clutch thee!
I have thee not, and yet I see thee still.
Art thou not, fatal vision, sensible
To feeling as to sight? Or art thou but
A dagger of the mind, a false creation,
Proceeding from the heat-oppressed brain?
MACB: Lady Macbeth, II, 1, 33.

dagger of lath, wooden or false weapon; prop carried by Vice in morality plays (to beat the Devil).

1H4: Falstaff, II, 4, 151.
TwN: Clown, IV, 2, 136.
2H4: Falstaff, III, 2, 344—Vice's dagger, an allusion to Shallow's lean physique.

Daintry, Daventry, Northamptonshire, central England.

3H6: 2Messenger, V, 1, 6.

daisy, low scapose herb with mul-ti-petaled flower, known in the United States as the *English daisy;* famed in English literature; symbol of "pure virginity," "spring or light of life and love."

HAM: Ophelia, IV, 5, 184.
LLL: Spring, V, 2, 904.

dalliance

. . . do not give dalliance
Too much the rein. The strongest oaths are straw
To the fire i' the blood.
TEMP: Prospero, IV, 1, 51.

Dalmatians, tribe of Adriatic Sea; conquered by Romans (34 BC); revolted (AD 6).

CYM: Cymbeline, III, 1, 74.
See PANNONIANS.

Damascus, believed to have been the place where Cain slew his brother Abel.

1H6: Winchester, I, 3, 39.

damask, red, pink and white; rose-colored.

COR: Brutus, II, 1, 232.
LLL: Boyet, V, 2, 296.
TwN: Viola, II, 4, 115.

damask cheek

. . . She never told her love,
But let concealment, like a worm i' th' bud,
Feed on her damask cheek.
TwN: Viola, II, 4, 114.

damned

(A fellow almost damn'd in a fair wife)
OTH: Iago, I, 1, 21.

Damon, one of the famed pair of faithful friends, Damon and Pythias; Damon, sure of Pythias' loyalty, stayed as a hostage in prison, while Pythias returned to Syracuse to put his affairs in order; when Pythias returned in time to be put to death and release Damon, Dionysius was so astounded by this show of devotion and trust that he released them both.

HAM: Hamlet, III, 2, 292.

dance barefoot, refers to elder unmarried sisters who were humiliated by having to dance barefoot at their younger sister's wedding.

SHREW: Katherina, II, 1, 33.

Dancer, speaks the Epilogue. 2H4.

dancing horse, famous performing horse owned by a man named Banks; called Morocco, he was trained to tap out numbers with his hoof; performed in circus shows in England in the 1590's.

LLL: Moth, I, 2, 57.

danger

. . . Danger knows full well
That Caesar is more dangerous than he.
We are two lions littered in one day,
And I the elder and more terrible,
And Caesar shall go forth.

JC: Caesar, II, 2, 44.

dangerous. See OPPOSITES.

Daniel, judge in story of Susanna in the Apocrypha; Susanna, falsely accused of adultery by two elders, is cleared by Daniel.

MERV: Shylock, IV, 1, 223.

Daniel, Samuel (1562-1619). English poet, dramatist; appointed licenser of the plays of the Queen's Revels (1604); Gentleman Extraordinary of Queen Anne's Privy Chamber; wrote pastoral tragi-comedies, *Vision of the Twelve Goddesses,* a masque, sonnets and narrative poems; influenced by his rival and friend, Shakespeare.

Dansker, Danish form of Danes.

HAM: Polonius, II, 1, 7.

Daphne, nymph pursued by Apollo; turned into a laurel tree (from OVID's *Metamorphoses*).

SHREW: 2Manservant, Induction, 2, 59.
MND: Helena, II, 1, 231.
T&C: Troilus, I, 1, 101.

dapples

Before the wheels of Phoebus, round about
Dapples the drowsy east with spots of grey.

ADO: Pedro, V, 3, 27.

Dardan, Trojan.

T&C: Prologue, 13.
MERV: Portia, III, 2, 58.
LUCRECE: 1436.

Dardanius, servant of Brutus; refuses to kill his master after his defeat at Philippi; runs away at Octavius' and Antony's approach.

JC: V, 5.

dare

I dare do all that may become a man.
Who dares do more is none.

MACB: Macbeth, I, 7, 46.

What man dare, I dare.
Approach thou like the rugged Russian bear,
The armed rhinoceros, or th' Hyrcan tiger;
Take any shape but that, and my firm nerves
Shall never tremble. Or be alive again,
And dare me to the desert with thy sword;
If trembling I inhabit then, protest me
The baby of a girl. Hence, horrible shadow
Unreal mock'ry, hence!

MACB: Macbeth, III, 4, 99. See HYRCAN.

dark

Finish, good lady. The bright day is done,
And we are for the dark.

A&C: Iras, V, 2, 193.

darkling, in the dark.

MND: Helena, II, 2, 86.

darkness

Is't night's predominance, or the
day's shame,
That darkness does the face of
earth entomb
When living light should kiss
it?
MACB: Ross, II, 4, 8.

dark night

Deep night, dark night, the
silent of the night,
The time of night when Troy
was set on fire;
The time when screech owls
cry and bandogs howl
And spirits walk and ghosts
break up their graves—
That time best fits the work we
have in hand.
2H6: Bolingbroke, I, 4, 19. See
BANDOGS.

Dark night, that from the eye
his function takes,
The ear more quick of apprehension makes.
Wherein it doth impair the seeing sense,
It pays the hearing double recompense.
MND: Hermia, III, 2, 177.

darnel, destructive weed; biblical
tares; rye grass.
HEN5: Burgundy, V, 2, 45.
LEAR: Cordelia, IV, 4, 5.
1H6: Pucelle, III, 2, 44.

darting Parthia, refers to successful tactics of Parthian horse-
men, who defeated the heavily
armed and slower moving
Romans by flinging darts and
riding off before they could be
attacked; shot arrows backward
as they fled.
A&C: Ventidius, III, 1, 1.

Datchet Mead, village on the
Thames near Windsor.
MWW: Mrs. Ford, III, 3, 15.

daub, pretend, dissemble, dis-
guise; taken from plastering
mortar.
LEAR: Edgar, IV, 1, 52.
RICH3: Richard, III, 5, 29.
MWW: Ford, IV, 2, 186—

daub'ry, false show, vulgar
imposture.

daughter

"One fair daughter, and no
more,
The which he loved passing
well."
HAM: Hamlet, II, 2, 426—refers to daughter of Jephthah.

Daughter of Antiochus, the evil
king of Antioch; described as
buxom and beautiful.
PER: I, 1.

Dauphin. See CHARLES VII.
HEN5: II, 4; 1H6: I, 2.

Davy, servant in Justice Shallow's
employ; makes a very clever defense of William Visor of Won-
cot against Clement Perkes o'
the hill.
2H4: V, 1.

daw, jackdaw, stupid, foolish
bird.
OTH: Iago, I, 1, 65. See HEART.
COR: 3Servingman, IV, 5, 47.

dawn. See LARK.

day

Let Hercules himself do what
he may,
The cat will mew, and dog will
have his day.
HAM: Hamlet, V, 1, 314. See
HERCULES.

Men judge by the complexion
of the sky
The state and inclination of the
day.
RICH2: Scroop, III, 2, 194. See
COMPLEXION.

dead, deadly; deathly pale; dark,
dreary.
RICH2: Bagot, IV, 1, 10.
MND: Hermia, III, 2, 57.

dead

He is dead and gone, lady,
He is dead and gone;
At his head a grass-green turf,
At his heels a stone.
HAM: Ophelia, IV, 5, 29. See
TRUE-LOVE.

dead shepherd

Dead shepherd, now I find thy
saw of might,

"Who ever lov'd that lov'd not
at first sight?"
AYL: Phebe, III, 5, 82—refers
to line from MARLOWE's *Hero
and Leander*.

dear, heavy; costly, valuable;
great.
RICH2: Mowbray, I, 1, 130.
TwN: Toby, III, 2, 58.
MND: Helena, I, 1, 249.

dearest, most vital or of most
concern.
HAM: Hamlet, I, 1, 182—most
hated.
TEMP: Alonso, II, 1, 135—
most grievous.

dearth, rareness, of uncommon
value or excellence; famine.
HAM: Hamlet, V, 2, 123.
RICH2: Richard, III, 3, 163.
COR: Menenius, I, 1, 69.

dear to fancy, exquisitely or
handsomely designed; appealing
to the fancy.
HAM: Osric, V, 2, 159.

death
Death is the fairest cover for her
shame
That may be wished for.
ADO: Leonato, IV, 1, 117.

Death, death, O amiable lovely
death!
Thou odoriferous stench! sound
rottenness!
Arise forth from the couch of
lasting night,
Thou hate and terror to prosperity,
And I will kiss thy detestable
bones,
And put my eyeballs in thy
vaulty brows,
And ring these fingers with thy
household worms,
And stop this gap of breath with
fulsome dust,
And be a carrion monster like
thyself.
JOHN: Constance, III, 4, 25.

That we the pain of death would
hourly die
Rather than die at once!
LEAR: Edgar, V, 3, 185.

. . . Nothing in his life
Became him like the leaving it.
He died
As one that had been studied in
his death
To throw away the dearest thing
he owed
As 'twere a careless trifle.
MACB: Malcolm, I, 4, 7. See
STUDIED.

For death remembered should
be like a mirror,
Who tells us life's but breath, to
trust it error.
PER: Pericles, I, 1, 45.

. . . nothing can we call our own
but death
And that small model of the
barren earth
Which serves as paste and cover
to our bones.
RICH2: Richard, III, 2, 152.
See PASTE, TALK OF GRAVES.

Death lies on her like an untimely frost
Upon the sweetest flower of all
the field.
R&J: Capulet, IV, 5, 28.

Then what could death do if
thou shouldst depart,
Leaving thee living in posterity?
SONNET: VI, 11.

So shalt thou feed on Death,
that feeds on men,
And Death once dead, there's
no more dying then.
SONNET: CXLVI, 13.

Come away, come away,
death . . .
TwN: Clown, II, 4, 52—beginning of song.

death. See COWARD, WOMEN, CRY
WOE.

death of Antony
The breaking of so great a thing
should make
A greater crack. The round
world
Should have shook lions into
civil streets
And citizens to their dens. The
death of Antony

Is not a single doom; in the name lay
A moiety of the world.
  A&C: Caesar, V, 1, 14. See MOIETY.

death of Falstaff
For after I saw him fumble with the sheets, and play with flowers, and smile upon his finger's end, I knew there was but one way; for his nose was as sharp as a pen, and 'a babbled of green fields.
  HEN5: Hostess, II, 3, 14.

death of kings
And tell sad stories of the death of kings:
How some have been deposed, some slain in war,
Some haunted by the ghosts they have deposed,
Some poisoned by their wives, some sleeping killed,
All murthered . . .
  RICH2: Richard, III, 2, 156.

death's conquest
. . . for thou art much too fair
To be death's conquest and make worms thine heir.
  SONNET: VI, 13.

debatement, discussion, argument, deliberation.
  HAM: Hamlet, V, 2, 45.

Deborah, war heroine and Hebrew prophetess of the Bible (Judges: 4, 4-6).
  1H6: Dauphin, I, 2, 105.

deboshed, debauched, corrupted, disgraced.
  TEMP: Trinculo, III, 2, 30.

deceit
Sweet, sweet, sweet poison for the age's tooth;
Which, though I will not practise to deceive,
Yet, to avoid deceit, I mean to learn;
For it shall strew the footsteps of my rising.
  JOHN: Bastard, I, 1, 213.

deceive
For having traffic with thyself alone,

Thou of thyself thy sweet self dost deceive:
  SONNET: IV, 9.

deception
To have what we would have, we speak not what we mean.
  MEAS: Isabella, II, 4, 118.

declension, depreciation, decline, deterioration, falling from standard.
  HAM: Polonius, II, 2, 149.

declining, bending or leaning toward.
  HAM: Player, II, 2, 500.

decoct, warm or heat up.
  HEN5: Constable, III, 5, 20.

deed
Ill deed is doubled with an evil word.
  COFE: Luciana, III, 2, 20.

deep, occult; serious.
  1H4: Glendower, III, 1, 49.

defeat thy favor, disguise your face.
  OTH: Iago, I, 3, 346.

defend, forbid.
  RICH2: Mowbray, I, 3, 18.
  A&C: Charmian, III, 3, 46.
  ADO: Hero, II, 1, 98.

defense
To kill, I grant, is sin's extremest gust;
But, in defence, by mercy, 'tis most just.
  TIMON: Alcibiades, III, 5, 54.

definement, delineation, description, portrait, depiction, explanation.
  HAM: Hamlet, V, 2, 151.

degree
. . . O, when degree is shaked,
Which is the ladder to all high designs,
The enterprise is sick!
  T&C: Ulysses, I, 3, 101.

degree. See DISCORD.

degree in hope, heir presumptive.
  RICH2: Richard I, 4, 36.

degrees of the lie
. . . The first, the Retort Courteous; the second, the Quip Modest; the third, the Reply

Churlish; the fourth, the Reproof Valiant; the fifth, the Countercheck Quarrelsome; the sixth, the Lie with Circumstance; the seventh, the Lie Direct, . . . you may avoid that too, with an If.
AYL: Touchstone, V, 4, 96.

Deiphobus, Trojan soldier in Greek legend; Priam and Hecuba's son; Troilus' brother.
T&C: IV, 1.

delimns, effaces, obliterates, blots or paints out.
A&C: Antony, IV, 14, 10.

deliver, report, communicate, relate.
MACB: Lady Macbeth, I, 5, 10.
1H4: Northumberland, I, 3, 26.

Delphos, island of Delos, smallest of the islands called Cyclades, in the Aegean Sea; famous in antiquity as the birthplace and holy seat of worship of Apollo.
WINT: Leontes, II, 1, 183.

demerits, deserts, values, merits.
OTH: Othello, I, 2, 22.
COR: Sicinius, I, 1, 276.

demesnes, domains, region, territory.
CYM: Belarius, III, 3, 70.—
R&J: Capulet, III, 5, 182—estates.

Demetrius, Athenian in love with Hermia; with the help of the fairies he falls in love with Helena.
MND: I, 1.

Demetrius, friend of Antony.
A&C: I, 1.

Demetrius. See CHIRON.
TITUS: I, 1.

demi-cannon, cannon with 6½-inch bore; sleeve tapered from shoulder to cuff with stiff inner lining to keep its shape.
SHREW: Petruchio, IV, 3, 88.

demi-puppets, very small creatures, probably fairies or elves, half the size of puppets.
TEMP: Prospero, V, 1, 36.

denier, small French coin worth one-twelfth of a sou (penny).
1H4: Falstaff, III, 3, 91.
SHREW: Sly, Induction, 1, 9.
RICH3: Richard, I, 2, 251—copper coin worth 1/10th of an English penny of the time.

Dennis, Oliver's servant.
AYL: I, 1.

Denny, Sir Anthony, gentleman of the court; commanded by the King to bring Cranmer to see him.
HEN8: V, 1.

denotement, careful scrutiny, notation.
OTH: Iago, II, 3, 323.

depose, necessitate his taking an oath, take his sworn testimony.
RICH2: Richard, I, 2, 30.
3H6: Richard, I, 2, 26.

deputation, office of a substitute; act as my representative or in my behalf.
A&C: Cleopatra, III, 13, 74.
1H4: Hotspur, IV, 1, 32.
MEAS: Isabella, II, 2, 60—*deputed sword,* sword of Justice, symbol of power of the Deputy and carried before him.

deracinate, uproot; destroy.
HEN5: Burgundy, V, 2, 47.
T&C: Ulysses, I, 3, 99.

Derby, one of the titles of Henry Bolingbroke.
RICH2: Bolingbroke, I, 3, 113.

Derby, Earl of. See STANLEY, THOMAS, LORD.

Dercetas, friend of Antony; when Antony stabs himself, Dercetas takes his sword to Caesar.
A&C: IV, 14.

dern, dark, wild, dreary; secret.
PER: Gower, Prologue, III, 15.
LEAR: Gloucester, III, 7, 63—*stern.*

descant, addition of part or parts to tenor or melody; forerunner of modern counterpoint and harmony; variations on an air.
2GENT: Lucetta, I, 2, 94.
RICH3: Richard, I, 1, 27.

Desdemona, innocent, artless, beautiful heroine; daughter of Brabantio, Venetian senator; secretly marries Othello, a Moor and general in the service of the Venetian republic; unjustly accused of unfaithfulness and killed by her husband.

OTH: I, 3.

deserts. See SLIPPERY PEOPLE.

designed. See CARRIAGE.

designment, strategy, plan, undertaking.

OTH: 3Gentleman, II, 1, 22.
COR: Aufidius, V, 6, 34.

desire

Naught's had, all's spent
Where our desire is got without content.
'Tis safer to be that which we destroy
Than by destruction dwell in doubtful joy.

MACB: Lady Macbeth, III, 2, 4.

The sea hath bounds, but deep desire hath none;
Therefore no marvel though thy horse be gone.

VENUS: 389.

desires

. . . Stars, hide your fires!
Let not light see my black and deep desires.
The eye wink at the hand; yet let that be.
Which the eye fears, when it is done, to see.

MACB: Macbeth, I, 4, 50.

despite, in spite of; scorn, contempt, disdain, defiance.

HAM: Hamlet, III, 4, 192.
COR: Coriolanus, III, 1, 164.
TwN: Toby, III, 4, 243.

determine, come to an end, terminate; fix limits for, finish.

A&C: III, 13, 161.
RICH2: Richard, I, 3, 150.

Deucalion, Greek mythological character who, with his wife, Pyrrha, survived the great flood created by Jove and was able to repopulate the earth with stones

turned into men; similar to Noah in Genesis.

COR: Menenius, II, 1, 101.

devil

The devil can cite Scripture for his purpose.
An evil soul, producing holy witness,
Is like a villain with a smiling cheek,
A goodly apple rotten at the heart.
O, what a goodly outside falsehood hath!

MERV: Antonio, I, 3, 99.

. . . you are one of those that will not serve God if the devil bid you.

OTH: Iago, I, 1, 108.

devils

When devils will the blackest sins put on,
They do suggest at first with heavenly shows,
As I do now.

OTH: Iago, II, 3, 357. See PUT ON.

devouring, the act or performance of making the banquet disappear was cleverly or splendidly accomplished.

TEMP: Prospero, III, 3, 84.

dewberries, fruit of certain blackberries or brambles.

MND: Titania, III, 1, 169.

dewdrops

I must go seek some dewdrops here,
And hang a pearl in every cowslip's ear.

MND: Fairy, II, 1, 14.

dewlapped, having loose folds of skin hanging from the neck or throat; possible reference to the goitrous condition of Swiss mountaineers.

TEMP: Gonzalo, III, 3, 45.
MND: Theseus, IV, 1, 125.

dexter, right.

T&C: Hector, IV, 5, 128.

Dian, Diana (Artemis), goddess of the moon and night; virgin

goddess of the hunt, of chastity and maidens.
OTH: Othello, III, 3, 387.
SHREW: Petruchio, II, 1, 260.
TWN: Duke, I, 4, 31.

Diana, goddess appears to Pericles in a dream and tells him to visit her temple at Ephesus.
PER: V, 1.

Diana, daughter of the Florentine widow with whom Helena lodges; wooed by Bertram, she helps Helena trick him.
ALL'sW: III, 5.

Diana in the fountain, refers to the legend of Actaeon; popular fountain figure.
AYL: Rosalind, IV, 1, 154. See ACTAEON.

Diana's Foresters, thieves who steal in the night.
1H4: Falstaff, I, 2, 29.

Dian's bud, herb or plant *Artemisia*, named for Artemis, Greek goddess of the hunt, called Diana by the Romans; or the *agnus castus* (chaste tree) which was believed to preserve chastity.
MND: Oberon, IV, 1, 76.

diaper, towel, linen napkin.
SHREW: Lord, Induction, 1, 57.

dibble, tool used for making holes in the earth for planting.
WINT: Perdita, IV, 4, 100.

dich, may it do.
TIMON: Apemantus, I, 2, 73.

Dick, butcher of Ashford; follower of Cade who makes skeptical aside remarks and then suggests "The first thing we do, let's kill all the lawyers."
2H6: IV, 2.

Dictynna, unusual title for Diana, Roman goddess of the moon; also Phoebe, Luna.
LLL: Holofernes, IV, 2, 37.

Dido, famous heroine of VERGIL's *Aeneid;* widow of Sychaeus; queen of Carthage, near site of modern Tunis; though she had pledged eternal faithfulness to

the memory of her husband, she falls in love with Aeneas when he stops at Carthage on his way from Troy to Italy; commits suicide when he deserts her.
TEMP: Gonzalo, II, 1, 76.
A&C: Antony, IV, 14, 53.
HAM: Hamlet, II, 2, 467.

die for love
. . . Men have died from time to time, and worms have eaten them, but not for love.
AYL: Rosalind, IV, 1, 106.

diet, feed, nurture; limit, restrict.
OTH: Iago, II, 1, 303.
ALL'sW: 1Lord, IV, 3, 35.

Fat paunches have lean pates, and dainty bits
Make rich the ribs but bankrout quite the wits.
LLL: Longaville, I, 1, 26.

Di faciant laudis summa sit ista tuae!, Latin, May the gods grant that this be the summit of thy glory (or your most famous action), from OVID, *Heroides*, II, 66.
3H6: Rutland, I, 3, 48.

differences, accomplishments, qualities or characteristics which set a person apart or are solely his; rank; variation in coats of arms.
HAM: Osric, V, 2, 112.
LEAR: Kent, I, 4, 100.
ADO: Beatrice, I, 1, 70.

diffidence, distrust, suspicion, doubt.
JOHN: Elinor, I, 1, 65.
LEAR: Edmund, I, 2, 161.

digested, organized, arranged.
HAM: Hamlet, II, 2, 461.

digestion. See TASTE.

digress, transgress, sin, err.
RICH2: Bolingbroke, V, 3, 66.

dig-you-den, give you good e'en (a good evening).
LLL: Costard, IV, 1, 42.

dilate, relate, detail, express in full.
OTH: Othello, I, 3, 153.
HAM: King, I, 2, 38.

OTH: Othello, III, 3, 123—emotions, accusations.

dildo and fading, refrain, word, burden of ballad or song; nonsense refrain.
WINT: Servant, IV, 4, 195.

diluculo surgere, part of quotation from Lily's *Latin Grammar: Diluculo surgere saluberrimum est*—to rise early is most healthful or, as Ben Franklin said, "Early to bed and early to rise makes a man healthy etc."
TWN: Toby, II, 3, 1.

Diomedes, Grecian commander; "false-hearted rogue" sent to conduct Cressida back to the Greek camp after her exchange for Antenor; seen making love to her by Troilus.
T&C: II, 3.

Diomedes, servant of Cleopatra; sent to tell Antony the truth, that she is not dead, but it is too late; takes the dying Antony to Cleopatra's monument.
A&C: IV, 14.

Diomedes. See ULYSSES.
3H6: Warwick, IV, 2, 19.

Dion, lord of Sicilia.
WINT: III, 1. See CLEOMENES.

Dionyza, wicked wife of Cleon, Governor of Tarsus; jealous of Marina, she plots her murder; burned to death.
PER: I, 4.

dipping, gilding, turning into gold.
HAM: King, IV, 7, 19.

directions, actual behavior or intentions; truths, facts.
HAM: Polonius, II, 1, 66.

Dis. See DUSKY DIS.
WINT: Perdita, IV, 4, 118.
TEMP: Ceres, IV, 1, 89.

discandy, melt, dissolve.
A&C: Cleopatra, III, 13, 165.

discase, disrobe, undress.
WINT: Camillo, IV, 4, 648.
TEMP: Prospero, V, 1, 85—take off my magic cloak.

disclose, open, uncover, hatch.

HAM: King, III, 1, 174—*doubt the hatch and the disclose,* fear the hatching of a snake from its egg.

discontent
Now is the winter of our discontent
Made glorious summer by this sun of York,
And all the clouds that low'rd upon our house
In the deep bosom of the ocean buried.
RICH3: Richard, I, 1, 1. See SUN OF YORK.

discord
Take but degree away, untune that string,
And hark what discord follows!
T&C: Ulysses, I, 3, 109.

discourse, thought, reflection, reason.
HAM: Hamlet, I, 2, 150—*wants discourse of reason,* lacks ability to reason or is unable to think. See WANTS.

disedged, satiety, dulled the appetite for.
CYM: Imogen, III, 4, 96.

disgrace with Fortune
When, in disgrace with Fortune and men's eyes,
I all alone beweep my outcast state,
And trouble deaf heaven with my bootless cries,
And look upon myself and curse my fate . . .
SONNET: XXIX, 1.

disguise, drinking bout, revel.
A&C: Caesar, II, 7, 129.

dish of wood, clack-dish of a beggar which had a cover that he clacked to attract attention.
RICH2: Richard, III, 3, 150. See GIVE.

dishonest, unchaste.
HEN5: Canterbury, I, 2, 49.
TWN: Olivia, I, 5, 46.

dislike, displease; is unpleasant to.
OTH: Iago, II, 3, 49.

dismal, ominous, threatening disaster.
MACB: Ross, I, 2, 53.

disme, tenth man sacrificed.
T&C: Hector, II, 2, 19.

dispark, throw open, open up.
RICH2: Bolingbroke, III, 1, 23.

dispersedly, from different angles or directions.
TEMP: Ariel, I, 2, 381—S.D., to come from different places.

displant, dismiss, remove (from office or position).
OTH: Iago, II, 1, 284.

disport, diversion, entertainment, form of relaxation.
OTH: Othello, I, 3, 272.

dispose, demeanor, temperament, bearing; come to terms, agreed.
OTH: Iago, I, 3, 403.
A&C: Diomedes, IV, 14, 123.

dissemble, delude, deceive, disguise.
MND: Helena, II, 2, 98.

distaff-women, women who spin and hold the staff of the spinning wheel.
RICH2: Scroop, III, 2, 118.

distemper, physical or mental illness or disorder; confused, perturbed; intoxicated, drunk.
HAM: King, II, 2, 55.
TWN: Olivia, I, 5, 97. See SELF-LOVE.
HEN5: King, II, 2, 54.

distilled, to obtain the essence of, by the process of distillation, to make perfumes; melted, dissolved.
MND: Theseus, I, 1, 76. See ROSE.
SONNET: V, 9.
HAM: Horatio, I, 2, 204.

distinctly, separately; simultaneously.
COR: Volsce, IV, 3, 48.
OTH: Cassio, II, 3, 290.
TEMP: Ariel, I, 2, 200.

distract, insane, out of one's mind, mad; violent; confused.
HAM: Gentleman, IV, 5, 2.
TEMP: Prospero, III, 3, 90.

distraction, division, scattered units, small detachments.
A&C: Soldier, III, 7, 77.

distrust, to be concerned for; anxious about.
HAM: Player Queen, III, 2, 175.

diurnal ring, daily round.
ALL'SW: Helena, II, 1, 165.

dive-dapper, dabchick or little grebe; shy water bird; lives in rushes.
VENUS: 86.

Dives, rich man in parable of Dives and Lazarus (Luke: 16, 19-31).
1H4: Falstaff, III, 3, 36.

division, ornamental elaboration of a simple melodic line for voice or instrument; modulation, harmony.
1H4: Mortimer, III, 1, 210.
R&J: Juliet, III, 5, 29.

docks or mallows, weeds of a common English variety.
TEMP: Sebastian, II, 1, 144.

Doctor, Cordelia brings a doctor to see her "mad" father.
LEAR: IV, 4.

Doctor, English, gives report to Malcolm on Macbeth's condition.
MACB: IV, 3.

Doctor, Scottish, examines Lady Macbeth when she walks in her sleep.
MACB: V, 1.

document, training lesson, instruction.
HAM: Laertes, IV, 5, 178.

dog
. . . Mine enemy's dog,
Though he had bit me, should have stood that night
Against my fire.
LEAR: Cordelia, IV, 7, 36.

Thou call'dst me dog before thou hadst a cause;
But, since I am a dog, beware my fangs.
MERV: Shylock, III, 3, 6.

dog. See DAY.

dog-apes, dog-faced male baboons.
AYL: Jaques, II, 5, 27.

Dogberry, pompous, blundering constable of Messina; sets the Watch that captures Borachio and Conrade.
ADO: III, 3.

dogfish, small shark; considered one of the lowest forms or order of fish.
1H6: Talbot, I, 4, 107.

dog's leather, used for making gloves; Shakespeare's father was a glover.
2H6: Bevis, IV, 2, 26.

doit, early Dutch coin; small, worth about a cent (half a farthing).
TEMP: Trinculo, II, 2, 34.
A&C: Antony, IV, 12, 37.
TIMON: Apemantus, I, 1, 217.

Dolabella, friend of Caesar; sent by him to bid Antony yield, but Antony is dead; tells Cleopatra that Octavius Caesar intends leading her in triumph through Rome; when he returns for her, she is dead. [Publius Cornelius Dolabella (c70-43 BC), Roman patrician; son-in-law of Cicero; commanded Julius Caesar's fleet in the Adriatic (49); became consul after Caesar's death (44); given province of Syria by Antony; defeated at Laodicea by Cassius; had one of his soldiers kill him so as not to be taken captive.]
A&C: III, 12.

dole, sorrow, grief, unhappiness.
HAM: King, I, 2, 13.
MND: Pyramus, V, 1, 283.

dole, lot, destiny, luck.
1H4: Falstaff, II, 2, 81.
WINT: Leontes, I, 2, 163—
happy man be's dole, proverbial expression meaning "Good luck to you" or "May it be his luck to be happy."

Doll Tearsheet, call girl at Boar's Head Tavern; goes to supper with Falstaff and Mistress

Quickly; dragged off to prison; does not appear in *Henry V*, although mentioned by Pistol.
2H4: II, 4.

dolour, grief, sorrow, unhappiness.
RICH2: Bolingbroke, I, 3, 257.
LEAR: Fool, II, 4, 55—pun on Spanish coin.
MACB: Macduff, IV, 3, 8—
Like syllable of dolour, similar cries of anguish.

Dolphin chamber, room in Mistress Quickly's inn of that name.
2H4: Hostess, II, 1, 95.

domineer, have a riotous time, swagger, "live it up."
SHREW: Petruchio, III, 2, 226.

Donalbain, younger son of Duncan; goes to Ireland following the murder of his father.
MACB: II, 3.

done
If it were done when 'tis done, then 'twere well
It were done quickly.
MACB: Macbeth, I, 7, 1.

. . . What's done cannot be undone.
MACB: Lady Macbeth, V, 1, 75.

Don John. See JOHN, Don.

Don Pedro. See PEDRO, Don.

doom, judgment, legal sentence; day of final judgment, doomsday.
SONNET: CXVI, 12. See LOVE.

And by the doom of death end woes and all.
CofE: Aegeon, I, 1, 2.

Dorcas, shepherdess, in love with the Clown.
WINT: IV, 4.

Doricles, name assumed by Prince Florizel when disguised as a shepherd.
WINT: IV, 4.

Dorset, Marquis of, eldest son of Elizabeth Woodville, later queen of Edward IV, by her first husband, Sir John Grey; joins Richmond in Brittany after Richard kills his brother, Lord Grey, and uncle, Earl Rivers; not present at Bosworth. [Thomas Grey (1451-1501), created Earl of Huntingdon (1471), 1st Marquis of Dorset (1475); participated in the murder of Henry VI's son, Edward (1471).]

RICH3: I, 3.

Dorset Garden Theatre, opened November, 1671; occupied by the DUKE'S COMPANY (1671-95); elaborately decorated Restoration theater having a music-room above the proscenium arch.

dotant, man in his dotage; dotard or old codger.

COR: 1Watch, V, 2, 47.

do themselves homage, serve only their own interests.

OTH: Iago, I, 1, 54.

doubled down his throat, accusation returned in kind to accuser's face.

RICH2: Mowbray, I, 1, 57.

double double

Double, double toil and trouble;
Fire burn, and cauldron bubble.

MACB: 3 Witches, IV, 1, 10. See WITCHES' CURSE.

double-fatal yew, so called because its wood was used for arrows and its leaves contain a poison.

RICH2: Scroop, III, 2, 117.

doublet, short, close-fitting jacket, with or without sleeves, laced to the hose or trousers; worn by men from 14th to 18th century.

HAM: Ophelia, II, 1, 78.
TWN: Clown, II, 4, 76.
ADO: Benedick, II, 3, 19.

double tongue, forked tongue, untruthfully.

RICH2: Richard, III, 2, 21.

doubt, to suspect, fear, be apprehensive about.

HAM: Hamlet, I, 2, 256.
OTH: Desdemona, III, 3, 19.

doubt

"Doubt thou the stars are fire;
Doubt that the sun doth move;

Doubt truth to be a liar;
But never doubt I love."

HAM: Polonius, II, 2, 116—quoting Hamlet's letter to Ophelia.

. . . Our doubts are traitors
And make us lose the good we oft might win
By fearing to attempt.

MEAS: Lucio, I, 4, 77.

. . . To be once in doubt
Is once to be resolved.

OTH: Iago, III, 3, 179.

. . . no hinge nor loop
To hang a doubt on—

OTH: Othello, III, 3, 365.

doughty-handed, bold, sturdy, stalwart in battle.

A&C: Antony, IV, 8, 5.

Douglas, Archibald, 4th Earl of, Scottish nobleman; after being defeated by Hotspur at Holmedon, joins his rebellion and fights with him at Shrewsbury; kills Blunt and almost kills the King; captured; freed by Prince Henry. [Known as "Tyneman" (c1369-1424); fought at Shrewsbury (1403), captured and kept prisoner (until 1408); fought with French against the English; created 1st Duke of Touraine by Charles VII of France; killed in battle of Verneuil.]

1H4: IV, 1.

dout, quench, drown, put out; abolish.

HAM: Laertes, IV, 7, 193.
HEN5: Dauphin, IV, 2, 11.

dove-drawn, Venus' chariot was drawn by doves.

TEMP: Iris, IV, 1, 94.

Dowland, John (c1563-c1626), well-known composer of the period; published music for the lute.

PASSPIL: VIII, 5.

dowlas, coarse woven linen, named from Doulas in Brittany.

1H4: Falstaff, III, 3, 79.

dowle, soft, downy, a feather; Harpies were not wounded when

attacked by Aeneas and his companions.
TEMP: Ariel, III, 3, 65.

down-gyved, hanging or falling down around his ankles like gyves or fetters worn by prisoners.
HAM: Ophelia, II, 1, 80.

Downs, rendezvous for ships, off the coast of Kent, within the Goodwin Sands.
2H6: Lieutenant, IV, 1, 9.
See GOODWIN SANDS.

doxy, female tramp or beggar; prostitute, wench; rogue's slang for beggar's mistress or moll.
WINT: Autolycus, IV, 2, 2.

dozy, made dizzy, confuse, giddy.
HAM: Hamlet, V, 2, 119.

drab, whore, wench, harlot, prostitute.
HAM: Polonius, II, 1, 26.
MACB: 3Witch, IV, 1, 31.
WINT: Autolycus, IV, 3, 27.

drachma, Greek coin; ancient silver coin.
COR: Marcius, I, 5, 6.
JC: Brutus, IV, 3, 73.

draff, swill, hog's wash, refuse.
1H4: Falstaff, IV, 2, 40.

dragon
. . . though I go alone,
Like to a lonely dragon, that his fen
Makes feared and talked of more than seen—
COR: Coriolanus, IV, 1, 29.

dram, apothecary's weight of ⅛ of an ounce (fluid); very small quantity; minute.
TwN: Malvolio, III, 4, 88.
TIMON: 2Senator, V, 1, 154.
WINT: Camillo, I, 2, 320.

draught, privy, cesspool, sewer.
TIMON: Timon, V, 1, 105.
T&C: Thersites, V, 1, 83.

draw, gather, collect, assemble, muster.
COR: Brutus, II, 3, 261.
JOHN: King, IV, 2, 118.
JC: Casca, I, 3, 22.

drawer, tapster, bartender; originally a barmaid.

1H4: Prince, II, 4, 7.
2H4: Poins, II, 2, 191.

drawn, healthy swig of the bottle, strong draught; with an unsheathed and drawn sword.
TEMP: Trinculo, II, 2, 151.
MND: Puck, III, 2, 402.

draws dry-foot, hunts by tracking the scent of the foot.
COFE: Dromio S., IV, 2, 39.

dream
A dream itself is but a shadow.
HAM: Hamlet, II, 2, 266. See AMBITION, BEGGARS.

I have had a dream, past the wit of man to say what dream it was.
MND: Bottom, IV, 1, 207.

The eye of man hath not heard, the ear of man not seen, man's hand is not able to taste, his tongue to conceive, nor his heart to report what my dream was.
MND: Bottom, IV, 1, 214.

dreaming
. . . in dreaming,
The clouds methought would open and show riches
Ready to drop upon me, that, when I waked,
I cried to dream again.
TEMP: Caliban, III, 2, 149.

dreams
. . . merciful powers
Restrain in me the cursed thoughts that nature
Gives way to in repose!
MACB: Banquo, II, 1, 8.

. . . Now o'er the one half-world
Nature seems dead, and wicked dreams abuse
The curtained sleep.
MACB: Macbeth, II, 1, 49. See ABUSE.

. . . I talk of dreams;
Which are the children of an idle brain
Begot of nothing but vain fantasy . . .
R&J: Mercutio, I, 4, 96.

All days are nights to see till I see thee,

And nights bright days when dreams do show thee me.
SONNET: CXIII, 13.

. . . We are such stuff
As dreams are made on, and our little life
Is rounded with a sleep.
TEMP: Prospero, IV, 1, 156.

drench, dose, bran and water, laxative, purge used for horses.
1H4: Prince, II, 4, 120.

dressed, groomed, combed, rubbed; equipped, prepared for, made ready.
RICH2: Groom, II, 5, 80.
OTH: 1Senator, I, 3, 26.

drift, intention, plan, aim, idea.
HAM: King, IV, 7, 152.
TEMP: Prospero, V, 1, 29.
ADO: Pedro, II, 1, 405.

drink. See SACK.

drinking oceans dry, proverb for the impossible.
RICH2: Green, II, 2, 145.

drink the air, swallow the distance or space.
TEMP: Ariel, V, 1, 101.

drive, drift.
TWN: Captain, I, 2, 11.

driven, process of refining or sifting down, which separates the heavy from the softest feathers.
OTH: Othello, I, 3, 232.

drollery, puppet show, usually comedy.
TEMP: Sebastian, III, 3, 21.

Dromio of Ephesus, slave to Antipholus of Ephesus; twin brother of Dromio of Syracuse; beaten by Antipholus of Syracuse when mistaken for his twin.
COFE: I, 2.

Dromio of Syracuse, twin brother of above; slave to Antipholus of Syracuse; beaten by Antipholus of Ephesus when mistaken for his twin.
COFE: I, 2.

drossy, worthless, trivial, frivolous.
HAM: Hamlet, V, 2, 196.

drovier, drover, cattle-driver.
ADO: Benedick, II, 1, 202.

drown
. . . if I drown myself wittingly, it argues an act; and an act hath three branches—it is to act, to do, and to perform; argal, she drowned herself wittingly.
HAM: Clown, V, 1, 10. See ARGAL.

. . . If the man go to this water and drown himself, it is, will he nill he, he goes—mark you that. But if the water come to him and drown him, he drowns not himself. Argal, he that is not guilty of his own death shortens not his own life.
HAM: Clown, V, 1, 16. See WILL HE NILL HE, ARGAL.

drowning
. . . methought what pain it was to drown!
What dreadful noise of water in mine ears,
What sights of ugly death within mine eyes!
Methoughts I saw a thousand fearful wracks;
A thousand men that fishes gnawed upon;
Wedges of gold, great anchors, heaps of pearl
Inestimable stones, unvalued jewels,
All scattered in the bottom of the sea.
RICH3: Clarence, I, 4, 21.

drumble, dawdle, stumble along.
MWW: Mrs. Ford, III, 3, 155.

drunkenness
. . . One draught above head makes him a fool, the second mads him, and a third drowns him.
TWN: Clown, I, 5, 140—*above head,* more than enough to warm him through.

Drury Lane Theatre, one of the important London theaters; opened by Killigrew and the KING'S COMPANY (May, 1663); destroyed by fire (1672); rebuilt by Sir Christopher Wren and again occupied by the KING'S COMPANY (1674); "revised or improved" versions of Shakespeare were produced; enlarged (1794); destroyed by fire (1809); present theater opened (1812).

dry-beaten, badly beaten but not bloody.
LLL: Berowne, V, 2, 263.
R&J: Mercutio, III, 1, 82.

ducat, gold coin having various values; used in most European countries at that time; silver coin in Italy.
SHREW: Tranio, II, 1, 371.
2GENT: Speed, I, 1, 144.
HAM: Hamlet, III, 4, 23—*Dead for a ducat, dead!*

Duchess of Bedford, Jacquetta, married a man of lower birth, Richard Woodville, a squire.
RICH3: Richard, I, 3, 102—refers to Lord Rivers' grandmother.

dudgeon, hilt or handle; originally, kind of wood used for handle of knives and daggers.
MACB: Macbeth, II, 1, 46.

duello, established code or rules of dueling.
LLL: Armado, I, 2, 185.
TWN: Toby, III, 4, 337.

duer, more duly or more promptly.
2H4: Falstaff, III, 2, 330.

dug, mother's nipple.
HAM: Hamlet, V, 2, 194—implies that Osric acted peculiarly, or in this absurd manner, from infancy.

Duke Frederick. See FREDERICK, Duke.

Duke of Milan. See MILAN, Duke of.

Duke of York's (Prince Charles') **Men,** company of the future Charles I; first appeared (1608); at Court (Feb., 1610); leading dramatist of the company was William Rowley; joined by Christopher Beeston (1619), moved to the COCKPIT.

Duke's Company, named for the Duke of York (James II); issued patent (1660) by Charles II, led by D'Avenant; joined by Betterton (1661); performed at LINCOLN'S INN FIELDS; moved to DORSET GARDEN THEATRE (1671); granted exclusive right to revise and perform many of Shakespeare's plays.

Duke "Senior," Rosalind's father; driven into exile by his brother, Duke Frederick; lives in a pastoral "paradise" in the Forest of Arden with his faithful followers.
AYL: II, 1.

Dull, Anthony, constable whose "intellect is not replenished"; Armado gets him to arrest Costard for courting Jacquenetta.
LLL: I, 1.

Dumain, one of the three charming young lords attending the King of Navarre; falls in love with the "most divine Kate."
LLL: I, 1.

dumb show, prior to a play or act in Senecan or neo-classical drama, actors would pantomime the forthcoming scene or action.
HAM: Hamlet, III, 2, 14.
ADO: Pedro, II, 3, 226.
TITUS: Titus, III, 1, 131.

dump, mournful, sad or doleful melody or tune.
2GENT: Proteus, III, 2, 85.
R&J: Peter, IV, 5, 108.

Duncan, King of Scotland, "his virtues / Will plead like angels, trumpet-tongued, against / The deep damnation of his taking-off" (I, 7, 16); murdered by Macbeth. [Duncan I, succeeded to the throne (c1034) on the death of Malcolm II, his grandfather; killed (c1040) near Elgin by Macbeth.]
MACB: I, 2.

Dunsinane (now Dunsinnan), Scottish town seven miles northeast of Perth; site of Macbeth's castle.

MACB: Third Apparition, IV, 1, 93. See BIRNAM, LION-METTLED.

dup, open.

HAM: Ophelia, IV, 5, 53.

durance, jailed, confinement, imprisonment.

TwN: Viola, V, 1, 283.
LLL: Armado, III, 1, 130.
CofE: Dromio S., IV, 3, 27.

durance, sturdy or durable material; of lasting quality.

1H4: Prince, I, 2, 49—pun on above meaning.

Dursley, old market town and parish in southwestern Gloucestershire; at the foot of the western escarpment of the Cotswolds; 19 miles northeast of Bristol. See DAVY.

dusky Dis, Pluto, god of the lower (dusky) regions or underworld; husband of Persephone, beautiful daughter of Ceres (Demeter) and Zeus, whom Pluto (Hades) had carried down to his kingdom by force; considered dark or black by OVID.

TEMP: Ceres, IV, 1, 89.

duty, act of kneeling or paying homage.

RICH2: York, II, 3, 84.

duty

Think'st thou that duty shall have
    dread to speak
When power to flattery bows?
    To plainness honour's bound
When majesty falls to folly.
    LEAR: Kent, I, 1, 149.

dwarf

A stirring dwarf we do allow-
    ance give
Before a sleeping giant.
    T&C: Agamemnon, II, 3, 146.

E

eager, sharp, biting, crisp; pungent, sour, acrid.
Ham: Horatio, I, 4, 2.
Sonnet: CXVIII, 2.
3H6: Clarence, II, 6, 68.

eagle
More pity that the eagle should be mewed,
While kites and buzzards prey at liberty.
Rich3: Richard, I, 1, 132. See kite, mew.

ean, bring forth offspring; give birth.
Per: Thaisa, III, 4, 6.
3H6: King, II, 5, 34.

eanlings, young or newborn lambs.
MerV: Shylock, I, 3, 80.

ear, plow, till.
Rich2: Richard, III, 2, 212.
A&C: Antony, I, 2, 115.
All'sW: Clown, I, 3, 47.

ear, window, loophole.
Rich2: Bolingbroke, III, 3, 34.

earnest, money paid in advance to seal an agreement or bind a bargain.
Lear: Lear, I, 4, 104.
CofE: Dromio S., II, 2, 42.
Macb: Ross, I, 3, 104.

Eastcheap, part of London where Boar's Head Tavern, kept by Dame Quickly, was located.
1H4: Poins, I, 2, 145.

eaves of reeds, a thatched roof.
Temp: Ariel, V, 1, 17.

ebbed man. See POPULARITY.

ecce signum, Latin, behold this proof or evidence; behold the sign or token.
1H4: Falstaff, II, 4, 187.

ecstasy, delirium, frenzy, madness.
Ham: Polonius, II, 1, 102.
Temp: Gonzalo, III, 3, 108.
Macb: Macbeth, III, 2, 22.

Edgar, legitimate elder son of Gloucester; without guile; innocent of his father's accusation that he is plotting to murder him and gain his estates; acts as his blind father's guide; reconciled with him before his death; kills Edmund, his bastard brother; with Kent and Albany, takes over the kingdom.
Lear: I, 2.

edge, reassurance, encouragement, i.e., whet his appetite further.
Ham: King, III, 1, 26.

Edmund, illegitimate son of Gloucester; "toad-spotted traitor" who convinces his father that Edgar is plotting his murder; gives evidence to Cornwall proving Gloucester is aiding Lear and Cordelia and is, therefore, responsible for his being blinded; becomes commander-in-chief of the English forces against the French and, capturing Lear and Cordelia, secretly orders their execution; loved by Goneril; arrested by Albany for treason; killed by Edgar.
Lear: I, 1.

Edmund. See RUTLAND, Earl of.

Edward, Earl of March, became Edward IV; appears (2H6) as eldest son of Richard Plantagenet, 3rd Duke of York; tells his father (3H6) how he killed Buckingham at St. Albans, and

106

helps to persuade him to break his oath to King Henry; after the murder of his father at Wakefield, defeats the Lancastrians at Towton and is crowned Edward IV (1461); marries Lady Grey; captured; escapes and returns to win battles of Barnet and Tewkesbury (1471); Richard tells him of Clarence's murder (RICH3); his death reported in next scene of play. [1442-83, son of Richard Plantagenet and Cecily Neville, daughter of the Earl of Westmoreland; defeated the Lancastrians at battle of Mortimer's Cross; secretly married Elizabeth Grey, daughter of Richard Woodville, Baron Rivers, a leader of Warwick's rebellion; fled to France; returned to successfully suppress uprisings; relatively peaceful reign (1461-83); Jane Shore one of his many mistresses.]

2H6: V, 1; 3H6: I, 1; RICH3: II, 1.

Edward (Plantagenet), Prince of Wales, only son of Henry VI; "young, valiant, wise," protests his father's promising the crown to York; betrothed to Warwick's daughter; captured at Tewkesbury and stabbed by Edward IV and his brothers.

3H6: I, 1.

Edward V, son of Edward IV and Elizabeth Woodville; appears as a baby (last scene, 3H6); as young Edward V, he and his brother, York, are put in the Tower and murdered on orders of their uncle, Richard, Duke of Gloucester, who has seized power. [1470-83, King of England (April-June, 1483) under the regency of Richard.]

RICH3: III, 1.

Edward shovel-board, shilling coined in time of Edward VI and used in game of shovegroat. MWW: Slender, I, 1, 159. See SHOVEGROAT.

Edwards, Richard (c1523-66).

English dramatist and musician; appointed Master of the Children of the Chapel (1561); wrote *Palamon and Arcite,* performed before Queen Elizabeth I at Oxford (1566), and *Damon and Pithias* (printed, 1571), now lost.

Egeus, adamant father of Hermia; appeals to Theseus to force his daughter to marry Demetrius, his choice for her; finally consents to her marriage to Lysander.

MND: I, 1.

eggshell, useless or worthless fragment, trifle or bagatelle. HAM: Hamlet, IV, 4, 53.

Eglamour, Sir, courtier; joins Silvia in her escape from Milan. 2GENT: IV, 3.

eglantine, sweetbrier. MND: Oberon, II, 1, 252. CYM: Arviragus, IV, 2, 223.

Egyptian, gypsy. OTH: Othello, III, 4, 56.

Egyptian thief, Theagenes; character in story by Heliodorus, who tried to kill Chariclea, the woman he loved, rather than lose her to others. TWN: Duke, V, 1, 121.

eight and six, alternate lines of eight and six syllables; meter most commonly used for ballads and songs. MND: Quince, III, 1, 25.

eke, also, too. MND: Thisby, III, 1, 97.

Elbow, stupid, blundering constable. MEAS: II, 1.

elder-gun, popgun, made by removing the pith from a piece of elder wood; harmless weapon. HEN5: Williams, IV, 1, 210.

Eleanor. See GLOUCESTER, Duchess of.

election, the king of Denmark was elected to the throne; he

did not rule by divine right.
HAM: Hamlet, V, 2, 366.

element, sky, heavens, air.
TwN: Valentine, I, 1, 26.

Elephant, famed inn on south side of the Thames in London; now called the Elephant and Castle.
TwN: Antonio, III, 3, 39.

elephant
The elephant hath joints, but none for courtesy; his legs are legs for necessity, not for flexure.
T&C: Ulysses, II, 3, 113. See FLEXURE.

elf, twisted, matted, tangled.
LEAR: Edgar, II, 3, 10.

elf-locks, knots or snarls in horses' manes and human hair were attributed to the fairies or elves.
R&J: Mercutio, I, 4, 90.

eliade (oeillad), eye, ogle, amorous or languishing glance.
LEAR: Regan, IV, 5, 25.
MWW: Falstaff, I, 3, 68—
illiads.

Elinor (Eleanor or Aliénor of Aquitaine), Queen of England and France; mother of King John; aware that his claim to the throne is not completely justified, she supports him against Arthur; recognizes Falconbridge as the son of Richard I (her eldest son), and he becomes her devoted follower; accompanies John on his French campaign, stays (and dies) in France. [c1122-1204, daughter of William X, Duke of Aquitaine; married Louis VII of France; divorced by him, she marries Henry of Anjou (Plantagenet), who became Henry II of England (1154); mother of Richard I, Geoffrey (father of Arthur), John, and Eleanor (mother of Blanch); backed her sons in their revolt against Henry (1173); kept in seclusion until his death (1189); acted as adviser to her sons; helped ransom Richard from France; leader of a brilliant court at Poitiers.]
JOHN: I, 1.

Elizabeth, Queen of Edward IV (1437-92); tries to save her children by taking them into sanctuary; although her husband and three sons were murdered by Richard, she agrees to try to persuade her daughter to marry him.
RICH3: I, 3. See GREY, Lady.

Elizabeth I, Queen of England (1533-1603). Succeeded to the throne (1558); only surviving child of Henry VIII (Tudor) and Anne Boleyn; her reign marks one of the most brilliant periods in English history; a great patron of literature and the theater, she encouraged the development of the arts; her birth is mentioned in *Henry VIII,* otherwise she is only indirectly referred to in the plays of Shakespeare; a great admirer of his work, several of Shakespeare's plays were performed for her, and it has been suggested that she was so fond of the character Falstaff that *The Merry Wives of Windsor* was written especially for her; she gave her name to an age.

Ely, Bishop of, used as a sounding board for Canterbury's speech, actually directed at the audience; cynical supporter of the war against France. [John Fordham (d.1425), Bishop of Ely (1388). See MORTON, John.]
HEN5: I, 1.

Ely House, the Bishop of Ely's London palace.
RICH2: Bushy, I, 4, 58.

Elysium, Elysian fields, paradise; classical abode of the blessed in the lower world; in HOMER, Elysium is not a part of the realm of the dead, but a perfect land on an island in the western ocean.
HEN5: King, IV, 1, 291.
CYM: Jupiter, V, 4, 97.

3H6: Richard, I, 2, 30.

embassage, message, dispatch, communication.

RICH2: Queen, III, 4, 93.

embattle, take up battle stations: draw up in battle array.

A&C: Sentry, IV, 9, 3.

embayed, sheltered in a bay or harbor.

OTH: Montano, II, 1, 18.

ember-eve, evening before an ember day—period of three-day fast; Catholic observance four times each year.

PER: Gower, I, Prologue, 6.

embossed, enraged, savagely angry; driven to extremes, as a hunted animal; foaming at the mouth.

A&C: Cleopatra, IV, 13, 3.
1H4: Prince, III, 3, 177.
SHREW: Lord, Induction, 1, 17.

embrew. See IMBRUE.

TITUS: Martius, II, 3, 222.

Emilia, wife of Iago and companion to Desdemona; innocent pawn in Iago's plot to make Othello jealous; exposes him and he kills her.

OTH: II, 2.

Emilia, accompanies Hermione to prison; tells Paulina of the birth of Perdita.

WINT: II, 2.

Emilia, sister of Hippolyta, beloved by Palamon and Arcite.

2NK: I, 1.

Emmanuel, God with us, piously written at the head of letters, deeds, etc.

2H6: Clerk, IV, 2, 106.

Emperor, refers to Sigismund, Emperor of the Holy Roman Empire, who acted as mediator on visit to England (May 1, 1416).

HEN5: Chorus, V, 38.

empery, empire; imperial domain; territory of an absolute ruler; absolute power, sovereignty.

CYM: Iachimo, I, 6, 120.

HEN5: King, I, 2, 226.

empiric, quack; ancient group of physicians (empirics) whose work or rules of practice was based on experience (empiricists).

ALL'SW: King, II, 1, 125.
COR: Menenius, II, 1, 128—*empiricutic.*

emulate, ambitious, jealous, aspiring.

HAM: Horatio, I, 1, 183—*emulate pride,* pride of rivalry.

Enceladus, one of the Titans.

TITUS: Aaron, IV, 2, 93.

enchafed, enraged, furious.

OTH: 2Gentleman, II, 1, 17.
CYM: Belarius, IV, 2, 174.

enchanted trifle, illusion, hallucination or phantasm (ghost) created by sorcery or magic.

TEMP: Alonso, V, 1, 112.

encompassment, going roundabout, encircling, "beating around the bush."

HAM: Polonius, II, 1, 10.

encumbered, folded (arms).

HAM: Hamlet, I, 5, 174.

end crowns all
. . . The end crowns all,
And that old common arbitrator, Time,
Will one day end it.

T&C: Hector, IV, 5, 224.

endeavor keeps in the wonted pace, their efforts continue at their accustomed speed.

HAM: Rosencrantz, II, 2, 353.

ending
. . . Now I want
Spirits to enforce, art to enchant;
And my ending is despair
Unless I be relieved by prayer,
Which pierces so that it assaults
Mercy itself and frees all faults.
As you from crimes would pardoned be,
Let your indulgence set me free.

TEMP: Prospero, Epilogue, 13.

end justifies the means
The fault unknown is as a thought unacted.

A little harm done to a great
   good end
For lawful policy remains en-
   acted.
   LUCRECE: 527.

endurance
The wonder is, he hath endured
   so long.
He but usurped his life.
   LEAR: Kent, V, 3, 316.

endure. See PATIENCE.

Endymion, beloved of Selene
   (Diana), goddess of the moon,
   sister of Helios, god of the sun,
   who watched him sleeping on
   Mount Latmus in Caria and
   fell in love with him; every night
   she came down from the skies
   to kiss him.
   MERV: Portia, V, 1, 109.

enemy in their mouths
. . . O God, that men should put
   an enemy in their mouths to
   steal away their brains!
   OTH: Cassio, II, 3, 291.

enew, old hawking term, to drive
   fowl or bird into the water; pursue.
   MEAS: Isabella, III, 1, 91.

enfeoff, surrender, deliver (as a
   fief), become a vassal; legal
   term meaning to turn over all
   property.
   1H4: King, III, 2, 69.

enforce, strongly urge, stress,
   press hard, confront vigorously.
   A&C: Maecenas, II, 2, 99.
   COR: Brutus, III, 3, 3.
   JC: Brutus, III, 2, 43.

enfranchisement, liberty, freedom.
   RICH2: Mowbray, I, 3, 90.
   A&C: Antony, III, 13, 149—
   enfranched.
   RICH2: Northumberland, III,
   3, 114—meaning reprieve from
   exile or banishment.

engage, pledge; hostage, pawn;
   enmesh, involve, entangle.
   OTH: Othello, III, 3, 462.
   TIMON: Steward, II, 2, 155.
   HAM: King, III, 3, 69. See
   SOUL.

engine, weapon, instrument of

warfare, machine, contrivance.
   TEMP: Gonzalo, II, 1, 161.
   COR: Menenius, V, 4, 19.
   VENUS: 367.

England
O England! model to thy inward
   greatness,
Like little body with a mighty
   heart,
What mightst thou do that hon-
   our would thee do,
Were all thy children kind and
   natural!
   HEN5: II, Prologue, 16.
This England never did, nor
   never shall,
Lie at the proud foot of a con-
   queror
But when it first did help to
   wound itself.
Now these her princes are come
   home again,
Come the three corners of the
   world in arms,
And we shall shock them.
   Naught shall make us rue
If England to itself do rest but
   true.
   JOHN: Bastard, V, 7, 112.

England's private wrongs, the
   wrongs suffered by private English citizens.
   RICH2: York, II, 1, 166.

English Ambassadors, announce
   that Guildenstern and Rosencrantz were killed as requested
   in Hamlet's forged letter.
   HAM: V, 2.

englut, consume, swallow, devour.
   OTH: Brabantio, I, 3, 56.

engross, collect, accumulate,
   amass.
   1H4: Prince, III, 2, 148.
   A&C: Enobarbus, III, 7, 37—
   ingrossed.

enlarge, free, release, set at liberty.
   TWN: Olivia, V, 1, 285.
   HEN5: King, II, 2, 40.
   CYM: Cloten, II, 3, 125—*en-
   largement,* freedom of action
   or choice.

Enobarbus, Antony's trusted

friend; a cynic yet an absolutely honest soldier, the symbol of sanity and common sense; gives Maecenas and Agrippa the famous description of Cleopatra in her barge (II, 2, 196); when Antony's judgment wanes he tries to join Caesar; when Antony sends his treasure after Enobarbus, he realizes his own treachery, and dies of a broken heart. [Gnaeus Domitius Ahenobarbus, consul (32 BC).]

    A&C: I, 2.

enow, enough.

    MACB: Porter, II, 3, 7.

enseam, smear with grease.

    HAM: Hamlet, III, 4, 92.

ensear, dry up, wither.

    TIMON: Timon, IV, 3, 187.

ensteep, submerge, immerse.

    OTH: Cassio, II, 1, 70.

entail, right of succession.

    ALL'SW: Parolles, IV, 3, 313.

enterlude, interlude or short play; usually the light stage presentation given between the acts of long plays.

    MND: I, 2, 5.

entertain, employ, hire, take into service.

    ADO: Borachio, I, 3, 60.

    A&C: Enobarbus, IV, 6, 17.

    COR: Volsce, IV, 3, 49.

entreat, treat, entertain; negotiate, petition; appoint, interview.

    RICH2: Bolingbroke, III, 1, 37.

    A&C: Antony, III, 13, 140.

    HAM: Polonius, I, 3, 122.

envenom, poison, destroy by poison.

    HAM: King, IV, 7, 104.

envy, malice, ill-will, hate.

    RICH2: Gaunt, II, 1, 49.

    1H4: Northumberland, I, 3, 27.

    HAM: Queen, IV, 7, 175—*envious sliver*, malicious small branch.

envy

Such men as he be never at heart's ease

Whiles they behold a greater than themselves,

And therefore are they very dangerous.

    JC: Caesar, I, 2, 208—refers to Cassius.

. . . she bore a mind that envy could not but call fair.

    TwN: Sebastian, II, 1, 30.

enwheel, encircle, surround, enclose.

    OTH: Cassio, II, 1, 87.

Ephesian, pal, bosom companion, good fellow.

    2H4: Page, II, 2, 164.

    MWW: Host, IV, 5, 19.

Ephesus, Ancient Ionian city near the coast of the Aegean Sea in western Asia Minor; conquered by the Persians, it was recaptured by Alexander the Great (334 BC); became capital of Roman province of Asia; known for famous temple to Diana.

    COFE: Duke, I, 1, 16.

Epicurian, Epicurean, sensual, luxurious.

    MWW: Ford, II, 2, 298.

    A&C: Pompey, II, 1, 24.

Epidamnum (Epidamnus), port on the eastern coast of the Adriatic Sea; called Dyrrachium by the Romans, now Durazzo (Durrës), Albania; founded by Corcyra and Corinth (c625 BC); quarrel over territory a cause of the Peloponnesian War; under Romans (after 229 BC).

    COFE: Duke, I, 1, 41.

Epidaurus, Ancient Greek seaport town in Argolis on Saronic Gulf; famed site of theater (4th century BC) and temple dedicated to Aesculapius, Greek god of healing and medicine.

    COFE: Aegeon, I, 1, 93.

Erebus, hell; place of unfathomable darkness beneath the earth, through which the shades pass on their way to Hades.

    2H4: Pistol, II, 4, 171.

    JC: Brutus, II, 1, 84.

    MERV: Lorenzo, V, 1, 87.

erewhile, short time ago, little while past.

    MND: Hermia, III, 2, 274.

eringo, candied root of the sea-holly; believed to be an aphrodisiac.

MWW: Falstaff, V, 5, 23. See POTATOES.

ern, yearn, grieve.

HEN5: Pistol, II, 3, 3.
JC: Brutus, II, 2, 129.
RICH2: Groom, V, 5, 75.

Eros, faithful servant (freed slave) of Antony; when ordered by his master to kill him, after he learns of Cleopatra's death, Eros kills himself instead.

A&C: III, 5.

Erpingham, Sir Thomas, officer in the English army; lends the king his cloak before the battle at Agincourt. [1357-1428, helped Bolingbroke to the throne.]

HEN5: IV, 1.

erring, roaming, wandering, roving.

OTH: Iago, I, 3, 362.

error

If this be error and upon me proved,
I never writ nor no man ever loved.

SONNET: CXVI, 13.

Escalus, Prince of Verona, threatens the Capulets and Montagues with death if they disturb the peace in the streets again; banishes Romeo; effects reconciliation of families at the end of the play.

R&J: I, 1.

Escalus, elderly lord, adviser to Angelo; privately disapproving of his severity, pleads for Claudio; dismisses Froth and Elbow with a warning; however, on the basis of Lucio's testimony, sends the disguised Duke to prison.

MEAS: I, 1.

Escanes, lord of Tyre, appears with Helicanus.

PER: I, 3.

escape, insolent adventure, escapade; sally or flash of wit.

OTH: Brabantio, I, 3, 197.

MEAS: Duke, IV, 1, 63.

escoted, provided for, sustained, supported, paid for, maintained.

HAM: Hamlet, II, 2, 362.

esill, vinegar, old French *aisil;* associated with vinegar and gall taken by Christ at crucifixion (Matthew: 27:34); was added torment, although it was supposed to be an anaesthetic.

HAM: Hamlet, V, 1, 299.

esperance, hope; motto of Percy family; used as a battle cry.

LEAR: Edgar, IV, 1, 4.
1H4: Hotspur, II, 3, 74.

espial, spy.

1H6: Master Gunner, I, 4, 8.
HAM: King, III, 1, 32.

espy. See SECURELY I ESPY.

Essex, Earl of, announces the Faulconbridge brothers to John. [Geoffrey Fitzpeter (d.1213); opposed church's land policies; became Earl of Essex (1189) through marriage; excommunicated for seizure of church lands; helped John gain crown at council of Northampton (1199).]

JOHN: I, 1.

estate, grant, bestow upon, donate; high rank, position.

TEMP: Ceres, IV, 1, 85.
MND: Egeus, I, 1, 98.
HAM: Hamlet, V, 1, 244.

estimation, conjecture, surmise; fame.

1H4: Worcester, I, 3, 272.
OTH: Othello, I, 3, 275.

estridge, goshawk or falcon; ostrich.

A&C: Enobarbus, III, 13, 197.

et bonum quo antiquius, eo melius, Latin, and the older a good thing is, the better it is.

PER: Gower, Prologue, 10.

eternal blazon, unveiling of eternity.

HAM: Ghost, I, 5, 21.

eternity

Eternity was in our lips and eyes,

Bliss in our brows' bent . . .
A&C: Cleopatra, I, 3, 35.

Ethiope, Ethiopian.
MND: Lysander, III, 2, 257—
refers to Hermia's dark hair
and complexion; might suggest
the possibility that one of the
boy actors was not fair-
skinned, but a negro or a mu-
latto. See BEAUTY.

Et tu, Brute?
Et tu, Brute? Then fall Caesar!
JC: Caesar, III, 1, 77.

eunuch, singer; one of the cas-
trati (popular in Italy) who
were castrated in early youth in
order to retain high tenor voices.
TwN: Viola, I, 2, 56.

Euphronius, ambassador; Antony,
following his defeat at Actium,
sends him to Caesar to beg that
he be allowed to live in exile and
Cleopatra remain Queen; Caesar
refuses.
A&C: III, 12.

Europa, in mythology, Jove in the
form of a white bull abducted
a mortal, Europa; her name
given to the area where he took
her.
ADO: Claudio, V, 4, 45.
MWW: Falstaff, V, 5, 4.

Evans, Sir Hugh, simple, med-
dling, flannel-mouthed Welsh
parson; disguised as a satyr,
leads the baiting of Falstaff in
Windsor Park.
MWW: I, 1.

even, candid, straightforward.
HAM: Hamlet, II, 2, 298.

even-Christen or even Christian,
fellow Christian or neighbor.
HAM: Clown, V, 1, 32.

even-pleached, carefully, smooth-
ly cut and intertwined or plaited.
HEN5: Burgundy, V, 2, 42.

ever-fixed mark
O, no! it is an ever-fixed mark
That looks on tempests and is
never shaken . . .
SONNET: CXVI, 5—lighthouse
or signal point. See MARK.

evil
No evil lost is wailed when it is
gone.
CofE: Luciana, IV, 2, 24.

evil manners
Men's evil manners live in brass;
their virtues
We write in water.
HEN8: Griffith, IV, 2, 45.

evitate, avoid, bypass.
MWW: Fenton, V, 5, 241.

except before excepted, legal
term, including all previous ex-
ceptions.
TwN: Toby, I, 3, 7—Sir Toby
thinks it is permissible for his
niece to object, but he will do
as he pleases.

exception, irritation, resentment,
displeasure, enmity.
HAM: Hamlet, V, 2, 241.

excess
Heat not a furnace for your foe
so hot
That it do singe yourself. We
may outrun
By violent swiftness that which
we run at,
And lose by overrunning. Know
you not
The fire that mounts the liquor
till't run o'er
In seeming to augment it wastes
it?
HEN8: Norfolk, I, 1, 140.
To gild refined gold, to paint
the lily,
To throw perfume on the violet,
To smooth the ice, or add
another hue
Unto the rainbow, or with taper
light
To seek the beauteous eye of
heaven to garnish,
Is wasteful and ridiculous ex-
cess.
JOHN: Salisbury, IV, 2, 11.

excrement, outgrowth of the
body, such as hair, nails.
HAM: Queen, III, 4, 121.
LLL: Armado, V, 1, 110.

excursion, used in stage directions only, to indicate that

groups of soldiers run across the stage; usually to simulate a battle.

   1H6: III, 2, following line 35.
   JOHN: II, 1, following line 299.
   T&C: V, 1, following line 4.

executor. See WILLS.

exequies, obsequies, funeral rites.
   1H6: Talbot, III, 2, 133.

exercise, religious devotion; penance.
   HAM: Polonius, III, 1, 45.

Exeter, Duke of, supports Henry in the Wars of the Roses. [Henry Holland (1430-73) died in poverty.]
   3H6: I, 1. See BEAUFORT, Thomas.

exhalation, meteor.
   1H4: Bardolph, II, 4, 352.
   JC: Brutus, II, 1, 44.
   JOHN: Pandulph, III, 4, 153.

exhibition, allowance or grant of money, pension; gift, present.
   LEAR: Gloucester, I, 2, 25.
   OTH: Othello, I, 3, 238.
   OTH: Emilia, IV, 3, 76.

exigent, crisis, pressing or compelling need, exigency, emergency.
   A&C: Antony, IV, 14, 63.
   JC: Antony, V, 1, 19.

expectancy, glowing, bright hope.
   HAM: Ophelia, III, 1, 160—*expectancy and rose of the fair state,* pride and hope; the rose symbolized beauty and perfection.

expectation
Oft expectation fails, and most oft there
Where most it promises; and oft it hits
Where hope is coldest and despair most fits.
   ALL'sW: Helena, II, 1, 145.

expedience, alacrity, speed.
   RICH2: Northumberland, II, 1, 287.
   MACB: Macbeth, II, 3, 116.

experience
Experience is by industry achieved

And perfected by the swift course of time.
   2GENT: Antonio, I, 3, 22.

express, perfectly formed, exact.
   HAM: Hamlet, II, 2, 318.

exsufflicate, inflated.
   OTH: Othello, III, 3, 182.

extend, praise, magnify; seize.
   CYM: 1Gentleman, I, 1, 25.
   A&C: Messenger, I, 2, 105.

extent, courtesy, showing kindness or justice; ceremony.
   HAM: Hamlet, II, 2, 390.
   A&C: Caesar, V, 2, 125.

extenuate, mitigate, lessen.
   MND: Theseus, I, 1, 120.

extirp, root out, eradicate.
   MEAS: Lucio, III, 2, 110.
   1H6: Charles, III, 3, 24.

Exton, Sir Pierce of, member of Bolingbroke's party; murders Richard II in Pomfret (Pontefract) at the sly suggestion of the new king, Henry IV.
   RICH2: V, 5.

extravagant, roving, wandering.
   HAM: Horatio, I, 1, 154.
   OTH: Roderigo, I, 1, 137.
   TwN: Sebastian, II, 1, 12—*extravagancy.*

eyas, young or nestling hawk.
   HAM: Rosencrantz, II, 3, 355.

eyas-musket, nestling male sparrow hawk; bright, lively youngster.
   MWW: Mrs. Ford, III, 3, 22.

eye, spot, tinge (of color); presence.
   TEMP: Sebastian, II, 1, 55.
   HAM: Fortinbras, IV, 4, 6.

eye (as a mirror)
I do protest I never loved myself
Till now infixed I beheld myself
Drawn in the flattering table of her eye.
   JOHN: Dauphin, II, 1, 501—in courtly love the lover speaks of love for himself as reflected in the one he loves.

. . . for the eye sees not itself
But by reflection, by some other things.

JC: Brutus, I, 2, 52.

eye-glass, lens of the eye.
WINT: Leontes, I, 2, 268.

eye of heaven, the sun.
RICH2: Gaunt, I, 3, 275.

. . . when the searching eye of
heaven is hid
Behind the globe, that lights the
lower world . . .
RICH2: Richard, III, 2, 37.

eyes
Mine eyes are made the fools o'
th' other senses,
Or else worth all the rest.
MACB: Macbeth, II, 1, 44.

If I could write the beauty of
your eyes
And in fresh numbers number
all your graces,

The age to come would say,
"This poet lies!
Such heavenly touches ne'er
touch'd earthly faces."
SONNET: XVII, 5.

eyes, like lamps
These eyes, like lamps whose
wasting oil is spent,
Wax dim, as drawing to their
exigent.
1H6: Mortimer, II, 5, 8. See
EXIGENT.

eyne, eyes, used in poetry.
MND: Helena, I, 1, 242.
LLL: King, V, 2, 206.

eyrie, nest.
HAM: Rosencrantz, II, 2, 354.

eysell (eisel). See ESILL.
SONNET: CXI, 10.

F

Fabian, servant in Olivia's household; angry with Malvolio, joins in the plot against him.
TwN: II, 5.

Fabyan, Robert (d. 1513). English chronicler; member of the Drapers' Company; sheriff of London (1493); *The New Chronicles of England and France* (pub., 1516; new editions, 1533, 1542, 1559); probably used by Shakespeare for material for *Henry VI.*

face
But there is never a fair woman has a true face.
A&C: Enobarbus, II, 6, 102.

. . . Was this the face
That like the sun did make beholders wink?
Was this the face that faced so many follies
And was at last outfaced by Bolingbroke?
A brittle glory shineth in this face.
As brittle as the glory is the face . . .
RICH2: Richard, IV, 1, 283.
See GLASS.

Look in thy glass and tell the face thou viewest
Now is the time that face should form another.
SONNET: III, 1.

face, adorn, trim, ornament, decorate; conceal the real purpose or meaning.
1H4: King, V, 1, 74.
SHREW: Grumio, IV, 3, 123—pun on defied.

faced (feazed), patched, worn, tattered.
1H4: Falstaff, IV, 2, 35.

faces
All men's faces are true, whatsome'er their hands are.
A&C: Menas, II, 6, 101.

facinerious, error, probably facinorous; infamous, wicked, evil.
ALL'sW: Parolles, II, 3, 35.

fact, evil deed, crime.
MACB: Lennox, III, 6, 10.
1H6: Gloucester, IV, 1, 30.
LUCRECE: 349.

factious, partisan; form a party or faction.
JC: Casca, I, 3, 118.
COR: Menenius, V, 2, 30—*factionary,* supporter, partisan.

factor, agent, representative.
1H4: Prince, III, 2, 147.
A&C: Pompey, II, 6, 10.
CYM: Iachimo, I, 6, 188.

fadge, suitable; pass, succeed.
LLL: Armado, V, 1, 154.
TwN: Viola, I, 2, 34.

fain, be pleased, willingly, gladly.
HAM: Laertes, IV, 7, 192.
2GENT: Speed, I, 1, 127.
LEAR: Cordelia, IV, 7, 38—obliged.

fair, beautiful.
MND: Helena, I, 1, 182.
She that was ever fair, and never proud;
Had tongue at will, and yet was never loud
OTH: Iago, II, 1, 149.

fair appointments, ironic expression for splendid and frightening arms or equipment.

116

RICH2: Bolingbroke, III, 3, 53.

fairest creatures

From fairest creatures we desire increase,

That thereby beauty's rose might never die . . .

SONNET: I, 1. See BEAUTY'S ROSE.

fairing, gift bought at a fair; complimentary present.

LLL: Princess, V, 2, 2.

fair stars, noble birth and rank.

RICH2: Aumerle, IV, 1, 21.

fairy toys, unimportant or ridiculous stories about fairies.

MND: Theseus, V, 1, 3.

falchion, curved sword.

RICH3: Anne, I, 2, 94.

LEAR: Lear, V, 3, 276.

LUCRECE: 176.

falcon

A falcon towering in her pride of place

Was by a mousing owl hawked at and killed.

MACB: Old Man, II, 4, 12—in falconry, towering means flying higher and higher in ever widening circles; place is greatest height attained in flight.

fall, happen; let fall; cadence (music).

MND: Pyramus, V, 1, 188.

TEMP: Prospero, V, 1, 64.

TwN: Duke, I, 1, 4.

falling in love

His heart, like an agate with your print impressed,

Proud with his form, in his eye pride expressed,

His tongue, all impatient to speak and not see,

Did stumble with haste in his eyesight to be;

All senses to that sense did make their repair,

To feel only looking on fairest of fair.

Methought all his senses were locked in his eye,

As jewels in crystal for some prince to buy,

Who, tendering their own worth

from where they were glassed,

Did point you to buy them along as you passed.

His face's own margent did quote such amazes

That all eyes saw his eyes enchanted with gazes.

LLL: Boyet, II, 1, 236. See MARGENT.

fall of a sparrow, from the Bible (Matthew 10:29): "Are not two sparrows sold for a farthing? and one of them shall not fall to the ground without your Father."

HAM: Hamlet, V, 2, 231.

fall off, desert, revolt.

1H4: Hotspur, I, 3, 94.

LEAR: Gloucester, I, 2, 116.

fall of kings

Rich men look sad, and ruffians dance and leap—

The one in fear to lose what they enjoy,

The other to enjoy by rage and war.

These signs forerun the death or fall of kings.

RICH2: Welsh Capt., II, 4, 12.

fallow, pale brownish-yellow, fawn-colored, pale reddish-brown.

MWW: Slender, I, 1, 91.

false

Heaven truly knows that thou art false as hell.

OTH: Othello, IV, 2, 39.

false face (deceit)

False face must hide what the false heart doth know.

MACB: Macbeth, I, 7, 82.

falsehood

. . . falsehood

Is worse in kings than beggars.

CYM: Imogen, III, 6, 13.

false soul

O this false soul of Egypt! this grave charm,

Whose eye beck'd forth my wars and called them home,

Whose bosom was my crownet, my chief end,

Like a right gipsy hath at fast
and loose
Beguil'd me to the very heart of
loss!
A&C: Antony, IV, 12, 25.

Falstaff, Sir John, most famous
comic character in Shakespeare;
obese, witty, bawdy old knight;
heavy-drinking, lying, thieving,
boastful drinking companion of
Prince Henry (1H4); robs travelers at Gadshill and is himself
robbed; talks himself out of a
charge of cowardice during the
Hotspur rebellion; leads a company of foot soldiers, misuses
the king's press; at Shrewsbury,
pretends to have killed Hotspur
himself; insults the Lord Chief
Justice (2H4); defrauds Mistress Quickly; sups with Doll
Tearsheet; captures the rebel
Colevile; borrows money from
Justice Shallow; disowned and
banished by Prince Hal, now
Henry V; death reported by
Mistress Quickly (HEN5); a
buffoon (in MWW), talks love
to Mistresses Page and Ford;
escapes Ford's jealous search,
once in a buck-basket, which is
thrown into the Thames, another
time as an old witch; persuaded
to dress as Herne, the Hunter,
he is baited in Windsor Forest
by Pistol, Quickly, Sir Hugh
Evans and his fairies. See
FASTOLFE.
1H4: I, 2; 2H4: I, 2; MWW:
I, 1.

fame, rumor, gossip, common
talk; from Vergilian goddess,
Fama.
ADO: Benedick, II, 1, 221.

fame
Let fame, that all hunt after in
their lives,
Live regist'red upon our brazen
tombs
And then grace us, in the disgrace of death,
When, spite of cormorant devouring Time,

Th' endeavour of this present
breath may buy
That honour which shall bate
his scythe's keen edge
And make us heirs of all eternity.
LLL: King, I, 1, 1.

famine
Making a famine where abun-
dance lies,
Thyself thy foe, to thy sweet self
too cruel.
SONNET: I, 7.

fan, winnow (chaff from corn);
test.
CYM: Iachimo, I, 6, 177.

fancies, thoughts, ideas or imag-
inings of love; impromptu tunes.
MND: Theseus, I, 1, 118.
2H4: Falstaff, III, 2, 343.

fancies (loves)
Our fancies are more giddy and
unfirm,
More longing, wavering, sooner
lost and worn,
Than women's are.
TwN: Duke, II, 4, 33.

fancy, love.
MND: Hermia, I, 1, 155.
Tell me, where is fancy bred,
Or in the heart, or in the head?
MERV: III, 2, 63—song sung
while Bassanio contemplates
the caskets.

fane, temple.
COR: Aufidius, I, 10, 20.
CYM: Guiderius, IV, 2, 242.

Fang, sheriff's officer; sent to
arrest Falstaff and Mistress
Quickly.
2H4: II, 1.

fangled, foppish, showy, fantastic; given to folly.
CYM: Posthumus, V, 4, 134.

fangs. See DOG.

fantasy, imagination, illusion,
hallucination; whim, caprice;
love.
HAM: Marcellus, I, 1, 23.
MND: Egeus, I, 1, 32.
OTH: Emilia, III, 3, 299.

fap, drunk, "loaded."
MWW: Bardolph, I, 1, 183.

farborough (tharborough), third-borough; constable.
LLL: Dull, I, 1, 185.

farced, stuffed, puffed up; usually with pompous phrases.
HEN5: King, IV, 1, 280.

fardingale (farthingale), hooped petticoat.
SHREW: Petruchio, IV, 3, 56.
2GENT: Julia, II, 7, 51.
MWW: Falstaff, III, 3, 69—one that doesn't join in front.

farewell
Farewell! thou art too dear for my possessing,
And like enough thou know'st thy estimate.
SONNET: LXXXVII, 1.

Farewell, dear heart etc., from song "Corydon's Farewell to Phyllis."
TwN: Toby, II, 3, 109.

farm our royal realm, practice of allowing a noble to collect taxes for a percentage of the total.
RICH2: Richard, I, 4, 45.

farthel (fardel) load, burden, bundle, peasant's pack.
HAM: Hamlet, III, 1, 76.
WINT: Shepherd, IV, 4, 728.

fashions, corruption of farcy, disease similar to glanders in horses; swellings on lymph glands.
SHREW: Biondello, III, 2, 53.

fast and loose, gambler's or conjurer's trick with a false knot that would easily pull loose; cheating game.
LLL: Moth, I, 2, 162.
A&C: Antony, IV, 12, 28. See FALSE SOUL.

Fastolfe, Sir John, cowardly knight; deserts Talbot and flees in terror; Talbot tears the Garter from his leg and the King banishes him. [The real Sir John Fastolf (c1378-1459) was governor of Maine and Anjou (1423); created Knight of the Garter (1426); did desert Talbot at Patay (1429), but only when the cause was lost; deprived of the Garter, but it was reinstated; owned a Boar's Head Tavern in Southwark; had been in the service of Thomas Mowbray, Duke of Norfolk, and accused of cowardice (over the Talbot episode), therefore, believed to be the original of Shakespeare's character.]
1H6: III, 2.

fat, gross, thick; slimy, nauseating.
HAM: Queen, V, 2, 298.
TwN: Olivia, V, 1, 112.
HAM: Ghost, I, 5, 32.

fate
The fate o'errules, that, one man holding troth
A million fail, confounding oath on oath.
MND: Puck, III, 2, 92.

Fate, show thy force! Ourselves we do not owe.
What is decreed must be—and be this so!
TwN: Olivia, I, 5, 329.

fates
Men at some time are masters of their fates.
The fault, dear Brutus, is not in our stars,
But in ourselves, that we are underlings.
JC: Cassius, I, 2, 139.

father
"Full fadom five thy father lies;
Of his bones are coral made;
Those are pearls that were his eyes;
Nothing of him that doth fade
But doth suffer a sea-change
Into something rich and strange.
Sea nymphs hourly ring his knell:"
TEMP: Ariel, I, 2, 396.

fathers. See FORTUNE.

fathom, ability, capacity, depth (of intellect).
OTH: Iago, I, 1, 153.

fathoms. See OATH.

fat-room, vat or tap room.
1H4: Prince, II, 4, 1.

fat woman of Brainford, actual person, known as the "witch of Brainford," notorious tavern keeper in Brentford on the Thames.
MWW: Mrs. Ford, IV, 2, 77.

Faulconbridge, Lady, mother of the Bastard (Philip) and Robert; Philip forces her to admit that Richard I was his father.
JOHN: I, 1.

Faulconbridge, Philip the Bastard, knighted by John when Queen Elinor recognizes him as her grandson; serves the King loyally.
JOHN: I, 1.

Faulconbridge, Robert, legitimate son; successfully appeals to John to let him have his father's inheritance.
JOHN: I, 1.

fault, misfortune, loss, lack.
MWW: Shallow, I, 1, 95.

fault, hunting term meaning a break or interruption in the line of scent; loss of scent.
TwN: Fabian, II, 5, 140.
SHREW: Lord, Induction, 1, 20.

faults
His faults, in him, seem as the spots of heaven,
More fiery by night's blackness; hereditary
Rather than purchased; what he cannot change
Than what he chooses.
A&C: Lepidus, I, 4, 12.

If she be made of white and red,
Her faults will ne'er be known;
For blushing cheeks by faults are bred
And fears by pale white shown.
Then if she fear, or be to blame,
By this you shall not know;
For still her cheeks possess the same
Which native she doth owe.
LLL: Moth, I, 2, 104.

Men's faults do seldom to themselves appear;

Their own transgressions partially they smother.
LUCRECE: 633.

His worst fault is that he is given to prayer; he is something peevish that way. But nobody but has his fault.
MWW: Quickly, I, 4, 13.

Fauste, precor gelida quando pecus omne sub umbra Ruminat, Latin, I pray you when all your flock lies feeding under the cool shade—opening lines from the *Eclogues* of Battista Spagnuoli Mantuanus (Mantuan, d. 1516) known for pastoral poetry.
LLL: Holofernes, IV, 2, 95.

favour, face, appearance, complexion, guise, countenance; charm, beauty.
A&C: Cleopatra, II, 5, 38.
HAM: Laertes, IV, 5, 189.
MACB: Lady Macbeth, I, 6, 73.

favour, pardon, indulgence, excuse.
MACB: Macbeth, I, 3, 149.

favours, personal colors or insignia.
1H4: Prince, V, 4, 96—probably a scarf with his colors or plume of his helmet.

fay, faith.
HAM: Hamlet, II, 2, 272.
SHREW: Sly, Induction, 2, 83.

fear
. . . if any fear
Lesser his person than an ill report;
If any think brave death outweighs bad life
And that his country's dearer than himself,
Let him alone, or so many so minded,
Wave thus to express his disposition,
And follow Marcius.
COR: Marcius, I, 6, 69.

. . . defect of judgment
Is oft the cause of fear.
CYM: Belarius, IV, 2, 111.

Of all base passions fear is most accursed.
1H6: Pucelle, V, 2, 18.

Let me still take away the harms
   I fear,
Not fear still to be taken.
LEAR: Goneril, I, 4, 35.

But cruel are the times, when
   we are traitors,
And do not know ourselves;
   when we hold rumour
From what we fear, yet know
   not what we fear,
But float upon a wild and vio-
   lent sea
Each way . . .
MACB: Ross, IV, 2, 18.

Is it for fear to wet a widow's
   eye
That thou consum'st thyself in
   single life?
SONNET: IX, 1.

fear no colours, proverbial expression, "Truth fears no colours" (enemy standards); fear
nothing; "I dare anyone."
TwN: Clown, I, 5, 6.

fear no more
Fear no more the heat o' th' sun
   Nor the furious winter's
   rages:
CYM: Guiderius, IV, 2, 258—
beginning of funeral song.

feast
. . . The feast is sold
That is not often vouched, while
   'tis a-making,
'Tis given with welcome. To feed
   were best at home.
From thence, the sauce to meat
   is ceremony;
Meeting were bare without it.
MACB: Lady Macbeth, III, 4,
33.

Feast of Crispian, October 25,
birthday of St. Crispinus and St.
Crispianus, patron saints of
shoemakers. [Brothers, fled from
Rome to Soissons in the time of
Diocletian; suffered martyrdom
(287 AD).]
HEN5: King, IV, 3, 40.

feater, trimmer, neater, more
gracefully.
TEMP: Antonio, II, 1, 272.

feather. See LEONTES.

feathers, plumes used as part of
an actor's costume.
HAM: Hamlet, III, 2, 286.

fee, payment made a public officer for performance of duty;
prisoners paid jailers upon their
release for their keep.
WINT: Hermione, I, 2, 53.
2H6: Warwick, III, 2, 217.

Feeble, Francis, woman's tailor;
one of the men supplied by Justice Shallow to Falstaff for the
army.
2H4: III, 2.

feeder, servant, menial, one who
depends on others for food; beg-
gar; parasite.
A&C: Antony, III, 13, 109.
WINT: Perdita, IV, 4, 11.
AYL: Corin, II, 4, 99.

feeding, pasture land for sheep
(or cattle).
WINT: Shepherd, IV, 4, 169.

fee-farm, in perpetuity; refers to
tenure held on land in fee
simple (at a fixed rent) in perpetuity.
T&C: Pandarus, III, 2, 53. See
FEE SIMPLE.

fee-grief, personal sorrow.
MACB: Macduff, IV, 3, 196.

feere (fere) mate, spouse, part-
ner.
PER: Gower, Prologue, 21.
TITUS: Marcus, IV, 1, 89.

fee simple, legal term meaning
absolute, complete possession or
ownership; belonging to heirs
of estate in perpetuity.
MWW: Mrs. Page, IV, 2, 225.
R&J: Benvolio, III, 1, 35.
ALL'sW: Parolles, IV, 3, 311.

felicity
Absent thee from felicity
   awhile . . .
HAM: Hamlet, V, 2, 358. See
WOUNDED NAME.

fell, cruel, fierce, violent, merci-
less.
COR: Virgilia, I, 3, 48.
OTH: Lodovico, V, 2, 362.
HAM: Hamlet, V, 2, 61. See
OPPOSITES.

fell, fleece, pelt, covering of hair or wool.
AYL: Corin, III, 2, 55.
MACB: Macbeth, V, 5, 11.

fellies, felloes, segments or pieces of the rim of a wooden wheel.
HAM: Player, II, 2, 517.

fellow, equal, peer; rival, match.
TEMP: Antonio, II, 1, 273.
MND: Bottom, IV, 1, 36.

fencing, it was often thought a young man who was an avid fencer was also arrogant, aggressive and flighty.
HAM: Polonius, II, 1, 25.

fennel, fragrant yellow-flowered perennial; used as seasoning herb; symbol of flattery and deceit.
HAM: Ophelia, IV, 5, 180.

fenny, from the fens or marshes.
MACB: 2Witch, IV, 1, 12. See WITCHES' CURSE.

Fenton, young man in love with Anne Page; her father objects to his suit; bribes the Host to help him elope with her.
MWW: I, 4.

Fenton, Sir Geoffrey (c1539-1605). Irish-English translator and political figure; principal secretary of state in Ireland; knighted for his services to Queen Elizabeth (1589); important for his translation of BOAISTEAU and BELLEFOREST used by Shakespeare.

feodary (fedary), confederate, accomplice.
WINT: Leontes, II, 1, 50.
CYM: Pisanio, III, 2, 21.
MEAS: Isabella, II, 4, 122.

fercel, male peregrine falcon; small hawk.
T&C: Pandarus, III, 2, 55.

Ferdinand, son of Alonso, King of Naples; with his father, he is among those shipwrecked on Prospero's island; falls in love with Miranda; Prospero makes him prove himself worthy of his daughter, but eventually permits their engagement.
TEMP: I, 2.

Ferdinand, King of Navarre, determined to have a court of scholars; falls in love with the Princess of France and pleads for her hand.
LLL: I, 1. See HENRY IV.

fernseed, believed to be visible only on St. John's (Midsummer) Eve, June 23rd, and if a person gathers it, he would become invisible.
1H4: Gadshill, II, 1, 98.

ferret, worry (as a ferret does its prey); red (like a ferret's eyes).
HEN5: Pistol, IV, 4, 30.
JC: Brutus, I, 2, 186.

ferryman. See CHARON.
RICH3: Clarence, I, 4, 46.

Feste, Olivia's fool; disguised as the parson, Sir Topas, he takes part in baiting Malvolio; sings famous songs including "O Mistress Mine."
TwN: I, 5.

festinate, hurried, hasty, precipitate.
LEAR: Cornwall, III, 7, 11.
LLL: Armado, III, 1, 6.

fet, fetched; derived.
HEN5: King, III, 1, 18.

fetch, trick, excuse, pretext, device.
LEAR: Lear, II, 4, 90.
HAM: Polonius, II, 1, 38—*fetch of warrant*, trick which is justified.

fetches, vetches, leguminous plants, climbing herbs.
TEMP: Iris, IV, 1, 61.

fetch off, retrieve, rescue; fleece, get the better of.
TEMP: Stephano, IV, 1, 213.
2H4: Falstaff, III, 2, 324.

fettle, get ready, prepare, adjust.
R&J: Capulet, III, 5, 154.

fico, Italian, fig; insulting hand gesture.
MWW: Pistol, I, 3, 33. See FIG.

fiddlestick, rapier, sword.
R&J: Mercutio, III, 1, 51.

fidiused, trounced, beaten.
COR: Menenius, II, 1, 144—coined phrase referring to expected treatment of Aufidius by Marcius in a death struggle; play on his name.

field of Golgotha
Disorder, horror, fear, and mutiny
Shall here inhabit, and this land be called
The field of Golgotha and dead men's skulls.
RICH2: Carlisle, IV, 1, 142. See GOLGOTHA, CONFOUND.

fiends, Flibbertigibbet (prince of grimacing and making faces), Smulkin, Modo (murder), Mahu (stealing), Frateretto, Hoppedance (Hop-dance) or Hobbididence (dumbness) and Obidicut (lust); material probably adapted from Samuel HARSNETT's *A Declaration of Egregious Popish Impostures* (1603), an anti-Catholic work.
LEAR: III, IV.

fierce
And though she be but little, she is fierce.
MND: Helena, III, 2, 325.

fiery portal, gate or place of the rising sun.
RICH2: Bolingbroke, III, 3, 64.

fiery Trigon, triangle formed by three signs (Aries, Leo and Sagittarius) of the Zodiac.
2H4: Poins, II, 4, 288.

fig, figo, fig of Spain; insulting and obscene gesture made by thrusting the thumb between the index and third fingers or between the teeth.
2H4: Pistol, V, 3, 123.
HEN5: Pistol, III, 6, 60.

fight
And fight and die is death destroying death,
Where fearing dying pays death servile breath.
RICH2: Carlisle, III, 2, 184.

fights, canvas screens put up to protect the crew during naval engagements.
MWW: Pistol, II, 2, 142.

figure, rhetorical means of expression, figure of speech; decorate with low relief designs, emboss; metaphor, simile.
HAM: Polonius, II, 2, 98.
RICH2: III, 3, 150.
LLL: Holofernes V, 1, 67.

file, list, roll; rank of soldiers.
MACB: Macbeth, III, 1, 95.
COR: Aufidius, V, 6, 33.
2H4: Hastings, I, 3, 10.

file of the subject, rank and file, mass of people.
MEAS: Lucio, III, 2, 144.

fillop (fillip), beat, assault; snap.
COR: Coriolanus, V, 3, 59.
2H4: Falstaff, I, 2, 255—*fillip me with a three-man beetle!* See BEETLE.

fills, shafts (of a cart).
T&C: Pandarus, III, 2, 48.

fine, perfectly, exquisitely made; short, brief; end.
HAM: Hamlet, II, 2, 468.
HAM: King, IV, 7, 134.
ALL'sW: Helena, IV, 4, 35.

fineless, unbounded, limitless, infinite.
OTH: Iago, III, 3, 173.

fines, legal process by which an estate tail was converted into a fee simple; which means transferred from one owner to another for complete possession or absolute ownership; conveyances.
HAM: Hamlet, V, 1, 114.

finger, measurement (breadth or length of a finger).
1H4: Prince, IV, 2, 80.

Finsbury, fields outside Moorgate; archery grounds and favorite recreation center for Londoners; popular for Sunday walks.
1H4: Hotspur, III, 1, 256.

firago, virago, violent woman, fury.
TWN: Toby, III, 4, 302.

fire, will-o'-the-wisp.
MND: Puck, III, 1, 112.

fire

Fire that's closest kept burns most of all.
2GENT: Lucetta, I, 2, 30.

A little fire is quickly trodden out;
Which, being suffered, rivers cannot quench.
3H6: Clarence, IV, 8, 8.

And where two raging fires meet together,
They do consume the thing that feeds their fury,
Though little fire grows great with little wind,
Yet extreme gusts will blow out fire and all.
SHREW: Petruchio, II, 1, 133.

fire and water, lightning and clouds; ancient explanation of thunder was fire hitting a cloud.
RICH2: Bolingbroke, III, 3, 56.

firebrand, will-o'-the-wisp.
TEMP: Caliban, II, 2, 6.

fire-drake, fiery dragon; meteor; man with a red nose.
HEN8: Man, V, 4, 45.

fire-ey'd maid of smoky war, reference to Bellona, Roman goddess of war.
1H4: Hotspur, IV, 1, 114.

fire-new, brand-new, fresh from the mint or forge, freshly coined.
LLL: Berowne, I, 1, 179.

fire of love

Thou wouldst as soon go kindle fire with snow
As seek to quench the fire of love with words.
2GENT: Julia, II, 7, 19.

fires

You sulph'rous and thought-executing fires,
Vaunt-couriers to oak-cleaving thunderbolts,
Singe my white head!
LEAR: Lear, III, 2, 4.

fires. See BLAZE OF RIOT.

firk, beat, trounce, drub, thrash.
HEN5: Pistol, IV, 4, 29.

fishmonger, pimp, procurer of whores.

HAM: Hamlet, II, 2, 174—cant term used by Hamlet to bait Polonius.

fistula, ulcer, abscess.
ALL'sW: Lafew, I, 1, 39.

fitchew, polecat, contemptuous word implying harlot, prostitute.
LEAR: Lear, IV, 6, 124.
OTH: Cassio, IV, 1, 50.
T&C: Thersites, V, 1, 66—fitchook.

fits, parts or divisions of a song.
T&C: Paris, III, 1, 62.

Fitzwater, Lord, member of Bolingbroke's faction; with Bagot, accuses Aumerle of complicity in the murder of the Duke of Gloucester. [c1368-1407.]
RICH2: IV, 1.

five moons, phenomenon which was believed to portend disaster.
JOHN: Hubert, IV, 2, 182.

fives, corruption of vives, swelling of the submaxillary glands in horses.
SHREW: Biondello, III, 2, 5.

five wits, mental ability or faculties listed in Stephen Hawes, *The Pastime of Pleasure* (1509), as common wit (or sense), imagination, fantasy, estimation and memory.
LEAR: Edgar, III, 4, 59.
SONNET: CXLI, 9.
R&J: Mercutio, I, 4, 47.

flags, flown from the tops of the theaters as a signal that performances were being given there; no flags were flown if the theater was closed, as during epidemics of the plague, for Lent or by order of the crown.

flail, two heavy stocks joined by leather thong used for threshing wheat.
3H6: Warwick, II, 1, 131.

flamed amazement, caused terror by turning into flames.
TEMP: Ariel, I, 2, 198—refers to St. Elmo's fire, flamelike phenomenon, sometimes observed during storms; at sea, it is usu-

ally seen as jets of flame extending from projecting points on a vessel, such as the tip of the mast.

flamen, priest of ancient Rome dedicated to a specific or special deity.

COR: Brutus, II, 1, 229.

TIMON: Timon, IV, 3, 155. See HOAR.

flame of love

There lives within the very flame of love

A kind of wick or snuff that will abate it;

And nothing is at a like goodness still,

For goodness, growing to a plurisy,

Dies in his own too-much.

HAM: King, IV, 7, 115. See SNUFF, PLURISY.

Flaminius, Timon's faithful servant; flings money in Lucullus' face, when he refuses to help his master.

TIMON: III, 1.

flapdragon, lighted or flaming raisin floated on top of liquor, which had to be snapped at and swallowed in game of snapdragon; similar to "ducking for apples."

LLL: Costard, V, 1, 45.

2H4: Falstaff, II, 4, 268.

WINT: Clown, III, 3, 100—*flapdragoned*, swallowed whole.

flatlong, hit with the flat side of the sword rather than the edge.

TEMP: Sebastian, II, 1, 181.

flattery

'Tis holy sport to be a little vain

When the sweet breath of flattery conquers strife.

COFE: Luciana, III, 2, 27. See VAIN.

That unicorns may be betrayed with trees

And bears with glasses, elephants with holes,

Lions with toils, and men with flatterers;

But when I tell him he hates flatterers,

He says he does, being then most flattered.

JC: Decius, II, 1, 204.

Fair cousin? I am greater than a king;

For when I was a king, my flatterers

Were then but subjects; being now a subject,

I have a king here to my flatterer.

Being so great, I have no need to beg.

RICH2: Richard, IV, 1, 305.

. . . He that loves to be flattered is worthy o' th' flatterer.

TIMON: Apemantus, I, 1, 232.

O that men's ears should be

To counsel deaf but not to flattery!

TIMON: Apemantus, I, 2, 256.

flattery. See TRUTH.

Flavius, Timon's faithful steward; tries to warn his master against reckless generosity, but is ignored; visits Timon in his cave and is the only one Timon doesn't abuse.

TIMON: I, 2.

Flavius. See MARULLUS.

JC: I, 1.

flaw, broken piece, fragment; gust or blast of wind, squall; colloquial word for sliver of ice formed around the edge of water; flake of snow.

LEAR: Lear, II, 4, 288.

HAM: Hamlet, V, 1, 239. See CAESAR.

2H4: King, IV, 4, 35.

Fleance, Banquo's son; escapes when his father is murdered at Macbeth's order.

MACB: II, 1. See BANQUO.

fleer, grin contemptuously, sneer, jeer.

LLL: Boyet, V, 2, 109.

OTH: Iago, IV, 1, 83.

ADO: Leonato, V, 1, 58.

flesh, enraged, made fierce and anxious for blood; hunting dogs were trained by feeding them the blood of game.

2H4: Northumberland, I, 1, 149.

HEN5: French King, II, 4, 50.

flesh

O that this too too solid flesh would melt,

Thaw, and resolve itself into a dew,

Or that the Everlasting had not fixed

His canon 'gainst self-slaughter.
HAM: Hamlet, I, 2, 129. See CANON.

. . . Lay her i' th' earth;

And from her fair and unpolluted flesh

May violets spring.
HAM: Laertes, V, 1, 261.

fleshed, had enough taste of blood or experienced enough bloodshed; hardened or inured to bloodshed.

TwN: Toby, IV, 1, 43.

RICH3: Tyrrel, IV, 3, 6.

Fletcher, John (1579-1625). English dramatist; collaborated with BEAUMONT, MASSINGER, Ben JONSON, Nathan FIELD, William ROWLEY and others; wrote *The Two Noble Kinsmen* with Shakespeare, possibly *Cardenio* (now lost) and the major part of *Henry VIII*; wrote (alone) *The Faithful Shepherdess* (printed, c1609), *Wit Without Money* (c1614), *The Mad Lover* (c1616) etc.

flewed, having hanging chaps, cheeks or dewlaps.

MND: Theseus, IV, 1, 123.

flexure, bowing, bending, obeisance.

HEN5: King, IV, 1, 272.

Flibbertigibbet. See FIENDS.
LEAR: Edgar, III, 4, 120.

flies

As flies to wanton boys are we to the gods.

They kill us for their sport.
LEAR: Gloucester, IV, 1, 36.

flight (of Adonis)

With this he breaketh from the sweet embrace

Of those fair arms which bound him to her breast

And homeward through the dark laund runs apace;

Leaves Love upon her back, deeply distress'd.

Look how a bright star shooteth from the sky—

So glides he in the night from Venus' eye.

VENUS: 811.

Flint Castle, the castle in Wales where Richard II and his adversary Bolingbroke confront one another.

RICH2: III, 2, 209.

flirt-gill, loose, flighty woman.
R&J: Nurse, II, 4, 162.

flock, piece, tuft, wisp of wool.
1H4: 1Carrier, II, 1, 7.

Flora, Roman goddess of flowers and spring; appears in April (festival, Floralia, celebrated April 28 to May 3).

WINT: Florizel, IV, 4, 2.

Florence, Duke of, pleads his cause in the war against Siena; appoints Bertram general of his horse.

ALL'sW: III, 1.

Florentius, Florent, hero in GOWER's *Confessio Amantis;* in order to learn the answer to the riddle "What do women most desire?" he agreed to marry an old hag; theme used by CHAUCER in *Tale of the Wife of Bath.*

SHREW: Petruchio, I, 2, 69.

Florio, Giovanni (c1553-1625). English lexicographer and author; son of Italian Protestant refugees; teacher of Italian and French; published *A World of Words* (1598), an English-Italian dictionary; famous translation of the *Essays* of MONTAIGNE (3 vols., 1603), still a standard work; Shakespeare (who was acquainted with Florio) undoubtedly used the latter as a source of material.

Florizel, Prince of Bohemia, son of Polixenes; in love with Perdita; succeeds, with the help of

Camillo, in eloping with her.
WINT: IV, 4.

flote, sea, wave, billows.
TEMP: Ariel, I, 2, 234.

flourish, trumpet or fanfare of
trumpets sounded to announce
the entrance of a character, person or persons of importance.
HAM: S.D., I, 2.
LEAR: S.D., I, 1.

flout, disdain, mock, scorn.
TEMP: Stephano, III, 2, 730.
MND: Helena, II, 2, 128.

flower. See SERPENT.

flower-de-luce, fleur-de-lis, the
iris; emblem of French kings;
first set in coat of arms of English kings by Edward I; English
kings from Edward III had
quartered emblem with English
lions.
WINT: Perdita, IV, 4, 127.
HEN5: King, V, 2, 224.
1H6: Messenger, I, 1, 80.

flowers. See WEEDS.

Fluellen, loyal, honest but pedantic, humorless Welsh officer;
quarrels with Irish captain Macmorris; forces Pistol to eat a leek
for insulting the Welsh; King involves him in a fight with Williams.
HEN5: III, 2.

flush, robust, vigorous, virile,
lusty.
HAM: Hamlet, III, 3, 81.

flute, wind instrument of very
early origin; referred to any
"pipe," whether it was single or
double reed or true flute; end-
blown flute first appeared and
was known as beat flute, flageolet, recorder, English or common
flute; side-blown or transverse
flute appeared in 13th century
and was most popular from
1400-1700; in Tudor times the
cross-blown flute, which was
purely a treble instrument, was
played (it was the favorite of
Henry VIII who owned 78 of
them), but the recorder or English flute was the more popular

and came in four sizes—treble,
alto, tenor and bass.

Flute, Francis, Athenian bellows-
mender; cast as Thisby to Bottom's Pyramus in the interlude.
MND: I, 2.

fly-blowing, being bothered or
contaminated by flies.
TEMP: Trinculo, V, 1, 284—
Trinculo was so pickled that he
didn't have to worry about flies,
as they did not bother meats
that were preserved. See
PICKLE.

foe
Would I had met my dearest foe
in heaven
Or ever I had seen that day,
Horatio.
HAM: Hamlet, I, 2, 182. See
DEAREST.

foil, flattering background which
sets something off or makes it
shine; such as gold leaf or tin
foil behind a jewel to add to its
luster.
HAM: Hamlet, V, 2, 266—pun
on weapon.
RICH2: Gaunt, I, 3, 266.

foil and target, lightweight fencing weapon or sword, probably
a rapier, and small shield.
HAM: Hamlet, II, 2, 334.

foin, thrust, in fencing.
LEAR: Edgar, IV, 6, 251.
ADO: Antonio, V, 1, 84.
MWW: Host, II, 3, 24.

foison, ample or plentiful crop or
harvest; abundance.
TEMP: Gonzalo, II, 1, 163.
A&C: Antony, II, 7, 23.
MEAS: Lucio, I, 4, 43.

folly, lasciviousness, licentiousness.
OTH: Iago, II, 1, 138.

folly
None are so surely caught, when
they are catched,
As wit turned fool; folly, in wis-
dom hatched,
Hath wisdom's warrant, and the
help of school.
LLL: Princess, V, 2, 69.

Folly in fools bears not so strong
a note
As fool'ry in the wise when wit
doth dote;
Since all the power thereof it
doth apply
To prove, by wit, worth in sim-
plicity.
LLL: Maria, V, 2, 75.

. . . But I remember now
I am in this earthly world, where,
to do harm
Is often laudable, to do good
sometime
Accounted dangerous folly.
MACB: Lady Macduff, IV, 2,
74.

folly. See NETTLE.

fond, foolish; infatuated (usually
with oneself); "head over heels"
in love, doting upon.
OTH: Desdemona, II, 1, 139.
SONNET: III, 8.
MND: Oberon, II, 1, 266.

fond many
An habitation giddy and unsure
Hath he that buildeth on the vulgar heart.
O thou fond many, with what
loud applause
Didst thou beat heaven with
blessing Bolingbroke
Before he was what thou
wouldst have him be!
2H4: Archbishop, I, 3, 89.

food
The food that to him now is as
luscious as locusts shall be to
him shortly as bitter as coloquintida.
OTH: Iago, I, 3, 354. See LO-
CUSTS, COLOQUINTIDA.

fool
. . . what a wasp-stung and impatient fool
Art thou to break into this
woman's mood,
Tying thine ear to no tongue but
thine own!
1H4: Northumberland, I, 3,
236.

fool. See WEEP.

Fool, realizes Lear's tragic blunder; tries to keep the King happy
by jesting, but only reminds him
of his mistakes; very unhappy
and unbalanced after Cordelia
goes to France; dies shortly after
following Lear out into the
storm.
LEAR: I, 4—character not included in the performances of
the play in the late 17th and
18th centuries, because he
wasn't understood by his audience.

Fool, servant of a courtesan; ex-
changes ribald remarks with
Apemantus and servants of
Timon's creditors.
TIMON: II, 2.

foolery
. . . the little foolery that wise
men have makes a great show.
AYL: Celia, I, 2, 96.

foolery. See MANHOOD.

fools
The more pity that fools may
not speak wisely what wise men
do foolishly.
AYL: Touchstone, I, 2, 92.

If it do come to pass
That any man turn ass—
AYL: Jaques, II, 5, 52—begin-
ning of song.

Well, thus we play the fools
with time, and the spirits of the
wise sit in the clouds and mock
us.
2H4: Prince, II, 2, 154.

Fools had ne'er less grace in a
year,
For wise men are grown foppish;
They know not how their wits to
wear,
Their manners are so apish.
LEAR: Fool, I, 4, 181—*foppish,*
foolish.

Lord, what fools these mortals
be!
MND: Puck, III, 2, 115.

. . . God give them wisdom that
have it, and those that are fools,
let them use their talents.
TwN: Clown, I, 5, 14.

fools of nature, dupes deceived by nature; men made to realize how helpless they are in nature's presence.
HAM: Hamlet, I, 4, 54.

fools of time. See TIME'S FOOL.

foot, grasp, clutch, seize with talons.
CYM: Sicilus Leonatus, V, 4, 116.

footcloth, ornamental cloth of trappings covering a horse and hanging to the ground on either side.
RICH3: Hastings, III, 4, 83.
2H6: Suffolk, IV, 1, 54.

footing, dancing; landing, disembarking.
TEMP: Iris, IV, 1, 137.
OTH: Cassio, II, 1, 76.

foot land-rakers, vagabonds who travel on foot and steal for a living; footpads.
1H4: Gadshill, II, 1, 81.

fop, fool, dupe.
OTH: Roderigo, IV, 2, 197.

forbear, depart, withdraw, retire.
CYM: 1Gentleman, I, 1, 68.
LEAR: Edmund, I, 2, 182.
OTH: Iago, I, 2, 10—leave alone.

forbid, accursed, under a ban.
MACB: 1Witch, I, 3, 21.

forbidden usury, charging very high rates of interest for money loaned was considered immoral (un-Christian); the law allowed an interest rate of ten percent.
SONNET: VI, 5.

forced marriage
For what is wedlock forced but a hell,
An age of discord and continual strife?
1H6: Suffolk, V, 5, 62.

forcing of his disposition, trying hard to be amenable, showing constraint.
HAM: Guildenstern, III, 1, 12.

for country
. . . I have done
As you have done—that's what I can; induced

As you have been—that's for my country.
COR: Marcius, I, 9, 15.

Ford, jealous of his wife; disguises himself as Master Brook and offers Falstaff money to woo her on his behalf.
MWW: II, 1.

Ford, Mistress, with Mistress Page teaches Falstaff a lesson; cures her husband of his jealousy.
MWW: II, 1.

fordo, destroy, undo.
HAM: Hamlet, V, 1, 244.
LEAR: Edmund, V, 3, 255.
OTH: Iago, V, 1, 129.

Fordun, John of (d. c1384). Scottish chronicler; author of the *Chronica gentis Scotorum* (5 vols., continued in the middle of the 15th century by Walter Bower; whole work known as the *Scotichronicon*), first (largely legendary) history of Scotland; used by BOECE.

foredone, done in, exhausted, worn out.
MND: Puck, V, 1, 381.

forgery, invention, imagination.
HAM: King, IV, 7, 90.

fork, twin-pronged arrow head; hairdress or style.
LEAR: Kent, I, 1, 146.

forked, horned (cuckold).
WINT: Leontes, I, 2, 186.
OTH: Othello, III, 3, 276.

form, likeness, image; manner; array, military formation; bench.
SONNET: IX, 6.
OTH: Iago, I, 1, 50.
2H4: Messenger, IV, 1, 20.
LLL: Costard, I, 1, 211.

Forres, town about 25 miles from Inverness, in northeastern Scotland; 11 miles from Elgin.
MACB: Banquo, I, 3, 39.

forset-seller (fosset), dealer in wooden faucets, wine or barrel taps.
COR: Menenius, II, 1, 79.

for shame
> For shame! deny that thou bear'st love to any,
> Who for thyself art so unprovident.
> SONNET: X, 1.

forspoken, spoken against, opposed.
> A&C: Cleopatra, III, 7, 3.

Fortinbras, Prince of Norway, nephew of the king, whose father was slain in single combat by old Hamlet; prevented by Claudius from invading Denmark, he is instead permitted to cross the country in a campaign against the Poles; after his victory, he appears at the Danish court and sees a political advantage to himself in the confusion brought on by the deaths of the Danish royal family; the dying Hamlet lends his support to his claim to the Danish crown.
> HAM: I, 2.

fortress
> This fortress built by Nature for herself
> Against infection and the hand of war . . .
> RICH2: Gaunt, II, 1, 43. See SCEPTERED ISLE.

fortune
> . . . Fortune knows
> We scorn her most when most she offers blows.
> A&C: Antony, III, 2, 73.

> Who this had seen, with tongue in venom steeped,
> 'Gainst Fortune's state would treason have pronounced.
> HAM: Player, II, 2, 533.

> Will Fortune never come with both hands full,
> But write her fair words still in foulest letters?
> She either gives a stomach, and no food
> (Such are the poor, in health), or else a feast,
> And takes away the stomach—such are the rich

> That have abundance and enjoy it not.
> 2H4: King, IV, 4, 103.

> There is a tide in the affairs of men
> Which, taken at the flood, leads on to fortune;
> Omitted, all the voyage of their life
> Is bound in shallows and in miseries.
> On such a full sea are we now afloat,
> And we must take the current when it serves
> Or lose our ventures.
> JC: Brutus, IV, 3, 218.

> . . . when Fortune means to men most good,
> She looks upon them with a threatening eye.
> JOHN: Pandulph, III, 4, 119.

> This is the excellent foppery of the world, that, when we are sick in fortune, often the surfeit of our own behaviour, we make guilty of our disasters the sun, the moon, and the stars; as if we were villains on necessity; fools by heavenly compulsion; knaves, thieves, and treachers by spherical predominance; drunkards, liars, and adulterers by an enforc'd obedience of planetary influence; and all that we are evil in, by a divine thrusting on. . . . I should have been that I am, had the maidenliest star in the firmament twinkled on my bastardizing.
> LEAR: Edmund, I, 2, 125.

> Fathers that wear rags
> Do make their children blind;
> But fathers that bear bags
> Shall see their children kind.
> Fortune, that arrant whore,
> Ne'er turns the key to th' poor.
> LEAR: Fool, II, 4, 48.

> When Fortune in her shift and change of mood
> Spurns down her late beloved, all his dependants,
> Which laboured after him to the mountain's top

Even on their knees and hands,
  let him slip down,
Not one accompanying his declining foot.
  TIMON: Poet, I, 1, 84.

fortune. See WISDOM.

Fortune, The, London theater
built for the ADMIRAL'S MEN by
Edward Alleyn and Philip
Henslowe (1599); about half a
mile from the CURTAIN on the
north side of the city, in the
parish of St. Giles Cripplegate;
wooden structure (80 ft. outside,
55 ft. inside); destroyed by fire
(1621); rebuilt of brick (1623);
pulled down (1649).

forty winters
When forty winters shall besiege
  thy brow
And dig deep trenches in thy
  beauty's field,
Thy youth's proud livery, so
  gaz'd on now,
Will be a tattered weed, of small
  worth held.
  SONNET: II, 1. See WEED.

for why, because.
  RICH2: Richard, V, 1, 46.

foul deeds
. . . Foul deeds will rise,
Though all the earth o'erwhelm
  them, to men's eyes.
  HAM: Hamlet, I, 2, 257.

foundation, charitable institution;
house of worship where alms
were distributed; security.
  CYM: Imogen, III, 6, 7.

foutra, indecent or coarse word
showing contempt.
  2H4: Pistol, V, 3, 103.

fox, sword; name derived from
trademark of wolf (later more
like a fox) that was imprinted
on the blade of Passau swords
by their maker.
  HEN5: Pistol, IV, 4, 9.

fox
A fox, when one has caught her,
And such a daughter,
Should sure to the slaughter,
If my cap would buy a halter.
  LEAR: Fool, I, 4, 340.

Foxe, John (1516-87). English
Protestant translator, writer, editor; author of *Book of Martyrs*
(actual title *Actes and Monuments,* Latin version, 1559, English, 1563); attack on Cranmer
in Shakespeare's *Henry VIII*
based on Foxe.

foxship, evil cunning; ingratitude.
  COR: Volumnia, IV, 2, 18.

fracted, broken, cracked, frac-
tured.
  HEN5: Pistol, II, 1, 130.
  TIMON: Senator, II, 1, 22.

fractions, broken sentences; separation; dissension.
  TIMON: Steward, II, 2, 220.

frailty
Frailty, thy name is woman.
  HAM: Hamlet, I, 2, 146.

Alas, our frailty is the cause, not
  we!
For such as we are made of,
  such we be.
  TWN: Viola, II, 2, 32.

frame, sensible order, logical or
cohesive thought; design, plan,
system; device, invention.
  ADO: Leonato, IV, 1, 129.
  HAM: Guildenstern, III, 2, 321.
  See OUT OF FRAME.

frampold (frampal), disagreeable,
ill-tempered, quarrelsome; wor-
ried.
  MWW: Quickly, II, 2, 94.

France, King of, cured by Helena,
he arranges her marriage to
Bertram; when he sees the ring
he had given Helena on Bertram's finger, he suspects him of
having murdered her; Helena
appears with the widow and all
is well.
  ALL'SW: I, 2.

France, King of, agrees to marry
dowerless Cordelia; see PHILIP
II (JOHN) and CHARLES IV
(HEN5).
  LEAR: I, 1.

France, Princess of, upsets the
peace and quiet of the court of
the King of Navarre; supposedly

came to settle a debt, but falls in love with the King.
LLL: II, 1.

franchised, free from blame, not bound by guilt.
MACB: Banquo, II, 1, 28.

Francis, tavern drawer; made fun of by Prince Henry and Poins.
1H4: II, 4.

Francisca, nun of the order of St. Clare; welcomes Isabella when she begins her novitiate.
MEAS: I, 4.

Francisco, typical soldier; guard at Elsinore; relieved of watch by Bernardo and does not appear again.
HAM: I, 1.

Francisco, a lord attending Alonso, King of Naples.
TEMP: II, 1.

frank, liberal, bounteous, of a giving nature; free.
SONNET: IV, 4.

frank, sty, enclosure for pigs or hogs; shut up, penned.
2H4: Prince, II, 2, 160.
RICH3: Derby, IV, 5, 3.

franklin, rich yeoman, freeholder, rank just below the gentry.
WINT: Clown, V, 2, 173.
1H4: Chamberlain, II, 1, 60.
CYM: Imogen, III, 2, 79.

Frateretto. See FIENDS.
LEAR: Edgar, III, 6, 7.

fraught, full, stored, freighted; burden, load, cargo; endowed.
LEAR: Goneril, I, 4, 241.
CYM: Cymbeline, I, 1, 126.
TITUS: Titus, I, 1, 71.

fray, frighten, terrify.
T&C: Pandarus, III, 2, 34.

Frederick, Duke, father of Celia; has usurped the position of his older brother, Duke "Senior"; banishes Rosalind; finally "sees the light" and returns all he has stolen.
AYL: I, 2.

freedom
. . . I had as lief have the fop-
pery of freedom as the morality of imprisonment.
MEAS: Lucio, I, 2, 137.

French crown, coin (*écu*); sarcastic allusion to the loss of hair caused by the "French" disease (syphilis).
MEAS: Lucio, I, 2, 52.
MND: Quince, I, 2, 99.

French falconers, the art of hawking or falconry was of particular interest to the French, who were very expert at it.
HAM: Hamlet, II, 2, 450— Hamlet is disparaging of the French methods.

fret, harass, irritate, annoy, disturb.
HAM: Hamlet, III, 2, 388.
SHREW: Tranio, II, 1, 330— going to waste.

frets, guides to fingering on stringed instruments; formerly rings of gut, now a bar of wood.
SHREW: Hortensio, II, 1, 150.
LUCRECE: 1140.

fretted, ornamented, decorated with fretwork, an angular, interlaced design; dug out, made by wearing away or digging out.
HAM: Hamlet, II, 2, 314. See CANOPY.
JC: Cinna, II, 1, 104.
RICH2: Richard, III, 3, 167.

friar, refers to Friar Tuck, member of Robin Hood's band.
2GENT: 3Outlaw, IV, 1, 36.
See ROBIN HOOD.

Friar Francis, suggests to Hero that she pretend she has died of grief, in order to change Claudio's slander to love; performs the marriage ceremonies.
ADO: IV, 1.

Friar John, Franciscan; sent by Friar Laurence to Mantua to tell Romeo to come and take the apparently dead Juliet from the Capulet tomb; suspected by the constables of having been infected with the plague, he is prevented from leaving.
R&J: V, 2.

Friar Laurence, Franciscan priest who befriends and secretly marries the lovers.
R&J: II, 3.

Friar Lodowick, name assumed by Duke Vincentio.
MEAS: II, 3.

Friar Peter, helps the disguised Duke of Vienna to carry out his plans; marries Angelo to Mariana.
MEAS: IV, 6.

Friar Thomas, permits the Duke of Vienna to disguise himself as a friar, so that he may spy on Angelo.
MEAS: I, 3.

friend
For who not needs shall never lack a friend,
And who in want a hollow friend doth try,
Directly seasons him his enemy.
HAM: Player King, III, 2, 217.

friends
I count myself in nothing else so happy
As in a soul rememb'ring my good friends.
RICH2: Bolingbroke, II, 3, 46.

He hath no friends but what are friends for fear,
Which in his dearest need will fly from him.
RICH3: Blunt, V, 2, 20.

friendship
Friendship is constant in all other things
Save in the office and affairs of love.
Therefore all hearts in love use their own tongues;
Let every eye negotiate for itself
And trust no agent.
ADO: Claudio, II, 1, 182.

. . . Friendship's full of dregs.
Methinks false hearts should never have sound legs.
Thus honest fools lay out their wealth on curtsies.
TIMON: Apemantus, I, 2, 239.

Friends, Romans, countrymen
Friends, Romans, countrymen, lend me your ears;
I come to bury Caesar, not to praise him.
The evil that men do lives after them;
The good is oft interred with their bones.
So let it be with Caesar.
JC: Antony, III, 2, 79—opening of Antony's famed oration.

frize, frieze; rough cloth, usually woolen, with a nap.
OTH: Iago, II, 1, 127.
MWW: Falstaff, V, 5, 46.

frippery, thrift shop, place where old or secondhand clothes are bought and sold.
TEMP: Trinculo, IV, 1, 226.

Frogmore, in Little Park, Windsor.
MWW: Host, II, 3, 78.

Froissart, Jean (1338-1410), renowned French chronicler; wrote about the wars of Edward III in France.
1H6: Alençon, I, 2, 29.

front, forehead, brow, face.
HAM: Hamlet, III, 4, 56.
OTH: Othello, I, 3, 80.
A&C: Philo, I, 1, 6—*tawny front,* swarthy complexion or face; although of pure Greek background, Cleopatra was thought to be dark-skinned.

frost. See DEATH.

froth, to draw beer with a big head, thereby giving less.
MWW: Host, I, 3, 14.

Froth, foolish gentleman; arrested with Pompey, who had been "using" him; dismissed by Escalus with a warning.
MEAS: II, 1.

fruit
The ripest fruit first falls.
RICH2: Richard, II, 1, 153.

frush, smash, break up, batter, destroy.
T&C: Hector, V, 6, 29.

fubbed, cheated, foiled, baffled.
1H4: Falstaff, I, 2, 68.

fullam, loaded dice.
MWW: Pistol, I, 3, 94.

Fulvia, Antony's wife; thought to be a shrewish woman; he finds her "good, being gone."
A&C: Cleopatra, I, 1, 20.

fumitory, weed.
HEN5: Burgundy, V, 2, 45.
LEAR: Cordelia, IV, 4, 3—*fumiter.*

furbish, restore to original luster; polish, clean armor of its rust.
RICH2: Bolingbroke, I, 3, 76.

furniture, equipment, provisions.
1H4: Prince, III, 3, 225.
SHREW: Petruchio, IV, 3, 182 —outfit, dress, clothing.

furzes. See BROWN FURZE, LONG HEATH.

fust, grow stale, musty, molded.
HAM: Hamlet, IV, 4, 39.
COR: Cominus, I, 9, 7.

fustian, nonsense, bombastic ranting, gibberish.
OTH: Cassio, II, 3, 282.
TWN: Fabian, II, 5, 119.
2H4: Doll, II, 4, 203.

fustian, coarse material of cotton and flax.
SHREW: Grumio, IV, 1, 49.

fustilarian, fat pig, frowsy, musty old wench or creature.
2H4: Falstaff, II, 1, 66.

G

gabardine, loose-fitting cloak or mantle; smock.

TEMP: Trinculo, II, 2, 42.

gad, spur, sharp spike, stylus, goad.

TITUS: Titus, IV, 1, 103.

LEAR: Gloucester, I, 2, 26— *Upon the gad,* on the spur of the moment.

Gadshill, village in North Kent, three miles northwest of Rochester, England; the hill there, on the road to Gravesend, was the hangout of highwaymen and the scene of many robberies; Falstaff Inn and Gadshill Place, home of Charles Dickens (1856-70), are there.

1H4: Poins, I, 2, 139.

Gadshill, thief; helps Falstaff, Bardolph and Peto to waylay the travelers from the Rochester inn and rob them; robbed in turn by the disguised prince and Poins; encourages Falstaff in his lies, when they explain their adventure in the Boar's tavern.

1H4: II, 1.

gage, pledge to fight in support or affirmation of ideas; a glove is usually thrown on the ground in challenge.

RICH2: Bolingbroke, I, 1, 69.

1H4: Hotspur, I, 3, 173.

HEN5: King, IV, 1, 223.

gage, stake, risk, pledge, gamble.

HAM: Horatio, I, 1, 91.

LUCRECE: 144.

gainsgiving, premonition of trouble, apprehension, foreboding, misgiving.

HAM: Hamlet, V, 2, 227.

gait, progress, advancement, moving ahead.

HAM: King, I, 2, 31.

Galen, famous Greek physician (c130-c200 AD); wrote many important works; highly regarded in Shakespeare's time.

COR: Menenius, II, 1, 128.

2H4: Falstaff, I, 2, 133.

MWW: Host, II, 3, 30.

gall, irritate, annoy, anger; make sore; break the skin with a weapon, draw blood, wound, scratch.

RICH2: Richard, V, 5, 94.

HAM: Hamlet, II, 2, 604.

JOHN: Salisbury, IV, 3, 94.

gall, "oak-apples," parasitic growth on oak tree from which ink was made.

CYM: Posthumus, I, 1, 101— pun on bitterness.

galleys, large, low Venetian vessels, propelled by both oars and sails, usually having one deck; used in Mediterranean waters for war and other purposes; typical warship was 100 to 200 feet long, having 20 oars to each side and each oar manned by many slaves.

OTH: Cassio, I, 2, 40.

Gallia, France.

MWW: Host, III, 1, 99.

1H6: Talbot, IV, 6, 15.

HEN5: Pistol, V, 1, 94.

galliard, lively dance in (quick) triple time; five-step.

TWN: Toby, I, 3, 127.

HEN5: Ambassador, I, 2, 252.

gallias, fast, merchant ship; heavier and slightly larger than a galley.

   SHREW: Tranio, II, 1, 380.

gallimaufry, medley, jumble, hodgepodge; hash.

   WINT: Servant, IV, 4, 335.

   MWW: Pistol, II, 1, 119.

gallow, frighten, terrify.

   LEAR: Kent, III, 2, 44.

galloway nags, Irish horses of low quality; common jades.

   2H4: Pistol, II, 4, 215. See JADES.

gallowglasses, regular Irish soldiers; more heavily armed and better trained than kerns; used pole-ax; fought on horseback. See KERNS, SLEDDED POLACKS.

   2H6: Messenger, IV, 9, 26.

   MACB: Sergeant, I, 2, 13.

gallows, a person who merits hanging; rogue.

   TEMP: Gonzalo, I, 1, 32—reference to an old proverb, "He that's born to be hanged need fear no drowning."

   LLL: Katherine, V, 2, 12.

Gallus, friend of Caesar; one of those who captures Cleopatra in her monument.

   A&C: V, 1.

gambol, shy away from, sidestep, evade.

   HAM: Hamlet, III, 4, 144.

gammon, leg, side, flitch, thigh; used today for ham (gammon of bacon—cured ham).

   1H4: 2Carrier, II, 1, 26.

gamouth (gamut) musical scale; devised by Guido d'Arezzo (Aretinus, c990-1050).

   SHREW: Hortensio, III, 1, 67.

Ganymede, beautiful young Trojan prince seized by Jove (Zeus), in the shape of an eagle, and brought to Olympus to be cupbearer to the gods.

   AYL: Rosalind, I, 3, 127—name assumed by Rosalind.

garb, manner; clothing, fashion, style.

   OTH: Iago, II, 1, 315.

   HAM: Hamlet, II, 2, 390.

garboil, commotion, upheaval, brawl.

   A&C: Antony, I, 3, 61.

Gardener, compares his garden to the way a kingdom should be run; overheard by the Queen.

   RICH2: III, 4.

Gardiner, Bishop of Winchester; leader of the attack on Cranmer; student of Wolsey; made to embrace Cranmer by the King. [Stephen Gardiner (1483?-1555), sent to Pope by Henry VIII on mission to discuss divorce from Catherine (1528); made Bishop of Winchester (1531); wrote learned defense of the Act of Supremacy (pub., 1535); committed to Tower of London (1552); appointed lord high chancellor by Queen Mary Tudor (1553); prosecuted Protestants.]

   HEN8: V, 1.

Gargrave, Sir Thomas, leading officer in the English army besieging Orleans; killed by a French sniper.

   1H6: I, 4.

garners, granaries; stored up, treasured.

   COR: Marcius, I, 1, 254.

   OTH: Othello, IV, 2, 58.

Gascoigne, George (c1535-77). English poet; *The Posies of G. G.* (1575) includes *Jocasta,* tragedy in blank verse and *Certayne Notes of Instruction concerning the making of verse or ryme in English* (1575), considered the earliest English critical essay; *The Steele Glas* (1576), first regular English satire; his adaptation of ARIOSTO's *I Suppositi,* earliest play in English prose; subplot of *The Taming of the Shrew* taken from this play.

gaskins, loose breeches, hose.

   TwN: Maria, I, 5, 27.

gastness, terror, terrified expression.

   OTH: Iago, V, 1, 106.

gathering head, a boil that is forming a head.
  RICH2: Richard, V, 1, 58.

gaud (gawd), trifle, playtoy, gee-gaw, trinket, jeweled ornament.
  MND: Egeus, I, 1, 33.
  SHREW: Bianca, II, 1, 3.
  T&C: Ulysses, III, 3, 176.

gaudy, festive, joyous revel; feast days are still called "gaudy days" at Oxford.
  A&C: Antony, III, 13, 183.

Gaunt. See JOHN OF GAUNT.

Gawlia, Wales.
  MWW: Host, III, 1, 99.

gaze, that which is seen, object of one's gaze, glance or sight.
  SONNET: V, 2. See HOURS.

gear, business, affair, matter.
  T&C: Pandarus, I, 1, 6.
  MERV: Launcelot, II, 2, 175.

geck, simpleton, fool, dupe.
  TWN: Malvolio, V, 1, 351.
  CYM: Sicilius Leonatus, V, 4, 67—*geek.*

gelded, deprived, cut off from; mutilated.
  RICH2: Ross, II, 1, 237.
  LLL: Ferdinand, II, 1, 149.

gelidus timor occupat artus, Latin, cold fear seizes my limbs.
  2H6: Suffolk, IV, 1, 117—inaccurate quote from Vergil.

geminy, pair (of twins).
  MWW: Falstaff, II, 2, 10.

general, the masses, common people, public in general.
  HAM: Hamlet, II, 2, 458.

generally, individually, singly.
  MND: Bottom, I, 2, 2.

generations. See YOUTH.

generous, noble, aristocratic, of gentle lineage.
  HAM: Polonius, I, 3, 74.
  OTH: Desdemona, III, 3, 280.

genius, man's guardian angel or spirit.
  T&C: Troilus, IV, 4, 52.
  TWN: Toby, III, 4, 142.
  MACB: Macbeth, III, 1, 56.

genius, personification.
  2H4: Falstaff, III, 2, 337.

gennet (jennet) small Spanish horse; possibly pony bred by the Moors.
  OTH: Iago, I, 1, 114.

gentleness
  If ever you have looked on better days,
  If ever been where bells have knolled to church,
  If ever sat at any good man's feast,
  If ever from your eyelids wiped a tear
  And know what 'tis to pity and be pitied,
  Let gentleness my strong enforcement be
  AYL: Orlando, II, 7, 113.

gentle thou art
  Gentle thou art, and therefore to be won,
  Beauteous thou art, therefore to be assail'd.
  SONNET: XLI, 5.

Geoffrey of Monmouth (c1000-54). English chronicler; author of *Historia regum Britanniae* (12 vols, 1147); extremely popular and influential source of the Arthurian and other legends; used by HOLINSHED and in turn by Shakespeare.

George Bevis. See BEVIS, George.

George, Duke of Clarence. See CLARENCE, Duke of.

german, from Latin *germanus,* kinsman, near relative.
  OTH: Iago, I, 1, 114.

Gerrold, schoolmaster; teaches the country folk the dance they perform before Theseus and his companions.
  2NK: III, 5.

Gertrude, weak-willed mother of Hamlet, Queen of Denmark, wife of Claudius; though she may have been guilty of adultery, she was not involved in the murder of her first husband, Hamlet's father; well-meaning but shallow, she perceives Claudius' guilt only after drinking the poisoned cup intended by him for Hamlet; in Scandinavian history, her name was Geruth or Gerutha.

HAM: I, 2.

gest, deed, exploit; time, usually of a halt in a royal procession.

A&C: Antony, IV, 8, 2.
WINT: Hermione, I, 2, 41.

Ghost of Hamlet's father, appears twice to Marcellus and Bernardo, and on several occasions to Horatio and Hamlet; reveals to his son the details of his own murder at the hands of his brother, Claudius; goads Hamlet into avenging his death, but instructs him not to harm his mother, but to "Leave her to Heaven"; later intervenes in her behalf and prevents Hamlet from killing her.

HAM: I, 1.

ghosts, used by Elizabethans in tragedies; borrowed from SENECA; the ghost in *Hamlet* might be compared to Tantalus in Seneca's *Thyestes;* thought to be bloodless corpses that rose from their graves, returning at cockcrow, and not hallucinations; demons and angels could also take human form; appear in *Hamlet, Macbeth, Julius Caesar, Cymbeline, Richard III, Henry VI.*

gib, tomcat; nickname for Gilbert, common cat's name.

HAM: Hamlet, III, 4, 190.
1H4: Falstaff, I, 2, 83.

gibbet, hang; gallows.

CYM: Jailer, V, 4, 207.
2H4: Falstaff, III, 2, 282—*gibbets on the brewer's bucket,* brewer's man had a wooden yoke on his shoulder with a bucket hanging from a chain and hook at either end.

giddy
He that is giddy thinks the world turns round.

SHREW: Widow, V, 2, 20.

gifts
The gifts she looks from me are packed and locked
Up in my heart, which I have given already,
But not delivered.

WINT: Florizel, IV, 4, 369.

gig, whirling top, spun by snapping or whipping.

LLL: Berowne, IV, 3, 167.

giglet (giglot), wanton, strumpet, harlot, trollop.

CYM: Queen, III, 1, 31.
MEAS: Escalus, V, 1, 352.
1H6: Pucelle, IV, 7, 41.

gild, to smear, color, cover with yellowish or red iridescent scum; make glow or flush; get drunk.

A&C: Caesar, I, 4, 62.
MACB: Lady Macbeth, II, 2, 56.
TEMP: Alonso, V, 1, 280.

gilded monuments. See RHYME.

gill, measure (½ pint) for drinks.

SHREW: Grumio, IV, 1, 52—pun on Jill (Gillian; girl or maidservant).

gillyvors, clove-scented pinks; favorite flower for garlands and spicing wine.

WINT: Perdita, IV, 4, 82.

gimmaled, jointed, hinged.

HEN5: Grandpré, IV, 2, 49.

gimmers, corruption of gimmals; mechanism, especially in a clock.

1H6: Reignier, I, 2, 41.

gin, trap, snare.

TWN: Fabian, II, 5, 51.

Giovanni (Fiorentino), Ser. Florentine author of a collection of stories (in the BOCCACCIO tradition) called *Il Pecorone* (written 1378, pub. 1558); Shakespeare used the story of Gianetto in *The Merchant of Venice.*

gird, taunt; sharp, bitter epithets.

COR: Brutus, I, 1, 260.
2H4: Falstaff, I, 2, 7.
SHREW: Lucentio, V, 2, 58.

girdle
I'll put a girdle round about the earth
In forty minutes.
MND: Puck, II, 1, 175.

Gis, Jesu, Jesus; popular contraction used as modern "Jeez."
HAM: Ophelia, IV, 5, 58—part of song.

give, heraldic term, display.
MWW: Slender, I, 1, 15.

give
I'll give my jewels for a set of beads,
My gorgeous palace for a hermitage,
My gay apparel for an almsman's gown,
My figured goblets for a dish of wood.
RICH2: Richard, III, 3, 147.
See SET OF BEADS, ALMSMAN, FIGURED, DISH OF WOOD, NAME OF KING.

give back, stand back, retreat, fall away.
2GENT: Valentine, V, 4, 126.

give me the lie, call me a liar.
TEMP: Stephano, III, 2, 85.

give me your hands, applaud.
MND: Puck, V, 1, 444.

give off, end, finish.
A&C: 1Soldier, IV, 3, 21.

giving and receiving
I gave it freely ever; and there's none
Can truly say he gives, if he receives.
If our betters play at that game, we must not dare
To imitate them. Faults that are rich are fair.
TIMON: Timon, I, 2, 10.

glanders, very serious, highly contagious disease of horses, infecting glands beneath and within the lower jaws.
SHREW: Biondello, III, 2, 51.

Glansdale, Sir William, leading officer in the English army at the siege of Orleans.
1H6: I, 4.

glass, image, reflection, mirror.

SONNET: III, 9.
HAM: Ophelia, III, 1, 161.
Give me the glass, and therein will I read.
No deeper wrinkles yet? Hath sorrow struck
So many blows upon this face of mine
And made no deeper wounds? O flattering glass,
Like to my followers in prosperity,
Thou dost beguile me!
RICH2: Richard, IV, 1, 276.

glasses, eyeballs, lenses, mirrors; hour; sandglasses or hourglasses, turned over to designate the passage of an hour of time.
RICH2: Richard, I, 3, 208.
TwN: Duke, V, 1, 272.
TEMP: Prospero, I, 2, 240—Shakespeare is regarded as imprecise here, since *The Tempest* takes place in a nautical setting and seamen in his day reckoned the time by half-hour glasses.

gleek (glike), biting or sarcastic comment or jest; gibe, jeer, mock.
MND: Bottom, III, 1, 149.
HEN5: Gower, V, 1, 78.
R&J: Peter, IV, 5, 115.

Glendower, Owen, defeats and captures Hotspur's brother-in-law, Mortimer, who marries his daughter; joins Hotspur's rebellion, but was not present when he is killed. [Welsh rebel, Lord of Glyndwr (c1359-c1415), educated in England, defeated with Henry Percy (Hotspur) at Shrewsbury (1403); joined the French, defeated by Henry, Prince of Wales (1405).]
1H4: III, 1.

glib, castrate, geld.
WINT: Antigonus, II, 1, 149.

globe, head.
HAM: Hamlet, I, 5, 97.

Globe, the, public theater built by Richard and Cuthbert Burbage and group (1599), just south of Maid Lane and southeast of the

Rose; model for the Fortune built by Alleyn (1600) except that the latter was rectangular while the Globe was octagonal; thatched roof led to fire (June 29, 1613)—burned to the ground during a performance of *Henry VIII;* rebuilt with a tiled roof and opened (June, 1614); pulled down by the Puritans (1644).

globy, swollen, bulging.
  2NK: Palamon, V, 1, 113.

glories
> O mighty Caesar! dost thou lie so low?
> Are all thy conquests, glories, triumphs, spoils,
> Shrunk to this little measure?

  JC: Antony, III, 1, 148.

glory
> Glory is like a circle in the water,
> Which never ceaseth to enlarge itself
> Till by broad spreading it disperse to naught.

  1H6: Pucelle, I, 2, 133.

> I have touched the highest point of all my greatness,
> And from that full meridian of my glory
> I haste now to my setting. I shall fall
> Like a bright exhalation in the evening,
> And no man see me more.

  Hen8: Cardinal, III, 2, 223.

> Glory grows guilty of detested crimes
> When for game's sake, for praise, an outward part,
> We bend to that the working of the heart.

  LLL: Princess, IV, 1, 31.

> I see thy glory, like a shooting star,
> Fall to the base earth from the firmament,
> Thy sun sets weeping in the lowly west,
> Witnessing storms to come, woe, and unrest.

  Rich2: Salisbury, II, 4, 19.

Gloucester, Duchess of, appeals in vain to Gaunt to avenge her husband's murder; dies of grief. [Eleanor de Bohun (d. 1399), widow of Thomas Woodstock, Duke of Gloucester (murdered by Mowbray), brother of John of Gaunt; aunt of Richard II.]
  Rich2: I, 2.

Gloucester, Duchess of, wished to be queen; with the help of Roger Bolingbroke, a practitioner of black magic, tries to kill the king; discovered and banished; sets out for the Isle of Man after warning Gloucester against Suffolk, York and the Bishop of Winchester. [Eleanor Cobham (d. c1443), second wife of Humphrey, Duke of Gloucester; actually imprisoned and sentenced to walk the streets for three days, carrying a burning taper in her hand; believed to have stayed in Peel Castle the rest of her life.]
  2H6: I, 2.

Gloucester, Earl of, father of Edgar, whom he distrusts, and the illegitimate Edmund, whom he unfortunately believes; faithful to the King and Cordelia, for which Cornwall puts out his eyes.
  Lear: I, 1.

Gloucester, Humphrey, Duke of (1391-1447), appears as Prince Humphrey, fourth son of Henry IV (2H4); Duke of Gloucester, brother of the king (Hen5); King's uncle; Protector of the Realm during his infancy; quarreled with Henry Beaufort, Cardinal of Winchester (1H6); when his wife is banished for sorcery, he is deprived of the Protectorship (2H6); his enemies succeed in having him arrested and murdered.
  2H4: IV, 4; Hen5: III, 7; 1H6: I, 1; 2H6: I, 1.

Gloucester, Richard, Duke of, fourth son of Richard Plantagenet, 3rd Duke of York and future Richard III; kills Somerset (2H6) in fight at St. Albans (although historically he was only eight years old at the time); created Duke of Gloucester by his brother Edward (3H6); thinking ahead, he supports his brother when he is deserted by Warwick and Clarence; stabs the Prince of Wales after the Battle of Tewkesbury, rushes to London; stabs Henry VI in the Tower, thereby getting rid of all the Lancastrians; eliminates rival Yorkists (RICH3); defeated and killed by Richmond at Bosworth. [1452-85, King (1483-85).]

2H6: V, 1; 3H6: I, 1; RICH3: I, 1.

glowworm. See MORNING.

gloze (glose), speak pleasantly but insincerely; flatter.
RICH2: Gaunt, II, 1, 10.
LLL: Longaville, IV, 3, 370.

gloze, interpret, gloss, comment on.
HEN5: Canterbury, I, 2, 40.
T&C: Hector, II, 2, 165.

glut, swallow, gulp.
TEMP: Gonzalo, I, 1, 63.
HEN5: Mountjoy, IV, 3, 83—*englutted.*

glutton, Dives in parable of Dives and Lazarus (Luke: 16:24).
2H4: Falstaff, I, 2, 39.

gnarling, growling, snarling.
RICH2: Gaunt, I, 3, 292.

goatish, licentious, lustful, lewd.
LEAR: Edmund, I, 2, 139.

gobbet, piece or chunk of raw flesh.
2H6: Lieutenant, IV, 1, 85.

Gobbo, Launcelot, "clown," servant of Shylock; leaves his service for that of Bassanio; helps Lorenzo carry off Jessica; accompanies Bassanio to Belmont; acts as messenger and buffoon.
MERV: II, 2.

Gobbo, Launcelot's (see above) father, called "sand-blind" Old Gobbo; appears with a present for Shylock, but, confused by his son, is persuaded to give it to Bassanio.
MERV: II, 2.

goddess of the night
Pardon, goddess of the night,
Those that slew thy virgin knight;
ADO: V, 3, 12—opening lines of song.

God-dild (God 'ild, God 'eild), may God reward or repay you; God yield; "thank you."
HAM: Ophelia, IV, 5, 41.
MACB: Duncan, I, 6, 132.

Godfrey of Viterbo (Gotfried von) (c1120-c96). German poet-historian; secretary to Emperor Frederick I; wrote history of the world in verse (revised as *Pantheon,* printed 1559); the source of *Pericles, Prince of Tyre* was GOWER, who took his version of *Apollonius of Tyre* from this work by Godfrey.

god kissing carrion, sun god, Apollo, shining on dead flesh.
HAM: Hamlet, II, 2, 182.

gods
The gods are just, and of our pleasant vices
Make instruments to scourge us.
LEAR: Edgar, V, 3, 170.

The gods are deaf to hot and peevish vows.
T&C: Cassandra, V, 3, 16.

gods. See FLIES.

God's bodykin, by God's little body; corruption of oath "by God's body."
HAM: Hamlet, II, 2, 554.

gogs-woons, corruption of God's (Christ's) wounds.
SHREW: Gremio, III, 2, 162.

gold
Gold were as good as twenty orators,
And will, no doubt, tempt him to anything.
RICH3: Page, IV, 2, 38.

There is thy gold—worse poison to mens' souls,

Doing more murther in this loathsome world,
Than these poor compounds that thou mayst not sell.
R&J: Romeo, V, 1, 80.

golden age, from OVID's *Metamorphoses* (I:89-112), the period at the beginning of time, under the rule of Saturn, when all was innocent and perfect.
TEMP: Gonzalo, II, 1, 168.

golden fee, the crown.
RICH3: Buckingham, III, 5, 96.

Golden Fleece, order of knights founded (1429) by Philip, Duke of Burgundy.
1H6: Lucy, IV, 7, 69.

golden sleep
Care keeps his watch in every old man's eye,
And where care lodges sleep will never lie;
But where unbruised youth with unstuffed brain
Doth couch his limbs, there golden sleep doth reign.
R&J: Friar, II, 3, 35.

golden world
. . . fleet the time carelessly as they did in the golden world.
AYL: Charles, I, 1, 124.

Golding, Arthur (c1536-c1605). English translator; famous for translation of OVID's *Metamorphoses* into English verse (1567); Shakespeare may have used this work as a source of *Venus and Adonis,* but as he knew Latin it is possible he relied on the original.

Golgotha, literally "the place of the skull" where criminals were tortured; Christ was crucified on the hill of Calvary, also called Golgotha.
RICH2: Carlisle, IV, 1, 144.
MACB: Sergeant, I, 2, 40.

Golias, form of Goliath, strong man in the Bible (I Samuel: 17:23-24).
1H6: Alençon, I, 2, 33.
MWW: Falstaff, V, 1, 24—
Goliah.

Goneril, evil, ungrateful eldest daughter of the King; wife of the mild Duke of Albany, whom she loathes; treats her father miserably and pushes him out; poisons her sister Regan; when Edmund, her lover, is killed, she stabs herself.
LEAR: I, 1.

Gonzaga, family name of Renaissance Dukes of Mantua; Vincentio Gonzaga was Duke of Mantua (1587-1612); used by Hamlet for his play within the play; in *Measure for Measure,* the Duke of Vienna is Vincentio.

Gonzalo, honest counselor in the government of Milan; when Antonio took over the duchy of Milan, setting the rightful duke, his brother, Prospero, and Prospero's daughter, Miranda, adrift at sea, Gonzalo supplied them with clothing, provisions, and Prospero's treasured books on magic.
TEMP: I, 1.

good cause
God and our good cause fight upon our side.
RICH3: Richmond, V, 3, 241.

good deed. See CANDLE, PRAISE.

good hands, applause, clapping hands.
TEMP: Prospero, Epilogue, 10.

good-nights, good-night songs, serenades, lullabies, farewells.
2H4: Falstaff, III, 2, 343.

good wine
. . . good wine needs no bush . . .
AYL: Rosalind, Epilogue, 4—
refers to custom of hanging a bush (or bunch) of ivy over the door of an alehouse.

Goodwin Sands, off the coast of Kent; treacherous spot in the English Channel.
MERV: Salerio, III, 1, 4.

goodyears, vague reference to evil or malevolent spirit; pox.
LEAR: Lear, V, 3, 24.

goose, tailor's pressing iron with

handle that looks like a goose's neck; swelling caused by venereal disease.
MACB: Porter, II, 3, 17.

goosequills, pens of satirists; perhaps a reference to Ben JONSON, whose *Poetaster*, acted in 1601 by the children's company, was part of the current stage war.
HAM: Rosencrantz, II, 2, 359.

gorbellied, fat-bellied, heavypaunched, gross.
1H4: Falstaff, II, 2, 93.

Gordian knot, insoluble problem or task; refers to knot tied in piece of bark to hold together the pole and yoke of the chariot of King Gordius of Phrygia; whoever could untie the knot, it was believed, would rule Asia; when Alexander the Great failed to untie it, he cut it with his sword and claimed he had fulfilled the prophecy.
HEN5: Canterbury, I, 1, 46.
CYM: Iachimo, II, 2, 34.

gorge, stomach, throat; vomit.
HAM: Hamlet, V, 1, 207.
TIMON: Timon, IV, 3, 40.

gorgeous
All plumed like estridges that with the wind
Bated like eagles having lately bathed;
Glittering in golden coats like images;
As full of spirit as the month of May
And gorgeous as the sun at midsummer;
Wanton as youthful goats, wild as young bulls.
1H4: Vernon, IV, 1, 98. See ESTRIDGES.

gorget, armor to protect the throat.
T&C: Ulysses, I, 3, 174.

Gorgon, Greek mythological monster with snakes for hair (most often Medusa), so horrible that the sight of her turned people to stone.

MACB: Macduff, II, 3, 77.
A&C: Cleopatra, II, 5, 116.

goss, gorse, a prickly shrub.
TEMP: Ariel, IV, 1, 180. See BROWN FURZE.

gossip, godparent, sponsor.
COFE: Aemilia, V, 1, 405.
WINT: Paulina, II, 3, 41.
RICH3: Richard, I, 1, 83.

gossip, crony; old woman, given to spreading rumors; friend.
MND: Puck, II, 1, 47.
2H4: Hostess, II, 1, 103.

go to, modern equivalent, come now or come, come; phrase of annoyance.
LLL: Berowne, III, 1, 203.

gourd, false dice (hollow or loaded).
MWW: Pistol, I, 3, 93.

gout, (large) drop.
MACB: Macbeth, II, 1, 46.

government, well executed, performed skillfully; proper control or management; behavior.
MND: Hippolyta, V, 1, 124.
1H4: Hotspur, IV, 1, 19.

government
For government, though high, and low, and lower,
Put into parts, doth keep in one consent,
Congreeing in a full and natural close,
Like music.
HEN5: Exeter, I, 2, 180.

Governor of Harfleur, yields the town to Henry.
HEN5: III, 3.

Governor of Paris, kneels before the King to take his oath of loyalty; doesn't speak.
1H6: IV, 1.

Gower, John (c1327-1408). English poet; friend of CHAUCER; best known work, *Confessio Amatis,* probably the source of themes used by Shakespeare in *The Comedy of Errors, Pericles, Prince of Tyre* (in which he appears as Chorus) and possibly *The Merchant of Venice.*

Gower, poet; acts as Chorus; speeches illustrated by dumbshows in several places.
PER: Chorus.

Gower, poet, admirer of the king.
2H4: II, 1.

Gower, captain; at Agincourt, important in restraining Fluellen's temper.
HEN5: III, 2.

grace, honor, favor granted to a person by a king or God.
HAM: Horatio, I, 1, 132.
MACB: Banquo, I, 3, 55.
1H4: Prince, V, 4, 161.

grace, pardon, forgiveness, reprieve.
TEMP: Caliban, V, 1, 295.
A&C: Ambassador, III, 12, 19.

grace
Angels are bright still, though the brightest fell.
Though all things foul would wear the brows of grace,
Yet grace must still look so.
MACB: Malcolm, IV, 3, 22.

graces. See VIRTUES.

Gracious, your majesty; form of address to the king.
HAM: Polonius, III, 1, 43.

gracious light (sun)
Lo, in the orient when the gracious light
Lifts up his burning head, each undereye
Doth homage to his new-appearing sight,
Serving with looks his sacred majesty.
SONNET: VII, 1. See UNDEREYE.

grain, veins and fibers of wood; dye obtained from cochineal.
COR: Aufidius, IV, 5, 113.
TWN: Olivia, I, 5, 240.

grained, of fast dye, dyed in grain, ingrained.
HAM: Queen, III, 4, 90.

gramercy, God-a-Mercy, or God have mercy; expression of gratitude; many thanks.
SHREW: Lucentio, I, 1, 41.
TIMON: Servants, II, 1, 70.
MERV: Bassanio, II, 2, 128.

Grandpré, French lord; described the ragged English army as a "beggar'd host" on the morning of Agincourt; killed in the battle.
HEN5: IV, 2.

grandsire. See EDWARD III.
RICH2: Northumberland, III, 3, 106.

grange, farmhouse, country house.
OTH: Brabantio, I, 1, 106.

Gratiano, friend of Antonio and Bassanio who "talked an infinite deal of nothing"; marries Nerissa.
MERV: I, 1.

Gratiano, brother of Brabantio, uncle of Desdemona; aids Cassio when Roderigo attacks him; attempts to help Emilia.
OTH: V, 2.

gravalled (graveled), stuck, run aground; nonplused, perplexed.
AYL: Rosalind, IV, 1, 74.

grave
My sceptre for a palmer's walking staff,
My subjects for a pair of carved saints,
And my large kingdom for a little grave,
A little little grave, an obscure grave; . . .
RICH2: Richard, III, 3, 151.
See NAME OF KING, PALMER.

graves
The graves stood tenantless, and the sheeted dead
Did squeak and gibber in the Roman streets.
HAM: Horatio, I, 1, 115. See SHEETED.

graymalkin (grimalkin), small gray cat.
MACB: 1Witch, I, 1, 8—demon or familiar spirit serving this witch in the form of a cat.

grazing, ricochet, rebounding, glancing off.
HEN5: King, IV, 3, 105.

great belly doublet, doublet with two thicknesses and the lower part, called the "belly," was often stuffed and hung down in the front.

HEN5: Fluellen, IV, 7, 51—probably refers to Falstaff's natural size.

great charge, heavy burden, massive weight.

HAM: Hamlet, V, 2, 43.

greatness

. . . Your virtue is
To make him worthy whose offence subdues him,
And curse that justice did it.
Who deserves greatness
Deserves your hate; and your affections are
A sick man's appetite, who desires most that
Which would increase his evil. He that depends
Upon your favours swims with fins of lead
And hews down oaks with rushes.

COR: Marcius, I, 1, 178.

Be great in act, as you have been in thought.
Let not the world see fear and sad distrust
Govern the motion of a kingly eye.
Be stirring as the time; be fire with fire;
Threaten the threatener and outface the brow
Of bragging horror.

JOHN: Bastard, V, 1, 45.

'Tis certain, greatness, once fallen out with fortune,
Must fall out with men too.

T&C: Achilles, III, 3, 75.

. . . Some are born great, some achieve greatness, and some have greatness thrust upon 'em.

TWN: Malvolio, II, 5, 157.

Greek, jester, merry, foolish fellow; Greeks of the period had a reputation for being featherbrained; the clown's language is "Greek" to Sebastian.

TWN: Sebastian, IV, 1, 19.

. . . but for mine own part, it was Greek to me.

JC: Casca, I, 2, 287.

green, immature, inexperienced, childish, foolish, callow.

OTH: Iago, II, 1, 250.
HAM: King, IV, 5, 83.
HEN5: King, V, 2, 149.

Green, Sir Henry, of Drayton, Northants, favorite of Richard II; beheaded by Bolingbroke (1399).

RICH2: I, 3.

Greene, Robert (1558-92). English dramatist, poet; one of the UNIVERSITY WITS; rivaled MARLOWE as a leading playwright; attacked his contemporary dramatists, including the young Shakespeare; many of his plays extant; his novel, *Pandosto, or, The Triumph of Time* (1588) is the source of *The Winter's Tale;* some scholars suggest he may have written the original of *Henry VI* which Shakespeare revised or rewrote; considered one of the most interesting of the Elizabethan writers.

green-eyed monster. See JEALOUSY.

green eyes, considered very beautiful in romantic literature, usually hazel-green in color.

MND: Thisby, V, 1, 342.

green sickness, a form of anemia (chlorosis), commonly contracted by teenage girls who are lovesick.

A&C: Enobarbus, III, 2, 6.
2H4: Falstaff, IV, 3, 100.

Greensleeves, popular love song with ribald lyrics.

MWW: Mrs. Ford, II, 1, 64.

green sour ringlets, fairy rings; inedible circles of grass believed to be caused by the fairies dancing in a ring; caused by mycelium (underground part) of the toadstools, which affected the roots of the grass.—(Arden.)

TEMP: Prospero, V, 1, 37.

greenwood tree
Under the greenwood tree
Who loves to lie with me . . .

AYL: Amiens, II, 5, 1—beginning of song.

Gregory, Capulet's servant; with fellow-servant, Sampson, begins the fight with the Montagues.
R&J: I, 1.

Gremio, rich, old suitor of Bianca in subplot; employs Lucentio, disguised as a scholar, as Bianco's tutor; superbly describes the marriage of Petruchio and Katherina.
SHREW: I, 1.

grew together
. . . So we grew together
Like a double cherry, seeming parted,
But yet an union in partition,
Two lovely berries moulded on one stem . . .
MND: Helena, III, 2, 208.

Grey, Lady, requests Edward IV restore estates lost by her husband, Sir Richard (John) Grey, killed at St. Albans; Edward falls in love with her; their marriage costs him the support of Warwick; with their infant son, reclaims throne at end of play. [1437-92, daughter of Richard Woodville, Earl Rivers.] See ELIZABETH.
3H6: III, 2.

Grey, Lord, youngest son of Elizabeth, Queen of Edward IV, by former husband, Sir John Grey; with Earl Rivers, the Queen's brother, executed by order of Richard. [Historically, Sir Richard Grey, youngest brother of Thomas Grey, Marquis of Dorset, who fled to the continent to join Richmond and stayed there until Richard was beaten at Bosworth.]
RICH3: I, 3.

Grey, Sir Thomas, one of the conspirators against the King; plot discovered; executed for treason. [d. 1415, knight of Northumberland.]
HEN5: II, 2.

grief
. . . every one can master a grief but he that has it.
ADO: Benedick, III, 2, 29.

. . . men
Can counsel and speak comfort to that grief
Which they themselves not feel; but, tasting it,
Their counsel turns to passion, which before
Would give preceptial medicine to rage,
Fetter strong madness in a silken thread,
Charm ache with air and agony with words.
ADO: Leonato, V, 1, 20.

Moderate lamentation is the right of the dead; excessive grief the enemy of the living.
ALL'sW: Lafew, I, 1, 63.

O, grief hath changed me since you saw me last.
And careful hours with time's deformed hand
Have written strange defeatures in my face.
CofE: Aegeon, V, 1, 297.

I will instruct my sorrows to be proud;
For grief is proud, and makes his owner stoop.
To me, and to the state of my great grief,
Let kings assemble; for my grief's so great
That no supporter but the huge firm earth
Can hold it up.
JOHN: Constance, III, 1, 68.

Honest plain words best pierce the ear of grief.
LLL: Berowne, V, 2, 762.

True grief is fond and testy as a child,
Who wayward once, his mood with naught agrees.
LUCRECE: 1094.

. . . Let grief
Convert to anger; blunt not the heart, enrage it.
MACB: Malcolm, IV, 3, 228.

Each substance of a grief hath twenty shadows
Which shows like grief itself, but is not so . . .
RICH2: Bushy, II, 2, 14.

. . . O that I were as great
As is my grief, or lesser than
   my name!
Or that I could forget what I
   have been!
Or not remember what I must
   be now!
RICH2: Richard, III, 3, 136.

. . . Some grief shows much of
   love;
But much of grief shows still
   some want of wit.
R&J: Lady, III, 5, 73.

. . . What's gone and what's
   past help
Should be past grief.
WINT: Paulina, III, 2, 223.

griefs
You may my glories and my state
   depose,
But not my griefs. Still I am
   king of those.
RICH2: Richard, IV, 1, 192.

Griffith, gentleman-usher to Queen
Katherine; describes the death
of Wolsey to the dying queen.
HEN8: IV, 2.

griffon, mythical, legendary,
amazing beast who was half
eagle, half lion.
MND: Helena, II, 1, 232.

grim alarm, desperate call to
arms.
MACB: Menteith, V, 2, 4.

gripe. See GRIFFON.
LUCRECE: 543—vulture.

Grissel, patient Griselda, heroine
of BOCCACCIO's tale in the *Decameron* and CHAUCER's *Clerk's
Tale;* prototype of loyal and
obedient wife.
SHREW: Petruchio, II, 1, 297.

grize (grise), step, stair; to a de-
gree or measure.
TWN: Viola, III, 1, 135.
OTH: Duke, I, 3, 200.
TIMON: Timon, IV, 3, 16.

grizzled, gray; black hair streaked
with gray or white.
HAM: Hamlet, I, 2, 240.
A&C: Antony, III, 13, 17.
TWN: Duke, V, 1, 168.

groat, coin equal to fourpence.
COR: Coriolanus, III, 2, 10.
RICH2: Richard, V, 5, 68.
2H4: Page, I, 2, 263.

Groom, comforts the imprisoned
King.
RICH2: V, 5.

gross and scope, overall concept,
general range; view, conclusion,
drift.
HAM: Horatio, I, 1, 68.

groundlings, those in the audience who could only afford a
penny for the privilege of standing in the yard or the pit of the
theater.
HAM: Hamlet, III, 2, 12.

grown into a hoop, become doubled or bent over, hunched.
TEMP: Prospero, I, 2, 259.

Grumio, Petruchio's "ancient"
servant; gives amusing description of the journey of his master
and Katherina from Padua to
their country house.
SHREW: I, 1.

guard, embroidery, ornamental
trimming of velvet, braid, etc.;
decoration.
LLL: Berowne, IV, 3, 58.
ADO: Benedick, I, 1, 289.
2H4: Westmoreland, IV, 1, 34.

guardant, protector, guard; heraldic term, referring to lion standing on its hind legs brandishing
a sword.
1H6: Talbot, IV, 7, 9.
COR: Menenius, V, 2, 68.

Guards, the, the two stars in constellation Ursa Minor (Little Bear).
OTH: 2Gentleman, II, 1, 15.

gudgeon, small fish, easily caught;
implies gullible person.
MERV: Gratiano, I, 1, 102.

guerdon, reward, recompense.
LLL: Berowne, III, 1, 170.
ADO: Claudio, V, 3, 5.
2H6: York, I, 4, 49.

Guiderius, elder son of the King;
brother of Imogen and Arviragus.
CYM: III, 3. See ARVIRAGUS.

guidon, small flag; standard, banner.
HEN5: Constable, IV, 2, 60.

Guildenstern. See ROSENCRANTZ.

guilder, gold coin; silver coin in the Netherlands (gulden).
CofE: Duke, I, 1, 8.

Guildford, Sir Henry, acts as host for Wolsey at banquet given at York Place.
HEN8: I, 4.

guilt
So full of artless jealousy is guilt
It spills itself in fearing to be spilt.
HAM: Queen, IV, 5, 19.

guilt. See CRUEL ACT.

Guinover (Guinever), King Arthur's queen; beloved by Lancelot.
LLL: Boyet, IV, 1, 125.

gules, heraldic term for red.
HAM: Hamlet, II, 2, 479.
TIMON: Timon, IV, 3, 59.

gulf, whirlpool, vortex, eddy.
HEN5: Mountjoy, IV, 3, 82.
RICH3: Buckingham, III, 7, 128.
3H6: King Henry, V, 6, 25.

gulf, gullet, voracious stomach or appetite.
MACB: 3Witch, IV, 1, 23.
COR: Menenius, I, 1, 101.

gull, nestling, unfledged bird.
1H4: Worcester, V, 1, 60.
TIMON: Senator, II, 1, 31.

gull, dupe, trick, fool.
TwN: Maria, II, 3, 146.
ADO: Benedick, II, 3, 123.
OTH: Emilia, V, 2, 163.

gummed velvet, inferior quality material treated with gum to give it gloss.
1H4: Poins, II, 2, 3.

gunstone, cannonball made of stone.
HEN5: King, I, 2, 282.

gurnet, small fish with large head and tapering body.
1H4: Falstaff, IV, 2, 13.

Gurney, James, servant of Lady Faulconbridge.
JOHN: I, 1.

gust, taste, perceive, realize.
WINT: Leontes, I, 2, 219.
SONNET: CXIV, 11.

Guynes and Arde, two towns in Picardy, on either side of the valley Andren; neutral territory; Guynes belonged to the English and Arde to the French (now spelled Ardres).
HEN8: Norfolk, I, 1, 7.

gypsy. See FALSE SOUL.

gyve, shackle, fetter, leg-iron.
HAM: King, IV, 7, 21.
OTH: Iago, II, 1, 171.
CYM: Posthumus, V, 4, 74.

habiliments, from the French for costume; attire, gear, equipment.
  RICH2: Richard, I, 3, 28.
  A&C: Caesar, III, 6, 17.

hackney, available for hire; prostitute.
  LLL: Moth, III, 1, 33.

hag, nightmare.
  R&J: Mercutio, I, 4, 92—associates Queen Mab with the demon that caused nightmares.

Hagar's offspring, Ishmaelite, term of derision.
  MERV: Shylock, II, 5, 44.

haggard, wild, intractable; from falconry, wild hawk (usually female).
  OTH: Othello, III, 3, 260.
  TWN: Viola, III, 1, 71.
  ADO: Hero, III, 1, 36.

haggle, to mangle, hack.
  HEN5: Exeter, IV, 6, 11.

hag-seed, born of or offspring of a hag or witch.
  TEMP: Prospero, I, 2, 365.

hair, character, nature, kind; grain.
  1H4: Worcester, IV, 1, 61.
  MWW: Shallow, II, 3, 40.

Hakluyt, Richard (c1552-1616). English geographer; great collection of exploration and travel, *Principa; Navigations, Voiages, and Discoveries of the English Nation* (first appeared, 1589; enlarged to 3 vols., 1598-1600). See TEMPEST, THE.

halberd, long-handled (5 to 7 ft.) weapon with sharp-edged pointed blade and spearhead mounted on a handle.
  RICH2: S.D., I, 2.

CofE: Duke, V, 1, 185.
  3H6: 1Watchman, IV, 3, 20.

halcyon, bird identified with the kingfisher; according to legend it bred during the winter solstice in a nest on the sea and produced a calm for 14 days; thus halcyon days was a period of calm.
  1H6: Pucelle, I, 2, 131.
  LEAR: Kent, II, 2, 84.

hale, haul, drag, pull; mistreat, abuse.
  A&C: S.D., II, 5, 64.
  SHREW: Vincentio, V, 1, 111.

Hall, Arthur (c1540-1604). English scholar; published the first English translation of HOMER; *The Bookes of Homer's Illiades* (I-X); based on the French work by Hugues Salel (1555); possibly a source of Shakespeare's *Troilus and Cressida.*

Hall, reference to Westminster Hall, adjacent to the Houses of Parliament; formerly seat of High Court of Justice.
  HEN8: 2Gentleman, II, 1, 2.

Halle, Edward (c1498-1547). English historian; author of *The Union of the Noble and Illustre Famelies of Lancastre and York* (covers the period 1399-1532); probably source of *Henry VI* and *Richard III.*

Hallowmas, All Saints' Day, November 1.
  RICH2: Richard, V, 1, 80.
  MEAS: Pompey, II, 1, 128.
  2GENT: Speed, II, 1, 27.

halt, limp, hobble, go lame.
  HAM: Hamlet, II, 2, 339.
  TEMP: Prospero, IV, 1, 10.

Hamlet (*The Tragicall Historie of Hamlet, Prince of Denmark*). One of Shakespeare's greatest tragedies, *Hamlet* is regarded by many as his finest work. Probably written 1601, performed by July, 1602, published 1603. The story of Hamlet, as we now know it, first appeared in the *Historia Danica*, a Latin work by the 12th-century Danish chronicler, SAXO GRAMMATICUS; translated into French prose by François de BELLEFOREST, used in the fifth book of his *Histoires tragiques* (published, 1576); more direct source, an Elizabethan tragedy, now lost, probably by Thomas Kyd, in which the hero feigns madness, the Senecan ghost tells his story, the play within the play, the suicide of Ophelia, the fight in her grave, the fencing match, the friend Horatio, and the bloody ending had all been worked into the plot; Shakespeare, in rewriting this tragedy of revenge, made his own unique contribution in the portrayal of the tragic intensity of Hamlet's nature, the parallel situations, and the ironic contrasts.

PLOT: Essentially, Hamlet is a play of revenge in which three sons—Hamlet, Laertes and Fortinbras—each try to avenge a murdered father. The scene is the Danish royal castle at Elsinore, where Claudius has seized the throne by murdering his brother, the King, and hastily marrying Gertrude, his brother's wife. Hamlet, son of the slain king and Gertrude, learns of the murder from his father's ghost who desires and urges revenge. Hamlet's brooding melancholy, his reflective turn of mind, and his fear that the ghost may be the Devil cause him to hesitate in accomplishing his desired end. Although he has loved Ophelia, his love for her, one of helpless regret, plays a subordinate role in the essential development of his character and the play.

Hamlet feigns madness to conceal his planned revenge. Learning that a troupe of actors have come to the castle, he asks them to stage a play paralleling the murder of his father. Tormented by conscience and fear as he watches the play, Claudius storms from the hall followed by his retinue. When, soon afterward, Hamlet sees Claudius in prayer, though convinced of his guilt, he hesitates to kill him. Reproaching Gertrude for her hasty marriage to her husband's brother, Hamlet alarms her with his passionate intensity and she screams for help.

Polonius, the King's chamberlain and father of Ophelia, spying behind a tapestry, echoes her cries. Believing it to be Claudius, Hamlet thrusts his sword through the arras and kills the old counselor. When Hamlet turns again to his mother, the Ghost of his father appears to intercede for her ("leave her to heaven," I, 5) and spurs Hamlet against Claudius. Gertrude, unable to see the Ghost, concludes finally that her son is mad.

Claudius, now well aware of Hamlet's knowledge, sends him to England with Rosencrantz and Guildenstern, with secret orders that he be killed there. Ophelia, meanwhile, crushed by her father's death and Hamlet's apparent rejection, becomes mad and drowns herself. Her brother, Laertes, returns to Denmark vowing vengeance. Hamlet also returns, having persuaded the pirates who intercepted his ship to return him to Denmark. On his homecoming, he sees Ophelia's funeral procession; he and Laertes, overcome with grief, grapple in her grave.

Laertes allows Claudius to involve him in a plot against Hamlet in which, during a "friendly" fencing match, Laertes' foil is to be unblunted and poisoned. If this plan fails, Hamlet's drink is to be poisoned. The plot backfires; Gertrude drinks the poisoned cup, and Laertes, after scratching Hamlet with the deadly blade, is himself wounded by the poisoned sword. Laertes, dying, reveals the King's guilt and asks Hamlet's forgiveness. Mortally wounded, Hamlet is at last aroused to act decisively; he stabs the King and forces him to drink the last of the poisoned wine.

Hamlet, Prince of Denmark, son of the former king and nephew of the present monarch; though reputedly irresolute, he is sometimes capable of decisive action: confronts the Ghost, lays a trap for Claudius, sends Rosencrantz and Guildenstern to the death intended for him, accepts the challenge of Laertes to a fencing match, and kills Claudius; witty and sardonic, yet he will not permit others to tease Polonius and demands courteous treatment of the actors; prototype of the ideal Renaissance prince "The courtier's, soldier's, scholar's eye, tongue, sword . . . The glass of fashion and the mould of form" (Ophelia, III, 1); Hamlet's "tragic flaw" has been variously analyzed by critics as extreme sensitivity (Goethe), excessive introspection (Coleridge and Schlegel), melancholy brooding (Bradley) and the Oedipus complex (Ernest Jones); the need to avenge his father's death, which is acting contrary to his nature, is only one aspect of Hamlet's dilemma; he is also faced with the possibility of his mother's adultery, the corruption of the social order ("The time is out of joint," I, 5), his extreme individualism, and his tendency to question the medieval codes.

Ham: I, 2.

hammered of, persistently or constantly thought about or deliberated.
WINT: Emilia, II, 2, 49.
2GENT: Antonio, I, 3, 18.

hams, knee joints.
HAM: Hamlet, II, 2, 203.

hand, engage in, pledge, handle.
WINT: Polixenes, IV, 4, 359.

hand
. . . What if this cursed hand
Were thicker than itself with
    brother's blood,
Is there not rain enough in the
    sweet heavens
To wash it white as snow?
HAM: King, III, 3, 43.

Full gently now she takes him
    by the hand,
A lily prison'd in a jail of
    snow . . .
VENUS: 361.

handfast, marriage contract; close custody.
CYM: Queen, I, 5, 78.

handling. See ABIDE.

handsaw, either a carpenter's tool used with one hand or a corruption of heron or "heronshaw."
HAM: Hamlet, II, 2, 397. See HAWK.

handsome
O, what a world of vile ill-favoured faults
Looks handsome in three hundred pounds a year!
MWW: Anne, III, 4, 32.

hanger, strap by which scabbard or sword is suspended or hung from the belt.
HAM: Osric, V, 2, 157.

hangman's hands, bloody business of executioner who tore vital organs from victim's body before drawing and quartering him.
MACB: Macbeth, II, 2, 28.

Hannibal (c249-183 BC), Carthaginian general who defeated the Romans.
1H6: Talbot, I, 5, 21.

hap, luck, chance.
RICH2: Mowbray, I, 1, 23.
ADO: Hero, III, 1, 106.

happily (haply), by good fortune, perchance, perhaps.
HAM: Horatio, I, 1, 134.
TWN: Malvolio, IV, 2, 56.

happiness
Happiness courts thee in her best array;
But, like a misbehaved and sullen wench,
Thou pout'st upon thy fortune and thy love.
Take heed, take heed, for such die miserable.
R&J: Friar, III, 3, 142.

happiness, appropriate or apt expression, well-chosen turn of phrase.
HAM: Polonius, II, 2, 213.

harbinger, forerunner; officer of the court, usually sent ahead to make the necessary arrangements for the traveling court party, expedition or group.
HAM: Horatio, I, 1, 122.
MACB: Macbeth, I, 4, 45.
COFE: Luciana, III, 2, 12.

Harcourt, officer in royal army; reports the defeat of the Earl of Northumberland and Lord Bardolph by the sheriff of Yorkshire to the King.
2H4: IV, 4.

hard-favored, ugly, sorrowful.
RICH2: Queen, V, 1, 14.

hardiment, bold or valiant blows; brave exploit.
1H4: Hotspur, I, 3, 101.

hardock, hardhack, shrub with rusty hairy leaves, panicles of pink.
LEAR: Cordelia, IV, 4, 4.

hare, considered a melancholy animal.
1H4: Prince, I, 2, 87.

Harflew, Harfleur, opposite Le Havre at the mouth of the Seine River.
HEN5: Chorus, Prologue, III, 17.

Harington, Sir John (1561-1612).

English poet; most important work, translation of ARIOSTO'S *Orlando Furioso* (1591), which may have been used by Shakespeare for the Claudio-Hero plot in *Much Ado*.

harmony. See TONGUES.

harness, armor, armed men.
1H4: King III, 2, 101.
MACB: Macbeth, V, 5, 52.
TIMON: Apemantus, I, 2, 53.

harpy, loathsome, odious creature with the face and body of a woman and the claws and wings of a bird of prey.
ADO: Benedick, II, 1, 80.
PER: Cleon, IV, 3, 46.
TEMP: S.D., III, 3—scene suggested by episode in Vergil's *Aeneid* when these monsters of vengeance destroy or spoil the food of Aeneas and his followers.
. . . Thou art like the harpy,
Which, to betray, dost, with thine angel's face,
Seize with thine eagle's talents.
PER: Cleon, IV, 3, 46.—*talents,* talons.

Harrison, William, 1534-93. English topographer, historian; author of *Description of England* (1577), important source of information on English institutions, people, etc.; collaborated with HOLINSHED on *The Chronicles of England, Scotland and Ireland* (1577, 1586-87).

Harry
. . . mean and gentle all,
Behold, as may unworthiness define,
A little touch of Harry in the night.
HEN5: Chorus, IV, 45.

Harry Monmouth, Prince Henry; born at Monmouth.
2H4: Rumor, Induction, 29.

Harry ten-shillings, coined by Henry VII.
2H4: Bullcalf, III, 2, 236.

Harsnett, Samuel (1561-1631).

English scholar; Vice-Chancellor of Pembroke Hall, Cambridge; Bishop of Chichester (1609), Archbishop of York (1629); his *Declaration of Egregious Popish Impostures* (1603) source of material for *King Lear*.

hart, male red deer; Elizabethan pun—heart.
TwN: Duke, I, 1, 21. See ACTAEON.

Harvey, originally Bardolph; when Shakespeare changed Oldcastle's name to Falstaff, he changed Harvey to Bardolph.
2H4: I, 2.

haste-post-haste, as quickly as possible; as quickly as a special messenger or postboy could ride.
OTH: Cassio, I, 2, 37.

Hastings, Lord, one of the rebel leaders; wants to fight on without Northumberland's help, but agrees to coming to terms with Prince John; through treachery, arrested and executed with the Archbishop and Mowbray. [Sir Ralph Hastings.]
2H4: I, 3.

Hastings, Lord, supporter of the King; helps him to escape capture by Warwick; when he refuses to join Richard in his seizure of the throne, he is executed. [William (c1430-83), Yorkist; made Lord Chamberlain by Edward IV.]
3H6: IV, 1; RICH3: I, 1.

hatchment, coat of arms displayed on a square or diamond-shaped tablet, usually carried during the funeral procession and then hung over the tomb, or a gate in front of the residence of the deceased.
HAM: Laertes, IV, 5, 214.

hate
In time we hate that which we often fear.
A&C: Charmian, I, 3, 12.
For thou art so possessed with murd'rous hate—
SONNET: X, 5.

haud credo, Latin, I don't believe it.
LLL: Holofernes, IV, 2, 11.

haught, arrogant, proud.
RICH2: Richard, IV, 1, 254.

haunt, society, group; resort.
HAM: King, IV, 1, 18.
A&C: Antony, IV, 14, 54.

haunt
I'll haunt thee like a wicked conscience still,
That mouldeth goblins swift as frenzy's thoughts.
T&C: Troilus, V, 10, 28.

haunted
The kindred of him hath been fleshed upon us;
And he is bred out of that bloody strain
That haunted us in our familiar paths.
HEN5: French King, II, 4, 50.

hautboy, wooden double-reed instrument of high pitch, oboe; English equivalent of French *hautbois* and Italian *oboe;* made in various sizes, similar to the recorder, the hautboy, sometimes called shawm or wait, was smaller and shriller; the *groisbois* or bassoon was the larger instrument of the same family.
HAM: S.D., III, 2.
COR: S.D., V, 4.
A&C: S.D., IV, 3.

hawk, probably a "hack," a type of pickaxe, mattock or hoe; play on the bird.
HAM: Hamlet, II, 2, 397—*I know a hawk from a handsaw,* "I'm not as mad as you think." See HANDSAW.

hawthorn buds, fops, dandies, gay young blades; hawthorn flower that blooms in early spring.
MWW: Falstaff, III, 3, 78.

hay, fencing term, final thrust home.
R&J: Mercutio, II, 4, 27.

hay, country dance similar to a

reel; dancers move in snakelike or winding fashion.

LLL: Dull, V, 1, 162.

Haymarket Theatre, built 1720; taken over by Foote, 1747, who was granted a royal patent, 1766, making it the Theatre Royal; many of Shakespeare's plays were performed at the Haymarket, including the famous productions under Tree at the end of the 19th century.

hazard, hole or opening in the wall; in tennis a point was scored when the ball was hit into a hazard; tennis court had both wall and floor.

HEN5: King, I, 2, 263.

hazard, risk, chance; pawn; dice game.

HEN5: Rambures, III, 7, 93.
RICH3: Richard, V, 4, 10.
1H4: Hotspur, I, 3, 128.

hazard all

. . . Men that hazard all
Do it in hope of fair advantages.
A golden mind stoops not to shows of dross.

MERV: Morocco, II, 7, 18.

head, armed force of advancing hostile rebels; title.

HAM: Messenger, IV, 5, 101.
1H4: Worcester, I, 3, 284.
RICH2: York, III, 3, 14.

head

The head is not more native to the heart,
The hand more instrumental to the mouth,
Than is the throne of Denmark to thy father.

HAM: King, I, 2, 47.

headborough, parish officer with functions of petty or local constable.

ADO: S.D., III, 5.

head-lugged, bear with head pulled or torn by hounds; surly.

LEAR: Albany, IV, 2, 42.

heady currance, violent torrent, current or flood.

HEN5: Canterbury, I, 1, 34—

refers to Hercules' cleansing of the Augean stables by diverting a river to run through them.

heart

My heart prays for him, though my tongue do curse.

COFE: Adriana, IV, 2, 28.

. . . I have one part in my heart
That's sorry yet for thee.

LEAR: Lear, III, 2, 72.

. . . But his flawed heart
(Alack, too weak the conflict to support!)
'Twixt two extremes of passion, joy and grief,
Burst smilingly.

LEAR: Edgar, V, 3, 196.

. . . for a light heart lives long.

LLL: Katherine, V, 2, 18.

A heavy heart bears not a nimble tongue.

LLL: Princess, V, 2, 746.

. . . my heart
Is true as steel.

MND: Helena, II, 1, 196.

. . . I will wear my heart upon my sleeve
For daws to peck at.

OTH: Iago, I, 1, 64. See DAWS.

heart. See HEAD, PASSION'S SLAVE.

heart of elder, coward; elder being a soft, useless wood with a center of pith (in contrast to a heart of oak).

MWW: Host, II, 3, 30.

heat, desire, passion, lust; to run across.

OTH: Othello, I, 3, 264.
WINT: Hermione, I, 2, 96.

heaven

. . . Leave her to heaven.

HAM: Ghost, I, 5, 85—refers to Gertrude.

hebona, yew or henbane, thought to be a poisonous plant; ebony.

HAM: Ghost, I, 5, 62.

Hecate, Greek goddess of witchcraft; power of the underworld and goddess of the crossroads; unusual triple goddess of moon, earth and evil, black magic.

HAM: Lucianus, III, 2, 269.

LEAR: Lear, I, 1, 112.
MACB: Macbeth, II, 1, 52.

Hecate's team, dragons that draw night's curtain across the sky.
MND: Puck, V, 1, 391.

Hector, eldest son of Priam, King of Troy; husband of Andromache; challenges all Greeks to single combat in defense of Helen; fights a draw with Ajax; murdered by a jealous Achilles and his Myrmidons.
LLL: King, V, 2, 537.
A&C: Antony, IV, 8, 7.
COR: Volumnia, I, 3, 45.

Hecuba, Queen of Troy, wife of Priam, mother of Hector, Cassandra, Paris and others; appears in two plays by Euripides.
HAM: Hamlet, II, 2, 524.
COR: Volumnia, I, 3, 43.
CYM: Imogen, IV, 2, 313.

hedge, shut, bar.
T&C: Helen, III, 1, 65.

hedge-born, of low birth; born under a hedge; hobo.
1H6: Talbot, IV, 1, 43.

hedgehog, cold, heartless person.
RICH3: Anne, I, 2, 103.

hedge-priest, illiterate priest of inferior or lower order.
LLL: Berowne, V, 2, 546.

heir
His tender heir might bear his memory . . .
SONNET: I, 4. See DEATH'S CONQUEST.

Helen, beautiful wife of Menelaus, King of Sparta; her flight to Troy with Paris was the immediate cause of the Trojan War; returned home after the war.
T&C: III, 1.

Helen, mother of Constantine the Great; believed to have been led by a vision to Mount Calvary where she discovered the true cross buried there.
1H6: Dauphin, I, 2, 142.

Helen, lady attending Imogen.
CYM: mentioned in II, 2.

Helena, daughter of a doctor, she cures the king and he grants her wish to marry Bertram, who leaves her; with the help of the widow of Florence and her lovely daughter, Diana, she manages to trick Bertram; her devotion finally wins him over; considered by Coleridge to be Shakespeare's "loveliest character."
ALL'sW: I, 1.

Helena, with the help of Puck's magic, she wins Demetrius, the man she loves.
MND: I, 1.

Helenus, priest, one of the sons of King Priam of Troy; debates with Troilus over Helen; in Vergil's *Aeneid,* a prophet, only son of Priam to survive the fall of Troy; marries Andromache, Hector's widow; in legend, became King of Epirus.
T&C: II, 2.

Helicanus, faithful lord of Tyre; manages Pericles' dominions while the latter travels to Tarsus.
PER: I, 2.

Helicons, muses from Mount Helicon.
2H4: Pistol, V, 3, 108.

Hellespont, Dardanelles, narrow strait in Turkey.
OTH: Othello, III, 3, 456.

hempen homespuns, rough fabrics for clothing spun at home; country bumpkins or rude country clowns.
MND: Puck, III, 1, 79.

hempseed, one destined for the gallows (to swing on the end of a hemp rope).
2H4: Hostess, II, 1, 64.

hems, clears her throat; usually an Elizabethan encouragement to "drink up" beer or wine.
HAM: Gentleman, IV, 5, 5.

henchman, page or servant; considered an honor.
MND: Oberon, II, 1, 121.

Henri (Henry) IV, King of Navarre and France (1553-1610);

became King upon the assassination of Henri III (August, 1589), but as a Protestant, he had to fight for the throne against the Catholic League; married Margaret of Valois, sister of Charles IX (1572); escaped St. Bartholomew massacre; became a Catholic (July 25, 1593), having decided that "Paris is worth a Mass"; crowned King at Chartres (February 27, 1594); published the Edict of Nantes (April 13, 1598), granting religious freedom to Protestants; assassinated by a Roman Catholic fanatic; succeeded by his son, Louis XIII; alluded to in several plays.

Henry, Prince (1207-72), young son of John; upon his father's death (1216), ascends the throne as Henry III.

JOHN: V, 7.

Henry, Prince of Wales, eldest son of Henry IV (Bolingbroke); with Poins, robs Falstaff, Bardolph, Peto and Gadshill of what they have stolen from the travelers; rehearses with Falstaff what he will say to the King; promises his father to reform; given command of the army against the rebels; kills Hotspur in single combat at Shrewsbury; disowns Falstaff (2H4) and has him imprisoned.

1H4: I, 2; 2H4: II, 2. See below.

Henry the Fourth, The First Part of King, written 1597, registered and published 1598 and performed 1600; HOLINSHED's *Chronicles* was the basic source, while an old play, *The Famous Victories of Henry the Fifth,* supplied several comic details.

PLOT: The basic action takes place from June, 1402 to July, 1403 in Scotland and Wales where Hotspur (Henry Percy), his father, Northumberland, and his uncle, Worcester, join Mortimer, Glendower and Douglas in rebellion against the King.

Only Douglas and Worcester are at Shrewsbury with Hotspur, who is killed by Henry, Prince of Wales. Worcester and Vernon are executed, Douglas freed.

Young Henry (later Henry V) is introduced in the company of Sir John Falstaff and a group of lively companions who plot to rob a group of travelers. After the Prince and Poins, disguised in buckram, rob the robbers at Gadshill, they meet the others at Boar's Head Tavern and the practical joke is revealed. The Prince is summoned to appear before the King. He agrees to reform and to lead the royal forces against Hotspur.

Falstaff, placed in charge of some foot soldiers, makes a famous speech on Honor at the battle of Shrewsbury, where he also claims credit for the death of Hotspur, who was killed by the Prince of Wales after he had rescued his father from Douglas. The King sends Prince John of Lancaster against Northumberland and Scroop, while he goes with his son to fight Glendower and the Earl of March in Wales.

Henry the Fourth, The Second Part of King, written 1598; registered and published 1600; HOLINSHED and *The Famous Victories* were used as sources (see Part I).

PLOT: The action covers the period from the victory at Shrewsbury (July 21, 1403) until the death of Henry IV (1413). When the Earl of Northumberland learns of Hotspur's defeat and receives word that the forces of the Prince of Lancaster and the Earl of Westmoreland are advancing against him, he joins forces with the Archbishop of York in an attempt to stop them. Meanwhile, in London, Falstaff bids farewell to his cronies in the Boar's Head Tavern and starts north in an attempt to recruit soldiers for the King's army. This saves him from being arrested for a debt he owes Mistress Quickly. Pistol and Doll Tearsheet are also present.

In the North, the wife and daughter-in-law (Hotspur's widow) of the Earl of Northumberland persuade him to flee to Scotland instead of fighting against the King. This news is not very well received in the rebel camp where the Archbishop finally persuades Mowbray and Hastings to present a schedule of their grievances to John of Lancaster, upon whose "princely word" the rebel armies are disbanded. They are tricked by John and executed.

Meanwhile, Falstaff persuades Justice Shallow to lend him a thousand pounds on the guarantee that he will pay it back when Prince Hal becomes king. When Falstaff learns that the King is dead and his young companion is now Henry V, he rushes to London. But the new king is now a serious young man, not the idle reveler of before, and Falstaff is banished from his presence and sent to prison. An invasion of France is predicted at the end of the play.

Henry IV. See BOLINGBROKE.

Henry the Fifth, The Life of King, written 1599; registered and published 1600; sources HOLINSHED and *Famous Victories* (see 1H4).

PLOT: Given verbal ammunition by the Archbishop of Canterbury, and annoyed by the French ambassadors, Henry decides to win the French crown by invading France. He learns at Southampton that Cambridge, Scrope and Grey had planned to assassinate him and has them executed. After taking the French city of Harfleur, he marches toward Calais. Met at Agincourt by a French army larger than his own under the Dauphin and the Constable of France, he defeats them. After signing the Treaty of Troyes, he marries Katherine, daughter of the French king.

Meanwhile, Quickly has married Pistol, who sets out with Bardolph and Nym to fight in the campaign. Falstaff's death is reported; Pistol is beaten by Fluellen for insulting the Welsh; Bardolph and Nym are hanged for looting. King Henry, wandering around the camp in disguise trying to get closer to his men, involves Fluellen in a quarrel with the English soldier Williams. In the Epilogue, the Chorus (*Henry V* is the only play in which Shakespeare prefaces every act with a chorus) announces the birth of a son, Henry VI.

Henry V (1397-1422), King of England (1413-22); eldest son of Henry IV and Mary, daughter of the Earl of Hereford; the character of Henry V is quite different from the Prince of Wales in the two parts of Henry IV; he is serious, more religious, strong and intelligent but not witty, exuberant nor brilliant.

HEN5: I, 2. See 1H4 and 2H4.

Henry the Sixth, The First Part of King, probably written 1591-92; mentioned by Nashe in *Pierce Penilesse,* performed 1592; registered and published 1623; although HOLINSHED, HALLE and FABYAN were the sources used, much of the play is not historically accurate.

PLOT: Part I covers the period from the death of Henry V to the marriage of young King Henry to Margaret, daughter of the King of Naples. The basic theme involves the struggle between the righteous English leader Talbot and Joan of Arc, who represents the evil of France. There is a struggle for power between the Protector Gloucester and Henry Beaufort, Bishop of Winchester and Cardinal. The play opens with the funeral procession of King Henry V during which messengers bring news of French victories and the wounding of Talbot, commander of the British forces. Joan la Pucelle (d'Arc) makes herself known to Charles, the Dauphin, and promises to raise the siege of Orleans and lead France to victory. Talbot counters with a daring night attack upon the city and recaptures it. Richard Plantagenet and the Earl of Somerset quarrel in the Temple Garden and those who side with Plantagenet and the House of York pluck white roses and those with Somerset and the House of Lancaster, red; the Wars of the Roses have begun.

The King restores his titles to Plantagenet and creates him Duke of York. The court sets out for France so that Henry of Windsor can be crowned in Paris. Talbot, created Earl of Shrewsbury, is trying to take Bordeaux from the Duke of Burgundy, who has been persuaded by Joan to switch allegiance to the French side; but without the necessary reinforcements, which the quarreling English factions neglect to send, he is defeated and killed, with his son, in the battle. Joan is captured by the Duke of York and burned at the stake.

Meanwhile the Earl of Suffolk, having captured Margaret of Anjou and fallen in love with her, decides to marry her to the King (as he himself is already married) and thus extend his influence. Peace is declared and the young King agrees to break his arrangement with Charles to marry the daughter of Armagnac, and takes Margaret back to England, much against the

wishes and the better judgment of Gloucester and Exeter.

Henry the Sixth, The Second Part of King, probably written 1590-91; registered and published 1594; HOLINSHED, HALLE, FABYAN and possibly Grafton and Stow were the sources; chronologically inaccurate since Richard (Gloucester) distinguishes himself in battle at a time when he was not yet three years old.

PLOT: Action of the play covers Margaret's arrival from France (1445) and ends with York's victory at St. Albans (1455). Margaret, Suffolk, York and Cardinal Beaufort are in a power struggle with the Protector Gloucester and succeed in having his Duchess banished for practicing "black magic" and employing conjurers to work against the King, and in having the Duke himself murdered. Suffolk, blamed for the murder, is banished and then murdered by pirates. Meanwhile York is sent to suppress the Irish revolt and now has an army under his command. Jack Cade's rebellion (sponsored by York) takes place in London, but the fickle mob, skillfully persuaded by Lord Clifford, turns on their leader and Cade, forced to flee, is killed by Iden in his garden. York, aided by Salisbury, Warwick and his sons, is victorious at the battle of St. Albans in which Somerset is slain by Richard (Gloucester) and Clifford is killed by York. The King flees to London with York in pursuit.

Henry the Sixth, The Third Part of King, written c1590; performed 1592; published 1595; sources, see above.

PLOT: The play opens in Parliament House (1460) following the Battle of St. Albans (May 22, 1455) and the Yorkist victory at Northampton (July

10, 1460). Henry is granted the crown for life on the condition that the title passes to Richard of York and his heirs. Civil war follows when Queen Margaret joins the northern lords in an attempt to keep the succession in the house of Lancaster. The Earl of Rutland, York's youngest son, is killed by Clifford (in revenge for his father's death); York is captured by the Queen's army, tortured and killed (although he actually died in battle). Edward and Richard join Warwick against them and the coronation of Edward is planned. King Henry flees to Scotland but returns to England only to be imprisoned in the Tower by Edward (now King Edward IV).

The King tries to make Lady Grey his queen but is persuaded by Warwick, upon his return from France, to marry Lady Bona. However, Edward marries Elizabeth Woodville (Lady Grey) much to the embarrassment of Warwick, who then joins Margaret's forces and arranges the betrothal of his daughter to Prince Edward. Warwick releases Henry and captures Edward, who is, however, set free by a force led by his brother Richard, the Duke of Gloucester. Henry is recaptured and Warwick is defeated and killed at the battle of Barnet (1471).

The Lancastrians are finally defeated at Tewkesbury (1471), the Prince of Wales is slain, and Margaret is banished to France after Edward restrains Richard from killing her. Finding the King reading in the tower, Gloucester stabs him to death and soliloquizes about his future ambitions. Edward, his Queen and young son are, temporarily, in power again.

Henry VI (1421-71), son of Henry V and Katherine of Valois, daughter of Charles VI of France; King of England (1422), crowned at Westminster (1426) and again in Paris (1431); married Margaret of Anjou (1445); Christian mystic "whose church-like humours fits not for a crown"; mild, scholarly, patient, passive almost negative king unable to prevent the civil strife of the Wars of the Roses or hold France as an English possession; subject to fits of insanity (from 1455); probably murdered in the Tower after the battle of Tewkesbury (1471).

1H6: III, 1; 2H6: I, 1; 3H6: I, 1.

Henry VII. See RICHMOND, Earl of.

Henry the Eighth, The Famous History of the Life of, written 1612-13; performed June 29, 1613 at the GLOBE (when the theater burned down); registered and published 1623; sources, HOLINSHED and FOXE'S *Book of Martyrs* for the scenes on Cranmer in the fifth act; it has been assumed that Shakespeare did not write much of *Henry VIII* and that FLETCHER completed an unfinished play under his direction; however, this is conjecture and constantly debated by Shakespearean scholars.

PLOT: The Duke of Buckingham is about to expose the ambitious Cardinal Wolsey to the King when he is arrested on charges of high treason, tried and, despite the efforts of the Queen to save him, executed. At a banquet at York Place, that the Cardinal has arranged for the entertainment of the King, Henry meets and dances with Anne Bullen for the first time. She is created the Marchioness of Pembroke and the machinery for Henry's divorce from Katherine is put into operation.

At the public trial, the King backs Wolsey against the

Queen's charges of having instigated the divorce; however, the Cardinal, hoping for a royal marriage with the Duchess of Alençon and an alliance with France, appeals to the Pope for assistance and offers to help Katherine, who, distrusting him, rejects his offer.

When the King learns of Wolsey's deception, he is dismissed and forced to leave court. Cranmer, Archbishop of Canterbury, annuls the marriage and takes Wolsey's place with the King; Katherine of Aragon dies shortly after becoming the Princess Dowager and moving to Kimbolton; Cranmer, supported by the King against the nobles, acts as godfather at the baptism of Princess Elizabeth for whom he predicts a glorious future.

Henry VIII (1491-1547), second son of Henry VII and Elizabeth of York; succeeded to the throne 1509; famous for his many wives, his quarrel with the Catholic Church, his wars with France, the execution of Stafford, Duke of Buckingham, the power and the fall of his chief minister, Cardinal Wolsey, and his successful suppression of the northern rebellions. Henry was a strong ruler despite his personal weaknesses and appetites, and England enjoyed comparative peace and prosperity during his reign.
    HEN8: I, 2.

Henryson (Henderson), Robert (c1430-c1506). Scottish poet; wrote *Testament of Cresseid* (tragic sequel to CHAUCER'S *Troilus and Cressida*) which was known to Shakespeare and referred to in *Twelfth Night* and *Henry V;* also wrote *Robene and Makyne*, believed to be the earliest English pastoral poem.

hent, occasion, opportunity, moment; occupied, taken positions at, seized.
    HAM: Hamlet, III, 3, 88.

    MEAS: Peter, IV, 6, 14.
    WINT: Autolycus, IV, 3, 133.

hep (hip), fruit of wild rose.
    TIMON: Timon, IV, 3, 422.

herald. See SILENCE.

heraldry, heraldic device, armorial bearings.
    HAM: Hamlet, II, 2, 478. See LAW AND HERALDRY.

herald's coat, tabard, sleeveless tunic embroidered with royal coat of arms; worn by herald.
    1H4: Falstaff, IV, 2, 50.

heralds' laws of combat. See LAW AND HERALDRY.

Herbert, Sir Walter, supporter of Henry Richmond.
    RICH3: V, 2.

herb of grace. See RUE.

Hercules, Roman name of famous hero of classical Greek mythology, Heracles; son of Zeus and Alcmene, wife of Amphitryon; born in Thebes; symbol of physical strength and courage for having performed 12 great tests of endurance.
    HAM: Hamlet, I, 2, 153. See DAY.
    COR: Coriolanus, IV, 1, 17.
    LLL: Moth, I, 2, 69—it has been suggested that Shakespeare knew that the kings of Navarre claimed descent from this Greek hero.

Hercules and his load, probably a reference to the globe Hercules carried on his shoulder which was the sign of the GLOBE playhouse.
    HAM: Rosencrantz, II, 2, 379.

heredity. See HAUNTED.

Hereford, Duke (Earl) of. See BOLINGBROKE.

heresies
    . . . the heresies that men do leave
    Are hated most of those they did deceive.
    MND: Lysander, II, 2, 139.

Hermes, in Greek mythology, herald and messenger of the

gods; called Mercury by the Romans; son of Zeus and Maia, daughter of Atlas; believed to have invented the shepherd's pipe or syrinx with which he charmed the monster Argus; also god of the roads who protected travelers.
HEN5: Dauphin, III, 7, 19.

Hermia, in love with Lysander; when her father insists she marry Demetrius, they run away to the forest where Puck, by mistake, uses magic to make him fall in love with Helena; the lovers finally marry when the fairies get them straightened out.
MND: I, 1.

Hermione, faithful, patient, wife of Leontes, King of Sicilia; falsely accused of infidelity by her husband and imprisoned; lived in seclusion while believed dead; reunited with her husband and her daughter at the end of the play.
WINT: I, 2.

hermit, beadsman who prayed for the soul of his benefactor.
MACB: Lady Macbeth, I, 6, 20.

Herne the Hunter, legendary figure said to haunt the great oaks in Windsor Forest; appeared at midnight at Herne's Oak, a six-hundred-year-old tree near the castle; blown down in a storm (1863).
MWW: Mrs. Page, IV, 4, 28.

Hero, quiet daughter of Leonato, governor of Messina; relatively colorless cousin and friend of Beatrice; although unjustly accused of infidelity by Claudio, she marries him.
ADO: I, 1.

Herod, actually the reigning dynasty in Palestine at the time of Christ, generally used to refer to the tyrant, Herod Antipas, in Biblical literature.
HAM: Hamlet, III, 2, 16.
A&C: Alexas, III, 3, 3.
MWW: Mrs. Page, II, 1, 20.

Hesperides, the golden apples, which Gaea had given to Hera as a wedding gift, were to be found in the garden of the Hesperides; guarded by a dragon and nymphs; getting these apples was the twelfth task of Hercules.
LLL: Berowne, IV, 3, 341.
PER: Antiochus, I, 1, 27.

Hesperus, the evening star.
ALL'sW: Helena, II, 1, 167.

hest, order, command, instruct, dictate; old form, behest.
TEMP: Miranda, III, 1, 37.
LLL: Rosaline, V, 2, 65.
1H4: Lady, II, 3, 65.

hexes, hamstrings (cuts the tendons behind the knee), disables, cripples.
WINT: Leontes, I, 2, 244.

Hibocrates, famous Greek physician, Hippocrates (5th century, BC).
MWW: Evans, III, 1, 66.

hic et ubique, Latin, here and everywhere.
HAM: Hamlet, I, 5, 156.

hic jacet, Latin, here lies.
ALL'sW: Parolles, III, 6, 66.

hide fox and all after, signal for all to scatter in a game similar to hide-and-seek.
HAM: Hamlet, IV, 2, 32.

Hiems, winter (personified).
MND: Titania, II, 1, 109.

Higgins, John (c1545-1602). English poet, historian; his fable in verse of *King Lear,* included as the *Firste parte* (added in 1574) to *The Mirrour for Magistrates* (1559), was probably used by Shakespeare.

high-battled, leader of large, victorious armies.
A&C: Enobarbus, III, 13, 29.

high cross, cross set in a high place in the center of the marketplace or town.
SHREW: Gremio, I, 1, 137.

high-lone, on one's own feet.
R&J: Nurse, I, 3, 36.

high-stomached, stubborn, haughty.
RICH2: Richard, I, 1, 18.

hight, called, is named, known as.
MND: Quince, Prologue, V, 1, 140.
LLL: Ferdinand, I, 1, 171.
PER: Gower, IV, Prologue, 18.

high tides, festival days, important season or occasions.
JOHN: Constance, III, 1, 86.

hilding, worthless, good for nothing.
2H4: Lord Bardolph, I, 1, 57.
CYM: Cloten, II, 3, 128.
SHREW: Baptista, II, 1, 26—wretch.

hills
. . . hills whose heads touch heaven . . .
OTH: Othello, I, 3, 141.

hind, doe, female red deer; peasant, rustic, servant, boor.
MND: Helena, II, 1, 232.
COFE: Dromio S., III, 1, 77.
LLL: Armado, I, 2, 124.

hint, occasion, reason, opportunity.
TEMP: Miranda, I, 2, 134.
OTH: Othello, I, 3, 142.

hipped, lamed in the hip, refers to a horse.
SHREW: Biondello, III, 2, 49.

Hippolyta, Queen of the Amazons; betrothed to Theseus.
MND: I, 1.

Hippolyta, wife of Theseus, sister of Emilia, heroine of play; persuades Theseus to punish Creon and to spare Palamon and Arcite. See above.
2NK: I, 1.

hirelings or hired men, employed and paid by the actor-sharers of a company; earned about six shillings a week; extra actors, stagehands, property men, musicians, tireman or wardrobe-master, bookkeeper or prompter were all hirelings.

Hiren, disputed word; possibly character from George Peele's play *The Turkish Mahomet and*
Hiren the Fair Greek (c1594); later meant whore or harlot.
2H4: Pistol, II, 4, 173.

his, its.
SONNET: IX, 10.
HAM: Bernardo, I, 1, 37.
MND: Titania, II, 1, 95.

hit it, name of an old dance tune.
LLL: Rosaline, IV, 1, 123.

hoar, grayish-white or gray; ghastly white; cover with white blotches (leprosy).
HAM: Queen, IV, 7, 169. See WILLOW.
TIMON: Timon IV, 3, 155.

Hobbididence (Hoppedance). See FIENDS.
LEAR: Edgar, III, 6, 32 and IV, 1, 60.

hobby-horse, used during the morris dance or May games; an imitation horse, made of a light material and worn about the waist of a performer whose antics were objected to by the Puritans of the period as ungodly or pagan; antic-figure, buffoon, simpleton; prostitute.
HAM: Hamlet, III, 2, 143.
ADO: Benedick, III, 2, 75.
LLL: Moth, III, 1, 30.

hob nob, have or have not, give or take, hit or miss.
TWN: Toby, III, 4, 263.

Hoby, Sir Thomas (1530-66). English translator of Castiglione's *The Courtyer of Count Baldessar Castilio* (or the *Cortegiano*) 1561; concerning European chivalry, possibly used by Shakespeare, who most certainly knew the book.

Holborn, former palace (seat) of the Bishops of Ely in London.
RICH3: Richard, III, 4, 31.

holding, refrain, burden of a song.
A&C: Enobarbus, II, 7, 116.

hold, or cut bowstrings, live up to your promise or suffer the consequences; proverbial phrase whose meaning is not certain.
MND: Bottom, I, 2, 113.

hold the mortise, stay joined together.
OTH: Montan, II, 1, 9.

holidam (halidom, holidame), oath meaning "holy relics"; salvation, holiness.
SHREW: Baptista, V, 2, 99.
2GENT: Host, IV, 2, 136.
HEN8: King, V, 1, 116.

holidays
If all the year were playing holidays,
To sport would be as tedious as to work;
But when they seldom come, they wish'd-for come,
And nothing pleaseth but rare accidents.
1H4: Prince, I, 2, 228. See BEHAVIOUR, REFORMATION.

Holinshed, Raphael (c1529-c80), famous as the author of *The Chronicles of England, Scotland and Ireland* from which Shakespeare took most of the material for his English historical plays, *Macbeth,* part of *Cymbeline* and perhaps *King Lear;* second, enlarged edition, edited by John Hooker, published posthumously (1587).

Holland, John, follower of Jack Cade.
2H6: IV, 2.

holland, fine lawn or linen.
1H4: Hostess, III, 3, 82.
2H4: Prince, II, 2, 26.

Holland, Philemon (1552-1637). English translator of Pliny's *Natural History* (1601) used as a source of *Othello.*

holloaed, shouted loudly.
RICH2: Another Lord, IV, 1, 54.

hollow crown
. . . for within the hollow crown
That rounds the mortal temples of a king
Keeps Death his court . . .
RICH2: Richard, III, 2, 160.
See ANTIC, DEATH OF KINGS.

Holmedon, in Northumberland near the border of Scotland; now Humbleton.
1H4: Westmoreland, I, 1, 55.

Holofernes, pedantic village schoolmaster who has "been at a great feast of languages and stolen the scraps"; plays Judas Maccabaeus in "The Nine Worthies," which he had suggested to Don Armado as the proper presentation for the princess.
LLL: IV, 2.

Holy-rood Day, September 14; feast of the Exaltation of the Holy Cross.
1H4: Westmoreland, I, 1, 52.

holy writ. See VILLANY.

home, to the full, thoroughly, entirely; to the point, directly, bluntly.
TEMP: Prospero, V, 1, 71.
LEAR: Gloucester, III, 3, 13.
OTH: Cassio, II, 1, 166.

Homer (fl. c700 BC). Poet credited with the writing of the *Iliad* and the *Odyssey;* translations of the works of Homer by HALL and Chapman were used by Shakespeare in the writing of *Troilus and Cressida.*

honest, chaste, virtuous.
HAM: Hamlet, III, 1, 103.
AYL: Celia, I, 2, 42.
OTH: Othello, III, 3, 225.

honesty
. . . honesty coupled to beauty is to have honey a sauce to sugar.
AYL: Touchstone, III, 3, 30.
. . . Rich honesty dwells like a miser, sir, in a poor house, as your pearl in your foul oyster.
AYL: Touchstone, V, 4, 62.
Nor are those empty-hearted whose low sounds
Reverb no hollowness.
LEAR: Kent, I, 1, 155—based on the proverb "Empty vessels make the most noise."
. . . O wretched fool,
That livest to make thine honesty a vice!

O monstrous world, take note,
take note, O world,
To be direct and honest is not
safe.
OTH: Iago, III, 3, 375. See
PROFIT.

I should be wise; for honesty's
a fool
And loses that it works for.
OTH: Iago, III, 3, 382.

honey
They surfeited with honey and
began
To loathe the taste of sweetness,
whereof a little
More than a little is by much
too much.
1H4: King, III, 2, 71.

honeybees. See OBEDIENCE.

honi soit qui mal y pense, French,
evil to him who thinks evil;
motto of the Knights of the
Garter.
MWW: Quickly, V, 5, 73.

honorificabilitudinitatibus, abla-
tive plural of medieval Latin
honorificabilitudo meaning hon-
orableness; Latin scholar's joke
as longest word in that language
and meaning loaded with honors.
LLL: Costard, V, 1, 44.

honour
. . . If I lose mine honour,
I lose myself.
A&C: Antony, III, 4, 22.

By heaven, methinks it were an
easy leap,
To pluck bright honour from
the pale-faced moon,
Or dive into the bottom of the
deep,
Where fadom line could never
touch the ground,
And pluck up drowned honour
by the locks,
So he that doth redeem her
thence might wear
Without corrival all her digni-
ties . . .
1H4: Hotspur, I, 3, 201. See
CORRIVAL.

What is honour? A word. What

is the word honour? Air. A trim
reckoning.
1H4: Falstaff, V, 1, 136.

Honour is a mere scutcheon—
and so ends my catechism.
1H4: Falstaff, V, 1, 142. See
SCUTCHEON.

But if it be a sin to covet honour,
I am the most offending soul
alive.
HEN5: King, IV, 3, 28.

Mine honour is my life. Both
grow in one;
Take honour from me, and my
life is done.
RICH2: Mowbray, I, 1, 182. See
REPUTATION.

Who bates mine honour shall
not know my coin.
TIMON: Sempronius, III, 3,
26.

. . . For honour,
'Tis a derivative from me and
mine,
And only that I stand for.
WINT: Hermione, III, 2, 44.

honourable men
Here, under leave of Brutus and
the rest
(For Brutus is an honourable
man;
So are they all, all honourable
men) . . .
JC: Antony, III, 2, 87.

hood, blindfold or cover for falcon's (or hawk's) head placed
on to calm it before going after
game.
HEN5: Constable, III, 7, 121—
hooded valour.

hoodman-blind, blind-man's buff.
HAM: Hamlet, III, 4, 77.
ALL'sW: 1Lord, IV, 3, 136.

hoodwink, blindfold, cover, make
invisible.
TEMP: Caliban, IV, 1, 206.
ALL'sW: 2Lord, III, 6, 26.

hope
True hope is swift and flies with
swallow's wings;
Kings it makes gods, and mean-
er creatures kings.

RICH3: Richmond, V, 2, 23.

Hope Theatre, built for Philip Henslowe (in partnership with Jacob Meade) on the BANKSIDE, Southwark (1613); originally a Bear Garden owned jointly by Henslowe and Alleyn (1604).

Horatio, loyal, serene, close friend of Hamlet; although his actions do not directly affect the plot, he is important as a dramatic foil and support for Hamlet (escially in the "MOUSETRAP"); sees Ghost of Hamlet's father and is the only one to whom Hamlet confides the story of his father's murder; used throughout as an echo of Hamlet's thoughts, he is his confidant and crutch; dying, Hamlet begs Horatio not to commit suicide, but to report his story as he would want it told.

HAM: I, 1.

hornbook, first reading book; children learned their ABC's from printed sheets, mounted on wooden paddles or handles and covered with thin translucent or transparent horn.

LLL: Moth, V, 1, 48.

Horner, Thomas, armorer, accused by his apprentice Peter Thump of backing Richard, Duke of York, as the rightful king; Gloucester orders a trial by combat; after a drinking bout, Horner confesses treason as Peter is about to kill his master.

2H6: I, 3.

horn-mad, like an enraged, horned animal, furious; mad because of being a cuckold.

MWW: Quickly, I, 4, 52.

COFE: Dromio E., II, 1, 57.

horns, sign of the cuckold; a husband whose wife is unfaithful.

LLL: Boyet, IV, 1, 114—*horns that year miscarry,* popular Elizabethan joke meaning in this instance that Rosaline will be an unfaithful wife.

horologe, clock.

OTH: Iago, II, 3, 135.

horse

A horse! a horse! my kingdom for a horse!

RICH3: Richard, V, 4, 7.

horse-drench, medicinal dose or draught for a horse; purge or crude remedy.

COR: Menenius, II, 1, 130.

horsehair, used for bow strings.

CYM: Cloten, II, 3, 33.

horsemanship

As if an angel dropped down from the clouds

To turn and wind a fiery Pegasus

And witch the world with noble horsemanship.

1H4: Vernon, IV, 1, 108. See PEGASUS.

Hortensio, in his attempt to win Bianca, he is forced to persuade his friend Petruchio to woo and marry her elder sister Katherina.

SHREW: I, 1.

Hortensius, servant of one of Timon's creditors.

TIMON: III, 4.

Host, takes Julia to find Proteus.

2GENT: IV, 2.

Host of the Garter Inn, tricks Evans and Caius, who avenge themselves by robbing him of his horses; helps Fenton win Anne Page.

MWW: I, 3.

Hostess, wants to arrest the drunken Sly; possibly Marian Hacket.

SHREW: Induction; HEN5: II, 1. See QUICKLY.

hostler (ostler), groom (who takes care of horses).

COR: Coriolanus, III, 3, 32.

hot minion, passionate or ardent mistress or lover.

TEMP: Iris, IV, 1, 98—refers to Venus, Mars' mistress.

Hotspur. See PERCY, Henry.

hounds of Sparta, famed in the ancient world as hunting dogs.

MND: Hippolyta, IV, 1, 110.
See ACTAEON.

hours

Those hours, that with gentle
work did frame
The lovely gaze where every eye
doth dwell,
Will play the tyrants to the very
same
And that unfair which fairly
doth excel . . .
SONNET: V, 1.

house

He that has a house to put's
head in has a good headpiece.
LEAR: Fool, III, 2, 26.

house against this house, the
royal houses of York and Lancaster set against one another,
leading to the Wars of the
Roses.
RICH2: Carlisle, IV, 1, 145.
See YORK, LANCASTER.

household coat, family coat of
arms in stained-glass windows.
RICH2: Bolingbroke, III, 1, 24.

housekeepers, name given to own-
ers or shareholders of a theater;
they received the money taken
in for entrance to the galleries,
although later it was reduced to
half; they were responsible for
the upkeep of the theater and
the payment of ground-rent.

Howard, Charles. See ADMIRAL'S
MEN.

Hoy-day! exclamation of surprise or disapproval.
TIMON: Apemantus, I, 2, 137.

Hubert de Burgh, King's chamberlain; ordered by John to put
Arthur to death; about to "blind
the boy," he yields to Arthur's pleading and releases
him; tells John he is dead; suspected later by Salisbury and
others of Arthur's subsequent
death; saved by the Bastard. [d.
1243, descendant of Charlemagne; with the king at Runnymede (1215), mentioned in the
Great Charter as one of those
who advised the granting of the

document; regent and chief min-
ister for Henry III, Duke of
Kent.]
JOHN: III, 3.

hugger-mugger, secretly and with
undue haste.
HAM: King, IV, 5, 84.

hull, drift along, lie becalmed,
float without sail.
TWN: Viola, I, 5, 217.
RICH3: Ratcliffe, IV, 4, 438.
HEN8: King, II, 4, 199.

humanity

Humanity must perforce prey
on itself,
Like monsters of the deep.
LEAR: Albany, IV, 2, 48.

humblebee, bumblebee.
MND: Titania, III, 1, 171.

Full merrily the humblebee doth
sing
Till he hath lost his honey and
his sting;
And being once subdued in
armed tail,
Sweet honey and sweet notes together fail.
T&C: Pandarus, V, 10, 42.

Hume, John, priest; bribed by
Cardinal Beaufort and Suffolk
to encourage the Duchess of
Gloucester in her interest in
black magic; discovered at their
ceremonies, he is sentenced to
hang.
2H6: I, 2.

humorous, melancholy.
LLL: Berowne, III, 1, 177.

humour, inclination toward
whimsy, fancy; capricious, fickle;
moist, damp.
HAM: Hamlet, II, 2, 335.
MND: Bottom, I, 2, 31.
JC: Portia, II, 1, 262.

humours, there were four bodily
fluids or humours: blood, producing a sanguine or optimistic
temperament; black bile, producing a melancholy or sad personality; yellow bile, producing
a choleric or angry one; and
phlegm, producing a dull or indifferent person; good health

was thought to come from a balance of the four, and bad health meant a predominance of any one; the symptoms of an imbalance of the humours are frequently used by Shakespeare.

RICH2: Richard, V, 5, 10.

LLL: Ferdinand, I, 1, 234.

WINT: Paulina, II, 3, 38.

Humphrey. See GLOUCESTER, Duke of.

Humphrey. See SINKLO.

Humphrey Hour, possibly "to go without dinner"; indigent gallants walked into St. Paul's Cathedral hoping to get a free meal.

RICH3: Richard, IV, 4, 176.

Hundred Merry Tales, very popular joke book (on the bawdy side), first published (1526).

ADO: Beatrice, II, 1, 135.

hurdle, rough wooden frame (sledge) on which condemned criminals were taken to be executed.

R&J: Capulet, III, 5, 156.

hurly, ado, commotion, tumult.

2H4: King, III, 1, 25.

JOHN: Pandulph, III, 4, 169.

hurricano, waterspout.

LEAR: Lear, III, 2, 2.

husband, manager or master of a household or farm.

2H4: Falstaff, V, 3, 12.

SHREW: Lord, Induction, 1, 68.

husband

Thy husband is thy lord, thy life, thy keeper,
Thy head, thy sovereign; one that cares for thee
And for thy maintenance; commits his body
To painful labour both by sea and land,
To watch the night in storms, the day in cold,
While thou li'st warm at home, secure and safe . . .

SHREW: Katherina, V, 2, 146.

husbandry, economy, thrift, frugality.

HAM: Polonius, I, 3, 77.

MACB: Banquo, II, 1, 4.

SHREW: Vincentio, V, 1, 71.

huswife, hussy, wanton, woman, harlot.

A&C: Cleopatra, IV, 15, 44.

2H4: Falstaff, III, 2, 341.

AYL: Celia, I, 2, 34.

Hybla, mountain and town in Sicily famous for its honey.

JC: Cassius, V, 1, 34.

1H4: Prince, I, 2, 47.

Hydra, nine-headed monster of the marsh area of Lerna in the Peloponnesus; destroyed by Hercules as the second of his tasks or labors; as each head was cut off, two appeared in its place until Iolaus thrust a burning torch into the bleeding stump.

OTH: Cassio, II, 3, 308.

COR: Coriolanus, III, 1, 93.

HEN5: Canterbury, I, 1, 35.

Hymen, Greek god or personification of marriage; appears frequently in Elizabethan and Jacobean masques.

AYL: V, 4.

HAM: Player King, III, 2, 169.

ADO: Claudio, V, 3, 32.

Hymen's torch, on the wedding night the torch of the god of marriage led the bride and groom to bed.

TEMP: Iris, IV, 1, 97.

Hyperion, son of Uranus and father of the sun-god Helios, with whom he is often confused.

HEN5: King, IV, 1, 292.

TIMON: Timon, IV, 3, 184.

HAM: Hamlet, I, 2, 140—refers to Apollo, usually the Titanic sun god.

Hyrcan, refers to desert area near Caspian Sea known as Hyrcania, where, according to Pliny, wild tigers roamed.

MACB: Macbeth, III, 4, 101.

HAM: Hamlet, II, 2, 472—*Hyrcanian beast,* tiger described by Vergil in the *Aeneid.*

MERV: Morocco, II, 7, 41—*Hyrcanian deserts.*

Iachimo, Roman courtier; meets the banished Posthumus at the house of his friend, Philario, and makes a bet with him that he can make Imogen unfaithful; accomplishes this by a ruse; confesses his villainy when captured during the invasion of Britain; pardoned.
CYM: I, 4.

Iago, arch villain; young Venetian; plays on Othello's jealousy until the Moor kills Desdemona; "character of Iago is one of the supererogations of Shakespeare's genius"—(Hazlitt); "a man without passions"—(Spencer); "Iago desires self-destruction"—(W. H. Auden).
OTH: I, 1.

I am I
Something about, a little from the right,
In at the window, or else o'er the hatch.
Who dares not stir by day must walk by night;
And have is have, however men do catch.
Near or far off, well won is still well shot,
And I am I, howe'er I was begot.
JOHN: Bastard, I, 1, 170.

Icarus, in Greek mythology, son of Daedalus, famed architect, who made wings for them both so that they could fly and thus escape the wrath of the King of Minos; flew too near the sun, which melted the wax that held the wings together, and he plunged into the Aegean Sea; Daedalus landed safely in Sicily.
1H6: Talbot, IV, 6, 55.

ice brook's temper, tempered or hardened in ice-cold water; tempered at Innsbruck, noted for fine armorer's steel at that time; Spanish swords were produced by this method.
OTH: Othello, V, 2, 253.

Iceland dog, shaggy, pointed-eared, long-haired, heavy-coated (usually white) lapdog with an unpleasant disposition.
HEN5: Pistol, II, 1, 43.

Iden, Alexander, Kentish gentleman; kills Cade in self-defense when he discovers him hiding in his garden; takes his head to the King; knighted.
2H6: IV, 10.

ides of March
Beware the ides of March.
JC: Soothsayer, I, 2, 18—March 15.

idle, absurd, mad, foolish, senseless.
HAM: Hamlet, III, 2, 95.
LEAR: Goneril, I, 3, 16.
MND: Puck, V, 1, 434.

idolatry. See SWEAR.

If
. . . Your If is the only peacemaker. Much virtue in If.
AYL: Touchstone, V, 4, 107.

i'fecks, in faith.
WINT: Leontes, I, 2, 120.

ignis fatuus, Latin, will-o'-the-wisp.
1H4: Falstaff, III, 3, 45.

ignorance. See KNOWLEDGE.

Ilion, Troy.

LLL: Armado, V, 2, 658—refers to Hector, *heir of Ilion.*
LUCRECE: 1370. See ILIUM.

Ilium, the tower, fortress, citadel of Troy; King Priam's palace.
HAM: Player, II, 2, 496.
T&C: Troilus, I, 1, 104.

ill deeds
How oft the sight of means to do ill deeds
Make deeds ill done!
JOHN: King, IV, 2, 219.

ill-erected, built for evil and causing woe.
RICH2: Queen, V, 1, 2—*To Julius Caesar's ill-erected tower,* the Tower of London was said to have been built by Julius Caesar.

ill-favoured thing
. . . A poor virgin, sir, an ill-favour'd thing, but mine own.
AYL: Touchstone, V, 4, 60. See AUDREY.

illness, wickedness, ruthlessness; fault.
MACB: Lady Macbeth, I, 5, 21.

illo, ho, ho, also hillo, the falconer's cry to signal his hawk.
HAM: Marcellus, I, 5, 115.

illustrate, illustrious.
LLL: Boyet, IV, 1, 65.

Illyria, city on the east coast of the Adriatic; Shakespeare chose the name for an imaginary kingdom.
TWN: Captain, I, 2, 2.

And what should I do in Illyria?
TWN: Viola, I, 2, 3.

image
Die single, and thine image dies with thee.
SONNET: III, 14.

imagery, as if hung or covered with tapestries or wall coverings.
RICH2: York, V, 2, 16.

imagination
And so, with great imagination, Proper to madmen, led his powers to death

And, winking, leapt into destruction.
2H4: Lord Bardolph, I, 3, 31.

The lunatic, the lover, and the poet
Are of imagination all compact.
MND: Theseus, V, 1, 7. See COMPACT.

imbost. See EMBOSSED.

imbrue, stain or cover with blood.
MND: Thisby, V, 1, 351.
2H4: Pistol, II, 4, 210.

immanity, savage ferocity, atrocious barbarity.
1H6: King, V, 1, 13.

immediately, expressly, clearly.
MND: Egeus, I, 1, 45.

immortal longings.
Give me my robe, put on my crown. I have
Immortal longings in me.
A&C: Cleopatra, V, 2, 283.

immure, wall.
T&C: Prologue, 9.
RICH3: Queen, IV, 1, 100—*immured,* closed or walled in.

Imogen, "impulsive" (Shaw) heroine; wife of Posthumus, daughter of the king; "at times a human being, at times a Griselda of the medieval imagination"— (Tillyard), "the woman best beloved in all the world of song and all the tide of time"— (Swinburne).
CYM: I, 1.

imp, to graft new feathers on the broken wing of a falcon to improve its flight; scion, heir, youngster.
RICH2: Northumberland, II, 1, 292.

impale (empale), surround, encircle the head (with a crown).
3H6: Richard, III, 2, 171.

impasted, turned into a crust or paste by the heat of the burning city; "burned to a crisp."
HAM: Hamlet, II, 2, 481.

impawn, pledge as security, as evidence of my good faith; as hostage to my intentions.

Wint: Camillo, I, 2, 436.
1H4: Hotspur, IV, 3, 108.
Hen5: King, I, 2, 21.

impeach, discredit, suspect, dishonor.
MND: Demetrius, II, 1, 214.
1H4: Blunt, I, 3, 75.
Rich2: Bolingbroke, I, 1, 189.

impeachment, hindrance, obstacle.
Hen5: King, III, 6, 151.

impediments. See MARRIAGE.

imperceiverant, not discerning or perceptive; possibly obstinate.
Cym: Cloten, IV, 1, 16.

impertinent, not relevant, out of place.
Temp: Prospero, I, 2, 138.

impeticos, in pocket or petticoats; pocketed.
TwN: Clown, II, 3, 27.

implorator, solicitor.
Ham: Polonius, I, 3, 129.

impone, bet, stake, wager.
Ham: Osric, V, 2, 171.

importance, request, desire, importunity.
John: France (King Philip), II, 1, 7.

imposthume, abscess, swelling caused by internal ulcer or infection.
Ham: Hamlet, IV, 4, 27.
T&C: Thersites, V, 1, 24.
Venus: 743.

imprese, allegorical animal or heraldic device used on family coats of arms.
Rich2: Bolingbroke, III, 1, 25.

impress, conscript, recruit, enforce.
Lear: V, 3, 50.
Ham: Marcellus, I, 1, 75.
1H4: King, I, 1, 21—enlisted.

imputation, reputation, public esteem; opinion, inference, probability.
Ham: Osric, V, 2, 149.
T&C: Nestor, I, 3, 339.
Oth: Iago, III, 3, 406.

in a spleen, outburst of anger, or impulsive display of temper; the spleen was believed to be the organ of the body that governed such actions.
MND: Lysander, I, 1, 146.

in capite, Latin, legal term, by direct grant from the crown.
2H6: Cade, IV, 7, 131.

incarnadine, stain or turn blood-red.
Macb: Macbeth, II, 2, 62.

Inch, small island.
Macb: Ross, I, 2, 61—*Saint Colme's Inch,* island of Saint Columba in the Firth of Forth; an Irish monk founded monasteries in Scotland and the Hebrides; now known as Inchcolm.

inchmeal, inch by inch, little by little, piecemeal.
Temp: Caliban, II, 2, 3.

incony, fine, rare, delicate, darling.
LLL: Costard, III, 1, 136—*incony Jew,* complimentary phrase.

incorporal, bodiless, incorporeal.
Ham: Queen, III, 4, 118.

incorporate, intimately or closely bound together, united in one body.
MND: Helena, III, 2, 208.
Oth: Iago, II, 1, 268.

incorpsed, embodied, made into one body.
Ham: King, IV, 7, 88.

indenture, deed, contract, legal agreement drawn up in duplicate on a single sheet, and then cut apart in an indented or zig-zag line.
Ham: Hamlet, V, 1, 120.
1H4: King, I, 3, 87.
John: Austria, II, 1, 20.

index, table of contents which preceded the actual material or body of the book; prologue; forerunner.

HAM: Queen, III, 4, 52.
OTH: Iago, II, 1, 262.

indifferent, moderate, average, ordinary; impartial, equally.

HAM: Rosencrantz, II, 2, 231.
RICH2: Bolingbroke, II, 3, 116.
HEN5: Canterbury, I, 1, 72.

indign, undeserving, disgraceful.

OTH: Othello, I, 3, 274.

indirection, devious course or suggestion, pretended action; crooked means.

HAM: Polonius, II, 1, 66.
JC: Brutus, IV, 3, 75.

indiscretion
Our indiscretion sometime serves us well
When our deep plots do pall; and that should learn us
There's a divinity that shapes our ends,
Rough-hew them how we will.

HAM: Hamlet, V, 2, 8.

indue (endue), furnish, endow, provide; suited or adapted by nature.

HEN5: King, II, 2, 139.
HAM: Queen, IV, 7, 181.
JOHN: King, IV, 2, 43.

indulgence. See ENDING.

in fee, owned or possessed outright, possession as a freeholder.

HAM: Captain, IV, 4, 22.

infest, torture, worry, harass.

TEMP: Prospero, V, 1, 246.

infirmity
Infirmity, that decays the wise, doth ever make the better fool.

TWN: Malvolio, I, 5, 82.

infusion, natural characteristics or temperament; essence.

HAM: Hamlet, V, 2, 122.

ingener (engener), inventor, one who engineers.

OTH: Cassio, II, 1, 65. See BEAUTY.

in good time, phrase or expression of anger, contempt or indignation; "fat chance for me" or "rotten timing."

OTH: Iago, I, 1, 32.

ingraft, firmly or securely fixed, engrafted.

OTH: Montano, II, 3, 145.

ingratitude
Blow, blow, thou winter wind,
Thou art not so unkind
As man's ingratitude.

AYL: Amiens, II, 7, 174—beginning of song.

Ingratitude, thou marble-hearted fiend,
More hideous when thou show'st thee in a child
Than the sea-monster.

LEAR: Lear, I, 4, 281.

inhabitable, uninhabitable, unendurable.

RICH2: Mowbray, I, 1, 65.

in hac spe vivo, Latin, in this hope I live; motto on Pericles' (sixth knight) shield.

PER: Thaisa, II, 2, 44.

inhooped, fighting cocks and quails were enclosed in a ring or hoop.

A&C: Antony, II, 3, 38.

injoint, join, unite, combine.

OTH: Messenger, I, 3, 35.

injurious, offensive, insulting, malicious; unjust.

RICH2: Bolingbroke, I, 1, 91.
MND: Helena, III, 2, 195.

inkle, type of linen tape.

LLL: Costard, III, 1, 140.
WINT: Servant, IV, 4, 208.
PER: Gower, V, Prologue, 8.

inky blots, reference to the blank charters and tax leases employed by the King; contemptuous term.

RICH2: Gaunt, II, 1, 64.

innocence
The silence often of pure innocence
Persuades when speaking fails.

WINT: Paulina, II, 2, 41.

innocents
Some innocents scape not the thunderbolt.
A&C: Cleopatra, II, 5, 77.

innovation, commotion, riot, change for the worse, upheaval.
OTH: Cassio, II, 3, 42.
HAM: Rosencrantz, II, 2, 347—reference to the companies of child actors of the Queen's Chapel Royal and the theater at the BLACKFRIARS, which competed with the adult companies such as the Chamberlain's Men.

Inns o' Court, legal societies, named after four buildings they occupied—Inner Temple, Middle Temple, Lincoln's Inn and Gray's Inn—that had the exclusive right to call or admit students to the bar.
2H4: Shallow, III, 2, 14.
1H6: setting of, II, 4.

inprimis (imprimis), Latin for first, in the first place; usually the beginning of inventory.
SHREW: Grumio, IV, 1, 68.
2GENT: Launce, III, 1, 274.
2H6: Gloucester, I, 1, 43.

in respect of, compared to.
HAM: Hamlet, V, 2, 120.

insane root, possible reference to the mandrake root which was in the shape of a man's legs, and when ripped from the ground was believed to make a human sound, a shrieking noise; the eating of the root of the mandrake, hemlock, henbane and deadly nightshade was believed to cause insanity.
MACB: Banquo, I, 3, 84.

insinuate, interpose, intrude, "worm one's way in"; ingratiate.
HAM: Hamlet, V, 2, 59.
LLL: Holofernes, V, 1, 28.

insisture, regularity, steady motion toward.
T&C: Ulysses, I, 3, 87.

instance, enticement, motive, precedent.
HAM: Queen, III, 2, 192.
TwN: Sebastian, IV, 3, 12.

instinct. See LION, SUSPICION.

instrumental, useful, practical, naturally serviceable.
HAM: King, I, 2, 48.

insulting, proudly exultant or contemptuously triumphant.
1H4: Prince, V, 4, 54.
TITUS: Titus, III, 2, 71.

insurrection
. . . never yet did insurrection want
Such water colours to impaint his cause,
Nor moody beggars, starving for a time
Of pell-mell havoc and confusion.
1H4: King, V, 1, 79.

Integer vitae scelerisque purus / Non eget Mauri iaculis nec arcu, Latin, He who is pure or upright in life and free from crime has no need of a Moor's javelins or bows and arrows; from Horace's *Odes* (Book I, 22).
TITUS: Demetrius, IV, 2, 20.

integrity
. . . Your dishonor
Mangles true judgment, and bereaves the state
Of that integrity which should becom't,
Not having the power to do the good it would
For th' ill which doth control't.
COR: Coriolanus, III, 1, 157.

intelligence, information, report; spies, espionage.
MND: Helena, I, 1, 248.
WINT: Polixenes, IV, 2, 51.
1H4: Hotspur, IV, 3, 98.

intemperance
Boundless intemperance
In nature is a tyranny. It hath been
Th' untimely emptying of the happy throne
And fall of many kings.
MACB: Macduff, IV, 3, 66.

intend, incline, tend; plan, purpose; pretend.
MND: Demetrius, III, 2, 333.

HEN5: King, I, 2, 144—*intendment*.
OTH: Roderigo, IV, 2, 206.

intentively, completely engrossed in, intently.
OTH: Othello, I, 3, 155.

intermit, delay, withhold, omit.
JC: Marullus, I, 1, 59.

intestine, domestic, internal, civil.
1H4: King, I, 1, 12.
COFE: Duke, I, 1, 11—*intestine jars,* deadly internal strife, bitter civil wars.

intrenchant, not able to be cut, invulnerable.
MACB: Macbeth, V, 8, 9.

Inverness, Macbeth's castle in northwestern Scotland.

investments, clothes, garments, attire.
HAM: Polonius, I, 3, 128.

invitis nubibus, Latin, in spite of the clouds.
2H6: Lieutenant, IV, 1, 99.

Io, daughter of Inachus; beloved by Jupiter who captured her and turned her into a cow to protect her from the jealousy of his wife, Juno; from OVID's *Metamorphoses.*
SHREW: Lord, Induction, 2, 56.

Ionia, ancient area on western coast of Asia Minor bordering on Aegean Sea; received name from Ionians, branch of ancient Greeks, who probably migrated from mainland; freed from Persians by Alexander of Macedon (334 BC); became part of Roman province of Asia.
A&C: Messenger, I, 2, 107.

ira furor brevis est, Latin, anger is a brief fury or madness; from Horace, *Epistles,* I, 2, 62.
TIMON: Timon, I, 2, 28.

Iras, attendant to Cleopatra; dies with her mistress.
A&C: I, 2.

Iris, one of the spirits led by Ariel; appears in masque celebrating the engagement of Ferdinand and Miranda as the "many-colored messenger" of Juno; calls Ceres, the Nymphs, and the Reapers to the festivities; in ancient Greek mythology, virgin goddess of the rainbow, female messenger of the gods, counterpart of Hermes, serving Zeus and Hera.
TEMP: IV, 1.
ALL'SW: Countess, I, 3, 158.
T&C: Ulysses, I, 3, 380.

iron tongue
The iron tongue of midnight hath told twelve.
MND: Theseus, V, 1, 370.

iron-witted, insensitive, unemotional.
RICH3: Richard, IV, 2, 28.

irregular, lawless; probably refers to guerrilla tactics.
1H4: Westmoreland, I, 1, 40.

Isabel, Queen of Charles VI of France; gives her blessing to the coming marriage of her daughter, Katherine, to Henry. [Isabeau of Bavaria (1370-1435), married Charles (1385); crowned with him (1389); acted as regent when Charles went insane (1392); mistress of Louis, Duke of Orléans; sided with English and the Burgundians in Hundred Years' War; largely responsible for Treaty of Troyes (1420); mother of Katherine and Isabel, queens of England.]
HEN5: V, 2.

Isabel or Isabella, Queen, second wife of Richard II; daughter of the king of France; although she was actually a child at the time of her marriage, Shakespeare makes her a sensitive adult; throughout the play she foresees doom for Richard. [1389-1409, daughter of Charles VI and Isabeau of Bavaria; married Richard II (1396); after Richard's death, she returned to France (1401); married Charles d'Orléans, Count of Angoulême (1404).
RICH2: II, 1.

Isabella, saintly heroine; sister of Claudio; entered a nunnery; object of Angelo's lust; rescued by and married to the Duke, after being used as bait to catch Angelo; "continues to be un-amiable"—(Coleridge).

Meas: I, 4.

Isidore, Timon owes him money; sends his servant to collect.

Timon: II, 2.

Isis, Egyptian goddess of the moon; originally goddess of the earth and fertility; sister and wife of Osiris, mother of Horus; sometimes shown with the head of a cow.

A&C: Charmian, I, 2, 70.

iwis, certainly, assuredly.

Shrew: Katherina, I, 1, 62.
MerV: Aragon, II, 9, 68.
Per: Gower, II, Prologue, 2—*i-wis*.

J

jack, knave, rogue, lowly rascal.
TEMP: Stephano, IV, 1, 198.
A&C: Antony, III, 13, 93.
COR: Menenius, V, 2, 67.

jack, leather drinking jug.
SHREW: Grumio, IV, 1, 51—
pun on boy or manservant.

jack, bowling term; small bowl
or ball known as the "jack" or
"mistress" is the target at which
players aim their bowl or bowling ball.
CYM: Cloten, II, 1, 2.

jack, key of virginal, a musical
instrument.
SONNET: CXXVIII, 5.

jack-a-Lent, decorated puppet,
set up for the boys to throw
things at during Lent; despic-
able person; butt.
MWW: Mrs. Page, III, 3, 27.

jackanapes, ape; performing
monkeys rode horseback; con-
ceited, base coxcomb.
HEN5: King, V, 2, 148.
ALL'SW: Diana, III, 5, 88.
CYM: Cloten, II, 1, 4.

Jack o' th' clock, a mechanical
figure which strikes the hours
of a clock at set intervals.
RICH2: Richard, V, 5, 60.
TIMON: Timon, III, 6, 107.
RICH3: Richard, IV, 2, 116.

Jack-slave, low fellow.
CYM: Cloten, II, 1, 22. See
JACK and JACKANAPES.

Jacob, story from Genesis (30:
35-43).
MERV: Shylock, I, 3, 72.

jade, nag, term for a horse that

has been ill-treated or is old
and wornout; trick, fool.
HAM: Hamlet, III, 2, 253.
RICH2: Richard, III, 3, 179.
TWN: Malvolio, II, 5, 179.

jade's trick, evasion; slipping out
of the halter; quitting just when
the race is getting under way;
vicious action of bad-tempered
nag.
ADO: Beatrice, I, 1, 145.
ALL'SW: Clown, IV, 5, 64.

Jailer, keeper of Palamon and
Arcite; father of the girl who
frees the former.
2NK: II, 1.

Jailer's Daughter, loves Palamon,
whom she frees from prison;
goes mad when she thinks that
she has caused the deaths of
Palamon and her father; saved
by her "wooer" who pretends
to be Palamon.
2NK: II, 1.

jakes, privy, WC; pronunciation
of Jaques.
LEAR: Kent, II, 2, 72.

Jamy, Scottish captain; talks with
Fluellen and Macmorris at the
siege of Harfleur.
HEN5: III, 2.

jangling, wrangling, boisterous
arguments or quarreling.
MND: Puck, III, 3, 353.

Janus, two-faced Roman god;
guardian of doors, gates and
entrances; faces, one smiling
and one frowning, look in opposite directions.
MERV: Solanio, I, 1, 50.
OTH: Iago, I, 2, 33.

Japhet, Japheth, son of Noah;

believed common ancestor of all European peoples.

2H4: Prince, II, 2, 128.

Jaquenetta, country wench; Costard, rival of Don Armado for her affections, is imprisoned for "consorting" with her.

LLL: I, 2.

Jaques, cynical lord attending the banished Duke; insists on Touchstone's marriage to Audrey; "can suck melancholy out of a song as a weasel sucks eggs"; "only purely contemplative character in Shakespeare. He thinks, and does nothing. . . . He is the prince of philosophical idlers; his only passion is thought; he sets no value upon anything but as it serves as food for reflection."—(Hazlitt.)

AYL: II, 5.

Jaques de Boys, second son of Sir Rowland de Boys, elder brother of Orlando; appears at end of play to announce restoration of his lands to the banished Duke.

AYL: V, 4.

jar, make them tick; to tick.

RICH2: Richard, V, 5, 51.
WINT: Hermione, I, 2, 43.

jauncing, bobbing or running up and down; constant or nervous prancing which causes a horse to tire.

R&J: Nurse, II, 5, 26.
RICH2: Richard, V, 5, 94.

jay, strumpet, harlot, loose or showy woman.

CYM: Imogen, III, 4, 51.
MWW: Mrs. Ford, III, 3, 43.

jealous, suspicious, skeptical, mistrustful; anxious or apprehensive.

OTH: Iago, III, 3, 147.
MND: Theseus, IV, 1, 147.
TwN: Antonio, III, 3, 8.
. . . Trifles light as air
Are to the jealous confirmations strong
As proofs of holy writ.
OTH: Iago, III, 3, 322.

jealous. See MONSTER.

jealousy
The venom clamours of a jealous woman
Poisons more deadly than a mad dog's tooth.
COFE: Lady Abbess, V, 1, 69.

O, beware, my lord, of jealousy!
It is the green-ey'd monster, which doth mock
The meat it feeds on.
OTH: Iago, III, 3, 165.

. . . the souls of all my tribe defend
From jealousy!
OTH: Iago, III, 3, 175.

. . . This jealousy
Is for a precious creature. As she's rare,
Must it be great; and as his person's mighty,
Must it be violent; and as he does conceive
He is dishonoured by a man which ever
Professed to him, why, his revenges must
In that be made more bitter.
WINT: Polixenes, I, 2, 451. See PRECIOUS.

jennet. See GENNET.
VENUS: 260.

Jephthah, famed character in the Bible (Judges II); promises Jehovah that if he is successful in his fight against the Ammonites, he would sacrifice the first person to greet him upon his return; met by his daughter, he is compelled to sacrifice her as he had vowed.

HAM: Hamlet, II, 2, 422.
3H6: Clarence, V, 1, 91.

jerkin, close-fitting leather jacket or coat.

1H4: Prince, I, 2, 48—*buff jerkin,* worn by sheriff's officers.
SHREW: Biondello, III, 2, 44.

jesses, short leather straps or thongs (sometimes made of silk or other material) which are attached to the hawk's legs and used to train and control the bird.

OTH: Othello, III, 3, 261.

Jessica, daughter of Shylock; disguises herself as a boy and elopes with Lorenzo, making sure to take some of her father's money along.

MERV: II, 3.

jest, sport; to act in a masque or play.

RICH2: Mowbray, I, 3, 95.

jest
A jest's prosperity lies in the ear
Of him that hears it, never in the tongue
Of him that makes it.

LLL: Rosaline, V, 2, 870.

jet, swagger, strut; walking with tail feathers up; bejeweled.

TWN: Fabian, II, 5, 36.
CYM: Belarius, III, 3, 5.
PER: Cleon, I, 4, 26.

jet, encroach.

TITUS: Aaron, II, 1, 64.

Jew
Hath not a Jew eyes? Hath not a Jew hands, organs, dimensions, senses, affections, passions? fed with the same food, hurt with the same weapons, subject to the same diseases, healed by the same means, warmed and cooled by the same winter and summer as a Christian is? If you prick us, do we not bleed? If you tickle us, do we not laugh? If you poison us, do we not die? And if you wrong us, shall we not revenge? If we are like you in the rest, we will resemble you in that. If a Jew wrong a Christian, what is his humility? Revenge. If a Christian wrong a Jew, what should sufferance be by Christian example? Why, revenge. The villany you teach me I will execute, and it shall go hard but I will better the instruction.

MERV: Shylock, III, 1, 61.

jewel
A jewel in a ten times barred-up chest
Is a bold spirit in a loyal breast.

RICH2: Mowbray, I, 1, 180.
See REPUTATION.

Jeweller, comes to sell his wares to Timon.

TIMON: I, 1.

Jezebel, wicked biblical queen (II Kings: 9:30) whose pride led to her own death.

TWN: Andrew, II, 5, 46.

jig, common song and dance; move with a rapid, dancing gait.

HAM: Hamlet, III, 1, 150.

jigging, rhyming; writers of doggerel.

JC: Brutus, IV, 3, 137.

Joan, common name for a country wench; originally popular name in royal families, but by the Elizabethan period it had become rustic; whore or any girl of lower class.

LLL: Berowne, III, 1, 207.
JOHN: Bastard, I, 1, 184.

Joan of Arc (la Pucelle), introduced to the Dauphin as "a holy maid"; after rejecting his love, she raises the siege of Orléans; persuades Burgundy to desert the English cause and take the side of the French; conjuring up evil spirits, she offers her body and soul for France; captured by the Duke of York; disowns her father and claims to be of royal descent and an immaculate virgin; however, upon being sentenced to burn, she reveals that she is pregnant and is carried off cursing England and the English. [Famed French heroine (c1412-31), met the Dauphin at Chinon (1429); burned at the stake as a heretic (May 30, 1431); beatification by Pope Pius X (1909), canonization by Pope Benedict XV (1920).]

1H6: I, 2.

John, Don, silent, unpleasant bastard brother of Don Pedro,

Prince of Arragon; falls in with Borachio's plan to cause trouble for the prince, Claudio, Hero etc.

ADO: I, 1.

John, King, youngest son of Henry II and Elinor of Aquitaine; seized the throne on the death of his eldest brother, Richard I (1199), in spite of the claims of Arthur, young son of his elder brother Geoffrey (whom he had killed, 1203). [Called John Lackland (1167-1216); forced to sign the Magna Carta at Runnymede (1215); died during war with France; son, Henry III, succeeded him.]

JOHN: I, 1. See KING JOHN.

john-a-dreams, simple, sleepy or dreamy character; "Sleepy Sam!"

HAM: Hamlet, II, 2, 595.

John Drum's entertainment, common phrase meaning giving a man a beating or throwing him out of doors.

ALL'SW: 1Lord, III, 6, 41.

John of Gaunt, Duke of Lancaster; father of Bolingbroke (Henry IV), first of the Lancastrian kings; loyal, yet critical of Richard; accuses the King of extravagance and folly on his deathbed; Richard seizes his estates upon his death. [1340-99, fourth son of Edward III, called "time-honored Gaunt" from Gand or Ghent, Flanders, where he was born; Earl of Richmond (1342); Duke of Lancaster (1361); created Duke of Aquitaine by Richard II (1390); by his third wife, Katherine Swynford, ancestor of the Beaufort-Tudor line (Henry VII).]

RICH2: I, 1.
2H4: Shallow, III, 2, 49.

John of Lancaster, Prince, third son of Henry IV and Mary, daughter of the Earl of Hereford; first appears at battle of Shrewsbury (1H4); captures leaders of northern rebellion (2H4) on promise to redress

their wrongs, but instead has them executed; as Regent of France (1H6) takes Orleans and Rouen, where he dies and is buried. [1389-1435; created Duke of Bedford (1414), later made Earl of Richmond; married Anne, daughter of Philip, Duke of Burgundy (1423); when Anne died (1432) married Jacqueline, daughter of Pierre, Count of St.-Pol (1433), turning Philip against him and ending French control of the English king.]

1H4: V, 1; 2H4: IV, 2; HEN5: I, 2; 1H6: I, 1.

joint. See TIME.

jointress, widow who owns joint property or estate through her marriage; equal possessor; dowager.

HAM: King, I, 2, 9.

jointure, marriage settlement given to wife; widow's share.

3H6: Lewis, III, 3, 136.
AYL: Rosalind, IV, 5, 6.
R&J: Capulet, V, 3, 297.

jolly, arrogant, insolent, brazen.

SHREW: Katherina, III, 2, 215.

jolthead, blockhead, stupid dunce.

SHREW: Petruchio, IV, 1, 169.

Jonson, Ben (Benjamin) (1572-1637). English dramatist, poet, actor, essayist; friend of Shakespeare; wrote for Henslowe, the ADMIRAL'S and Chamberlain's companies and the Children of the Chapel (1598-1602); Shakespeare acted in his first successful comedy, *Every Man in his Humour* (1598); engaged in the War of the Theatres against Marston and Dekker (1600-02) for which he wrote *Poetaster* (1601); imprisoned (again) for *Satiromastix* (1605); outstanding plays include *Volpone, or the Fox* (1606), *Epicoene, or the Silent Woman* (1609), *The Alchemist* (1610), *Bartholomew Fair* (1614) and several sucessful Court Masques; author of *A Tale of a Tub* (1633), a title used later by Swift; paid tribute to Shakespeare in several works; buried in Westminster Abbey.

jordan, chamber pot.
  1H4: 2Carrier, II, 1, 21.
  2H4: Falstaff, II, 4, 37.

Jourdain, Margery, witch; conjures up spirit for the Duchess of Gloucester; burned at the stake at Smithfield.
  2H6: I, 4.

Jourdan, Sylvester (d. 1650). English explorer; accompanied Sir George Somers, admiral of the Virginia Company, on voyage (1609); wrote *A Discovery of the Barmudas, otherwise called the Ile of Divels* (1610), used by Shakespeare for *The Tempest.*

journeymen, workers who have not mastered their trade; apprentices; used as a term of derision.
  HAM: Hamlet, III, 2, 38.
  RICH2: Bolingbroke, I, 3, 274.

Jove, Roman god, also known as Jupiter; equivalent of Greek god of gods, god of all power, Zeus. See JUPITER.
  HAM: Hamlet, III, 2, 294.
  WINT: Florizel, IV, 4, 16.
  TEMP: Prospero, V, 1, 45. See RIFTED.

jowl, dash, hurl, knock.
  HAM: Hamlet, V, 1, 84.

joys
  My plenteous joys,
  Wanton in fullness, seek to hide themselves
  In drops of sorrow.
  MACB: King, I, 4, 33.

Judas Maccabaeus, son of Mattathias the Hasmonaean; headed religious revolt against Antiochus IV (175-165 BC), resulting in a period of freedom for the Jewish people.
  LLL: Holofernes, V, 1, 125. See NINE WORTHIES.

judgment
  O judgment, thou art fled to brutish beasts,

And men have lost their reason.
  JC: Antony, III, 2, 110.

  . . . But in these cases
  We still have judgment here,
    that we but teach
  Bloody instructions, which being taught return
  To plague th' inventor.
  MACB: Macbeth, I, 7, 7.

judgments
  . . . I see men's judgments are
  A parcel of their fortunes, and
    things outward
  Do draw the inward quality
    after them
  To suffer all alike.
  A&C: Enobarbus, III, 13, 31.

Julia, continues to love the unfaithful Proteus; follows him disguised as Sebastian, a page; forgives him and they are reunited.
  2GENT: I, 2.

Juliet, daughter of Capulet; beautiful, romantic, imaginative child who dies for love.
  R&J: I, 3.

Juliet, has a child by Claudio, for which he is condemned to die; Duke finally orders Claudio to marry her.
  MEAS: I, 2.

Juliet is the sun
  But soft! What light through
    yonder window breaks?
  It is the East, and Juliet is the
    sun!
  Arise, fair sun, and kill the
    envious moon,
  Who is already sick and pale
    with grief
  That thou her maid art far more
    fair than she.
  R&J: Romeo, II, 2, 2.

Julius Caesar, The Tragedy of, written and performed c1599; registered and published 1623; source, NORTH's translation of PLUTARCH's *Lives* (1579) from the French of Jacques AMYOT (1559).

  PLOT: Upon Caesar's triumphant return from the war with Pompey, Cassius plans with

Casca, Cinna and others to win Brutus to their cause and then to assassinate the ambitious Caesar, who has been warned by a soothsayer to "beware the Ides of March." Calpurnia dreams of blood and refuses to leave her house. She pleads with her husband not to go to the Capitol, but, persuaded by Decius Brutus, he goes and is stabbed to death crying "Et tu, Brute?" to his friend Marcus Brutus.

Antony obtains permission to speak at the funeral. He manages to incense the crowd against the conspirators and they are driven from Rome. A triumvirate of Octavius, Antony and Lepidus is formed while Brutus and Cassius go to Asia Minor and join forces at Sardis. There they quarrel until news arrives that Portia, Brutus' wife, upon hearing that Octavius and Antony are advancing against the conspirators, has killed herself. The ghost of Caesar enters Brutus' tent to warn him that they will meet at Philippi (in Macedonia). Their forces defeated (42 BC), Brutus and Cassius commit suicide.

Julius Caesar, Roman Emperor. See CAESAR, Julius.
> HAM: Polonius, III, 2, 108.

jump, agree, correspond.
> OTH: 2Senator, I, 3, 5.
> TWN: Viola, V, 1, 259.
> SHREW: Tranio, I, 1, 195.

jump, uncertain chance, risk, hazard.
> A&C: Caesar, III, 8, 6.
> MACB: Macbeth, I, 7, 7.

jump, precisely, exactly.
> HAM: Marcellus, I, 1, 65.
> OTH: Iago, II, 3, 392.

junkets, dainties, sweetmeats, delicacies.
> SHREW: Baptista, III, 2, 250.

Juno, character in the masque celebrating the engagement of Ferdinand and Miranda; in ancient Roman mythology, queen of the heavens, wife and sister of Jupiter; among other functions attributed to her was her role as the goddess of womanhood, protecting women in marriage; counterpart of Hera in Greek mythology.
> TEMP: IV, 1.
> WINT: Perdita, IV, 4, 121.
> CYM: Pisanio, III, 4, 168.

Jupiter, god of the sky; chief divinity of the Romans; took the form of a bull to carry off Europa; counterpart of Jove in Greek mythology.
> WINT: Florizel, IV, 4, 27. See EUROPA.
> MWW: Falstaff, V, 5, 7.
> COR: Menenius, II, 1, 115.

just equinox, exactly equal; literally, the times when the length of days and nights are equal.
> OTH: Iago, II, 3, 129.

justice
Through tattered clothes small vices do appear;
Robes and furred gowns hide all. Plate sin with gold,
And the strong lance of justice hurtless breaks;
Arm it in rags, a pygmy's straw does pierce it.
> LEAR: Lear, IV, 6, 168.

. . . This even-handed justice
Commends th' ingredience of our poisoned chalice
To our own lips.
> MACB: Macbeth, I, 7, 10.

justice. See OFFENSE.

justs, jousts, tilting matches with lances.
> RICH2: York V, 2, 52.

jutty, projection; projecting part of a building or wall.
> MACB: Banquo, I, 6, 6.

juvenal, youth, lad.
> MND: Thisby, III, 1, 97.
> 2H4: Falstaff, I, 2, 23.
> LLL: Armado, I, 2, 8.

K

kam, wrong, in error, askew.
COR: Sicinius, III, 1, 304.

kates. See CATES.

Katherina, spirited, witty heroine; eldest daughter of Alfonso, who wants to marry her off before allowing Bianca, his favorite pampered younger daughter, to wed; cleverly establishes a relationship with Petruchio ("tamed" in public) that will lead to a successful marriage.
SHREW: I, 1.

Katherine, one of the ladies attending the Princess of France; falls in love with Dumain.
LLL: II, 1.

Katherine, Princess, daughter of Charles VI of France, marries Henry V; mother of Henry VI. [Katherine of Valois (1401-37), married Henry V (1420), after his death (1422) married Owen Tudor (c1425).]
HEN5: III, 4.

Katherine, Princess of France. See FRANCE, Princess of.

Katherine, Queen, first wife of Henry VIII; pleads for a fair trial for Buckingham; distrusts Wolsey; dies soon after Henry succeeds in divorcing her. [Katherine of Aragon, (1485-1536), daughter of Ferdinand and Isabella of Spain; married Henry's elder brother Arthur (1501) and Henry (1509); divorced (1533); Mary Tudor (Bloody Mary), who became queen (1553-58), was her only surviving child.]
HEN8: I, 2.

kecksies, kexes, plants with dry hollow stems or stalks.
HEN5: Burgundy, V, 2, 52.

keech, lump of suet or fat of slaughtered animal.
HEN8: Buckingham, I, 1, 55—allusion to the fact that Wolsey was a butcher's son.
2H4: Hostess, II, 1, 102—refers to butcher's wife.

keel, cool; prevent pot from boiling over by adding cool liquid; stirring; skim.
LLL: Winter, V, 2, 930.

keep, live, dwell, inhabit.
HAM: Polonius, II, 1, 8.

keep a farm and carters, become a country squire.
HAM: Polonius, II, 2, 167.

keep up, leave in the sheath, sheathed.
OTH: Othello, I, 2, 59.

ken, range of sight; marine measurement of 20 to 21 miles; view.
2H4: Westmoreland, IV, 1, 151.
CYM: Imogen, III, 6, 6.
LUCRECE: 1114.

Kendal green, coarse cloth made in Kendal, Westmorland; worn by working class; associated with Robin Hood and his men.
1H4: Falstaff, II, 4, 246.

kennel, gutter.
SHREW: Petruchio, IV, 3, 98.
2H6: Lieutenant, IV, 1, 71.

Kent, Earl of, honest, noble, loyal courtier; banished by the King for siding with Cordelia; disguises himself and gets into service with Lear as Caius; beats

Oswald and put in the stocks; follows Lear into the storm and manages to take him to Cordelia in the French camp at Dover; dies after the battle, saying goodbye to his beloved king; "nearest to perfect goodness of all Shakespeare's characters, and yet the most individualized"—(Coleridge).

LEAR: I, 1.

kept my square, followed a straight line or kept to the straight and narrow path; a square is a footrule in carpenter's tools.

A&C: Antony, II, 3, 7.

kern, "wild" Irish foot soldier; lightly armed; sometimes applied to Scottish highlanders.

RICH2: Richard, II, 1, 156.
HEN5: Dauphin, III, 7, 56.
MACB: Sergeant, I, 2, 13.

kersey, plain, coarse homespun cloth.

LLL: Berowne, V, 2, 413.
SHREW: Biondello, III, 2, 68.
MEAS: 1Gentleman, I, 2, 34.

kettle, abbreviated form of kettledrum.

HAM: King, V, 2, 286.

kibe, chilblain on the knee.

HAM: Hamlet, V, 1, 153.
TEMP: Antonio, II, 1, 276.
LEAR: Fool, I, 5, 9.

kickshawses, trifles, fanciful toys or amusements; from French, *quelque chose* (something).

TwN: Toby, I, 3, 122.
2H4: Shallow, V, 1, 29.

kill with kindness

This is a way to kill a wife with kindness.

SHREW: Petruchio, IV, 1, 211.

kiln-hole, fireplace; fire-hole of kiln or oven; used for making malt.

WINT: Clown, IV, 4, 247.

kin

A little more than kin, and less than kind.

HAM: Hamlet, I, 2, 65—used elsewhere in Elizabethan litera-

ture as a proverbial expression; in this case kin means nephew. See KIND, PEACE.

kind, natural in feeling or relation.

HAM: Hamlet, I, 2, 65.
SHREW: Lord, Induction, 1, 66.

kindle, bring forth, give birth, bear.

AYL: Rosalind, III, 2, 358.

kindness

Kindness in women, not their beauteous looks,
Shall win my love.

SHREW: Hortensio, IV, 2, 41.

king

A king of shreds and patches!
HAM: Hamlet, III, 4, 102.

Ay, every inch a king!
LEAR: Lear, IV, 6, 109.

"King and the Beggar," old ballad or song about King Cophetua and Zenelophon, the beggar maid he loved and married.

LLL: Armado, I, 2, 115.

King Cambyses, leading character in a melodramatic, bombastic tragedy by Thomas Preston, *Cambyses, King of Persia* (1570).

1H4: Falstaff, II, 4, 425.

kingdoms

Kingdoms are clay; our dungy earth alike
Feeds beast as man. The nobleness of life
Is to do thus [embracing]; when such a mutual pair
And such a twain can do't, in which I bind,
On pain of punishment, the world to weet
We stand up peerless.

A&C: Antony, I, 1, 35. See WEET.

The greater cantle of the world is lost
With very ignorance. We have kissed away
Kingdoms and provinces.

A&C: Scarus, III, 10, 7. See CANTLE.

King Gorboduc, legendary British king (invented by early chroniclers); portrayed in early English tragedy.

TWN: Clown, IV, 2, 16.

King John, The Life and Death of, written 1594-96; published 1623; source, *The Troublesome Raigne of Iohn King of England,* an anonymous play published in two parts, 1591, entirely rewritten by Shakespeare.

PLOT: King Philip of France sends an ambassador to King John of England demanding surrender of his crown to Arthur, Duke of Bretagne, whom he considers the rightful king. John refuses and prepares for war. The two kings meet before Angiers, prepared to fight, but war is averted by the arrangement of a marriage between the Dauphin of France and Lady Blanch, the King's niece.

However, the peace is almost immediately broken when Pandulph, the "holy legate of the Pope," threatens excommunication for Philip if he makes an alliance with the heretic John, who opposes Stephen Langton, Archbishop of Canterbury. In the battle which follows, the French are defeated, the Bastard kills Austria and John takes Arthur prisoner and sends him to England, ordering Hubert de Burgh to blind him. Hubert is unable to carry out the order, but Arthur is killed trying to escape. The nobles defect to France when they discover Arthur's body.

John is forced to yield to the Pope in an attempt to stop the Dauphin's invasion. When the English nobles learn of the Dauphin's planned treachery, they return to help the English king. However, John is poisoned by a monk and dies at Swinstead Abbey. He is succeeded by his son, Henry III.

King Lear, The Tragedy of, written and performed 1606; published 1608; sources: the old folk-tale of three daughters and the impetuous old king, their father, first appeared in GEOFFREY OF MONMOUTH's *Historia Britonum* (c1135), then in HOLINSHED's *Chronicles,* later in Spenser's *Faerie Queene* and John HIGGINS' *The Mirrour for Magistrates* (1574 edition); the anonymous play *King Leir,* performed early 1590's, registered 1594 and printed 1605; the outline of the Gloucester story from SIDNEY's *Arcadia.*

PLOT: King Lear of Britain, about to divide his kingdom equally among his three daughters, Goneril, Regan and Cordelia, is forced to change his plans when Cordelia, his youngest, refuses to make a public declaration of her love for him. He disinherits her and banishes Kent for siding with her. The King of France marries the dowerless Cordelia anyway. The Earl of Gloucester, also unperceptive, gives his land and title to Edmund, his bastard son, instead of to his natural son, Edgar, who rightfully deserves it. When Goneril and Regan refuse to keep their father, with his retinue, in their homes, the brokenhearted Lear goes out into the storm followed by the disguised Kent and the loyal Gloucester. They are met by Lear's fool and Edgar, disguised as mad Tom o' Bedlam. Gloucester warns the King's friends that his daughters are planning to take his life and urges that he be taken to Dover where invading French forces are coming to his aid.

Meanwhile, Edmund furnishes Cornwall with evidence that proves Gloucester is assisting the King and directing Cordelia's invasion and, when Edmund leaves, Cornwall puts out the old man's eyes, but is stabbed to death by a servant. Edgar finds his blind father and, without revealing his identity, becomes his guide. Cordelia finds her father and they are reconciled. However, defeated in battle, they are captured and Edmund orders Cordelia be hanged. Goneril poisons Regan in a fit of jealous rage over Edmund and when Edgar kills her lover, she stabs herself. Lear comes in with the dead Cordelia in his arms and dies in his attempt to revive her. Edgar, Albany and Kent are left to try to restore order to the kingdom.

"It is therefore, Shakespeare's greatest work, but it is not what Hazlitt called it, the best of his plays; and its comparative unpopularity is due, not merely to the extreme painfulness of the catastrophe, but in part to its dramatic defects—" (A. C. Bradley). "*King Lear* . . . is the only one of Shakespeare's plays in which personal relationship is treated as an end and not as a means; . . . to determine character rather than to have an effect upon character."—(Arthur Sewell.) "Among the tragedies of Shakespeare, *King Lear* stands out as, in the Aristotelian sense of the word, the most tragic."—(E. K. Chambers.)

King Lear, spoiled by a life of absolute power, full of pride, vanity and childish stubbornness, lacking perception in human relationships, given to violence in frustration and, in old age, losing the dignity of "kingship," Lear has created his own tragedy. Critics have likened his suffering to that of Job. "He unlearns hatred, and learns love and humility. He loses the world and gains his soul."—(Kenneth Muir.)
     LEAR: I, 1.

kings
Kings are earth's gods; in vice their law's their will;

And if Jove stray, who dares say Jove doth ill?
     PER: Pericles, I, 1, 103.

kings. See CEREMONY.

King's Company, formed by Thomas Killigrew on a patent from Charles II (1660); occupied the newly built Theatre Royal, DRURY LANE (1663); when this burned down (1672), a new theater was built by Sir Christopher Wren (1674); joined by the DUKE'S COMPANY (1682); produced *Othello, 1-Henry IV, The Merry Wives* and *Julius Caesar.*

King's Men. See Chamberlain's-King's Men in Appendix.

kings of snow
O that I were a mockery king of snow,
Standing before the sun of Bolingbroke
To melt myself away in water drops!
     RICH2: Richard, IV, 1, 260.

King Stephano, reference is to old ballad which began "King Stephen was and a worthy peer."
     TEMP: Trinculo, IV, 1, 222.
     OTH: Iago, II, 3, 92—song.

kinred (kindred), relation, cousin.
     RICH2: Bolingbroke, I, 1, 70.

kirtle, skirt, dress, gown.
     2H4: Falstaff, II, 4, 297.

kiss
Give me one kiss, I'll give it thee again,
And one for int'rest, if thou wilt have twain.
     VENUS: 209. See TWAIN.

kite, lowly or despised bird of prey; often applied to wanton women; rapacious person.
     A&C: Antony, III, 13, 89.
     WINT: Antigonus, II, 3, 185.
     HEN5: Pistol, II, 1, 80—*lazar kite of Cressid's kind,* diseased whore like Cressida who in Robert Henryson's *Testament of Cresseid* died of leprosy.

kites. See EAGLE.

knack, knickknack, trinket, plaything, trifling thing.
MND: Egeus, I, 1, 34.
WINT: Polixenes, IV, 4, 439.

knap, chew, bite; snap off bit by bit; rap, crack.
MERV: Solanio, III, 1, 10.
LEAR: Fool, II, 4, 125.

knave
. . . An honest man, sir, is able to speak for himself, when a knave is not.
2H4: Davy, V, 1, 50.

knife
. . . Come, thick night,
And pall thee in the dunnest smoke of hell,
That my keen knife see not the wound it makes,
Nor heaven peep through the blanket of the dark
To cry "Hold, hold!"
MACB: Lady Macbeth, I, 5, 51.

knitters. See SPINSTERS.

knot, company, group, band.
MWW: Ford, III, 2, 52.
JC: Cassius, III, 1, 117.

knot. See TIME.

knotgrass, common, tough weed that was believed to have stunted the growth of animals and children; got in the way of the plow.
MND: Lysander, III, 2, 329.

knots, patterned flower beds in Elizabethan formal garden.
RICH2: Gardener, III, 4, 46.

knowledge
. . . ignorance is the curse of God,
Knowledge the wing wherewith we fly to heaven . . .
2H6: Lord Say, IV, 7, 78.

Too much to know is to know naught but fame.
LLL: Berowne, I, 1, 92.

know thee not
I know thee not, old man. Fall to thy prayers,
How ill white hairs become a fool and jester!
2H4: Prince, V, 5, 51—beginning of famous speech in which Hal rejects Falstaff.

L

Labienus, Quintus Labienus, sent by Brutus and Cassius to gain the cooperation of the King of Parthia against Antony and Octavius Caesar. [Commanded army for King Orodes of Parthia.]
  A&C: Messenger, I, 2, 103.

labras, from Latin, lips.
  MWW: Pistol, I, 1, 166.

laced mutton, prostitute, strumpet, possibly tightly laced.
  2Gent: Speed, I, 1, 102.

Lacedaemon, Sparta.
  Timon: Timon, II, 2, 160.

ladder, leading off gallows platform.
  1H4: Prince, I, 2, 42.

ladder. See ambition.

Lady Lucy, Elizabeth Lucy, a mistress of Edward IV.
  Rich3: Buckingham, III, 7, 6—mistaken identity. See bastardy of Edward's children.

lady-smocks, common English wildflower, *cardamine pratensis.*
  LLL: Spring, V, 2, 905.

Laertes, son of Polonius, brother of Ophelia; young, hot-headed, impulsive and popular with the "mob," returns to Denmark from Paris to avenge the death of his father; further stirred to vengeance by his sister's madness and suicide; becomes party to Claudius' plot to kill Hamlet with a poisoned blade; both are killed, Laertes begging forgiveness for his actions as he dies.
  Ham: I, 2.

Laertes. See Ulysses.
  Titus: Marcus, I, 1, 380.

Lafew (Lafeu), aged lord, friend of the Countess; presents Helen to the King; quarrels with Parolles, warning Bertram not to trust him.
  All'sW: I, 1.

la fin couronne les œuvres, French, the end crowns the work (or justifies the means.)
  2H6: Clifford, V, 2, 28.

lamentation. See grief.

Lammastide, August 1.
  R&J: Nurse, I, 3, 15.

lampass, disease causing swelling of the palate in horses, resulting in loss of appetite.
  Shrew: Biondello, III, 2, 52.

Lancaster, Duke of. See John of Gaunt.

Lancaster, Prince John of. See John of Lancaster.

Landsdowne, Lord. See Granville, George.

Langley, Edmund of. See York, Duke of.

lanthorn, lantern; turret with windows; dome set in the roof of a building to give added light.
  MND: Moon, V, 1, 244.
  R&J: Romeo, V, 3, 84.

lap, clad, wrap.
  Macb: Ross, I, 2, 54.
  Cym: Belarius, V, 5, 360.

Lapland, legendary home in the dark north of witches and other creatures of magic.
  CofE: Antipholus S., IV, 3, 11.

lapsed, surprised and attacked, caught unawares, pounced upon.
TwN: Antonio, III, 3, 36.

lapwing, refers to the plover, a spirited bird that tries to run almost before it is hatched.
HAM: Horatio, V, 2, 193.
CofE: Adriana, IV, 2, 27.
ADO: Hero, III, 1, 24.

lard, embellish, adorn, garnish, fatten.
HAM: Ophelia, IV, 5, 37.

large, loose, free, unrestrained.
LLL: Rosaline, V, 2, 851.

lark
Hark, hark, the lark at heaven's gate sings . . .
CYM: Cloten, II, 3, 22—opening lines of song.
LLL: Spring, V, 2, 914.

Lo here the gentle lark, weary of rest,
From his moist cabinet mounts up on high
And wakes the morning, from whose silver breast
The sun ariseth in his majesty;
Who doth the world so gloriously behold
That cedar tops and hills seem burnish'd gold.
VENUS: 853.

larron, thief, robber.
MWW: Caius, I, 4, 71.

'larum, trumpet call to arms; signal for battle to begin. See ALARUM.
COR: Marcius, I, 4, 9.

lasslorn, spurned, forsaken or deserted by his love or sweetheart.
TEMP: Iris, IV, 1, 68.

latch, catch, charm, hold fast by magic or a spell.
MND: Oberon, III, 2, 36.
MACB: Ross, IV, 3, 195.
SONNET: CXVI, 6.

latten, made of latten (tin plate); soft brass.
MWW: Pistol, I, 1, 165.

Launce, clown; Proteus' servant; goes with him to Milan; known for scenes with Valentine and with his dog, Crab.

2GENT: II, 3.

Launcelot Gobbo. See GOBBO.

laund (land), glade, open space in a wood.
3H6: Sinklo, III, 1, 2.

Laura, lady to whom Petrarch wrote his love sonnets.
R&J: Mercutio, II, 4, 41. See PETRARCH.

laus Deo, bone intelligo, Latin, praise God, I understand well.
LLL: Nathaniel, V, 1, 30.

Lavatche, clown; servant of the Countess of Rossillion.
ALL'sW: I, 3.

Lavinia, chaste daughter of Titus; heroine; beloved of Bassianus who is killed; ravaged by Tamora's sons.
TITUS: I, 1.

lavish, uncontrolled, unrestrained, insolent, undisciplined.
MACB: Ross, I, 2, 57.

lavolta, lively dance for two persons; with arms intertwined, they take two steps followed by a high leap.
HEN5: Bourbon, III, 5, 33.
T&C: Troilus, IV, 4, 88—*lavolt.*

law
We must not make a scarecrow of the law,
Setting it up to fear the birds of prey,
And let it keep one shape till customs make it
Their perch, and not their terror.
MEAS: Angelo, II, 1, 1.

law and heraldry, laws; signed agreements of both common law and those regulating combat were often stamped with heraldic seals.
HAM: Horatio, I, 1, 87.

lawless resolutes, thieving ruffians, desperadoes or in modern terms gangsters.
HAM: Horatio, I, 1, 98.

lawn
Lawn as white as driven snow...
WINT: Autolycus, IV, 4, 220—beginning of selling song.

law of arms, fighting (swordplay) in the king's palace (or in the royal presence) was punishable by death; Blackstone's *Commentaries* (IV, 124).
1H6: Basset, III, 4, 38.

law of writ, following of the classical rules of the drama; possibly rehearsed performances as contrasted with extemporaneous dialogue used particularly in comedy.
HAM: Polonius, II, 2, 420. See LIBERTY.

Law Salique, Salic Law, originally folk laws and customs of the Salian Franks; term later applied to succession (to the throne) when French nobles elected Philip of Valois in order to prevent rule by a female.
HEN5: King, I, 2, 11—Henry's claim was through Isabella, daughter of Henry IV of France and wife of Edward II (Henry's great-great-grandfather).

lay, bet, wager.
LLL: Berowne, I, 1, 311.
CYM: Queen, I, 1, 174.
TwN: Olivia, III, 4, 222.

lay home to, "let him have it," be forceful or strict with, don't "mince words with."
HAM: Polonius, III, 4, 1.

lay on
. . . Lay on, Macduff,
And damned be him that first cries "Hold, enough."
MACB: Macbeth, V, 8, 33.

lazar, leper; diseased, poor person.
HEN5: Canterbury, I, 1, 15.
HAM: Hamlet, I, 5, 72.
T&C: Thersites, II, 3, 37.

lead, inner coffin or lining of the wooden coffin used in the burial of important people; to weight with lead.
1H6: Bedford, I, 1, 64.
MERV: Morocco, II, 7, 49.

lead apes in hell, proverbial expression referring to the fate of spinsters or old maids.

SHREW: Katherina, II, 1, 34.
ADO: Beatrice, II, 1, 43.

leads, rooftops covered with lead.
COR: Brutus, II, 1, 227.

league, distance of three miles.
TEMP: Stephano, III, 2, 17.
MND: Lysander, I, 1, 165.
ADO: Messenger, I, 1, 4.

leaguer, camp.
ALL'sW: 2Lord, III, 6, 28.

lean, agree, defer, submit to.
CYM: Queen, I, 1, 78.

lean and hungry look
Let me have men about me that are fat,
Sleek-headed men, and such as sleep a-nights.
Yond Cassius has a lean and hungry look.
He thinks too much. Such men are dangerous.
JC: Caesar, I, 2, 192.

Leander, lovesick young man who swam the Hellespont every night to visit the beautiful Hero; drowned in a storm; MARLOWE's poem, *Hero and Leander* (published, 1598).
ADO: Benedick, V, 2, 30.
AYL: Rosalind, IV, 1, 99.
2GENT: Valentine, I, 1, 22.

leaping house, brothel.
1H4: Prince, I, 2, 10.

Lear. See KING LEAR.

learn, teach, instruct.
HAM: Hamlet, V, 2, 9.
OTH: Desdemona, I, 3, 183.

learning
For where is any author in the world
Teaches such beauty as a woman's eye?
Learning is but an adjunct to ourself,
And where we are our learning likewise is.
Then when ourselves we see in ladies' eyes,
Do we not likewise see our learning there?
LLL: Berowne, IV, 3, 312.

learn to love
O, learn to love! The lesson is but plain,
And once made perfect, never lost again.
VENUS: 407.

leash, three; set of three greyhounds (or other dogs).
1H4: Prince, II, 4, 7.

leather-coats, russet apples.
2H4: Davy, V, 3, 43.

Le Beau, affected courtier attending Duke Frederick; announces wrestling match; advises Orlando to leave the palace.
AYL: I, 2.

Leda, wife of Tyndareus, King of Sparta; embrace by Zeus, in the shape of a swan, resulted in the birth of Pollux and Helen of Troy; also mother of Castor and Clytemnestra by her husband.
MWW: Falstaff, V, 5, 8.
SHREW: Tranio, I, 2, 244—refers to Helen.

leech, physician, doctor.
TIMON: Alcibiades, V, 4, 84.

leese, lose.
SONNET: V, 14.

leet, session of court held by the lord of the manor; court leet, district court.
SHREW: 1Manservant, Induction, 1, 89.
OTH: Iago, III, 3, 140—*leets and law days,* days when the court was literally in session.

legerity, vigor, nimbleness, alertness.
HEN5: King, IV, 1, 23.

Legh, Gerard (d. 1563). English writer on heraldry; author of *Accedens of Armorie* (1563); contains material used by Shakespeare for *King Lear* and *Love's Labour's Lost.*

Legion, Biblical reference (Mark, 5:9) to man from the tombs possessed by a host or troop of devils or fiends . . . "their name is Legion."
TWN: Toby, III, 4, 95.

leiger (lieger), resident, ambassador, representative in the court.
CYM: Queen, I, 5, 80.
MEAS: Isabella, III, 1, 59.

leman, sweetheart, lady love, paramour.
TWN: Andrew, II, 3, 26.
2H4: Silence, V, 3, 49.
MWW: Ford, IV, 2, 171.

lender. See BORROWER.

lendings, money advanced to soldiers when regular pay cannot be given to them.
RICH2: Bolingbroke I, 1, 89.

Lennox, Scottish nobleman; approves Macbeth's murder of the drunken grooms; however, after Banquo's murder and Macbeth's unusual behavior, recognizes the true situation and joins the rebellion against the king.
MACB: I, 2.

lenten entertainment, plain, bare, scanty, meager welcome; no meat was eaten during Lent.
HAM: Rosencrantz, II, 2, 328.

Leonardo, Bassanio's servant.
MERV: II, 2.

Leonato, Governor of Messina, father of Hero, uncle of Beatrice.
ADO: I, 1.

Leonatus. See POSTHUMUS.

Leonine, Dionyza's servant; persuaded by his master to kill Marina; interrupted by pirates; tells Dionyza Marina is dead; she poisons him.
PER: IV, 1.

Leontes, jealous, tyrannical King of Sicilia; husband of Hermione, father of Perdita; "I am a feather for each wind that blows" (II, 3, 153).
WINT: I, 2.

Lepidus, Marcus Aemilius, Roman political leader; "barren-spirited fellow" who witnesses Caesar's assassination (JC); tries to keep peace between Antony and Octavius (A&C); one of the triumvirate (43 BC), overthrown and imprisoned by

Octavius. [d. 13 BC; Consul (46); deposed (36)].
   JC: IV, 1; A&C: I, 4.

Le Port Blanc, the modern Port Le Blanc.
   RICH2: Northumberland, II, 1, 277.

let, impede, hinder, prevent.
   HAM: Hamlet, I, 4, 85.

lethe, death.
   JC: Antony, III, 1, 206.

Lethe, river of forgetfulness in Hades; in Greek mythology it was believed the drinking of the waters of this river would make the person forget his past life.
   HAM: Ghost, I, 5, 33.
   A&C: Pompey, II, 1, 27.
   TwN: Sebastian, IV, 1, 66.

letting blood, blood-letting or the giving of blood through a vein in the body; it was thought that the body could be purged of impurities or disease by draining out the "bad" blood on certain days and months of the year.
   RICH2: Richard, I, 1, 153.

level, clearly, plainly; guess, aim.
   HAM: King, IV, 5, 151.
   A&C: Caesar, V, 2, 339.

Leviathan, whale (Job: 41).
   MND: Oberon, II, 1, 174.

Lewis (dauphin and king of France). See LOUIS.

liable, suitable, appropriate.
   LLL: Holofernes, V, 1, 97.

libbard, old form of leopard; possibly refers to heraldic leopard on Pompey's shield or symbolic costume.
   LLL: Boyet, V, 2, 551.

liberal, lewd, obscene, licentious.
   OTH: Desdemona, II, 1, 165.
   HAM: Queen, IV, 7, 172.
   ADO: Pedro, IV, 1, 93.

liberal conceit, imaginatively and superbly created or designed, exquisitely or highly wrought, artistically conceived.
   HAM: Osric, V, 2, 160.

liberty, disputed meaning; an area outside the jurisdiction of the London corporation; evil or wicked transgressor.
   CofE: Antipholus S., I, 2, 102.
   HAM: Polonius, II, 2, 421—freedom of rules in the writing or acting of plays. See LAW OF WRIT.

liberty
A man is master of his liberty.
   CofE: Luciana, II, 1, 7.

. . . headstrong liberty is lashed to woe.
There's nothing situate under heaven's eye
But hath his bound in earth, in sea, in sky.
The beasts, the fishes, and the winged fowls
Are their males' subjects and at their controls;
Man, more divine, the master of all these,
Lord of the wide world and wild wat'ry seas,
Indued with intellectual sense and souls,
Or more preëminence than fish and fowls,
Are masters to their females, and their lords.
   CofE: Luciana, II, 1, 15.

Libya, ancient name for Africa.
   A&C: Caesar, III, 6, 69.

Lichas, servant, page or attendant to Hercules (Alcides).
   MERV: Morocco, II, 1, 32.

lictor, official, usually of lower birth or class, who worked for Roman magistrate; probably equivalent to Elizabethan beadle, who was, with other duties, in charge of prostitutes.
   A&C: Cleopatra, V, 2, 214.
   COR: S.D., II, 2.

lie. See DEGREES OF THE LIE.

liege, lord to whom allegiance and loyal service was due.
   RICH2: Mowbray, I, 1, 59.

lie i' th' throat, worst, bitterest of insults.
   HAM: Hamlet, II, 2, 601.

Lieutenant
   COR: IV, 7 (to Aufidius).

2H6: IV, 1 (navy).

Lieutenant of the Tower, when the King is rescued by Warwick, the Lieutenant begs his pardon for having kept him prisoner.
3H6: IV, 6.

life
I do not set my life at a pin's fee,
And for my soul, what can it do to that,
Being a thing immortal as itself?
HAM: Hamlet, I, 4, 65.

Give me life; which if I can save, so; if not, honour comes unlooked for, and there's an end.
1H4: Falstaff, V, 3, 62.

To-morrow, and to-morrow, and to-morrow
Creeps in this petty pace from day to day,
To the last syllable of recorded time;
And all our yesterdays have lighted fools
The way to dusty death. Out, out, brief candle!
Life's but a walking shadow, a poor player
That struts and frets his hour upon the stage,
And then is heard no more. It is a tale
Told by an idiot, full of sound and fury,
Signifying nothing.
MACB: Macbeth, V, 5, 19.

life-rendering pelican, refers to the fable, legend or belief that a pelican feeds her young with her own blood; symbol of family devotion.
HAM: Laertes, IV, 5, 146.

Ligarius, Caius, joins conspiracy against Caesar; not present at assassination. [Really Quintus Ligarius, Roman commander; follower of Pompey; defended by CICERO in plea to Caesar. PLUTARCH calls him Caius and Shakespeare copied the mistake —(Halliday).]
JC: II, 1.

liggens, dialect word meaning

drinking capacity or hollow leg; with God's, an oath.
2H4: Shallow, V, 3, 69.

light
Why, all delights are vain, but that most vain
Which, with pain purchased, doth inherit pain:
As, painfully to pore upon a book
To seek the light of truth while truth the while
Doth falsely blind the eyesight of his look.
Light, seeking light, doth light of light beguile.
So, ere you find where light in darkness lies,
Your light grows dark by losing of your eyes.
LLL: Berowne, I, 1, 72.

Lilies that fester. See POWER TO HURT.

lily. See HAND.

Limander, mistaken reference to Leander, of Leander and Hero, the lovers.
MND: Pyramus, V, 1, 199. See LEANDER.

limbeck, the cap (alembic) of a still which catches the fumes as they rise during distillation.
MACB: Lady Macbeth, I, 7, 67.
SONNET: CXIX, 2.

limber, feeble, limp, flabby; flexible.
WINT: Hermione, I, 2, 47.

limbmeal, limb from limb.
CYM: Posthumus, II, 4, 147.

lime, put into wine to make it taste better, give it sparkle and preserve it; wine, doctored or adulterated, by lime.
1H4: Falstaff, II, 4, 137.
MWW: Host, I, 3, 14.

lime, birdlime, which was a sticky substance, good for people who drop things and for thieves; thus the expression "sticky fingers."
TEMP: Trinculo, IV, 1, 246.
2GENT: Proteus, III, 2, 68.
HAM: King, III, 3, 68—*limed,*

snared, trapped or caught with lime.

limit, appoint.
MACB: Macduff: II, 3, 56.

limn, picture, paint.
AYL: Duke Senior, II, 7, 194.

Lincoln, Bishop of, reminded by the King that he advised his divorce from Katherine. [John Longland.]
HEN8: II, 4.

Lincoln's Inn Fields, area laid out by Inigo Jones (c1620) west of the city; theater built there for D'Avenant's DUKE'S COMPANY (1661); KING'S COMPANY occupied the theater (1672); used by Betterton and other companies (1695-1705); another small theater was opened in Lincoln's Inn Fields (1714) built by Christopher Rich and opened by John Rich (1714); Italian operas were given there (1734); demolished (1848); with the DRURY LANE, considered the most important theater in London.

line, lime or linden tree; possibly a clothesline made of hair.
TEMP: Prospero, IV, 1, 193.

line, support, aid, reinforce, strengthen.
1H4: Lady, II, 3, 86.
MACB: Angus, I, 3, 112.
HEN5: French King, II, 4, 7.

lineaments, features.
AYL: Rosalind, III, 5, 56.
RICH3: Buckingham, III, 7, 12.

ling, salted cod fish.
ALL'sW: Countess, III, 2, 14.

link, small torch (of pitch).
1H4: Falstaff, III, 3, 48.
SHREW: Grumio, IV, 1, 137—smoke used for blacking.

linsey-woolsey, jargon, nonsense, hodgepodge; literally cloth made of linen and wool or wool and flax.
ALL'sW: 2Lord, IV, 1, 13.

linstock, gunner's staff or long stick (3 ft.) with forked head

that held lighted match or torch that set off the cannon.
HEN5: Chorus, Prologue, III, 33.
1H6: S.D., I, 4, following line 56.

lion, reference to the lion as the symbol of the kings of England.
RICH2: Richard, I, 1, 174—*Lions make leopards tame,* kings outrank nobles.

Lion, in interlude.
MND: V, 1. See SNUG.

lion
'Tis better playing with a lion's whelp
Than with an old one dying.
A&C: Enobarbus, III, 13, 94.

The lion will not touch the true prince. Instinct is a great matter.
1H4: Falstaff, II, 4, 300—popular belief.

. . . a lion among ladies is a most dreadful thing.
MND: Bottom, III, 1, 31.

lion-mettled
Be lion-mettled, proud, and take no care
Who chafes, who frets, or where conspirers are.
Macbeth shall never vanquish'd be until
Great Birnam Wood to high Dunsinane Hill
Shall come against him.
MACB: 3rd Apparition, IV, 1, 90.
See CROWNED CHILD, BIRNAM WOOD, DUNSINANE, METAL.

Lipsbury Pinfold, explained as Liptown (lips, jaw) Pinfold (pound), an enclosure for stray cattle or other animals; between my teeth or "in my power"; also a good spot for a fight because neither opponent could get away.
LEAR: Kent, II, 2, 10.

liquor, grease, oil, waterproofed (boots).
1H4: Gadshill, II, 1, 94.
MWW: Falstaff, IV, 5, 101.

liquors

> Though I look old, yet I am
> strong and lusty;
> For in my youth I never did
> apply
> Hot and rebellious liquors in my
> blood . . .

AYL: Adam, II, 3, 47.

list, urge, desire, wish, like.
    OTH: Iago, II, 1, 105.
    ADO: Margaret, III, 4, 83.
    SHREW: Gremio, III, 2, 167.

list, end, boundary, limit, objective; barrier enclosing a course, combat ground.
    TWN: Viola, III, 1, 86.
    RICH2: Duchess of Gloucester, I, 2, 52.
    1H4: Hotspur, IV, 1, 51.

list, selvage, strip of cloth at border; waste material at end of weaving.
    SHREW: Biondello, III, 2, 69.
    MEAS: Lucio, I, 2, 31.

lists, roster or roll call of soldiers.
    HAM: King, I, 2, 32.

lither, yielding, supple, pliant, soft.
    1H6: Talbot, IV, 7, 21.

live (lief), as soon as, leave.
    HAM: Hamlet, III, 2, 4.

liver, desire, ardor; the liver was believed the source of sexual passion.
    TEMP: Ferdinand, IV, 1, 56.
    TWN: Duke, I, 1, 37.
    LLL: Berowne, IV, 3, 74—
    liver vein, style of love.

Livia, wife of Octavius Caesar.
    A&C: Cleopatra, V, 2, 169.

Livy (Titus Livius) (59 BC-AD 17). Roman historian; considered the most important prose writer in the age of Augustus; his history of Rome, the *Annales* (142 books, only 35 remain) contains the story of *Lucrece* (I:56-60) and the fable of the belly told by Menenius in *Coriolanus*.

loach, small fish carrying parasites; believed to breed fleas.
    1H4: 2Carrier, II, 1, 23.

loam, mixture of clay and sand; also used in plastering walls.
    HAM: Hamlet, V, 1, 233.
    RICH2: Mowbray, I, 1, 179.

lob, droop, hang.
    HEN5: Grandpré, IV, 2, 47.

lob of spirits, Puck, though he could "put a girdle round the earth in forty minutes," was heavy and sluggish (or the country lout) compared to the other fairies; he was the lubber of the spirit group; Shakespeare's "lob of spirits" is the same as "lubbar fiend," used by Milton in *L'Allegro*.
    MND: Fairy, II, 1, 16.

lockram, coarse linen fabric.
    COR: Brutus, II, 1, 225.

locusts, fruit of the carob tree; exact meaning not known.
    OTH: Iago, I, 3, 354. See FOOD.

lodestar, guiding star; the lodestar is the polestar which is used by mariners as a guide.
    MND: Helena, I, 1, 183.

lodge, thresh, beat until flat.
    RICH2: Richard, III, 3, 162.

Lodge, Thomas (c1558-1625). English dramatist, novelist, poet, physician; one of the UNIVERSITY WITS; his novel, *Rosalynde: Euphues Golden Legacy* (1590), written during his voyage to the Canaries (1588), the source of *As You Like It*; *Venus and Adonis* probably owes something to his *Scilla's Metamorphosis* (pub., 1589), a volume of poetry.

Lodovico, Venetian noble; kinsman of Desdemona's father, Brabantio; helps Cassio when he is attacked by Roderigo; discovers Iago's guilt and promises to make him pay heavily for his crimes.
    OTH: IV, 1.

Lodowick, Friar. See FRIAR LODOWICK.

loggets, game in which little logs or small pieces of wood are thrown at a stake stuck into the ground or on a floor or at a wooden wheel; similar to modern game of quoits or horseshoes.

HAM: Hamlet, V, 1, 101.

London Stone, ancient rounded block of stone; landmark in Cannon Street, London; parts of it were built into the street wall of St. Swithin's Church.

2H6: Cade, IV, 6, 2.

Longaville, one of the three lords attending the King of Navarre; falls in love with Maria. [Henry, Duc de Longueville, supporter of Henry of Navarre in his fight for the French crown (1589-93).]

LLL: I, 1.

long heath, a form of tall heather or rough grass that grows on wastelands.

TEMP: Gonzalo, I, 1, 69.

long purples, early purple orchids thought to represent the "cold hand of death."

HAM: Queen, IV, 7, 171.

long-staff sixpenny strikers, petty thieves, using long cudgels or staves, who hold up (or knock down) a traveler for sixpence.

1H4: Gadshill, II, 1, 82.

loofed (luffed), bring ship's head up into the wind.

A&C: Scarus, III, 10, 18.

lop, small branches and twigs of trees.

HEN8: King, I, 2, 96.

Lord Admiral's Men. See ADMIRAL'S MEN.

Lord Chamberlain, at Wolsey's feast, presents Anne Bullen to the King; arranges Elizabeth's christening. [Lord Chamberlains at the time were Charles Somerset, Earl of Worcester (1509-26) and Lord Sands (1526-43).]

HEN8: I, 3.

Lord Chamberlain's Men. See Chamberlain-King's Men in Appendix.

Lord Chancellor, president of the

Council before whom Cranmer is arraigned. [Actually Sir Thomas Audley, Lord Chancellor (1533-44); Speaker of House of Commons (1529), presided over "Black Parliament" which abolished papal authority in England. Sir Thomas More had resigned the chancellorship, May, 1532.]

HEN8: V, 3.

Lord Chief Justice, ordered by young Henry V to banish Falstaff. [Sir William Gascoigne (c1350-1419), appointed by Henry IV (c1400); imprisoned the young prince when he struck him.]

2H4: I, 2.

Lord Scroop, William Scrope, Earl of Wiltshire; executed (1399) for treason; HOLINSHED mistaken in making him the Archbishop's brother.

1H4: Worcester, I, 3, 271.

Lorenzo, musician friend of Bassanio; elopes with Shylock's daughter, Jessica.

MERV: I, 1.

lose your voice, in modern terms, to waste your breath.

HAM: King, I, 2, 45.

lots to blanks, the odds are in your favor, more than likely, practically certain; lots were lottery tickets.

COR: Menenius, V, 2, 10.

Louis, the Dauphin, son of Philip II of France. [1187-1226, called Le Lion; happily married to Blanche of Castile, granddaughter of Henry II of England (1200); offered English crown by nobles who opposed John; lost out to Henry III; returned to France (1217); succeeded as Louis VIII (1223).]

JOHN: II, 1.

Louis, the Dauphin, son of Charles VI; boasts of his coming victory, but is defeated at

Agincourt (although actually he
was not there). [1396-1415.]
Hen5: II, 4.

Louis XI, King of France; promises to help Margaret against
Edward IV; then, persuaded by
Warwick that Edward should
marry Lady Bona, he switches
his allegiance. [1423-83, succeeded his father, Charles VII
(1461); grandson of Charles
VI, first cousin of Henry VI and
Queen Margaret; unhappily married to Margaret of Scotland,
daughter of James I; as Dauphin, involved in plots against
the King; quarreled with Agnes
Sorel, the king's mistress; fled
to Burgundy (1456); nobles
under Charles the Bold rebelled
against him (1465); truce declared; supported Lancastrians
in England.]
3H6: III, 3.

love

. . . loving goes by haps;
Some Cupid kills with arrows,
some with traps.
Ado: Hero, III, 1, 106. See
hap.

There's beggary in love that can
be reckoned.
A&C: Antony, I, 1, 15.

Let love, being light, be drowned
if she sink.
CofE: Antipholus S., III, 2, 52.

I shall be loved when I am
lacked.
Cor: Coriolanus, IV, 1, 15.

Love's reason's without reason.
Cym: Arviragus, IV, 2, 22.

This is the very ecstasy of love,
Whose violent property fordoes
itself
And leads the will to desperate
undertakings
As oft as any passion under
heaven
That does afflict our natures.
Ham: Polonius, II, 1, 102. See
property fordoes.

Where love is great, the littlest
doubts are fear;

Where little fears grow great,
great love grows there.
Ham: Player Queen, III, 2,
181.

For 'tis a question left us yet to
prove,
Whether love lead fortune, or
else fortune love.
Ham: Player King, III, 2, 212.

Nature is fine in love, and where
'tis fine,
It sends some precious instance
of itself
After the thing it loves.
Ham: Ophelia, IV, 5, 161—
does not appear in Quarto.

. . . Love's not love
When it is mingled with regards
that stand
Aloof from th' entire point. Will
you have her?
She is herself a dowry.
Lear: Burgundy, I, 1, 236.

And how can that be true love
which is falsely attempted? Love
is a familiar; Love is a devil.
There is no evil angel but Love.
LLL: Armado, I, 2, 176. See
familiar.

Love, whose month is ever May,
Spied a blossom passing fair
Playing in the wanton air.
LLL: Dumain, IV, 3, 102.

But love, first learned in a lady's
eyes,
Lives not alone immured in the
brain,
But with the motion of all elements
Courses as swift as thought in
every power,
And gives to every power a
double power
Above their functions and their
offices.
LLL: Berowne, IV, 3, 327.

As love is full of unbefitting
strains,
All wanton as a child, skipping
and vain,
Formed by the eye and therefore, like the eye,
Full of straying shapes, of habits, and of forms,

Varying in subjects as the eye
doth roll
To every varied object in his
glance.
LLL: Berowne, V, 2, 769. See
STRAIN.

The love that follows us some-
time is our trouble,
Which still we thank as love.
MACB: King, I, 6, 11.

Love looks not with the eyes,
but with the mind;
And therefore is winged Cupid
painted blind.
MND: Helena, I, 1, 234.

"Love like a shadow flies when
substance love pursues,
Pursuing that that flies, and flying what pursues."
MWW: Ford, II, 2, 215.

In love the heavens themselves
do guide the state;
Money buys lands, and wives
are sold by fate.
MWW: Ford, V, 5, 245.

(. . . base men being in love have
then a nobility in their natures
more than is native to them) . . .
OTH: Iago, II, 1, 217.

Love is a smoke raised with the
fume of sighs;
Being purged, a fire sparkling in
lovers' eyes;
Being vexed, a sea nourish'd
with lovers' tears.
What is it else? A madness most
discreet,
A choking gall, and a preserv-
ing sweet.
R&J: Romeo, I, 1, 197.

. . . I love thee in such sort
As, thou being mine, mine is thy
good report.
SONNET: XXXVI, 13; XCVI, 13.

This thou perceiv'st, which
makes thy love more strong,
To love that well which thou
must leave ere long.
SONNET: LXXIII, 13.

. . . Love is not love
Which alters when it alteration
finds,

Or bends with the remover to
remove.
SONNET: CXVI, 2. See MAR-
RIAGE.

Love's not Time's fool, though
rosy lips and cheeks
Within his bending sickle's com-
pass come.
SONNET: CXVI, 9. See TIME'S
FOOL.

Love alters not with his brief
hours and weeks
But bears it out even to the edge
of doom.
SONNET: CXVI, 11.

Love, love, nothing but love,
still love, still more!
T&C: Pandarus, III, 1, 125—
beginning of song.

O spirit of love, how quick and
fresh art thou!
That, notwithstanding thy ca-
pacity
Receiveth as the sea, naught
enters there,
Of what validity and pitch
soe'er,
But falls into abatement and
low price
Even in a minute!
TwN: Duke, I, 1, 9.

What is love? 'Tis not hereafter;
Present mirth hath present
laughter . . .
TwN: Clown, II, 3, 48—part
of song.

. . . If ever thou shalt love,
In the sweet pangs of it remem-
ber me . . .
TwN: Duke, II, 4, 15.

Love sought is good, but given
unsought is better.
TwN: Olivia, III, 1, 168.

To be in love, where scorn is
bought with groans;
Coy looks with heart-sore sighs;
one fading moment's mirth
With twenty watchful, weary,
tedious nights: . . .
2GENT: Valentine, I, 1, 29.

Love is a spirit all compact of
fire,

Not gross to sink, but light, and
    will aspire.
    VENUS: 149.

love (compared to a snail)
Or as the snail, whose tender
    horns being hit,
Shrinks backward in his shelly
    cave with pain,
And there, all smooth'red up, in
    shade doth sit,
Long after fearing to creep forth
    again . . .
    VENUS: 1033.

love-in-idleness, one of many
names for the wild flower—the
pansy; it is also suggested that
the lines may come from the
change of mulberries from white
to purple by the blood of Pyramus (OVID, *Metamorphoses*, IV,
125-27).
    MND: Oberon, II, 1, 168. See
    BOLT OF CUPID.

love is blind
But love is blind, and lovers
    cannot see
The pretty follies that them-
    selves commit . . .
    MERV: Jessica, II, 6, 36.

Lovel, Lord, willing agent of
Richard; ordered to execute
Hastings, he returns with his
head. [d. c1487. Sir Francis
Lovel, created Viscount (1483).]
    RICH3: III, 4.

Lovell, Sir Thomas, Chancellor
of the Exchequer; courtier in
the King's confidence; sides with
Gardiner against Cranmer. [d.
1524.]
    HEN8: I, 3.

love of country. See ROME.

lover
It was a lover and his lass—
    AYL: Pages, V, 2, 17—begin-
    ning of song.

If thou rememb'rest not the
    slightest folly
That ever love did make thee
    run into,
Thou hast not loved.
Or if thou hast not sat as I do
    now,

Wearing thy hearer in thy mis-
    tress' praise,
Thou hast not loved.
Or if thou hast not broke from
    company
Abruptly, as my passion now
    makes me,
Thou hast not loved.
    AYL: Silvius, II, 4, 33.

A lover may bestride the gossa-
    mer
That idles in the wanton summer
    air,
And yet not fall; so light is
    vanity.
    R&J: Romeo, II, 6, 18.

lovers
Lovers can see to do their amo-
    rous rites
By their own beauties; or, if love
    be blind,
It best agrees with night.
    R&J: Juliet, III, 2, 8.

lovers and madmen
Lovers and madmen have such
    seething brains,
Such shaping fantasies, that ap-
    prehend
More than cool reason ever
    comprehends.
    MND: Theseus, V, 1, 4. See
    SEETHING, FANTASY.

Lover's Complaint, A, poem published in Thomas Thorpe's edition of the *Sonnets* (1609);
Shakespeare's authorship of the
poem has been generally rejected.

lover's eyes
It adds a precious seeing to the
    eye:
A lover's eyes will gaze an eagle
    blind.
    LLL: Berowne, IV, 3, 333.

lover's fee, usually three kisses.
    MND: Puck, III, 2, 113.

love's feeling
Love's feeling is more soft and
    sensible
Than are the tender horns of
    cockled snails.
    LLL: Berowne, IV, 3, 337.

Love's heralds

. . . Love's heralds should be thoughts,

Which ten times faster glide than the sun's beams

Driving back shadows over lowering hills.

Therefore do nimble-pinioned doves draw Love,

And therefore hath the windswift Cupid wings.

R&J: Juliet, II, 5, 4. See LOWERING.

Love's Labour's Lost, written 1594-95; published 1598; although several characters are inspired by the Italian *commedia dell'arte,* the play seems to be entirely Shakespeare's own.

PLOT: Ferdinand, King of Navarre, and three of his attending lords: Biron, Longaville and Dumain, take an oath to study for three years and to completely avoid the company of women. However, the Princess of France arrives at the court and the King promptly falls in love with her, while the others are immediately attracted to ladies of her retinue. There is much writing of poetry and expressions of love. Don Armado and Costard, rivals for the love of Jaquenetta, join Holofernes and Nathaniel in presenting the interlude of the NINE WORTHIES. The Princess is forced to return home when learning that her father has died, but the women promise to return in a year and a day to marry their lovers.

love's light wings

With love's light wings did I o'erperch these walls;

For stony limits cannot hold love out,

And what love can do, that dares love attempt.

R&J: Romeo, II, 2, 66.

love's mind

Nor hath Love's mind of any judgment taste;

Wings, and no eyes, figure unheedy haste.

And therefore is Love said to be a child,

Because in choice he is so oft beguil'd.

MND: Helena, I, 1, 236.

love speaks

And when Love speaks, the voice of all the gods

Make heaven drowsy with the harmony.

Never durst poet touch a pen to write

Until his ink were temp'red with Love's sighs.

LLL: Berowne, IV, 3, 344.

love vs lust

"Call it not love, for Love to heaven is fled

Since sweating Lust on earth usurp'd his name;

* * *

"Love comforteth like sunshine after rain,

But Lust's effect is tempest after sun.

Love's gentle spring doth always fresh remain;

Lust's winter comes ere summer half be done.

Love surfeits not, Lust like a glutton dies;

Love is all truth, Lust full of forged lies. . . ."

VENUS: 793, 799.

low, one of humble birth or rank.
MND: Hermia, I, 1, 136.

low countries, tail end, lower or private parts of the body.
2H4: Prince, II, 2, 25.

lowereth (loureth), threatens, darkens.
COFE: Luciana, II, 2, 86.

lowering (louring), threatening, foreboding; frowning.
RICH2: Richard, I, 3, 187.
R&J: Juliet, II, 5, 6.

lown (loon) lout, knave, rascal.
OTH: Iago, II, 3, 95.

loyalty

My heart doth joy that yet in all my life

I found no man but he was true to me.

JC: Brutus, V, 5, 34.

lozel, rascal, scoundrel, rogue.

WINT: Leontes, II, 3, 108.

lubber. See LOB OF SPIRITS.

TWN: Clown, IV, 1, 15.

Lubber's Head in Lumbert Street, the Leopard's Head in Lombard Street; the silkman's shop had a leopard head sign.

2H4: Hostess, II, 1, 31.

Lucan (Marcus Annaeus Lucanus) (39-65). Roman poet; author of the *Pharsalia* (10 books, incomplete), an epic poem on the civil war between Caesar and Pompey, possibly used as a source by Shakespeare.

luce, pike (fish).

MWW: Slender, I, 1, 16—refers to arms of Sir Thomas Lucy of Charlecote, Stratford.

Luce, Adriana's servant.

CofE: III, 1.

Lucentio, son of Vincentio of Pisa; successful suitor of Bianca.

SHREW: I, 1.

Lucetta, Julia's caustic lady-in-waiting; supports Proteus in his suit for her hand.

2GENT: I, 2.

Lucian (c120-c200). Greek satirist; known for satirical dialogues, *Auction of Philosophers* and *Timon the Misanthrope*, which may have been used (in a Latin or French translation) by Shakespeare.

Luciana, unmarried sister of Adriana; confuses Antipholus of Syracuse with her twin brother, her sister's husband, and is shocked when he makes love to her.

CofE: II, 1.

Lucianus, king's nephew in MOUSETRAP play.

HAM: III, 2.

Lucilius, friend of Brutus and Cassius; captured at Philippi.

JC: IV, 2.

Lucilius, servant to Timon, who gives him enough money to become a suitor to the girl he loves.

TIMON: I, 1.

Lucina, goddess of childbirth.

CYM: Mother, V, 4, 43.
PER: Antiochus, I, 1, 8.

Lucio, dissolute friend of Claudio; asks Isabella to intercede for her brother with Angelo; slanders the Duke.

MEAS: I, 2.

Lucius, eldest son of Titus; after the havoc wrought on his family, he goes to the Goths to raise an army to fight against Saturninus; kills the Emperor and is hailed as ruler; orders Tamora's body thrown to the beasts and Aaron tortured.

TITUS: I, 1.

Lucius, young, son of above, gives the ravishers of Lavinia a present of arrows wrapped in a threatening note from Titus.

TITUS: III, 2.

Lucius, boy servant to Brutus; sent by Portia to see that all is well with her husband; falls asleep on duty.

JC: II, 1.

Lucius, lord, refuses to lend Timon money, although he had given Lucius a present of horses, trapped in silver.

TIMON: III, 2.

Lucius, servant of above, called by his name.

TIMON: III, 4.

Lucius Tarquinius (Superbus), last legendary king of Rome (534-510 BC); tyrant; rape of Lucretia by his son caused people to revolt; Tarquins expelled from the city.

LUCRECE: Argument, 1.

Lucrece, portrait head of Lucrece appeared on Olivia's seal (intaglio).

TWN: Malvolio, II, 5, 104.
SHREW: Petruchio, II, 1, 298.

Lucrece, The Rape of, narrative poem probably written between April, 1593 and May, 1594; dedicated to the Right Honourable Henry Wriothesley, Earl of Southampton and Baron of Titchfield; registered and published 1594; source, OVID's *Fasti* (II, 711-852) and Livy (I, 56-60); novella by BANDELLO translated by BELLEFOREST; CHAUCER, *The Legend of Good Women;* used by PAINTER in *Palace of Pleasure* (1566-67). (Although Shakespeare knew Latin and actually owes nothing to Painter or Chaucer.)

PLOT: Lucrece, the virtuous, faithful wife of Collatine, is raped in his absence by his lecherous friend, Tarquin. Upon her husband's return, she tells him what has happened and then stabs herself. Brutus (Lucius Junius) urges not grief but revenge. The weakness of the tragedy is in the heroine's remorseless eloquence; she talks too much. Although there are passages of great brilliance, atmosphere and power, *Lucrece* has been considered, by most critics, an artistic failure.

Lucullus, lord; "trencher-friend" who refuses to lend Timon money, although he had given him prize greyhounds; one of those invited to Timon's mock banquet.
TIMON: III, 1.

Lucy, Sir Thomas (1532-1600); English landowner in Warwickshire; justice of the peace; alleged (by Nicholas Rowe, 1710) to have prosecuted Shakespeare (c1585) for stealing deer in his park at Charlecote; it is believed that Shakespeare retaliated by modeling his character Justice Shallow after Lucy.

Lucy, Sir William, English leader; accuses York and Somerset of causing Talbot's death.
1H6: IV, 3.

Ludlow, castle in Shropshire, seat of the Lord President of Wales.
RICH3: Buckingham, II, 2, 121.

Ludovico. See LODOVICO.

Lud's town, London; originally Troynovant, it was renamed Caerlud or Lud's town after Cymbeline's grandfather, King Lud.
CYM: Queen, III, 1, 32.

lug, bait, led.
1H4: Falstaff, I, 2, 83—refers to bear torn by mastiff.

luggage, excess baggage, burdens.
TEMP: Caliban, IV, 1, 231.

lunes, fits of frenzy, lunacy or madness; reference to Luna, goddess of the moon, who was believed to cause madness (moon-mad).
WINT: Paulina, II, 2, 30.

Lupercal, feast of Lupercalia was held on February 15 in Rome in honor of Lupercus (Pan) protector of shepherds and farmers.
JC: Marullus, I, 1, 72.

lurch, go off with, rob, steal.
COR: Cominius, II, 2, 105.

lust

Fie on sinful fantasy!
Fie on lust and luxury!
Lust is but a bloody fire,
Kindled with unchaste desire,
Fed in heart, whose flames aspire
As thought do blow them, higher and higher.
Pinch him, fairies, mutually;
Pinch him for his villany;
Pinch him and burn him and turn him about
Till candles and starlight and moonshine be out.
MWW: Queen, V, 5, 97—song.

lustick (lustig), from Dutch, lively, brisk, lustily.
ALL'sW: Lafew, II, 3, 47.

lux tua vita mihi, Latin, thy light is life to me; motto on the shield of a knight of Sparta.
PER: Thaisa, II, 2, 21.

luxury, lust, passionate desire.
HAM: Ghost, I, 5, 83.
A&C: Antony, III, 13, 120—
luxuriously.
HEN5: Dauphin, III, 5, 6.

Lychorida, Marina's nurse.
PER: III, 1.

Lycurguses, lawgivers or law-makers; Lycurgus, responsible for the constitution and the laws of Sparta, credited with being an unusually wise man.
COR: Menenius, II, 1, 60.

Lydgate, John (c1370-c1451). English poet; considered himself a disciple of CHAUCER; ordained as a priest (1397); his *Troy Book,* in heroic couplets (1412-20, first printed, 1513) may have been the source of the Greek scenes in *Troilus and Cressida.*

Lydia, one of the most important powers in western Asia Minor (7th to 6th centuries BC.).
A&C: Messenger, I, 2, 107.

Lyly, John (c1554-1606). English dramatist, novelist; most important work, *Euphues, or the Anatomy of Wit* (1579) and its sequel, *Euphues and his England* (1580); brought into popularity his "new style"—euphuism, an exaggerated, affected use of figures of speech; wrote for Paul's boys; *Love's Labour's Lost* shows Shakespeare's indebtedness to Lyly.

lym, lymmer, species of bloodhound.
LEAR: Edgar, III, 6, 72.

Lymoges. See AUSTRIA, Duke of.

Lysander, Athenian; in love with Hermia; runs off with her to the forest.
MND: I, 1.

Lysimachus, governor of Mytilene; finds Marina in the brothel; gets her to see the speechless Pericles, assured she can help him; Pericles announces Lysimachus and Marina will be married at Pentapolis.
PER: IV, 6.

Mab, Queen, fairy queen; also appears in JONSON'S *Althorp Entertainment* (1603).

R&J: Mercutio, I, 4, 53.

Macbeth, The Tragedy of, written 1605-6; performed 1611; registered and published 1623; source, HOLINSHED (Scottish history comes from Latin *Scotorum Historiae* of Hector BOECE) with changes made for dramatic effect.

PLOT: Macbeth and Banquo, generals in the army of Duncan, King of Scotland, are returning from the successful suppression of Scottish (Macdonwald) and Norwegian rebels when they meet three witches. Macbeth is hailed as Thane of Glamis and Cawdor and "king hereafter" by the witches, while Banquo is told he will be the begetter of kings, though he will never rule himself. News arrives that Macbeth has indeed been made Thane of Cawdor and he reveals his ambition to make the rest of the prophecy come true.

At Inverness, Lady Macbeth, after receiving a letter from her husband telling her of the prophecy, determines to fortify his will to take violent action which, she foresees, will be necessary. The King and his sons arrive for a stay at the castle. After Lady Macbeth drugs the grooms of the King's bedchamber, Macbeth stabs Duncan. When the deed is discovered, Macbeth, feigning great grief, stabs the grooms and places the blame on them. The King's sons, Malcolm and Donalbain, flee the country, aware that they might face a similar fate, and Macbeth is crowned king.

Macbeth, uneasy about the witches' prophecy to Banquo, plots to have him and his son, Fleance, killed. Banquo is slain but Fleance escapes. At a banquet honoring the slain general, the ghost of Banquo, seen only by Macbeth, appears and takes a seat. The terrified Macbeth begins to reveal his guilt and the Queen dismisses the assembly. News is received that Malcolm has joined Macduff, a powerful Scottish lord, in England, and together they are planning to overthrow Macbeth.

Meanwhile, Hecate and the witches plot his downfall. When Macbeth visits them, they warn him to beware Macduff. They prophesy that "none of woman born shall harm Macbeth" and promise that he shall be safe until Birnam Wood shall move against him.

When Macbeth has Macduff's wife and children killed, Lady Macbeth goes mad in the famed "sleepwalking scene." The English forces, under Malcolm and the Earl of Northumberland, join the Scottish army near Birnam Wood. There they cut and carry boughs to conceal their movement and word is brought to Macbeth that Birnam Wood is moving against him.

This and the news of his wife's suicide send him into battle with a foolhardy recklessness. He kills young Siward, son of the English general, but when he meets Macduff, who reveals that he was "not of woman born," the tyrant, though fighting desperately, falls. Malcolm is hailed King of Scotland. "Darkness, we may even say blackness, broods over this tragedy. . . . Lady Macbeth is marked by her fear of darkness."—(A. C. Bradley.) "Macbeth is a statement of evil . . . not of a philosophy but ordered emotion."—(L. C. Knights.)

Macbeth, Scottish king; the ruler of Moray and Ross, became King of Scotland succeeding Duncan, whom he murdered (c1040), his claim to the throne being through his wife, Gruach; defeated, killed by Siward and Duncan's son, Malcolm III; tragic figure of Shakespeare's play (see above).
MACB: I, 3.

Macbeth, Lady, ambitious wife of above; taunts Macbeth and spurs him into action; finally, tortured by guilt, she commits suicide.
MACB: I, 5.

Macduff, Scottish Thane of Fife; discovers the murdered Duncan; distrusts and suspects Macbeth; goes to England where he is joined by Malcolm; kills Macbeth.
MACB: II, 3.

Macduff, Lady, wife of above; murdered, with her children, by order of Macbeth.
MACB: IV, 2.

Macduff's son. See above.
MACB: IV, 2.

mace, sergeant's staff of office; weapon.
CoFE: Dromio S., IV, 3, 28.
JC: Brutus, IV, 3, 268.

machine, body; not used prior to

Shakespeare and considered an affected use of the word.
HAM: Polonius, II, 2, 124.

Machivel (Machiavelli), Niccolò, (1469-1527), famed Florentine author of *The Prince* (1513); synonymous with unscrupulous schemer or intriguer.
MWW: Host, III, 1, 104.
3H6: Richard, III, 2, 193.
1H6: York, V, 4, 74—*Machiavel.*

Macmorris, Irish officer in King Henry's army; quarrels with Fluellen.
HEN5: III, 2.

maculate, stained, impure, spotted.
LLL: Moth, I, 2, 97.

mad
Mad as the sea and wind when both contend
Which is the mightier.
HAM: Queen, IV, 1, 7.

made a push, made a fearless or brave attempt to stand against; scoffed at, pooh-poohed.
ADO: Leonato, V, 1, 38.

mad world
Mad world! mad kings! mad composition!
JOHN: Bastard, II, 1, 561. See COMPOSITION.

Maecenas, Gaius (Caius) Cilnius, friend of Octavius Caesar; tries to heal the breach between Antony and Octavius; present at conference and feast with Pompey; supports Octavius in his attack on Antony. [Maecenas (d. 8 BC) famous as patron of Vergil and Horace; administered Rome while Octavian fought against Pompey (36); acted as adviser to Emperor Augustus (Octavian).
A&C: II, 2.

magnanimous, courageous, exceptionally brave, heroic.
HEN5: Fluellen, III, 6, 6.

magnifico, title given to nobles, leaders or grandees of Venice.
OTH: Iago, I, 2, 12—refers to Brabantio.

Mahu. See FIENDS.
LEAR: Edgar, III, 4, 149.

maiden, in warfare or battle means bloodless, never been taken.
T&C: Achilles, IV, 5, 87.

Maid Marian, hero's sweetheart in tales of Robin Hood; character in May games and Morris dances, opposed by Puritans as bawdy.
1H4: Falstaff, III, 3, 129. See ROBIN HOOD.

maids
. . . Men are April when they woo, December when they wed. Maids are May when they are maids, but the sky changes when they are wives.
AYL: Rosalind, IV, 1, 147.

mail, wallet, purse; budget.
LLL: Costard, III, 1, 74.

mail, wrap, cover, conceal.
2H6: Eleanor, II, 4, 31.

main, stake; term from hazard, a dice game (modern equivalent, main chance).
1H4: Hotspur, IV, 1, 47.
2H6: Salisbury, I, 1, 208.

mainly, powerfully, forcefully.
1H4: Falstaff, II, 4, 222.

majesty
. . . The cesse of majesty
Dies not alone, but like a gulf doth draw
What's near it with it.
HAM: Rosencrantz, III, 3, 15.
See CESSE, GULF.

make a leg, courtesy (curtsy), bow.
RICH2: Richard, III, 3, 175.

makeless, one without a mate; widowed.
SONNET: IX, 4.

makes mouths, dares, makes faces of scorn.
HAM: Hamlet, IV, 4, 50.

malapert, impudent, saucy.
TwN: Toby, IV, 1, 47.
RICH3: Queen Margaret, I, 3, 255.
3H6: Clarence, V, 5, 32.

Malcolm, elder son of Duncan, King of Scotland; Prince of Cumberland, heir to the throne; flees after his father is killed; returns to assume control after Macbeth is killed. [Malcolm III MacDuncan, called Canmore (d. 1093); ascended throne after defeat of Macbeth at Lumphanan in Aberdeenshire (1054); crowned at Scone (1057); forced to submit to William the Conqueror (1072); four sons became kings of Scotland; daughter Matilda became Queen of Henry I of England.]
MACB: I, 2.

malefactions, evil crimes; not used prior to Shakespeare.
HAM: Hamlet, II, 2, 620.

malkin, filthy servant or kitchen maid, slut, slattern; used generally for lower class girls.
COR: Brutus, II, 1, 224.
PER: Dionyza, IV, 3, 34—*mawkin.*

mallard, wild drake.
A&C: Scarus, III, 10, 20.

malmsey, rich, sweet wine; strong; considered a relatively vulgar drink from Spain, Cyprus etc.
LLL: Berowne, V, 2, 233.
2H4: Hostess, II, 1, 42.
RICH3: 1Murderer, I, 4, 161.

maltworm, toper, soak, sot, tippler.
2H4: Falstaff, II, 4, 362.
1H4: Gadshill, II, 1, 83—*mustachio purple-hued maltworms,* red-faced heavy drinkers with mustaches dyed with ale.

Malvolio, Olivia's haughty, humorless, ambitious steward; an "affectioned ass," the butt of tricky, practical jokes; made to look ridiculous.
TwN: I, 5.

Mamillius, young son of Leontes and Hermione; following Leontes' rejection of the oracle, news comes of Mamillius' death.
WINT: I, 2.

mammering on, wavering, hesitating about, being indecisive.
OTH: Desdemona, III, 3, 70.

mammet, doll, puppet.
1H4: Hotspur, II, 3, 95.
R&J: Capulet, III, 5, 186.

mammock, tear to pieces.
COR: Valeria, I, 3, 71.

man
He was a man, take him for all in all.
I shall not look upon his like again.
HAM: Hamlet, I, 2, 187.

What a piece of work is man . . .
HAM: Hamlet, II, 2, 316.

. . . to know a man well were to know himself.
HAM: Hamlet, V, 2, 146—"No man can completely know another, but by knowing himself, which is the utmost extent of human wisdom."—(Dr. Samuel Johnson.)

Thou art the thing itself; unaccommodated man is no more but such a poor, bare, forked animal as thou art.
LEAR: Lear, III, 4, 111.

man. See NOTHING.

manage, term from riding school, short gallop at full speed; exercise.
LLL: Boyet, V, 2, 482.
1H4: Lady, II, 3, 52.

man as beast
. . . If thou wert the lion, the fox would beguile thee. If thou wert the lamb, the fox would eat thee. If thou wert the fox, the lion would suspect thee when peradventure thou wert accus'd by the ass. If thou wert the ass, thy dulness would torment thee, and still thou liv'dst but as a breakfast to the wolf. If thou wert the wolf, thy greediness would afflict thee, and oft thou shouldst hazard thy life for thy dinner. Wert thou the unicorn, pride and wrath would confound thee and make thine own self the conquest of thy fury.

Wert thou a bear, thou wouldst be kill'd by the horse; wert thou a horse, thou wouldst be seiz'd by the leopard; wert thou a leopard, thou wert germane to the lion, and the spots of thy kindred were jurors on thy life.
TIMON: Timon, IV, 3, 330.

mandragora, mandrake, plant with strong narcotic qualities; root used for sleeping potions; its forked root was thought to resemble the human form and when pulled it was believed to shriek; herb, when eaten by women, (so went the old wives' tale) would induce conception. See SLEEP.
A&C: Cleopatra, I, 5, 4.
OTH: Iago, III, 3, 330.
2H4: Falstaff, I, 2, 17.

mandrake. See above.
2H6: Suffolk, III, 2, 310.
R&J: Juliet, IV, 3, 48—sound of mandrake shrieking was supposed to drive the hearer insane.

manhood
And manhood is called foolery when it stands
Against a falling fabric.
COR: Cominius, III, 1, 246.

Manningtree, town in Essex; noted for cattle fairs where a whole ox was roasted.
1H4: Prince, II, 4, 499.

Marcellus, officer of the guard; with Bernardo, sees Ghost of Hamlet's father; later swears to Hamlet not to reveal what he has seen.
HAM: I, 1.

March-chick, literally, chicken hatched prematurely; precocious youngster.
ADO: John, I, 3, 58.

marches, borders, frontier.
HEN5: Canterbury, I, 2, 140.

marchpane, marzipan; almond paste sweet or small cake.
R&J: 1Servant, I, 5, 9.

Marcius, young son of Coriolanus; goes with Volumnia and

Virgilia to beg his father to spare Rome.

COR: V, 3.

Marcus Andronicus, brother of Titus; tribune of the people; discovers the ravished Lavinia; helps his brother in avenging the foul deeds of his enemies.

TITUS: I, 1.

Marcus Crassus, with Pompey and Caesar formed first triumvirate; defeated by Surenas, general in the army of Orodes, King of Parthia, on the plains of Mesopotamia (53 BC); killed by treachery during conference proposed by the victor; Orodes poured molten gold down the dead man's throat giving him his fill of what he had wanted so much in life.

A&C: Ventidius, III, 1, 2.

Mardian, eunuch attending Cleopatra; sent by her to tell Antony she had killed herself.

A&C: I, 5.

Margarelon, bastard son of Priam; fights with Thersites.

T&C: V, 7.

Margaret, gentlewoman attending Hero; infatuated with Borachio, who manages to make love to her at Hero's window so that Claudio and the Prince mistake her for her mistress; Borachio's confession absolves her of any complicity in the plan.

ADO: II, 1.

Margaret of Anjou, Suffolk manages to make her Henry's queen and his mistress (1H6); quarrels with the Duchess of Gloucester and gets her husband dismissed; persuades Suffolk to murder the Duke; confesses her love for him after he is banished and killed; flees with Henry to London after Lancastrian defeat at St. Albans (2H6); continues the struggle against York (3H6); defeats York at Wakefield and stabs him; defeated at Towton, goes to France for aid and is joined by War-

wick; defeated at Tewkesbury; after the murder of her husband and son, she is ransomed by her father and sent home; prophesies disaster (RICH3), cursing the House of York (historically inaccurate, she never returned to England); characterized by York (3H6) as "O tiger's heart wrapped in a woman's hide." [1430-82, daughter of René of Anjou and Isabella of Lorraine, wife of Henry VI, mother of Edward.]

1H6: V, 3; 2H6: I, 1; 3H6: I, 1; RICH3: I, 3.

Margaret Plantagenet, Lady. See PLANTAGENET, Margaret.

margent, margin, border, edge, shore.

HAM: Horatio, V, 2, 163.
LLL: Boyet, II, 1, 246.
MND: Titania. II, 1, 85.

Maria, one of the ladies attending the Princess of France; falls in love with Longaville.

LLL: II, 1.

Maria, Olivia's witty gentlewoman; writes the love-letter and leaves it where Malvolio can find it; marries Sir Toby.

TwN: I, 3.

Mariana, Florentine, friend of the mother of Diana, whom she warns against Bertram and Parolles.

ALL'sW: III, 5.

Mariana, betrothed to Angelo; deserted by him when her dowry is lost; visits him in place of Isabella; Duke arranges marriage between them.

MEAS: IV, 1.

marigold, flower, symbol of constancy in love.

WINT: Perdita, IV, 4, 105.
LUCRECE: 397.

Marina, beautiful daughter of the King and Thaisa; left by her father in the care of Cleon and Dionyza; saved by pirates when the queen arranges her murder; taken to Mytilene where she is

sold to a brothel-keeper; saved
by Lysimachus, who eventually
marries her.
PER: IV, 1.

Mariners, crew members of the
ship wrecked in the tempest
caused by the magic of Prospero.
TEMP: I, 1; one also appears
in WINT: III, 3.

mark, buoy, sea mark, object
used to mark a spot on the
ocean.
SONNET: CXVI, 5. See EVER-
FIXED MARK.

mark, outer boundary or reach,
limit.
A&C: Caesar, III, 6, 87.

mark, worth two-thirds of a
pound or 13 shillings and fourpence.
2H4: Falstaff, I, 2, 217.
MEAS: Pompey, IV, 3, 7.
HEN8: King, V, 1, 170.

market, profits, gain, compensa-
tion.
HAM: Hamlet, IV, 4, 34.

mark prodigious, unnatural birth-
mark which foretold evil.
MND: Oberon, V, 1, 419.

marl, clay, earth.
ADO: Beatrice, II, 1, 66.

Marlowe, Christopher (1564-93).
English poet, dramatist; one of
the UNIVERSITY WITS; wrote
Tamburlaine (produced, 1587),
Dr. Faustus (produced, 1588),
The Jew of Malta (1589), *Edward II* (c1593); with Thomas
Nashe *The Tragedy of Dido,
Queen of Carthage* (c1593);
The Massacre at Paris (alone
or in collaboration, c1593);
known for *The Passionate Shepherd to His Love.* His early
death robbed the Elizabethan
theater of one of its greatest
dramatists, and there are those
who claim that had he lived,
he would have surpassed Shakespeare; it has been conjectured
that he wrote Shakespeare's
plays, but this claim, along with

others, has been ridiculed by the
experts.

marmoset, small monkey; any
one of several species of South
American midoid monkeys; historically the monkeys, with dia-
mond-studded collars, were
worn as opulent decoration by
the wealthy women of the court.
TEMP: Caliban, II, 2, 174.

marriage
. . . If men could be contented
to be what they are, there were
no fear in marriage.
ALL'SW: Clown, I, 3, 54.

Marriage is a matter of more
worth
Than to be dealt in by attorney-
ship.
1H6: Suffolk, V, 5, 55.

. . . O curse of marriage,
That we can call these delicate
creatures ours,
And not their appetites! I had
rather be a toad
And live upon the vapour of a
dungeon
Than keep a corner in the thing
I love
For others' uses.
OTH: Othello, III, 3, 268.

Let me not to the marriage of
true minds
Admit impediments.
SONNET: CXI, 1.

Many a good hanging prevents
a bad marriage . . .
TWN: Clown, I, 5, 20.

marry, indeed; literally an oath:
Mary, by the Virgin Mary.
HAM: Polonius, I, 3, 90.
MND: Quince, I, 2, 11.
RICH2: Aumerle, I, 4, 16.

marry
Or if thou wilt needs marry,
marry a fool; for wise men
know well enough what monsters you make of them.
HAM: Hamlet, III, 1, 143. See
MONSTERS.

Mars, Roman god of war (Ares,
in Greek mythology); beloved
of Venus (Aphrodite).

HAM: Hamlet, III, 4, 57.
TEMP: Iris, IV, 1, 98.
A&C: Philo, I, 1, 4.

marshal, high officer of the state, now called earl marshal.
1H4: Archbishop, IV, 4, 2—*Lord Marshal,* refers to Thomas Mowbray, son of the Duke of Norfolk, who had been exiled by Richard II (RICH2: I, 3).

Marshalsea, prison in Southwark; dealt with offenders belonging to the King's household; abolished 1842.
HEN8: Chamberlain, V, 4, 90.

Martext, Sir Oliver, vicar, about to perform a mock marriage ceremony for Touchstone and Audrey, when Jaques intervenes.
AYL: III, 3.

Martius, one of the four sons of Titus; accused, with brother Quintus, of the murder of Bassianus and executed.
TITUS: I, 1.

Martlemas, beef (from ox) fattened, killed and then salted on Martinmas Day (November 11).
2H4: Poins, II, 2, 110—refers to Falstaff.

martlet, martin; swallow-like bird, often built its nest in church spires.
MACB: Banquo, I, 6, 4.
MERV: Arragon, II, 9, 28.

Marullus, tribune; fears the growing power of Caesar and urges the people not to celebrate his victory over Pompey; silenced by Caesar.
JC: I, 1.

Mary-bud. See MARIGOLD.
CYM: Cloten, II, 3, 26.

Mass, by the mass, a common oath.
HAM: Other Clown, V, 1, 62.

Massinger, Philip (1583-1640). English dramatist; collaborated with Dekker in the writing of *The Virgin Martyr* (1622); succeeded FLETCHER as chief dramatist for the KING'S MEN (1625); best known for *A New Way to Pay Old Debts* (c1625-26); some critics suggest that Massinger wrote *The Two Noble Kinsmen* and the non-Fletcher parts of *Henry VIII*.

massy, weighty, massive, huge.
TEMP: Ariel, III, 3, 67.
HAM: Rosencrantz, III, 3, 17—*massy wheel,* might be development of Fortune's wheel.

mast, fruit of various trees used as food for pigs.
TIMON: Timon, IV, 3, 422—acorns.

Master, master or commander of a ship.
TEMP: I, 1; 2H6: IV, 1.

Master Gunner of Orleans, his son kills Lord Salisbury and Sir Thomas Gargrave with his gun.
1H6: I, 4.

masters
We cannot all be masters, nor all masters
Cannot be truly followed.
OTH: Iago, I, 1, 43.

mastic, abusive, scourging, snarling.
T&C: Agamemnon, I, 3, 73.

Masuccio da Salerno (Tomaso Guardato) (c1415-c77). Italian novelist in service of the Duke of Milan; wrote 50 novels in the Neapolitan dialect (printed in Naples, 1476); one of these may be the source of *Romeo and Juliet*.

matched in mouth like bells, each hound in a perfect pack had a different voice or note and harmonized like a chime of bells.
MND: Theseus, IV, 1, 126.

mate, amaze, astonish, daze, confound.
MACB: Doctor, V, 1, 86.
COFE: Antipholus S., III, 2, 54.

matin. See MORNING.
HAM: Ghost, I, 5, 89.

matter, significance, of serious concern, sense.
HAM: King, IV, 1, 1.
TEMP: Sebastian, II, 1, 230.

ADO: Benedick, I, 1, 281.

mattock, tool like a pickaxe with a broad end.
R&J: Romeo, V, 3, 22.

maugre, in spite of, despite.
LEAR: Edgar, V, 3, 131.
TWN: Olivia, II, 1, 163.
TITUS: Aaron, IV, 2, 110.

maxim of love
. . . Women are angels, wooing;
Things won are done; joy's soul
lies in the doing.
That she beloved knows naught
that knows not this:
Men prize the thing ungained
more than it is.
That she was never yet that ever
knew
Love got so sweet as when de-
sire did sue.
Therefore this maxim out of
love I teach:
Achievement is command; un-
gained, beseech.
T&C: Cressida, I, 2, 312.

Mayor of London, stops the
fighting in the city between
Gloucester's and the Bishop of
Winchester's men; begs the
King to intervene (1H6: John
Coventry, Lord Mayor, 1425);
supports Richard's actions and
claim to the throne (RICH3:
Sir Edmund Shaw, Lord Mayor,
1482); present at the christen-
ing of Elizabeth (HEN8: Sir
Stephen Pecocke).
1H6: I, 3; RICH3: III, 1;
HEN8: V, 5.

Mayor of St. Albans, helps carry
Simpcox to present him to the
King.
2H6: II, 1.

Mayor of York, King Edward
takes his keys to the gates.
3H6: IV, 7.

mazzard, slang or cant expression
for head, literally meaning
"drinking bowl."
HAM: Hamlet, V, 1, 97.
OTH: Cassio, II, 3, 155.

meacock, milksop, cowardly or
effeminate fellow.

SHREW: Petruchio, II, 1, 315.

mead, meadow.
TEMP: Gonzalo, III, 3, 3.

mealed, tainted, spotted, stained.
MEAS: Duke, IV, 2, 86.

mean, tenor or alto part; between
treble and bass.
LLL: Berowne, V, 2, 328.
WINT: Clown, IV, 3, 46.

mean, lament, moan.
MND: Demetrius, V, 1, 330.

meaning
We are not the first
Who with the best meaning
have incurred the worst.
LEAR: Cordelia, V, 3, 3.

measure, pace out, travel over.
RICH2: Richard, III, 2, 125.

measure, stately or formal dance.
R&J: Benvolio, I, 4, 10.
RICH2: Gaunt, I, 3, 291.
RICH3: Richard, I, 1, 8—dance
steps.

measure
Haste still pays haste, and lei-
sure answers leisure;
Like doth quite like, and Mea-
sure still for Measure.
MEAS: Duke, V, 1, 415.

Measure for Measure, written
and performed 1604; registered
and published 1623; sources,
Promos and Cassandra by
George Whetstone (pub. 1578),
based on novella in Geraldi
CINTHIO's *Hecatommithi* or
Hundred Tales (1565), with the
addition of the character Mariana and other changes.
PLOT: Vincentio, the kindly
Duke of Vienna, disguised as a
friar, remains in the city, although he is believed to have
departed, leaving the affairs of
state in the hands of Angelo and
Escalus and expecting a strict
enforcement of the laws against
immorality. The Deputy's first
act is to revive the death penalty
for fornication and Claudio, his
first victim, is paraded through
the streets in disgrace. He begs
his friend Lucio to get his sister

Isabella to plead for him. Escalus, a Justice, and Isabella all plead in vain for Claudio. However, Angelo is smitten with the beautiful novice and attempts to exchange her brother's life for her virtue. She refuses.

The Duke, as Friar Lodowick a confessor, has learned Claudio and Juliet's story and plans to help. He suggests to Isabella that she agree to an assignation with Angelo and substitute Mariana, the girl he jilted years before, for herself. This is worked out but Angelo demands Claudio's head. The Friar (Duke) arranges the substitution of a dead prisoner's head for Claudio's but allows Isabella to think that her brother is dead and suggests that she seek justice from the returning Duke.

When the Duke returns and is met by Angelo, Isabella accuses him of his crimes. The Duke, pretending not to believe her, has her arrested. Mariana demands recognition as Angelo's wife. The Duke, again disguised as the Friar, acts as the witness for the two women before Angelo. Accused as a false witness, the Duke reveals himself. Angelo is spared if he will marry Mariana, Claudio and Juliet are reunited and the Duke asks Isabella to marry him.

meat

Upon what meat doth this our
    Caesar feed
That he is grown so great?
    JC: Cassius, I, 2, 149.

Medea, helped Jason gain the Golden Fleece and refused to leave him; Aeson was Jason's father.
    MerV: Jessica, V, 1, 13.

Media, country in Asia Minor (or South Asia); originally in plateau region corresponding to northwestern part of modern Iran; part of Assyrian Empire (8th century to 626 BC); conquered by Cyrus, founder of

Persian Empire (550 BC); bounded on north by Elburz Mountains, on the northwest by Armenia, on the northeast by Hyrcania, on the east by Parthia, on the west by Assyria, on the south by Persis and Susiana, and on the southwest by Babylonia.
    A&C: Silius, III, 1, 7.

Medice, teipsum, Latin, proverbial expression, Physician cure or heal yourself; from Luke (4: 23); only quotation from the Vulgate.
    2H6: Cardinal, II, 1, 53.

medicine, potion, philter, love potion, philosopher's stone, alchemist's tincture.
    1H4: Falstaff, II, 2, 19.

medicine potable, gold in solution known as *aurum potabile;* thought to have great medicinal value.
    2H4: Prince, IV, 5, 163.

medlar, fruit of tree *Mespilus germanica,* eaten when decayed to soft pulp; resembles small brown-skinned apple; usually with pun on meddler; licentious.
    TIMON: Apemantus, IV, 3, 305.
    AYL: Rosalind, III, 2, 125.
    MEAS: Lucio, IV, 3, 184—prostitute.

meed, importance, merited portion, reward.
    HAM: Osric, V, 2, 149.
    COR: Cominius, II, 2, 101.
    CYM: Pisanio, III, 5, 168.

meered (mered) question, limited or sole argument, subject or ground of quarrel or hostility; meers, in Shakespeare's day, were the boundaries in the common fields.
    A&C: Enobarbus, III, 13, 10.

meet, even, quits; apt, suitable; sufficient, gain.
    ADO: Leonato, I, 1, 47.
    A&C: Caesar, II, 6, 2.

mehercle, by Hercules.
    LLL: Holofernes, IV, 2, 80.

meiny (meinie), common herd, multitude.

Cor: Coriolanus, III, 1, 66.

meiny, retinue, servants, followers.

Lear: Kent, II, 4, 35.

melancholy

. . . I can suck melancholy out a song as a weasel sucks eggs.

AYL: Jaques, II, 5, 12. See SIMPLES.

I have neither the scholar's melancholy, which is emulation; nor the musician's, which is fantastical; nor the courtier's, which is proud; nor the soldier's, which is ambitious; nor the lawyer's, which is politic; nor the lady's, which is nice; nor the lover's, which is all these; but it is a melancholy of mine own, compounded of many simples, extracted from many objects, and indeed the sundry contemplation of my travels, in which my often rumination wraps me in a most humorous sadness.

AYL: Jaques, IV, 1, 10.

mell, deal, mingle, meddle, embrace.

All'sW: Parolles (letter), IV, 3, 257.

Melun, French lord; acts as intermediary between Salisbury and the Dauphin; when dying, warns the English against the Dauphin's double-dealing.

John: V, 4.

memento mori, Latin, reminder of death; probably a symbol such as a skull and crossbones.

1H4: Falstaff, III, 3, 35.

memory. See QUARRELS, SINNER.

men

. . . Know thou this, that men Are as the time is; to be tender-minded Does not become a sword.

Lear: Edmund, V, 3, 30.

If we imagine no worse of them than they of themselves, they may pass for excellent men.

MND: Theseus, V, 1, 218.

But men are men; the best sometimes forget.

Oth: Iago, II, 3, 241.

Men should be what they seem; Or those that be not, would they might seem none!

Oth: Iago, III, 3, 126.

Men's natures wrangle with inferior things, Though great ones are their object.

Oth: Desdemona, III, 4, 144.

men. See SIGH NO MORE.

Menas and **Menecrates,** pirates; friends of Pompey.

A&C: II, 1.

mend, outdo, improve upon, surpass; supplement, remedy.

LLL: Berowne, V, 2, 329.
Shrew: Gremio, I, 2, 151.
AYL: Celia, II, 4, 94.

Menecrates. See MENAS.

Menelaus, King of Sparta, husband of Helen of Troy, brother of Agamemnon; with the help of the Greeks, captured Troy and took Helen back to Sparta.

T&C: I, 3.

Menenius Agrippa, patrician, friend of Coriolanus; pleads the patrician cause to the people; tries to get Coriolanus to treat them without contempt; appeals to him in vain not to attack Rome.

Cor: I, 1.

men of Rome

. . . What conquest brings he home?
What tributaries follow him to Rome
To grace in captive bonds his chariot wheels?
You blocks, you stones, you worse than senseless things!
O you hard hearts, you cruel men of Rome,
Knew you not Pompey?

JC: Marullus, I, 1, 37.

men of war, soldiers, not ships.

Rich2: Northumberland, II, 1, 286.

Menteith, Scottish nobleman; leads Scottish forces to join Malcolm and Siward against Macbeth.

MACB: V, 2.

me pompae provexit apex, Latin, the crown of glory (triumph) has led me on; motto on the shield of a knight of Antioch.

PER: Thaisa, II, 2, 30.

Mercade, messenger; brings word to the Princess of France that her father has died.

LLL: V, 2.

mercatante, old Italian, merchant.

SHREW: Biondello, IV, 2, 63.

Merchant of Venice, The, written 1597; registered 1598; published 1600; sources, Ser GIOVANNI Fiorentino's *Il Pecorone* (*The Simpleton,* IV, 1; printed 1558), the Casket theme from Richard Robinson's version of the *Gesta Romanorum* (1577), some influence seen in MARLOWE'S *Jew of Malta* and a possible anonymous lost play *The Jew,* described in Stephen Gosson's *The School of Abuse* (1579).

PLOT: When Bassanio cannot get the loan he needs to woo Portia from his friend Antonio, he is forced to borrow the money from Shylock, who, in turn, demands Antonio's capital in ships and merchandise as security and a pound of Antonio's flesh. The bond is signed and Bassanio, with his companion Gratiano, sets out for Belmont where he passes Portia's casket test, selecting the leaden casket containing her portrait. She gives him a ring and agrees to marry him. Gratiano wins Nerissa, Portia's gentlewoman.

Meanwhile, Shylock's daughter Jessica has eloped with Lorenzo and her father's ducats. When word comes that Antonio's ships failed to make port, Bassanio and Gratiano go to his aid. Portia disguises herself as a lawyer and Nerissa as her clerk and, unknown to the men, they go to plead in Antonio's behalf. Portia demands that Shylock take the pound of flesh without shedding one drop of Antonio's blood, or his life as well as his fortune will be forfeited. The Duke grants Shylock his life, giving his fortune to Antonio who, in turn, gives half to Shylock on the condition that he become a Christian and give the money to Jessica and Lorenzo.

Portia and Nerissa are satisfied to demand the rings they gave their husbands as reward for their efforts, knowing full well they can charge them with infidelity when they meet them back in Belmont. All ends happily for everyone, except of course for Shylock, as Antonio's ships come safely into harbor.

merchants

Let us, like merchants, show our foulest wares,
And think perchance they'll sell; if not,
The lustre of the better yet to show,
Shall show the better.

T&C: Ulysses, I, 3, 359.

Mercury, Roman god of business or commerce; corresponds to Greek god Hermes, messenger of the gods; honored by a festival in May; one of the handsomest of the gods, he had as his symbol a sacred branch of peace; wore winged sandals.

A&C: Cleopatra, IV, 15, 35.

HAM: Hamlet, III, 4, 58.

WINT: Autolycus, IV, 3, 25— Autolycus in classical mythology was the son of Mercury, god of thieves and other dishonest people, and Chione; noted for clever thefts; father of Odysseus; the hero for whom this Autolycus is named.

A station like the herald Mercury

New lighted on a heaven-kissing hill.

Ham: Hamlet, III, 4, 58. See STATION.

Mercutio, kinsman of the Prince of Verona; witty, sophisticated, courageous friend of Romeo; famous for "Queen Mab" speech; killed in quarrel when Tybalt when Romeo, secretly married to Juliet, tries to stop the fight.

R&J: I, 4.

mercy

Mercy is not itself that oft looks so.

Pardon is still the nurse of second woe.

Meas: Escalus, II, 1, 297.

The quality of mercy is not strain'd;

It droppeth as the gentle rain from heaven

Upon the place beneath. It is twice blest—

It blesseth him that gives, and him that takes.

MerV: Portia, IV, 1, 184—beginning of famous speech.

Wilt thou draw near the nature of the gods?

Draw near them then in being merciful.

Titus: Tamora, I, 1, 117.

mercy. See ENDING.

merely, totally, absolutely, entirely, purely.

Cor: Brutus, III, 1, 305.

Ham: Hamlet, I, 2, 137.

A&C: Enobarbus, III, 7, 9.

mere words

Words, words, mere words, no matter from the heart . . .

T&C: Troilus, V, 3, 108.

merit

A dearer merit, not so deep a maim

As to be cast forth in the common air,

Have I deserved at your highness' hands.

Rich2: Mowbray, I, 3, 156.

Merlin, old magician of King Arthur's court.

Lear: Fool, III, 2, 95.

Merlin's prophecy. See Lear: Fool, III, 2, 80.

mermaid

. . . heard a mermaid, on a dolphin's back,

Uttering such dulcet and harmonious breath

That the rude sea grew civil at her song,

And certain stars shot madly from their spheres

To hear the sea-maid's music.

MND: Oberon, II, 1, 150—possibly an allusion to one of the elaborate spectacles presented for Queen Elizabeth's entertainment.

Mermaid Tavern, taken over by William Johnson as landlord (1603); friend and trustee of Shakespeare's will; in Bread Street, to the east of St. Paul's Cathedral, London; with an entrance in Friday Street, it was the meeting place of the Friday Street Club, founded by Sir Walter Raleigh; Shakespeare, Donne, Fletcher, Beaumont, Johnson and Coryate were all members.

merry

I am not merry; but I do beguile

The thing I am by seeming otherwise.

Oth: Desdemona, II, 1, 123.

Merry Wives of Windsor, The, written 1600-01; performed 1602; registered and published 1602; plot essentially Shakespeare's; possible that he wrote the play by order of the Queen; there were various previous works that contained elements of the play, but it is not definite which source, if any, Shakespeare used.

Plot: Shallow and Slender complain bitterly over the wrongs done them by Falstaff and his cronies, Bardolph, Nym and Pistol. Falstaff meets Mrs.

Ford and Mrs. Page and, imagining they have flirted with him, decides to send them love letters which he gives to Pistol and Nym to deliver. They refuse and he entrusts them to Robin, his page, instead. Out of spite Nym and Pistol decide to tell the husbands of the ladies.

Meanwhile, Mistress Page's daughter, Anne, is being sought by three suitors. Sir Hugh Evans, a Welsh parson, is her father's choice, Dr. Caius, a French doctor, her mother's and Slender is supported by his uncle, Shallow. Fenton, a friend of Prince Hal, is trying to win her on his own. The women compare Falstaff's letters and decide to teach him a lesson. Page isn't jealous but Mr. Ford is. He disguises himself as Master Brook and asks Falstaff to act as a go-between for him with Mistress Ford, claiming he wants to prove Ford a cuckold. When Falstaff arrives for his meeting with Mrs. Ford, she is sorting the dirty linen to send to the wash. The wooing is interrupted by Mrs. Page who warns of Mr. Ford's arrival. The women convince Falstaff to hide in the buck-basket. They cover him with dirty clothes and send him to be dumped into a muddy ditch. The bedraggled Falstaff is comforted by Mrs. Quickly with the assurance of another meeting. Ford surprises them at a second meeting and Falstaff flees disguised as Mother Prat, the fat woman of Brainford. Although he escapes, he is beaten by the angry husband. The women convince Falstaff that he should disguise himself as Herne the hunter and meet them in Windsor Park at night. Meanwhile all three suitors of Anne Page are urged by their backers to elope with her from the meeting at the Park. Falstaff is burned by the tapers of Sir Hugh Evans disguised as a satyr and generally made the laughing stock of the party, while Slender and Dr. Caius steal away with "fairies in green" who turn out to be boys, and Fenton gets his Anne.

mess, group at a king's table or banquet, four people usually included.
HAM: Hamlet, V, 2, 90. See BEAST.
LLL: Berowne, IV, 3, 207.
SHREW: Tranio, IV, 4, 70—course, dish.

Messala, friend of Brutus and Cassius; brings them the news of Portia's and Cicero's deaths; captured at Philippi.
JC: IV, 3.

metal (mettle), the quality, substance or "stuff" of a person; disposition, temperament.
TEMP: Gonzalo, II, 1, 182.
ADO: Beatrice, II, 1, 63.

metal of India, fine gold.
TwN: Toby, II, 5, 16.

mete, aim; measure.
LLL: Boyet, IV, 1, 134.

Metellus Cimber, conspirator; his appeal to Caesar on behalf of his banished brother, Publius, is the signal for assassination.
JC: II, 1.

mete-yard, measuring rod, yardstick.
SHREW: Grumio, IV, 3, 153.

metheglin, mead; a spiced Welsh drink made from fermented honey, water, herbs and other ingredients.
LLL: Berowne, V, 2, 233.
MWW: Evans, V, 5, 167.

mew, cage, confine, shut or coop up; caged area or building where falcons were kept were called mews.
MND: Theseus, I, 1, 71.
SHREW: Gremio, I, 1, 87.
JOHN: Pembroke, IV, 2, 57.

Michael, follower of Cade.
2H6: IV, 2.

Michael, Sir, somehow connected with the Church; sent by his friend, the Archbishop of York, with letters to the Lord Marshal and his cousin Scrope.
1H4: IV, 4.

Michaelmas, St. Michael's Day, September 29th.
MWW: Simple, I, 1, 212.

micher, truant; sneak.
1H4: Falstaff, II, 4, 451.

miching malhecho, lurking, sneaking, skulking trouble or mischief; miching (see above); malhecho believed to be from Spanish word meaning misdeed.
HAM: Hamlet, III, 2, 147.

mickle, great, mighty, much.
HEN5: Pistol, II, 1, 70.
R&J: Friar, II, 3, 15.
COFE: Dromio E., III, 1, 45.

microcosm, man was considered a microcosm or little world as compared to the macrocosm or universe.
COR: Menenius, II, 1, 69.

Midas, King of Phrygia; forgot to exclude food from his wish that everything he touched should turn to gold.
MERV: Bassanio, III, 2, 102.

midnight mushrumps (mushrooms), at midnight, it was thought, the fairies caused the mushrooms, which grow in a single night, to come forth.
TEMP: Prospero, V, 1, 39.

mid season, the noon hour.
TEMP: Ariel, I, 2, 239.

Midsummer Night's Dream, A, written 1596; registered and published 1600; though the play is certainly Shakespeare's own creation, there are elements which suggest the use of PLUTARCH's *Life of Theseus,* OVID's *Metamorphoses* (for Titania, Pyramus and Thisbe), SCOT's *Discovery of Witchcraft* and GREENE's *James IV* (for Oberon).

PLOT: To celebrate the forthcoming marriage of Theseus, Duke of Athens, to Hippolyta, Queen of the Amazons, a group of Athenian workmen are preparing a production of the play, *Pyramus and Thisbe,* in a wood near Athens. Lysander and Hermia, who are running away together because Egeus, her father, insists she marry Demetrius, arrive at the same wood, closely followed by Demetrius, who is enamored of Hermia, and Helena, who wants him. There too are Oberon and Titania, King and Queen of the Fairies; after they quarrel, Oberon manages to squeeze a magic juice on Titania's eyes so that she will fall in love with the first creature she sees upon waking. The lucky fellow is Bottom, the Weaver, whose head has been changed into that of an ass by Puck, the mischievous servant of Oberon. Puck has also mistakenly poured the magic juice into Lysander's eyes and he falls in love with Helena. Oberon pours the juice into Demetrius' eyes and he too falls for Helena. After much quarreling and confusion the various charms are removed and Theseus, upon finding the sleeping lovers, arranges the marriages of Lysander to Hermia and Demetrius to Helena and invites them to join his wedding party. They watch the remarkable performance of Bottom and his friends.

mighty Caesar
O Julius Caesar, thou art mighty yet!
Thy spirit walks abroad and turns our swords
In our own proper entrails.
JC: Brutus, V, 3, 94.

Milan, Duke of, father of Silvia; when Proteus tells him that his friend, Valentine, is planning to elope with his daughter, the Duke orders him to leave the court; when Silvia follows Valentine, the Duke pursues her;

captured by pirates, rescued by his daughter's lover, he agrees to their marriage.
2GENT: II, 4.

milch, milky, tearful.
HAM: Player, II, 2, 540.

Mile-end (Green), exercise ground of the citizen-militia of London.
ALL'sW: Parolles, IV, 3, 310.
2H4: Shallow, III, 2, 298.

mill-sixpences, sixpence stamped by mill and press; coins with raised borders.
MWW: Slender, I, 1, 158.

Milo, Milo of Crotona was a famed Greek athlete who carried a bull on his shoulders at the Olympic games; well-known statue of him at the Acropolis, Athens.
T&C: Ulysses, II, 3, 258.

mind
Whether 'tis nobler in the mind to suffer
The slings and arrows of outrageous fortune
Or to take arms against a sea of troubles,
And by opposing end them.
HAM: Hamlet, III, 1, 57. See TO BE, OUTRAGEOUS FORTUNE.

If your mind dislike anything, obey it.
HAM: Horatio, V, 2, 228.

. . . When the mind's free,
The body's delicate. The tempest in my mind
Doth from my senses take all feeling else
Save what beats there.
LEAR: Lear, III, 4, 11.

The mind I sway by and the heart I bear
Shall never sag with doubt, nor shake with fear.
MACB: Macbeth, V, 3, 9.

Canst thou not minister to a mind diseased,
Pluck from the memory a rooted sorrow,
Raze out the written troubles of the brain,

And with some sweet oblivious antidote
Cleanse the stuffed bosom of that perilous stuff
Which weighs upon the heart?
Doctor: Therein the patient
Must minister to himself.
MACB: Macbeth, V, 3, 40.

minds. See MARRIAGE.

mineral, mine.
HAM: Queen, IV, 1, 26.

Minerva, Roman goddess of handicrafts, health and wisdom; identified with Greek Athena; also guided men in war, thus wore a helmet, shield and coat of mail; believed to be the inventor of musical instruments.
CYM: Iachimo, V, 5, 164.
SHREW: Lucentio, I, 1, 84.

minim, half-note in music; note equal to one-half a semibreve.
MWW: Nym, I, 3, 31.
R&J: Mercutio, II, 4, 23.

minimus, tiniest creature; very small or little thing.
MND: Lysander, III, 2, 329.

minion, darling, pet, plaything, favorite; mistress, hussy.
CYM: Cymbeline, II, 3, 46.
TwN: Duke, V, 1, 128.
CofE: Antipholus E., III, 1, 54.

minister, provide, supply; agent.
OTH: Iago, II, 1, 277.
HAM: Hamlet, III, 4, 175.
TEMP: Prospero, I, 2, 131.

Minotaur, monster or creature—half man, half beast, lived in Crete; maidens were sacrificed to the Minotaur; lived in center of labyrinth (maze); slain by Theseus.
1H6: Suffolk, V, 3, 189.

mint. See SLANDER.

minute's mirth
Who buys a minute's mirth to wail a week?
Or sells eternity to get a toy?
LUCRECE: 213.

mirable, marvelous, wonderful.
T&C: Hector, IV, 45, 142.

miraculous harp, in legend (OVID), Amphion, son of Zeus, was able to raise or pull together the walls of Thebes by playing his miraculous harp.

   TEMP: Antonio, II, 1, 86—implication is that Gonzalo has performed an even greater miracle by building Carthage at Tunis where it never existed.

Miranda, daughter of Prospero, rightful Duke of Milan; lives with her father on a lonely island where they had drifted twelve years earlier; falls in love with Ferdinand, the first young man she has ever seen; after Ferdinand has proven himself worthy of her, Prospero permits their engagement.

   TEMP: I, 2.

mirror of kings
   . . . the mirror of all Christian kings . . .

   HEN5: Chorus, II, Prologue, 6.

mirth
   . . . I show more mirth than I am mistress of . . .

   AYL: Rosalind, I, 2, 2.

   Mirth cannot move a soul in agony.

   LLL: Berowne, V, 2, 866.

Misanthropos, hater of mankind.
   TIMON: Timon, IV, 3, 53.

miscarry, come to harm, perish.
   TWN: Olivia, III, 4, 69.

mischief, adversity, misfortune; disease.
   OTH: Duke, I, 3, 204.
   ADO: John, I, 3, 13—*mortifying mischief,* deadly disease.

   To mourn a mischief that is past and gone
   Is the next way to draw new mischief on.

   OTH: Duke, I, 3, 204.

mischiefs
   The secret mischiefs that I set abroach
   I lay unto the grievous charge of others.

   RICH3: Richard, I, 3, 325. See ABROACH.

miscreant, heretic; vile villain or rascal.
   RICH2: Bolingbroke, I, 1, 39.
   LEAR: Lear: I, 1, 163.

misdoubts, suspects, misgivings.
   LLL: Jaquenetta, IV, 3, 195.

Misenum, naval base under Augustus; constructed by Agrippa (31 BC) on the Bay of Naples.
   A&C: Caesar, II, 2, 163.

misery
   . . . Nothing almost sees miracles
   But misery.

   LEAR: Kent, II, 2, 173.

   Misery acquaints a man with strange bedfellows.

   TEMP: Trinculo, II, 2, 43.

misfortunes
   . . . Full oft 'tis seen,
   Our means secure us, and our mere defects
   Prove our commodities.

   LEAR: Gloucester, IV, 1, 19.

misgraffed, misgrafted, imperfectly matched, misapplied.
   MND: Lysander, I, 1, 137.

misprise (misprize), despise, disdain, undervalue.
   ADO: Hero, III, 1, 52.
   ALL'sW: Countess, III, 2, 33.

misprision, mistake, error; contempt.
   TWN: Clown, I, 5, 61.
   1H4: Northumberland, I, 3, 27.
   ADO: Friar, IV, 1, 186.

Misshapen Time
   Misshapen Time, copesmate of ugly Night,
   Swift subtle post, carrier of grisly care,
   Eater of youth, false slave to false delight,
   Base watch of woes, sin's packhorse, virtue's snare!
   Thou nursest all, and murth'rest all that are.

   LUCRECE: 925. See COPESMATE.

missive, messenger.
   A&C: Caesar, II, 2, 74.
   MACB: Lady Macbeth, I, 5, 7.

mistress mine
   O mistress mine, where are you roaming?

TwN: Clown, II, 3, 40—beginning of song.

Mistress Shore, Jane, wife of a London goldsmith; mistress of Edward IV; upon his death, she became Hastings' mistress.
RICH3: Richard, I, 1, 98.

mobled, concealed, muffled, muted; with the head wrapped up.
HAM: Player, II, 2, 525.

mocking wenches
The tongues of mocking wenches are as keen
As is the razor's edge invisible,
Cutting a smaller hair than may be seen,
Above the sense of sense: so sensible
Seemeth their conference; their conceits have wings,
Fleeter than arrows, bullets, wind, thought, swifter things.
LLL: Boyet, V, 2, 256. See SENSIBLE, CONCEITS.

Modena, province of north central Italy; ancient Etruscan city of Mutina which withstood the siege by Mark Antony (44-43 BC).
A&C: Caesar, I, 4, 57.

modern, ordinary, commonplace, trite.
OTH: Duke, I, 3, 109.

modest doubt
. . . but modest doubt is called
The beacon of the wise, the tent that searches
To the bottom of the worst.
T&C: Hector, II, 2, 15. See TENT.

modesty, moderation, reasonableness.
HAM: Hamlet, II, 2, 462.

Modo. See FIENDS.
LEAR: Edgar, III, 4, 149.

module, mere model, image; counterfeit.
JOHN: King, V, 7, 58.
ALL'SW: Bertram, IV, 3, 114.

moe, more; not an abbreviated form of word.

RICH2: Northumberland, II, 1, 239.
TEMP: Sebastian, II, 1, 133.
OTH: Brabantio, I, 1, 167.

moiety, share, part, portion.
LEAR: Gloucester, I, 1, 7.
A&C: Caesar, V, 1, 19.
WINT: Leontes, II, 3, 8.

moist star, refers to the moon which controlled or influenced the tides.
HAM: Horatio, I, 1, 118.

moldwarp, mole, animal that bores underground and tosses up the dirt.
1H4: Hotspur, III, 1, 149.

mollis aer, Latin, tender air.
CYM: Soothsayer, V, 5, 447.

mome, blockhead, dolt, simpleton.
COFE: Dromio S., III, 1, 32.

momentany, momentary, transitory.
MND: Lysander, I, 1, 143.

monarch
. . . who would not make her husband a cuckold to make him a monarch? I should venture purgatory for't.
OTH: Emilia, IV, 3, 77.

Monarcho, name of well-known Italian, who was probably mentally disturbed; "fantastic" hanger-on at Elizabeth's court.
LLL: Boyet, IV, 1, 101.

monarchs
Who has a book of all that monarchs do,
He's more secure to keep it shut than shown . . .
PER: Pericles, I, 1, 94.

money
. . . nothing comes amiss, so money comes withal.
SHREW: Grumio, I, 2, 82.

monster, cuckold; man made to wear horns by the actions of his unfaithful wife.
HAM: Hamlet, III, 1, 144. See MARRY.

monster

But jealous souls will not be answered so.

They are not ever jealous for the cause,

But jealous for they are jealous. 'Tis a monster

Begot upon itself, born on itself.

OTH: Emilia, III, 4, 159.

Montague, father of Romeo.

R&J: I, 1.

Montague, Lady, mother of Romeo, wife of above; dies of grief over her son's exile.

R&J: I, 1.

Montague, Marquess of, Yorkist who joins (with Warwick, his brother) the Lancastrians when Edward IV marries Lady Grey; killed at Barnet. [Sir John Neville (c1430-71), 3rd son of Richard Neville (1400-60), Earl of Salisbury; Earl of Northumberland; created Marquess of Montague (1470).]

3H6: I, 1.

Montaigne, Michel Eyquem de (1533-92). French essayist; famous for his *Essais* (1580), a literary form he originated; translated into English by John FLORIO (1603); influenced Shakespeare, particularly in the writing of *The Tempest.*

Montano, former Governor of Cyprus.

OTH: II, 1.

Montano. See REYNALDO.

Montemayor, Jorge de (c1521-61). Spanish writer; author of the pastoral prose romance *Diana Enamorada* (English translation published, 1598); source of *The Two Gentlemen of Verona.*

Montgomery, Sir John, persuades Edward, Duke of York, to proclaim himself Edward IV. [Sir Thomas Montgomery, d. 1495.]

3H6: IV, 7.

month's mind, strong inclination toward, longing, desire.

2GENT: Julia, I, 2, 137.

Montjoy, title of chief herald of France; not the name of the character.

HEN5: III, 6.

monument

If a man do not erect in this age his own tomb ere he dies, he shall live no longer in monument than the bell rings and the widow weeps.

ADO: Benedick, V, 2, 79.

Your monument shall be my gentle verse,

Which eyes not yet created shall o'erread.

SONNET: LXXXI, 9.

monument. See PATIENCE.

moody-mad, furiously angry; hot-tempered.

1H6: Talbot, IV, 2, 50.

moon

The moon is down; I have not heard the clock.

MACB: Fleance, II, 1, 2.

. . . the moon like a silver bow New-bent in heaven.

MND: Hippolyta, I, 1, 9.

To live a barren sister all your life,

Chanting faint hymns to the cold fruitless moon.

MND: Theseus, I, 1, 72—singing hymns without warmth or passion to Diana, the maiden goddess of chastity and single women.

The moon, methinks, looks with a wat'ry eye;

And when she weeps, weeps every little flower,

Lamenting some enforced chastity.

MND: Titania, III, 1, 203.

Romeo: Lady, by yonder blessed moon I swear,

That tips with silver all these fruit-tree tops—

Juliet: O, swear not by the moon, th' inconstant moon,

That monthly changes in her circled orb,

Lest that thy love prove likewise variable.
R&J: II, 2, 107.

moon. See TIDES.

mooncalf, misshapen creature, monster, freak; deformities were believed to have been caused by the moon.
TEMP: Stephano, II, 2, 111.

Moonshine, part played by Robin Starveling in the interlude.
MND: V, 1.

moonshine. See CALENDAR.

Moor Ditch, filthy open sewer or ditch outside the city walls; marshy Moorfields drained into Moor Ditch.
1H4: Prince, I, 2, 87.

Moorfields, holiday, summer area; reclaimed marshland, lying just to the north of city walls and south of Finsbury, drained in 16th century and laid out as a park or public grounds (1606); CURTAIN THEATRE said to have been there; animal parades were held outside Moorgate.
HEN8: Porter, V, 4, 33.

mop, contorted facial expression, grimace.
TEMP: Ariel, IV, 1, 47.

mope, act bewildered, dazed, dull.
HAM: Hamlet, III, 4, 81.
TEMP: Boatswain, V, 1, 240.

Mopsa, shepherdess; sings and dances.
WINT: IV, 4.

moral, symbolic, allegorical; hidden meaning; maxim.
TIMON: Painter, I, 1, 90.
HEN5: Fluellen, III, 6, 36.
SHREW: Biondello, IV, 4, 79.

Mordake, Earl of Fife; actually Duke of Albany's son; Shakespeare was misled by HOLIN-SHED.
1H4: King, I, 1, 71.

More, Sir Thomas (1478-1535). English statesman and author; executed for high treason; refused to accept the Act of Supremacy (Henry VIII became head of the Church of England); author of *Utopia* (written in Latin, 1516); his *Richard III* 1513) was the indirect source of Shakespeare's play.

more deaf than adders, from Psalms (58:4-5).
T&C: Hector, II, 2, 172.

more measure, a kiss; a dance was started with the exchange of bows, a handclasp and a kiss.
LLL: King, V, 2, 222.

Morisco, morris dancer.
2H6: York, III, 1, 365.

morn
But look, the morn, in russet mantle clad,
Walks o'er the dew of yon high eastward hill.
HAM: Horatio, I, 1, 166. See RUSSET.

The grey-eyed morn smiles on the frowning night,
Checkering the eastern clouds with streaks of light;
And flecked darkness like a drunkard reels
From forth day's path and Titan's fiery wheels.
R&J: Friar, II, 3, 1.

morning (matin)
The glowworm shows the matin to be near
And 'gins to pale his uneffectual fire.
HAM: Ghost, I, 5, 89.

Full many a glorious morning have I seen . . .
SONNET: XXXIII, 1.

morning. See LARK.

Morning's love, Cephalus; Aurora loved him and carried him away with her, but because he was in love with his wife, Procris, she returned him to her; from OVID's *Metamorphoses* (VII:690-861).
MND: Oberon, III, 2, 389.

Morocco, Prince of, unsuccessful suitor for Portia's hand (and wealth); chooses the golden casket.
MERV: II, 1.

morris, traditional English folk-dance performed in fantastic costume; possibly evolved from the sword-dance; popular characters from legend or story were often represented; may have been included in Court Revels.
HEN5: Dauphin, II, 4, 25. See WHEESON.

morris-pike, large pike (weapon) believed to have been invented by the Moors.
COFE: Dromio S., IV, 3, 27.

mortal, deadly.
OTH: Cassio, II, 1, 72.
CYMS Posthumus, V, 3, 51—
mortal bugs, deadly fiends or terrors.

mortality
When I consider every thing that grows
Holds in perfection but a little moment,
That this huge stage presenteth naught but shows
Whereon the stars in secret influence comment . . .
SONNET: XV, 1.

mortals. See FOOLS.

Mort du vinaigre!, meaningless oath in misunderstood French, literally, death of vinegar.
ALL'SW: Parolles, II, 3, 50.

Mortimer, Edmund, 5th Earl of March; old man who tells Richard Plantagenet that his father, the late Earl of Cambridge, was not a traitor; claims to be the true heir of Richard II. [1391-1424; not historically accurate (confused with uncle, Sir Edmund, see below); had a better claim to the throne, but was a friend of Henry V; died of the plague.]
1H6: II, 5.

Mortimer, Sir Edmund, Earl of March; confused with above; defeated and captured by the Welsh rebel Glendower; marries his daughter; joins Hotspur. [1376-1409; brother of Lady Percy.]
1H4: III, 1.

Mortimer, Lady, daughter of Owen Glendower, wife of Edmund (above); speaks only Welsh.
1H4: III, 1.

Mortimer, Sir John and Sir Hugh, illegitimate sons of Roger Mortimer, Earl of March; uncles of Richard Plantagenet, Duke of York; support his claim to the throne; killed at Wakefield.
3H6: I, 2.

mort of the deer, hunter's call on the horn announcing the kill.
WINT: Leontes, I, 2, 118.

Morton, brings news of the defeat and death at Shrewsbury of his son Hotspur to Northumberland.
2H4: I, 1.

Morton, John, Bishop of Ely under Edward IV; arrested by order of Richard III, escapes, joins Richmond. [c1420-1500, Archbishop of Canterbury, Cardinal and Lord Chancellor during reign of Henry VII; Sir Thomas MORE was brought up as a page in his household; Shakespeare used More as his source for the play; More got his material from Morton, a Tudor apologist and a very partial observer.]
RICH3: III, 4.

mot, motto, inscription, device.
LUCRECE: 830.

mote, minute particle, usually a speck of dust.
HAM: Horatio, I, 1, 112.
MND: Demetrius, V, 1, 324.

Moth, page to Don Armado; Hercules in the interlude of the NINE WORTHIES.
LLL: I, 2.

Moth, one of Titania's fairies.
MND: III, 1.

moth. See MOTE.

mother
. . . There's no man in the world
More bound to's mother; yet here he lets me prate
Like one i' th' stocks. Thou hast never in thy life

Showed thy dear mother any
courtesy,
When she (poor hen), fond of
no second brood,
Has clucked thee to the wars,
and safely home
Loaden with honour.
  Cor: Volumnia, V, 3, 158.
Taint not thy mind, nor let thy
soul contrive
Against thy mother aught. Leave
her to heaven,
And to those thorns that in her
bosom lodge
To prick and sting her.
  Ham: Ghost, I, 5, 85.

Mother Prat. See FAT WOMAN OF
BRAINFORD.
  MWW: Mrs. Page, IV, 2, 191.

mother's glass
Thou art thy mother's glass, and
she in thee
Calls back the lovely April of
her prime.
  SONNET: III, 9. See GLASS.

moth of peace, useless parasite
living a life of idleness and luxury.
  OTH: Desdemona, I, 3, 257.

motion, motive, reason, impulse,
incitement; desire, strong emotion, passion; offer, propose,
suggest.
  Cor: Menenius, II, 1, 55.
  MND: Helena, I, 1, 193.
  TwN: Toby, III, 4, 316.

motion, puppet or puppet show.
  Wint: Autolycus, IV, 3, 103.
  Meas: Lucio, III, 2, 119.
  2Gent: Speed, II, 1, 100.

motive, tool, instrument, moving
organ.
  Rich2: Bolingbroke, I, 1, 193
—refers to tongue.

motley, multicolor costume of
professional fool or jester.
  Lear: Fool, I, 4, 160.
  TwN: Clown, I, 5, 63.
  AYL: Jaques, II, 7, 13.

Mouldy, Ralph, Cotswold peasant; buys his release from service from Falstaff for 40 shillings.
  2H4: III, 2.

mountant, rising, uplifted, raised.
  Timon: Timon, IV, 3, 135.

mountanto (montant), fencing
term, a thrust, upward cut or
blow.
  Ado: Beatrice, I, 1, 30.
  MWW: Host, II, 3, 27.

mountebank, fraudulent or quack
doctor who journeyed from
place to place selling forbidden
poisons and miracle drugs or
remedies; to gain by clever chatter.
  Ham: Laertes, IV, 7, 142.
  Oth: Brabantio, I, 3, 61.

Mount Misena (Misenum), promontory at the west of the Bay
of Naples; port.
  A&C: Caesar, II, 2, 163. See
MISENUM.

mourn in ashes, to wear ashes on
the head and face as a sign of
repentance.
  Rich2: Richard, V, 1, 49.

mouse, tear and shake as a cat
bites and destroys a mouse.
  MND: Theseus, V, 1, 274.
  John: Bastard, II, 1, 354.

mouse-hunt, chaser of women
(cat and mouse); in modern
parlance a "wolf."
  R&J: Lady, IV, 4, 11.

mousetrap, refers to the play
within the play; the means by
which he would "catch the conscience of the king."
  Ham: Hamlet, III, 2, 247.

mouth. See HEAD.

mouthed, gaping, open-mouthed;
Shakespeare pictured wounds as
looking like mouths.
  1H4: Hotspur, I, 3, 97.

moveable, piece of furniture; re-
placeable property.
  Shrew: Katherina, II, 1, 198.

mow, make faces, grimace, sneer.
  Temp: Caliban, II, 2, 9.
  Cym: Iachimo, I, 6, 41.
  Ham: Hamlet, II, 2, 382.

Mowbray, Lord (1386-1405), eldest son of the 1st Duke of Norfolk (see below); joins rebellion

of Scrope and Hastings; arrested with them by Prince John and executed.

2H4: I, 3.

Mowbray, Thomas, 1st Duke of Norfolk, unjustly accused of treason by Bolingbroke for complicity in the murder of the Duke of Gloucester and misappropriation of public funds; ordered by Richard to meet Bolingbroke at Coventry to defend his honor in combat; before the joust can take place, however, Richard banishes Mowbray from England for life; later absolved from guilt in Gloucester's murder. [c1366-99, Earl of Nottingham (1383), Duke of Norfolk (1397), died in Venice.]

RICH2: I, 1.

Much Ado About Nothing, written 1598-99; registered and published 1600; sources, 22nd story in BANDELLO'S *Novelle* (1554), either in the original or BELLEFOREST'S translation (1569), gives the Claudio-Hero plot, as does ARIOSTO'S *Orlando Furioso* (cantos IV-VI) and Spenser's *Faerie Queene* (II, 4, 17-36); the rest is primarily Shakespeare's own.

PLOT: Benedick and Claudio return with Don Pedro of Arragon to Messina to join the governor, Leonato, accompanied by Don John, the bastard brother of the prince. While Benedick continues his war of wit with Beatrice, Claudio falls in love with Hero, her gentle cousin. Don Pedro offers to woo Hero for Claudio while in disguise at the masquerade. Don John arranges to have Claudio and Don Pedro see Borachio making love to Margaret, Hero's gentlewoman, at the window, so that they will think that Hero is a loose woman. Thus when the wedding ceremony at the church is to begin, Claudio refuses to marry an unchaste woman and Hero faints.

Friar Francis spreads the news that she is dead, hoping to rescue her reputation. Beatrice believes her cousin has been unjustly accused and Benedick, in agreeing with her, declares his love for her. Beatrice wants him to kill Claudio in a duel. Meanwhile Dogberry and his watch have captured a drunken Borachio, who confesses his part in the crime. Claudio, to make amends, arranges to marry Leonato's niece, who, of course, turns out to be none other than Hero. When Claudio, who previously had repented, is forgiven by Beatrice the duel with Benedick is off and, instead, the four decide to make it a double wedding. Don John, responsible for all this, is captured as he attempts to escape.

muddied, agitated, confused, stirred up.

HAM: King, IV, 5, 81.

muddy, stupid, muddleheaded, dull.

1H4: Gadshill, II, 1, 106.
WINT: Leontes, I, 2, 325.

muddy-mettled, dim or colorless in spirit, lackluster.

HAM: Hamlet, II, 2, 594.

mulled, dull, drowsy, dispirited.

COR: 1Servingman, IV, 5, 239.

Mulmutius, according to HOLINSHED, Mulmucius Dunwallon was the first to wear a crown in Britain (as king not tribal chief); his father Cloton, King of Cornwall, probably influenced Shakespeare's choice of Cloten as the name for that character.

CYM: Cymbeline, III, 1, 59.

mummer, pantomime actor in dumbshow or rustic play; dancer who masquerades and performs often ribald or rowdy antics.

COR: Menenius, IV, 1, 84.

mummy, drug, supposedly with magic power, made from the liquid of an embalmed corpse, pieces of a fresh corpse (heart, see text) chemically treated or liquid from a dead body.
OTH: Othello, III, 4, 74.

muniments, defenses, furnishings, minor fortifications.
COR: 1Citizen, I, 1, 122.

mural, wall.
MND: Theseus, V, 1, 209.

murder
For murther, though it have no tongue, will speak
With most miraculous organ.
HAM: Hamlet, II, 2, 621.

Murderers, hired assassins of Gloucester (2H6); Banquo and Macduff's family (MACB) and Clarence (RICH3).
2H6: III, 2; MACB: III, 1; RICH3: I, 3.

murdering piece, small cannon or mortar loaded with grapeshot or slugs that would scatter when fired; also called "murderer."
HAM: King, IV, 5, 95.

Murder of Gonzago, play-within-a-play, dumbshow.
HAM: III, 2.

mure, wall.
2H4: Clarence, IV, 4, 119—*wrought the mure,* worn away the wall.

murrain, plague, disease of cattle; used as a curse.
TEMP: Trinculo, III, 2, 88.
COR: 3Roman, I, 5, 3.
MND: Titania, II, 1, 97—*murrion,* stricken with murrain.

muse, be amazed by, wonder, marvel at.
TEMP: Alonso, III, 3, 36.
2H4: Westmoreland, IV, 1, 167.
COR: Coriolanus, III, 2, 7.

muse of fire
O for a Muse of fire, that would ascend
The brightest heaven of invention,

A kingdom for a stage, princes to act,
And monarchs to behold the swelling scene!
HEN5: Prologue, opening lines.

music
Give me some music; music, moody food
Of us that trade in love.
A&C: Cleopatra, II, 5, 1.

. . . music oft hath such a charm
To make bad good, and good provoke to harm.
MEAS: Duke, IV, 1, 13.

The man that hath no music in himself,
Nor is not moved with concord of sweet sounds,
Is fit for treasons, stratagems, and spoils;
The motions of his spirit are dull as night,
And his affections dark as Erebus.
Let no such man be trusted.
MERV: Lorenzo, V, 1, 83. See EREBUS.

. . . How sour sweet music is
When time is broke and no proportion kept!
So is it in the music of men's lives.
RICH2: Richard, V, 5, 42.

This music mads me. Let it sound no more;
For though it have holp madmen to their wits,
In me it seems it will make wise men mad.
RICH2: Richard, V, 5, 61.

Music to hear, why hear'st thou music sadly?
Sweets with sweets war not, joy delights in joy.
SONNET: VIII, 1. See MUSIC TO HEAR.

If music be the food of love, play on,
Give me excess of it, that, surfeiting,
The appetite may sicken, and so die.
TWN: Duke, I, 1, 1.

Musicians, appear in R&J: IV, 5; OTH: III, 1; 2GENT: IV, 2; and MERV: V, 1.

music to hear, you, your voice, resemble the sound of music; you, who are like a melody. SONNET: VIII, 1. See MUSIC.

musit (muset), gap or hole in a hedge, through which the escaping hare runs. VENUS: 683.

muss, scramble; game to retrieve scrambled objects. A&C: Antony, III, 13, 91.

mussel-shell, one who gapes; simpleton. MWW: Falstaff, IV, 5, 28.

Mustardseed, one of Titania's fairies. MND: III, 1.

mutine, mutiny, rise in rebellion. HAM: Hamlet, III, 4, 83.

mutines in the bilboes, sailors who mutinied were placed in shackles (bilboes) which slide on an iron bar fastened or locked to the floor of the ship. HAM: Hamlet, V, 2, 6.

Mutius, youngest son of Titus; attempts to stop his father when he interferes in Bassianus' abduction of Lavinia, and is stabbed by him. TITUS: I, 1.

mutton, loose woman, tart, prostitute. LLL: Costard, I, 1, 305. MEAS: Lucio, III, 2, 192.

Myrmidons, Thessalian troops of Achilles at the siege of Troy. TwN: Clown, II, 3, 29. T&C: Ulysses, I, 3, 378.

mystery, trade, craft, profession, art. TIMON: Timon, IV, 1, 18. OTH: Othello, IV, 2, 30. MEAS: Abhorson, IV, 2, 30.

Naiades, water nymphs associated with brooks, lakes and rivers.
TEMP: Iris, IV, 1, 128.

nail, cloth measure of 2¼ inches.
SHREW: Petruchio, IV, 3, 109.

nail
Even as one heat another heat expels
Or as one nail by strength drives out another,
So the remembrance of my former love
Is by a newer object quite forgotten.
2GENT: Proteus, II, 4, 192.

naked, unarmed; destitute, needy.
OTH: Othello, V, 2, 259.
HAM: King, IV, 7, 46.

naked to mine enemies
Had I but served my God with half the zeal
I served my king, he would not in mine age
Have left me naked to mine enemies.
HEN8: Cardinal, III, 2, 455.

name
. . . no man that hath a name,
But falsehood and corruption doth it shame.
COFE: Adriana, II, 1, 112.

Good name in man and woman, dear my lord,
Is the immediate jewel of their souls.
OTH: Iago, III, 3, 155.

Who steals my purse steals trash; 'tis something, nothing;
'Twas mine, 'tis his, and has been slave to thousands;
But he that filches from me my good name

Robs me of that which not enriches him
And makes me poor indeed.
OTH: Iago, III, 3, 157.

What's in a name? That which we call a rose
By any other name would smell as sweet.
R&J: Juliet, II, 2, 43.

name of action. See ACTION.

name of king
What must the king do now? Must he submit?
The king shall do it. Must he be depos'd?
The king shall be contented. Must he lose
The name of king? a God's name, let it go.
RICH2: Richard, III, 3, 143.

napkin, handkerchief.
OTH: Othello, III, 3, 287.
1H4: Falstaff, IV, 2, 49.
HAM: Queen, V, 2, 299.

Naples, refers to Italian city where venereal disease was prevalent; "Neapolitan" disease.
OTH: Clown, III, 1, 4.

napless, threadbare.
COR: Brutus, II, 1, 250.

Narcissus, unusually handsome youth in Greek mythology loved by the nymphs; Echo died in a vain attempt to win his love and Nemesis punished his indifference by causing him to fall in love with his own reflection in the water; drowning, he is changed into the flower which bears his name.
A&C: Cleopatra, II, 5, 96.

226

Venus: 161.
Lucrece: 265.

Nathaniel, Petruchio's servant.
Shrew: IV, 1.

Nathaniel, Sir, curate (hedge-priest); sententious friend of Holofernes; falters when playing Alexander in the *Nine Worthies.*
LLL: IV, 2.

native, legitimate, hereditary, genuine; intimately related.
Rich2: Richard, III, 2, 25.
Ham: King, I, 2, 47.

natural, a born idiot or fool.
Temp: Trinculo, III, 2, 57.

nature
Nature teaches beasts to know their friends.
Cor: Sicinius, II, 1, 6.

. . . of a free and open nature
That thinks men honest that but seem to be so . . .
Oth: Iago, I, 3, 405.

Yet nature is made better by no mean
But nature makes that mean. So, over that art
Which you say adds to nature, is an art
That nature makes.
Wint: Polixenes, IV, 4, 89.

nature. See LOVE, STRANGE FELLOWS.

nature's bastards, grown artificially by cross-breeding.
Wint: Perdita, IV, 4, 83.

nature's bequest
Nature's bequest gives nothing, but doth lend . . .
Sonnet: IV, 3.

nature's livery, inherent, inborn or natural attribute.
Ham: Hamlet, I, 4, 32.

nature's second course, sleep (main course of a meal); the first course being food.
Macb: Macbeth, II, 2, 39.

naught, mischievous, wanton, indecent, disgusting, wicked.
Ham: Ophelia, III, 2, 157.
Lear: Lear, II, 4, 136.

MND: Flute, IV, 2, 14.

nave, navel; hub or center of a wheel.
Macb: Captain, I, 2, 22.
Ham: Player, II, 2, 518.

Nazarite, Nazarene; the reference is to Christ driving the devils out of men and into swine (Luke, 7: 32-33).
MerV: Shylock, I, 3, 35.

neaf, fist.
MND: Bottom, IV, 1, 20.
2H4: Pistol, II, 4, 200.

Neapolitan bone-ache, venereal disease.
T&C: Thersites, II, 3, 21.

neat, ox, cow.
1H4: Falstaff, II, 4, 27.
Shrew: Grumio, IV, 3, 17.
Wint: Servant, IV, 4, 332— *neatherd,* cowboy.

neat's leather, cowhide, leather from cattle of the ox variety; shoes.
Temp: Stephano, II, 2, 73.
JC: Cobbler, I, 1, 29.

neb, originally beak; later, mouth, nose, face.
Wint: Leontes, I, 2, 183.

Nebuchadnezzar, "did eat grass as oxen" from Daniel (4: 28-37).
All'sW: Clown, IV, 5, 21.

necessities
The art of our necessities is strange,
That can make vile things precious.
Lear: Lear, III, 2, 70.

necessity
Necessity will make us all forsworn
Three thousand times within this three years' space;
For every man with his affects is born,
Not by might mastered but by special grace.
LLL: Berowne, I, 1, 150. See AFFECTS, GRACE.

There is no virtue like necessity.
Rich2: Gaunt, I, 3, 278—proverb used earlier by Chaucer.

To make a virtue of necessity . . .
2GENT: 2Outlaw, IV, 1, 62.

needle's eye. See CAMEL.

neeze, to sneeze.
MND: Puck, II, 1, 56.

ne intelligis, domine?, Latin, do you understand, sir?
LLL: Holofernes, V, 1, 29.

Nemean lion's nerve; sinew, tendon from the savage lion, whelp of Typhon, a hundred-headed monster, and Echidna, half-woman and half-serpent, that lived in Nemea, a valley in Argolis; Hercules slew the beast as one of his tasks of strength and courage, known as the Twelve Labors of Heracles (Hercules).
HAM: Hamlet, I, 4, 83.
LLL: Boyet, IV, 1, 90.
2NK: Theseus, I, 2, 68.

Nemesis, goddess of justice; punished arrogance and pride; retribution.
1H6: Lucy, IV, 7, 78.

nephew, cousin, most common Elizabethan usage; grandson.
1H6: Mortimer, II, 5, 64.
T&C: Alexander, I, 2, 13.
OTH: Iago, I, 1, 113.

Neptune, Roman god of the sea, equivalent of Greek god, Poseidon.
TEMP: Prospero, V, 1, 35.
A&C: Menas, II, 7, 136.
WINT: Florizel, IV, 4, 28—reference to Neptune's wooing of Theophane disguised as a ram.

Nereides, sea nymphs or mermaids; according to Steevens, the fifty daughters of Nereus and Doris, gods of the Aegean Sea, were unlike mermaids in that they had complete human forms.
A&C: Enobarbus, II, 2, 211.

Nerissa, Portia's lady-in-waiting; marries Gratiano.
MERV: I, 2.

Nero (Nero Claudius Caesar), 37-68 AD; ruled as Roman emperor (54-68); killed his mother, Agrippina; believed to have played on his lute (fiddle) while Rome burned; noted for cruelty.
HAM: Hamlet, III, 2, 412.
1H6: Talbot, I, 4, 95.
3H6: King, III, 1, 40.

nerve, sinew, tendon, where strength of the body lies.
TEMP: Prospero, I, 2, 484.

Nervii, Belgian tribe conquered by Caesar during his campaigns in Gaul.
JC: Antony, III, 2, 178.

Nessus, centaur; killed by a poisoned arrow shot by Hercules in defense of his wife Deianira, whom Nessus tried to rape when he carried her across the river Evenus.
A&C: Antony, IV, 12, 43.
ALL'SW: Parolles, IV, 3, 281.

Nestor, wise man, aged counselor; old King of Pylos; joined Greek expedition against Troy; supports Ulysses in trying to get Achilles angry at Ajax (T&C).
T&C: I, 3.
LLL: Berowne, IV, 3, 169.
MERV: Solanio, I, 1, 56.

nether-stocks, stockings, made of material; upper-stocks were breeches.
1H4: Falstaff, II, 4, 130.

nettle
We call a nettle but a nettle and
The faults of fools but folly.
COR: Menenius, II, 1, 207.

nettles, coarse herbs with stinging hairs; referred to in expression nettled or "stung to the quick."
HAM: Queen, IV, 7, 171.

neuter, neutral, impartial; unconcerned, indifferent.
RICH2: York, II, 3, 159.
HAM: Player, II, 2, 503.

new customs
New customs,
Though they be never so ridiculous
(Nay, let 'em be unmanly), yet are followed.
HEN8: Lord Sandys, I, 3, 3.

Newgate, London prison.
1H4: Bardolph, III, 3, 104.

news, a plural noun in Shakespeare's time.
RICH2: Queen, III, 4, 100.

nice, accurately detailed, exact, precise.
MACB: Macduff, IV, 3, 174.
LLL: Berowne, V, 2, 232.

nice, trivial, flimsy, unimportant.
2H4: Mowbray, IV, 1, 191.
R&J: Friar, V, 2, 18.
OTH: Cassio, III, 3, 15.

nice, wanton, lustful, lascivious.
CYM: Posthumus, II, 5, 26.
LLL: Moth, III, 1, 24.
A&C: Antony, III, 13, 180.

nicely, by the use of sophistry, unscrupulously, underhanded.
HEN5: King, I, 2, 15.

nick, beyond estimation or reckoning; cut short, snip, get the better of.
2GENT: Host, IV, 2, 76.
A&C: Enobarbus, III, 13, 8.

nickname, give things erroneous or indecent names, mark with folly, disgrace.
HAM: Hamlet, III, 1, 151.

niggard, slight, put off; hoard.
JC: Brutus, IV, 3, 228.
SONNET: I, 12. See CHURL.
HAM: Rosencrantz, III, 1, 13.

night

O comfort-killing Night, image of hell!
Dim register and notary of shame!

* * *

O hateful, vaporous, and foggy Night!

* * *

O Night, thou furnace of foul reeking smoke . . .
LUCRECE: 764, 771, 799—series of images built around night.

. . . Come, seeling night,
Scarf up the tender eye of pitiful day,
And with thy bloody and invisible hand

Cancel and tear to pieces that great bond
Which keeps me pale! Light thickens, and the crow
Makes wing to th' rooky wood.
Good things of day begin to droop and drowse,
Whiles night's black agents to their preys do rouse.
MACB: Macbeth, III, 2, 46. See SEELING.

The night is long that never finds the day.
MACB: Malcolm, IV, 3, 240.

The dragon wing of night o'er-spreads the earth . . .
T&C: Achilles, V, 8, 17.

nighted color, black, then as now, the color of mourning.
HAM: Queen, I, 2, 68—unlike the gayly clad members of the court, Hamlet, mourning his father, wears black.

nightingale. See ROAR, SINGING BIRDS.

night owls shriek, omen of death.
RICH2: Richard, III, 3, 183.

night-rule, devilment, mischief or diversions in the night.
MND: Oberon, III, 2, 5.

night's swift dragons, dragons pulled the chariot of Hecate, goddess of the night; in OVID's *Metamorphoses* (VII, 218-21), Medea is rescued by a team of dragons after she appeals to Hecate.
MND: Puck, III, 2, 379.

Nilus' slime, richly productive mud of the Nile River.
A&C: Cleopatra, I, 3, 69.

nim, steal, thief.
HEN5: Pistol, II, 1, 115—pun on Nym (character).

nine men's morris, game played on a square cut in the turf by two players using nine "men" (counters, pebbles, pins, disks or pegs) that are moved until one player has "taken" all the pieces of his opponent; similar to checkers.
MND: Titania, II, 1, 98.

Nine Worthies, interlude generally presented with Hector, Alexander the Great, Julius Caesar, Joshua, King David, Judas Maccabaeus, King Arthur, Charlemagne and either Guy of Warwick or Godfrey of Bouillon; Shakespeare included Hercules and Pompeus.

LLL: V, 2—presented before the King of Navarre and his guests. See COSTARD, HOLOFERNES, SIR NATHANIEL, MOTH and ARMADO.

2H4: Doll, II, 4, 239.

Niobe, daughter of Tantalus, wife of Amphion, mother of seven sons and seven daughters; angered the gods by her arrogant belittling of Leto (Roman, Latona), mother of only two children, Apollo and Artemis; Apollo slew the sons and Artemis the daughters of Niobe; she wept so pitifully that the gods, taking pity on her, turned her to stone upon Mount Sipylus in Lydia; stone or rock continued to pour forth everlasting water (tears).

HAM: Hamlet, I, 2, 149.
T&C: Troilus, V, 10, 19.

nobility

True nobility is exempt from fear.
More can I bear than you dare execute.

2H6: Suffolk, IV, 1, 129.

noble, gold coin worth six shillings, eight pence.

RICH2: Bolingbroke, I, 1, 88.
HEN5: Pistol, II, 1, 112.
1H6: Shepherd, V, 4, 23.

noble. See PEOPLE.

noble minds

. . . Therefore it is meet
That noble minds keep ever with their likes;
For who so firm that cannot be seduced?

JC: Cassius, I, 2, 314.

nobleness. See KINGDOMS.

noblest Roman

This was the noblest Roman of them all.
All the conspirators save only he
Did that they did in envy of great Caesar;
He only, in a general honest thought
And common good to all, made one of them.

J.C.: Antony, V, 5, 68.

noddy, simpleton.

2GENT: Proteus, I, 1, 119.

noise, band of musicians.

2H4: Francis, II, 4, 13.

noises (music)

Be not afeared. The isle is full of noises,
Sounds and sweet airs that give delight and hurt not.
Sometimes a thousand twangling instruments
Will hum about mine ears; and sometime voices
That, if I then had waked after long sleep,
Will make me sleep again.

TEMP: Caliban, III, 2, 144.

noisome, unwholesome, offensive.

RICH: Gardener, III, 4, 38.
ADO: Beatrice, II, 2, 53.

nole, head, "noodle," pate.

MND: Puck, III, 2, 17.

nonage, minority, boyhood.

RICH3: 2Citizen, II, 3, 13.

nonce, purpose, occasion.

HAM: King, IV, 7, 161.
1H4: Poins, I, 2, 201.

nonpareil, unequaled, unparalleled (for loveliness).

TEMP: Caliban, III, 2, 108.
MACB: Macbeth, III, 4, 19.
A&C: Enobarbus, III, 2, 11.

nonsuits, disdains, rejects the claim or petition of; throws the suit out of court.

OTH: Iago, I, 1, 16.

nook-shotten, running out into corners; remote, godforsaken place.

HEN5: Dauphin, III, 5, 14.

Norfolk, Duke of, supporter of York. [John, 3rd Duke (1415-61); 5th Earl of Nottingham.]
3H6: I, 1.

Norfolk, Duke of, killed with Richard at Bosworth. [John, called Jack of Norfolk (c1430-85); 1st Duke of Howard line (1483).]
RICH2: V, 3.

Norfolk, Duke of, son of above; appears as the Earl of SURREY (RICH3); bitter foe of Wolsey. [Thomas Howard (1443-1524), 2nd Duke of Norfolk; defeated Scots at Flodden Field (1513).]
HEN8: I, 1.

Norfolk, Duke of. See MOWBRAY.

North, Sir Thomas (c1535-c1601), English scholar; important translator of PLUTARCH's *Lives* from the French version of Jacques AMYOT (pub., 1579 as *The Lives of the Noble Grecians and Romans*); source of *Julius Caesar, Timon of Athens, Coriolanus* and *Antony and Cleopatra*.

north, north wind.
OTH: Emilia, V, 2, 220.

northern star. See CONSTANT.

Northren man, border thief; used long stick, pole or staff as a weapon.
LLL: Costard, V, 2, 701.

Northumberland, 1st Earl of, father of Hotspur; principal noble favoring the ascendancy of Bolingbroke; functions as his chief aide; presents Richard with the list of criminal charges in Parliament (RICH2); promises to join his son, Hotspur, and his brother Worcester in rebellion against Bolingbroke (1H4); however, not present at the critical battle of Shrewsbury when Hotspur is killed and Worcester captured; after encouraging Archbishop Scrope in his rebellion (2H4), hides in Scotland. [Sir Henry Percy (1342-1408), 1st Earl of Northumberland.]

RICH2: III, 1; 1H4: I, 3; 2H4: I, 1.

Northumberland, 3rd Earl of, grandson of Hotspur; supports Henry and the Lancastrian cause; killed at Towton. [Henry Percy, 1421-61.]
3H6: I, 1.

Northumberland, Lady, persuades her husband (1st Earl, see above) to take refuge in Scotland.
2H4: II, 3.

nose
And will as tenderly be led by th' nose
As asses are.
OTH: Iago, I, 3, 407.

note, mark of dishonor, brand of infamy; news, information, knowledge.
RICH2: Bolingbroke, I, 1, 43.
LEAR: Kent, III, 1, 18.
TEMP: Antonio, II, 1, 248.

note of expectation, list of expected or anticipated guests.
MACB: 2Murderer, III, 3, 10.

nothing
Nothing can be made out of nothing.
LEAR: Lear, I, 4, 146.

. . . But whate'er I be,
Nor I, nor any man that man is,
With nothing shall be pleased till he be eased
With being nothing.
RICH2: Richard, V, 5, 38.

not-pated, notted hair (cut short), close-cropped.
1H4: Prince, II, 4, 79.

nouns, corruption of wounds.
MWW: Quickly, IV, 1, 26—
'Od's nouns, God's wounds.

nouzle (nousle), train; coddle, pamper.
PER: Cleon, I, 4, 42.

novi hominem tanquam te, Latin, I know the man as well as I know you.
LLL: Holofernes, V, 1, 10.

noyance, damage, injury, harm.
HAM: Rosencrantz, III, 3, 13.

Numa, Numa Pompilius, second king of Rome; legendary figure who founded the temple of Janus.
Cor: Brutus, II, 3, 247.

numbers, verses, rhythm.
Ham: Polonius, II, 2, 120.
LLL: Longaville, IV, 3, 57.

numbers, cannot try the cause, an arena too small to hold the men who would fight it out or settle the issue by combat.
Ham: Hamlet, IV, 4, 63.

numbering sands, proverb for the impossible.
Rich2: Green, II, 2, 145.

nuncio, messenger.
TwN: I, 4, 28.

nunnery
Get thee to a nunnery.
Ham: Hamlet, III, 1, 122—also a house of prostitution, indicating Hamlet's bitterness toward women.

Nurse, first important comic character of the plays; "all the garrulity of old age, and all its fondness . . . also the arrogance of ignorance"—(Coleridge); acts as go-between for the lovers.
R&J: I, 3.

Nurse, one of three witnesses to the birth of Aaron's bastard son, he kills her.
Titus: IV, 2.

nurse
This nurse, this teeming womb of royal kings,
Feared by their breed and famous by their birth,
Renowned for their deeds as far from home . . .
Rich2: Gaunt, II, 1, 51. See SCEPTERED ISLE.

nuthook, hooked stick used to pull down branches of nut tree, usually synonymous with beadle or constable.
2H4: Doll, V, 4, 8.
MWW: Nym, I, 1, 171—"cop."

Nym, angry at being fired by Falstaff, tells Page and Ford of his love-letters to their wives (MWW); corporal; reconciled with Pistol after losing to him in the wooing of Mistress Quickly; goes on French campaign; hanged with Bardolph for looting (Hen5). See NIM.
MWW: I, 1; Hen5: II, 1.

Nymphs, the naiads, spirits appearing in the masque celebrating the betrothal of Miranda and Ferdinand; in ancient Greek mythology, the nymphs were semidivine creatures, beautiful maidens who personified the natural regions where they lived, such as forests, lakes, mountains, springs and fountains.
Temp: IV, 1.

O

oak, garland of oak leaves; symbol of great deeds; Roman equivalent of the Congressional Medal of Honor.
COR: Volumnia, I, 3, 17.

oath
Not for Bohemia nor the pomp that may
Be thereat gleaned, for all the sun sees or
The close earth wombs or the profound seas hide
In unknown fathoms, will I break my oath
To this my fair beloved.
WINT: Florizel, IV, 4, 499.

ob, halfpenny, from Greek *obolus.*
1H4: Peto, II, 4, 589.

obedience
To which is fixed as an aim or butt
Obedience; for so work the honeybees,
Creatures that by a rule in nature teach
The act of order to a people kingdom.
HEN5: Exeter, I, 2, 186. See STATE OF MAN.

Oberon, King of the Fairies; quarrels with Titania over a changeling; anoints her eyes with a magic juice that makes her fall in love with Bottom; leads the fairy masque in honor of the wedding of Theseus and Hippolyta.
MND: II, 1.

Obidicut. See FIENDS.
LEAR: Edgar, IV, 1, 60.

objectivity
Indeed it is a strange-disposed time.
But men may construe things after their fashion,
Clean from the purpose of the things themselves.
JC: Cicero, I, 3, 33.

oblivion
Time hath, my lord, a wallet at his back,
Wherein he puts alms for oblivion,
A great-sized monster of ingratitudes.
Those scraps are good deeds past, which are devoured
As fast as they are made, forgot as soon
As done.
T&C: Ulysses, III, 3, 145.

obloquy, disgrace, reproach.
1H6: Richard, II, 5, 49.
ALL'sW: Bertram, IV, 2, 48.
LUCRECE: 523.

obscure bird, the owl.
MACB: Lennox, II, 3, 64.

obsequious sorrow, dutiful, though not always sincere, evidence of sorrow, usually shown at funerals.
HAM: King, I, 2, 92.

observation, observance of ceremonial rites.
MND: Theseus, IV, 1, 107.

occasion, advantage, convenience, opportunity.
A&C: Enobarbus, II, 6, 140.
HAM: Laertes, I, 3, 54.
TEMP: Antonio, II, 1, 207.

occulted, secreted, undisclosed, hidden.
HAM: Hamlet, III, 2, 85.

occurrents, events, incidents, circumstances.
HAM: Hamlet, V, 2, 368.

Octavia, sister of Octavius Caesar; marries Antony in an attempt to bring the two together, but his desertion of her leads to war between them.
A&C: III, 2.

Octavius Caesar. See CAESAR, Octavius.

odd-even, about midnight; possibly from the gambling expression "take odds or even" and meaning "give or take" either side of midnight.
OTH: Roderigo, I, 1, 124.

'Od's heartlings, God's little heart, mild oath.
MWW: Slender, III, 4, 59.

oeillads. See ELIADES.

o'ercrows, subdues, overpowers, term from cockfighting.
HAM: Hamlet, V, 2, 364.

o'er ears, "in the soup," over or up to my ears in the water.
TEMP: Stephano, IV, 1, 214.

o'erleaven, knead together, changing throughout; pervade and modify.
HAM: Hamlet, I, 4, 29.

o'erlook, bewitch.
MWW: Pistol, V, 5, 88.

o'erparted, given too difficult a role to play.
LLL: Costard, V, 2, 589.

o'erraught, caught up with, overtook, cheated out of.
HAM: Rosencrantz, III, 1, 17.

o'ersized with coagulate gore, covered with a gluelike substance used for sizing of plaster; covered with congealed blood.
HAM: Hamlet, II, 2, 484.

o'erteemed, worn out with the bearing of children or childbirth.
HAM: Player, II, 2, 531—she had borne fifty-two.

oes, small round spangles; circles; pun on "o" and "i" or "o's" and eyes.
MND: Lysander, II, 2, 188.

offend
If we offend, it is with our good will.

That you should think, we come not to offend,
But with good will. To show our simple skill,
That is the true beginning of our end.
MND: Prologue (Quince), V, 1, 108.

offense
In the corrupted currents of this world
Offense's gilded hand may shove by justice,
And oft 'tis seen the wicked prize itself
Buys out the law. But 'tis not so above.
HAM: King, III, 3, 57.

office, service, duty, function.
A&C: Philo, I, 1, 5.
TEMP: Prospero, V, 1, 156.

offices, workrooms, servants quarters, household areas such as kitchens, larders.
RICH2: Duchess of Gloucester, I, 2, 69.
MACB: Banquo, II, 1, 14.
TIMON: Steward, II, 2, 167.

oily palm, a moist palm was believed to be an indication of an amorous or wanton disposition.
A&C: Charmian, I, 2, 52.

old, plenty of, many or much (general intensive).
TEMP: Prospero, I, 2, 367.
MACB: Porter, II, 3, 2.

old age
As you are old and reverend, you should be wise.
LEAR: Goneril, I, 4, 261.

Nature in you stands on the very verge
Of her confine.
LEAR: Regan, II, 4, 119.

The oldest hath borne most; we that are young
Shall never see so much, nor live long.
LEAR: Edgar, V, 3, 325.

Old Athenian, requests Timon's consent to the marriage of Lucilius and his daughter.
TIMON: I, 1.

old fashions

Old fashions please me best; I
am not so nice
To change true rules for odd in-
ventions.

SHREW: Bianca, III, 1, 80. See
NICE.

Old Hamlet. See GHOST OF HAM-
LET'S FATHER.

Old Lady, excellent minor character who talks Shakespearean
bawdy to Anne Bullen.

HEN8: II, 3.

old Vice, comic character in old
morality plays; armed with a
wooden dagger, he tried to cut
the Devil's nails.

TwN: Clown, IV, 2, 134.

Oliver, eldest son of Sir Rowland
de Boys; treats his brother Orlando badly and threatens to kill
him; when he follows him into
the forest, Orlando saves his life;
has a change of heart and promises his estates to his brother;
marries Celia.

AYL: I, 1.

Oliver and Rowland, two famed
knights of Charlemagne; heroes
of legend.

1H6: Alençon, I, 2, 30.

Olivia, young, lovely and wealthy
Illyrian countess; falls in love
with Viola, disguised as the
Duke's page; mistakes Sebastian
for his twin and agrees to marry
him.

TwN: I, 5.

Olympus, mountain in Thessaly,
Greece; at almost ten thousand
feet, it is the highest point in the
country; legends sometimes put
Olympus in heaven and not on
earth; hidden from sight by
clouds, it was the home of the
gods.

HAM: Laertes, V, 1, 276.

omen, catastrophe, disaster, calamity.

HAM: Horatio, I, 1, 123.

omit, pass by, neglect, ignore.

TEMP: Prospero, I, 2, 183.

omne bene, Latin, all's well.

LLL: Nathaniel, II, 2, 33.

on mount, at the highest point.

HAM: Laertes, IV, 7, 28.

on the hip, in an unfavorable or
disadvantageous position; in
one's power; wrestling term.

OTH: Iago, II, 1, 314.

on the top, the highest level or
balcony of the stage, which probably can be seen by the audience
and not by members of the cast.

TEMP: S.D., III, 3.

operant, vital, potent, active.

HAM: King, III, 2, 184.

Ophelia, daughter of Polonius,
sister of Laertes; forced to obey
her father and brother, she rejects Hamlet's advances, though
she loves him; innocent and
childlike, she is caught up in
something she cannot understand; repulsed and verbally
abused by Hamlet, after he kills
her father, she goes mad and
drowns herself.

HAM: I, 3.

opportunity

Who seeks, and will not take
when once 'tis offered,
Shall never find it more.

A&C: Menas, II, 7, 89.

O Opportunity, thy guilt is great!
'Tis thou that execut'st the
traitor's treason . . .

LUCRECE: 876 — beginning of
section on opportunity.

opposites

'Tis dangerous when the baser
nature comes
Between the pass and fell incensed points
Of mighty opposites.

HAM: Hamlet, V, 2, 60. See
PASS, FELL.

orbs, fairy rings or circles of tall
dark grass in the meadows or
pastures.

MND: Fairy, II, 1, 9.

order

The heavens themselves, the
planets, and this centre

Observe degree, priority, and place,

Insisture, course, proportion, season, form,

Office, and custom, in all line of order . . .

T&C: Ulysses, I, 3, 85. See IN-SISTURE.

ordinant, in control, directing, controlling.

HAM: Hamlet, V, 2, 48.

ordinary, supper or meal served at an eating-house or public tavern for a fixed price; important institution in Shakespeare's time and a central place for discussion, gossip etc.

A&C: Enobarbus, II, 2, 230.
ALL'sW: Lafew, II, 3, 211.

ordure, manure, fertilizer.

HEN5: Constable, II, 4, 39.

organ, instrument; means by which something is accomplished; agent.

HAM: Laertes, IV, 7, 71.
MEAS: Duke, I, 1, 21.

orgillous (orgulous), proud, haughty.

T&C: Prologue, 2.

orient, particularly lustrous, with the special sheen of priceless pearls.

MND: Oberon, IV, 1, 57.

orient. See GRACIOUS LIGHT.

orison, prayer, devotion, appeal.

HAM: Hamlet, III, 1, 89.
HEN5: King, II, 2, 53.
CYM: Imogen, I, 3, 32.

Orlando, youngest son of Sir Rowland de Boys; escapes to the forest after learning that his brother Oliver threatens his life; falls in love with Rosalind; rescues his brother, gets his estates back and wins Rosalind.

AYL: I, 1.

Orleans, Bastard of, Jean Dunois, the illegitimate son of Louis, Duke of Orleans; serves as a lieutenant to Joan of Arc; introduces the Dauphin to her.

1H6: I, 2.

Orleans, Duke of (Duc d'Orléans), friend and cousin of the Dauphin; captured at Agincourt (1415). [Charles d'Orléans (1391-1465), French poet; kept prisoner in England; ransomed (1440); married Isabella, widow of Richard II of England (1406) and Mary of Cleves, daughter of Philip the Good of Burgundy (1440); their son became Louis XII.]

HEN5: III, 7.

ornament

The world is still deceived with ornament.

In law, what plea so tainted and corrupt

But, being seasoned with a gracious voice,

Obscures the show of evil? In religion,

What damned error but some sober brow

Will bless it, and approve it with a text,

Hiding the grossness with fair ornament?

MERV: Bassanio, III, 2, 74.

Orpheus, legendary pre-Homeric poet; son of Oeagrus, king of Thrace, and Calliope, muse of epic poetry; famed for his playing of the golden lyre which could control the forces of nature as well as humans and beasts; hero of legend portraying his love for Eurydice and his visit to Hades.

MERV: Lorenzo, V, 1, 80.
2GENT: Proteus, III, 2, 78.
LUCRECE: 553.

Orpheus with his lute made trees
And the mountain tops that freeze
  Bow themselves when he did sing.

HEN8: Queen and Ladies, III, 1, 3—beginning of song.

Orsino, Duke of Illyria; unsuccessful in his suit to win Olivia; finally falls in love with Viola, who has been disguised as his page.

TwN: I, 1.

ort, scrap, fragment (leftover food).

TIMON: Bandit, IV, 3, 400.
T&C: Troilus, V, 2, 158.
LUCRECE: 985.

o's, round spots, smallpox scars, very common marks in the 16th century.

LLL: Rosaline, V, 2, 45.

osier, willow.

AYL: Celia, IV, 3, 80.
R&J: Friar, II, 3, 7.
PASSPIL: VI, 5.

osprey, large bird of prey (sea eagle) that feeds on fish.

COR: Aufidius, IV, 7, 34.

Osric, foppish courtier; informs Hamlet of the King's proposed fencing match with Laertes; characterization believed to be satire of young nobles of the court.

HAM: V, 2.

Ossa, mountain in Thessaly, Greece; almost 6,500 feet high.

HAM: Hamlet, V, 1, 306. See PELION.

ostent, show, display, appearance.

MERV: Gratiano, II, 2, 205.

Oswald, Goneril's steward; beaten by Kent; when carrying a love-letter from Goneril to Edmund, meets and attempts to kill the blind Gloucester; killed by Edgar.

LEAR: I, 3.

Othello, the Moor of Venice, The Tragedy of, written and performed 1604; registered 1621; published 1622; source, the seventh novella in CINTHIO'S (Giovanni Battista Giraldi) *Hecatommithi* (1565), with plot changes and the introduction of the character Iago.

PLOT: Othello, the Moor, a general in the service of the Venetian republic, falls in love with and secretly marries Desdemona, the daughter of Brabantio, a Venetian senator. When Othello picks Cassio as his lieutenant instead of Iago, the latter vows to ruin them both. While the Moor is explaining his love and marriage to the Duke and the Senate, a Turkish attack on Cyprus is threatened and Othello is sent to defend the island. Desdemona declares her love for her husband and leaves her father to accompany him.

Iago takes advantage of every opportunity and, succeeding in getting Cassio drunk while on duty, he has him demoted to the ranks. He also implants the idea in Othello's head that his wife has been unfaithful with Cassio and cleverly suggests to the latter that he get Desdemona to plead for him. Iago manages to "plant" on Cassio a handkerchief that Othello had given to his wife. Now certain of her infidelity, the Moor smothers her. Emilia, Iago's wife, discovers the murdered Desdemona and proves her innocence to Othello before Iago stabs her to insure her silence. Meanwhile, Iago persuades Roderigo to murder Cassio, but when he fails, Iago kills him to silence him. However, incriminating letters are found on the luckless Roderigo that prove Iago's guilt, and he is arrested. Othello fails in his attempt to kill Iago and commits suicide. Cassio, made lord governor, orders Iago tortured and executed.

Othello, "magnanimous, artless and credulous" — (Johnson); "Othello's nobility, his apparent control of his passions, was directed, until Iago got hold of him, to good purposes"—(Spencer); "Othello's marriage is important to him . . . as a symbol of being loved and accepted as a person"—(Auden).

OTH: I, 2.

othergates, otherwise, in another way.

   TwN: Andrew, V, 1, 197.

Ottomites, Ottoman Turks.

   OTH: Messenger, I, 3, 33.

ounce, lynx; wild animal of cat family.

   MND: Oberon, II, 2, 30.

ouph, elf, goblin.

   MWW: Mrs. Page, IV, 4, 50.

ourselves

   . . . 'Tis in ourselves that we are thus or thus. Our bodies are our gardens, to the which our wills are gardeners.

   OTH: Iago, I, 3, 322.

out of frame, disorganized, out of order.

   HAM: King, I, 2, 20.

out of his guard, from fencing term meaning unable to defend himself; at a loss for a witty reply.

   TwN: Malvolio, I, 5, 93.

out of warrant, illegal, prohibited.

   OTH: Brabantio, I, 2, 79.

outvenoms. See SLANDER.

outward habit of encounter, façade or shallow mannerisms of society.

   HAM: Hamlet, V, 2, 197.

outward watch, face of a clock.

   RICH2: Richard, V, 5, 52.

overconfidence. See SECURITY.

Overdone, Mistress, bawd; rants against strict Viennese laws aimed at immorality; sent to prison.

   MEAS: I, 2.

over-proud, very or too productive, fruitful, luxuriant.

   RICH2: Gardener, III, 4, 59.

overscutched, worn-out, broken-down, stale.

   2H4: Falstaff, III, 2, 341.

overture, discovered, disclosure.

   LEAR: Regan, III, 7, 89.

   WINT: Antigonus, II, 1, 172.

overween, presumptuous, arrogant.

   2H4: Westmoreland, IV, 1, 149.

Ovid (Publius Ovidius Naso), 43 BC–AD 17; famous poet; noted particularly for *Metamorphoses,* a narrative poem in 15 books, written in hexameters, based on Greek and Roman mythology.

   TITUS: Boy, IV, 1, 42.

   AYL: Touchstone, III, 3, 8— refers to Ovid's banishment from Rome by patron, the Emperor Augustus, for intrigue with his daughter.

owe, own, possess, have.

   CofE: Antipholus E., III, 1, 42.

   OTH: Roderigo, I, 1, 66.

   TEMP: Ferdinand, I, 2, 407.

owl, the hoot of the owl was believed to be an omen of death.

   RICH3: Richmond, IV, 4, 507.

   1H6: Captain, IV, 2, 15.

   3H6: Edward, II, 6, 56.

owl was a baker's daughter, refers to the legend of the baker's daughter who, having scolded her mother for having generously given Christ too much bread, was turned into an owl.

   HAM: Ophelia, IV, 5, 412.

Oxford, Earl of, supports Margaret and the Lancastrian cause; captured at Tewkesbury (3H6); joins Richmond and fights at Bosworth (RICH3). [John de Vere, 13th Earl of Oxford (1443-1513); helped consolidate Henry VII's position.]

   3H6: III, 3; RICH3: V, 2.

oxlips, hybrid primrose, crossed with cowslip.

   MND: Oberon, II, 1, 250.

oyes, call of the town (court, public) crier, from French *oyez,* here ye.

   T&C: Hector, IV, 5, 143.

   MWW: Queen, V, 5, 41—here used as roll-call.

oyster

   . . . the world's mine oyster, Which I with sword will open.

   MWW: Pistol, II, 2, 3.

oyster-wench, female fishmonger.

   RICH2: Richard, I, 4, 31.

pack, conspire, plot.
  CofE: Antipholus E., V, 1, 219.
  Cym: Cloten, III, 5, 80.
  Shrew: Gremio, V, 1, 122.

paction, agreement, concord, compact.
  Hen5: Queen, V, 2, 393.

paddle, play gently with the fingers; caress.
  Oth: Iago, II, 1, 259.
  Wint: Leontes, I, 2, 115.
  Ham: Hamlet, III, 4, 185.

paddock, toad.
  Ham: Hamlet, III, 4, 190.
  Macb: 2Witch, I, 1, 9—familiar (demon) of this witch takes the form or guise of a toad.

pagan, whore, harlot.
  2H4: Prince, II, 2, 168.

Page, Anne, although her father wants her to marry Slender and her mother Dr. Caius, she runs away with Fenton.
  MWW: I, 1.

Page, Master, called Thomas and George; father of Anne and William; trusts his wife and advises Ford to have more faith in his.
  MWW: I, 1.

Page, Mistress, one of the merry wives; husband calls her Meg; helps fool Falstaff.
  MWW: II, 1.

Page, William, young brother of Anne.
  MWW: IV, 1.

pageant, fake or feigned show, pretense; to mimic.
  Oth: 1Senator, I, 3, 18.

Page to Falstaff, after Falstaff's death (Hen5), serves as boy to Bardolph, Pistol and Nym; killed at Agincourt while guarding the "luggage"; presumed to be Robin (MWW).
  2H4: I, 2; Hen5: II, 1; MWW: I, 3.

pain, labor, trouble, effort.
  MND: Philostrate, V, 1, 80.

pain of life, pain of execution.
  Rich2: Richard, I, 3, 140.

painted, fallacious, specious, false.
  Ham: King, III, 1, 53.

painted, referring to a poster, sign or board painted for display outside a booth or tent at a fair.
  Temp: Trinculo, II, 2, 30.

Painter, sells his painting to Timon.
  Timon: I, 1.

Painter, William (c1540-94). English translator; published *The Palace of Pleasure* (first volume, 1566; second, 1567; second edition, 1575), which contained 100 stories from Plutarch, Livy, Boccaccio, Bandello, Cinthio, Straparola etc.; the source of material used by Shakespeare in the writing of *All's Well* and probably *Romeo and Juliet* and *Timon of Athens*.

painting
  Painting is welcome.
  The painting is almost the natural man;
  For since dishonour traffics with man's nature,
  He is but outside; these pencilled figures are
  Even such as they give out.
  Timon: Timon, I, 1, 156.

paint the lily. See EXCESS.

pajock, sometimes thought to be a peacock, a cruel and lecherous bird; others believe it refers to a scarecrow, because of the "king of shreds and patches" later in the play; several editors refer to Spenser's use in the form "patchock" or "patchocke" to deplore the degenerate English in Ireland.
HAM: Hamlet, III, 2, 295.

palabras, from Spanish *pocas palabras,* meaning few words.
ADO: Dogberry, III, 5, 18.

Palamon, nephew of Creon, King of Thebes; with cousin (later rival) Arcite, imprisoned by Theseus; falls in love with Emilia; ordered to fight in tournament against Arcite, loses; however, Arcite is thrown from his horse and, dying, gives Emilia to Palamon.
2NK: I, 2.

pale, fence, enclosure, barrier.
HAM: Hamlet, I, 4, 28.
MND: Fairy, II, 1, 4.
A&C: Menas, II, 7, 74.

pale, sad, melancholy; pallor.
MND: Theseus, I, 1, 15.

palfrey, saddle-horse.
HEN5: Dauphin, III, 7, 29.
2H6: Cade, IV, 2, 75.
TITUS: Titus, V, 2, 50.

palisado, defensive protection (wall, fence) made of iron-pointed stakes in the ground.
1H4: Lady, II, 3, 55.

pall, cover, shroud; fail, grow weak.
MACB: Lady Macbeth, I, 5, 52.
HAM: Hamlet, V, 2, 9. See IN-DISCRETION.

Pallas Athena. See MINERVA.
TITUS: Marcus, IV, 3, 55.

palliament, white ceremonial robe worn by a candidate for the Roman consulship.
TITUS: Marcus, I, 1, 182.

palmer, pilgrim who wandered from shrine to shrine; name de-rived from palm branch carried as a symbol that the bearer had made a pilgrimage to the Holy Sepulchre in Jerusalem.
R&J: Juliet, I, 5, 102.
2H6: York, V, 1, 97.
LUCRECE: 791.

palmy, prosperous, flourishing.
HAM: Horatio, I, 1, 113.

palsy, paralysis.
RICH2: York, II, 3, 104.

palter, use trickery, equivocate, hedge; shuffle.
A&C: Antony, III, 2, 63.
COR: Cominius, III, 1, 58.
JC: Brutus, II, 1, 126.

Pandar, owner of the brothel in Mytilene to which Marina is taken.
PER: IV, 2.

Pandarus, uncle of Cressida; acts as a go-between for the lovers; "let all pitiful goers-between be called to the world's end after my name: call them all Pan-dars" (III, 2); in Greek legend an archer, Lycian leader.
T&C: I, 1.
TwN: Clown, III, 1, 57.

pander, to satisfy or gratify the desires or passions of another; pimp.
HAM: Hamlet, III, 4, 88.
WINT: Leontes, II, 1, 46.
HEN5: Bourbon, IV, 5, 14.

Pandulph, Cardinal, papal legate; excommunicates John and forces French king to break alliance with England; persuades the Dauphin to invade England. [Italian cardinal; sent to England by Pope Innocent III (1211); supported John against the nobles during crisis over Magna Carta; virtual ruler of the kingdom during minority of Henry III; made Bishop of Nor-wich (1216), died there (1226).]
JOHN: III, 1.

pannier, basket.
1H4: 1Carrier, II, 1, 29.

Pannonians, Hungarian tribe; rebelled against the Romans (AD 6).

CYM: Cymbeline, III, 1, 74.

pansies, garden plants bearing many-colored flowers; the flower of thoughts, dreams; cupid's flower; also called heartsease and love-in-idleness.

HAM: Ophelia, IV, 5, 177.

MND: Titania, IV, 1, 76.

pantaloon, foolish old man of Italian *commedia dell'arte;* dotard.

AYL: Jaques, II, 7, 158.

SHREW: Lucentio, III, 1, 37.

Pantheon, temple in Rome dedicated to all the gods.

TITUS: Saturninus, I, 1, 242.

Panthino, Antonio's servant; suggests that Proteus, his master's son, go with Valentine to the king's court.

2GENT: I, 3.

pantler, pantryman, servant in charge of the pantry.

2H4: Falstaff, II, 4, 258.

CYM: Cloten, II, 3, 129.

WINT: Shepherd, IV, 4, 56.

Paphos, ancient town of Cyprus, probably founded by the Phoenicians; center of the cult or worship of Aphrodite (Venus), who was believed to have risen from the waves; doves were sacred to the goddess.

TEMP: Iris, IV, 1, 93.

VENUS: 1193.

PER: Gower, IV, Prologue, 32.

Paracelsus, Philippus Aureolus (real name Theophrastus Bombastus von Hohenheim, 1493-1541); German-Swiss physician, alchemist, philosopher; introduced many new drugs, important in the development of pharmaceutical chemistry; opposed GALEN'S views of the cause of disease.

ALL'sW: Lafew, II, 3, 12.

paramour

A paramour is (God bless us!) a thing of naught.

MND: Flute, IV, 2, 13. See NAUGHT.

Parca, Fate; Parcae, the Three Fates, in classical legend, wove the web of man's destiny and determined when it was to be cut or ended.

HEN5: Pistol, V, 1, 21.

parcel, part, portion, item, detail.

OTH: Othello, I, 3, 154.

2H4: Hostess, II, 1, 94.

1H4: Prince, II, 4, 113.

parcel-bawd, pimp.

MEAS: Elbow, II, 1, 63.

pard, leopard or panther.

AYL: Jaques, II, 7, 150.

MND: Oberon, II, 2, 31.

T&C: Cressida, III, 2, 201.

Paris, son of Hecuba and King Priam of Troy; also called Alexander; married Oenone, daughter of river god Cebren; in dispute between goddesses gave golden apple to Aphrodite, under whose protection he sailed for Sparta; succeeded in carrying off Helen, wife of Menelaus, causing the Trojan War.

T&C: II, 2.

SHREW: Tranio, I, 2, 247.

Paris, young nobleman related to the Prince of Verona; suitor for Juliet's hand approved by her parents; killed at the tomb by Romeo.

R&J: I, 2.

Paris balls, tennis balls.

HEN5: Dauphin, II, 4, 131.

Parish (Paris) Garden, arena for bear-baiting, near the GLOBE theater at BANKSIDE, Southwark.

HEN8: Porter, V, 4, 2.

parish top, large top kept by the parish, usually at the marketplace, for the enjoyment and exercise of the local parishioners.

TwN: Toby, I, 3, 44.

paritor, apparitor or officer of ecclesiastical court who served summonses on persons charged with sexual or moral offenses.

LLL: Berowne, III, 1, 188.

Park-ward, toward Windsor Great Park.

MWW: Simple, III, 1, 5.

parle, trumpet signal to announce a conference; parley, meeting.
RICH2: Bolingbroke, I, 1, 192.
HAM: Polonius, I, 3, 123.

parlous, shocking, awful, perilous.
MND: Snout, III, 1, 14.
AYL: Touchstone, III, 2, 45.

parlous, mischievous, precocious, clever.
RICH3: Queen, II, 4, 35.

parmacity, spermaceti, fatty or waxy substance extracted from the head of a sperm whale; used in ointments.
1H4: Hotspur, I, 3, 58.

Parolles, famous braggart, coward; follower of Bertram; "A very tainted fellow, and full of wickedness"; captured and blindfolded in mock ambush, gives information that would harm his companions; exceptional characterization; lacks sense of humor.
ALL'SW: I, 1.

part, personal quality or attribute; action, deed; ability.
LLL: Maria, II, 1, 44.
OTH: Othello, I, 2, 31.
MND: Helena, III, 2, 153.

Parthia, kingdom southeast of the Caspian Sea; ruled by Persians, Alexander the Great and the Seleucidae; independent (250 BC); fought off Roman attacks until reconquered by the Persians (226 AD); people of Turkoman stock; famed fighters on horseback using bow as only weapon.
A&C: Messenger, I, 2, 104.
CYM: Iachimo, I, 6, 20.

partial slander, unbecoming partiality to one's own son or heir.
RICH2: Gaunt, I, 3, 241.

parti-coated, wearing cloak of the fool.
LLL: Berowne, V, 2, 775. See MOTLEY.

particular, personal, of private concern, individual.
OTH: Brabantio, I, 3, 55.

COR: 3Citizen, II, 3, 48.
HAM: Polonius, II, 1, 12—*particular demands,* direct questions.

parting
Goodnight, goodnight! Parting is such sweet sorrow,
That I shall say goodnight till it be morrow.
R&J: Juliet, II, 2, 186.

partisan, 16-17th century weapon used by the infantry in defense against the cavalry; long-handled spear with a blade having one or more lateral cutting projections; pike.
HAM: Marcellus, I, 1, 140.
A&C: 2Servant, II, 7, 14.
CYM: Lucius, IV, 2, 399.

Partlet, from Pertelote, the traditional name for the hen (rooster, Chanticlere); in CHAUCER'S *Nuns' Priest's Tale,* the hen almost ruins her husband by her complete dominance over him; nagging hen in *Reynard the Fox.*
WINT: Leontes, II, 3, 75.
1H4: Falstaff, III, 3, 60.

party-verdict, one opinion among many, together forming a legal verdict.
RICH2: Richard I, 3, 234.

pass, thrust or lunge, fencing term.
HAM: Hamlet, V, 2, 61. See OPPOSITES.
MWW: Shallow, II, 1, 234.

passado, forward thrust with the sword in fencing; Italian, *passata,* Spanish, *pasada;* pass.
LLL: Armado, I, 2, 185.
R&J: Mercutio, II, 4, 27.

passage, descent, source; people passing or going by.
HEN5: Canterbury, I, 1, 86.
OTH: Cassio, V, 1, 37.
COFE: Balthazar, III, 1, 99.

passant, heraldic term for walking.
MWW: Evans, I, 1, 20.

passenger, pedestrian, wayfarer, traveler.
RICH2: Bolingbroke, V, 3, 9.

passing fell, exceedingly angry, fierce, cruel, hot tempered.
MND: Puck, II, 1, 20.

passion, feel deep emotion; grieve; passionate.
TEMP: Prospero, V, 1, 24.
LLL: Ferdinand, I, 1, 263.
JOHN: Dauphin, II, 1, 544.

This passion, and the death of a dear friend, would go near to make a man look sad.
MND: Theseus, V, 1, 293.

Passionate Pilgrim, The, twenty-one poems published in octavo by W. Jaggard (1599); five (I, II, III, V, XVI) are definitely by Shakespeare, the others debated.

passion's slave
. . . Give me that man
That is not passion's slave, and I will wear him
In my heart's core, ay, in my heart of heart,
As I do thee.
HAM: Hamlet, III, 2, 76.

pass of pate, razor-sharp expression of wit; pointed or clever witticism.
TEMP: Stephano, IV, 1, 244.

passy measures pavin, debated meaning, possibly refers to eight-bar double-slow stately dance; *passamezzo,* Italian for slow measure.
TwN: Toby, V, 1, 206.

past. See GRIEF.

past and present
. . . O thoughts of men accursed!
Past, and to come, seems best; things present, worst.
2H4: Archbishop, I, 3, 107.

paste, top or covering like pie-crust.
RICH2: Richard, III, 2, 154.

pastern, hoof; part of the horse's foot between the fetlock and the coffin bone.
HEN5: Dauphin, III, 7, 13.

pat, precisely on time, on the dot.
MND: Quince, III, 1, 2.

patch, fool, clown.
TEMP: Caliban, III, 2, 71.
COFE: Dromio S., III, 1, 32.
MACB: Macbeth, V, 3, 15.

patchery, knavery, chicanery.
TIMON: Timon, V, 1, 99.
T&C: Thersites, II, 3, 76.

patches
As patches set upon a little breach
Discredit more in hiding of the fault
Than did the fault before it was so patched.
JOHN: Pembroke, IV, 2, 32.

pate, head; usually top or bald area.
HAM: Hamlet, II, 2, 599.
LLL: Longaville, I, 1, 26.
OTH: Iago, II, 1, 127.

paten, tile; thin plate or disk of metal.
MERV: Lorenzo, V, 1, 59.

pathetic fallacy, a poetic mode in which animals or inanimate objects are given human characteristics or qualities.
RICH2: Richard, III, 2, 6.

patience
. . . 'Tis all men's office to speak patience
To those that wring under the load of sorrow,
But no man's virtue nor sufficiency
To be so moral when he shall endure
The like himself.
ADO: Leonato, V, 1, 27.

Patience unmoved, no marvel though she pause;
They can be meek that have no other cause.
A wretched soul bruised with adversity
We bid be quiet when we hear it cry;
But were we burdened with like weight of pain,
As much, or more, we should ourselves complain.
COFE: Adriana, II, 1, 32.

Though patience be a tired mare,
yet she will plod . . .
HEN5: Nym, II, 1, 26.

Patience is for poltroons . . .
3H6: Clifford, I, 1, 62. See
POLTROON.

How poor are they that have
not patience!
What wound did ever heal but
by degrees?
OTH: Iago, II, 3, 376.

. . . Yet thou dost look
Like Patience gazing on kings'
graves and smiling
Extremity out of act.
PER: Pericles, V, 1, 138.

. . . like Patience on a monument . . .
TwN: Viola, II, 4, 117.

Patience, Queen Katherine's
woman-in-waiting.
HEN8: IV, 2.

Patroclus, Grecian commander;
friend of Achilles; his death at
the hands of the Trojans finally
stirs Achilles to action.
T&C: II, 1.

pauca, few; see PALABRAS.
HEN5: Pistol, II, 1, 83.
SHREW: Beggar (Sly), Induc-
tion, 1, 5—say no more.
LLL: Holofernes, II, 2, 171—
pauca verba, let's forget it.

Paulina, honest, clever, fearless
wife of Antigonus; defends
Hermione against Leontes'
charges; brings him prison-born
Perdita; announces Hermione's
death; eventually reconciles the
king and the "restored" Hermione; marries Camillo.
WINT: II, 2.

Paul's, St. Paul's Cathedral, London.
1H4: Prince, II, 4, 576.
RICH3: Anne, I, 2, 30.
2H4: Falstaff, I, 2, 58—servants were hired there.

paunch, stab in the abdomen, dis-
embowel.
TEMP: Caliban, III, 2, 98.

pawn, pledge, gage, stake.

RICH2: Bolingbroke, I, 1, 74.
LEAR: Kent, I, 1, 157.
TIMON: Old Athenian, I, 1,
147.

pax, piece of metal with Crucifixion stamped on it; small tablet with picture of Christ, the
Virgin or a saint that was passed
around during Mass to be kissed
by the communicants.
HEN5: Pistol, III, 6, 42.

pay, lease or rent on a yearly
basis.
HAM: Captain, IV, 4, 20.

peace
I speak of peace while covert
enmity
Under the smile of safety
wounds the world.
2H4: Rumour, Induction, 9.

Our peace will, like a broken
limb united,
Grow stronger for the breaking.
2H4: Archbishop, IV, 1, 222.

A peace is of the nature of a
conquest;
For then both parties nobly are
subdued,
And neither party loser.
2H4: Archbishop, IV, 2, 89.

. . . Better be with the dead,
Whom we, to gain our peace,
have sent to peace,
Than on the torture of the mind
to lie
In restless ecstasy.
MACB: Macbeth, III, 2, 19.

Peace shall go sleep with Turks
and infidels,
And in this seat of peace tumul-
tuous wars
Shall kin with kin and kind with
kind confound.
RICH2: Carlisle, IV, 1, 139.

peach, inform, turn king's evidence; denounce.
MEAS: Pompey, IV, 3, 13.
1H4: Falstaff, II, 2, 47.

peacocks, these birds were sacred
to Juno and pulled her chariot.
TEMP: Iris, IV, 1, 74.

peak, brood, mope; sneak.
HAM: Hamlet, II, 2, 594.

peascod, full or mature pea pod.
MND: Bottom, III, 1, 191.

Peaseblossom, one of Titania's fairies.
MND: III, 1.

peat, little pet; common expression (1570-1640).
SHREW: Katherina, I, 1, 78.

pebbled shore. See TIME.

peculiar, private, personal, individual.
OTH: Desdemona, III, 3, 79.
HAM: Rosencrantz, III, 3, 11.
MEAS: Pompey, I, 2, 91.

Pedant, frightened by Tranio into pretending to be Vicentio, father of the real Lucentio; discusses marriage of his "son" with Bianca's father.
SHREW: IV, 2.

Pedro, Don, Prince of Arragon; arranges marriage of Claudio to Hero; later supports him in exposing her infidelity; makes amends when he discovers his mistake.
ADO: I, 1.

peep, look over, peer across and over rather than through a barrier or hedge.
HAM: King, IV, 5, 124.

peep (pip), spot on a card or die.
SHREW: Grumio, I, 2, 33—refers to card game "Trentuno."

peevish, foolish, silly, senseless.
OTH: Emilia, IV, 3, 92.

Pegasus, in mythology, born of the Gorgon Medusa's blood after she was killed by Perseus; winged horse of the Muses.
1H4: Vernon, IV, 1, 109.
HEN5: Dauphin, III, 7, 15.

peise (peize), balance, poise; hold back, weight or slow down, retard.
JOHN: Bastard, II, 1, 575.
MERV: Portia, III, 2, 22.
RICH3: Richmond, V, 3, 106.

pelf, possessions, property; profit, booty.
TIMON: Apemantus, I, 2, 63.
PER: Gower, II, Prologue, 35.
PASSPIL: XIV, 12.

pelican, bird reputed to nourish its young with its own blood.
RICH2: Gaunt, II, 1, 126.
LEAR: Lear, III, 4, 77.

Pelion, mountain in Thessaly, near the Aegean coast of Greece; according to legend, the Aloadae, two giants named Otus and Ephialtes, attempted to reach heaven and make war upon the gods by piling Mount Ossa on Mount Olympus and Pelion upon Ossa; they almost succeeded, but were slain by Apollo.
HAM: Laertes, V, 1, 276.
MWW: Mrs. Page, II, 1, 82.

Peloponnesus, southern peninsula of Greece, between Ionian and Aegean Seas; connected with the central part of the country by the Isthmus of Corinth; conquered by the Romans (146 BC).

pelting, paltry, meager, petty, worthless.
MND: Titania, II, 1, 91.
MEAS: Isabella, II, 2, 112.
RICH2: Gaunt, II, 1, 60.

Pembroke, Earl of, disapproves of John's submission to the Pope and accuses him of Arthur's murder; joins Dauphin's army of invasion; returns to the English side when he learns that the Dauphin plans to have them killed. [William Marshal (c1146-1219), Earl of Pembroke and Strigul; placed in charge of Henry II's oldest son (1170); went on crusade (1185-87); sided with King against his sons; present at Runnymede; fought off French (Lincoln, 1217); remained loyal.]
JOHN: IV, 2.

Pembroke, Earl of, Yorkist leader. [William Herbert, 1st Earl (1468); captured and beheaded by rebel supporters of Henry VI (1469).]
3H6: IV, 1.

Pembroke, Henry Herbert, 2nd Earl of (c1534-1601), succeeded his father (1570); appointed

President of Wales (1586); Mary, Sir Philip SIDNEY's sister (c1561-1621), was his third wife and the mother of William Herbert, 3rd Earl; noted as patron of Pembroke's Men who performed at Court (1592).

Pembroke, in Wales; seat of Jasper Tudor, Richmond's uncle.
RICH3: Christopher, IV, 5, 10.

pencilled, painted.
LLL: Rosaline, V, 2, 43.

pendent, hanging down over the water.
HAM: Queen, IV, 7, 174.

Pendragon, refers to Uther Pendragon, father of King Arthur, legendary hero, or his brother; title of ancient British chief in command of other chiefs.
1H6: Bedford, III, 2, 95.

Penelope, incredibly faithful wife of Ulysses who waited in Ithaca for ten years for her husband's return from Troy; put off suitors by claiming she had to finish a piece of weaving, which she was supposed to have unraveled every night.
COR: Valeria, I, 3, 92.

Penker, Friar, popular priest.
RICH3: Richard, III, 5, 104.

pensioner, royal bodyguard; of high birth, usually handsome with an excellent physique; wore magnificent uniforms.
MND: Fairy, II, 1, 10.

Pentecost. See WHEESON.
2GENT: Julia, IV, 4, 163.

Penthesilea, queen of the Amazons. See AMAZONS.
TWN: Toby, II, 3, 193.

penthouse lid, eyelid, which slopes like the roof of a penthouse or lean-to.
MACB: 1Witch, I, 3, 20.
LLL: Moth, III, 1, 18.

people
Faith, there hath been many great men that have flattered the people who ne'er loved them; and there be many that they have loved, they know not

wherefore; so that, if they love they know not why, they hate upon no better a ground. Therefore, for Coriolanus neither to care whether they love or hate him manifests the true knowledge he has in their disposition, and out of his noble carelessness lets them plainly see't.
COR: 2Officer, II, 2, 7.

Pepin, founder of the Carlovingian dynasty of French kings; son of Charles Martel and father of Charlemagne; King of the Franks (751-68); fought against the Moors and the Saxons; conquered Aquitaine and subdued Bavaria.
HEN8: Lord Chamberlain, I, 3, 10.
HEN5: Canterbury, I, 2, 65.
LLL: Rosaline, IV, 1, 123—Pippen.

pepper gingerbread, spicecake.
1H4: Hotspur, III 1, 258—mild oath.

peradventure, perchance, by chance.
MND: Bottom, IV, 1, 217.

Percy, Henry, called Hotspur because of his fiery temperament; son of the Earl of Northumberland; member of Bolingbroke's party; broke with Henry over exchange of Douglas for Mortimer and joined Owen Glendower in fighting against the King; deserted by his allies at Shrewsbury, killed. [1364-1403, son of Northumberland, nephew of the Earl of Worcester; fought at Homildon Hill, captured the Earl of Douglas; married Elizabeth Mortimer, daughter of the 3rd Earl of March.]
RICH2: II, 3; 1H4: I, 3.

Percy, Henry, Earl of Northumberland. See NORTHUMBERLAND.

Percy, Lady, wife of Hotspur, sister of Roger Mortimer, 4th Earl of March; pleads with her husband to tell her what bothers him; follows him to Wales

(1H4); urges her father-in-law
to revenge her dead husband
(2H4).

1H4: II, 3; 2H4: II, 3.

Percy, Thomas. See WORCESTER,
Earl of.

perdie (perdy), from French *par dieu,* by God; mild oath; indeed,
certainly.

HAM: Hamlet, III, 2, 305.
TWN: Clown, IV, 2, 81.
HEN5: Pistol, II, 1, 52.

Perdita, lost daughter of King
Leontes and Queen Hermione of
Sicily; brought up as a shep-
herd's daughter, she captivates
Florizel and, fleeing with him to
Sicily, is reconciled with her
parents.

WINT: IV, 4.

perdition, loss, destruction, ruin.

HAM: Hamlet, V, 2, 117.
OTH: Herald, II, 2, 3.
TEMP: Ariel, III, 3, 77.

perdu, sentry; soldier in dangerous post or position.

LEAR: Cordelia, IV, 7, 35.

perdurable, enduring, durable,
lasting.

OTH: Iago, I, 3, 344.
HEN5: Dauphin, IV, 5, 7.

peregrinate, manner or air of one
who has traveled; foreigner;
affected.

LLL: Holofernes, V, 1, 15.

peremptory, determined, resolute;
domineering, imperious.

COR: Sicinius, III, 1, 286.

perforce, by force, with violence;
of necessity.

RICH2: Bolingbroke, II, 3, 121.
HEN5: King, IV, 6, 33—against
my will.

perge, Latin word meaning pro-
ceed, go on.

LLL: Nathaniel, II, 1, 55.

periapt, amulet, charm, magic
girdle.

1H6: Pucelle, V, 3, 2.

Pericles, Prince of Tyre, partially
written by Shakespeare (probably in 1608, when it was registered); source, John GOWER's
Confessio Amantis (1393, VIII,
271-2008) which retells the
story from the Latin *Historia
Apollonii Regis Tyri* presumed
to be based on an early Greek
romance; Laurence Twine's *The
Patterne of Painefull Aduen-
tures* (registered 1576) was possibly another source; the name
Pericles, substituted for Apollonius in the original story, may
have been inspired by Pyrocles
in SIDNEY's *Arcadia* (pub. 1590).

PLOT: Gower, serving as
chorus, introduces Pericles,
Prince of Tyre, who succeeds in
answering the riddle put to him
by King Antiochus of Antioch
and wins his daughter. However,
afraid that he will be killed, having discovered the secret of their
incestuous relationship, Pericles
decides to sail for home. Forced
to escape Antiochus' vengeance,
he leaves his kingdom in the
hands of the faithful Helicanus
and flees to Tarsus. Warned that
he isn't safe there either, he
again sets sail only to be shipwrecked off Pentapolis. There he
enters the tournament celebrating the birthday of Thaisa, lovely
daughter of King Simonides, who
promptly falls in love with him
and he marries her.

Informed of Antiochus' death,
he sails for Tyre. Thaisa, appearing to have died in childbirth, is put into a chest and
buried at sea. She is washed
ashore at Ephesus, restored to
life by Cerimon, and, in gratitude, enters the Temple of
Diana. Pericles, meanwhile,
stops at Tarsus where he leaves
his daughter, Marina, to be
reared by Cleon, the governor,
and Dionyza, his wife.

Sixteen years later, having
turned into a beauty and out-
shining Dionyza's own daughter,
Marina is about to be murdered
by order of the jealous mother,

when she is carried off by pirates. At Mytilene, she is sold to a brothel-keeper but Lysimachus, the governor, falls in love with her and gives her the necessary gold to buy her freedom.

Meanwhile Pericles, told in Tarsus that his daughter is dead, is on his way home when his ship is driven ashore at Mytilene. There he is restored to health by Lysimachus and Marina, whom he recognizes as his long-lost daughter. In a vision, the goddess Diana calls him to Ephesus, where he is reunited with his wife. Marina, after being reunited with her mother, marries Lysimachus and they become the rulers of Tyre. Pericles and Thaisa go off to rule Pentapolis, while Gower informs the audience that the wicked Cleon and his wife have been put to the stake by the people of Tarsus.

periwig-pated, wearing a wig.
HAM: Hamlet, III, 2, 11.

perpend, reflect, weigh, ponder.
HAM: Polonius, II, 2, 105.
TwN: Clown, V, 1, 307.
AYL: Touchstone, III, 2, 69.

perpetual wink, eternal sleep.
TEMP: Antonio, II, 1, 285.

Perseus' horse. See PEGASUS.
T&C: Nestor, I, 3, 42.

perspective, Renaissance toy, in which a single image could depict several different objects when viewed (foreshortened) from the side.
RICH2: Bushy, II, 2, 18.

per Styga, per manes vehor, Latin, I am borne across the Styx, among the shades (or spirits of the dead); in modern terms, I will go through hell to get what I want.
TITUS: Demetrius, II, 1, 135—quotation from SENECA's *Hippolytus.*

pert, quick, lively, brisk, animated.
MND: Theseus, I, 1, 13.
TEMP: Prospero, IV, 1, 58.

pertaunt-like, from card game Post and Pair, suggesting a combination of winning cards; tyrant-like.
LLL: Rosaline, V, 2, 66.

pester, crowd, throng, infest.
COR: Sicinius, IV, 6, 7.

petar, small bomb, land mine, petard; modern equivalent, hand grenade.
HAM: Hamlet, III, 4, 207.

Peter, servant of Juliet's nurse.
R&J: II, 4.

Peter of Pomfret, imprisoned and hanged for prophesying that King John would lose his crown before the next Ascension Day.
JOHN: IV, 2.

Peter Thump, accuses his master, Horner, of saying that York is the rightful king; kills him in trial by combat (using sandbags); later hanged as a criminal.
2H6: I, 3.

Peto, helps Falstaff rob the travelers; brings news of the rebellion to the Prince.
2H4: II, 4.

Petrarch, reference to Francesco Petrarca (1304-74), considered the greatest purely lyric poet in Italian literature; famed for sonnets to Laura.
R&J: Mercutio, II, 4, 41.

Petruchio, dashing, witty, good-natured gentleman of Verona; an admitted fortune-hunter, he marries and tames (in a fashion) Katherina (the Shrew); "very honest fellow, who hardly speaks a word of truth and succeeds in all his tricks and impostures"—(Hazlitt).
SHREW: I, 1.

pettitoes, toes, trotters, pig's feet, human feet.
WINT: Autolycus, IV, 4, 619.

Phaethon, in Greek mythology, son of Helios, the sun god, and Clymene (wife of Merops); granted permission to drive the chariot of the sun, lost control and almost burned heaven and earth; Jupiter slew him with a thunderbolt; symbol of impetuous youth.
R&J: Juliet, III, 2, 3.
3H6: Clifford, I, 4, 33.
2GENT: Duke, III, 1, 153.

Pharamond, legendary king of the Salian Franks (ruled c420-28); known in Arthurian cycle of romance.
HEN5: Canterbury, I, 2, 37.

Pheazar, invented comic name; probably vizier, awesome person or one who frightens others away. See PHEEZE.
MWW: Host, I, 3, 10.

Phebe, shepherdess, loved by Silvius; falls in love with the disguised Rosalind.
AYL: III, 5.

pheeze (pheese), settle, take care of; frighten, beat.
SHREW: Beggar (Sly), Induction, 1, 1.
T&C: Ajax, II, 3, 215.

Philario, friend of Posthumus' father; Iachimo and the banished Posthumus meet at his home in Rome; tries to prevent the latter from wagering on Imogen's chastity.
CYM: I, 4.

Philemon, Cerimon's servant.
PER: III, 2.

Philemon, old peasant who, with his wife Baucis, unknowingly entertained the gods Jupiter (Jove) and Mercury in their cottage; story in OVID's *Metamorphoses.*
ADO: Pedro, II, 1, 99.

Philip II, King of France, supports Arthur's claim to the English throne. [1165-1223, son of Louis VII; succeeded to the throne (1180); greatest of Capetian kings; greatly enlarged

France during his reign; seized all English possessions in France (by 1208); built the Louvre, chartered the University of Paris; attacked Henry II and supported his sons against him.]
JOHN: II, 1.

Philip and Jacob, festival day of St. Philip and St. James, May 1st.
MEAS: Bawd (Overdone), III, 2, 214.

Philippi, city in Macedon; scene of battles between the forces of Antony and Octavius Caesar and those of Brutus and Cassius (42 BC).
JC: Brutus, IV, 3, 170.
A&C: Cleopatra, II, 5, 23—*Philippan,* sword with which Antony conquered Brutus and Cassius at Philippi.

Philip's daughters, virgin daughters of Philip the Evangelist who had the power of prophecy (Acts: 21:9).
1H6: Dauphin, I, 2, 143.

Philip sparrow, Philip (pronounced Phip) was a common name for a sparrow.
JOHN: Bastard, I, 1, 231.

Philip the Bastard. See FAULCONBRIDGE.

Philo, Antony's friend.
A&C: I, 1.

Philomel, Philomela, character in OVID's *Metamorphoses* who is turned into a nightingale.
CYM: Iachimo, II, 2, 46. See TEREUS.
MND: 1Fairy, II, 2, 13.
TITUS: Aaron, II, 3, 43.

philosophy
There are more things in heaven and earth, Horatio,
Than are dreamt of in your philosophy.
HAM: Hamlet, I, 5, 166.
Adversity's sweet milk, philosophy . . .
R&J: Friar, III, 3, 55.

Philostrate, Master of the Revels.
MND: V, 1.

Philoten, daughter of Cleon and Dionyza; only mentioned in the Chorus (Act IV) by Gower.
PER: IV.

Philotus, servant of one of Timon's creditors; asks Timon to pay his master.
TIMON: III, 4.

Phoebe, another name for the moon goddess, Diana.
LLL: Nathaniel, II, 2, 39. See DICTYNNA.

Phoebus, god of the sun, light and youth was also Apollo; known by either name or Phoebus Apollo.
HAM: Player King, III, 2, 165.
A&C: Cleopatra, I, 5, 28.
ADO: Pedro, V, 3, 26.

phoenix, mythical bird endowed with the ability to breed by nesting on spices and, after setting fire to the nest by beating its wings, a new phoenix is born out of the ashes of the old; only one phoenix was believed to be alive at one time, and that one lived for 500 years.
TEMP: Sebastian, III, 3, 23.
TIMON: Senator, II, 1, 32.
AYL: Rosalind, IV, 3, 17.

Phoenix and Turtle, The, printed with Shakespeare's signature in Robert Chester's *Loves Martyr: Or, Rosalins Complaint. Allegorically shadowing the truth of Loue, in the constant Fate of the Phoenix and Turtle* (1601); the volume contains poems by JONSON, Chapman, and Marston; *Let the bird of loudest lay,* Shakespeare's poem, is the fifth in the series.

Phoenix, The, theater in Drury Lane; roofed cockpit converted by Beeston (1616-17) into a private theater; first occupied by Queen Anne's Men (1617-19); pulled down by the Puritans (1649); *Pericles* produced there after the Restoration (1660); superseded by newer theaters.

Phrygia, area in Asia minor; Troy located there.

TWN: Clown, III, 1, 58.
T&C: Prologue, 7.
LUCRECE: 1502.

Phrynia, Alcibiades' mistress.
TIMON: IV, 3.

physician (precisian), strict spiritual adviser; puritan.
MWW: Mrs. Page, II, 1, 5.

physics the subject, acts as a stimulant; brings vigor to the people or nation.
WINT: Camillo, I, 1, 43.

pia mater, the brain.
T&C: Thersites, II, 1, 78.
LLL: Holofernes, II, 2, 72.
TWN: Clown I, 5, 124.

pick, pitch, throw.
COR: Marcius, I, 1, 204.

pickaxes, fingers.
CYM: Imogen, IV, 2, 389.

picked, cultured, refined, choice.
LLL: Holofernes, V, 1, 14.
HAM: Hamlet, V, 1, 152.

pickers and stealers, hands or ten fingers of my hands; taken from catechism of Church of England wherein the Christian is admonished to keep his hands from "picking (pilfering) and stealing."
HAM: Hamlet, III, 2, 349.

pickthanks, men who curry favor by flattery or telling tales.
1H4: Prince, III, 2, 25.

Pickt-hatch, district of London known for houses of prostitution (which had hatches or half-doors protected by spikes), thieves and other disreputable characters.
MWW: Falstaff, II, 2, 19.

picture, portrait, most likely a miniature; painted faces, make-up.
HAM: Hamlet, III, 4, 53.
OTH: Iago, II, 1, 110.

picture of No-body, a sign with an illustration of a man with a head, neck, arms and legs, but no body; used by John Trundle on a sign and on the title page of a play *No-body and Some-body* published in 1606.

TEMP: Trinculo, III, 2, 131.

pie, magpie; loud, unpleasant, un-lucky bird.

3H6: King, V, 6, 48.

piece, perfect specimen, paragon; enlarge, augment; heal, cure, mend.

TEMP: Prospero, I, 2, 56. See MAN.

A&C: Alexas, I, 5, 45.

OTH: Brabantio, I, 3, 219. See WORDS.

piece of him, a droll, ironic re-mark suggesting that Horatio is skeptical of what he was brought there to see; only "a part of" him is present.

HAM: Horatio, I, 1, 19.

Pie Corner, inn; according to John Stow's *Survey of London* (1598) "now divided into tene-ments, and over against the said Pie Corner lieth Cock Lane, which runneth down to Holborn conduit."

2H4: Hostess, II, 1, 29.

pied ninny, fool in patched, or parti-colored costume; jester's motley.

TEMP: Caliban, III, 2, 71.

Pierce, Sir, of Exton. See EXTON.

pigeon-livered, gentle, meek; pigeons were thought to be gentle because they were not possessed of gall.

HAM: Hamlet, II, 2, 604.

pight, pitched; determined.

T&C: Troilus, V, 10, 24.

pignuts, earthnuts, edible tubers with a nutlike flavor; also called hawknuts.

TEMP: Caliban, II, 2, 172.

Pigrogromitus ("of the Vapians passing the equinoctial of Queu-bus"); meaningless words; mock learned phrase or tomfoolery.

TwN: Andrew, II, 3, 23.

Pilate, Roman governor who ceremoniously washed his hands of the guilt of Christ's crucifix-ion (Matthew 27:24).

RICH2: Richard, IV, 1, 239.

RICH3: 2Murderer, I, 4, 278.

pilch, outer coat of leather or skin.

PER: 1Fisherman, II, 1, 12.

pilcher, scabbard; pilchard, small fish of the herring family.

R&J: Mercutio, III, 1, 84.

TwN: Clown, III, 1, 40.

pill, plunder, pillage, rob.

RICH2: Ross, II, 1, 246.

TIMON: Timon, IV, 1, 12.

Pillicock, part of an old rhyme; origin possibly in pelican; term of endearment; also used as a synonym for phallus.

LEAR: Edgar, III, 4, 78.

pin, trifle, insignificant.

MWW: Shallow, I, 1, 117.

pin and web, cataract; disease of the eye.

WINT: Leontes, I, 2, 291.

LEAR: Edgar, III, 4, 122—*web and the pin.*

pinch, torment, torture, gall.

WINT: Leontes, II, 1, 51.

Pinch, a schoolmaster and "doc-tor"; beaten by Antipholus of Ephesus when he attempts to cure him at the request of his wife Adriana; declares Antiph-olus and his servant Dromio mad and orders them put away.

CofE: IV, 4.

Pindarus, Cassius' servant; when Titinius has been captured and Cassius feels the battle of Phil-ippi lost, he promises Pindarus his freedom if he will kill him with the sword that stabbed Caesar; Pindarus stabs his master and flees.

JC: IV, 2.

pine, erode, wear away; starve.

RICH2: Richard, V, 1, 77.

VENUS: 602.

pines
He fires the proud tops of the eastern pines . . .

RICH2: Richard, III, 2, 42— the pine or cedar was con-sidered the king of trees.

pinfold, pound, enclosure for stray animals.
2GENT: Proteus, I, 1, 113.

pinion, flight-feather.
A&C: Dolabella (Thyreus), III, 12, 4.

pink, half-shut, winking; tired.
A&C: Enobarbus, II, 7, 119.

pin's fee. See LIFE.

pioned, disputed meaning with general opinion favoring dug, trenched or furrowed.
TEMP: Iris, IV, 1, 64.

pioner, miner, digger; military menial.
HAM: Hamlet, I, 5, 163.
HEN5: Gower, III, 2, 92.
OTH: Othello, III, 3, 346.

pipe, small flageolet with three stops; played with tabor or drum.
TEMP: S.D., III, 2, 134.

pipes of corn, musical instrument of shepherds, made of grain stalks.
MND: Titania, II, 1, 67.

pipe-wine, wine from the pipe (small cask).
MWW: Ford, III, 2, 90—pun on dancing to the music of the pipe (or canary).

Pippen. See PEPIN.

Pirates, save Marina from Leonine, who is about to murder her on orders from Dionyza.
PER: IV, 1.

Pirithous, Athenian general.
2NK: I, 1.

Pisanio, Posthumus' servant; Imogen is left in his care by his master; when ordered to kill her, helps her disguise herself and escape; reveals true identity of Fidele, Lucius' page.
CYM: I, 1.

pismire, ant.
1H4: I, 3, 240.

pissing conduit, popular name of fountain (conduit) near the Royal Exchange and Stokes Market, London, where lower classes tried to get water from its very small flow.
2H6: Cade, IV, 6, 3.

Pistol, braggart, rascally coward, who used incredible language; first appears as Falstaff's ensign (2H4); taken to prison; dismissed, he refuses to deliver Falstaff's love-letters, and in retaliation tells Ford about them; decides to marry Mistress Quickly (MWW); host of Boar's Head (HEN5), with Bardolph and Nym, goes on Agincourt campaign; scenes with Fluellen.
2H4: II, 4; MWW: I, 1; HEN5: II, 1.

pit, grave, pit or deep trench into which wild animals are driven and captured.
JC: Brutus, V, 5, 23.

pitch, height in terms of elevation; in falconry, the highest point in the flight of the falcon or hawk.
SONNET: VIII, 9.
TWN: Duke, I, 1, 12.
RICH3: Buckingham, III, 7, 188.

pitch and pay, cash on the line, no credit, nothing "on the cuff."
HEN5: Pistol, II, 3, 51.

pitched a toil, set or laid a trap, prepared a net or snare.
LLL: Berowne, IV, 3, 2.

pith, strength; essence, core. See PITCH.
OTH: Othello, I, 3, 83. See SPEECH.
SHREW: Tranio, I, 1, 171.
RICH2: Richard, I, 1, 109.

pitiful. See STORY.

pity

And pity, like a naked new-born babe,
Striding the blast, or heaven's cherubin, hors'd
Upon the sightless couriers of the air,
Shall blow the horrid deed in every eye,
That tears shall drown the wind.
MACB: Macbeth, I, 7, 21.

For pity is the virtue of the law,
And none but tyrants use it
cruelly.
  TIMON: Alcibiades, III, 5, 8.

piu por dulzura que por fuerza,
Spanish phrase meaning more
by gentleness than by force;
motto on the shield of the prince
of Macedon.
  PER: Thaisa, II, 2, 27.

placket, opening or slit in petticoat made for a pocket; pocket
itself; in Elizabethan bawdy a
"skirt."
  LLL: Berowne, III, 1, 186.
  WINT: Clown, IV, 4, 245.
  T&C: Thersites, II, 3, 22.

plague
A plague o' both your houses!
  R&J: Mercutio, III, 1, 103.

plainer, flatter; make smoother,
more level.
  MND: Puck, III, 2, 404.

plain-song, simple melody or
theme sung without elaborate
or varying pitch and intonation.
  MND: Bottom, III, 1, 134.

planched, boarded, made of
planks.
  MEAS: Isabella, IV, 1, 30.

planets strike, planets (stars)
were believed to exert an evil
influence and bring disaster.
  HAM: Marcellus, I, 1, 162.

plant, sole of the foot.
  A&C: 1Servant, II, 7, 1—pun
on double meaning of the
word; refers to their heavy
drinking and unsteadiness on
their feet.

Plantagenet, Lady Margaret, last
of the Plantagenets; young
daughter of Clarence; with her
brother, Edward, Earl of Warwick, mourns her father's death.
[1473-1541; created Countess of
Salisbury (1513); beheaded.]
  RICH3: II, 2.

Plantagenet, Richard. See YORK,
3rd Duke of.

plantain, broad-leafed weed used
for care and soothing of bruises.
  LLL: Costard, III, 1, 74.

plantation, colonizing, settling.
  TEMP: Gonzalo, II, 1, 143—
taken by Antonio to mean
planting.

plash, shallow pool, puddle.
  SHREW: Lucentio, I, 1, 23.

Plashy, Duke of Gloucester's
country estate in Essex.
  RICH2: Duchess of Gloucester,
I, 2, 66.

plate, silver coin; probably refers
to Spanish coin *real de plata.*
  A&C: Cleopatra, V, 2, 92.

plated, clothed or covered with
armor.
  RICH2: Richard, I, 3, 28.
  A&C: Philo, I, 1, 4.

platform, level area or paved construction on the ramparts where
cannon or guns were mounted.
  HAM: S.D., I, 1.
  OTH: Montano, II, 3, 125.

plausive, congenial, pleasing,
agreeable.
  HAM: Hamlet, I, 4, 30.

Plautus, Roman dramatist, (fl.
3rd century BC); noted for outstanding comedies; ranked with
TERENCE.
  HAM: Polonius, II, 2, 420.

play
. . . The play's the thing
Wherein I'll catch the conscience
of the King.
  HAM: Hamlet, II, 2, 632.

You would play upon me; you
would seem to know my stops;
you would pluck out the heart
of my mystery; you would sound
me from my lowest note to the
top of my compass; and there
is much music, excellent voice,
in this little organ, yet cannot
you make it speak.
  HAM: Hamlet, III, 2, 380.

players. See WORLD'S A STAGE.

play it off, drink or toss it down;
get on with it.
  1H4: Prince, II, 4, 19.

play the men, according to some
interpreters, "ply" the men, see
that they attend to their duties;
according to others, "act like

men," which implies a note of reproach—that those addressed are not performing to full capacity.

TEMP: Alonso, I, 1, 11.

pleached, folded; crossed and tied together as is a prisoner.

A&C: Antony, IV, 14, 73.

pleached, sheltered, fenced or covered with intertwining or interlocked boughs.

ADO: Antonio, I, 2, 10.

pleasure. See PROFIT.

plume, plumage or wing.

TEMP: Ariel, III, 3, 65.

plumed like estridges. See GORGEOUS.

plume-plucked, stripped of feathers, crestfallen, humbled; helmets usually had a plume of feathers.

RICH2: York, IV, 1, 108.

plume up, adorn, dignify, glorify.

OTH: Iago, I, 3, 399.

plummet, lead weight placed at the end of a cord and dropped into the water to determine its depth.

TEMP: Alonso, III, 3, 101.

plurisy, excess, overflow, plethora.

HAM: King, IV, 7, 118. See FLAME OF LOVE.

Plutarch (c50-130). Greek historian; author of the 46 "Parallel Lives" of Greeks and Romans; an exceptionally influential work; translated by Sir Thomas NORTH from the French version of Jacques AMYOT, it was the source of several of the plays.

Pluto, king of the underworld; god of Hades. See DIS.

JC: Cassius, IV, 3, 102.

2H4: Pistol, II, 4, 169—*Pluto's damned lake,* river Styx.

T&C: Ulysses, III, 3, 197—*Pluto's gold,* Pluto mistaken for Plutus, god of wealth.

pocket up, conceal; accept or take without protest.

TEMP: Sebastian, II, 1, 67.

poem unlimited, drama not limited to the rules of neo-classical writing.

HAM: Polonius, II, 2, 419.

poesy

Our poesy is as a gum, which oozes

From whence 'tis nourished. The fire i' th' flint

Shows not till it be struck. Our gentle flame

Provokes itself and like the current flies

Each bound it chafes.

TIMON: Poet, I, 1, 21.

Poet, comes to sell his verses to Timon.

TIMON: I, 1.

Poet, tries to get Cassius and Brutus to "love and be friends."

JC: IV, 3.

poet's eye

The poet's eye, in a fine frenzy rolling,

Doth glance from heaven to earth, from earth to heaven;

And as imagination bodies forth

The forms of things unknown, the poet's pen

Turns them to shapes, and gives to airy nothing

A local habitation and a name.

MND: Theseus, V, 1, 12.

Poins, Prince Henry's companion; "practical joker" who "swears with a good grace"; proposes to Henry (1H4) they rob Falstaff and his friends of the booty they have stolen from the travelers; suggests plan to expose Falstaff (2H4) in his "true colors."

1H4: I, 2; 2H4: II, 2.

point, tagged lace for fastening various parts or garments together; Elizabethan doublet or jacket was thus attached to the hose or breeches; buttons now used for similar purposes.

2H4: Lord Bardolph, I, 1, 53.

SHREW: Biondello, III, 2, 49.

A&C: Antony, III, 13, 158—*ties his points,* acts as valet.

point, pinnacle; reaching full maturity.
  MND: Lysander, II, 2, 119.

point-devise (device), exceedingly precise or particular.
  LLL: Holofernes, V, 1, 21.

pointing stock, laughingstock, butt of ridicule.
  2H6: Eleanor, II, 4, 46.

point of war, sound of trumpet as call to battle.
  2H4: Westmoreland, IV, 1, 52.

poise, weight, prize; importance; offset, counterbalance.
  OTH: Desdemona, III, 3, 82.
  LEAR: Regan, II, 1, 122.
  OTH: Iago, I, 3, 331.

poison
  Dangerous conceits are in their natures poisons
  Which at the first are scarce found to distaste,
  But with a little act upon the blood
  Burn like the mines of sulphur.
  OTH: Iago, III, 3, 326. See CONCEIT.

poison. See GOLD.

poke, pouch, pocket, purse, wallet.
  AYL: Jaques, II, 7, 20.

poking stick, metal rod, heated and used to stiffen or iron pleats in starched ruffs.
  WINT: Autolycus, IV, 4, 228.

Polacks. See SLEDDED.

pole, pole star, north or guiding star.
  OTH: 2Gentleman, II, 1, 15.
  A&C: Cleopatra, IV, 15, 65.

polecat, slang for prostitute.
  MWW: Quickly, IV, 1, 29.

pole-clipt, poles or stakes that surround or hedge a vineyard upon which the vines climb.
  TEMP: Iris, IV, 1, 68.

policy, clever politics, political acumen or villainy; strategy or scheme; the word was usually associated with Machiavelli, who had an evil reputation in England.

RICH2: Northumberland, V, 1, 84.
  1H4: Hotspur, I, 3, 108.
  TwN: Fabian, III, 2, 31.

politic, politically adroit.
  SHREW: Petruchio, IV, 1, 191.
  HAM: Hamlet, IV, 3, 21—*convocation of politic worms,* perhaps a reference to the Diet of Worms, a meeting of high Church officials summoned by Charles V, Holy Roman Emperor, and held on January 28, 1521, to question and condemn Martin Luther.

politician
  . . . Get thee glass eyes
  And, like a scurvy politician, seem
  To see the things thou dost not.
  LEAR: Lear, IV, 6, 174.

Polixenes, noble King of Bohemia; father of Florizel; close friend of Leontes; unjustly accused by him of committing adultery with his wife; escapes his wrath by returning home.
  WINT: I, 2.

poll, head.
  HAM: Ophelia, IV, 5, 196.
  2H4: Prince, II, 4, 282.

polled, cleared, cropped, shorn, bald.
  COR: 3Servingman, IV, 5, 215.

Polonius, lord chamberlain; father of Laertes and Ophelia, determined to rule their lives; petty despot; though with some dignity, he is old, pompous and meddlesome; advice to his son is paralleled in John LYLY's *Euphues: the Anatomy of Wit* (1580), and other sources; adept at intrigue, it has been suggested that he was involved with Claudius in the murder of the King; killed by Hamlet while behind the arras in the Queen's room; called Corambis in the first quarto.
  HAM: I, 2.

poltroon, lazy coward, dastard, cur.
  2H6: Clifford, I, 1, 62.

Polydore, name given to Guiderius by Belarius (Morgan); in classical mythology, the youngest son of Priam and Hecuba, killed by Achilles.
CYM: III, 3.

Polyxena, daughter of Priam and Hecuba; beloved by Achilles; killed by Neoptolemus (see PYRRHUS).
T&C: Ulysses, III, 3, 208.

pomander, ball of perfume, scent-ball.
WINT: Autolycus, IV, 4, 609.

Pomfret, Pontefract Castle, in Yorkshire; partially destroyed during the English civil war.
RICH2: Northumberland, V, 1, 52.
2H4: Morton, I, 1, 205.
JOHN: Bastard, II, 2, 148.

Pomgarnet, Pomegranate; name of room in Boar's Head Tavern.
1H4: Francis, II, 4, 42.

pomp, festive ceremonial procession; pageant.
MND: Theseus, I, 1, 15.

Pompey, younger son of Pompey the Great; continues his father's fight against Rome; concludes treaty with the triumvirs at Misenum; finally defeated by Octavius after changing his mind and fighting again. [Pompeius Magnus Sextus (75-35 BC) called Pompey the Younger; defeated by Caesar at Munda (45); commander of fleet on coasts of Sicily and Italy; defeated by Agrippa in naval battle (36); fled to Asia Minor; captured and executed.]
A&C: II, 1.

Pompey (Bum), clown; servant to Mistress Overdone; arrested twice by Elbow and sent to prison; becomes assistant to Abhorson the hangman. See PARCEL-BAWD.
MEAS: I, 2.

Pompey's Porch, portico or entrance to Pompey's Theater in the Campus Martius; built by Pompey (55 BC).
JC: Cassius, I, 3, 126.

Pompion, pumpkin, slip of the tongue for Pompey.
LLL: Costard, V, 2, 504.

pomwater (pomewater), variety of large sweet apple.
LLL: Holofernes, IV, 2, 4.

poniard, dagger; usually slender with triangular or square blade.
ADO: Benedick, II, 1, 255.

Pontic, Black Sea, the Euxine.
OTH: Othello, III, 3, 453.

poop, deceive; play a mean trick.
PER: Boult, IV, 2, 25.

poor but honest
My friends were poor but honest; so's my love.
ALL'sW: Helena, I, 3, 201.

poor-John, dried and salted hake, a type of fish.
TEMP: Trinculo, II, 2, 28.
R&J: Gregory, I, 1, 37.

Popilius Lena, senator whose speech almost reveals the assassination plot.
JC: III, 1.

popingay (popinjay), old name for parrot; showy but senseless bird.
1H4: Hotspur, I, 3, 50.

popularity
. . . he which is was wished until he were; `
And the ebbed man, ne'er loved till ne'er worth love,
Comes deared by being lacked.
A&C: Caesar, I, 4, 42.

porches, entrances.
HAM: Ghost, I, 5, 63.

port, gate, portal; appearance, carriage, bearing; social position, state.
COR: Lartius, I, 7, 1.
HEN5: I, prologue, 6.
SHREW: Lucentio, I, 1, 208.

portage, portholes; cargo.
HEN5: King, III, 1, 10—eye-sockets.

portcullised, closed off by bars or a grating; enclosed, shut in.

RICH2: Mowbray, I, 3, 167.

Porters: MACB: II, 3; 2H4: I, 1; 1H6: II, 3; HEN8: V, 4.

Portia, beautiful, brilliant heiress in love with Bassanio; noted for her defense of Antonio in court scene; "Portia has a certain degree of affectation and pedantry about her."—(Hazlitt.)
MERV: I, 2.

Portia, devoted, noble wife of Brutus; Cato's daughter; anxiety for her husband's safety drives her to suicide.
JC: II, 1.

portly, stately, majestic, dignified.
1H4: Worcester, I, 3, 13.

possess, inform, acquaint, communicate.
TWN: Toby, II, 3, 150.
COR: Menenius, II, 1, 146.

posset, to curdle.
HAM: Ghost, I, 5, 68.

posset, hot, spiced nightcap.
MACB: Lady Macbeth, II, 2, 6.
MWW: Quickly, I, 4, 8.

post, pillar in tavern or shop upon which accounts were marked or scored by chalk lines or notches.
COFE: Dromio E., I, 2, 64.

post, speed, hasten, usually on horseback.
CYM: Iachimo, I, 5, 192.
LLL: Berowne, IV, 3, 188.
A&C: Cleopatra, I, 5, 61.

post, messenger, courier.
TWN: Viola, I, 5, 303.
MACB: Ross, I, 3, 98.
2H4: Falstaff, IV, 3, 40—horses.

postern, narrow gate; small back or side door.
WINT: Camillo, I, 2, 438.
2GENT: Silvia, V, 1, 9.
RICH2: Richard, V, 5, 17.

post-haste and romage, with unusual speed and excitement, great dispatch and disturbance, pressing activity and commotion.
HAM: Horatio, I, 1, 107.

Posthumus Leonatus, poor but noble husband of Imogen; easily tricked into believing her unfaithful; reconciled with her at end of play.
CYM: I, 1.

posy, short rhyming motto or message in "poesy" which was inscribed inside a ring.
HAM: Hamlet, III, 2, 162.
MERV: Gratiano, V, 1, 148.

pot (to the pot), to destruction or certain death.
COR: All, I, 4, 47.

potato, Spanish or sweet potato was believed to stimulate sexual desire.
T&C: Thersites, V, 2, 56.
MWW: Falstaff, V, 5, 21.

potatoes
. . . Let the sky rain potatoes; let it thunder to the tune of "Greensleeves," hail kissing comfits, and snow eringoes.
MWW: Falstaff, V, 5, 20. See ERINGOES.

potch, to thrust at, stab or poke.
COR: Aufidius, I, 10, 15.

potential, powerful.
OTH: Iago, I, 2, 13.

potting, drinking, tippling, imbibing.
OTH: Iago, II, 3, 79.

pottle, large goblet or tankard holding two quarts of liquid.
MWW: Ford, II, 1, 223.
2H4: Bardolph, II, 2, 84—*pottle-pot.*
OTH: Iago, II, 3, 56—*pottle-deep,* "bottoms up."

pouncet box, small perforated container, jar or box for perfume; pomander; used to counteract foul odors and possibly protect oneself against infection.
1H4: Hotspur, I, 3, 38.

pourquoi, French, why.
TWN: Toby, I, 3, 95.

powder, salt, pickle.
1H4: Falstaff, V, 4, 112.

powdering tub, salting or pickling tub; slang for steam bath or tub used as a cure for venereal disease.

HEN5: Pistol, II, 1, 79.

MEAS: Lucio, III, 2, 62—*powdered bawd,* pickled whore.

power

So that his power, like a fangless lion,
May offer, but not hold.

2H4: Hastings, IV, 1, 218.

power. See VIRTUES.

power of wit

Upon her wit doth earthly honour wait,
And virtue stoops and trembles at her frown.

TITUS: Aaron, II, 1, 10. See WIT.

power to hurt

They that have power to hurt and will do none,
That do not do the thing they most do show,
Who, moving others, are themselves as stone,
Unmoved, cold, and to temptation slow—
They rightly do inherit heaven's graces
And husband nature's riches from expense; . . .

* * *

For sweetest things turn sourest by their deeds;
Lilies that fester smell far worse than weeds.

SONNET: XCIV, 1, 13.

Powl's, St. Paul's Church.

HEN8: Man, V, 4, 16.

pow, waw, expression of contempt; pooh, pooh; to doubt the truth of the statement.

COR: Volumnia, II, 1, 157.

pox, plague, usually syphilis or venereal disease.

TEMP: Antonio, II, 1, 77.

practice, plan, plot, intrigue; treason.

LEAR: Edmund, I, 2, 198.
OTH: Desdemona, III, 4, 141.
COR: Coriolanus, IV, 1, 33.

practice

. . . The foul practice

Hath turned itself on me.

HAM: Laertes, V, 2, 328.

praemunire, writ by which a person may be apprehended on a charge of appealing to the Pope in an action against an English subject; punishment was forfeiture of goods and imprisonment.

HEN8: Suffolk, III, 2, 340.

praetor, magistrate, official of ancient Rome next in rank to the consul.

JC: Cassius, I, 3, 143.

praise

I never loved you much; but I ha' praised ye
When you have well deserved ten times as much
As I have said you did.

A&C: Enobarbus, II, 6, 77.

For we, which now behold these present days,
Have eyes to wonder, but lack tongues to praise.

SONNET: CVI, 13.

. . . One good deed dying tongueless
Slaughters a thousand waiting upon that.
Our praises are our wages. You may ride 's
With one soft kiss a thousand furlongs ere
With spur we heat an acre.

WINT: Hermione, I, 2, 92.

praised the vile

"When we for recompense have praised the vile,
It stains the glory in that happy verse
Which aptly sings the good."

TIMON: Poet, I, 1, 15.

prank, dress up, show off, adorn.

COR: Coriolanus, III, 1, 23.
TwN: Duke, II, 4, 89.
WINT: Perdita, IV, 4, 10.

prattle

. . . (as you know
What great ones do, the less will prattle of) . . .

TwN: Captain, I, 2, 32.

preambulate, go before, precede.

LLL: Armado, V, 1, 84.

precedent, original document or agreement; first draft; specimen.
JOHN: Dauphin, V, 2, 3.
1H4: Prince, II, 4, 37.

precept, writ, order, summons.
2H4: Davy, V, 1, 15.

precious, exceptional, rare; non-conforming or errant.
WINT: Polixenes, I, 2, 452.
OTH: Othello, V, 2, 235.

precisian. See PHYSICIAN.

precurse, hint of warning; announce in terms of an omen.
HAM: Horatio, I, 1, 121.

preech, breech, whip.
MWW: Evans, IV, 1, 81.

prefer, recommend, commend.
JC: Strato, V, 5, 62.
CYM: Queen, II, 3, 51.
SHREW: Baptista, I, 1, 97.

pregnant, meaningful, commonly used in phrase "pregnant with meaning"; quick-witted, clever, expert; evident, obvious, apparent.
HAM: Polonius, II, 2, 212.
MEAS: Duke, I, 1, 12.
OTH: Iago, II, 1, 237.

prenominate, previously mentioned, aforesaid.
HAM: Polonius, II, 1, 43.

preparation, accomplishment.
MWW: Ford, II, 2, 238.

presage, foreboding, presentiment, omen.
RICH2: Bagot, II, 2, 141.
JC: Cassius, V, 1, 78.

prescience, foreknowledge, sagacity, foresight.
TEMP: Prospero, I, 2, 180.
A&C: Alexas, I, 2, 20.

prescript, order, instructions, mandate.
HAM: Polonius, II, 2, 142.
A&C: Caesar, III, 8, 5.
HEN5: Dauphin, III, 7, 49—appropriate.

presence, assembled group, royal company; audience chamber.
HAM: Hamlet, V, 2, 217.
RICH2: Gaunt, I, 3, 289.

present, immediate, instantaneous.
OTH: Othello, I, 2, 90.
HAM: King, IV, 3, 67.
2H4: John, IV, 3, 80.

present horror, terrible silence of midnight.
MACB: Macbeth, II, 1, 59.

press, conscript, draft, call into service.
RICH2: Richard, III, 2, 58.
COR: Aufidius, I, 1, 9.
1H4: Falstaff, IV, 2, 14.

press, wardrobe, clothes-closet.
MWW: Evans, III, 3, 226.

pressed to death, tortured by the ancient method of *peine forte et dure;* in England those who refused to plead guilty or innocent were tortured under heavy weights.
RICH2: Queen, III, 4, 72.

pressure, imprint or impression produced by pressure, usually on a seal; idea.
HAM: Hamlet, III, 2, 28. See TIME.

prest, ready, prepared.
PER: Gower, IV, Prologue, 45.

Prester John, fabled king and Christian priest in the Far East (during the middle ages); from 15th century, believed king of Ethiopia or Abyssinia.
ADO: Benedick, II, 1, 276.

prevailment, persuasive, overpowering force.
MND: Egeus, I, 1, 35.

prevent, forestall or anticipate an event.
HAM: Hamlet, II, 2, 305.
2H4: Falstaff, I, 2, 259.
RICH2: York, II, 1, 167—Richard II forestalled the marriage of Bolingbroke to the daughter of the Duc de Berri for political reasons.

Priam, aged king of Troy; father of Hector, Troilus and Paris; husband of Hecuba.
T&C: II, 2.
HAM: Hamlet, II, 2, 470.

2H4: Northumberland, I, 1, 72.

Priapus, god of fertility and copulation; son of Dionysus and Aphrodite; to Elizabethans the representation of lechery.
PER: Bawd, IV, 4, 4.

prick, incite, urge, spur on.
HAM: Horatio, I, 1, 83.
OTH: Iago, III, 3, 412.
1H4: Falstaff, V, 1, 131.

prick, center of target, bull's-eye; mark off, indicate or check.
LLL: Boyet, IV, 1, 134.
2H4: Falstaff, II, 4, 359.

prick, point or mark on the sundial showing the time.
3H6: Clifford, I, 4, 34.
LUCRECE: 781.

pricket, buck in its second year; 2-year-old red deer.
LLL: Dull, II, 2, 21.

pricksong, melody accompanying a plainsong; music "pricked" or written as notes.
R&J: Mercutio, II, 4, 21.

pride, prime, best condition; height, highest pitch.
RICH2: Richard, V, 5, 22.

pride, heat, sexual desire.
OTH: Iago, III, 3, 404.

pride
. . . pride
Which out of daily fortune ever taints
The happy man . . .
COR: Aufidius, IV, 7, 37.

. . . He that is proud eats up himself. Pride is his own glass, his own trumpet, his own chronicle; and whatever praises itself but in the deed, devours the deed in the praise.
T&C: Agamemnon, II, 3, 163.

. . . Pride hath no other glass
To show itself but pride; for supple knees
Feed arrogance and are the proud man's fees.
T&C: Ulysses, III, 3, 47.

Priest, "churlish" character who at the obsequies of Ophelia ex-

plains that although she may be buried in consecrated ground, no Requiem Mass may be sung for her, as her death may have been a suicide.
HAM: V, 1.
RICH2: Richard, IV, 1, 173. See CLERK.

prig, thief.
WINT: Clown, IV, 3, 108.

primal, literally primeval, primitive; reference to Genesis (4: 11), the story of Cain and Abel.
HAM: King, III, 3, 37.

prime, sensual, lustful.
OTH: Iago III, 3, 403.

prime. See MOTHER'S GLASS.

primero, popular card game, early version of poker.
MWW: Falstaff, IV, 5, 104.
HEN8: Gardiner, V, 1, 7.

prince
. . . Good night, sweet prince,
And flights of angels sing thee to thy rest.
HAM: Horatio, V, 2, 370.

Prince of Cats, Tibert (Tybalt or Tibalt), a character in *Reynard the Fox*, was the prince or king of the cats.
R&J: Mercutio, II, 4, 19.

princes
For princes are the glass, the school, the book
Where subjects' eyes do learn, do read, do look.
LUCRECE: 615. See 2H4: II, 3, 31.

Princess of France. See FRANCE, Princess of.

princox, saucy, conceited boy; whippersnapper.
R&J: Capulet, I, 5, 88.

Priscian, famed Latin grammarian whose texts were well known; "to break Priscian's head" meant to speak poor Latin.
LLL: Holofernes, V, 1, 31.

pristine, ancient, old, former, early.
HEN5: Fluellen, III, 2, 88.

private, personal, intimate, favorite, pun or play on "private parts" and private referring to personal life as compared with public life or politics.
HAM: Guildenstern, II, 2, 237.

private wrongs. See ENGLAND'S PRIVATE WRONGS.

privy to, in possession of secret information concerning.
HAM: Horatio, I, 1, 133.
CofE: Dromio S., III, 2, 146.

prizer, one who fights (or wrestles) for a prize; champion; professional athlete.
AYL: Adam, II, 3, 8.

probal, probable.
OTH: Iago, II, 3, 344.

probation, verification, proof.
OTH: Othello, III, 3, 365.
HAM: Horatio, I, 1, 156.
MACB: Macbeth, III, 1, 80.

process, tale, story; conversation, course of events.
OTH: Othello, I, 3, 142.
HAM: Polonius, III, 3, 29.

process, summons to appear before a court of law; formal command.
A&C: Cleopatra, I, 1, 28.
COR: Menenius, III, 1, 314—due process of law.

Proculeius, Caesar's friend; sent to capture Cleopatra in the monument where she has taken refuge following Antony's death.
A&C: V, 1.

prodigal, extravagant, unnecessarily lavish; the parable of the prodigal son was an Elizabethan favorite.
HAM: Polonius, I, 3, 116.
RICH2: Gardener, III, 4, 31.

prodigy, monster, freak; unnatural, deformed; marvel, phenomenon.
RICH2: Queen, II, 2, 63.
SHREW: Petruchio, III, 2, 98.
JOHN: Constance, III, 1, 46—prodigious.

prodigy, omen, portent.

JC: Cassius, II, 1, 198.
1H4: King, V, 1, 20.

proditor, traitor, betrayer.
1H6: Winchester, I, 3, 31.

proface, to your health, cheers etc; a toast.
2H4: Davy, V, 3, 30.

profane, worldly, unspiritual, unreligious; hypocritical.
RICH2: Richard, V, 1, 25.

profit, progress; proficient.
1H4: Mortimer, III, 1, 166.
TEMP: Prospero, I, 2, 172.
OTH: Iago, III, 3, 379. See HONESTY.

No profit grows where is no pleasure ta'en.
In brief, sir, study what you most affect.
SHREW: Tranio, I, 1, 39.

progress, state or formal journey by a ruling monarch.
HAM: Hamlet, IV, 3, 33.

projection, scale, design; planning.
HEN5: Dauphin, II, 4, 46.

prolixious, superfluous, long-drawn-out, tedious.
MEAS: Angelo, II, 4, 162.

prolong, defer, put off, postpone.
ADO: Friar, IV, 1, 255.

Prometheus, in mythology, known as the founder of civilization; stole fire from the heavens and gave it to men; allusions to him represent creativity, the inspiration of life.
TITUS: Aaron, II, 1, 17.
LLL: Berowne, IV, 3, 304—Promethean fire, creative inspiration or imagination.
OTH: Othello, V, 2, 12—Promethean heat, divine fire.

promises
. . . Promising is the very air o' th' time; it opens the eyes of expectation. Performance is ever the duller for his act; and, but in the plainer and simpler kind of people, the deed of saying is quite out of use. To promise is most courtly and fashionable; performance is a kind of

will or testament which argues
a great sickness in his judgment
that makes it.
Timon: Painter, V, 1, 24.

proof, experience, test, trial; armor; ability to resist attack of
weapons as if protected by the
stoutest armor, impenetrable.
Ado: Leonato, IV, 1, 46.
Ham: Hamlet, III, 4, 38.
Rich2: Bolingbroke, I, 3, 73.

proper, private, pesonal, one's
own; handsome, personable.
2H6: Gloucester, III, 1, 115.
Temp: Ariel, III, 3, 60.
MND: Quince, I, 2, 88.

propertied, made a tool of, used.
TwN: Malvolio, IV, 2, 99.

property, unique, distinctive, natural qualities or characteristics.
Rich2: Scroop, III, 2, 135.
Oth: Brabantio, I, 1, 173.
Ham: Polonius, II, 1, 103.

prophesy
There is a history in all men's
lives,
Figuring the nature of the times
deceas'd,
The which observ'd, a man may
prophesy,
With a near aim, of the main
chance of things
As yet not come to life, which
in their seeds
And weak beginnings lie intreasured.
2H4: Warwick, III, 1, 80.
And if you crown him, let me
prophesy
The blood of English shall
manure the ground
And future ages groan for this
foul act; . . .
Rich2: Carlisle, IV, 1, 136.

Propontic, Sea of Marmora.
Oth: Othello, III, 3, 456.

proportion, military requirement,
size of force and amount of supplies; preponderance.
Ham: King, I, 2, 32.
Hen5: King, I, 2, 137.
Macb: Duncan, I, 4, 19.

propose, discuss, talk, converse.

Oth: Iago, I, 1, 25.
Ado: Hero, III, 1, 3.

propriety, identity, individuality,
one's own self.
TwN: Olivia, V, 1, 150.
Oth: Othello, II, 3, 176. See
BELL.

prorogue, defer, postpone, put off.
R&J: Romeo, II, 2, 78.
A&C: Pompey, I, 1, 26.

Proserpina, daughter of Ceres,
seized while picking flowers by
Dis and carried off in his chariot
to be his queen. See DUSKY DIS
(Persephone).
Wint: Perdita, IV, 4, 116.
T&C: Thersites, II, 1, 37.

prospect, sight, appearance.
Oth: Iago, III, 3, 398.

prosperity
. . . Besides, you know
Prosperity's the very bond of
love,
Whose fresh complexion and
whose heart together
Affliction alters.
Wint: Camillo, IV, 4, 583.

Prospero, rightful Duke of Milan;
student and practitioner of magic; robbed of his dukedom by
his brother, Antonio, aided by
the king of Naples; set adrift in
a leaky boat, Prospero and his
daughter Miranda eventually
reach a desolate island; creates
tempest that shipwrecks boat
carrying Antonio, the King of
Naples, and his son Ferdinand,
and they land on the island;
after subjecting his enemies to
many harassments, he makes
himself known to them, forgives
Antonio in exchange for the return of his domain, and permits
Ferdinand to become engaged
to Miranda; as he prepares to
leave the island, Prospero breaks
his wand and renounces the art
of magic; some Shakespearean
scholars have identified Prospero's renunciation of the art of
magic with Shakespeare's farewell to the theater.
Temp: I, 2.

prosperous, favorable, friendly, propitious.
OTH: Desdemona, I, 3, 245.

protest, vow, solemn promise.
MND: Theseus, I, 1, 89.

The lady doth protest too much, methinks.
HAM: Queen, III, 2, 240.

Proteus, typical charming, flighty young blade of the period; falls in love with Silvia, his friend's love; finally realizes he had a "gem" in Julia; named after sea deity. See below.
2GENT: I, 1.

Proteus, early sea deity; able to change form and disguise himself; when Menelaus was returning from the Trojan War, his ship was becalmed; he succeeded in capturing Proteus and forcing him to get the ship sailing again; word "protean," meaning changing rapidly, comes from his name.
3H6: Richard, III, 2, 192.

proud-pied (April), brilliantly varied in color; magnificently multi-colored.
SONNET: XCVIII, 2.

provand, provender, feed, fodder.
COR: Brutus, II, 1, 267.

prove, attempt, try, test.
ADO: John, I, 3, 75.
COR: Coriolanus, IV, 5, 98.

prove none, refers to notion that one is not a number.
SONNET: VIII, 14.

provincial roses, large rosettes, imitating damask rose; named after Provins, French town forty miles from Paris, famed for its roses.
HAM: Hamlet, III, 2, 288.

Provost, prison governor, persuaded by the disguised Duke to execute Barnardine instead of Claudio; however, when Ragozine, the pirate, dies in prison, the Duke agrees to have the Provost send his head to Angelo instead of Claudio's and Barnardine is spared.

MEAS: I, 2.

prune, preen, primp up.
LLL: Berowne, IV, 3, 183.
1H4: Westmoreland, I, 1, 98—preen his feathers as a bird of prey (hawk) does before an attack.

psaltery, stringed instrument; played with both hands by plucking with the fingers or a plectrum; similar to zither or dulcimer.
COR: Messenger, V, 4, 52.

Ptolemy, Cleopatra's dead brother-husband; she had been married to him in accordance with Egyptian royal custom.
A&C: Caesar, I, 4, 6.

publican, collector of Roman taxes; term of scorn and abuse.
MERV: Shylock, I, 3, 42.

Publicola, outstanding consul of Rome.
COR: Coriolanus, V, 3, 64.

Publius, son of Marcus Andronicus; helps his uncle Titus in his revenge on Demetrius and Chiron.
TITUS: IV, 3.

Publius, senator.
JC: II, 2.

Pucelle, maid, virgin. See JOAN OF ARC.
1H6: Messenger, I, 4, 101.

Puck, originally an evil spirit, but associated by Shakespeare with a mischievous sprite of English folklore, Hobgoblin or Robin Goodfellow; serves as jester to King Oberon; fond of playing tricks on mortals (the fools); but he too can make mistakes, which makes him appealing to mere humans.
MND: II, 1.

pudding, sausage, stuffing.
MWW: Mrs. Page, II, 1, 32.
1H4: Prince, II, 4, 499.
PER: 1Fisherman, II, 1, 87.

puddled, muddied, sullied, stirred up.
OTH: Desdemona, III, 4, 143.

pudency, modesty, prudency.
CYM: Posthumus, II, 5, 11.

pueritia, child, little one.
LLL: Holofernes, V, 1, 52.

puffed, panting, swelled with over-doing.
HAM: Ophelia, I, 3, 49.

pugging, possibly thieving or pilfering; thievish.
WINT: Autolycus, IV, 3, 7.

puissance, power, strength; armed forces.
2H4: Mowbray, I, 3, 9.
HEN5: I, Prologue, 25.
JOHN: King, III, 1, 339.

puissant, overwhelming, strong, powerful.
LEAR: Edgar, V, 3, 216.
JC: Metellus Cimber, III, 1, 33.

puke, dark gray or blue-black woollen cloth.
1H4: Prince, II, 4, 78.

puling, whimpering, simpering, whining.
R&J: Capulet, III, 5, 185.
COR: Volumnia, IV, 2, 52.

pumpion, pumpkin.
MWW: Mrs. Ford, III, 3, 42.
See POMPION.

pun, to pound (early form).
T&C: Thersites, II, 1, 42.

punk, strumpet, harlot.
MWW: Pistol, II, 2, 141.
MEAS: Lucio, V, 1, 179.
ALL'sW: Clown, II, 2, 24.

punto, fencing term, thrust or stroke with the point of the sword.
MWW: Host, II, 3, 26.
R&J: Mercutio, II, 4, 27.

puppet, doll-like, small of stature.
MND: Helena, III, 2, 288.
HAM: Hamlet, III, 2, 257—refers to puppet or marionette master who interpreted the action in the Elizabethan puppet shows seen at the fairs.

purchase, plunder, spoils, booty, loot.
1H4: Gadshill, II, 1, 101.

RICH3: Buckingham, III, 7, 187.

purgation, cleansing of sin or guilt from the soul; cleansing the system for medical or health reasons by the use of cathartics.
HAM: Hamlet, III, 3, 318.
AYL: Duke, I, 3, 55.
WINT: Leontes, III, 2, 7—acquittal.

purgatory. See WORLD.
OTH: Emilia, IV, 3, 79.

purl, rise in a spiral.
LUCRECE: 1407.

purlieu, tract of land on border or boundary of a forest.
AYL: Oliver, IV, 3, 77.

purple, red as blood; bloodstain.
RICH2: Richard, III, 3, 94.
JC: Antony, III, 1, 158.

purple-in-grain, dyed purple; colored with dye from dried bodies of female cochineal insects, which look like grain.
MND: Bottom, I, 2, 97.

purpose
Purpose is but the slave to memory,
Of violent birth, but poor validity;
Which now, like fruit unripe, sticks on the tree,
But fall unshaken when they mellow be.
HAM: Player King, III, 2, 198.

purse
Our purses shall be proud, our garments poor;
For 'tis the mind that makes the body rich;
And as the sun breaks through the darkest clouds
So honour peereth in the meanest habit.
SHREW: Petruchio, IV, 3, 174.

purse. See NAME.

Pursuivant, heraldic officer, king's messenger.
RICH3: III, 2.

pursy, distended, corpulent; short-winded.
HAM: Hamlet, III, 4, 153.

TIMON: Alcibiades, V, 4, 12.

purveyor, officer who makes advance arrangements to secure lodgings and supplies for the royal household.
MACB: Duncan, I, 6, 22. See PROGRESS.

pussel (puzzel), slut, harlot, prostitute, drab, whore.
1H6: Talbot, I, 4, 107.

put, entrusted.
TEMP: Prospero, I, 2, 69.

put it to the foil, defeated or made it worthless, brought it to disgrace or shame.
TEMP: Ferdinand, III, 1, 46.

put on, incite, urge or impel to action.
OTH: Iago, II, 1, 313.

puts on this confusion, acts distracted; does not have modern connotation of a false or assumed attitude.
HAM: King, III, 1, 2.

putter-on, scheming plotter, inciter, instigator.
WINT: Antigonus, II, 1, 141.
HEN8: Queen, I, 2, 24.

puttock, kite; carrion-eating hawk.
CYM: Imogen, I, 1, 140.
T&C: Thersites, V, 1, 67

2H6: Warwick, III, 2, 191.

Pygmalion, figure in classical legend; created statue of a woman and loved it so passionately that Aphrodite brought it to life; appeared in *Pygmalion's Image* by Marston (1598).
MEAS: Lucio, III, 2, 47.

Pyramus. See BOTTOM.
MND: V, 1.

Pyrrhus, Achilles' son; also known as Neoptolemus; joined the war to avenge his father's death; one of the Greeks concealed in the famous wooden horse taken within the gates of Troy.
T&C: Ulysses, III, 3, 209.
HAM: Hamlet, II, 2, 472.
LUCRECE: 1449.

Pythagoras, Greek philosopher and mathematician (d. c497 BC); important in mathematics, primarily founding the theory of numbers, and in the study of acoustics and music; quantitative study of nature; mystic; doctrine of transmigration of souls (soul could pass into a beast or bird after death) attributed to him.
MERV: Gratiano, IV, 1, 131.
TWN: Clown, IV, 2, 54.

Q

quail, courtesan, mistress, wanton.
T&C: Thersites, V, 1, 57.

quail, defeat, overpower; repress, intimidate; fail, slacken.
MND: Pyramus, V, 1, 292.
AYL: Duke, II, 2, 20.

quaint, elegant, elaborate; delicate, dainty, fine; curious, odd, queer.
TEMP: Prospero, I, 2, 317.
ADO: Margaret, III, 4, 22.
MND: Titania, II, 1, 99.

quaint, clever, wily, shrewd; skillful, ingenious, adroit, deft.
SHREW: Tranio, III, 2, 149.
2H6: Suffolk, III, 2, 274.
TEMP: S.D., III, 3—ingenious mechanism or machinery

qualify, appease, assuage, pacify, conciliate, mitigate; dilute.
WINT: Camillo, IV, 4, 543.
OTH: Iago, II, 1, 283.
OTH: Cassio, II, 3, 40.

quality, character, nature; resource, special feature or property.
TEMP: Antonio, II, 1, 199.
OTH: Othello, III, 3, 259.
TEMP: Caliban, I, 2, 337.

quality, profession, occupation, skill; party, company.
HAM: Hamlet, II, 2, 363.
TEMP: Ariel, I, 2, 193.
1H4: Hotspur, IV, 3, 36.

qualm, sudden pain, faintness.
ADO: Margaret, III, 4, 75.

quantity, proportion, share, dimension; fragment, small amount.
HAM: Player Queen, III, 2, 177.

MND: Helena, I, 1, 232.
2H4: Falstaff, V, 1, 70.

quare, Latin, why.
LLL: Holofernes, V, 1, 36.

quarrels
Be it thy course to busy giddy minds
With foreign quarrels, that action, hence borne out,
May waste the memory of the former days.
2H4: King, IV, 5, 214.

quarry, term used in deer hunting for heap of dead carcasses piled one on top of the other at the end of the hunt.
COR: Marcius, I, 1, 202.
HAM: Fortinbras, V, 2, 375. See CRY HAVOC.

quarter, amicability or friendliness; combine arms of two families, adding coat of arms to one quarter of a shield.
OTH: Iago, II, 3, 180.
MWW: Slender, I, 1, 24.

quat, literally a pimple or small boil; an irritant; term of contempt.
OTH: Iago, V, 1, 11.

quatch, squat, fat.
ALL'SW: Clown, II, 2, 18.

quean, hussy, strumpet, slut.
2H4: Falstaff, II, 1, 51.
MWW: Ford, IV, 2, 180.
ALL'SW: Clown, II, 2, 27.

Queen, evil wife of Cymbeline; mother of Cloten by a former marriage; hopes to arrange his marriage to Imogen; attempts to poison her, the king and Pisanio;

266

goes mad; dies confessing her sins.

CYM: I, 1.

Queen Elizabeth's Men, most important of the adult companies (1583-90); Edmund Tilney, Master of the Revels (1583) was asked by her majesty to form the company; ELIZABETH had shown a preference for the Boys' companies, but following the construction of THE THEATRE and CURTAIN (1576), she preferred to have her own adult company; some of the leading actors who joined the company included Robert Wilson, Richard Tarlton, John Towne, John Dutton, John Laneham, Leonell Cooke, John Bentley and William Johnson; they may have been joined by Shakespeare when they appeared at Stratford (1587).

Queen of Troy, Hecuba; after the fall of her city, she was taken as a slave by the Thracian Polymnestor; she slew his two sons and put out his eyes, in revenge for the slaying of her son, Polydorus.

TITUS: Demetrius, I, 1, 136.

queen o' th' sky, Juno, Roman goddess of the heavens, wife of Jupiter; equivalent of Greek goddess, Hera.

TEMP: Iris, IV, 1, 70.

queens. See under first name.

quell, kill, slay, slaughter, destroy.
MND: Pyramus, V, 1, 292.
MACB: Lady Macbeth, I, 7, 72.

quern, hand mill for grinding wheat, pepper, mustard, malt etc.
MND: Fairy, II, 1, 36.

quest, inquest; group of persons appointed to hold an inquiry.
HAM: Clown, V, 1, 25.

question, talk or conversation rather than interrogation.
HAM: Rosencrantz, III, 1, 13.
MACB: Banquo, I, 3, 43.

question. See LOVE.

quick, sensitive part of the flesh;

used in modern expression "cut to the quick."
HAM: King, IV, 7, 124.

quicken, rouse to life, enliven; revive; refresh.
TEMP: Ferdinand, III, 1, 6.
OTH: Othello, III, 3, 277.

Quickly, Mistress, hostess of the Boar's Head tavern in Eastcheap (1H4); claims Falstaff, whom she has known for 29 years, has promised to marry her (2H4); he talks her out of having him arrested for debt; sent to prison with Doll Tearsheet; describes Falstaff's death (HEN5); marries Pistol who goes off to war; housekeeper for Dr. Caius (MWW), helps suitors of Anne Page.
1H4: II, 4; 2H4: II, 1; HEN5: II, 1; MWW: I, 4.

quiddits, subtleties, hair-splitting, hedging; from scholastic philosophy.
HAM: Hamlet, V, 1, 107.
1H4: Falstaff, I, 2, 51—*quiddities*.

quietus, a release from debt; document of adjustment or settlement.
HAM: Hamlet, III, 1, 75.
SONNET: CXXVI, 12—discharge.

quill, note, referring here to pipe made of a reed or stalk, thus a thin piping note.
MND: Bottom, III, 1, 131.
2H6: 1Petitioner, I, 3, 4—all together.

quillet, quibble, legal subtlety, clever verbal usage or distinction.
OTH: Cassio, III, 1, 24.
HAM: Hamlet, V, 1, 108.

Quinapalus, mythical character, wise man, invented for the occasion.
TwN: Clown, I, 5, 39.

Quince, Peter, carpenter; produces the interlude of *Pyramus and Thisbe.*
MND: I, 2.

quintain, post or wooden dummy used as a mark or target for tilting or other military practice.
AYL: Orlando, I, 2, 262.

quintessence, perfection; literally the fifth essence, which would be left if the four elements were taken away; term in alchemy; substance of the heavenly bodies and latent in all things, according to ancient and medieval philosophy.
HAM: Hamlet, II, 2, 322.

Quintus, one of the four sons of Titus; accused of murder. See MARTIUS.
TITUS: I, 1.

qui passa, a certain tune.
2NK: Daughter, III, 5, 86.

quire, company, usually jolly; choir; harmonize.
MND: Puck, II, 1, 55.

quirk, ingenious or subtle turn of phrase; quip.
OTH: Cassio, II, 1, 63. See BEAUTY.

quis, Latin, who? what?
LLL: Holofernes, V, 1, 55.

quit, release, discharge; pay back, reward.
TwN: Duke, V, 1, 329.
A&C: Antony, III, 13, 123.
HEN5: King, II, 2, 34.

quite, requite, repay equally or in kind.

RICH2: Richard, V, 1, 43.
COR: Coriolanus, IV, 5, 98.

quiver, nimble, quick, active.
2H4: Shallow, III, 2, 301.

quod me alit, me extinguit, Latin, who feeds or nourishes me, kills me; motto on the shield of the fourth knight.
PER: Thaisa, II, 2, 33.

quoif (coif), tight-fitting cap or headdress.
WINT: Autolycus, IV, 4, 226.
2H4: Northumberland, I, 1, 147—often worn by the ill.

quoit, toss, throw, chuck.
2H4: Falstaff, II, 4, 206.

quondam, Latin, previously, formerly.
LLL: Nathaniel, V, 1, 7.
ADO: Benedick, V, 2, 32.
HEN5: Pistol, II, 1, 82.

quoniam, Latin, seeing that, since, because.
LLL: Holofernes, V, 2, 596.

quote, scrutinize, observe, note, mark.
HAM: Polonius, II, 1, 112.
LLL: Rosaline, V, 2, 795—interpret.

quotidian, fever that recurs daily, daily feverish symptoms.
HEN5: Hostess, II, 1, 124.
AYL: Rosalind, III, 2, 384.

R

rabbit-sucker, unweaned suckling rabbit.
  1H4: Falstaff, II, 4, 480.

race (raze), root.
  WINT: Clown, IV, 3, 50.

rack, accumulation of clouds in the upper air, usually driven ahead by the winds; cloud drift.
  HAM: 1Player, II, 2, 506.
  TEMP: Prospero, IV, 1, 156.
  A&C: Antony, IV, 14, 10.

rack, stretch, strain, exaggerate; refers to rack used in torture.
  ADO: Friar, IV, 1, 221.

raddock (ruddock), English robin.
  CYM: Arviragus, IV, 2, 224.

rain. See WIT.

rake, very slender, thin person.
  COR: I, 1, 23.

Rambures, Lord, Master of the Crossbows; one of the French lords with the Dauphin's company; killed at Agincourt.
  HEN5: III, 7.

ramp, tramp, harlot, prostitute.
  CYM: Iachimo, I, 6, 134.

rampallian, female rascal.
  2H4: Falstaff, II, 1, 65.

ramping, rearing, standing on hind legs.
  1H4: Hotspur, III, 1, 153.
  3H6: King Edward, V, 2, 13.

range, rank; line or order of battle.
  A&C: Enobarbus, III, 13, 5.

rank, foul, diseased, corrupt, swollen with indulgence; in need of blood-letting, the usual remedy of that period.
  2H4: Westmoreland, IV, 1, 64.

rank, full, copious, overgrown, overflow, flood.
  JOHN: Salisbury, V, 4, 54.
  VENUS: 71.

rankle, to cause to fester.
  RICH2: Bolingbroke, I, 3, 302.

rapier, an Elizabethan weapon unknown in King Richard's time.
  RICH2: Fitzwater, IV, 1, 40.

rapier and dagger, used together in a fencing match; the dagger was held in the left hand and used to ward off thrusts or blows.
  HAM: Osric, V, 2, 152.

rascal, inferior, underdeveloped or worthless deer; not much of a challenge for a hunter.
  COR: Menenius, I, 1, 163. See BLOOD.
  1H4: Falstaff, II, 4, 383.
  AYL: Touchstone, III, 3, 60.

rase (raze), erase; blot or wipe out; destroy.
  CYM: Cymbeline, V, 5, 70.
  RICH2: Berkeley, II, 3, 75.

Ratcliffe, Sir Richard, accomplice of Richard; killed at Bosworth.
  RICH3: III, 2.

rate, worth, value, rank, esteem; estimate, appraise.
  MND: Titania, III, 1, 157.
  TEMP: Alonso, II, 1, 109.

rate, berate, scold, chide; drive away.
  1H4: Falstaff, I, 2, 95.
  SHREW: Tranio, I, 1, 165.

rated, allotted, apportioned share.
  A&C: Caesar, III, 6, 25.

JC: Antony, III, 1, 152.
AYL: Oliver, I, 1, 91.

raught, reached, grasped, laid hold of.
> LLL: Holofernes, II, 2, 41.
> A&C: Sentry, IV, 9, 29.
> HEN5: Exeter, IV, 6, 21.

raught. See REACH.

ravel, tangled; (out) untangle, make clear, reveal.
> MACB: Macbeth, II, 2, 37.
> HAM: Hamlet, III, 4, 186.
> RICH2: Richard, IV, 1, 228.

ravens
. . . he that doth the ravens feed, Yea, providently caters for the sparrow.
> AYL: Adam, II, 3, 43.

Ravenspurgh, English port, now submerged by sea, between Hull and Bridlington, in Yorkshire, on the Humber River.
> RICH2: Northumberland, II, 1, 296.

rawer breath, unskilled, inadequate or cruder speech.
> HAM: Hamlet, V, 2, 129.

rayed, befoul, muddied, dirtied.
> SHREW: Biondello, III, 2, 54.

raze (race), root. See RASE.
> 1H4: 2Carrier, II, 1, 27.
> MACB: Macbeth, V, 3, 42.

razed, ornamental pattern achieved through cutting or slashing.
> HAM: Hamlet, III, 2, 288.

reach, competence, resourcefulness.
> HAM: Polonius, II, 1, 64.

readiness. See SPARROW.

Reapers, group of "sunburnt sicklemen" who dance in the masque celebrating the engagement of Ferdinand and Miranda.
> TEMP: IV, 1.

reason
If there were reason for these miseries,
Then into limits could I bind my woes.
> TITUS: Titus, III, 1, 220.

I have no exquisite reason for't, but I have reason good enough.
> TWN: Andrew, II, 3, 157.

reasonable shore, return to understanding or sanity.
> TEMP: Prospero, V, 1, 81. See UNDERSTANDING.

reason and love
. . . reason and love keep little company together nowadays.
> MND: Bottom, III, 1, 147.

reasons, conversations, discourses.
> LLL: Nathaniel, V, 1, 2.

rebato, stiff, flaring high collar or ruff; usually starched or of wired lace.
> ADO: Margaret, III, 4, 6.

rebec, medieval pear-shaped instrument with a thin neck; played with a bow; Hugh Rebeck, one of the musicians.
> R&J: IV, 5.

rebellion
Unthread the rude eye of rebellion
And welcome home again discarded faith.
> JOHN: Melun, V, 4, 11.

recanting, causing to take back, retract, disavow.
> RICH2: Bolingbroke, I, 1, 193— *the slavish motive of recanting fear,* before he allows his tongue to retract his words out of fear, he will bite off his tongue and spit it in Mowbray's face.

recheat (rechate), call sounded on the hunting horn to bring back the dogs.
> ADO: Benedick, I, 1, 243—allusion to cuckold's horns.

reck, to care, pay attention to.
> HAM: Ophelia, I, 3, 51. See REDE.

reclusive, retired, cloistered, secluded (like a recluse).
> ADO: Friar, IV, 1, 243.

recognizance, token, keepsake, acknowledgment, bond. See STATUTES.
> OTH: Othello, V, 2, 214.

recommend, advise, inform, familiarize.
> OTH: Messenger, I, 3, 41.

recordation, memorial, commemorate.
2H4: Lady Percy, II, 3, 61.

Recorder, legal official of the city of London appointed by the mayor or aldermen; used as a witness.
RICH3: Buckingham, III, 7, 30.

recorder, wind instrument resembling the flageolet or flute; wooden pipe.
HAM: Hamlet, III, 2, 303.
MND: Hippolyta, V, 1, 123.

recoveries, transfers.
HAM: Hamlet, V, 1, 115. See FINES.

recover the wind, hunting expression which suggests that a beast can be overtaken or captured if the hunter approaches from the windward or with the wind against him.
HAM: Hamlet, III, 2, 361.

recreant, coward, traitor.
LEAR: Lear, I, 1, 170.
COR: Volumnia, V, 3, 114.
JOHN: Constance, III, 1, 129.

recreation
Sweet recreation barred, what doth ensue
But moody and dull melancholy,
Kinsman to grim and comfortless despair.
COFE: Lady Abbess, V, 1, 78.

Red Bull Theatre, built by Aaron Holland (c1604), north of Clerkenwell Green, west of St. John Street, Clerkenwell; occupied by Queen Anne's (Worcester's) Men (1609-17).

redime te captum quam queas minimo, Latin, redeem yourself from captivity as cheaply as you can; adapted from TERENCE'S *Eunuchus* (I, 1, 29).
SHREW: Tranio, I, 1, 167.

red dominical, red letters (*dies dominica*) used to mark Sunday in almanacs of the period; reference to Katherine's golden hair, implying that her coloring was artificial.
LLL: Rosaline, V, 2, 44.

rede, advice, counsel.
HAM: Ophelia, I, 3, 51.

red lattice, mark of an alehouse, tavern where lattice-windows were painted red.
MWW: Falstaff, II, 2, 28.

redoubted, dreaded, feared.
HEN5: Dauphin, II, 4, 14.
RICH2: Bolingbroke, III, 3, 198.

red plague, name given to the bubonic plague which covered the victim's body with red sores.
TEMP: Caliban, I, 2, 364.

reechy, putrid, filthy, greasy, grimy.
COR: Brutus, II, 1, 225.
HAM: Hamlet, III, 4, 184.
ADO: Borachio, III, 3, 143.

reels, revelry, revels.
A&C: Enobarbus, II, 7, 99.

refel, refute, refuse.
MEAS: Isabella, V, 1, 94.

refer, transfer, assign, hand over.
CYM: 1Gentleman, I, 1, 6.

refigure, recreate the appearance of, reproduce, regenerate.
SONNET: VI, 10.

reformation
And, like bright metal on a sullen ground,
My reformation, glittering o'er my fault,
Shall show more goodly and attract more eyes
Than that which hath no foil to set it off.
I'll so offend to make offence a skill,
Redeeming time when men think least I will.
1H4: Prince, I, 2, 236.

Regan, completely selfish, sadistic, evil, vengeful second daughter of Lear; married to the Duke of Cornwall.
LEAR: I, 1.

regard, an object of sight; consequence, reason, consideration.
OTH: Montano, II, 1, 39.
HAM: Hamlet, III, 1, 87.

regards of safety and allowance, terms arranged that will safe-

guard the passage of troops through the country; conditions of protection.
HAM: Voltemand, II, 2, 79.

region kites, vultures of the upper air or area of the sky.
HAM: Hamlet, II, 2, 606.

regreet, hail, salute.
RICH2: Bolingbroke, I, 3, 67.

regret
. . . Things without all remedy
Should be without regard.
What's done is done.
MACB: Lady Macbeth, III, 2, 11.

reguerdon, reward.
1H6: King, III, 1, 169.

Reignier (René), Duke of Anjou, supports the Dauphin and Joan of Arc; however, when his daughter, Margaret, is captured by Suffolk, he agrees to her marriage to Henry. [1434–80, Count of Maine, Duke of Anjou.]
1H6: I, 2.

reins, kidneys, possibly loins.
MWW: Falstaff, III, 5, 25.

rejourn, adjourn, postpone, put off.
COR: Menenius, II, 1, 79.

relish, feel, be sensitive or responsive to; appreciate, prefer; touch or taste of.
TEMP: Prospero, V, 1, 23.
OTH: Cassio, II, 1, 166.
HAM: Hamlet, III, 1, 120.

relish, sing.
2GENT: Valentine, II, 1, 20.
LUCRECE: 1126.

remedies
Our remedies oft in ourselves do lie,
Which we ascribe to heaven.
ALL'SW: Helena, I, 1, 231.

remiss, nonchalant, indifferent to.
HAM: King, IV, 7, 135.

remover, faithless person or disturbing cause.
SONNET: CXVI, 4. See LOVE.

rend an oak, a torture or punishment much more terrible than being imprisoned in a tree.

TEMP: Prospero, I, 2, 294.

render, surrender.
A&C: Canidius, III, 10, 33—
To Caesar will I render / My legions and my horse.

repair, return.
MND: Oberon, IV, 1, 70.

repeal, recall, call back.
OTH: Iago, II, 3, 363.
COR: Cominius, IV, 1, 41.
LEAR: Edgar, III, 6, 119.

repent
Woe that too late repents!
LEAR: Lear, I, 4, 279.

repent. See CONFESS.

repine, dislike, discontent, dissatisfied.
VENUS: 490.

replication, response, formal reply; echo.
HAM: Hamlet, IV, 2, 13.
JC: Marullus, I, 1, 51.

reprisal, prize, reward.
1H4: Hotspur, IV, 1, 118.

reprobance, reprobation; rejection by God; eternal damnation.
OTH: Gratiano, V, 2, 209.

repugn, oppose, reject, repel.
1H6: Basset, IV, 1, 94.

reputation
. . . Reputation is an idle and most false imposition, oft got without merit and lost without deserving.
OTH: Iago, II, 3, 268.

The purest treasure mortal times afford
Is spotless reputation. That away,
Men are but gilded loam or painted clay.
RICH2: Mowbray, I, 1, 177. See LOAM.

require, request, ask for.
HEN5: Exeter, II, 4, 101.

requit (requite), avenge, pay back; compensate, reward.
TEMP: Ariel, III, 3, 71.
MACB: Porter, II, 3, 44.
AYL: Oliver, I, 1, 144.

reremice, bats.
MND: Titania, II, 2, 4.

resolute. See LAWLESS RESOLUTES.

resolution

It makes us, or it mars us—think on that,

And fix most firm thy resolution.

OTH: Iago, V, 1, 4.

respects of thrift, thought for profit or gain.

HAM: Queen, III, 2, 193.

respice finem, Latin, look to or remember your end (death and salvation) and *respice funem,* remember the rope; popular pun; phrase taught to parrots.

COFE: Dromio E., IV, 4, 44.

rest, stakes, in card game primero.

LEAR: Lear, I, 1, 125.

COFE: Dromio S., IV, 3, 26.

restem, hold the course; steer again.

OTH: Messenger, I, 3, 37.

retrograde, contrary, repugnant.

HAM: King, I, 2, 114.

revenge

Blood and revenge are hammering in my head.

TITUS: Aaron, II, 3, 39.

revenge. See BLOODY THOUGHT.

reverence

Cover your heads, and mock not flesh and blood

With solemn reverence. Throw away respect,

Tradition, form, and ceremonious duty;

For you have but mistook me all this while.

RICH2: Richard, III, 2, 171.

reverend, room, chapel, place of meditation; faith, respect.

RICH2: Bolingbroke, V, 6, 25.

reverse, fencing term, backhanded stroke.

MWW: Host, II, 3, 27.

reversion, a property reverts back to the original owner after the death of the lessee or after a grant becomes void.

RICH2: Richard, I, 4, 35.

1H4: Douglas, IV, 1, 54.

revolt, unfaithfulness.

OTH: Othello, III, 3, 188.

revolted wives

. . . Should all despair

That have revolted wives, the tenth of mankind

Would hang themselves.

WINT: Leontes, I, 2, 198.

revolve, consider, ponder.

TWN: Malvolio, II, 5, 155.

Reynaldo, Polonius' servant; sent to Paris to spy on Laertes; called Montano in first Quarto.

HAM: II, 1.

rhapsody, meaningless or senseless stream or string.

HAM: Hamlet, III, 4, 48.

Rhesus, King of Thrace who aided the Trojans. See ULYSSES.

3H6: Warwick, IV, 2, 20.

rheum, discharge of water, such as tears; moisture secreted by glands; cold in the head, catarrh.

JOHN: Constance, III, 1, 22.

COR: Aufidius, V, 6, 45.

A&C: Enobarbus, III, 2, 58.

Rhodope, Greek courtesan, married an Egyptian king of Memphis and was supposed to have built the third pyramid.

1H6: Dauphin, I, 6, 22.

rhyme

Not marble nor the gilded monuments

Of princes shall outlive this pow'rful rhyme . . .

SONNET: LV, 1.

Rialto, famous bridge and street in Venice which is the Merchant's Exchange; men usually meet twice a day to make deals and gossip.

MERV: Shylock, I, 3, 20.

ribald-rid (ribaudred), wanton, foul, obscene; ridden by ribalds.

A&C: Scarus, III, 10, 10.

Rich, Barnabe (c1540–1617). English pamphleteer, writer of romances; author of *Riche his Farewell to Militarie Profession conteining verie pleasaunt discourses fit for a peacable tyme* (1581); source of *Twelfth Night* and other works.

Richard II, The Tragedy of, probably written 1595; only play entirely in verse; strong evidence that Richard II was written as the first of a tetralogy, the other parts being 1 and 2 Henry IV and Henry V; performances of 1601 were supported by the rebellious Essex faction as a propaganda weapon against the rule of Elizabeth I; registered and first printed 1597; sources, principally HOLINSHED'S *Chronicles;* Samuel DANIEL's *The First Four Books of the Civil Wars;* Berner's translation of FROISSART'S *Chronicles;* Edward HALLE's *The Union of Two Noble and Illustrious Families of Lancaster and York;* Jean Creton's *Histoire du Roi d'Angleterre Richard;* the anonymous *La Chronique de la Traison et Mort de Richard Roi d'Angleterre;* the anonymous play *Thomas of Woodstock,* also known as Richard II; scenes added or changed, characterization of queen differs from sources.

PLOT: Henry Lancaster, Duke of Hereford, surnamed Bolingbroke, son of John of Gaunt, Duke of Lancaster, in the presence of King Richard II accuses Thomas Mowbray, Duke of Norfolk, of treason for his part in the murder of Richard's uncle, the Duke of Gloucester. Richard judges that the two adversaries meet in combat at Coventry. However, when the time of the contest arrives, Richard interposes and decrees that Mowbray be exiled for life and Bolingbroke for a period of six years. Richard thus rids himself of his cousin, Bolingbroke, who has become very popular with both the nobility and the people.

John of Gaunt, Duke of Lancaster, on his deathbed warns the King of his extravagances and his intention of mortgaging England in order to pay for his Irish campaign. After Gaunt's death, Richard seizes the Duke's estates which rightfully belong to Bolingbroke. The injustice of Richard's appropriations gives Bolingbroke the excuse he needs to return to England with the aid of dissatisfied nobles. After an unsuccessful campaign in Ireland, Richard returns to Wales only to find that his Welsh army has deserted him and Bolingbroke has executed Bushy and Green, his favorites. Richard meets Bolingbroke, supported by an army of men, at Flint Castle and is forced to return with him to London, a prisoner in everything but name. The third act closes with the famous garden scene in which the gardener compares his garden to a well-run kingdom. Richard is forced to surrender his crown to Bolingbroke and is sent to the Tower. Richard is separated from his queen, whom he tells to return to France, and Bolingbroke is crowned as Henry IV. Richard is taken to Pomfret Castle where he is murdered by Sir Pierce Exton. Henry, whose subtle suggestion precipitated the murder, promises to do penance by journeying to Jerusalem.

Richard II, King, also called Richard of Bordeaux (1367-1400), son of Edward, the Black Prince, succeeded Edward III, his grandfather, as 8th king of the house of Plantagenet (1377); nephew to Gaunt and York, cousin of Bolingbroke and Aumerle; Shakespeare balances Richard against the formidable and subtle Bolingbroke; though Richard is weak, though he has mismanaged his kingdom through fancy and miscalculation, though the claims of Parliament are somewhat justified, he is made a sympathetic, tragic character; psychologically complex, self-aware, and extravagant in language. Shakespeare gives voice to the inwardness and suffering of his tragic protagonist, the man who sees himself fall, but who can do nothing about it, and as a king can neither fulfill his duties nor "wash off" the royal oil. "We feel neither respect nor love for the deposed monarch; for he is wanting in energy as in principle; but we pity him, for he pities himself. . . . The sufferings of the man make us forget that he ever was a king"—(Hazlitt).

RICH2: I, 1.

Richard III, The Tragedy of, written 1592, performed 1593, registered and published 1597; source, HOLINSHED, who used HALLE, and Sir Thomas MORE's *History of Richard III.*

PLOT: Richard is determined to become king though six people stand between him and his ambition. He first succeeds in turning King Edward against his brother, George, Duke of Clarence, and following his arrest sees to it that he is murdered in the Tower. Richard persuades Lady Anne, who had been betrothed to Henry VI's son, the Prince of Wales, whom he had stabbed at Tewkesbury, to marry him.

Queen Margaret, Henry VI's widow, warns the Yorkists against Richard and proves to be correct when, following Edward IV's death, Richard, backed by Buckingham attacks the Queen's supporters and has them imprisoned in Pomfret Castle. With the Prince of Wales and the Duke of York safely in the Tower, Buckingham persuades the people to proclaim Richard king. The Queen Mother, with the Duchess of York and Lady Anne, attempt to gain admission to the Tower, but fail. Richard is crowned and in order to secure his position suggests to Buckingham that he kill the little princes in the Tower. Buck-

ingham balks at this and asks for time to consider it. When he hesitates too long, Richard arranges to have Tyrrel murder his nephews.

To further strengthen his claim to the throne, Richard hastens the death of his wife Anne and marries Elizabeth, Edward's daughter. Buckingham, meanwhile, has decided he will be safer if he joins Henry Tudor, the Earl of Richmond, against Richard, but he is captured at Salisbury and executed. Richmond, joined by other nobles, lands at Milford and is marching inland when the two armies meet on Bosworth Field. The night before the battle, Richard is haunted by the ghosts of his victims who foretell his defeat. He is slain in personal combat by Richmond who, by accepting the crown as Henry VII and by marrying Elizabeth of York, unites the two families, and the Wars of the Roses is ended.

Richard III. See GLOUCESTER, Richard, Duke of.

Richard, Duke of York. See YORK, Duke of.

rich men. See FALL OF KINGS.

Richmond, Henry Tudor, Earl of; Henry VI predicts that Richmond will one day be king (3H6); lands with Lancastrian army to contest the title with Yorkist Richard, whom he defeats in personal combat at Bosworth Field (RICH3); crowned Henry VII. [1457-1509, son of Margaret Beaufort, great-granddaughter of John of Gaunt, and of Edmund Tudor, Earl of Richmond; founder of Tudor line; strong king.]

RICH3: V, 3.

ridge, horizontal crossbar of the gallows.

1H4: Prince, I, 2, 43.

rift, split, tear apart.

TEMP: Prospero, V, 1, 45.

riggish, wanton.
A&C: Enobarbus, II, 2, 245.

right-drawn, unsheathed for a just or reasonable cause.
RICH2: Bolingbroke, I, 1, 46.

right-hand file, aristocrats, patricians, upper-class citizens, ruling class.
COR: Menenius, II, 1, 25.

rights of memory, custom or unwritten laws that are remembered and observed.
HAM: Fortinbras, V, 2, 400.

rigoll, ring, circle.
2H4: Prince, IV, 5, 36.
LUCRECE: 1745.

rim, diaphragm, belly, midriff.
HEN5: Pistol, IV, 4, 15.

Rinaldo, Steward of the Countess of Rossillion; tells her of Helena's love for her son Bertram.
ALL'sW: I, 3.

ring-carrier, go-between.
ALL'sW: Mariana, III, 5, 95.

ringlet, fairy ring in the grass; round dance.
MND: Titania, II, 1, 86.
TEMP: Prospero, V, 1, 37.

Ringwood, popular name for a hound.
MWW: Pistol, II, 1, 122.

ripe, ready to be performed or used.
MND: Philostrate, V, 1, 42.

ripeness
. . . Men must endure
Their going hence, even as their coming hither;
Ripeness is all.
LEAR: Edgar, V, 2, 9.

The mellow plum doth fall, the green sticks fast,
Or being early pluck'd is sour to taste.
VENUS: 527.

risk. See WORLD.

rites. See DUTY'S RITES.

rivage, shore, banks.
HEN5: Chorus, Prologue, III, 14.

rival, partner, associate.
HAM: Bernardo, I, 1, 12.
A&C: Eros, III, 5, 8—*rivality,* partnership, equality.

rive, split, rupture.
A&C: Charmian, IV, 13, 5.
COR: Volumnia, V, 3, 153.
JC: Cassius, IV, 3, 85.

rivelled, wrinkled, dry and furrowed.
T&C: Thersites, V, 1, 26.

Rivers, Earl, told by Elizabeth of Edward's capture by Warwick (3H6); executed by order of Richard (RICH3). [Anthony Woodville (c1442-83), brother of Elizabeth (Lady Grey), 2nd Earl Rivers, Baron Scales; patron of William Caxton, who printed his translations from the French.]
3H6: IV, 4; RICH3: I, 3.

rivo, popular drinker's cry meaning "down the hatch," "cheers" etc.
1H4: Prince, II, 4, 124.

road, common passage or way; place where ships ride at anchor; whore.
2H4: Prince, II, 2, 183.

roar
. . . I will roar you as gently as any sucking dove; I will roar you an 'twere any nightingale.
MND: Bottom, I, 2, 84.

roarer, loud wave, indirect reference to bully or blusterer.
TEMP: Boatswain, I, 1, 18.

robbed
The robbed that smiles steals something from the thief;
He robs himself that spends a bootless grief.
OTH: Duke, I, 3, 208. See BOOTLESS.

He that is robbed, not wanting what is stolen,
Let him not know't, and he's not robbed at all.
OTH: Othello, III, 3, 342.

Robin, Falstaff's page; delivers Falstaff's letters to the merry wives.

MWW: I, 3. See PAGE TO FAL-STAFF.

Robin Goodfellow. See PUCK.

Robin Hood, famed legendary English outlaw whose band of men lived in Sherwood Forest, Nottinghamshire; "stole from the rich to help the poor"; many ballads and tales have been written of his exploits.
2NK: Prologue, 21, and else-where. See MAID MARIAN, FRIAR TUCK.

robustious, clamorous, noisy.
HAM: Hamlet, III, 2, 10.

Rock Tarpeian, rock face on Capitoline Hill from which all state criminals were hurled to their deaths.
COR: Sicinius, III, 1, 213.

Roderigo, Venetian gentleman; in love with Desdemona; used by Iago, who forces him into a drunken fight with Cassio; wounded, he is killed by Iago; incriminating letters against his murderer are found in his pocket.
OTH: I, 1.

Rogero, "Second Gentleman" of Sicily; reports that Perdita is found.
WINT: V, 2.

rogue
O what a rogue and peasant slave am I!
HAM: Hamlet, II, 2, 576.

romage. See POST-HASTE AND ROMAGE.

Roman Brutus, Lucius Junius Brutus (known as Brutus the Liberator) who feigned idiocy to conceal the conspiracy against his uncle Tarquinius Superbus (Tarquin).
HEN5: Constable, II, 4, 37.

Roman fashion
We'll bury him; and then, what's brave, what's noble,
Let's do it after the high Roman fashion

And make death proud to take us.
A&C: Cleopatra, IV, 15, 86.

Romano, Julio, reference to Giulio Romano (1499-1546), architect and painter of the Renaissance in Italy; pupil and assistant to Raphael; designed, built outstanding ducal church at Mantua.
WINT: 3Gentleman, V, 2, 106.

Romans, countrymen, and lovers
Romans, countrymen, and lov-ers, hear me for my cause, and be silent, that you may hear. Believe me for mine honour, and have respect to mine hon-our, that you may believe. Cen-sure me in your wisdom, and awake your senses, that you may the better judge.
JC: Brutus, III, 2, 13—open-ing of Brutus' famed oration.

Rome
Not that I loved Caesar less, but that I loved Rome more.
JC: Brutus, III, 2, 23.

Romeo, young heir of the Mon-tagues; falls madly in love with Juliet, daughter of the rival Capulets. "Romeo is Hamlet in love"—(Hazlitt).
R&J: I, 1.

Romeo
O Romeo, Romeo! wherefore art thou Romeo?
Deny thy father and refuse thy name!
Or, if thou wilt not, be but sworn my love,
And I'll no longer be a Capulet.
R&J: Juliet, II, 2, 33.

Romeo and Juliet, The Tragedy of, written 1595, published 1597, registered 1607; source, a poem by Arthur BROOKE (Broke), *The Tragical Historye of Ro-meus and Iuliet* (1562) which was taken from BOAISTEAU'S *Histoires Tragiques* (1559), the French version of the ninth story in Part II of BANDELLO'S *Novelle* (1554).
PLOT: Following a renewal

of the outbreak of fighting between the Montagues and the Capulets on the streets of Verona, the Prince orders them to stop on penalty of death. Romeo, a Montague, is in love with Rosaline, but Benvolio, attempting to prove she isn't the only fair maiden in the city, takes him to a masked ball at the home of the Capulets. There he meets and falls in love with Juliet, daughter of the host. There follows the famous love scene in the garden and they are secretly married the next afternoon by Friar Laurence.

Tybalt, a Capulet, picks a quarrel with Romeo and when the latter refuses to fight, his friend Mercutio accepts the challenge. After Tybalt kills Mercutio, Romeo draws his sword and kills the offender. He is banished by the Prince. With the aid of the Friar, Romeo manages to climb to Juliet's chamber, but at dawn must flee to Mantua.

Meanwhile the Capulets are planning Juliet's marriage to Paris, but she refuses him. She goes to the Friar and he decides on a dangerous plan. He gives her a potion which makes her appear dead (for 42 hours) while sending a message to Romeo to come and rescue her when she awakens. Juliet drinks the potion and is placed in the vault by the Friar who also sends the messenger to Mantua as planned.

However, the message isn't delivered to Romeo who hears only that she is dead. He goes to the tomb where he meets and kills Paris, who had attacked him. When he breaks into the tomb and finds Juliet dead, he drinks poison and dies beside her. The Friar is too late to save him but rushes to help Juliet, who upon awakening and discovering the dead Romeo, stabs

herself. The Montagues and the Capulets are reconciled over the dead bodies of their children.

ronyon (runnion), scabby, mangy person, good-for-nothing; hag.
MACB: 1Witch, I, 3, 6.

rood, cross, crucifix.
2H4: Shallow, III, 2, 3.
R&J: Nurse, I, 3, 36.
RICH3: Stanley, III, 2, 75.

roof, body.
SONNET: X, 7.

rook, crouch, squat; perch in huddled position; European corvine bird similar to a crow.
3H6: Henry, V, 6, 47. See CROW.

rope
. . . "beware the rope's end."
CofE: Dromio E., IV, 4, 46—refers to hangman's noose.

ropery, roguery, knavish talk.
R&J: Nurse, II, 4, 154.

Rosalind, beautiful, witty, carefree daughter of the banished Duke; friend and cousin of Celia, daughter of Duke Frederick; falls in love with Orlando; disguises herself as a young man (Ganymede) and flees to the Forest of Arden; wins Orlando. "Rosalind is not a complete human being: she is simply an extension into five acts of the most affectionate, fortunate, delightful five minutes in the life of a charming woman."—(G. B. Shaw.)
AYL: I, 2.

Rosaline, one of the ladies attending the Princess of France; agrees to marry Biron.
LLL: II, 1.

Rosaline, referred to by Mercutio in Act I of *Romeo and Juliet* as "a pale-hearted wench" but does not appear in the play.

Roscius, outstanding Roman actor whose unusual intellect and abilities gained him wider acceptance and prestige than was usu-

ally accorded members of his
profession.

HAM: Hamlet, II, 2, 410.

3H6: Henry, V, 6, 10.

rose

But earthlier happy is the rose
distilled

Than that which, withering on
the virgin thorn,

Grows, lives, and dies in single
blessedness.

MND: Theseus, I, 1, 76.

rose. See NAME, BEAUTY.

rosemary, fragrant shrub, used
as an herb in cooking.

HAM: Ophelia, IV, 5, 175—
*rosemary, that's for remem-
brance,* the perfume of the
flower was thought to help the
memory.

Rosencrantz, courtier, former
university friend of Hamlet;
with his close companion, Guildenstern, he is induced by Claudius to stay at the Danish court
to spy on Hamlet; later they are
both sent to England with Hamlet, carrying sealed orders from
the king ordering the Prince's
death; during the voyage, Hamlet substitutes a forged letter re-
questing the bearers be killed,
and they are subsequently put
to death. Rosencrantz and Guildenstern were names of noted
Danish families in Shakespeare's
period; appear in records of
Wittenberg University.

HAM: II, 1.

roses

Roses, their sharp spines being
gone,

Not royal in their smells alone,

But in their hue . . .

2NK: Boy, I, 1, opening lines
of flower song.

roses. See WOMEN.

Rose Theatre, Philip Henslowe's
(in partnership with John
Cholmley, until 1592) theater
on the BANKSIDE, between Maid
Lane and the river, Southwark,
London; built (April, 1587-88)

of timber and plaster with a
thatched roof; used by Strange's
company (1592) and others.

Ross, Thane of, visits Lady Macduff and defends her husband's
flight to England; reports to
Macduff that his family has been
killed; joins the rebellion against
Macbeth.

MACB: I, 2.

Ross, William, Lord, noble, dissatisfied with King Richard II's
reign; member of Bolingbroke
faction following the seizure of
the Lancastrian properties. [7th
Baron Ross of Hamlake, Yorkshire (d. 1414); became lord
treasurer upon the accession of
Henry IV to throne.]

RICH2: II, 3.

Rossillion, Count of. See BER-
TRAM.

Rossillion, Countess of, mother
of Bertram; friend and guardian
to Helena.

ALL'sW: I, 1.

rother, ox, horned beast; brother.

TIMON: Timon, IV, 3, 12.

Rotheram, Thomas, Archbishop
of York; resigns his seal to
Elizabeth, widow of Edward IV,
when he learns that both her
brother and son have been imprisoned by Richard. [1423-
1500, Chancellor (1475), Archbishop (1480); imprisoned for
supporting Elizabeth.]

RICH3: II, 4.

rotten

Something is rotten in the state
of Denmark.

HAM: Marcellus, I, 4, 90.

roughcast, mixture of lime and
gravel which is used to plaster
outside walls; rough plaster.

MND: Bottom, III, 1, 70.

round, straight from the shoulder, direct, not mincing words,
plain spoken.

HAM: Polonius, II, 2, 139.

OTH: Othello, I, 3, 90.

TwN: Malvolio, II, 3, 102.

round, whisper.
JOHN: Bastard, II, 1, 566.
WINT: Leontes, I, 2, 217.

roundel, dance that is performed in a circle; round.
MND: Titania, II, 2, 1.

roundly, brazenly, boldly, bluntly.
RICH2: Richard, II, 1, 122.
LEAR: Knight, I, 4, 58.

roundure (rondure), circumference, circle.
JOHN: France (Philip), II, 1, 259.

rouse, heavy drink of wine, usually as a toast; carouse.
HAM: King, I, 2, 127.
OTH: Cassio, II, 3, 66.

rout, common crowd or herd, rabble; riot, brawl, uproar, tumult.
JC: Cassius, I, 2, 78.
COFE: Balthazar, III, 1, 101.
OTH: Othello, II, 3, 210.

row, stanza, verse, line or column of print.
HAM: Hamlet, II, 2, 438.

rowel, spur.
CYM: Arviragus, IV, 4, 39.
2H4: Travers, I, 1, 46—*rowel-head*, prick of the spur.

Rowland. See OLIVER AND ROWLAND.

Rowley, Samuel (d. c1634). English actor-dramatist; with the ADMIRAL's-Prince's Men; only play in print: *When you See me, You Know Me* (1605), based on the life of Henry VIII; may have been used by Shakespeare and FLETCHER as the source of their play; *The Noble Soldier* (1634) has been attributed to Rowley; may have written the comic parts in *Taming of the Shrew* and *Henry V.*

Rowley, William (c1585-c1642). English actor-dramatist; with the DUKE OF YORK's-Prince Charles' Company (1610-19); KING's COMPANY (1623-25); wrote *A New Wonder: A Woman never Vext* (1632), A

Match at Midnight (1633) and others; Pope credited him with collaborating with Shakespeare on *King John*, and others ascribe parts of *Pericles* to Rowley.

royal, coin worth ten shillings (half a pound); usually referred to in puns.
RICH2: Groom, V, 5, 67.
1H4: Falstaff, I, 2, 157.

royalties, rights or honors granted to a member of the royal family.
RICH2: York, II, 1, 90.

roynish, scurvy, coarse; term of contempt.
AYL: 2Lord, II, 2, 8.

rub, impediment, obstacle, obstruction; Shakespeare often used terms from sports, and rubs were lumps that stopped or slowed down the bowling balls.
COR: Cominius, III, 1, 60.
JOHN: Pandulph, III, 4, 128.
HAM: Hamlet, III, 1, 65—*ay, there's the rub*, part of *to be* soliloquy.

rude, vulgar, rough-hewn.
OTH: Othello, I, 3, 81. See SPEECH.
RICH2: Bolingbroke, III, 3, 32 —*rude ribs*, rough-hewn stone of a castle.

rude mechanicals, stupid workmen or mechanics.
MND: Puck, III, 2, 9.

rudeness
This rudeness is a sauce to his good wit,
Which gives men stomach to digest his words
With better appetite.
JC: Cassius, I, 2, 304—refers to Casca.

rudesby, barbarian, ruffian, insolent, rude fellow.
TwN: Olivia, IV, 1, 55.
SHREW: Katherina, III, 2, 10.

rue, yellow-flowered, strong-scented perennial woody herb; formerly known as herb of grace; symbol of repentance and sorrow.

HAM: Ophelia, IV, 5, 181.
RICH2: Gardener, III, 4, 105.
WINT: Perdita, IV, 4, 74.

ruffians. See FALL OF KINGS.

ruffle, outrage, treat with violence.
LEAR: Gloucester, III, 7, 41.

ruffling, ostentatious, frilly, showy.
SHREW: Petruchio, IV, 3, 60.

Rugby, John, Dr. Caius' servant.
MWW: I, 4.

rug-headed, unkempt, shaggy.
RICH2: Richard, II, 1, 156.

ruined love
. . . Now I find true
That better is by evil still made better;
And ruin'd love, when it is built anew,
Grows fairer than at first, more strong, far greater.
SONNET: CXIX, 9.

rule the roast, domineer the feast, master of the situation.
2H6: Gloucester, I, 1, 109.

Rumour, "painted full of tongues"; tells Northumberland that Hotspur, his son, won the battle of Shrewsbury. [Popular allegorical figure in Jacobean masques.]
2H4: Induction; used as a link between Henry IV, Parts I and II.

rumour
. . . Rumour is a pipe
Blown by surmises, jealousies, conjectures;
And of so easy and so plain a stop
That the blunt monster with uncounted heads,

The still-discordant wavering multitude,
Can play upon it.
2H4: Rumour, Induction, 15.

. . . From Rumour's tongues
They bring smooth comforts false, worse than true wrongs.
2H4: Rumour, Induction, 39.

rumour. See PRATTLE.

runagate, renegade, deserter, traitor.
CYM: Iachimo, I, 6, 137.
RICH3: Richmond, IV, 4, 464.

runnion. See RONYON.

rush candle, made by dipping a rush into tallow or grease.
SHREW: Katherina, IV, 5, 14.

russet, reddish-brown or gray color usually associated with unpleasant or dull weather; also a coarse homespun cloth.
HAM: Horatio, I, 1, 166.
LLL: Berowne, V, 2, 143.

russet-pated, gray-headed.
MND: Puck, III, 2, 21. See CHOUGHS.

ruth, compassion, pity.
COR: Marcius, I, 1, 201.
T&C: Troilus, III, 3, 48.
RICH2: Gardener, III, 4, 106.

Rutland, Edmund, Earl of, murdered by Clifford. [1443-60, 3rd son of Richard Plantagenet, Duke of York, brother of Richard III.]
3H6: I, 3.
RICH3: Richard, I, 2, 157.

Rutland. See AUMERLE.

ruttish, lascivious, lustful, lewd.
ALL'sW: Parolles, IV, 3, 343.

S

Saba, Queen of Sheba, who visited King Solomon (I Kings 10:1-10).
HEN8: Cranmer, V, 5, 24.

sable, heraldic term, black.
HAM: Hamlet, II, 2, 474.
LUCRECE: 1074.

sack, dry white wine imported from Spain and the Canary Islands; sherry.
TEMP: Stephano, II, 2, 125.
TWN: Toby, V, 3, 206.
1H4: Prince, I, 2, 3.

. . . skill in the weapon is nothing without sack, for that sets it awork; and learning a mere hoard of gold kept by a devil, till sack commences it and sets it in act and use.
2H4: Falstaff, IV, 3, 124.

sackbut, instrument similar to the trombone, with a slide used to alter pitch; bass trumpet.
COR: Messenger, V, 4, 52.

Sackerson, famous bear exhibited and used in bear-baiting at Paris Garden on the Bankside.
MWW: Slender, I, 1, 307.

sacrament, Holy Communion.
RICH2: Abbot, IV, 1, 328—oaths were often affirmed by the participants receiving Holy Communion.

sacrifices
Upon such sacrifices, my Cordelia,
The gods themselves throw incense.
LEAR: Lear, V, 3, 20.

sacrificing Abel's, Abel sacrificed the fruits of the earth to God.
RICH2: Bolingbroke, I, 1, 104.

sacring bell, a bell rung at mass at the elevation of the host.
HEN8: Surrey, III, 2, 295—consecrating.

sad, serious, sober, grave, morose.
MND: Oberon, IV, 1, 98.
TWN: Olivia, III, 4, 5.
ADO: Benedick, II, 3, 230.

Sadler's Wells, famous London theater; opened April 23, 1753; a series of Shakespeare's plays were produced there by Samuel Phelps (1844-62); reopened by Lilian Baylis (1831) with a performance of *Twelfth Night;* associated with OLD VIC; now home of opera and ballet.

sadness
In sooth, I know not why I am so sad.
It wearies me; you say it wearies you;
But how I caught it, found it, or came by it,
What stuff 'tis made of, whereof it is born,
I am to learn;
And such a want-wit sadness makes of me
That I have much ado to know myself.
MERV: Antonio, I, 1, 1.

safed, provided safe conduct for.
A&C: Soldier, IV, 6, 26.

saffron, yellow-orange, orange-red; herb used to color pastry and fruit.
TEMP: Ceres, IV, 1, 78.
WINT: Clown, IV, 3, 48.
ALL'SW: Lafew, IV, 5, 2—

282

color of cowards and jealous men.

Sagittary, centaur, half-man, half-horse, who according to legend fought with the Trojans against the Greeks.

T&C: Agamemnon, V, 5, 14.

Sagittary, inn in Venice with the sign of Sagittarius (the Archer).

OTH: Iago, I, 1, 159.

St. Albans, scene of the battle between the Lancastrians and the Yorkists, February 17, 1461 (Wars of the Roses).

RICH3: Richard, I, 3, 130.

Saint Bennet, Saint Benedict's church in London.

TwN: Clown, V, 1, 42.

Saint Clare, order of nuns called Poor Clares and Minoresses; founded by St. Clare of Assisi (1212); teaching order.

MEAS: Isabella, I, 4, 5.

Saint Davy's day, March 1, in celebration of the Welsh victory over the Saxons, Welshmen wore a leek, their national symbol, in their hats; the King was born at Monmouth, Wales.

HEN5: Pistol, IV, 1, 55.

Saint Denis, patron saint of France.

HEN5: King, V, 2, 193.

1H6: Dauphin, I, 6, 28.

LLL: Princess, V, 2, 87.

Saint George, patron saint of England; part of the insignia of the Order of the Garter.

HEN5: King, III, 1, 34.

RICH3: Richard, IV, 4, 366.

1H6: Bedford, I, 1, 154—*St. George's feast,* April 23.

St. George's Field, open area on the south bank (Surrey side) of the Thames between Southwark and Lambeth; adjoined church of St. George the Martyr in Southwark; drilling ground.

2H6: York, V, 1, 46.

Saint Jaques le Grand, famous shrine at Compostela, Spain.

ALL'SW: Steward (reading), III, 4, 4.

Saint Lambert's Day, September 17.

RICH2: Richard, I, 1, 199.

Saint Martin's summer, Indian summer; period of warm weather following St. Martin's Day, November 11.

1H6: Pucelle, I, 2, 131.

Saint Michael, noted French order of knights.

1H6: Lucy, IV, 7, 69.

Saint Nicholas, patron saint of robbers; pictured in medieval period with three purses in his hand.

1H4: Gadshill, II, 1, 68—*Saint Nicholas' clerks,* highwaymen, thieves.

2GENT: Launce, III, 1, 310.

Saint Patrick, keeper of purgatory; patron saint of sinners and those who err; believed to have banished the snakes from Ireland.

HAM: Hamlet, I, 5, 136.

Saint Stephen, first Christian martyr.

TITUS: Clown, IV, 4, 42.

Saint Valentine's day, according to an old folk tale, February 14 was the day when a young maiden, seen in the morning by an eligible young man, became his true-love or valentine.

HAM: Ophelia, IV, 5, 48—part of song.

MND: Theseus, IV, 1, 142—the day the birds were to begin their mating.

salad days. See YOUTH.

salamander, kind of lizard, believed to live in fire.

1H4: Falstaff, III, 3, 53—refers to Bardolph's red face or nose.

Salerio and Solanio, friends of Antonio and Bassanio; Salerio helps Lorenzo to elope with Jessica.

MERV: I, 1.

Salisbury, Earl of, loyal member of Richard II's party; tries to

prevent the loss of the Welsh forces; joins the rebellion against Henry IV; captured and beheaded at Cirencester. [John de Montacute, 3rd Earl, d. 1400.]
RICH2: II, 4.

Salisbury, Earl of, illegitimate son of Henry II; disapproves of John's second coronation and suspects him of Arthur's death; joins Dauphin, but returns to the English side when he learns of the Dauphin's plan to have the English nobles killed. [William de Longspée, d. 1226.]
JOHN: III, 1.

Salisbury, Earl of, with King at Agincourt (HEN5); killed at Orleans (1H6). [Thomas de Montacute, 4th Earl (1388-1428), famous general.]
HEN5: IV, 3; 1H6: I, 4.

Salisbury, Earl of, enemy of Suffolk; joins the Duke of York, his brother-in-law, and fights at St. Albans. [Richard Neville, 1st Earl (1400-60), son of Ralph Neville, 1st Earl of Westmoreland; married the daughter of Thomas (above); their son being Warwick the Kingmaker; captured at Wakefield and beheaded by the Lancastrians.]
2H6: I, 1.

Salisbury Court Theatre, principal playhouse of London; built 1629; destroyed 1649; used by Queen Henrietta's and Prince's Men; replaced by the DORSET GARDEN THEATRE (Duke's Theatre, 1671).

sallet, spicy morsel, Elizabethan form of salad, highly seasoned.
HAM: Hamlet, II, 2, 463—spicy passage.
2H6: Cade, IV, 10, 9—pun on light, round helmet.

Salomon (Solomon), King of Israel (c973-c933 BC), son of David and Bathsheba; noted for great wisdom and magnificent reign; reputed author of *Proverbs, The Song of Songs* and *Ecclesiastes* in the Biblical canon; and of *The Wisdom of Solomon* in the Apocrypha.
LLL: Berowne, IV, 3, 168.

salt, lustful, wanton, bawdy; stinging.
A&C: Pompey, II, 1, 21.
TIMON: Timon, IV, 3, 85.
OTH: Iago, II, 1, 245.

Saltiers, for satyrs, jumpers.
WINT: Servant, IV, 4, 334.

salvages, savages, wild creatures.
TEMP: Stephano, II, 2, 60.

sampire (samphire), plant growing along the rocky seacoast, including the white cliffs of Dover; heavy aroma; used in making relishes, pickles.
LEAR: Edgar, IV, 6, 15.

Sampson, Capulet servant.
R&J: I, 1. See GREGORY.

Samson, famed Israelite strong man (Judges 13) who pulled down the temple of his enemies.
1H6: Alençon, I, 2, 33.
HEN8: Man, V, 4, 22.
LLL: Moth, I, 2, 73.

sanctimonious, sacred, holy, religious.
TEMP: Prospero, IV, 1, 16.

sanctuarize, give protection or sanctuary to.
HAM: King, IV, 7, 28.

sandal shoon, sandals worn by pilgrims.
HAM: Ophelia, IV, 5, 26. See TRUE-LOVE.

sanded, color of sand.
MND: Theseus, IV, 1, 123.

sands
The sands are numbered that make up my life . . .
3H6: York, I, 4, 25.

Sandys, Lord, flirts with Anne Bullen; as Sir William Sandys accompanies Buckingham on his way to execution. [d. 1540; created Baron (1523), Lord Chamberlain (1526).]
HEN8: I, 3.

sans, French, without.
HAM: Hamlet, III, 4, 79.

JOHN: Bastard, V, 6, 15—*sans compliment,* informally.

TEMP: Prospero, I, 2, 97—*sans bound,* without limit.

sarcenet (sarsanet), soft, very fine, silk material; flimsy, light.
1H4: Hotspur, III, 1, 254.
T&C: Thersites, V, 1, 36.

Sarum Plain, Salisbury Plain in the south of England.
LEAR: Kent, II, 2, 89.

satis quod sufficit, Latin, enough is as good as a feast; found in Heywood's *Proverbs* (1546).
LLL: Holofernes, V, 1, 1.

Saturn, farthest, most remote planet known to ancient astronomers; believed to cause people born under its influence to be grim, cold, morose or, appropriately, saturnine.
ADO: John, I, 3, 12.
CYM: Posthumus, II, 5, 12—father of Jupiter; synonymous with old age.

Saturninus, elected Emperor; marries Tamora; orders killing of two of Titus' sons, believing they murdered his brother, Bassianus; Titus kills Tamora at the banquet, Saturninus kills Titus and is himself killed by Lucius, Titus' son.
TITUS: I, 1.

satyr, mythological creature with upper body of a man, shaggy legs, goat's hoofs and small horns in curly hair; called a faun by the Romans; rural, lecherous; leader was Pan, son of Hermes.
HAM: Hamlet, I, 2, 140.

sauce, make a person pay dearly.
MWW: Host, IV, 3, 11.
AYL: Rosalind, III, 5, 69—rebuke.

Savoy, great guest house in London near the INNS OF COURT.
2H6: Cade, IV, 7, 2—mistaken dating here as the Savoy was destroyed by Wat Tyler at the time of his rebellion (1381) and was not rebuilt until 1505.

Saxo Grammaticus (c1150-c1206). Danish poet, historian; author of the Latin history of the Danish kings, *Historia Danica* (1514), which includes the legend of Hamlet (Amleth); used by BELLEFOREST in *Histoires Tragiques* (1576), the source of Shakespeare's play.

Say, Lord, Lord Treasurer, captured by Cade, who accuses him of extortion; beheaded, with his son-in-law, Sir James Cromer.
2H6: IV, 4.

say, silk cloth resembling serge.
2H6: Cade, IV, 7, 27—pun.

'Sblood, by God's blood, an oath.
HAM: Hamlet, II, 2, 384.
OTH: Iago, I, 1, 4.

scaffolage (scaffold), stage of a theater; wooden platform.
T&C: Ulysses, I, 3, 156.
HEN5: Chorus, I, 10—*scaffold.*

scald, scurvy, contemptible, scabby.
A&C: Cleopatra, V, 2, 215.
MWW: Evans, III, 1, 123—*scall.*

scale, to weigh, estimate, compare.
COR: Sicinius, II, 3, 257.

Scales, Lord, commander of the Tower during Cade's rebellion; had been reported captured at Patay (1H6: I, 1).
2H6: IV, 5.

scambling, quarrelsome, unruly.
ADO: Antonio, V, 1, 94.
HEN5: Canterbury, I, 1, 4.

scamel, much debated word, possibly a sea bird, sea-mel, seagull.
TEMP: Caliban, I, 2, 176.

scant my sizes, cut my allowances.
LEAR: Lear, II, 4, 178.

scape, escapade, prank.
WINT: Shepherd, III, 3, 74.

scarf, decoration; wreath; banner, flag.
JC: Casca, I, 2, 289.

HAM: Hamlet, V, 2, 13—
scarfed.

Scarus, loyal friend of Anthony.
A&C: III, 10.

scauld, scabby, scurfy, scaly.
HEN5: Fluellen, V, 1, 5.

scene individable, play which adheres to unities of time, place and action.
HAM: Polonius, II, 2, 418.

sceptered isle
This royal throne of kings, this
   sceptered isle.
This earth of majesty, this seat
   of Mars,
This other Eden, demi-Paradise.
RICH2: Gaunt, II, 1, 40.

schedule, note, document, paper,
scroll.
JC: Artemidorus, III, 1, 3.
2H4: Archbishop, IV, 1, 168.
LLL: Ferdinand, I, 1, 18.

scholar. See THOU ART A SCHOLAR.

school, advise, lecture, reprimand.
MND: Theseus, I, 1, 116.

schoolmaster, private tutor.
A&C: Antony, III, 11, 71.

schoolmasters. See WILFUL MEN.

scion. See SECT OR SCION.

sconce, small fort, earthwork, breastwork, part of a fortification.
HEN5: Gower, III, 6, 76.

sconce, slang or common term for head.
COFE: Antipholus E., I, 2, 79.
COR: Coriolanus, III, 2, 97.
HAM: Hamlet, V, 1, 110.

Scone, ancient royal city north of Perth, Scotland; possibly capital of old Pictish kingdom; Stone of Destiny, later stolen by Edward I (1269) and taken to Westminster Abbey, was stone upon which all Scottish kings were crowned.
MACB: Macduff, II, 4, 31.

scope, purpose, aim.
RICH2: Northumberland, III, 3, 112. See GROSS AND SCOPE.

score, account kept by tallies or markers on a door.
SHREW: Beggar (Sly), Induction, 2, 25.

Scot, Reginald (c1538-99). English author of *The Discouerie of Witchcraft . . .* (1584), the source of material for *Macbeth* and possibly of ROBIN GOODFELLOW; book ordered burned by James VI of Scotland.

scot and lot, municipal tax; in full; lock, stock and barrel.
1H4: Falstaff, V, 4, 115.

scotch, slash, gash, score, cut.
COR: 1Servingman, IV, 5, 197.
A&C: IV, 7, 10.

scour, scurry, hasten, hurry.
WINT: Lord, II, 1, 35.
TIMON: 3Senator, V, 2, 15.

scourge and minister, a scourge was a punisher of sin (like Tamerlaine) used by God and then destroyed by him for his human errors; a minister was a servant of God pure enough to carry out his mission and service.
HAM: Hamlet, III, 4, 175.

scout, deride, jeer at, possibly befool.
TEMP: Stephano, III, 2, 130.

screw, detach, pry loose; a jack that forces.
TWN: Duke, V, 1, 126.

scrimer, from French *escrimeur*, fencer.
HAM: King, IV, 7, 101.

scrip, script, written list; wallet or satchel.
MND: Bottom, I, 2, 3.
AYL: Touchstone, III, 2, 171
—*scrippage*, wallet with its contents.

scripture. See DEVIL.

scrivener, notary, professional clerk or writer who prepared legal documents or agreements.
SHREW: Tranio, IV, 4, 59.

Scrivener, prepares indictment of Lord Hastings.
RICH3: III, 6.

Scroop (Scrope), Lord, one of

Henry's most trusted advisers; plans, with Cambridge and Grey, to murder the King as he sets out for France; discovered and executed. [Henry le Scrope (d. 1415), 3rd Baron, eldest son of Sir Stephen Scrope (see below).]

HEN5: II, 2.

Scroop (Scrope), Richard, Archbishop of York; joins Hotspur's rebellion (1H4), but not present at Shrewsbury; tricked (2H4) by Prince John into dismissing his forces, executed. [Richard le Scrope (c1350-1405), 4th son of the 1st Baron.]

1H4: IV, 4; 2H4: I, 3.

Scroop (Scrope), Sir Stephen, member of Richard's party; announces the news of Bolingbroke's success in arms and the fates of Bushy, Green and the Earl of Wiltshire, his brother, to Richard; widow married Sir John Falsolfe (1409).

RICH2: III, 2.

scroyle, scurvy, scabby scoundrel or wretch.

JOHN: Bastard, II, 1, 373.

scruple, apothecaries' weight of ⅓ of a dram; very small part, bit.

TWN: Malvolio, III, 4, 88. See DRAM.

MEAS: Duke, I, 1, 38.

ADO: Antonio, V, 1, 93.

scruple, doubt, hesitate to admit.

2H4: Falstaff, I, 2, 149—*dram of a scruple,* trifle doubtful.

scullion, the lowest rank of servants, usually used in the kitchen for the dirtiest work.

HAM: Hamlet, II, 2, 615.

scurvy, wretched, diseased, "lousy."

TEMP: Stephano, II, 2, 46.

scut, deer's tail.

MWW: Falstaff, V, 5, 20.

scutcheon, escutcheon; coat of arms displayed at funerals; lowest form of heraldic ensign; usu-

ally of silk, buckram, metal or paper; hung in churches.

1H4: Falstaff, V, 1, 143.

Scylla and Charybdis, legendary sea monsters, believed to be in the Straits of Messina; ambushed and killed sailors.

MERV: Launcelot, III, 5, 19.

Scythian, ancient nomadic people mentioned by Herodotus and others; inhabited steppes north of the Black Sea and area east of the Aral Sea; considered wild and barbarous.

LEAR: Lear, I, 1, 118.

TITUS: Chiron, I, 1, 131.

Scythian Tomyris, Queen of the Massagetae (South Russia); Cyrus, King of Persia, had killed her son and when she defeated him in battle (529 BC), she had his head cut off and put into a wineskin of his own blood, so that he could have his fill.

1H6: Countess, II, 3, 6.

sea change. See FATHER.

Sea-Captain (Lieutenant), captures the Duke of Suffolk (2H6); captain of the ship wrecked off the coast of Illyria (TwN); promises to present Viola, disguised as a page, to Orsino.

2H6: IV, 1; TwN: I, 2.

sea-coal, bituminous coal, carried by sea from Newcastle to London, as distinguished from charcoal.

2H4: Hostess, II, 1, 96.

sea-gown, high collared, short-sleeved, heavy coat worn by men at sea.

HAM: Hamlet, V, 2, 13.

seal, sign or conclude an agreement or contract; confirm; stamp or mark for selection or possession.

A&C: Enobarbus, III, 2, 3.

HAM: Hamlet, III, 2, 70.

MND: Demetrius, III, 2, 144.

seam, fat, grease.

T&C: Ulysses, II, 3, 195.

sea-marge, margin of the sea or seashore.
TEMP: Iris, IV, 1, 69.

searching, intoxicating, powerful, strong.
2H4: Hostess, II, 4, 30.

season, mature, ripen; temper, qualify.
HAM: Polonius, I, 3, 81.
HAM: Horatio, I, 2, 193.

seat, throne; feudal estates; position.
RICH2: Scroop, III, 2, 119.
HEN5: King, III, 5, 47.
1H4: Worcester, V, 1, 45.

seated, fixed, embedded, set firmly.
MACB: Macbeth, I, 3, 136.

sea water
Sea water shalt thou drink, thy food shall be
The fresh-brook mussels, withered roots, and husks
Wherein the acorn cradled.
TEMP: Prospero, I, 2, 462.

Sebastian, treacherous brother of Alonso, King of Naples.
TEMP: I, 1.

Sebastian, twin brother of Viola; wins Olivia.
TwN: II, 1.

second accent, echo.
HEN5: Exeter, II, 4, 126.

sect or scion, cutting; detached shoot or slip, capable of propagation, taken from a tree or plant and prepared for grafting.
OTH: Iago, I, 3, 337.

secure, free from care, apprehension or anxiety; confident, sure; to guard.
RICH2: Carlisle, III, 2, 34.
OTH: Iago, III, 3, 198.
TEMP: Sebastian, II, 1, 310.

security
He shall spurn fate, scorn death, and bear
His hopes 'bove wisdom, grace, and fear;
And you all know, security
Is mortals' chiefest enemy.
MACB: Hecate, III, 5, 30.

sedge, a rush or grasslike plant; border, hedge.
TEMP: Iris, IV, 1, 129.
ADO: Benedick, II, 1, 210.
1H4: Hotspur, I, 3, 98.

seeds. See PROPHESY.

seel, in falconry, to sew the eyelids of a hawk with a fine thread to make the bird easier to train; close, blind, conceal.
MACB: Macbeth, III, 2, 46. See NIGHT.
A&C: Antony, III, 13, 112.
OTH: Othello, I, 3, 270.

seely. See SILLY.

Segar, Sir William (d. 1633). English author of *Booke of Honor and Armes* (pub., 1590); source of the dueling material in *Love's Labour's Lost* and *Romeo and Juliet*.

segregation, act of being scattered, dispersed or separated.
OTH: 2Gentleman, II, 1, 10.

seized of, legally in possession of.
HAM: Horatio, I, 1, 89.

Seleucus, Cleopatra's treasurer; warns Caesar that only half of Cleopatra's possessions are listed in the inventory.
A&C: V, 2.

self, same; one's own.
HEN5: Canterbury, I, 1, 1.
RICH2: Duchess of Gloucester, I, 2, 23.

self
To thine own self be true.
HAM: Polonius, II, 1, 114.

self. See HONOUR.

self-bounty, inherent or natural goodness of heart.
OTH: Iago, III, 3, 200.

self-charity, self-love, conceit.
OTH: Montano, II, 3, 202.

self-comparisons, actions that were equal with or matched his own.
MACB: Ross, I, 2, 55.

self-interest
Commodity, the bias of the world—

The world, who of itself is
   peised well,
Made to run even upon even
   ground
Till this advantage, this vile
   drawing bias,
This sway of motion, this Com-
   modity,
Makes it take head from all in-
   difference,
From all direction, purpose,
   course, intent—
  JOHN: Bastard, II, 1, 574. See
  COMMODITY, BIAS, PEISE.

self-love
Or who is he so fond will be the
   tomb
Of his self-love, to stop poster-
   ity?
  SONNET: III, 8.

Sin of self-love possesseth all
   mine eye
And all my soul and all my
   every part;
And for this sin there is no
   remedy,
It is so grounded inward in my
   heart.
  SONNET: LXII, 1.

O, you are sick of self-love,
Malvolio, and taste with a dis-
tempered appetite.
  TwN: Olivia, I, 5, 97.

self-neglect
Self-love, my liege, is not so vile
   a sin
As self-neglecting.
  HEN5: Dauphin, II, 4, 74.

semblable, resemblance, similar;
like or likeness.
  HAM: Hamlet, V, 2, 124.
  A&C: Antony, III, 4, 2.
  TwN: Duke, I, 4, 34.

Semiramis, legendary queen of
Assyria; wife of Ninus, infamous
for sensuous life; beautiful, wise,
builder of cities.
  SHREW: Lord, Induction, 2, 41.
  TITUS: Aaron, II, 1, 22.

semper idem, Latin, always the
same.
  2H4: Pistol, V, 5, 30.

Seneca, Lucius Annaeus (c4 BC–
65 AD), Roman dramatist, Stoic
philosopher; famous for great
tragedies; senator under Calig-
ula; banished under Claudius;
recalled to tutor Agrippina's son
Nero; extremely powerful when
Nero became emperor (54);
charged with treason, committed
suicide by order of the crazed
emperor; important influence on
Renaissance writers and Shakespeare.
  HAM: Polonius, II, 2, 419.

senna, purgative or cathartic herb.
  MACB: Macbeth, V, 3, 55.

sennet, special notes or call on the
trumpet to announce the approach and departure of processions or important personages;
used in stage directions.
  LEAR: I, 1.
  MACB: III, 1.
  A&C: II, 7.

s'ennight, seven nights, a week.
  OTH: Cassio, II, 1, 77.

Senoys, Siennese, inhabitants of
Siena, Italy.
  ALL'sW: King, I, 2, 1.

sense, emotional perception, sensual passion, feeling.
  HAM: Hamlet, III, 4, 71

sense. See QUAT.

senseless brands
. . . The senseless brands will
   sympathize
The heavy accent of thy moving
   tongue
And in compassion weep the fire
   out . . .
  RICH2: Richard, V, 1, 46.

senseless conjuration, attempt to
entreat or appeal to things which
have no feelings or do not comprehend; invocation of the inanimate.
  RICH2: Richard, III, 2, 3.

sensible, sensitive, impressible,
perceptive, keenly felt.
  TEMP: Gonzalo, II, 1, 174.
  LLL: Boyet, V, 2, 259.
  COR: Valeria, I, 3, 95.

sentence, proverbial or sententious saying or maxim; adage.
OTH: Duke, I, 3, 199.

se offendendo, Latin, in self-offense, which is a comic twist on *se defendendo* meaning in self-defense.
HAM: Clown, V, 1, 9.

Sepronius, another Lord who refuses Timon a loan.
TIMON: III, 3.

septentrion, the north; seven stars called the Big Dipper or Ursa Major.
3H6: I, 4, 136.

sequent, successive, following, subsequent, consequently, consecutive.
HAM: Hamlet, V, 2, 54.
OTH: Cassio, I, 2, 41.

sequestration, separation, estrangement, parting; imprisonment.
OTH: Iago, I, 3, 351.
AYL: 1Lord, II, 1, 33.
1H6: Mortimer, II, 5, 25.

sere. See TICKLE O' TH' SERE.

serpent
. . . To beguile the time,
Look like the time; bear welcome in your eye,
Your hand, your tongue; look like the innocent flower,
But be the serpent under't.
MACB: Lady Macbeth, I, 5, 64.

serpent's tongue, hissing (from the audience).
MND: Puck, V, 1, 440.

serpent's tooth. See THANKLESS CHILD.

serpigo (suppeago), disease of the skin.
MEAS: Duke, III, 1, 31.
T&C: Thersites, II, 3, 80.

service
. . . 'tis the curse of service.
Preferment goes by letter and affection,
And not by old gradation, where each second
Stood heir to th' first.
OTH: Iago, I, 1, 35.

Servilius, Timon's servant; sent to Lucius for money.
TIMON: III, 2.

session, regular court of justice.
OTH: Brabantio, I, 2, 86.

set, fixed, dazed, glassy, in a drunken stare.
TEMP: Stephano, III, 2, 10.
TwN: Clown, V, 1, 205.

set abroach, let loose, get started.
2H4: John, IV, 2, 14.

set a match, arrange or set up a theft.
1H4: Falstaff, I, 2, 118.

set down the pegs, loosen the pegs that keep the strings of the instrument in tune.
OTH: Iago, II, 1, 202—I'll change your tune.

Setebos, god or giant of the Patagonians; called "great devil" by Antonio Pigafetta in his report of Magellan's voyage around the globe; English version in Richard Eden's *The History of Trauayle in the West and East Indies* (1577).
TEMP: Caliban, I, 2, 373.

set off his head, notwithstanding, not charged or held against him.
1H4: Prince, V, 1, 88.

sets a blister, marks or brands with infamy, sin or degradation; harlots were branded by law.
HAM: Hamlet, III, 4, 44.

sets me, gambling term, wagers against me; challenges me.
RICH2: Aumerle, IV, 1, 57.

setter, thief who "sets up" the victim; decoyer; highwayman's helper.
1H4: Poins, II, 2, 53.

seven sons. See EDWARD III.
RICH2: Duchess of Gloucester, I, 2, 11.

several, distinct, individual, separate.
TEMP: Ferdinand, III, 1, 42.

Severn, river which divides England from Wales.
CYM: Cymbeline, III, 5, 17.

sewer, servant (butler) in charge of dinner arrangements.

MACB: S.D., I, 7.

Sextus Pompeius. See POMPEY.

Seyton, loyal officer of Macbeth; brings news of Lady Macbeth's death. "The Setons of Touch were (and still are) hereditary armour bearers to the Kings of Scotland," from French's *Shakespeare Genealog.*

MACB: V, 3.

shadow, protective roof built over the apron stage in the open public theaters.

shadow. See DREAM.

Shadow, Simon, one of the men recruited into service by Falstaff.

2H4: III, 2.

shadows

The best in this kind are but shadows; and the worst are no worse, if imagination amend them.

MND: Theseus, V, 1, 215— *shadows*, spirits, phantoms, creatures of no real substance.

Shadwell, Thomas (1642-92). English dramatist; adapted D'Avenant-Dryden version of *The Tempest* into an opera, *The Enchanted Island* (1673) with music by Purcell; wrote *History of Timon of Athens, the Man Hater* (1678) produced at DORSET GARDEN; poet laureate (1688); rival of Dryden.

Shafalus to Procurus, mistaken reference to Cephalus and Procris, husband and wife who were tested in their love by Eos, goddess of the dawn, who loved Cephalus.

MND: Pyramus, V, 1, 201.

Shakespeare Memorial Theatre, opened at Stratford (April 23, 1879); destroyed by fire (1926); reopened (April 23, 1932); plays produced in temporary theater at the time of the first Festival (1864); Charles Flower of Stratford sponsored the first Memorial Theatre and his nephew, Archibald, raised the money to rebuild the present theater.

Shallow, Robert, Justice of the Peace in the county of Gloucester; brags of his youth when he was a gay blade (mostly imaginary); supplies Falstaff with recruits; lends money to Falstaff on the security of Henry's accession to the throne (2H4); threatens to have him brought up on charges (MWW); tries to marry Anne Page to his cousin Slender.

2H4; III, 2; MWW: I, 1. See LUCY, Sir Thomas.

shambles, slaughterhouse.

OTH: Othello, IV, 2, 66.

shame

My life thou shalt command, but not my shame.

The one my duty owes; but my fair name,

Despite of death that lives upon my grave,

To dark dishonour's use thou shalt not have.

RICH2: Mowbray, I, 1, 166.

shame. See DEATH.

shape, envision, imagine, conceive of.

OTH: Cassio, II, 1, 55.

shard, potsherd, fragment or broken piece of crockery or pottery; horny, scaly, hard, shiny case or sheath of the beetle's wing; patch of cow dung.

HAM: Doctor, V, 1, 254.

CYM: Belarius, III, 3, 20.

A&C: Enobarbus, III, 2, 20— refers to tumblebug which breeds in dung.

shard-borne beetle

. . . Ere the bat hath flown

His cloister'd flight, ere to black Hecate's summons

The shard-borne beetle with his drowsy hums

Hath rung night's yawning peal, there shall be done

A deed of dreadful note.

MACB: Macbeth: III, 2, 40.

share, each regular member of a

theatrical company received a share of the profits; the shares were also subdivided and several players received half-shares.
HAM: Horatio, III, 2, 290.

shark (up), grab, gather rapaciously as a shark lunges at its prey.
HAM: Horatio, I, 1, 98—*sharked*.

Shaw, Doctor (Friar Ralph), popular preacher; first to speak publicly of the alleged precontract between Edward and Elizabeth Lucy.
RICH3: Richard, III, 5, 103.

shent, admonished, scolded severely, rebuked; disgraced.
HAM: Hamlet, III, 2, 416.
TwN: Clown, IV, 2, 112.
MWW: Quickly, I, 4, 38.

Shepherd, father rejected by Joan of Arc.
1H6: V, 4.

Shepherd, discovers the baby Perdita on the beach and brings her up as his daughter; condemned to death by Polixenes, he escapes with the young lovers to Sicilia.
WINT: III, 3.

sheriff's post, in Elizabethan England, a post, with a bulletin board for displaying notices, was set up in front of the local sheriff's house.
TwN: Malvolio, I, 5, 157.

shift, stratagem, trick; manage; change.
CofE: Antipholus S., III, 2, 187.
MACB: Porter, II, 3, 46.
ADO: Pedro, II, 3, 80.

ship-tire, elaborate, fashionable headdress, shaped like a ship.
MWW: Falstaff, III, 3, 60.

shive, slice; splinter.
RICH2: Richard, IV, 1, 289—*shivers*.

shog, jog, walk.
HEN5: Nym, II, 1, 47.

shooting star. See GLORY.

short, shorten, keep under control, confine, tether.
HAM: King, IV, 1, 18.
CYM: Iachimo, I, 6, 200.

shot-free, without paying the bill.
1H4: Falstaff, V, 3, 30.

shotten herring, fish that has spawned (shot its roe) and therefore thin and worthless.
1H4: Falstaff, II, 4, 144.

shough, rough or shaggy-haired dog.
MACB: Macbeth, III, 1, 94.

shovegroat, game played with coins slid toward a numbered space or mark; similar to shuffleboard (still played).
2H4: Falstaff, II, 4, 206.

showers, tears.
HAM: Ophelia, IV, 5, 39. See BLAZE OF RIOT.

shrewd, sharp, malicious, sly, evil.
OTH: Othello, III, 3, 429.
RICH2: Richard, III, 2, 59.
HEN5: Constable, III, 7, 52.

shrewd, stinging; sharp-tongued; bitter; shrewish.
HAM: Hamlet, I, 4, 1.
A&C: 1Watch, IV, 9, 5.
MND: Helena, III, 2, 323.

Shrewsbury, Earl of. See TALBOT.

shrieve, sheriff.
2H4: Harcourt, IV, 4, 99.
ALL'sW: Parolles, IV, 3, 212—*shrieve's fool*, idiot or feeble-minded girl, under the guardianship of the sheriff who was in charge of the indigent insane.

shrift, confession; confessional; absolution.
OTH: Desdemona, III, 3, 24.
RICH3: Ratcliff, III, 4, 94.
R&J: Friar, II, 3, 56.

shrive, to hear confession and grant absolution.
MERV: Portia, I, 2, 145.
HAM: Hamlet, V, 2, 47.
CofE: Adriana, II, 2, 210.

shrouds, sail-ropes, ropes running from the masthead; part of ship's rigging; take cover or shelter.

HEN8: 3Gentleman, IV, 1, 72.
JOHN: John, V, 7, 53.
TEMP: Trinculo, II, 2, 44.

Shrovetide, three days before Ash Wednesday; usually a gay time.
2H4: Silence, V, 3, 38.

shrowd. See SHREWD.
HEN5: Orleans, III, 7, 163.

shut doors
Men shut their doors against a setting sun.
TIMON: Apemantus, I, 2, 150.

Shylock, Jewish moneylender; father of Jessica; defeated in court by Portia. "Both the embodiment of an irrational hatred, and a credible human being"— (J. M. Murry); "made a scapegoat in the cruelest, most dishonest way"—(C. L. Barber); critics and actors have seen (or portrayed) him as a stony adversary, an inhuman wretch, a complete villain, a buffoon or a truly sympathetic figure.
MERV: I, 3.

Sibyl, mythological Cumaean prophetess; Apollo allowed her to live as long as she could hold grains of sand in her hand; consulted by Aeneas before his descent into hell.
SHREW: Petruchio, I, 2, 70.
1H6: Bastard, I, 2, 56.
OTH: Othello, III, 4, 70—prophetess.

Sibylla. See above.
MERV: Portia, I, 2, 116.

Sicinius Velutus, tribune of the people.
COR: I, 1.

sicle, shekel, an ancient coin.
MEAS: Isabella, II, 2, 149.

sic spectanda fides, Latin, thus is faith to be tested or faithfulness to be tried; motto on the shield of the fifth knight.
PER: Thaisa, II, 2, 38.

Sicyon, Ionian town in southern Greece where Antony had left Fulvia.
A&C: Antony, I, 2, 117.

side-sleeves, ornamental, second-ary sleeves hanging from the shoulder, open from the armhole.
ADO: Margaret, III, 4, 21.

Sidney, Sir Philip (1554-86). English poet, critic; son of Sir Henry and Lady Mary Dudley (Sidney); wrote *Arcadia* (1580-83, pub., 1590); *Apologie for Poetries* (pub., 1595); *Astrophel and Stella* (1591; 11 songs and 108 sonnets dedicated to Penelope Devereux); knighted, married Frances Walsingham (1583); *Arcadia* used as the source of the subplot for *King Lear* and for names in other plays; influenced the *Sonnets.*

siege, rank, seat, place.
HAM: King, IV, 7, 77—rank was determined by seating at table.
MEAS: Provost, IV, 2, 101.
OTH: Othello, I, 2, 22.

siege, excrement.
TEMP: Stephano, II, 2, 110.

sigh no more
Sigh no more, ladies, sigh no more!
Men were deceivers ever,
One foot in sea, and one on shore;
To one thing constant never.
ADO: Balthasar, II, 3, 64—beginning of song.

signiory, government of state of Venice.
OTH: Othello, I, 2, 18.

signory, domain of a nobleman, dukedom.
TEMP: Prospero, I, 2, 71.
RICH2: Bolingbroke, III, 1, 22.
2H4: Westmoreland, IV, 1, 111.

signs. See FALL OF KINGS.

silence
Silence is the perfectest herald of joy.
ADO: Claudio, II, 1, 317.
The rest is silence.
HAM: Hamlet, V, 2, 369.
. . . for silence is only commendable

In a neat's tongue dried and a maid not vendible.
   MerV: Gratiano, I, 1, 111. See NEAT.

silence. See INNOCENCE.

Silence, country justice; cousin of Shallow.
   2H4: III, 2.

silent love
O, learn to read what silent love hath writ!
To hear with eyes belongs to love's fine wit.
   SONNET: XXIII, 13.

Silius, officer in Ventidius' army; urges him to pursue the defeated Parthians.
   A&C: III, 1.

silken thread. See GRIEF.

silly (seely), innocent, harmless, simpleminded; poor, wretched.
   Rich2: Richard, V, 5, 25.

Silvia, beautiful, gentle daughter of the Duke of Milan; faithful to Valentine, she rejects Proteus.
   2Gent: II, 1.

Silvius, shepherd in love with Phebe.
   AYL: II, 4.

Simois, small river which flows from Mount Ida, joins the Scamander river and enters into the plain of Troy.
   LUCRECE: 1437.

Simonides, King of Pentapolis, father of Thaisa; crowns Pericles victor of the tournament; puts him to the test before giving his daughter.
   Per: II, 2.

simony, practice of buying and selling ecclesiastical offices and favors.
   Hen8: Katherine, IV, 2, 36.

Simpcox, Saunder, impostor, claiming to have been cured of blindness at St. Alban's shrine, when Gloucester exposes him.
   2H6: II, 1.

Simple, Peter, Slender's servant; butt of jokes.
   MWW: I, 1.

simple faith
When love begins to sicken and decay
It useth an enforced ceremony.
There are no tricks in plain and simple faith.
   JC: Brutus, IV, 2, 20.

simples, medicinal herbs or plants; ingredient or element in a compound; uncompounded.
   HAM: Laertes, IV, 7, 145.
   MWW: Caius, I, 4, 65.
   R&J: Romeo, V, 1, 40.

sin
Teach sin the carriage of a holy saint.
   CofE: Luciana, III, 2, 14.
I am a man
More sinned against than sinning.
   LEAR: Lear, III, 2, 58.
Some rise by sin, and some by virtue fall.
Some run from brakes of vice, and answer none;
And some condemned for a fault alone.
   MEAS: Escalus, II, 1, 38. See BRAKE.
Few love to hear the sins they love to act.
   PER: Pericles, I, 1, 92.
Nothing emboldens sin so much as mercy.
   TIMON: 1Senator, III, 5, 3.

Sinel, Macbeth's father.
   MACB: Macbeth, I, 3, 71.

sinew, strength, support.
   1H4: Archbishop, IV, 4, 17.

singing birds
The crow doth sing as sweetly as the lark
When neither is attended; and I think
The nightingale, if she should sing by day
When every goose is cackling, would be thought
No better a musician than the wren.
   MERV: Portia, V, 1, 102.

single, lonely, weak, feeble; undivided.

TEMP: Ferdinand, I, 2, 432.
COR: Menenius, II, 1, 41.
MACB: Macbeth, I, 3, 140.

singuled, separated, segregated.
LLL: Armado, V, 1, 86.

sinister, left, left-handed; illegitimate, irregular.
MND: Prologue (Quince), V, 1, 164.
T&C: Hector, IV, 5, 128.
HEN5: Exeter, II, 4, 85.

sink-a-pace (cinquepace), five steps, dance similar to the galliard. See GALLIARD.
TWN: Toby, I, 3, 139.
ADO: Beatrice, II, 1, 77.

Sinklo, with Humphrey, (game) keeper of the forest; arrests the disguised King. [John Sincler, an actor in the Chamberlain's-King's company, played tall, thin parts.]
3H6: III, 1.

sinner
Made such a sinner of his memory
To credit his own lie . . .
TEMP: Prospero, I, 2, 101.

Sinon, a Greek who pretended to desert to the Trojans; persuaded them to pull the wooden horse into the city; released the soldiers who captured Troy.
CYM: Imogen, III, 4, 61.
3H6: Richard, III, 2, 190.
TITUS: Marcus, V, 3, 85.

Sir, courtesy title given to the clergy; honored on the basis that they too had enough Latin learning to have earned a Bachelor of Arts degree at a university
RICH3: Hastings, III, 2, 109—
Sir John.
MWW: Shallow, I, 1, 1—*Sir Hugh.*
LLL: Holofernes, IV, 2, 11—
Sir Nathaniel.

sirrah, word of haughty address used to inferiors; often used in anger.
RICH2: York, II, 2, 89.

LLL: Berowne, I, 1, 312.
TWN: Duke, V, 1, 148.

Sisters Three, the Fates who were believed to spin out man's destiny.
MND: Thisby, V, 1, 343.
2H4: Pistol, II, 4, 213.
MERV: Launcelot, II, 2, 66.

sit at, expenses, cost; tenant at a fixed rent.
MWW: Falstaff, I, 3, 8.

sit fas aut nefas, Latin, be it right or wrong.
TITUS: Demetrius, II, 1, 133—
quotation from SENECA's *Hippolytus.*

sits on brood, literally sits hatching; concocting, inventing.
HAM: King, III, 1, 173.

sit sore, press badly.
RICH2: Northumberland, II, 1, 265.

Siward, Earl of Northumberland; Malcolm's uncle; leader of the English forces that conquer Macbeth; his son, young Siward, is slain in personal combat with the king (V, 7).
MACB: V, 4.

six and seven, utter confusion.
RICH2: York, II, 2, 121.

skipper, young, frivolous upstart, saucy lad, playboy.
SHREW: Gremio, II, 1, 341.

skirr, scour, scurry.
MACB: Macbeth, V, 3, 35.
HEN5: King, IV, 7, 64.

slab, thick, slimy, sticky, viscous.
MACB: 3Witch, IV, 1, 32.

slander, misuse; disgrace.
HAM: Polonius, I, 3, 133.

slander
For slander lives upon succession,
Forever housed where it gets possession.
COFE: Balthazar, III, 1, 105.
. . . 'tis slander,
Whose edge is sharper than the sword, whose tongue
Outvenoms all the worms of Nile, whose breath

Rides on the posting winds and
   doth belie
All corners of the world.
   CYM: Pisanio, III, 4, 35.

That thou art blam'd shall not
   be thy defect,
For slander's mark was ever yet
   the fair . . .
   SONNET: LXX, 1.

A slave whose gall coins slanders like a mint . . .
   T&C: Nestor, I, 3, 193.

slave

Being your slave, what should I
   do but tend
Upon the hours and times of
   your desire?

        *   *   *

So true a fool is love that in
   your will,
Though you do anything, he
   thinks no ill.
   SONNET: LVII, 1 and 13.

sledded Polacks (Pollax), it is suggested that either the king struck
his leaded pole-ax on the ice,
or attacked the Poles in their
sledges.
   HAM: Horatio, I, 1, 63.

sleep

. . . she looks like sleep,
As she would catch another
   Antony
In her strong toil of grace.
   A&C: Caesar, V, 2, 349.

. . . O sleep, O gentle sleep,
Nature's soft nurse, how have I
   frighted thee,
That thou no more wilt weigh
   my eyelids down
And steep my senses in forgetfulness . . .
   2H4: King, III, 1, 5—beginning of well-known soliloquy
on sleep.

Methought I heard a voice cry
   "Sleep no more!
Macbeth does murther sleep"—
   the innocent sleep,
Sleep that knits up the ravelled
   sleave of care,
The death of each day's life,
   sore labour's bath,

Balm of hurt minds, great na-
   ture's second course,
Chief nourisher in life's feast.
   MACB: Macbeth, II, 2, 35.

You lack the season of all natures, sleep.
   MACB: Lady Macbeth, III, 4,
141.

. . . Not poppy nor mandragora,
Nor all the drowsy syrups of the
   world,
Shall ever medicine thee to that
   sweet sleep
Which thou ow'dst yesterday.
   OTH: Iago, III, 3, 330. See
MANDRAGORA.

sleided, raw, unwrought, divided
into threads.
   PER: Gower, IV, Prologue, 21.

Slender, Abraham, half-witted
country cousin of Shallow; in-
articulate suitor of Anne Page;
supposed to run off with her, he
makes a mistake and runs off
with a boy.
   MWW: I, 1.

'Slid, by God's eyelid, a mild
oath.
   TwN: Andrew, III, 4, 426.

slip, counterfeit coin.
   R&J: Mercutio, II, 4, 51.

slip, leash, usually refers to a
greyhound.
   HEN5: King, III, 1, 31.
   CYM: Cymbeline, IV, 3, 22.
   SHREW: Tranio, V, 2, 52—
slipped, released, freed, un-
leashed.

slipper, slippery, shifty, untrust-
worthy.
   OTH: Iago, II, 1, 244.

slippery people

. . . Our slippery people,
Whose love is never link'd to the
   deserver
Till his deserts are past . . .
   A&C: Antony, I, 2, 192.

slippery place

And he that stands upon a
   slippery place
Makes nice of no vile hold to
   stay him up.
   JOHN: Pandulph, III, 4, 137.

slop, loose, baggy or full breeches; codpiece.
> LLL: Berowne, IV, 3, 58.
> ADO: Pedro, III, 2, 36.
> 2H4: Falstaff, I, 2, 34.

slough, skin; usually a reference to a snake that sheds its old skin.
> TwN: Malvolio, II, 5, 161.
> HEN5: King, IV, 1, 23.
> 2H6: Queen, III, 1, 229.

slubber, smudge, soil, tarnish, sully.
> OTH: Duke, I, 3, 227.
> MERV: Salerio, II, 8, 39.

Sly, Christopher, drunken tinker; "keeper of bears," made to believe he is the lord of the manor. [Possibly a well-known character of Wincot, near Stratford-on-Avon.]
> SHREW: Induction.

sly-slow hours, time passing so slowly it is not noticed.
> RICH2: Richard, I, 3, 150.

smatter, chatter, jabber, prattle.
> R&J: Capulet, III, 5, 172.

smiles
> Seldom he smiles, and smiles in such a sort
> As if he mocked himself and scorned his spirit
> That could be moved to smile at anything.
> JC: Caesar, I, 2, 204—refers to Cassius.

Smith, the Weaver, follower of Cade.
> 2H6: IV, 2.

Smithfield, cattle and livestock market of London; butchers' quarter.
> 2H4: Page, I, 2, 59.
> 2H6: Scales, IV, 5, 10.

smock, female undergarment, nightgown.
> LLL: Berowne, V, 2, 479.
> WINT: Servant, IV, 4, 211.
> ADO: Leonato, II, 3, 138.

smoke, fumigate; Elizabethan rooms were perfumed with the smoke of burning juniper; smell out, detect.

> ADO: Borachio, I, 3, 61.
> ALL'SW: Lord, III, 6, 111.

smoke, beat, thrash, make the dust fly in.
> JOHN: Bastard, II, 1, 139—smoke your skin-coat, tan your hide (lion's skin that Richard wore).

smooth path
> The path is smooth that leadeth on to danger.
> VENUS: 788.

smooth water. See BROOK.

Smulkin. See FIENDS.
> LEAR: Edgar, III, 4, 146.

snaffle, bridle bit without a curb, for use on a horse that is easy to handle.
> A&C: Antony, II, 2, 63.

snail. See LOVE.

Snare, one of two sergeants, sheriff's officers, who are no match for Falstaff. See FANG.
> 2H4: II, 1.

snatch, quip, repartee, wisecrack.
> MEAS: Provost, IV, 2, 6.

sneak-cup, low, sneaking thief; petty rascal; one who doesn't drink his share.
> 1H4: Falstaff, III, 3, 99.

sneap, rebuke, snub; bite, nip, pinch with cold.
> 2H4: Falstaff, II, 1, 133.
> WINT: Polixenes, I, 2, 13.
> LUCRECE: 333.

sneck up, go hang, be hanged.
> TwN: Toby, II, 3, 101.

snipe, insignificant, senseless fool.
> OTH: Iago, I, 3, 391.

snort, snore.
> OTH: Iago, I, 1, 90.

Snout, Tom, Athenian tinker, cast as Pyramus' father, but plays the Wall at the performance of the Interlude.
> MND: I, 2.

snow. See LAWN.

snuff, anger and resentment, huff; quarrel.
> 1H4: Hotspur, I, 3, 41.

MND: Demetrius, V, 1, 254—
pun (see below).
LEAR: Kent, III, 1, 26.

snuff, burnt-out or smoking wick
of a candle; created unpleasant
odor.
CYM: Iachimo, I, 6, 87.
HAM: King, IV, 7, 116. See
FLAME OF LOVE.

Snug, slow-witted Athenian joiner;
plays the part of the Lion in the
Interlude because all he has to
do is roar.
MND: I, 2.

sociable, compassionate, sympathetic.
TEMP: Prospero, V, 1, 63.

sodden, boiled.
HEN5: Constable, III, 5, 18.

so-hough (so-ho), hunter's cry
when following the hare.
2GENT: Launce, II, 1, 189.

soil, explanation.
SONNET: LXIX, 14.

soil. See ADDITION.

soiled, well-fed on green fodder.
LEAR: Lear, IV, 6, 124.

sola. See SOWLA.

soldier
You may relish him more in the
soldier than in the scholar.
OTH: Cassio, II, 1, 166. See
RELISH.

sole (sowl), pull by the ears; seize
roughly; drag.
COR: 3Servingman, IV, 5, 12.

solemnity, festival, celebration.
MND: Theseus, IV, 1, 137.

solicited, incite, move to action.
HAM: Hamlet, V, 2, 369.
MACB: Macbeth, I, 3, 130.

solidare, gold coin; Roman coin
solidus worth approximately a
pound, in England applied to the
shilling (now shilling-mark).
TIMON: Lucullus, III, 1, 46.

Solinus, Duke of Ephesus, condemns Aegeon of Syracuse to
death for landing in Ephesus
when their cities are on unfriendly terms; allows him the

day to raise 1,000-mark ransom.
COFE: I, 1.

Solon, Athenian lawgiver (c640-
559 BC); credited with saying
"Call no man happy till he is
dead."
TITUS: Marcus, I, 1, 177.

Somerset, Dukes of. See BEAU-
FORT.

Somerville, Sir John, informs
Warwick that Clarence and his
forces are on their way.
3H6: V, 1.

Sonnets, written 1592-98; registered 1600, published 1599; 1609;
there have been volumes written
to explain the mystery of the
Dark Lady and of W.H., and
many interpretations of meaning, chronology etc. See Introductory Reading List.

Son of Clarence. See WARWICK,
Earl of, and CLARENCE, Duke of.

sons. See WOMBS.

sonties, saints.
MERV: Gobbo, II, 2, 47—*Be
God's sonties,* oath.

sooth, truth.
TEMP: Trinculo, II, 2, 151.
MND: Helena, II, 2, 129.
MACB: Sergeant, I, 2, 36.

sooth (soothe), flattery, cajolery,
appeasement; to humor, indulge.
RICH2: Richard, III, 3, 136.
1H4: Hotspur, IV, 1, 7.
PER: Helicanus, I, 2, 44.

Soothsayer, tells Caesar to "beware the Ides of March." (JC);
tells Charmian and Iras that they
will outlive Cleopatra (A&C),
and warns Antony that Caesar is
destined to be the final victor;
foretells (CYM) the success of
the Romans for Lucius.
JC: I, 2; A&C: I, 2; CYM: IV,
2.

sop, cake floated in wine, usually
muscatel served at a bridal party.
SHREW: Gremio, III, 2, 178.

Sophy, the Shah of Persia.
TWN: Fabian, II, 5, 198.
MERV: Morocco, II, 1, 25.

sore, a buck in its fourth year.
LLL: Holofernes, II, 2, 59.
T&C: Pandarus, III, 1, 130.

sorel, sorrel, a buck in its third year; young buck.
LLL: Holofernes, II, 2, 61.

sorrow
. . . Our size of sorrow,
Proportioned to our cause, must be as great
As that which makes it.
A&C: Cleopatra, IV, 15, 4.

Bad is the trade that must play fool to sorrow,
Angering itself and others.
LEAR: Edgar, IV, 1, 39.

Sorrow would be a rarity most beloved,
If all could so become it.
LEAR: Gentleman, IV, 3, 25—refers to Cordelia.

To show an unfelt sorrow is an office
Which the false man does easy.
MACB: Malcolm, II, 3, 142.

Sorrow breaks seasons and reposing hours,
Makes the night morning and the noontide night.
RICH3: Brakenbury, I, 4, 76.

Sorrow concealed, like an oven stopped,
Doth burn the heart to cinders where it is.
TITUS: Marcus, II, 4, 36.

sorrow's eye
For sorrow's eye, glazed with blinding tears,
Divides one thing entire to many objects . . .
RICH2: Bushy, II, 2, 16.

sort, rank; conform, fit; proper; suitable.
ADO: Messenger, I, 1, 7.
HAM: Bernardo, I, 1, 109.
MND: Theseus, V, 1, 55.

soul
O limed soul, that, struggling to be free,
Art more engaged!
HAM: King, III, 3, 68.

souls. See BLOOD.

sour. See TASTE.

souse, swoop down upon.
JOHN: Bastard, V, 2, 150.

Southwell, John, priest who helps to conjure up a spirit for the Duchess of Gloucester; captured and hung.
2H6: I, 4.

south-west, wind that was believed to carry sickness or infection.
TEMP: Caliban, I, 2, 323.

sovereign, omnipotent, all-embracing power, overwhelming.
TEMP: Prospero, V, 1, 143.
A&C: Caesar, V, 1, 41.

sowla (sola), halloo, hello; hunting call in response to off-stage shout.
LLL: Costard, IV, 1, 151.
MERV: Launcelot, V, 1, 39.

sowter, literally a cobbler, contemptuous word meaning poor or clumsy bungler.
TWN: Fabian, II, 5, 135.

space
Let Rome in Tiber melt and the wide arch
Of the ranged empire fall! Here is my space.
A&C: Antony, I, 1, 33.

span, possibly the distance between the thumb and the little finger of an outstretched hand; about 9 inches; limited distance.
OTH: Iago, II, 3, 74—*life's but a span.*

span-counter, game played with marbles, coins, disks or counters in which the player tosses a counter to hit or come within the span (see above) of his opponent's toss.
2H6: Cade, IV, 2, 166.

spare, dodge, avoid, circumvent.
MND: Titania, II, 1, 142.

sparrow
There is a special providence in the fall of a sparrow. If it be now, 'tis not to come; if it be not to come, it will be now; if it be not now, yet it will come. The readiness is all.
HAM: Hamlet, V, 2, 230.

Spartan dog, renowned for tenacity, fierceness, speed and keen scent; relentless.

OTH: Lodovico, V, 2, 361.
MND: Theseus, IV, 1, 122.

spavin, disease causing swelling in the joints (in horses).

SHREW: Biondello, II, 2, 54.
HEN8: Lord Sandys, I, 3, 12.

speak

Speak low if you speak love.
ADO: Pedro, II, 1, 103.

Speak what we feel, not what we ought to say.
LEAR: Edgar, V, 3, 324.

speak of me

Speak of me as I am. Nothing extenuate,
Nor set down aught in malice.
Then must you speak
Of one that loved not wisely, but too well;
Of one not easily jealous, but, being wrought,
Perplexed in the extreme; of one whose hand,
(Like the base Indian) threw a pearl away
Richer than all his tribe . . .
OTH: Othello, V, 2, 342.

speak parrot, talk irrationally, babble nonsense.
OTH: Cassio, II, 3, 281.

speak unbonneted, talk as an equal; probably because those of lesser rank or class had to stand with their hat off when talking with a superior.
OTH: Othello, I, 2, 23.

specialty, particular, precise terms; special contract or guarantee.
LLL: Boyet, II, 1, 165.
SHREW: Petruchio, II, 1, 127.

speculation, informer, scout, spy.
LEAR: Kent, III, 1, 24.

speech

Speak the speech, I pray you, as I pronounced it to you, trippingly on the tongue.
HAM: Hamlet, III, 2, 1—opening lines of speech giving Shakespeare's ideas on the art of the actor and the method used by his company.

A knavish speech sleeps in a foolish ear.
HAM: Hamlet, IV, 2, 25.

If for I want that glib and oily art
To speak and purpose not, since what I will intend,
I'll do't before I speak—
LEAR: Cordelia, I, 1, 227.

His speech is like a tangled chain; nothing impaired, but all disordered.
MND: Theseus, V, 1, 124.

. . . Rude am I in my speech,
And little blessed with the soft phrase of peace;
For since these arms of mine had seven years' pith
Till now some nine moons wasted, they have used
Their dearest action in the tented field . . .
OTH: Othello, I, 3, 81.

Speed, Valentine's servant; goes with his master to Milan; warns him that Proteus is also in love with Silvia.
2GENT: I, 1.

spell backward, misconstrue, turn inside out, say the reverse of.
ADO: Hero, III, 1, 61.

spendthrift sigh, wasteful, improvident; it was believed that by sighing you drained blood from the heart.
HAM: King, IV, 7, 123.

sperr, shut, bar.
T&C: Prologue, 19.

sphere, orbit of the planets; according to the Ptolemaic concept, a planet or heavenly body moved in transparent revolving shells or spheres.
HAM: Ghost, I, 5, 17.
MND: Oberon, II, 1, 153.
WINT: Hermione, I, 2, 48.

sphery, starry or starlike.
MND: Helena, II, 2, 99.

Sphinx, a she-monster of mythology, born in the country of the Arimi; the Theban sphinx is said to have destroyed the passerby who couldn't answer a riddle she proposed (eventually solved by Oedipus); the Egyptian Sphinx has the figure of a lion and the upper part of the body and head of a woman; the Greek Sphinx has a winged body of a lion, the breast and head of a woman.

LLL: Berowne, IV, 3, 342.

spicery, refers to the nest of spices which the phoenix made into both a funeral pyre and the birthplace of a new bird.

RICH3: Richard, IV, 4, 424. See PHOENIX.

spider

Why strewest sugar on that bottled spider
Whose deadly web ensnareth thee about?

RICH3: Margaret, I, 3, 242.

spies, slang expression for eyes.

TEMP: Trinculo, V, 1, 259.

spinsters

The spinsters and the knitters in the sun,
And the free maids that weave their thread with bones,
Do use to chant it.

TWN: Duke, II, 4, 45. See BONES.

spirit

Be thou a spirit of health or goblin damned,
Bring with thee airs from heaven or blasts from hell . . .

HAM: Hamlet, I, 4, 40.

Spirit. See ASMATH.

spital, hospital.

HEN5: Pistol, II, 1, 78.
TIMON: Timon, IV, 3, 39—spital-house, hospital for venereal diseases.

splay, castrate.

MEAS: Pompey, II, 1, 243.

spleen, impulsiveness, impetuosity; excessive display of temper or anger; caprice, waywardness.

LLL: Boyet, V, 2, 117.
COR: Coriolanus, IV, 5, 96.
AYL: Rosalind, IV, 1, 217.

spleen, organ of the body believed to produce fits of laughter.

TWN: Maria, III, 2, 72.
SHREW: Lord, Induction, 1, 137.

splenitive, quick-tempered, irascible.

HAM: Hamlet, V, 1, 284.

splinter, wrap or bind in splints; mend.

OTH: Iago, II, 3, 330.

spoon, refers to proverb "He that would eat with the Devil needs a long spoon"—in order to get something for himself and keep away from the Devil's claws.

TEMP: Stephano, II, 2, 103.

sport

That sport best pleases that doth least know how:
Where zeal strives to content, and the contents
Dies in the zeal of that which it presents.
Their form confounded makes most form in mirth
When great things labouring perish in their birth.

LLL: Princess, V, 2, 516.

spot, embroidery pattern or stitch.

COR: Valeria, I, 3, 56.

spot, stain, deceive, disgrace, dishonor.

MND: Lysander, I, 1, 110.
TIMON: 2Senator, V, 4, 34—guilty.
RICH2: Mowbray, I, 1, 175—pun on spots of leopard.

Out, damned spot!

MACB: Lady Macbeth, V, 1, 39.

spots of heaven. See FAULTS.

sprag (sprack), alert, lively.

MWW: Evans, IV, 1, 84.

sprat, worthless thing or creature; small fish caught in shoals and sold for very little.

ALL'SW: 1Lord, III, 6, 113.

spray, offshoot, bastard.

HEN5: Dauphin, III, 5, 5.

spring, reference to several springs in England which have a heavy lime content.

HAM: King, IV, 7, 20.

spring
Spring comes to you at the farthest
In the very end of harvest.
TEMP: Ceres, IV, 1, 114.

springe, snare for birds.
HAM: Polonius, I, 3, 115.

spur, post, ride quickly.
RICH2: Duchess of York, V, 2, 112.

spurn, kick.
A&C: Eros, III, 5, 17.
HAM: Gentleman, IV, 5, 6.

spurs, main roots of a tree.
TEMP: Prospero, V, 1, 47.
CYM: Guiderius, IV, 2, 58.

squadron, troop of 25 men under the command of a corporal.
OTH: Iago, I, 1, 22.

square, quarrel, taken from boxing expression "to square off" or to assume a fighting stance.
MND: Puck, II, 1, 30.
A&C: Pompey, II, 1, 45.
ADO: Beatrice, I, 1, 82.

square, squadron in formation.
A&C: Antony, III, 11, 40.

square, piece of embroidered material that covered the bosom; bodice, facing of dress.
WINT: Servant, IV, 4, 212.

squash, unripe, young peapod; youngster.
MND: Bottom, III, 1, 191.
WINT: Leontes, I, 2, 160.

squire (squier), foot rule; carpenter's square; obsolete form of square.
LLL: Berowne, V, 2, 474.
WINT: Servant, IV, 4, 348.
1H4: Falstaff, II, 2, 13.

squirrel, small lapdog.
2GENT: Launce, IV, 4, 59.

staff, literally, the shaft of a spear or lance; spear.
JOHN: English Herald, II, 1, 318.
COFE: Dromio E., III, 1, 51—
set in my staff, make myself at home.

Stafford, Lord (of Southwick),

Yorkist, ordered by Edward IV to raise an army.
3H6: announced I, 1.

Stafford, Sir Humphrey and brother, William, attempt to stop Cade and his followers at Blackheath; killed.
2H6: IV, 2. See BUCKINGHAM.

stage
I hold the world but as the world, Gratiano—
A stage, where every man must play a part,
And mine a sad one.
MERV: Antonio, I, 1, 77.

stage. See WORLD'S A STAGE.

staggers, giddiness, dizziness; disease of cattle and horses.
CYM: Posthumus, V, 5, 233.

stain, overshadow, eclipse, surpass.
A&C: Antony, III, 4, 27.

Staines, village on the Thames on the road to Southampton.
HEN5: Hostess, II, 3, 2.

stale, lure, decoy, bait; laughingstock, dupe, butt.
TEMP: Prospero, IV, 1, 187.
COFE: Adriana, II, 1, 101.
3H6: Warwick, III, 3, 260.

stale, harlot, prostitute; urine (usually horses').
ADO: Borachio, II, 2, 26.
SHREW: Katherina, I, 1, 58.
MWW: Host, II, 3, 31.

stalking-horse, real or artificial horse used by hunter for cover while tracking game, to enable him to inch closer to his prey.
AYL: Duke Senior, V, 4, 111.

stall, dwell; install.
A&C: Caesar, V, 1, 39.

stamp, minting, coinage; make impression or mark.
1H4: Hotspur, IV, 1, 4.

stamped the leasing, authenticated a lie or falsehood.
COR: Menenius, V, 2, 22.

standard, standard-bearer, junior officer or ensign; support.
TEMP: Stephano, III, 2, 19.

stand upon points, pay attention

to punctuation marks, proper phrasing.

MND: Theseus, V, 1, 118.

staniel, inferior hawk; kestrel.

TwN: Toby, II, 5, 124.

Stanley, Sir John, brother of Thomas; escorts the Duchess of Gloucester into exile on the Isle of Man.

2H6: II, 4.

Stanley, Sir William, brother of Thomas; helps Edward IV to escape from Middleham Castle. [Supported Richmond at Bosworth.]

3H6: IV, 5.

Stanley, Thomas, Lord, Lancastrian; Richard doesn't trust him, though he professes loyalty, because his wife is Margaret Beaufort, mother of Richmond (Henry VII); remains neutral. [c1435-1504, created 1st Earl of Derby by Henry VII.]

RICH3: I, 3.

Star Chamber, high court of justice sitting in Westminster.

MWW: Shallow, I, 1, 2.

star-crossed lovers

A pair of star-crossed lovers take their life . . .

R&J: Chorus, I, Prologue, 6.

stars

When my good stars that were my former guides

Have empty left their orbs and shot their fires

Into th' abysm of hell.

A&C: Antony, III, 13, 145.

. . . It is the stars,

The stars above us, govern our conditions . . .

LEAR: Kent, IV, 3, 34.

starting hole, place of refuge for small animals; refuge, cover-up.

1H4: Prince, II, 4, 290.

Starveling, Robin, Athenian tailor; cast as Thisby's mother; plays Moonshine in the Interlude.

MND: I, 2.

state, bearing, attitude, demeanor, poise; rank.

LLL: Berowne, IV, 3, 185.

state. See INTEGRITY, LOVE.

state of man

. . . Therefore doth heaven divide

The state of man in divers functions,

Setting endeavour in continual motion.

HEN5: Exeter, I, 2, 183.

This is the state of man: to-day he puts forth

The tender leaves of hopes; tomorrow blossoms,

And bears his blushing honours thick upon him;

The third day comes a frost, a killing frost,

And when he thinks, good easy man, full surely

His greatness is a-ripening, nips his root,

And then he falls, as I do.

HEN8: Wolsey, III, 2, 352.

station, posture or attitude when standing.

HAM: Hamlet, III, 4, 58.

statist, statesman, politician.

HAM: Hamlet, V, 2, 33.

CYM: Posthumus, II, 4, 16.

statute, bond or note acknowledging a debt; legal term.

HAM: Hamlet, V, 1, 113.

statute cap, flat, plain woolen cap worn on Sundays and holidays by ordinary citizens and apprentices by act of parliament (1571).

LLL: Rosaline, V, 2, 281.

stave, lance.

2H4: Mowbray, IV, 1, 120.

stead, benefit, assist, support.

OTH: Iago, I, 3, 345.

MEAS: Lucio, I, 4, 17.

TEMP: Prospero, I, 2, 165.

stem, prow of a ship.

COR: Cominius, II, 2, 111.

Stephano, drunken butler shipwrecked on Prospero's island; worshiped by Caliban as a god; plot to kill Prospero and take over the island fails.

TEMP: II, 2.

Stephano, Portia's servant; tells

Lorenzo that she has returned to Belmont.
MERV: V, 1.

sterling, silver, legal currency having full value; metaphorical for legal.
HAM: Polonius, I, 3, 107.
RICH2: Richard, IV, 1, 264.

stew, brothel, house of prostitution.
2H4: Falstaff, I, 2, 60.
CYM: Imogen, I, 6, 152.
RICH2: Percy, V, 3, 16.

Steward. See RINALDO.

stickler-like, like the umpire in a duel who separates the fighters in a friendly battle.
T&C: Achilles, V, 8, 18.

sting, passionate desire, instinctive impulse.
OTH: Iago, I, 3, 335.

stinkard, term of derision applied to the occupants of the "cheapest seats in the house," the gallery or standing room in the yard. See GROUNDLING.

stithy, smithy; to forge.
HAM: Hamlet, III, 2, 89.
T&C: Hector, IV, 5, 255.

stoccado (stoccata), thrust in fencing.
MWW: Shallow, II, 1, 234.

stock, stoccado; blockhead, senseless block, post.
MWW: Host, II, 3, 26.
SHREW: Tranio, I, 1, 31—pun on stoic.

stockfish, dried and salted cod or hake which was beaten before cooking.
TEMP: Stephano, III, 2, 99. See POOR-JOHN.
1H4: Falstaff, II, 4, 272.
MEAS: Lucio, III, 2, 116.

stomach, adventuresomeness, courage to attempt; appetite; inclination, propensity toward.
HAM: Horatio, I, 1, 100.
1H4: Lady, II, 3, 44.
TEMP: Alonso, II, 1, 107.

stomach, anger, resentment, proud temper, quarrel.

A&C: Lepidus, II, 2, 9.
1H6: Mayor, I, 3, 90.

stomach
'Tis not a year or two shows us a man.
They are all but stomachs and we all but food;
They eat us hungerly, and when they are full,
They belch us.
OTH:Emilia, III, 4, 103.

stomacher, ornamental fabric or covering of some kind used over the breast (or stomach) in women's dresses.
WINT: Autolycus, IV, 3, 226.
CYM: Imogen, III, 4, 86.

stone (thunder-stone), thunderbolt, lightning.
OTH: Othello, V, 2, 234.

stone. See DEAD.

stone-bow, crossbow used to shoot stones; used for fowl or small game.
TwN: Toby, II, 5, 51.

stooping, bowing, reverential.
RICH2: Bolingbroke, III, 3, 48.

stop, mark of punctuation (period) and sudden or sharp check on a horse's rein to bring him up short.
MND: Lysander, V, 1, 120.

storms. SEE BLAZE OF RIOT.

story
. . . My story being done,
She gave me for my pains a world of sighs.
She swore in faith, 'twas strange, 'twas passing strange;
'Twas pitiful, 'twas wondrous pitiful.
OTH: Othello, I, 3, 158.

story. See WOUNDED NAME.

stoup (stope), large pot or mug, usually measuring two quarts; tankard.
HAM: Clown, V, 1, 68.
OTH: Iago, II, 3, 29.
TwN: Toby, II, 3, 14.

stout, haughty, arrogant, proud.
TwN: Malvolio, II, 5, 186.

stover, winter fodder or grass for cattle.
    TEMP: Iris, IV, 1, 63.

Strachey, William (fl. 1588-1620). English colonist, secretary of Virginia (c1610-12); wrecked, with Sir T. Gates, on the Bermudas (1609); account of experience published (1625), contradicting JOURDAN'S story; two works on the Virginia Colony, published by the Hakluyt Society (1849). See THE TEMPEST.

straight-pight, erect, having a tall and dignified carriage.
    CYM: Iachimo, V, 5, 164.

strain, impulse, emotion.
    LLL: Berowne, V, 2, 769. See LOVE.

strange fellows
Nature hath framed strange fellows in her time . . .
    MERV: Solanio, I, 1, 51.

strangeness, alienation, unapproachability, aloofness.
    OTH: Desdemona, III, 3, 12.

strappado, form of Spanish torture which jerks a man's shoulders or elbows out of joint.
    1H4: Falstaff, II, 4, 262.

stratagem, violent deed.
    2H4: Northumberland, I, 1, 8.

Strato, Brutus' servant; holds the sword on which Brutus kills himself; taken into Octavius' service.
    JC: V, 5.

strawberry
The strawberry grows underneath the nettle,
And wholesome berries thrive and ripen best
Neighboured by fruit of baser quality.
    HEN5: Ely, I, 1, 60.

strength
. . . O, it is excellent
To have a giant's strength; but it is tyrannous
To use it like a giant.
    MEAS: Isabella, II, 2, 107.

strewments, flowers which are thrown or strewn on the grave.
    HAM: Doctor, V, 1, 256.

strike sail, lower sails to show obedience or adherence to; salute.
    2H4: Warwick, V, 2, 18.
    RICH2: Northumberland, II, 1, 266.
    3H6: Margaret, III, 3, 5.

strike the vessel, possibly tap or broach the cask; nautical term meaning empty a vessel of its load; "bottoms up."
    A&C: Antony, II, 7, 102.

stripes, floggings, lashes.
    TEMP: Prospero, I, 2, 345.

strond, strand, shore, region.
    1H4: King, I, 1, 3.
    2H4: Northumberland, I, 1, 62.
    MERV: Bassanio I, 1, 171.

strow, strew, scatter.
    RICH2: Gaunt, I, 2, 289—Tudor chambers were usually covered with rushes. See PRESENCE.

strucken deer. See WORLD.

strutting player
And, like a strutting player—whose conceit
Lies in his hamstring, and doth think it rich
To hear the wooden dialogue and sound
'Twixt his stretched footing and the scaffolage—
    T&C: Ulysses, I, 3, 153. See SCAFFOLAGE.

stubborn, harsh, rough, rude; tight rein or firm control.
    JC: Cassius, I, 2, 35.

stuck, fencing term, thrust; same as STOCCADO.
    HAM: King, IV, 7, 162.

study
Berowne: What is the end of study? Let me know.
Ferdinand: Why, that to know which else we should not know.
Berowne: Things hid and barred (you mean) from common sense.

Ferdinand: Ay, that is study's godlike recompense.
LLL: I, 1, 55.

stuprum, Latin, rape.
TITUS: Titus, IV, 1, 78.

sty, enclose or confine in an area, pen up.
TEMP: Caliban, I, 2, 342.

Stygian, refers to river Styx which flows through Hell (Hades).
T&C: Troilus, III, 2, 10.

submission, admission of guilt or fault; confession.
1H4: Prince, III, 2, 28.

submission
Be not as extreme in submission as in offence.
MWW: Page, IV, 4, 11.

suborn, incite, instigate, hire a person to do something wrong or evil; bear false witness.
CofE: Antipholus E., IV, 4, 85.
MACB: Macduff, II, 4, 24.
2H4: Westmoreland, IV, 1, 90.

subscription, allegiance, submission.
LEAR: Lear, III, 2, 18.

subtleties, magical illusions, qualities of enchantment.
TEMP: Prospero, V, 1, 124.

suburbs, where the most notorious brothels of the London area were located.
MEAS: Pompey, I, 2, 98.

success, result or consequence of action whether good or bad; outcome.
OTH: Iago, III, 3, 222.
A&C: Enobarbus, III, 5, 6.

sue his livery, bring suit for the establishment of property rights.
RICH2: York, II, 1, 203.
1H4: Hotspur, IV, 3, 62.

suffer
Who alone suffers suffers most i' the mind,
Leaving free things and happy shows behind;
But then the mind much sufferance doth o'erskip

When grief hath mates, and bearing fellowship.
LEAR: Edgar, III, 6, 110.

sufferance, grave damage, disaster.
OTH: 3Gentleman, II, 1, 23.

Suffolk, Duke of, High Steward at the coronation of Anne Bullen; present at the christening of Princess Elizabeth. [Charles Brandon (c1484-1545), created Viscount Lisle (1513), Duke of Suffolk (1514); accompanied Henry to Field of Cloth of Gold (1520); commanded armies invading France (1523, 1544); favorite of King; married his sister, Mary Tudor, widow of Louis XII of France.]
HEN8: I, 1.

Suffolk, Earl of, Lancastrian; captures Margaret at Angiers; arranges her marriage to Henry VI; becomes her lover (1H6); plots disgrace of Duchess of Gloucester and murder of her husband (2H6); banished by King; captured and beheaded. [William de la Pole (1396-1450), 4th Earl (1415), created 1st Duke (1448); with Henry V in France; no proof exists that he was Margaret's lover; enemies arranged his exile and death.]
1H6: II, 4; 2H6: I, 1.

suggest, incite, induce, motivate, usually for evil; tempt.
RICH2: Bolingbroke, I, 1, 101.
SONNET: CXLIV, 2.
TEMP: Ferdinand, IV, 1, 26—*suggestion.*

suit
Suit the action to the word, the word to the action.
HAM: Hamlet, III, 2, 19.

suit of sables, equivocation or quibble on sable meaning black (from heraldry) and the fur, *mustela zibellina,* which adorned rich cloaks and gowns worn by the wealthy.
HAM: Hamlet, III, 2, 138.

sullied. See ADDITION.

sulphur, believed to be the source of lightning.

Cor: Volumnia, V, 3, 152.

summer's cloud

Can such things be,
And overcome us like a summer's cloud,
Without our special wonder?

Macb: Macbeth, III, 4, 110.

summer's day

Shall I compare thee to a summer's day?
Thou art more lovely and more temperate.

Sonnet: XVIII, 1.

sum my count, balance my records, even my score.

Sonnet: II, 11.

sumpter, pack animal, drudge.

Lear: Lear, II, 4, 219.

sun

When the sun shines let foolish gnats make sport,
But creep in crannies when he hides his beams.

CofE: Antipholus S., II, 2, 30.

sun breed maggots in a dead dog, generally accepted belief.

Ham: Hamlet, II, 2, 181.

sun of York, triple pun: Edward IV was the son of the Duke of York; leader or blazing sun of the York party in power; the sun was his emblem or badge.

Rich3: Richard, I, 1, 2.

superflux

Expose thyself to feel what wretches feel,
That thou mayst shake the superflux to them
And show the heavens more just.

Lear: Lear, III, 4, 34.

superscript, address (on a letter).

LLL: Holofernes, II, 2, 135.

supervise, read over, peruse, scan.

Ham: Hamlet, V, 2, 23.

supervisor, onlooker, spectator, eyewitness.

Oth: Iago, III, 3, 395.

supple knee, easily bent, implying flattery.

Rich2: Richard, I, 4, 33.

supply, reinforcements.

1H4: Hotspur, IV, 3, 3.
2H4: Hastings, I, 3, 12.

sur-addition, surname; additional title of honor.

Cym: 1Gentleman, I, 1, 33.

surcease, completion, cessation, as in death; to cease.

Macb: Macbeth, I, 7, 4.

surety, man who guarantees the presence of a prisoner at the time of his trial, bail bondsman.

Rich2: Bolingbroke, IV, 1, 159.

surfeit

As surfeit is the father of much fast,
So every scope by the immoderate use
Turns to restraint.

Meas: Claudio, I, 2, 130.

. . . they are as sick that surfeit with too much as they that starve with nothing. It is no mean happiness, therefore, to be seated in the mean. Superfluity comes sooner by white hairs, but competency lives longer.

MerV: Nerissa, I, 2, 6.

For, as a surfeit of the sweetest things
The deepest loathing to the stomach brings.

MND: Lysander, II, 2, 137.

surgeon

With the help of a surgeon he might yet recover, and yet prove an ass.

MND: Theseus, V, 1, 316—refers to Pyramus.

Surrey, Duke of, defends Aumerle against the accusations of Fitzwater; joins the plot against Bolingbroke; captured, killed and his head set on London Bridge. [Thomas Holand (or Holland), 3rd Earl of Kent (1374-1400).]

Rich2: I, 3.

Surrey, Earl of, appears but does not speak. [Thomas Fitzalan, Earl of Arundel and Surrey (1381-1415).]

2H4: III. 1.

Surrey, Earl of, fights for Richard at Bosworth. [Thomas Howard (1443-1524) succeeded his father, 2nd Duke of Norfolk.]
RICH3: V, 3.

Surrey, Earl of, opposes Wolsey and avenges Buckingham's death. [Thomas Howard (1473-1554), succeeded his father (above) as the 3rd Duke of Norfolk (1524); married Buckingham's daughter.]
HEN8: III, 2.

surveyor, overseer of an estate.
HEN8: Cardinal, I, 1, 115—here applies to Charles Knyvet, Buckingham's cousin (see below).

Surveyor, servant of the Duke of Buckingham whom he falsely accuses of threatening the King.
HEN8: I, 2.

suspicion
See what a ready tongue suspicion hath!
He that but fears the thing he would not know
Hath by instinct knowledge from others' eyes
That what he feared is chanced.
2H4: Northumberland, I, 1, 84.

Suspicion always haunts the guilty mind;
The thief doth fear each bush an officer.
3H6: Richard, V, 6, 11.

sustaining, buoyant in the water.
TEMP: Ariel, I, 2, 218.

sutler, seller or provider of provisions to the army.
HEN5: Pistol, II, 1, 116.

Sutton Co'fil', Sutton Coldfield, 20 miles beyond Coventry in Warwickshire, near Birmingham.
1H4: Falstaff, IV, 2, 3.

suum cuique, Latin, to each his own or his due.
TITUS: Marcus, I, 1, 280.

swabber, sailor or petty officer in charge of keeping the decks or ship clean.

TEMP: Stephano, II, 2, 48.
TWN: Viola, I, 5, 217.

swag-bellied, heavy, loose-bellied; with hanging paunch.
OTH: Iago, II, 3, 80.

swaggering upspring reels, whirl in a riotous or wild dance.
HAM: Hamlet, I, 4, 9.

swan
. . . 'Tis strange that death should sing!
I am the cygnet to this pale faint swan
Who chants a doleful hymn to his own death
And from the organ-pipe of frailty sings
His soul and body to their lasting rest.
JOHN: Henry, V, 7, 20.

swanlike end, it was believed that swans sing only once, just before they die.
MERV: Portia, III, 2, 44.
OTH: Emilia, V, 2, 247.
PHOENIX: 15.

swan's downfeather. See TIDE.

Swan Theatre, fourth of the London theaters in Paris Garden; built c1595-97 by Francis Langley at the western end of the BANKSIDE.

swasher, swaggerer, swashbuckler, bully, braggart.
HEN5: Boy, III, 2, 30.

swath, swaddling clothes.
TIMON: Timon, IV, 3, 252.

swear
Do not swear at all;
Or if thou wilt, swear by thy gracious self,
Which is the god of my idolatry,
And I'll believe thee.
R&J: Juliet, II, 2, 112.

sweat, a sweating sickness, form of the plague; treatment for venereal disease.
MEAS: Bawd (Overdone), I, 2, 84.
T&C: Pandarus, V, 10, 56.

sweet. See TASTE.

sweet breath
. . . eat no onions nor garlic, for we are to utter sweet breath.
MND: Bottom, IV, 2, 42.

swift as a shadow
Swift as a shadow, short as any dream,
Brief as the lightning in the collied night,
That, in a spleen, unfolds both heaven and earth . . .
MND: Lysander, I, 1, 144. See COLLIED, SPLEEN.

swing-buckler, one who strikes hard at a buckler; swashbuckler; dashing or flamboyant swordsman.
2H4: Shallow, III, 2, 24. See BUCKLER.

swinge, beat, thrash; impetus, sway.
2H4: Doll, V, 4, 21.
JOHN: Bastard, II, 1, 288.
2GENT: Speed, II, 1, 88.

Switzers, Swiss bodyguard, usually hired by foreign princes; the popes and kings of France used Switzers.
HAM: King, IV, 5, 98.

swoopstake, without discernment or discrimination; a gambling or gaming term meaning "sweep the board" or take all the stakes.
HAM: King, IV, 5, 142.

sword-and-buckler, weapons used by persons of low rank; rapier and dagger were used by gentlemen.
1H4: Hotspur, I, 3, 230. See BUCKLER, RAPIER AND DAGGER.

sword Philippan, the sword Antony wore at the battle of Phil-

ippi when he defeated Brutus and Cassius.
A&C: Cleopatra, II, 5, 23.

sworn brother, an allusion to the old practice of taking the oath of brotherhood between persons not related to one another; usually taken by knights embarking on a perilous adventure or going into battle.
RICH2: Richard, V, 1, 20.

'swounds, God's wounds, zounds.
HAM: Hamlet, II, 2, 603.

Sycorax, witch, mother of Caliban; found only in Shakespeare; believed to be derived from the Greek word for hawk from which Circe is also taken.
TEMP: Prospero, I, 2, 258.

Sylla, Lucius Cornelius Sulla (138-78 BC); waged civil war against Marius; dictator; known for mass slaughter of his opponents.
2H6: Lieutenant, IV, 1, 84.

sympathy, equality in rank or position; agreement, harmony.
RICH2: Fitzwater, IV, 1, 33.
LLL: Moth, III, 1, 52—*sympathized.*

synod, council, legislative assembly.
HAM: Player, II, 2, 516.
A&C: Scarus, III, 10, 4.

Syracusa, ancient Syracusae (Siracusa), seaport, southeast Sicily, separated from the mainland by a narrow canal, in the Ionian Sea; founded by Corinthian settlers (734 BC); fell to Rome (212) after resisting attack for three years.
CofE: Duke, I, 1, 3.

table, writing table or notebook.
HAM: Hamlet, I, 5, 98.
CYM: Imogen, III, 2, 39.
WINT: Autolycus, IV, 4, 610.

table, board or flat surface on which a picture was painted.
JOHN: Dauphin, II, 1, 502.

table-book. See above (notebook).

tables, backgammon; game believed to have been invented in the 10th century as a rival to chess.
LLL: Berowne, V, 2, 326.

tabor, small drum usually worn at the side and played with the right hand, while the pipe was played with the left.
TEMP: S.D., III, 2.
LLL: Dull, V, 1, 161.
TwN: S.D., III, 1.

tabourin (taborin), drum, usually small military drum.
A&C: Antony, IV, 8, 37.

tackle, rigging (of a ship).
JOHN: King, V, 7, 52.

tag, rabble.
COR: Cominius, III, 1, 248.

Tailor, makes Katherina's wedding gown.
SHREW: IV, 3.

taint, disparage, discredit; tarnish or slur a reputation.
OTH: Iago, II, 1, 274.

take, charm, bewitch, enchant.
HAM: Marcellus, I, 1, 163.

taken out, copied, make a duplicate of.
OTH: Emilia, III, 3, 296.

Take, O, take those lips away
Take, O, take those lips away
That so sweetly were forsworn;
And those eyes, the break of day,
Lights that do mislead the morn;
But my kisses bring again, bring again;
Seals of love, but sealed in vain, sealed in vain.
MEAS: Boy, IV, 1, 1—song.

take the wall, show superiority by taking the side of the walk next to the wall, which was the safest and least muddy; to yield this spot was to show courtesy.
R&J: Sampson, I, 1, 15.

Talbot, Lord, leader of the English armies; when Sir John Fastolfe deserts him, he is captured by Joan of Arc at Patay; escapes from the Countess of Auvergne's trap and retakes Rouen; exposes Fastolfe's cowardice; finally surrounded and killed, with his son John, near Bordeaux. [John Talbot (c1388-1453), 6th Baron, created 1st Earl of Shrewsbury (1442), Earl of Waterford; killed with his son, Lord Lisle, at Castillon, France.]
1H6: I, 4.

Talbot, John. See above.

tale
In winter's tedious nights sit by the fire
With good old folks, and let them tell thee tales
Of woeful ages long ago betid;
And ere thou bid good-night, to quite their griefs
Tell thou the lamentable tale of me,

And send the hearers weeping to their beds.
RICH2: Richard, V, 1, 40.

talk of graves
Let's talk of graves, of worms, and epitaphs;
Make dust our paper, and with rainy eyes
Write sorrow on the bosom of the earth.
RICH2: Richard, III, 2, 145.

talent, riches, treasures, sum of money; historically, various coins, i.e. Hebrew gold talent worth $29,380 (U.S.), silver, worth c$2,000 (U.S.).
TIMON: Messenger, I, 1, 95.

talkative wives
Leontes: . . . thou art worthy to be hanged
That wilt not stay her tongue.
Antigonus: Hang all the husbands
That cannot do that feat, you'll leave yourself
Hardly one subject.
WINT: II, 3, 108.

talkers
Talkers are no good doers.
RICH3: Villain, I, 3, 351.

tall, splendid, fine, gallant; valiant.
A&C: Caesar, II, 6, 7.
WINT: Clown, V, 2, 177.
2H4: Bardolph, III, 2, 67.

tamed piece, cask which has been left open too long and the wine has gone flat; woman who has lost her charm or been taken by another.
T&C: Diomedes, IV, 1, 62.

Taming of the Shrew, The, written c1594 and performed the same year; published 1623; sources, an anonymous play, A Shrew (published, 1594, but written earlier) and ARIOSTO's I Suppositi (translated by George GASCOIGNE as The Supposes, printed 1573).
PLOT: In the Induction, a nobleman comes upon the drunken tinker, Christopher Sly, and has him carried to a beautifully furnished room in his home where he is dressed in fine clothes. Sly is persuaded that he is, in reality, the owner of the house and a page, disguised as his wife, convinces him that he has merely been out of his mind for fifteen years. A company of itinerant players perform the comedy, The Taming of the Shrew, for his amusement.

Katherina, the shrew, is the eldest daughter of Baptista Minola, wealthy merchant of Padua, who has insisted she marry before he will consent to the marriage of his younger, gentler daughter Bianca. Lucentio, young student from Pisa, in love with Bianca, changes clothes with his servant, Tranio, and gets a job as her tutor. Gremio and Hortensio, suitors for Bianca's hand, join forces in the task of finding a husband for Katherina. Hortensio meets his friend Petruchio, a rogue from Verona, who, willing to help his friend, but particularly interested in her dowry, agrees to marry her.

He begins the "taming" process by humiliating her. He arrives, in disreputable clothes on a sway-backed horse, late for the marriage ceremony. Refusing to stay for the wedding feast, Petruchio carries Kate off to his country house where he won't allow her to eat or sleep. Tamed, she is taken back to Padua by Petruchio. Lucentio, meanwhile, elopes with Bianca. Hortensio consoles himself with a wealthy widow and at a triple-wedding feast, Petruchio demonstrates that his wife is the most obedient of the three brides.

Tamora, evil, vengeful Queen of the Goths; later Roman Empress responsible for many deaths; finally killed by Titus. [There was a Tamara, or Thamar,

Queen of Georgia (1184-1212).]
TITUS: I, 1.

tang, sharp note or ring.
TEMP: Stephano, II, 2, 52.

tanling, sunburned or tanned child.
CYM: Belarius, IV, 4, 29.

"Tantaene animis coelestibus irae?" Latin, Is there such resentment in the minds of the gods? from Vergil's *Aeneid* (I, 11).
2H6: Gloucester, II, 1, 24.

tanta est erga te mentis integritas, regina serenissima, Latin, so great is my integrity of mind toward you, most serene highness (or Queen).
HEN8: Wolsey, III, 1, 41.

Tantalus, son of Zeus and the nymph Pluto; father of Niobe; when he divulged the secrets entrusted to him by his father, he was punished in Hades by being placed in the middle of a lake, while suffering a raging thirst and an overpowering hunger; when he attempted to drink, the waters drew back; when he attempted to eat the fruit of the overhanging trees, they swung out of reach; a large rock was suspended over his head which threatened to crush him (HOMER, *Odyssey,* XI, 582).
VENUS: 599.
LUCRECE: 858.

targe (target), light shield, buckler.
LLL: Costard, V, 2, 556.
A&C: Pompey, II, 6, 39.
COR: Aufidius, IV, 5, 125.

Tarpeian. See ROCK TARPEIAN.

Tarquin (Tarquinius Superbus), in Roman legend, the 7th and last king of Rome (534-510 BC); although a tyrant, he was a great leader; ravisher of Lucrece in Shakespeare's poem, *The Rape of Lucrece.* [Actually it was his son Sextus who raped Lucretia,

the wife of his cousin Tarquinius Collatinus.]
MACB: Macbeth, II, 1, 55.
COR: Volumnia, II, 1, 166.

tarre, provoke, incite, usually associated with a dog fight.
HAM: Rosencrantz, II, 2, 371.
JOHN: Arthur, IV, 1, 117.
T&C: Nestor, I, 3, 392.

Tartar, in classical mythology, the prison or worst section of the infernal regions where the evil are punished; Tartarus or hell.
TWN: Toby, II, 5, 225.
HEN5: King, II, 2, 123.
COFE: Dromio S., IV, 2, 32—*Tartar limbo,* limbo is where the pure but unbaptized souls stay; Tartars were barbarous people of the East, so it is suggested that *Tartar limbo* means the savage hell of the East.

task, to test, challenge by demanding the performance of a task; challenge.
TEMP: Ariel, I, 2, 192.
LLL: Princess, V, 2, 126.
1H4: Hotspur, V, 2, 51.

task
Unarm me, Eros. The long day's task is done,
And we must sleep.
A&C: Antony, IV, 14, 35.

tassel-gentle. See TERCEL.
R&J: Juliet, II, 2, 160.

taste
Things sweet to taste prove in digestion sour.
RICH2: Gaunt, I, 3, 236.

taste of it, it was the usual habit of servants to taste the food before serving it to the royal family to see if it had been poisoned.
RICH2: Richard, V, 5, 99.

Tate, Nahum (1652-1715). Irish-English poet and playwright; wrote the libretto for Purcell's *Dido and Aeneas;* adapted *Richard III* (1680) and *Coriolanus* (1681-82) produced at DRURY LANE; his *The History of King Lear* (1681), performed at

Duke's Theatre, eliminates the Fool and ends happily.

Taurus, great mountain range of southern Turkey.
MND: Demetrius, III, 2, 141.

Taurus, zodiacal sign of the bull; according to contemporary astrologers, governing the neck and throat.
TwN: Toby, I, 3, 146—reference to legs and thighs incorrect.

Taurus, Statilius, commander of Caesar's army at Actium.
A&C: III, 8.

tawdry-lace, colored silk necktie or neckerchief; named for St. Audrey or Etheldreda, founder of Ely Cathedral; fair held on the saint's day (Oct. 17) at Ely noted for the wearing of colorful costumes and jewelry.
WINT: Mopsa, IV, 4, 253.

tawny, yellowish-brown, dark-skinned or dark-complected.
MND: Lysander, III, 2, 263.

tax, chastise, reprimand, scold; accuse.
HAM: Polonius, III, 3, 29.
ADO: Leonato, I, 1, 46.
ALL'sW: Countess, I, 1, 77.

tear a cat, rant and rage and generally overact or "ham it up."
MND: Bottom, I, 2, 32.

tears
Scorn and derision never come in tears.
Look, when I vow, I weep; and vows so born,
In their nativity all truth appears.
MND: Lysander, III, 2, 123.

Tears show their love, but want their remedies.
RICH2: Richard, III, 3, 203.

His tears run down his beard like winter's drops
From eaves of reeds.
TEMP: Ariel, V, 1, 16. See EAVES OF REEDS.

tears. See PITY.

Tearsheet, Doll, mistress of Fal-

staff; quarrels with Pistol; dragged off to prison as a prostitute; death mentioned in *Henry V.*
2H4: II, 4. See MISTRESS QUICKLY.

teeming date, time when a woman is able to bear children.
RICH2: Duchess of York, V, 2, 91.

teen, grief, misery, sorrow.
LLL: Berowne, IV, 3, 164.
RICH3: Duchess of York, IV, 1, 97.
TEMP: Miranda, I, 2, 64.

teeth and forehead, face to face with; the very face of.
HAM: King, III, 3, 63.

teeth on edge
I had rather hear a brazen canstick turned,
Or a dry wheel grate on the axletree,
And that would set my teeth nothing on edge,
Nothing so much as mincing poetry.
'Tis like the forced gait of a shuffling nag.
1H4: Hotspur, III, 1, 129—*canstick,* candlestick.

Telamon, refers to Ajax, son of Telamon, called Telamoniades, who went mad when the armor and famous shield of Achilles was awarded to Ulysses.
A&C: Cleopatra, IV, 13, 2. See AJAX.

tell, to count, enumerate, tally.
HAM: Horatio, I, 2, 237.
LEAR: Fool, II, 4, 55.
WINT: Servant, IV, 4, 185.

tell the clock, say that this is the right or appropriate moment or time.
TEMP: Antonio, II, 1, 289.

Tellus' orbed ground, spherical earth, globe; Tellus or more often Terra, equivalent of Greek goddess Gaea, was mother earth and the goddess of marriage and fertility; one of the deities of the lower world.

Ham: Player King, III, 2, 166.
Per: Marina, IV, 1, 14.

temper, hardness of steel, strong quality.
Rich2: Aumerle, IV, 1, 29.

temper, concoct, mix, compound.
Ham: Laertes, V, 2, 339.
Ado: Borachio, II, 2, 21.

temperance, climate, temperature.
Temp: Adrian, II, 1, 43.

temperance, chastity, continence; popular Puritan girl's name.
Temp: Antonio, II, 1, 44.

temperance
. . . Being once chafed, he cannot
Be reined again to temperance; then he speaks
What's in his heart, and that is there which looks
With us to break his neck.
Cor: Brutus, III, 3, 27.

tempest
If after every tempest come such calms,
May the winds blow till they have wakened death . . .
Oth: Othello, II, 1, 187.

Tempest, The, believed to be Shakespeare's last completed play, written 1611; probably first performed that year on Hallowmas Night by the King's Players in Whitehall; published 1623; sources, possibly *Die Schöne Sidea*, a contemporary German comedy by Jakob Ayrer (d. c1605); a story by Sylvester Jourdan of the wreck of Sir George Somer's Virginia Company ship, the *Sea Venture* (July, 1609) on the island of Bermuda, in *A Discovery of the Barmudas or Ile of Divels* (published, 1610); *Newes from Virginia* (1610) a ballad by Robert Rich; the official account, *A True Declaration of the estate of the Colonie in Virginia;* Giovanni Florio's translation of Montaigne's *Essays* (published, 1603), for the ideal commonwealth described by Gonzalo which follows closely "Of the Cannibals" (No. 30). It has been suggested that Shakespeare in *The Tempest* is himself speaking in the person of Prospero and saying a farewell to his art.

Plot: Prospero, a scholar skilled in the art of magic, lives with his lovely young daughter, Miranda, on an enchanted tropical island. A tempest, apparently caused by Prospero and the spirit, Ariel, beaches a ship carrying Antonio, Prospero's brother, who had usurped his power in Milan, and the rest of his party on the island. Prospero tells Miranda of the past and the loss of his dukedom. He casts spells on the various survivors of the wreck. Ferdinand, son of Alonso, King of Naples, thinking himself the sole survivor, finds his way to Prospero's cave. He falls in love with Miranda.

Meanwhile, Alonso and some of his party are lulled to sleep by Ariel's invisible music. Sebastian and Antonio plot to steal Alonso's crown by killing him and the faithful Gonzalo. Ariel frustrates their plans. In another part of the island, Trinculo and Stephano meet Caliban. They plan to kill Prospero and take over control of the island.

Prospero has Ariel present a lovely masque, acted by the spirits, to celebrate the engagement of Ferdinand and Miranda. Prospero and Ariel harass Caliban and his co-conspirators, while the King and his party are led to Prospero's cave. Prospero forgives Antonio, after revealing himself to them, but demands restoration of his dukedom. Alonso gives his blessing to the marriage of Ferdinand and Miranda and they all prepare to sail for Italy for the wedding ceremony. "*The Tempest* is one of the most original and perfect of Shakespeare's productions, and he has shown in it all the variety of his powers."—(Hazlitt.)

tempests. See EVER-FIXED MARK.

temple, the body; handsome or magnificent person.
HAM: Laertes, I, 3, 12.
TEMP: Miranda, I, 2, 457.

Temple Garden. See INNS O' COURT.

temptation
. . . Most dangerous
Is that temptation that doth goad us on
To sin in loving virtue.
MEAS: Angelo, II, 2, 181.

Those pretty wrongs that liberty commits
When I am sometime absent from thy heart,
Thy beauty and thy years full well befits,
For still temptation follows where thou art.
SONNET: XLI, 1.

And sometimes we are devils to ourselves,
When we will tempt the frailty of our powers,
Presuming on their changeful potency.
T&C: Troilus, IV, 4, 97.

tenable, kept firmly, held fast.
HAM: Hamlet, I, 2, 248.

Tenantius, King Cymbeline's father.
CYM: 1Gentleman, I, 1, 31.

tench, spotted fresh-water fish.
1H4: 2Carrier, II, 1, 17.

ten commandments, ten fingers.
2H6: Duchess, I, 3, 145.

tender, value highly, hold dearly.
HAM: King, IV, 3, 43.

tender, offer, give or hand over.
MND: Demetrius, III, 2, 87.
ADO: Pedro, II, 3, 186.
TEMP: Prospero, IV, 1, 5.

tender-hefted, gentle, womanly; stirred by tender feelings.
LEAR: Lear, IV, 4, 174.

Tenedos, modern Bozcaada, island in the Aegean Sea off the coast of Turkey; in Trojan legend, station of the Greek fleet; used by Xerxes in the Persian War.
T&C: Prologue, 11.

tenement, property leased to its occupant.
RICH2: Gaunt, II, 1, 60.

ten groats
Groom: Hail, royal prince!
Richard: Thanks, noble peer.
The cheapest of us is ten groats too dear.
RICH2: Richard, V, 5, 68—an allusion to the monetary differences between the coins, a royal, noble and groat, and since Richard thinks he is worth nothing, he is "ten groats too dear." See ROYAL, NOBLE, GROAT.

tenner, tenour, legal term meaning the substance or purport of a document; purpose of a speech.
2NK: Schoolmaster, III, 5, 123.
LUCRECE: 1310.

tennis, net game very popular with all classes in France and with the nobility or courtiers of England.
HAM: Polonius, II, 1, 59.

When we have matched our rackets to these balls,
We will in France (by God's grace) play a set
Shall strike his father's crown into the hazard.
HEN5: King, I, 2, 261. See HAZARD.

tent, small roll of linen or other absorbent material used to clean or probe a wound prior to binding; figuratively, a probe.
LEAR: Lear, I, 4, 322.
COR: Cominius, I, 9, 31.
CYM: Imogen, III, 4, 118.

tenure, legal term, property title or holding. See also TENNER.
HAM: Hamlet, V, 1, 108.

tercel, male peregrine falcon.
T&C: Pandarus, III, 2, 55.

Terence (Publius Terentius Afer) (c185-c159 BC); Roman poet; born in Carthage, brought to Rome as a slave; freed by his master, Terentius Lucanus; wrote six comedies, then left for Greece; influenced by Menander and Apollodorus; popular in England in the first half of the 16th century.

Tereus, Thracian king who raped his sister-in-law, Philomela, and had her tongue torn out so she couldn't tell about it; from OVID'S *Metamorphoses.*
    CYM: Iachimo, II, 2, 45.
    LUCRECE: 1134.

Termagant, portrayed as a raving tyrant, this imagined god of the Saracens or Moslems was used in mystery plays or medieval romance and drama.
    HAM: Hamlet, III, 2, 16.
    1H4: Falstaff, V, 4, 114.

terrene, earthly, terrestrial.
    A&C: Antony, III, 13, 154—*terrene moon,* earthly moon goddess; Cleopatra is the personification of the goddess Isis.

test. See TRY.

tester, sixpence; from French *teston.*
    2H4: Falstaff, III, 2, 296.
    MWW: Pistol, I, 3, 96.

testern, tip; give a sixpence.
    2GENT: Speed, I, 1, 153.

testril, little tester, also worth sixpence.
    TWN: Andrew, II, 3, 34.

tether, rope used to secure an animal to a peg.
    HAM: Polonius, I, 3, 125.

tetter, rash, skin eruption, scabby.
    T&C: Thersites, V, 1, 27.
    HAM: Ghost, I, 5, 71.
    COR: Coriolanus, III, 1, 79.

Tewkesbury, market town in Gloucestershire not far from Stratford-on-Avon; famous for its mustard and mustard-balls.
    2H4: Falstaff, II, 4, 262.

Thaisa, beautiful daughter of King Simonides, wife of Peri-

cles, mother of Marina; apparently dies in childbirth but is brought to life by Cerimon; becomes a priestess of Diana; reunited with her husband and daughter.
    PER: II, 2.

Thaliard, lord of Antioch; King Antiochus orders him to kill Pericles.
    PER: I, 1.

thane, chief of a Scottish clan; similar in rank to the son of an English earl.
    MACB: Malcolm, I, 2, 45.

thankless child
    How sharper than a serpent's tooth it is
    To have a thankless child!
    LEAR: Lear, I, 4, 310.

tharborough. See FARBOROUGH.

Thasos (Thasus), island in the Aegean Sea off the coast of Thrace near Philippi.
    JC: Brutus, V, 3, 104.

theater
    As in a theatre the eyes of men,
    After a well-graced actor leaves the stage,
    Are idly bent on him that enters next,
    Thinking his prattle to be tedious,
    Even so, or with much more contempt, men's eyes
    Did scowl on gentle Richard.
    RICH2: York, V, 2, 23—theaters were not built in London until about 1575 and certainly not in 1399, the time of the play.

Theatre, The, first London theater; built by James Burbage, father of Richard (1576), on the site of the priory of Saint John the Baptist, Shoreditch; a wooden structure; closed July, 1597; taken down December, 1598 by Cuthbert Burbage, his son, and its timber used to build the GLOBE.

"The Beggar and the King," refers to popular ballad, "King

Cophetua and the Beggar Girl."
RICH2: Bolingbroke, V, 3, 80.

theft
. . . There's warrant in that theft
Which steals itself when there's
no mercy left.
MACB: Malcolm, II, 3, 151.

Thersites, bawdy, cynical jester in
the Greek army that besieged
Troy; makes Ajax the butt of
his sarcasm; some critics think
he was meant to be Marston at-
tacking JONSON in the *Poeto-
machia.*
T&C: II, 1.
CYM: Guiderius, IV, 2, 252.

Theseus, Duke of Athens who
plans to marry Hippolyta
(MND); sanctions Hermia's
marriage to Lysander; married
to Hippolyta (2NK); conquers
Creon; imprisons Palamon and
Arcite; arranges for them to
fight for Emilia, his sister-in-
law; finally agrees to her marriage to Palamon.
MND: I, 1; 2NK: I, 1.

Theseus, hero of Attica and Athens; son of Aegeus, king of
Athens, and Aethra, daughter of
Pittheus, king of Troezen in
Argolis; performed many exploits similar to those of Heracles (Hercules); with the help
of Ariadne, escaped from the
labyrinth where he had slain
the Minotaur.
2GENT: Julia, IV, 4, 173.

the star, i.e., the North Star.
SONNET: CXVI, 7.

Thetis, mother of Achilles; one
of the Nereides; a sea nymph.
A&C: Antony, III, 7, 61.
T&C: Nestor, I, 3, 39.
PER: Gower, IV, 4, 39.

thews, bodily strength; muscles
and sinews.
HAM: Laertes, I, 3, 12.
1H4: Falstaff, III, 2, 277.
JC: Cassius, I, 3, 81.

thief
. . . A man may see how this
world goes with no eyes. Look

with thine ears. See how yond
Justice rails upon yond simple
thief. Hark, in thine ear. Change
places and, handy-dandy, which
is the Justice, which is the thief?
LEAR: Lear, IV, 6, 153—*handy-
dandy,* a children's version of
the "shell game."

thievery in nature
The sun 's a thief, and with his
great attraction
Robs the vast sea. The moon 's
an arrant thief,
And her pale fire she snatches
from the sun.
The sea 's a thief, whose liquid
surge resolves
The moon into salt tears. The
earth 's a thief;
That feeds and breeds by a
composture stolen
From the general excrement.
Each thing 's a thief.
The laws, your curb and whip,
in their rough power
Have unchecked theft.
TIMON: Timon, IV, 3, 439.

things
Things that are past are done
with me.
A&C: Antony, I, 2, 101.
Things bad begun make strong
themselves by ill.
MACB: Macbeth, III, 2, 55.
Things past redress are now
with me past care.
RICH2: York, II, 3, 171.

things. See PHILOSOPHY.

thin habits, flimsy appearances,
insubstantial evidence.
OTH: Duke, I, 3, 108.

thinking
. . . there is nothing either good
or bad but thinking makes it so.
HAM: Hamlet, II, 2, 256.

third, an important part or good
share.
TEMP: Prospero, IV, 1, 3.

thirdborough, town constable.
SHREW: Hostess, Induction, 1,
12.

thirty years, length of Clown's
service established Hamlet's age

and created a problem for the critics who had assumed Hamlet to be younger; the three-and-twenty, referring to Yorick's skull, several speeches later, confirmed the estimate, as Hamlet knew Yorick as a young boy.
HAM: Clown, V, 1, 177.

Thisby. See FLUTE.

this England
This blessed plot, this earth, this realm, this England . . .
RICH2: Gaunt, II, 1, 50. See SCEPTERED ISLE.

"This was a man!"
His life was gentle, and the elements
So mixed in him that Nature might stand up
And say to all the world, "This was a man!"
JC: Antony, V, 5, 73—refers to Brutus.

Thomas, Friar. See FRIAR THOMAS.

thorough, through.
MND: Fairy, II, 1, 3.

thou art a scholar, Latin religious formulas were necessary to protect oneself against evil spirits and as Horatio was a scholar of the University of Wittenberg, it was suggested he approach the apparition, thought to be the ghost of Hamlet's father, and address it in Latin.
HAM: Marcellus, I, 1, 42.

thought, sorrow, grief, melancholy.
A&C: Enobarbus, IV, 6, 35.
HAM: Hamlet, III, 1, 85.
AYL: Rosalind, IV, 1, 217.

thoughts
With thoughts beyond the reaches of our souls?
HAM: Hamlet, I, 4, 56.
Our thoughts are ours, their ends none of our own.
HAM: Player King, III, 2, 223.

Faster than springtime showers comes thought on thought.
2H6: York, III, 1, 337.

My brain I'll prove the female to my soul,
My soul the father; and these two beget
A generation of still-breeding thoughts;
And these same thoughts people this little world,
In humours like the people of this world,
For no thought is contented.
RICH2: Richard, V, 5, 6.

My thoughts are minutes; and with sighs they jar
Their watches on unto mine eyes, the outward watch,
Whereto my finger, like a dial's point,
Is pointing still, in cleansing them from tears.
RICH2: Richard, V, 5, 51.

thoughts. See WORDS.

thousand ships
. . . she is a pearl
Whose price hath launched above a thousand ships,
And turned crowned kings to merchants.
T&C: Troilus, II, 2, 81—refers to Helen; cf. MARLOWE's *Dr. Faustus,* "Was this the face that launched a thousand ships?"

thousand thousand, form of farewell.
TEMP: Ferdinand, III, 1, 91.

Thracian singer, Orpheus.
MND: Theseus, V, 1, 49—the Bacchantes (worshipers of Bacchus) tore Orpheus to pieces (OVID's *Metamorphoses,* XI, 1).

thrasonical, boastful; typical of Thraso, the bragging soldier in TERENCE's *Eunuchus.*
LLL: Holofernes, V, 1, 14.
AYL: Rosalind, V, 2, 34.

three-farthings, silver coin of Elizabeth's reign; very thin; bore profile portrait of the queen with a rose behind her ear.
JOHN: Bastard, I, 1, 143.

three-hooped pot, bands or hoops were placed at equal intervals on wooden pots.
2H6: Cade, IV, 2, 72.

three-man songmen, singers of catches and rounds.
WINT: Clown, IV, 3, 45.

three-nooked, three-cornered; refers to Europe, Asia and Africa, or perhaps to the world's having been divided between the Triumvirs.
A&C: Caesar, IV, 6, 6.

three-pile, thick (three-piled), heavy, costly velvet.
WINT: Autolycus, IV, 3, 14.

threne, anglicized form of *threnos* (Greek), funeral song or dirge.
PHOENIX: 49.

thrift, benefit, advantage, gain.
HAM: Hamlet, III, 2, 67.

throe, anguish, agony, extreme pain.
A&C: Canidius, III, 7, 81—*throes forth,* gives birth with difficulty.
TEMP: Sebastian, II, 1, 231—*throes thee much,* is very painful or agonizing to issue forth.

throne
In God's name I'll ascend the regal throne.
RICH2: Bolingbroke, IV, 1, 113.

throne. See HEAD.

throstle, song thrush, mavis, missel thrush.
MERV: Portia, I, 2, 65.
MND: Bottom, III, 1, 130.

throughly, thoroughly, completely.
HAM: Laertes, IV, 5, 136.
TEMP: Sebastian, III, 3, 14.

throw at all, dicing term, risk all by challenging all.
RICH2: Aumerle, IV, 1, 57.

thrum, end of warp thread in weaving; fringe.
MND: Pyramus, V, 1, 291.
MWW: Mrs. Page, IV, 2, 80—*thrummed,* ornamented with fringe or tufts.

thrust forth a vanity, show extravagance.
RICH2: York, II, 1, 24.

thunder, natural habitat of witches and demons.
MACB: 1Witch, I, 1, 2.

thunder
. . . And thou, all-shaking thunder,
Strike flat the thick rotundity o' th' world,
Crack Nature's moulds, all germens spill at once,
That make ingrateful man!
LEAR: Lear, III, 2, 6.

Thurio, unsuccessful suitor of Silvia; renounces her when Valentine threatens him.
2GENT: II, 4.

Thyreus, nobleman, ambassador; Caesar sends him to win Cleopatra from Antony; she is reacting favorably to his flattery and promises when Antony finds him and has him whipped.
A&C: III, 12.

thyself
It is thyself, mine own self's better part,
Mine eye's clear eye, my dear heart's dearer heart,
My food, my fortune, and my sweet hope's aim,
My sole earth's heaven, and my heaven's claim.
COFE: Antipholus S., III, 2, 61.

Tib, strumpet, "moll," low-class woman.
PER: Marina, IV, 6, 176.
ALL'SW: Clown, II, 2, 24.

tickle, unsteady, insecure, precarious.
MEAS: Lucio, I, 2, 177.
2H6: York, I, 1, 216.

tickle-brain, strong liquor or drink, or the dispenser of same.
1H4: Falstaff, II, 4, 439.

tickle o' th' sere, discharge, explode or "go off" at a touch; sere is the trigger or part of the gun-lock which keeps the hammer at full or half cock and is

easy to set off with a mere touch
or "tickle" if it is filed smooth.
HAM: Hamlet, II, 2, 338.

tide
Her tongue will not obey her
heart, nor can
Her heart inform her tongue—
the swan's downfeather
That stands upon the swell at
full of tide,
And neither way inclines.
A&C: Antony, III, 2, 47.

tide. See FORTUNE.

tide of times
O, pardon me, thou bleeding
piece of earth,
That I am meek and gentle with
these butchers!
Thou art the ruins of the noblest
man
That ever lived in the tide of
times.
JC: Antony, III, 1, 254.

tides
. . . you may as well
Forbid the sea for to obey the
moon
As or by oath remove or counsel
shake
The fabric of his folly.
WINT: Camillo, I, 2, 426.

tight, competent, skillful, adroit.
A&C: Antony, IV, 4, 15.

tilly-vally (-fally), nonsense word;
fiddlesticks; possibly "hoity-
toity."
TwN: Toby, II, 3, 83.
2H4: Hostess, II, 4, 90.

tilt, thrust.
LLL: Browne, V, 2, 483.

tilth, cultivated, tilled land.
TEMP: Gonzalo, II, 1, 152.

Timandra, Alcibiades' mistress to
whom Timon gives gold.
TIMON: IV, 3.

Time, acts as Chorus to bridge
passage of 16 years between
Acts III and IV.
WINT: IV, 1.

time
There's a time for all things.
CofE: Antipholus S., II, 2, 66.

Time is a very bankrout and
owes more than he's worth to
season.
CofE: Dromio S., IV, 2, 58.
See BANKROUT, SEASON.

The time is out of joint. O
cursed spite
That ever I was born to set it
right.
HAM: Hamlet, I, 5, 189.

. . . the very age and body of the
time his form and pressure.
HAM: Hamlet, III, 2, 27.

We have seen the best of our
time.
LEAR: Gloucester, I, 2, 119.

Had I but died an hour before
this chance,
I had lived a blessed time; for
from this instant
There's nothing serious in mortality;
All is but toys; renown and
grace is dead;
The wine of life is drawn, and
the mere lees
Is left this vault to brag of.
MACB: Macbeth, II, 3, 96—*lees,*
dregs.

Let every man be master of his
time . . .
MACB: Macbeth, III, 1, 41.

. . . What I believe, I'll wail;
What know, believe; and what
I can redress,
As I shall find the time to friend,
I will.
MACB: Malcolm, IV, 3, 8.

Like as the waves make towards
the pebbled shore,
So do our minutes hasten to
their end . . .
SONNETS LX, 1—beginning of
sonnet on passing time.

For Time is like a fashionable
host,
That slightly shakes his parting
guest by th' hand,
And with his arms outstretched
as he would fly
Grasps in the comer.
T&C: Ulysses, III, 3, 165.

O Time, thou must untangle
    this, not I;
It is too hard a knot for me t'
    untie!
    TwN: Viola, II, 2, 41.

Time is the nurse and breeder of
    all good.
    2Gent: Proteus, III, 1, 243.

I that please some, try all: . . .
    Wint: Time, IV, 1, 1.

time. See SERPENT.

timeless, untimely, inopportune.
    Rich2: Bolingbroke, IV, 1, 5.

time must have a stop
But thoughts the slaves of life,
    and life time's fool,
And time, that takes survey of
    all the world,
Must have a stop.
    1H4: Hotspur, V, 4, 81.

times, quarter- and half-hour in-
dications on a clock.
    Rich2: Richard, V, 5, 58.

time's fool, ridiculed, deceived or
mocked by time.
    Sonnet: CXVI, 9. See LOVE.

Time's glory
Time's glory is to calm contend-
    ing kings,
To unmask falsehood and bring
    forth truth to light
    Lucrece: 939—beginning of
    section on time.

Timon of Athens, The Life of,
written 1605-1608; registered
and published 1623; sources,
Plutarch's *Lives*, Painter's
Palace of Pleasure, Lucian's
Timon, or the Misanthrope
(c1585).

    Plot: Timon, a wealthy noble-
man of Athens (whom Wilson
calls the "stillborn twin" of
Lear) is ruining himself by entertaining his friends and giving
them money and gifts. Apemantus, a professional misanthrope,
and Flavius, his faithful servant,
warn Timon that he is a fool and
that his friends are false. When
his wealthy creditors seek to collect their loans, Timon asks his
friends for help and is turned

down. Finally recognizing them
for what they are, he invites
them all to a banquet at which
he serves warm water in elaborately covered dishes and throws
it in their faces.

    Meanwhile, Alcibiades, the
general, banished for having
pleaded for a poor soldier, is
gathering an army to attack
Athens. Timon retires to a cave
near the seashore where he finds
buried treasure. He is found by
Alcibiades and his two mistresses
who are kind to him. When
Timon hears that Alcibiades,
who offers him gold, is marching
against Athens, he shares his
treasure with him. The general
can now pay his soldiers, who
have been deserting him. Apemantus and Flavius also find
Timon. The former he curses
and drives off, but he finally
recognizes Flavius as the only
honest man.

    When the Senate sends dele-
gates offering Timon absolute
power if he will return to fight
off Alcibiades, he refuses. The
general, allowed to take the city
when he agrees to spare the innocent and only punish his
enemies, is told of Timon's
death. "It is the only play . . .
in which spleen is the predomi-
nant feeling of the mind. It is as
much a satire as a play: and
contains some of the finest pieces
of invective possible to be conceived"—(Hazlitt).

Timon, honest, good-hearted lord
with little judgment and no apparent sense of values "brought
low by his own heart, undone by
goodness" until, mentally ill, he
dies.
    Timon: I, 1.
    LLL: Berowne, IV, 3, 170.

Timon's Epitaph
Here lies a wretched corse, of
    wretched soul bereft.
Seek not my name. A plague
    consume you wicked caitiffs
    left!

Here lie I, Timon, who alive all
   living men did hate.
Pass by, and curse thy fill; but
   pass, and stay not here thy
   gait.
TIMON: Alcibiades, V, 4, 70—
PLUTARCH said Timon wrote
the last two lines and the poet
Callimachus the first two.

tinct, color.
HAM: Queen, III, 4, 91.

tinder, inflammable material, usually scorched linen, kept in a
box; ignited by striking flint on
steel.
OTH: Brabantio, I, 1, 141.
MWW: Falstaff, I, 3, 27—refers to Bardolph's flaming red
nose.

tipstaves, bailiffs; officers who
take persons into custody; so-
called because they carry staves
tipped with metal.
HEN8: S.D., II, 1.

tire, headdress, usually elaborately decorated.
A&C: Cleopatra, II, 5, 22.
ADO: Margaret, III, 4, 13.
2GENT: Julia, IV, 4, 190.

tire, devour, eat ravenously.
CYM: Imogen, III, 4, 97.
3H6: King, I, 1, 269.
VENUS: 56.

tire-valiant, fantastic, elaborate
headdress.
MWW: Falstaff, III, 3, 60.

tiring house, dressing room; in
Elizabethan theater it was di-
rectly behind the stage.
MND: Quince, III, 1, 4.

tirrits, for terrors; agitation.
2H4: Hostess, II, 4, 219.

tisick, cough; disease of the lungs.
T&C: Pandarus, V, 3, 101.

Titan, Hyperion, the sun (in
HOMER); sun god (Helios).
1H4: Prince, II, 4, 133.
CYM: Pisanio, III, 4, 166.
T&C: Troilus, V, 10, 25.

Titania, Queen of the Fairies;
quarrels with Oberon over a
"little changeling boy"; using

magic, he makes her fall in love
with Bottom.
MND: II, 1.

tithe, tenth part, a tenth; usually
a church tax, tenth of income.
HAM: Hamlet, III, 4, 97.
1H4: Hostess, III, 3, 66.
TIMON: 2Senator, V, 4, 31—
tithed death, killing of every
tenth man.

tithe-pig, every tenth pig was
given to the local parson as tax.
R&J: Mercutio, I, 4, 79.

Titinius, friend of Brutus and
Cassius; sent to discover whether
certain troops are friendly to
them at Philippi; they are Brutus' forces, but Cassius, thinking they are the enemy, persuades Pindarus to kill him;
Titinius, finding Cassius' body,
stabs himself with his friend's
sword.
JC: IV, 3.

titles
Princes have but their titles for
   their glories,
An outward honour for an in-
   ward toil;
And for unfelt imaginations
They often feel a world of rest-
   less cares;
So that between their titles and
   low name
There's nothing differs but the
   outward fame.
RICH3: Brakenbury, I, 4, 78.

Titus, servant of one of Timon's
creditors; comes to collect 50
talents.
TIMON: III, 4. See TALENT.

***Titus Andronicus, The Tragedy
of,*** written and performed
c1592; registered and published
1594; sources, SENECA's *Thyestes,* for the cannibalism, and
Troades for the sacrifice in the
first act; OVID's *Metamorphoses*
for the tale of Philomela.
PLOT: Titus Andronicus brings
Queen Tamora and her three
sons to Rome following his victory over the Goths. The eldest
of these boys is sacrificed by the

Andronici to the spirit of one of their brothers who had been slain in battle. Although Titus is offered the crown, he gives it to Saturninus, elder son of the late Emperor, who promises to marry Lavinia, Titus' daughter. However, she is engaged to his brother Bassianus, and with the help of her brothers, she escapes with him.

Titus is infuriated and in the battle that follows Titus kills his youngest son, Mutius, who had helped the runaways. Saturninus, calling Titus a traitor, marries Tamora. She persuades him to forgive them all so that they may one day massacre them. Aaron, the lover of Tamora, upon hearing Demetrius and Chiron, her sons, quarreling over Lavinia, urges them to rape her and then, to maintain her silence, tear out her tongue and cut off her hands. They have also managed to kill Bassianus. Quintus and Martius are thrown into the pit where they have tossed Bassianus, making certain that they will be accused of his murder.

Titus pleads for his sons in vain and they are sentenced to death, while Lucius, the third son, is banished for trying to help them. Aaron tells Titus that if he will chop off one of his hands and send it to the Emperor, the sons will be spared. Instead, his hand comes back with his sons' heads.

Titus, mad with grief and vengeance, sends Lucius to the Goths to enlist their help against Rome. Meanwhile Tamora gives birth to Aaron's son. They substitute a white baby for the son and send their baby to the Goths to be brought up. Meanwhile Saturninus and Tamora learn that Lucius and the Goths are advancing toward Rome and ask for a parley at Titus' home. Titus cuts the throats of Ta-

mora's sons as Lavinia catches their blood in a basin, and they are later served to the Empress baked in a pie. Then Titus kills both Lavinia and Tamora, Saturninus kills Titus and Lucius kills the Emperor. The winner of this game of "musical" murders becomes Emperor and orders Aaron tortured to death.

Titus Andronicus, Roman general; major victim in the tale of horror above.
    TITUS: I, 1.

Titus Lartius, one of the Roman generals who fights against the Volscians; takes part in the capture of Corioli; retires to Antium.
    COR: I, 1.

to, for, in comparison with.
    TEMP: Adrian, II, 1, 75.

toaze (touse), tear, rent; worry.
    WINT: Autolycus, IV, 4, 760.

to be

To be, or not to be—that is the question.
Whether 'tis nobler in the mind to suffer
The slings and arrows of outrageous fortune,
Or to take arms against a sea of troubles,
And by opposing end them. To die, to sleep—
No more; and by a sleep to say we end
The heartache and the thousand natural shocks
That flesh is heir to. 'Tis a consummation
Devoutly to be wished. To die, to sleep—
To sleep, perchance to dream. Ay, there's the rub,
For in that sleep of death what dreams may come
When we have shuffled off this mortal coil,
Must give us pause. There's the respect
That makes calamity of so long life.

For who would bear the whips
and scorns of time,
Th' oppressor's wrong, the
proud man's contumely
The pangs of despised love, the
law's delay,
The insolence of office, and the
spurns
That patient merit of th' un-
worthy takes,
When he himself might his
quietus make
With a bare bodkin? Who would
fardels bear,
To grunt and sweat under a
weary life,
But that the dread of something
after death,
The undiscovered country from
whose bourn
No traveller returns, puzzles the
will,
And makes us rather bear those
ills we have
Than fly to others that we know
not of?
Thus conscience does make
cowards of us all,
And thus the native hue of
resolution
Is sicklied o'er with the pale
cast of thought,
And enterprises of great pitch
and moment
With this regard their currents
turn awry
And lose the name of action.
  HAM: Hamlet, III, 1, 56. See
  RUB, CONTUMELY, QUIETUS,
  BODKIN, FARTHEL (fardel),
  BOURN, PITCH.

tod, old weight of 28 pounds of
wool.
  WINT: Clown, IV, 3, 33.

to die
  . . . To die, to sleep—
No more; and by a sleep to say
we end
The heartache and the thousand
natural shocks
That flesh is heir to. 'Tis a con-
summation
Devoutly to be wished.
  HAM: Hamlet, III, 1, 60—part
  of TO BE soliloquy.

to do
If to do were as easy as to know
what were good to do, chapels
had been churches, and poor
men's cottages princes' palaces.
  MERV: Portia, I, 2, 13.

toged, wearing a toga; gowns of
peace worn by the Romans.
  OTH: Iago, I, 1, 25.

toil, pitfall, snare, trap.
  HAM: Hamlet, III, 2, 362.

tokened pestilence, plague, when
its characteristic symptoms are
present or red spots which mean
certain death.
  A&C: Scarus, III, 10, 9.

told, counted, possibly tolled.
  MND: Theseus, V, 1, 370. See
  IRON TONGUE.

tomboy, wanton, strumpet, harlot.
  CYM: Iachimo, I, 6, 122.

to-morrow and to-morrow. See
LIFE.

tongs, by striking a pair of tongs
with a key or piece of metal
"music" was made.
  MND: Bottom, IV, 1, 31—
  tongs and the bones. See BONES.

tongue
That man that hath a tongue, I
say is no man
If with his tongue he cannot win
a woman.
  2GENT: Valentine, III, 1, 104.

tongueless, silent, uninhabited.
  RICH2: Bolingbroke, I, 1, 105—
  tongueless caverns of the earth.

tongues
. . . the tongues of dying men
Enforce attention like deep harmony.
Where words are scarce, they
are seldom spent in vain,
For they breathe truth that
breathe words in pain.
  RICH2: Gaunt, II, 1, 5.

top, forelock; cut off the top.
  ADO: Antonio, I, 2, 15—take
  the present time by the top,
  seize the opportunity.

tortive, twisted aside, distorted.
  T&C: Agamemnon, I, 3, 9.

to shallow rivers, opening words of a garbled, fragmentary version of MARLOWE's *The Passionate Shepherd to his Love.*
   MWW: Evans, III, 1, 17.

to sleep
To sleep, perchance to dream.
   HAM: Hamlet, III, 1, 65—part of TO BE soliloquy.

toss, impale on a pike.
   1H4: Falstaff, IV, 2, 71.

Tottel, Richard (d. 1593). English printer; granted a patent (1552) for printing law books; printed very popular *Miscellany: Songes and Sonnettes* (June, 1557) containing the works of Sir Thomas Wyatt and Henry Howard, Earl of Surrey; probably edited by Nicholas Grimald; first regular Elizabethan collection of English miscellaneous verse; referred to in *The Merry Wives* and *Hamlet.*

touch, characteristic, trait; feeling, concern; exploit or feat; test.
   MND: Hermia, III, 2, 70.
   A&C: Antony, I, 2, 187.
   MEAS: Duke, I, 1, 36.

touch, touchstone, used by jewelers to test the quality of gold.
   TIMON: Timon, IV, 3, 390.
   RICH3: Richard, IV, 2, 8.
   COFE: Adriana, II, 1, 111.

Touchstone, witty fool of Duke Frederick's court; accompanies Celia and Rosalind to the forest of Arden; meets and marries Audrey; famous for his speech on "the seven degrees of affront" (V, 4); critical of human folly.
   AYL: I, 2. See DEGREES OF THE LIE.

touse. See TOAZE.
   MEAS: Escalus, V, 1, 313.

toward, in preparation, impending.
   HAM: Marcellus, I, 1, 77.
   A&C: Enobarbus, III, 6, 74.
   MND: Puck, III, 1, 81.

Tower, the Tower of London was a residence, containing royal living quarters, and not the place of danger and imprisonment it became later; believed (erroneously) to have been built by Julius Caesar.
   RICH3: Richard, III, 1, 65.
   1H6: Gloucester, I, 1, 167.

toy, unimportant item, trifle, whim, fancy.
   OTH: Emilia, III, 4, 156.
   WINT: Antigonus, III, 3, 39.
   JOHN: Bastard, I, 1, 232—rumors.

toy in the blood, mere impulsive fancy.
   HAM: Laertes, I, 3, 6.

trace, follow in the footsteps of, track; roam; strive after, aim at.
   MND: Puck, II, 1, 25.
   ADO: Hero, III, 1, 16.
   HAM: Hamlet, V, 2, 125.

trade-fallen, bankrupt, ruined, unemployed, idle.
   1H4: Falstaff, IV, 2, 33.

traders, merchant or trading ships.
   MND: Titania, II, 1, 127.

traduce, slander, calumny, disgrace.
   HAM: Hamlet, I, 4, 18.

traffic. See DECEIVE.

traitor
And from th' extremest upward of thy head
To the descent and dust beneath thy foot,
A most toad-spotted traitor.
   LEAR: Edgar, V, 3, 136.

traitors. See ACTIONS.

trammel, enmesh, entangle, confine in a net.
   MACB: Macbeth, I, 7, 3.

Tranio, Lucentio's servant; impersonates his master so that he will be free to disguise himself as a teacher and woo Bianca; manages to get Baptista's consent to marry Bianca; unmasked, he flees.
   SHREW: I, 1.

tranquil mind
Farewell the tranquil mind, farewell content!
Farewell the plumed troop, and the big wars
That make ambition virtue!
OTH: Othello, III, 3, 348.

transfigured, excited, stimulated.
MND: Hippolyta, V, 1, 24.

translate, transform, change.
MND: Helena, I, 1, 191.

transparent, obvious, able to be seen through; brilliant, bright.
MND: Lysander, II, 2, 104.

trash, hold in check; hunting term referring to the holding back of a hound to keep him from outrunning the rest of the pack; clip the top branches of tall trees.
OTH: Iago, II, 1, 312.
TEMP: Prospero, I, 2, 81.

travelers
... now am I in Arden, the more fool I! When I was at home, I was in a better place; but travellers must be content.
AYL: Touchstone, II, 4, 16.

travelling lamp, the sun.
MACB: Ross, II, 4, 7.

Travers, Northumberland's retainer; brings news of Hotspur's defeat at Shrewsbury.
2H4: I, 1.

traverse, "step on it"; from the military, forward march; dodge; in fencing, advance.
OTH: Iago, I, 3, 379.
2H4: Bardolph, III, 2, 291.
MWW: Host, II, 3, 25.

traverse, fold, cross.
TIMON: Alcibiades, V, 4, 7—refers to arms.
AYL: Celia, III, 4, 45—to break one's lance across an adversary's shield was considered a disgrace; devious.

tray-trip, dice game, winner threw threes.
TwN: Toby, II, 5, 207.

treason
For treason is but trusted like the fox,

Who, ne'er so tame, so cherished and locked up,
Will have a wild trick of his ancestors.
1H4: Worcester, V, 2, 9.
Treason and murther ever kept together,
As two yoke-devils sworn to either's purpose,
Working so grossly in a natural cause
That admiration did not whoop at them ...
HEN5: King, II, 2, 105.

treasure
Where all the treasure of thy lusty days ...
SONNET: II, 6.

trebles thee o'er, triples your position; makes you three times as great as you are.
TEMP: Antonio, II, 1, 221.

Trebonius, Caius, one of the conspirators; agrees with Brutus that Antony should not be killed with Caesar; gets him out of the way at the time of the assassination.
JC: II, 1.

trencher, wooden plate.
TEMP: Caliban, II, 2, 187.
COR: Coriolanus, IV, 5, 55.
ADO: Beatrice, I, 1, 51—*trencherman,* eater; servant.

tribunal, high platform or throne; place or seat of importance.
A&C: Caesar, III, 6, 3.

trick, natural custom or habit, characteristic action; deceit, knavery.
HAM: Laertes, IV, 7, 189.
HAM: Gentleman, IV, 5, 5.

tricked, heraldic term meaning decorated with colors that are arranged in special dots and lines; spotted.
HAM: Hamlet, II, 2, 479.

tricksy, resourceful, clever; ornate.
TEMP: Prospero, V, 1, 226.

trident, three-pronged forklike scepter symbolizing sea power.
COR: Menenius, III, 1, 256.

trim, fine, usually said ironically meaning clever or subtle; elegantly clothed or attired.

    MND: Helena, III, 2, 157.

    OTH: Iago, I, 1, 50.

Trinculo, jester; one of the travelers shipwrecked on Prospero's island; with Stephano, a drunken butler, he joins in the unsuccessful plot to murder Prospero and "take over."

    TEMP: II, 2.

triple Hecate, the goddess Diana was referred to (OVID's *Metamorphoses,* VII, 94) as three-formed; worshiped as Luna, the moon, in heaven; Diana on earth; Proserpina or Persephone (Hecate) in Hades.

    MND: Puck, V, 1, 391. See HECATE.

triple pillar, one of the triumvirate; the other two being Octavius Caesar and Lepidus.

    A&C: Philo, I, 1, 12—reference to Antony.

triplex, triple time in music.

    TwN: Clown, V, 1, 41.

tristful, unhappy, melancholy, sorrowful.

    HAM: Hamlet, III, 4, 50.

    1H4: Falstaff, II, 4, 434.

Triton, trumpeter of Neptune, the Roman sea god; demigod who calmed the waves by playing on a trumpet made from a conch shell; in Greek mythology, trumpeter son of Poseidon and Amphitrite, who lived in a golden palace at the bottom of the sea; sometimes mentioned in the plural (Tritons) and imagined as being half-men, half-fish riding on sea-serpents.

    COR: Coriolanus, III, 1, 88.

triumph, public spectacle, celebration or festival.

    1H4: Falstaff, III, 3, 47.

    RICH2: York, V, 2, 52.

    MND: Theseus, I, 1, 19.

Troilus and Cressida, The Tragedy of, written 1598-1602; registered 1603; published 1609; sources, several versions of HOMER's *Iliad* (Hall and Chapman); CHAUCER's *Troilus and Criseyde* based on BOCCACCIO's *Filostrato;* Caxton's *The Recuyell of the Historyes of Troye;* LYDGATE's *Sege of Troye;* some authorities believe the uncomplimentary description of Ajax (I, 1) is aimed at Ben JONSON.

PLOT: Troilus, youngest son of Priam, King of Troy, loves Cressida and has arranged with her uncle Pandarus for a meeting with her. Although she feigns indifference, she is attracted to him. Calchas, her father, persuades Agamemnon, the Greek commander, to exchange the Trojan prisoner Antenor for his daughter. At the Greek camp, the generals are trying to whip up some enthusiasm in their soldiers. A group of Trojans, headed by Aeneas, brings a challenge from Hector to fight any Greek in single combat. The challenge is really meant for Achilles, who has turned temperamental and won't fight, and they are forced to give the honor to Ajax.

At a feast following a draw fought between the two, Achilles insults Hector and agrees to meet him in combat the following day. Meanwhile in Troy, Priam and his sons consider the conditions of the Greek peace offer which involves returning Helen to her husband and the paying of an indemnity. They decide to keep Helen, whom Paris carried off, starting the whole siege. Cassandra warns of the consequences of such an action, but is ignored. Pandarus arranges the meeting between Troilus and Cressida and they declare their love for one another. However, when he returns, guided by Ulysses, he finds her in the arms of Diomedes, who has been sent to conduct her safely to the Greek camp, and he watches as she gives him a token he had given to her.

In the battle the following day, he attempts to kill Diomedes, but fails. When Hector slays Patroclus, Achilles' friend, the latter, finding the unarmed Hector resting, orders his Myrmidons to kill him, and further dishonor the Trojans by dragging his body, tied to his horse's tail, around the city. Pandarus, snubbed by Troilus, speaks the epilogue.

Troilus, "the Prince of Chivalry"; rather colorless youngest son of Priam, King of Troy; more in love than loving, he embodies the virtue of faithfulness and suffers heartbreak unjustly.
T&C: I, 1.

Trojan horse, large wooden horse left by the Greeks on the beach at Troy as a gift to the city; filled with soldiers, it was taken into the city enabling the Greeks to capture it; synonymous with deceit; origin of the expression "Beware Greeks bearing gifts."
PER: Pericles, I, 4, 93.

troll-my-dames, game similar to bagatelle; from French *troumadame;* object was to roll balls through arches or hoops on a board.
WINT: Autolycus, V, 3, 92.

troll the catch, take up or catch his part in the round and sing the song. See CATCH.
TEMP: Caliban, III, 2, 126.

trophy, memorial or any form placed over a tomb or grave; monument.
HAM: Laertes, IV, 5, 214.
COR: Volumnia, I, 3, 43.

tropically, metaphorically, figuratively, using a trope or figure of speech; with a pun on trap.
HAM: Hamlet, III, 2, 247.

trot, hag, old woman.
SHREW: Grumio, I, 2, 80.

troth, truth, faith.
MND: Lysander, II, 2, 42.

troubled mind
My mind is troubled like a fountained stirred,
And I myself see not the bottom of it.
T&C: Achilles, III, 3, 310.

trow, think, believe; know; certain, sure.
RICH2: Richard, II, 1, 218.
SHREW: Petruchio, I, 2, 4.
ADO: Beatrice, III, 4, 59—wonder.

trowel
Well said! That was laid on with a trowel.
AYL: Celia, I, 2, 112.

Troyan (Trojan), hale fellow, gay chap.
LLL: King, V, 2, 640.
1H4: Gadshill, II, 1, 77.
HEN5: Pistol, V, 1, 20.

truckle-bed, trundle bed; pushed under a standing bed.
MWW: Host, IV, 5, 7.

true-love
How should I your true-love know
From another one?
By his cockle hat and staff
And his sandal shoon.
HAM: Ophelia, IV, 5, 23—song of "mad" scene.

. . . for aught that I could ever read,
Could ever hear by tale or history,
The course of true love never did run smooth . . .
MND: Lysander, I, 1, 132.

Conceit, more rich in matter than in words,
Brags of his substance, not of ornament.
They are but beggars that can count their worth;
But my true love is grown to such excess
I cannot sum up sum of half my wealth.
R&J: Juliet, II, 6, 30.

truepenny, honorable old fellow; nickname for the Devil.
  HAM: Hamlet, I, 5, 150.

trull, whore, harlot, strumpet.
  A&C: Maecenas, III, 6, 95.
  1H6: Burgundy, II, 2, 28.
  TITUS: Tamora, II, 3, 191.

trumpery, worthless, gaudy clothes or finery, trash.
  TEMP: Prospero, IV, 1, 186.

truncheon, staff, baton or mace carried by kings and military officers; general or commander's staff; to cudgel.
  HAM: Horatio, I, 2, 204.
  OTH: Iago, II, 1, 280.
  2H4: Doll, II, 4, 154.

trunk, body.
  COR: Coriolanus, V, 3, 23.
  WINT: Camillo, I, 2, 435.
  TIMON: Apemantus, IV, 3, 229.

trust
  I wonder men dare trust themselves with men.
  Methinks they should invite them without knives:
  Good for their meat, and safer for their lives.
  TIMON: Apemantus, I, 2, 44.

truth
  Who tells me true, though in his tale lie death,
  I hear him as he flattered.
  A&C: Antony, I, 2, 102.
  . . . Tell truth and shame the devil.
  1H4: Prince, III, 1, 59.
  Truth's a dog must to kennel; he must be whipped out, when Lady the brach may stand by th' fire and stink.
  LEAR: Fool, I, 4, 124. See BRACH.
  . . . Truth hath a quiet breast.
  RICH2: Mowbray, I, 3, 96.
  Did they not sometime cry "All Hail!" to me?
  So Judas did to Christ: but he in twelve,
  Found truth in all but one; I, in twelve thousand, none.
  RICH2: Richard, IV, 1, 169.

truth. See TONGUES.

truths
  . . . truths would be tales
  Where now half-tales be truths.
  A&C: Agrippa, II, 2, 136.

try
  Let the end try the man.
  2H4: Prince, II, 2, 50.

Tubal, Jewish friend who brings Shylock the sad news about Jessica and the welcome information about Antonio's lost argosy.
  MERV: III, 1.

tuck, rapier, sword.
  TwN: Toby, III, 4, 244.
  1H4: Falstaff, II, 4, 274.

tucket, personal trumpet call or flourish; generally used in stage directions.
  HEN5: S.D., III, 6.
  TIMON: S.D., I, 2.

tuition, protection; often used in 16th-century letters as a formal closing.
  ADO: Claudio, I, 1, 283.

Tullus Aufidius. See AUFIDIUS, Tullus.

Tully, Marcus Tullius Cicero [(106-43 BC); famed orator, writer, formerly known as Tully (later CICERO); murdered by order of Marcus Antonius (Antony).]
  2H6: Suffolk, IV, 1, 136.
  TITUS: Titus, IV, 1, 14.

tun, barrel.
  HEN5: Ambassador, I, 2, 255.
  COR: Coriolanus, IV, 5, 105.

tun-dish, funnel.
  MEAS: Lucio, III, 2, 182.

Turk Gregory, used to refer to any cruel man; possibly either Pope Gregory VII (Hildebrand) whose name was synonymous with violence, or Pope Gregory XIII who sanctioned the Massacre of St. Bartholomew's Eve.
  1H4: Falstaff, V, 3, 46.

Turnbull Street, red-light district; rough neighborhood.
  2H4: Falstaff, III, 2, 329.

turn his girdle, prepare for a

fight; possibly refers to a wrestling or fencing gesture.

ADO: Claudio, V, 1, 142.

turnips

Alas, I had rather be set quick i' th' earth,

And bowled to death with turnips.

MWW: Anne, III, 4, 90. See QUICK.

turn Turk, become a pagan (converted from Christian to Moslem); act the renegade; become false and cruel.

HAM: Hamlet, III, 2, 287.

ADO: Margaret, III, 4, 57.

turtle, turtle-dove; mated for life, they symbolized faithful love.

WINT: Florizel, IV, 4, 154.

MWW: Mrs. Page, II, 1, 83.

LLL: Berowne, IV, 3, 212.

Tutor, to Rutland, pleads for the boy's life.

3H6: I, 3.

twain, pair, couple.

TEMP: Ferdinand, I, 2, 438.

Twelfth Night; or, What You Will, written 1600-01; performed 1602; registered and published 1623; source, tale of *Apolonius and Silla* in Barnabe RICH's *Riche his Farewell to Militarie Profession* (pub. 1581); Siennese comedy, *Gl'Ingannati* (1531), used the theme which also appeared in a novella by BANDELLO (1554), translated into French by BELLEFOREST (1571).

PLOT: The Duke Orsino of Illyria loves the Countess Olivia, but she, having pledged to mourn her brother's death for seven years, ignores him. Viola, shipwrecked on the coast and believing her twin brother Sebastian has drowned, decides to disguise herself as a boy and try to gain employment as a page in the Duke's court. As Cesario, she falls in love with her master, who sends her as a messenger to Olivia to plead his suit.

The Countess, however, is not too deep in mourning not to fall in love with Viola-Cesario and later, when Sebastian appears, Olivia, mistaking him for Viola, asks him to marry her. Orsino is furious, but Viola, recognizing her brother, explains that she is his twin sister and sets things straight. The Duke realizes, of course, that it is Viola he really loves and marries her.

The subplot centers on Malvolio, Olivia's steward, who has so alienated the members of the household that they seek revenge. Olivia's uncle, Sir Toby Belch, Sir Andrew Aguecheek, her foolish suitor, and her gentlewoman, Maria, manage to have Malvolio find a letter, supposedly from Olivia but written by Maria, suggesting he take matters into his own hands and pay court to the Countess. When Malvolio, following the instructions in the letter, behaves very strangely, he is imprisoned as a madman and only released when Olivia discovers the trick the others have played on him. Sir Toby is so delighted with Maria's part in the plot that he decides to marry her. Pepys commented "one of the weakest plays that ever I saw on the stage"; "This play is, in the graver part, elegant and easy, and, in some of the lighter scenes, exquisitely humorous." —(Johnson); "This is justly considered one of the most delightful of Shakespeare's comedies." —(Hazlitt.)

twelve score, 240 yards.

1H4: Prince, II, 4, 598.

MWW: Ford, III, 2, 35.

twice-told tale

There's nothing in this world can make me joy.

Life is as tedious as a twice-told tale

Vexing the dull ear of a drowsy man;

And bitter shame hath spoiled
the sweet world's taste,
That it yields naught but shame
and bitterness.
JOHN: Dauphin, III, 4, 107.

twiggen bottle, large wine bottle
covered with wicker; demijohn.
OTH: Cassio, II, 3, 152.

twigs, twigs or branches smeared
with birdlime to catch birds;
snare.
ALL'sW: Mariana, III, 5, 26.

twilled. See PIONED.

twinned, exactly alike, twin.
WINT: Polixenes, I, 2, 67.
CYM: Iachimo, I, 6, 35—worth-
less.

twire, twinkle, peep.
SONNET: XXVIII, 12.

twofold balls and treble scepters,
emblems of sovereignty.
MACB: Macbeth, IV, 1, 121—
Kingdoms of Scotland, England, Ireland united (1603)
under James I of England
(James VI of Scotland), Banquo's descendant.

Two Gentlemen of Verona, The,
written 1594, registered and
published 1623; source, a prose
romance, *La Diana Enamorada,*
by Jorge de MONTEMAYOR
(translated from Spanish into
French by N. Colin, 1578, and
into English by B. YONGE,
1582) and published 1598.
PLOT: Proteus and Valentine,
two young gentlemen of Verona,
are friends about to part. Valentine goes to the court of the
Duke of Milan where he falls
in love with the Duke's daughter, Silvia. Proteus stays in
Verona to be near Julia, his
love, but his father sends him
to join Valentine. Proteus exchanges rings with Julia and,
swearing to be faithful, sets out
to join his friend in Milan.
Valentine asks Proteus to help
him elope with Silvia, but Proteus has fallen in love with her

and is determined to win her
for himself.
Proteus reveals Valentine's
elopement plans to the Duke,
who wants his daughter to
marry the wealthy fool, Thurio,
and Valentine is banished from
his dukedom. In a forest near
Mantua, he is captured by a
band of outlaws who are so impressed with him that they make
him their chief. Julia, disguised
as a page named Sebastian, has
followed her lover to Milan and
is taken into service by the un-
suspecting Proteus. He asks her
to carry the ring she had given
him to Silvia, who refuses it.
Silvia, with the help of Sir
Eglamour, escapes from Milan
and tries to find Valentine. She
is captured by an outlaw band
and rescued by Proteus and his
page, who have followed her.
When Proteus attempts to force
his attentions on Silvia, Valentine appears and comes to her
aid. However, he tells his good
friend that he can have her.
Julia (Sebastian) faints. Her
identity is revealed by the ring
on her finger. Proteus, of course,
realizes that he loves her best
after all. At this the Duke and
Thurio arrive, brought before
Valentine by his band of outlaws. Thurio, the coward, refuses to fight for Silvia, and the
Duke gives her to Valentine. He
pardons the outlaws and everyone returns happily to Milan.
Two Noble Kinsmen, The, written in collaboration with John
FLETCHER (1613); not included
in the Folio, first appeared in
print 1634 (18 years after
Shakespeare's death); source,
CHAUCER'S *Knight's Tale.*
PLOT: The two noble kins-
men, Palamon and Arcite, decide to leave the court of their
uncle Creon, King of Thebes.
They learn that he will be attacked by Theseus at the request
of three queens whose husbands

the cruel tyrant has killed. They fight for Thebes, however, and are captured and imprisoned by Theseus. From the window of the prison they see Emilia, sister of Hippolyta, Theseus' queen, and fall in love with her.

Arcite is released and banished from Athens. Disguised, he manages to get a job in Emilia's household. Palamon escapes, meets and fights with Arcite, who is now his rival for Emilia. Discovered by Theseus, they are sentenced to death. Hippolyta and Emilia intercede and Theseus orders instead that they return in a month, each with three knights as assistants, to participate in a tournament. The winner goes free and gets Emilia, the loser is beheaded. They return. Arcite is victorious, but is thrown from his horse. He saves Palamon, just as he is to be beheaded, by giving Emilia to his cousin. Theseus blesses the union.

The subplot involves the love of the jailer's daughter for Palamon, who, after releasing him, goes mad with fear that he will be eaten by wolves and her father hanged. A doctor suggests to the young man that loves her that he pretend to be Palamon and she is cured.

Tybalt, Lady Capulet's nephew; picks a quarrel with Romeo, who refuses to be baited; when Mercutio accepts the challenge and is fatally wounded by Tybalt, Romeo kills him.
R&J: I, 1.

Tyburn, noted place of execution for London criminals.
LLL: Berowne, IV, 3, 54—reference to three-cornered gallows located there.

tyke (tike), cur, mongrel, dog.
HEN5: Pistol, II, 1, 31.
LEAR: Edgar, III, 6, 73.

Typhon, son of Tartarus; red-eyed, fire-breathing giant with a roaring voice and the heads of a hundred snakes; defeated by Jove (Jupiter) and his thunderbolts when he attempted to dethrone him; imprisoned under Mount Aetna (in Tartarus).
T&C: Ulysses, I, 3, 160.
TITUS: Aaron, IV, 2, 94.

tyrants
'Tis time to fear when tyrants seem to kiss.
PER: Pericles, I, 2, 78.

Tyrian, dark-red, royal purple (from Tyre).
SHREW: Gremio, II, 1, 351.

Tyrrel, Sir James, agrees to arrange the murder of the princes in the Tower; gets Dighton and Forrest to kill them and tells Richard they are dead and buried. [Yorkist; knighted (1471); Master of the Horse to Richard III; Governor of Guisnes under Henry VII, who had him executed (1502).]
RICH3: IV, 2.

U

ugly to the thing that helps it, aided by make-up or cosmetics as well as the glow of sexual desire, the harlot's cheek is not more ugly than his deed.
HAM: King, III, 1, 52.

Ulysses (Odysseus), King of Ithaca in Greek legend; one of the heroes of the Trojan War; famous for wanderings and exploits told in the *Odyssey* (credited to HOMER); son of Laertes, husband of Penelope, father of Telemachus; courageous, clever, resourceful; suggests they will provoke Achilles to fight again by making him jealous of Ajax; attempts to comfort Troilus when he discovers Cressida's infidelity.
T&C: I, 3.
3H6: Warwick, IV, 2, 19—relates the story from the *Iliad* (Book 10) when Ulysses and Diomedes killed the Thracian, Rhesus, and stole his white horses.

umbrage, shadow, reflection, pale counterpart.
HAM: Hamlet, V, 2, 125.

unaneled, without having received extreme unction, the last rites of the church.
HAM: Ghost, I, 5, 77.

unbated, not blunted; with a sharp point.
HAM: King, IV, 7, 139.

unbitted, unrestrained, unbridled.
OTH: Iago, I, 3, 336.

unbraced, untied, unlaced, un-fastened; men relaxed by un-bracing their doublet.
HAM: Ophelia, II, 1, 78.

unbraided, untarnished; not faded or soiled, new not shopworn.
WINT: Clown, IV, 4, 204.

unbreathed, unpracticed, unexercised.
MND: Philostrate, V, 1, 74.

uncape, uncover, reveal; let loose hounds or ferret.
MWW: Ford, III, 3, 176.

uncharge the practice, not suspect that it was a planned and clever plot.
HAM: King, IV, 7, 68.

unchary, carelessly, heedlessly; unsparingly, generously.
TWN: Olivia, III, 4, 222.

unclasped my practice, revealed or disclosed my plot or evil plan.
WINT: Leontes, III, 2, 168.

unclew, unwind, undo; figuratively, ruin or destroy.
TIMON: Timon, I, 1, 168—metaphor refers to a ball of wool.

unconfirmed, inexperienced, untrained.
ADO: Borachio, III, 3, 124.
LLL: Holofernes, IV, 2, 19.

uncouth, strange, wild, dreadful.
TITUS: Quintus, II, 3, 211.
AYL: Orlando, II, 6, 6.

unction, salve or healing ointment.
HAM: Hamlet, III, 4, 145.

uncurrent, will not pass as legal tender or lawful coinage; improper; valueless.

HAM: Hamlet, II, 2, 448.

TwN: Sebastian, III, 3, 16.

WINT: Hermione, III, 2, 50.

underbear, endure, submit to; trim on the lower edge.

RICH2: Richard, I, 4, 29.

JOHN: Constable, III, 1, 65.

underborne, lined, stiffened from underneath, with undergarment.

ADO: Margaret, III, 4, 21.

undercrest, heraldic term, take the title as my crest and be worthy of it.

COR: Marcius, I, 9, 71.

undergoing stomach, spirit of enduring courage; the stomach was considered the base or center of fortitude and valor.

TEMP: Prospero, I, 2, 157.

under-skinker, apprentice or assistant bartender; skink is to draw wine or pour, from German *schenken*.

1H4: Prince, II, 4, 27.

understanding

. . . Their understanding
Begins to swell, and the approaching tide
Will shortly fill the reasonable shore,
That now lies foul and muddy.

TEMP: Prospero, V, 1, 79.

undertaker, protector, one who takes up a challenge; meddler.

TwN: Toby, III, 4, 350.

uneared, uncultivated, untilled, unplowed.

SONNET: III, 5.

uneath, with difficulty, scarcely, hardly.

2H6: Gloucester, II, 4, 8.

unfair, to strip of beauty, deprive of loveliness.

SONNET: V, 5. See HOURS.

unfellowed, incomparable, without an equal, beyond compare.

HAM: Osric, V, 2, 150.

unfledged, inexperienced, immature.

HAM: Polonius, I, 3, 65.

unfolding, revelation, disclosure; time to release sheep from sheepfold.

OTH: Desdemona, I, 3, 245.

MEAS: Duke, IV, 2, 219.

unfurnished, unprotected, not provided with defenses; deprived of.

HEN5: King, I, 2, 148.

ungalled, uninjured, unhurt, without a scratch.

COFE: Balthazar, III, 1, 102.

ungored, unscathed; free from or not disgraced.

HAM: Laertes, V, 2, 261.

unguem, to the nail or at the fingernail; correct latin would be *ad unguem*.

LLL: Holofernes, V, 1, 83.

unhoused, unmarried, not bound by domestic ties or responsibilities.

OTH: Othello, I, 2, 26.

unhouseled, without receiving Holy Communion or the Eucharist.

HAM: Ghost, I, 5, 77.

unimproved mettle, untried, unused courage; uncontrolled nature.

HAM: Horatio, I, 1, 96.

union, an exquisite large pearl.

HAM: King, V, 2, 283.

University Wits, name given (1580's) to group of playwrights associated with the universities, including GREENE, Nashe and MARLOWE from Cambridge and LYLY, LODGE and Peele of Oxford.

unkennel, come out of hiding (like a fox or weasel from its hole), reveal itself, bring to light.

HAM: Hamlet, III, 2, 86.

unkind

In nature there's no blemish but the mind;
None can be called deformed but the unkind.

TwN: Antonio, III, 4, 400— *unkind,* unnatural.

unkindest cut

This was the most unkindest cut of all;

For when the noble Caesar saw
    him stab,
Ingratitude, more strong than
    traitors' arms,
Quite vanquished him.
    JC: Antony, III, 2, 188—from
    Antony's famed oration, refers
    to Brutus.

unlace, undo, disgrace, cast off.
    OTH: Othello, II, 3, 194.

unlaid ope, concealed, undisclosed.
    PER: Pericles, I, 2, 88.

unlicked bear-whelp, popular belief that the bear cub was born a mass of unformed flesh and was licked into shape by its mother.
    3H6: Richard, III, 2, 161.

unmitigable, uncontrolled, unreasonable.
    TEMP: Prospero, I, 2, 276.

unowed interest, disputed or uncertain ownership or possession; accruing interest or power of nobility; questionable right to the crown.
    JOHN: Bastard, IV, 3, 147.

unpaved, castrated.
    CYM: Cloten, II, 3, 34.

unpeopled, without a retinue.
    RICH2: Duchess of Gloucester, I, 2, 69.

unpinked, not decorated or pinked (punched holes); without scallops.
    SHREW: Grumio, IV, 1, 136.

unplausive, disapproving; neglectful.
    T&C: Ulysses, III, 3, 43.

unpregnant, devoid of power; unready; not urged on by.
    HAM: Hamlet, II, 2, 595.

unproportioned, excessive, not within proper limits; not consistent with a plan of action.
    HAM: Polonius, I, 3, 60.

unreclaimed, sinful, untamed, naturally wild, undisciplined; usually refers to hawks.
    HAM: Polonius, II, 1, 34.

unsex
. . . Come, you spirits
That tend on mortal thoughts,
    unsex me here,
And fill me, from the crown to
    the toe, top-full
Of direst cruelty!
    MACB: Lady Macbeth, I, 5, 41.

unshaped, confused, disordered, incoherent.
    HAM: Gentleman, IV, 5, 8.

unshrubbed down, upland country of level ground, usually covered with grass and without shrubs; rolling open acreage, prairie.
    TEMP: Ceres, IV, 1, 81.

unsifted, untried.
    HAM: Polonius, I, 3, 102.

unsinewed, without strength, weak, flabby and lacking muscle.
    HAM: King, IV, 7, 10.

unsorted, unsuitable, unfit, ill-chosen.
    1H4: Hotspur, II, 3, 14.

unstaid, unbecoming.
    2GENT: Julia, II, 7, 60.

unthrift, wastrel, prodigal, spendthrift.
    RICH2: Bolingbroke, II, 3, 122.
    SONNET: IX, 9.

unthrifty loveliness
Unthrifty loveliness, why dost
    thou spend
Upon thyself thy beauty's legacy?
    SONNET: IV, 1. See BEAUTY'S LEGACY.

untutored youth
When my love swears that she
    is made of truth
I do believe her, though I know
    she lies,
That she might think me some
    untutor'd youth,
Unlearned in the world's false
    subtilties.
    SONNET: CXXXVIII, 1.

unvarnished tale
. . . little shall I grace my cause
In speaking for myself. Yet, by
    your gracious patience,

I will a round unvarnished tale
deliver
Of my whole course of love.
OTH: Othello, I, 3, 88. See
ROUND.

unwonted, unusual, rare, unique.
TEMP: Miranda, I, 2, 497.

unyoke, call it a day; finish a
day's work; unharnessing the
oxen signified the end of a
day's labor.
HAM: Clown, V, 1, 59.

upcast, bowling term, throw
which pushes the opponent's
ball away from the target. See
JACK.
CYM: Cloten, II, 1, 2.

uphoarded, it was believed that
when a person buried treasure,
usually gold, and had a magical
wish or charm said over it, the
spell had to be removed before
he would find peace after death
as a spirit or ghost.
HAM: Horatio, I, 1, 136.

uplifted, brandished.
RICH2: Green, II, 2, 50.

upon my sword, oath taken on
the sword because the hilt was
in the form of a cross; sword
sacred to the soldier in any case
and an oath taken was binding
in military honor as well as in
a religious sense.
HAM: Hamlet, I, 5, 147.

up-staring, standing on end.
TEMP: Ariel, I, 2, 213.

urchin, goblin in the form of a
hedgehog; mischievous sprite or
elf.
TEMP: Prospero, I, 2, 326.

TITUS: Tamora, II, 3, 101.
MWW: Mrs. Page, IV, 4, 50.

urn, container of ashes of the
dead; grave; tomb.
COR: 1Lord, V, 6, 145.

Ursula, one of Hero's gentle-
women.
ADO: II, 1.

Urswick, Christopher, the Earl
of Derby (Stanley) sends him
with a message to Richmond.
[Chaplain to Margaret Beaufort,
Richmond's mother.]
RICH3: IV, 5.

usance, usury, charging of excessive interest on a loan.
MERV: Shylock, I, 3, 46.

use, interest, profit.
SONNET: IV, 7.

use of metal, coinage of money,
use of exchange.
TEMP: Gonzalo, II, 1, 153.

uses, ways, customs, general or
habitual practice.
HAM: Hamlet, I, 2, 134.
MACB: Macbeth, I, 3, 137.

utis, form of "utas" which refers
to octave or 8th day after a
feast or festival; fun, merry-
making.
2H4: 1Drawer, II, 4, 21.

utter, sell, bring to market.
WINT: Autolycus, IV, 4, 330.
LLL: Princess, II, 1, 16.
R&J: Apothecary, V, 1, 67.

utterance, last extremity; in a
duel to the death.
CYM: Cymbeline, III, 1, 73.
MACB: Macbeth, III, 1, 72.

V

vagabond flag, wild iris.
  A&C: Caesar, I, 4, 45.

vail, lower, let fall; flag.
  MEAS: Isabella, V, 1, 20.
  LLL: Boyet, V, 2, 297.
  HAM: Queen, I, 2, 70.

vail, tip, gratuity; leftovers from
  a feast given to servants.
  PER: 2Fisherman, II, 1, 157.

vain, untrue, false, deceitful.
  COFE: Luciana, III, 2, 27.

valanced, bearded; probably from
  valance, which is draped material (usually fringed) that
  hangs as an overcurtain or from
  a bed.
  HAM: Hamlet, II, 2, 442.

Valentine, true friend; faithful
  lover of Silvia, daughter of the
  Duke of Milan, whom he marries.
  2GENT: I, 1.

Valentine, gentleman attending
  Orsino, Duke of Illyria.
  TwN: I, 4.

vale of years
  . . . I am declin'd
  Into the vale of years—
  OTH: Othello, III, 3, 265.

Valeria, loquacious friend of Virgilia.
  COR: I, 3.

Valerius, Theban nobleman;
  warns Palamon and Arcite of
  Theseus' planned attack on
  Thebes.
  2NK: I, 2.

valiant
  He's truly valiant that can wisely
  suffer
  The worst that man can breathe,
  and make his wrongs

His outsides, to wear them like
  his raiment, carelessly,
And ne'er prefer his injuries to
  his heart,
To bring it into danger.
  TIMON: 1Senator, III, 5, 31.

valour
In a false quarrel there is no
  true valour.
  ADO: Benedick, V, 1, 120.

. . . When valour preys on rea-
  son,
It eats the sword it fights with.
  A&C: Enobarbus, III, 13, 199.

He that is truly dedicate to war
Hath no self-love; nor he that
  loves himself
Hath not essentially, but by circumstance,
The name of valour.
  2H6: Clifford, V, 2, 37.

value
But value dwells not in particu-
  lar will:
It holds his estimate and dignity
As well wherein 'tis precious of
  itself
As in the prizer. 'Tis mad idol-
  atry
To make the service greater than
  the god . . .
  T&C: Hector, II, 2, 53.

vanity, powers of illusion; fiction.
  TEMP: Prospero, IV, 1, 41.

vanity
For there was never yet fair
  woman but she made mouths in
  a glass.
  LEAR: Fool, III, 2, 36. See
  GLASS.

vantage, advantage; opportune
  situation or position; superiority.
  RICH2: York, V, 3, 132.

HAM: Polonius, III, 3, 33.
MND: Lysander, I, 1, 102.

vantbrace, defensive armor for the forearm.
T&C: Nestor, I, 3, 297.

variety. See AGE.

varlet (varlot), rogue, rascal; knight's attendant.
ADO: Dogberry, IV, 2, 74.
1H4: Falstaff, II, 2, 26.
2H4: Shallow, V, 3, 13—menial.

varlotry, rabble; group of servants.
A&C: Cleopatra, V, 2, 56.

Varrius, friend of Pompey.
A&C: II, 1.

Varro, servant who slept in Brutus' tent before Philippi.
JC: IV, 3.

Varro, usurer who sends his servant to collect money from Timon.
TIMON: II, 2.

vassal, slave, wretched fellow, base subject.
TEMP: Caliban, I, 2, 374.
LEAR: Lear, I, 1, 163.
LLL: Ferdinand, I, 1, 256.

vast, great void or desolation, abyss.
TEMP: Prospero, I, 2, 327. See WASTE.

Vaughan, Sir Thomas, executed at Pomfret Castle by order of Richard.
RICH3: III, 3.

vaulted arch, the sky, heaven.
CYM: Iachimo, I, 6, 33.

vaunt, beginning, outset, first part.
T&C: Prologue, 27.

Vaux, Sir Nicholas, in charge of the condemned Buckingham. [Son of below; estates forfeited by his father, restored to him by Henry VII.]
HEN8: II, 1.

Vaux, Sir William, tells the Queen that Cardinal Beaufort is dying. [Lancastrian; killed at Tewkesbury (1471).]
2H6: III, 2.

vaward, literally vanguard, referring to the forefront or early part; advanced position.
MND: Theseus, IV, 1, 108.
COR: Cominius, I, 6, 53.
HEN5: York, IV, 3, 130.

vein, mood, disposition, humor.
MND: Demetrius, III, 2, 82.

veins, underground waters, streams.
TEMP: Prospero, I, 2, 255.

velvet guards, trimming of velvet on women's clothing; symbol of class.
1H4: Hotspur, III, 1, 259.

venereal, erotic, of love.
TITUS: Aaron, II, 3, 37.

veney (venew), venue; in fencing, a bout; sally.
MWW: Slender, I, 1, 296.
LLL: Armado, V, 1, 62.

Venice, Duke (Doge) of, presiding judge of the Court of Justice; spares Shylock's life (MERV) if he will become a Christian, give half his estate to Antonio and pay a fine to the state; appointed Othello to the command of Cyprus (OTH); tries to get Brabantio to accept him as Desdemona's husband.
MERV: IV, 1; OTH: I, 3.

Venice
Venetia, Venetia,
Chi non ti vede, non ti pretia.
LLL: Holofernes, IV, 2, 99—Italian, Venice, Venice, who has not seen you, does not prize (or value) you; or doesn't appreciate you.

ventages, air holes, stops, vents of wind instruments.
HAM: Hamlet, III, 2, 373.

Ventidius, although rescued by Timon from debtor's prison, he refuses to help him when he is needed.
TIMON: I, 2.

Ventidius, general in Antony's army; routed the Parthians.
A&C: III, 1.

Venus, Roman goddess of love, beauty and fertility; identified with the Greek goddess, Aphrodite; the worship of Venus was encouraged by Caesar who erected a magnificent temple to her honor; in the *Iliad* of HOMER, Aphrodite is the daughter of Zeus and Dione; wife of Hephaestus, she was unfaithful with Ares, god of war, and others; later poets suggested she was born or sprung from the foam of the sea; the most beautiful goddess, she received the golden apple from Paris; mother of Eros.

TEMP: Ceres, IV, 1, 87.

VENUS: see below.

Venus and Adonis, narrative poem written 1592-93; registered and published 1593; dedicated to the Right Honourable Henry Wriothesley, Earl of Southampton, and Baron of Titchfield; written in *sesta rima* (quatrain followed by a couplet) used by LODGE in his *Scilla's Metamorphosis* (1589) and Spenser in *Astrophel;* source, probably OVID'S *Metamorphoses* (X, 520-59, 705-39) and possibly MARLOWE'S *Hero and Leander* was read in manuscript. A sensual mythological tale of the goddess Venus in her pursuit of the handsome, self-centered young Adonis, interested only in hunting. Her attempts at seduction, by word and deed, are frustrated as Adonis goes off to hunt. Killed by a wild boar, he evaporates into air and his blood, turned into a flower, is plucked and worn by the sorrowing goddess. The poem is not, however, tragic, but a combination of romance, sexual desire, wit and humor, kept light with a fairy-tale quality, unique in Elizabethan poetry.

verdure, vitality, i.e. power of growth.

TEMP: Prospero, I, 2, 87.

verge, boundary, compass.

RICH2: Bolingbroke, I, 1, 93.

TIMON: Timon, V, 1, 219—shore, beach.

RICH3: Anne, IV, 1, 59—encircling.

Verges, headborough or petty constable; assistant to Dogberry.

ADO: III, 3.

Vergil (Virgil), Polydore (c1470-1555). Italian-English ecclesiastic historian; author of *Historia Anglica* (26 vols., 1534; 3rd edition, 1555); used by HALLE and HOLINSHED, from whom Shakespeare took material for *Richard III.*

Vernon, member of York faction; refused permission to fight in single combat against the Lancastrian, Basset.

1H6: II, 4.

Vernon, Sir Richard, joins Hotspur's rebellion; agrees with Worcester's decision not to tell Hotspur of the King's offer of peace; captured and executed.

1H4: IV, 1.

verse. See MONUMENT.

Vesper, night, evening.

A&C: Antony, IV, 14, 8.

vestal, priestess of Vesta or Hestia; takes a vow of chastity; duty to keep the vestal or sacred fire burning on the altar; probably an allusion to Elizabeth, the Virgin Queen.

MND: Oberon, II, 1, 158.

R&J: Romeo, II, 2, 8.

A&C: Caesar, III, 12, 31.

vestal. See WOMEN.

vesture

One that excels the quirks of blazoning pens,

And in the essential vesture of creation

Does tire the ingener.

OTH: Cassio, II, 1, 63. See INGENER.

via, Italian, come on, let's go, forward! Word used to get a horse moving faster.

LLL: Holofernes, V, 1, 156.

vice, to force (using a tool).

WINT: Camillo, I, 2, 416.

vice, buffoon, caricature, comic figure; the vice was the Devil's

servant who tempted Man or Everyman in the morality plays; the Elizabethan fool or jester was a later development of the vice.
HAM: Hamlet, III, 4, 98.

vice. See VIRTUE.

vicegerent, deputy; ruler by divine right.
LLL: Ferdinand, I, 1, 221.

videlicet, Latin, namely, that is to say.
HAM: Polonius, II, 1, 61.
AYL: Rosalind, IV, 1, 97.
MND: Demetrius, V, 1, 330.

vie, stake, give, offer repeatedly, wager, term from card games.
SHREW: Petruchio, II, 1, 311.

vile
Wisdom and goodness to the vile seem vile.
Filths savour but themselves.
LEAR: Albany, IV, 2, 38.

villain, serf, servant, bondman.
AYL: Oliver, I, 1, 57.
LEAR: Cornwall, III, 7, 78.
LUCRECE: 1338.

villain
And therefore, since I cannot prove a lover
To entertain these fair well-spoken days,
I am determined to prove a villain
And hate the idle pleasures of these days.
RICH3: Richard, I, 1, 28.

villany
And thus I clothe my naked villany
With odd old ends stolen forth of holy writ,
And seem a saint when most I play the devil.
RICH3: Richard, I, 3, 337.

Vincentio, Lucentio's father; told by Petruchio that his son has married Bianca; almost imprisoned in Padua; when his son confesses, Vincentio forgives him.
SHREW: IV, 5.

Vincentio, Duke of Vienna.
MEAS: I, 1.

Vintner, works in the Boar's Head Tavern.
1H4: II, 4.

viol, six-stringed member of the violin family.
RICH2: Mowbray, I, 3, 162.

Viola, appealing heroine, twin sister of Sebastian; assumes the name of Cesario and becomes a page to the Duke with whom she falls in love; obediently pleads his case with Olivia, but wins him for herself.
TWN: I, 2.

viol-de-gamboys, viol da gamba, early form of cello.
TWN: Toby, I, 3, 27.

Violenta, friend of the widow of Florence; does not speak.
ALL'SW: III, 5.

violent delights
These violent delights have violent ends
And in their triumph die, like fire and powder,
Which, as they kiss, consume.
R&J: Friar, II, 6, 9.

violet, flower; early violets were symbolic of transitory, passing or changing things; favorite of the court.
HAM: Ophelia, IV, 5, 184—faithfulness.
LLL: Spring, V, 2, 904.
RICH2: Duchess of York, V, 2, 46.
The forward violet thus did I chide:
Sweet thief, whence didst thou steal thy sweet that smells,
If not from my love's breath?
SONNET: XCIX, 1—beginning of sonnet about flowers.

Virgilia, gracious, modest, faithful wife; her gentle femininity contrasts sharply with Volumnia's (her mother-in-law) almost masculine forcefulness; helps to persuade Coriolanus to spare Rome. [Called Virgilia by PLUTARCH, but in legend, Volumnia was his wife and Veturia his mother.]
COR: I, 3.

virginity

. . . Virginity by being once lost may be ten times found; by being ever kept it is ever lost. 'Tis too cold a companion. Away with't!
ALL'SW: Parolles, I, 1, 142.

virgin patent, privilege or right to live as a virgin or maiden.
MND: Hermia, I, 1, 80.

vir sapit qui pauca loquitur, Latin, it's a wise man who speaks few words.
LLL: Holofernes, IV, 2, 82.

virtue, essence, essential nature or character; power.
OTH: Roderigo, I, 3, 320.
LLL: King, V, 2, 348.
MACB: Malcolm, IV, 3, 156.

virtue

Virtue itself turns vice, being misapplied,
And vice sometime's by action dignified.
R&J: Friar, II, 3, 21.

. . . The rarer action is
In virtue, than in vengeance.
TEMP: Prospero, V, 1, 27.

virtue. See GRACE.

virtues

. . . So our virtues
Lie in the interpretation of the time;
And power, unto itself most commendable,
Hath not a tomb so evident as a chair
T' extol what it hath done.
COR: Aufidius, IV, 7, 49.

. . . his virtues
Will plead like angels, trumpet-tongued, against
The deep damnation of his taking-off . . .
MACB: Macbeth, I, 7, 18.

. . . The king-becoming graces,
As justice, verity, temp'rance, stableness,
Bounty, perseverance, mercy, lowliness,
Devotion, patience, courage, fortitude,
I have no relish of them, but abound

In the division of each several crime,
Acting it many ways. Nay, had I power, I should
Pour the sweet milk of concord into hell,
Uproar the universal peace, confound
All unity on earth.
MACB: Malcolm, IV, 3, 91.

virtuous, essential, concentrated; medically powerful.
2H4: King, IV, 5, 76.

visages of duty, outward appearances of loyalty or service.
OTH: Iago, I, 1, 50.

vision

And, like the baseless fabric of this vision,
The cloud-capped towers, the gorgeous palaces,
The solemn temples, the great globe itself,
Yea, all which it inherit, shall dissolve,
And, like this insubstantial pageant faded,
Leave not a rack behind.
TEMP: Prospero, IV, 1, 151.
See BASELESS FABRIC, RACK.

visitation, seizure; also has medical implication of attack of the plague.
TEMP: Prospero, III, 1, 32.

visitor, spiritual guide, one who ministers or gives comfort to the distressed; ecclesiastical inspector or examiner.
TEMP: Antonio, II, 1, 11.

visor (vizor), mask.
LLL: Rosaline, V, 2, 227.
ADO: Pedro, II, 1, 99.
R&J: Mercutio, I, 4, 30.

vizaments, for advisements, i.e. careful consideration of; counsel.
MWW: Evans, I, 1, 39.

vizard, mask.
MACB: Macbeth, III, 2, 34.
1H4: Poins, I, 2, 142.
MWW: Ford, IV, 4, 70.

vlouting-stog, flouting or laughingstock.

MWW: Evans, III, 1, 121.

vocatur, Latin, is called.

LLL: Holofernes, V, 1, 26.

voice, vote, suffrage; approval.

HAM: Hamlet, V, 2, 367.

voice

I'll speak in a monstrous little voice. Thisne, Thisne?

MND: Bottom, I, 2, 54.

volley of words

A fine volley of words, gentlemen, and quickly shot off.

2GENT: Silvia, II, 4, 32.

Voltimand, Danish courtier; tells Claudius, Gertrude and Polonius of current political relations with Norway and Prince Fortinbras' desire to cross Danish territory in order to attack Poland.

HAM: 1, 2.

Volumnia, strong mother of Coriolanus, who advises him to conceal his contempt for the plebeians until he is consul; persuades him to spare Rome. [PLUTARCH calls her Volumnia, but legend has her as Veturia]. "A mother like Volumnia would be a liability to any boy. She was the most unfortunate of mothers for such a rare and sensitive child. . . . Congenitally he must have been closer to a young poet than a young warrior."—(Goddard.)

COR: I, 3.

Volumnius, Brutus' friend; refuses to help him commit suicide.

JC: V, 5.

Voragine, Jacobus de (c1230-98). Italian Archbishop of Genoa (from 1292); compiled a collection of the lives of the saints, *Legenda aurea* (English translation, *The Golden Legend,* by Caxton, 1483); the legend of St. Barlaam possible source of the casket theme in *The Merchant of Venice.*

votary, one who takes a vow.

TIMON: Timon, IV, 3, 27.

MND: Titania, II, 1, 123—*vot'ress.*

OTH: Roderigo, IV, 2, 190—*votarist.*

vouch, state, affirm, declare, assert; testify, witness, approve.

OTH: Brabantio, I, 3, 103.

TEMP: Sebastian, II, 1, 10.

HAM: Hamlet, V, 1, 114—*voucher,* guarantee a title to property.

vouchsafe, grant, allow.

TEMP: Ferdinand, I, 2, 422.

vow

'Tis not the many oaths that makes the truth,

But the plain single vow that is vowed true.

ALL'sW: Diana, IV, 2, 21.

vows

Vows are but breath, and breath a vapour is.

    Then thou, fair sun, which on earth dost shine,

Exhal'st this vapour-vow; in thee it is.

    If broken then, it is no fault of mine;

    If by me broke, what fool is not so wise

To lose an oath to win a paradise?

LLL: Longaville, IV, 3, 68.

Vulcan, Roman god of fire and furnaces or popularly, the blacksmith god; also known as Mulciber, the hammer god; in Greek mythology, the god of fire was Hephaestus, chief workman of the gods, son of Zeus and Hera; ugly and deformed, he was thrown out of heaven twice; had forges and shops in various places as well as in his palace on Olympus; married to the beautiful Venus, who betrayed him with Mars and others.

HAM: Hamlet, III, 2, 89.

T&C: Ulysses, I, 3, 168.

TITUS: Demetrius, II, 1, 89—*Vulcan's badge,* cuckold's horns.

vulgar, common, ordinary.

HAM: King, I, 2, 99.

W

waft, turn away or aside; beckon.
  WINT: Polixenes, I, 2, 372.

wag, go away, get packing; wave the beard in merry chatter; rogue.
  ADO: Leonato, V, 1, 16.
  MWW: Host, I, 3, 7.

waggish, playful, mischievous, roguish.
  MND: Helena, I, 1, 240.

wagtail, bird similar to a pipit; trim slender body and a long tail that it bobs up and down.
  LEAR: Kent, II, 2, 73.

wain, wagon.
  TWN: Toby, III, 2, 64.

waist, portion of a vessel between the quarter-deck or poop and the forecastle; girdle, belt.
  TEMP: Ariel, I, 2, 197.

wake and wage, attempt and risk; begin and chance or hazard.
  OTH: 1Senator, I, 3, 30.

Walloon, inhabitant of the border country between the Netherlands (which included Belgium) and France; now southern Belgium.
  1H6: Messenger, I, 1, 137.

walls of brass
  Nor stony tower, nor walls of beaten brass,
  Nor airless dungeon, nor strong links of iron,
  Can be retentive to the strength of spirit . . .
  JC: Cassius, I, 3, 93.

wanion, vengeance.
  PER: 1Fisherman, II, 1, 17.

want credit, to be unbelievable.

  TEMP: Antonio, III, 3, 25.

wanton, unrestrained, licentious; luxuriant; overindulged, spoiled or pampered child.
  MACB: Duncan, I, 4, 34.
  MND: Titania, II, 1, 99.
  HAM: Hamlet, V, 2, 310.

wantonness, wildness, lewdness; self-indulgence, lightheartedness.
  HAM: Hamlet, III, 1, 152.
  LLL: Rosaline, V, 2, 74.
  RICH2: Richard, III, 3, 164—*wantons.*

wappened, tired, faded, worn out.
  TIMON: Timon, IV, 3, 38.

ward, defense, guard, protect; defensive position in fencing.
  LLL: Armado, III, 1, 132.
  RICH3: Richmond, V, 3, 255.
  TEMP: Prospero, I, 2, 471.

ward, bar, bolt, lock; literally, the bar inside a lock which fit the key; part of a lock.
  TIMON: Servant, III, 3, 38.
  LUCRECE: 303.

ward, cell in a prison.
  HAM: Hamlet, II, 2, 252.
  2H6: York, V, 1, 112.

warden, large, delicious winter pear (or apple); named after fruit of the Cistercian abbey of Warden in Bedfordshire, England.
  WINT: Clown, IV, 3, 48.

warder, truncheon, staff, used to signal the beginning or end of a battle or tournament.
  RICH2: Marshal, I, 3, 118.
  2H4: Mowbray, IV, 1, 125.

Warkworth, seat of the Percys in Northumberland.
  1H4: II, 3.

warlikeness
Once more unto the breach,
dear friends, once more;
Or close the wall up with our
English dead.
In peace there's nothing so be-
comes a man
As modest stillness and humility;
And when the blast of war blows
in our ears,
Then imitate the action of the
tiger;
Stiffen the sinews, summon up
the blood,
Disguise fair nature with hard-
favoured rage . . .
HEN5: King, III, 1, 1.

warm, comfortable, "well-heeled,"
flush.
1H4: Falstaff, IV, 2, 19.

warp, deviate, swerve; to distort.
MEAS: Duke I, 1, 15.

warranted quarrel. Sée CHANCE
OF GOODNESS.

warrener, gamekeeper, keeper of
a rabbit warren.
MWW: Simple, I, 4, 28.

Wart, Thomas, pressed into army
service by Falstaff.
2H4: III, 2.

Warwick, Earl of, comforts the
King (2H4); defends the Prince
of Wales; helps Plantagenet recover his title of Duke of York;
involved in sending Joan of Arc
to the stake (1H6). [Richard
Beauchamp (1382-1439), fought
against Glendower; served as
Governor of Normandy (1437-
39), where he died; daughter
Anne, married Richard Neville
(see below).]
2H4: III, 1; HEN5: IV, 8;
1H6: II, 4.

Warwick, Earl of, accuses Suffolk
of the murder of Gloucester
(2H6); quarrels with Somerset; joins his father, Salisbury
and Yorkists in Wars of the
Roses; helps win the first battle
of St. Albans; supports claim to
the throne of the Duke of York;
after Battle of Towton has
York's son crowned Edward IV

(3H6); when he learns that Edward has married Lady Grey,
joins Queen Margaret and the
Lancastrians; captures Edward,
returns his crown to Henry VI;
defeated and killed at Barnet.
[Richard Neville (1428-71), son
of 1st Earl of Salisbury; married the daughter of the Earl
of Warwick and inherited the
earldom (above); daughter Isabel married the Duke of Clarence; referred to as "the Kingmaker."]
2H6: I, 1; 3H6: I, 1.

Warwick, Earl of, young son of
Clarence; imprisoned by Rich-
ard. [Edward (1475-99), son of
Edward IV; impersonated by
Lambert Simnel (c1475-1537),
executed by Henry VII.]
RICH3: II, 2.

Washford, old name for Wex-
ford, Ireland.
1H6: Lucy, IV, 7, 63.

waspish-headed, malicious, quick-
tempered, spiteful.
TEMP: Iris, IV, 1, 99.

wasp-stung. See FOOL.

wassail, revelry, drinking.
HAM: Hamlet, I, 4, 9.
MACB: Lady Macbeth, I, 7, 64.
LLL: Berowne, V, 2, 318.

Wat (Walter), nickname for a
hare.
VENUS: 697.

watch, wakeful condition, sleep-
lessness, insomnia.
OTH: Desdemona, III, 3, 285.
COR: Coriolanus, II, 3, 134.
RICH2: Gaunt, II, 1, 78.

watch, sentry or night watchman;
awake.
RICH2: King Henry, V, 3, 9.
MACB: Lady Macbeth, II, 2,
71.

watch him tame, tame him by
keeping him awake; method
used in taming falcons or wild
hawks.
OTH: Desdemona, III, 3, 23.

water, luster (of a diamond); reference to urinalysis, practiced by

qualified doctors, quacks and "witches" or wise women.
TIMON: Jeweller, I, 1, 19.
TWN: Fabian, III, 4, 114. See WISE WOMAN.

waterfly, worthless, futile creature who glides over the surface; vain, idle.
HAM: Hamlet, V, 2, 84.

water-gall, minor, secondary, faint rainbow, considered a sure sign of rain; called in America "sundogs."—(Porter.)
LUCRECE: 1588.

water-rug, shaggy dog, good in the water (retriever).
MACB: Macbeth, III, 1, 94.

waterwork, water color; used as wall hanging in place of (or in imitation of) tapestry.
2H4: Falstaff, II, 1, 158.

watery arch, the rainbow; Iris was the personification of the rainbow.
TEMP: Iris, IV, 1, 71.

watery star, the moon.
WINT: Polixenes, I, 2, 1.

waxen, as soft as wax; easy to pierce or penetrate; increase.
RICH2: Bolingbroke, I, 3, 75.

we, used by kings, usually when speaking officially; the royal "we" meant I, but also implied that he was speaking for all.
RICH2: Richard, III, 3, 72.

weakness
But I am weaker than a woman's tear,
Tamer than sleep, fonder than ignorance,
Less valiant than the virgin in the night,
And skilless as unpractised infancy.
T&C: Troilus, I, 1, 9.

weak supposal, low estimate, poor opinion.
HAM: King, I, 2, 18.

weal, well-being, welfare, affluence; commonwealth, the body politic.
HAM: Rosencrantz, III, 3, 14.
JOHN: Pembroke, IV, 2, 65.

wealsmen, statesmen.
COR: Menenius, II, 1, 59.

wealthily
I come to wive it wealthily in Padua;
If wealthily, then happily in Padua.
SHREW: Petruchio, I, 2, 75.

wear, adapt, mold, suit.
TWN: Duke, II, 4, 31.

weasel (Scot)
For once the eagle (England) being in prey,
To her unguarded nest the weasel (Scot)
Comes sneaking, and so sucks her princely eggs,
Playing the mouse in absence of the cat,
To spoil and havoc more than she can eat.
HEN5: Westmoreland, I, 2, 169.

weather, the windward.
TEMP: Ariel, V, 1, 10—
weather-fends, protects from the wind and storm.

weather
Many may brook the weather that love not the wind.
LLL: Nathaniel, IV, 2, 34.

weaver, noted as a group for their love of singing; popular singers of psalms, usually Puritans.
1H4: Falstaff, II, 4, 147.
TWN: Toby, II, 3, 61.

weaver's beam, wooden roller in a loom, once made of a solid tree trunk.
MWW: Falstaff, V, 1, 24—refers to story of David and Goliath (II Samuel 21:19).

web of our life
The web of our life is of a mingled yarn, good and ill together. Our virtues would be proud if our faults whipped them not, and our crimes would despair if they were not cherished by our virtues.
ALL'sW: 2Lord, IV, 3, 83.

weed, garment, attire, clothing, robe.
SONNET: II, 4.

weed

. . . O thou weed,
Who art so lovely fair, and
smell'st so sweet,
That the sense aches at thee,
would thou hadst ne'er been
born!
OTH: Othello, IV, 2, 67.

weeds

. . . O, then we bring forth
weeds
When our quick minds lie still,
and our ills told us
Is as our earing.
A&C: Antony, I, 2, 113.

Now 'tis the spring, and weeds
are shallow-rooted.
Suffer them now, and they'll
o'ergrow the garden
And choke the herbs for want
of husbandry.
2H6: Queen, III, 1, 31.

The noisome weeds which
without profit suck
The soil's fertility from whole-
some flowers.
RICH2: Gardener, III, 4, 38.
See NOISOME.

ween, think, imagine, expect.
1H6: Mortimer, II, 5, 88.

weep, refers to the sap or resin
which drips from the burning
logs and resembles tears.
TEMP: Miranda, III, 1, 19.

weep

Let us seek out some desolate
shade, and there
Weep our sad bosoms empty.
MACB: Malcolm, IV, 3, 1.

. . . I am a fool
To weep at what I am glad of.
TEMP: Miranda, III, 1, 73.

weep. See TEARS.

weeping philosopher, reference
to Heraclitus, Greek philosopher (533-475 BC), who believed that the essential characteristic of the universe was
change; believed to have wept
for mankind.
MERV: Portia, I, 2, 53.

weigh, balance; counterbalance
match in a value or esteem;
waver, hesitate.
LLL: Rosaline, V, 2, 26.
TEMP: Sebastian, II, 1, 130.

Weird Sisters, goddesses of destiny; hands of fate; the Fates.
MACB: I, 3, 32.

welcome

A table full of welcome makes
scarce one dainty dish.
COFE: Antipholus E., III, 1,
23.

Small cheer and great welcome
makes a merry feast.
COFE: Balthazar, III, 1, 26.

welkin, sky, heaven.
TEMP: Miranda, I, 2, 4.
TWN: Toby, II, 3, 59.
WINT: Leontes, I, 2, 136—sky
blue.

Welsh

Now I perceive the Devil under-
stands Welsh;
And 'tis no marvel, he is so
humorous.
1H4: Hotspur, III, 1, 231. See
HUMOROUS.

Welsh Captain, announces to
Salisbury that his men have dispersed because of ill omens and
the belief that the king is dead.
RICH2: II, 4.

Welsh hook, weapon, bill or pike
with a curved hook; kind of
Irish bull.
1H4: Falstaff, II, 4, 373.

wen, tumor, swelling, abnormal
growth.
2H4: Prince, II, 2, 115—reference to Falstaff.

wesand, windpipe, throat, gullet.
TEMP: Caliban, III, 2, 99.

Western Isles, the Hebrides, or
islands of northwestern Scotland.
MACB: Sergeant, I, 2, 12.

Westminster, Abbot of, plots with
Aumerle and the Bishop of Carlisle to kill Bolingbroke (Henry
IV) and restore Richard II to
the throne; plan is discovered
and he is killed. [Believed to

have been William de Colchester.]

RICH2: IV, 1.

Westminster Hall, convocation hall of the English parliament; scene of the abdication of Richard in favor of his cousin Bolingbroke; abdication speeches not included until after the accession of James I to the throne; the Essex faction used the play as a propaganda device against ELIZABETH I.

RICH2: IV, 1.

Westmoreland, Earl of, firm supporter of Henry (1H4); leader of his armies; arranges a meeting between Prince John and the rebel leaders (2H4); wishes for more men at Agincourt (HEN5). [Ralph Neville, 4th Baron (1365-1425), created 1st Earl of Westmoreland by Richard II; cousin of Henry IV by marriage with Joan Beaufort, his half-sister; actually not present at Agincourt.]

1H4: I, 1; 2H4: IV, 1; HEN5: I, 2.

Westmoreland, Earl of, Lancastrian; loses patience with Henry when he makes York his heir. [Ralph, 2nd Earl (c1404-84), grandson of above.]

3H6: I, 1.

wet, weep or cry for.

TEMP: Sebastian, II, 1, 127.

We Three, refers to satirical picture of two fools or asses and the inscription "We Three," assuming the onlooker to be the third idiot or ass; popular as an inn sign.

TWN: Clown, II, 3, 17.

what is done

. . . what is done cannot now be amended.

Men shall deal unadvisedly sometimes,

Which after-hours gives leisure to repent.

RICH3: Richard, IV, 4, 291.

wheaten garland, wreath of farm or fruitful products; symbol of peace as agriculture cannot flourish during a war.

HAM: Hamlet, V, 2, 41.

wheel, variously explained by editors as: spinning-wheel, turn in a dance, Fortune's wheel, burden, refrain.

HAM: Ophelia, IV, 5, 171.

wheeling, wandering, roaming.

OTH: Roderigo, I, 1, 137.

wheel of fire

. . . I am bound

Upon a wheel of fire, that mine own tears

Do scald like molten lead.

LEAR: Lear, IV, 7, 46.

wheel of fortune

The wheel is come full circle . . .

LEAR: Edmund, V, 3, 174.

Wheeson, Whitsun (day); Whitsuntide is the week starting the 7th Sunday after Easter; Pentecost.

2H4: Hostess, II, 1, 96.

whelk, pimple, swelling, knob.

HEN5: Fluellen, III, 6, 109.

whelked, twisted in spirals, convolved.

LEAR: Edgar, IV, 6, 71.

Whenas I sat in Pabylon. See TO SHALLOW RIVERS (from Psalm 137).

MWW: Evans, III, 1, 24.

whiffler, official or officer who clears the way for a procession (either royal or municipal).

HEN5: Chorus, V, 12.

"while the grass grows," refers to a proverb which ends with "the horse (or stead) starves (or serveth)."

HAM: Hamlet, III, 2, 359.

whinid'st (vinewed'st), moldy; unsalted.

T&C: Ajax, II, 1, 15.

whip

. . . put in every honest hand a whip

To lash the rascals naked through the world.

OTH: Emilia, IV, 2, 142.

whipster, whipping boy, whippersnapper.

OTH: Othello, V, 2, 244.

whist, calm and still, silent.
TEMP: Ariel, I, 2, 378.

white, circle at the center of the target.
SHREW: Petruchio, V, 2, 186—pun on Bianca (Italian for white).

Whitefriars Theatre in the district of that name in London; named for the convent of Carmelites or White Friars established in Fleet Street (1241); monastery given to a company of players to use as a private theater (1580); used by King's and Queen's Revels companies (1608-13); replaced by SALISBURY COURT (1629) and then by DORSET GARDEN (c1670).

Whitmore, Walter, captures Suffolk at sea; loses an eye; chops off Suffolk's head in revenge.
2H6: IV, 1.

whitster, bleacher of linen.
MWW: Mrs. Ford, III, 3, 15.

Whitsun pastorals, plays (Robin Hood), morris dances, presented as part of festivities of the feast of Whitsun (Pentecost). See WHEESON.
WINT: Perdita, IV, 4, 134.
HEN5: Dauphin, II, 4, 25.

whittle, small clasp-knife; carving knife.
TIMON: Timon, V, 1, 183.

Who is Silvia?
Who is Silvia? What is she,
That all our swains commend her?
2GENT: Proteus, IV, 2, 39—opening lines of song.

whoreson, vulgar epithet meaning bastard, dog, good-for-nothing.
HAM: Clown, V, 1, 189.
LLL: Berowne, IV, 3, 204.
SHREW: Petruchio, IV, 1, 132.

why
. . . every why hath a wherefore.
COFE: Dromio S., II, 2, 45.

wicked
Those wicked creatures yet do look well-favoured,
When others are more wicked; not being the worst
Stands in some rank of praise.
LEAR: Lear, II, 4, 259.

Widow, when Hortensio fails to win Bianca, he marries her.
SHREW: V, 2.

Widow, mother of Diana; Helena lives with her in Florence.
ALL'SW: III, 5.

widow's eye. See FEAR.

wight, person, man, fellow.
LLL: Berowne, I, 1, 178.
MWW: Pistol, I, 3, 20—Hungarian wight, ragged soldier returning from the wars fought between the Hungarians and the Turks.

wild, weald, forest.
1H4: Chamberlain, II, 1, 60.

wilful men
. . . to wilful men
The injuries that they themselves procure
Must be their schoolmasters.
LEAR: Regan, II, 4, 305.

will, lust, carnal desires.
A&C: Enobarbus, III, 13, 3.
LEAR: Edgar, IV, 6, 279.
CYM: Iachimo, I, 6, 47.

will. See OURSELVES.

will he, nill he, willy-nilly, will he or won't he, whether he wants to or not.
HAM: Clown, V, 1, 17. See DROWN.
SHREW: Petruchio, II, 1, 273.

William, peasant in love with Audrey; scared away by Touchstone.
AYL: V, 1.

Williams, Michael, soldier who quarrels with Henry walking disguised among his troops the night before Agincourt; the King gives his pledge (challenge) to Fluellen.
HEN5: IV, 1.

willing misery
. . . Willing misery
Outlives incertain pomp, is crowned before.

The one is filling still, never complete;
The other, at high wish. Best state, contentless,
Hath a distracted and most wretched being,
Worse than the worst, content.
TIMON: Apemantus, IV, 3, 242.

Willoughby, Lord William, noble dissatisfied with the King; member of Bolingbroke's faction. [5th Baron Willoughby de Eresby, d. 1409.]
RICH2: II, 1.

willow, used in a garland to symbolize disappointed, forsaken or unrequited love.
ADO: Benedick, II, 1, 194.
3H6: Bona, III, 3, 228.
OTH: Desdemona, IV, 3, 42. See below.

There is a willow grows aslant the brook,
That shows his hoar leaves in the glassy stream . . .
HAM: Queen, IV, 7, 168. See HOAR.

The poor soul sat sighing by a sycamore tree,
Sing all a green willow;
Her hand on her bosom, her head on her knee,
Sing willow, willow, willow.
The fresh streams ran by her and murmured her moans,
Sing willow, willow, willow;
Her salt tears fell from her, and soft'ned the stones.
Sing willow—
OTH: Desdemona, IV, 3, 41— song.

willow cabin
Make me a willow cabin at your gate
And call upon my soul within the house;
Write loyal cantons of contemned love
And sing them loud even in the dead of night.
TwN: Viola, I, 5, 287.

wills
. . . the power and corrigible authority of this lies in our wills.
OTH: Iago, I, 3, 329.

Let's choose executors and talk of wills.
And yet not so—for what can we bequeath,
Save our deposed bodies to the ground?
RICH2: Richard, III, 2, 148.

Wilson, Robert (c1550-1600). English actor, dramatist; played with Leicester's (1572-4) and QUEEN'S (1583) companies; collaborated with Dekker and Drayton in the writing of 16 plays (lost) for the ADMIRAL'S company (1598-1600); *Three Ladies of London* (pub., 1584), attributed to him, possible source of the Shylock plot in *The Merchant of Venice*.

Wiltshire, Earl of, Lord Treasurer, chief favorite of the King; eldest son of Richard, first Baron Scroop of Mosham; does not appear in the play.
RICH2: Richard, II, 1, 215.

wimpled, blindfolded, hooded; refers to Cupid, portrayed with a cloth over his eyes, to show that love is blind.
LLL: Berowne, III, 1, 181.

win
. . . nothing can seem foul to those that win.
1H4: King, V, 1, 8.

Winchester, Bishops of. See BEAUFORT, Henry, and GARDINER, Stephen.

Winchester goose, prostitute of the brothels of Southwark, under the jurisdiction of the Bishop of Winchester.
T&C: Pandarus, V, 10, 55.
1H6: Gloucester, I, 3, 53.

wind
The southern wind
Doth play the trumpet to his purposes
And by his hollow whistling in the leaves
Foretells a tempest and a blust'ring day.
1H4: Prince, V, 1, 3.

windgalls, disease of horses causing tumors on the fetlock joints or above the fetlocks.

SHREW: Biondello, III, 2, 53.

windlasses, circuitous, indirect or roundabout way or method.

HAM: Polonius, II, 1, 65.

Windmill, probably a brothel which stood in Paris Garden near St. George's Field, near the Church of St. George the Martyr; a low neighborhood west of Southwark in London.

2H4: Shallow, III, 2, 207.

windows, eyelids.

CYM: Iachimo, II, 2, 22.

winds

Blow, winds, and crack your
  cheeks! rage! blow!
You cataracts and hurricanoes,
  spout
Till you have drenched our
  steeples, drowned the cocks!

LEAR: Lear, III, 2, 1.

wine

. . . O thou invisible spirit of wine, if thou hast no name to be known by, let us call thee devil.

OTH: Cassio, II, 3, 283.

. . . good wine is a good familiar creature, if it be well used.

OTH: Iago, II, 3, 313.

win me and wear me, expression used in challenging someone to a duel.

ADO: Antonio, V, 1, 82.

winter

For never-resting time leads
  summer on
To hideous winter, and confounds him there;
Sap check'd with frost and lusty
  leaves quite gone,
Beauty o'ersnow'd and bareness
  everywhere.

SONNET: V, 5.

How like a winter hath my absence been
From thee, the pleasure of the fleeting year!

SONNET: XCVII, 1.

winter of our discontent. See DIS-CONTENT.

winter's ragged hand

Then let not winter's ragged
  hand deface
In thee thy summer ere thou be
  distill'd . . .

SONNET: VI, 1.

Winter's Tale, The, written 1610-11; performed May 15, 1611; registered and published 1623; source, the romance *Pandosto or The Triumph of Time* by Robert GREENE (1588; reprinted 1607 as *Dorastus and Fawnia*).

PLOT: The jealous Leontes, King of Sicilia, believes that his friend Polixenes, King of Bohemia, is the lover of his wife, Hermione, and he tries to poison him. Warned by Camillo, Polixenes escapes. His flight only confirms his guilt, as far as Leontes is concerned, and he publicly disgraces his wife as an adulteress and throws her into prison. She gives birth to a daughter whom Leontes orders Antigonus to take to some desert place and abandon.

Leontes sends to the oracle at Delphos for word that he has done the right thing, but word comes from there that Hermione is chaste, Polixenes blameless and Camillo a loyal subject. Leontes is also warned that unless he finds what he has lost he will have no heir. The King denies the oracle, but is shaken when Paulina, the Queen's gentlewoman, announces the deaths of the Queen and Mamillius, their young son. Meanwhile, Antigonus has named the baby Perdita and left her on the coast of Bohemia. She is found there by a shepherd who rears her as his own daughter.

Sixteen years later Florizel, Prince of Bohemia, son of Polixenes, falls in love with her, but their marriage is prevented by his father. The lovers, with the help of the faithful Camillo, escape by ship bound for Sicilia.

At Leontes' court, the King and Polixenes, who had followed the lovers, are reunited as friends, and Camillo is welcomed back. Perdita is established as Leontes' lost daughter, and Paulina restores to life the apparently dead Hermione, who had been living in secret seclusion all these years. Thus Leontes gets back everything he lost (or threw away), the lovers are wed, and even Paulina is married to Camillo.

winter wind. See INGRATITUDE.

wiry, strong; wire was a popular metaphor for hair among Elizabethan poets.
JOHN: France (Philip), III, 4, 64.

wisdom
Wisdom and fortune combating together,
If that the former dare but what it can,
No chance may shake it.
A&C: Thyreus (Thidias), III, 13, 79.

. . . wisdom cries out in the streets, and no man regards it. (From Proverbs 1:20-24.)
1H4: Prince, I, 2, 99.

Have more than thou showest,
Speak less than thou knowest,
Lend less than thou owest,
Ride more than thou goest,
Learn more than thou trowest,
Set less than thou throwest;
LEAR: Fool, I, 4, 131—*trowest*, believe; *set less than thou throwest*—don't bet all on the next throw of the dice.

wise father
It is a wise father that knows his own child.
MERV: Launcelot, II, 2, 80.

wise fellow, refers to the story of a poet called Philides (Philippides) and King Lysimachus; from Barnabe RICH's *Souldiers Wishe to Britons Welfare, or Captain Skill and Captain Pill* (1604).

PER: Thaliard, I, 3, 4.

wise men
When clouds are seen, wise men put on their cloaks;
When great leaves fall, then winter is at hand;
When the sun sets, who doth not look for night?
RICH3: 3Citizen, II, 3, 32.

wise woman, reference to a witch who dealt in magical herbs.
TWN: Fabian, III, 4, 114.

wise youth
So wise so young, they say do never live long.
RICH3: Richard, III, 1, 79.

wish
Thy wish was father, Harry, to that thought.
2H4: King, IV, 5, 93.

wishers
Wishers were ever fools.
A&C: Cleopatra, IV, 15, 37.

wishtly, longingly, wistfully, eagerly.
RICH2: Exton, V, 4, 7.

wish to be
And were I anything but what I am,
I would wish me only he.
COR: Marcius, I, 1, 235—refers to Aufidius.

wisp of straw, mark or badge of a scold (nag), who was forced to wear a crown of straw.
3H6: Edward, II, 2, 144.

wistly, intently, attentively.
VENUS: 343.

wit, intelligent or sound judgment, keen understanding.
HAM: Polonius, II, 2, 89—*brevity is the soul of wit.*

wit, imaginative and clever strategy, planned maneuver.
OTH: Iago, II, 3, 379.

wit
. . . there's many a man hath more hair than wit.
COFE: Antipholus S., II, 2, 85.
I am not only witty in myself, but the cause that wit is in other men.

2H4: Falstaff, I, 2, 11.

He that has and a little tiny
wit,
  With hey, ho, the wind and
  the rain,
Must make content with his fortunes fit,
  Though the rain it raineth
  every day.
LEAR: Fool, III, 2, 74.

For he hath wit to make an ill
shape good,
And shape to win grace though
he had no wit.
LLL: Katherine, II, 1, 59.

Your wit's too hot, it speeds too
fast, 'twill tire.
LLL: Berowne, II, 1, 120.

witch. See BEAUTY.

witchcraft
She loved me for the dangers I
had passed,
And I loved her that she did
pity them.
This only is the witchcraft I
have used.
OTH: Othello, I, 3, 167.

Witches, open the play; foretell
the future for Macbeth and
Banquo.
MACB: I, 1.

witches' curse
Round about the cauldron go;
In the poisoned entrails throw.
Toad, that under cold stone
Days and nights has thirty-one
Sweltered venom sleeping got,
Boil thou first i' th' charmed pot.
Double, double, toil and trouble;
Fire burn, and cauldron bubble.
Fillet of a fenny snake,
In the cauldron boil and bake;
Eye of newt, and toe of frog,
Wool of bat, and tongue of dog,
Adder's fork, and blindworm's
sting,
Lizard's leg and howlet's wing;
For a charm of powerful trouble
Like a hell-broth boil and bub-
ble.
Double, double, toil and trou-
ble;
Fire burn, and cauldron bubble.

MACB: 3 Witches, IV, 1, 4. See
FENNY, BLINDWORM.

withers, the high point or ridge
of a horse's back at the neck
between the shoulders.
HAM: Hamlet, III, 2, 253.

Withold (Saint), Saint Vitalis (Or-
dericus Vitalis), English historian and Benedictine monk
(1075-c1143).
LEAR: Edgar, III, 4, 125.

without, beyond the range of.
TEMP: Prospero, V, 1, 271.
MND: Lysander, IV, 1, 156.

with parted eye, eyes out of focus,
divided vision.
MND: Hermia, IV, 1, 192.

witness, evidence; vengeance.
MACB: Lady Macbeth, II, 2, 47.
SHREW: Gremio, V, 1, 122.

wit-old, enfeebled mentality; pun
on wittol.
LLL: Moth, V, 1, 66. See WIT-
TOL.

wit's regard, honored by reason
and wisdom.
RICH2: York, II, 1, 28.

Wittenberg, noted German university, founded 1502, center of
study and learning; where Luther opened his public dispute
of theological principles, suggesting skepticism and dissent.
HAM: Queen, I, 2, 119.

wittol, contented, stupid or willing cuckold.
MWW: Ford, II, 2, 311.

wives
We'll leave a proof by that
which we will do,
Wives may be merry, and yet
honest too.
We do not act that often jest
and laugh;
'Tis old but true: Still swine
eats all the draff.
MWW: Mrs. Page, IV, 2, 106.

woe, sorry, grieved about it.
TEMP: Prospero, V, 1, 139.

woes
When we our betters see bearing
our woes,

We scarcely think our miseries
our foes.
LEAR: Edgar, III, 6, 108.

And woes by wrong imaginations lose
The knowledge of themselves.
LEAR: Gloucester, IV, 6, 290—
wrong imaginations, illusions.

Wolsey, Cardinal, helps the King
get his divorce from Queen
Katherine; arranges the death of
Buckingham; opposes the King's
marriage to Anne Bullen; letters to the Pope used as evidence
of his opposition to the King
and cause his downfall. [Thomas
Wolsey (c1475-1530), Archbishop of York (1514); Cardinal (1515); appointed Lord
Chancellor; extremely influential; died on his way to London,
following his indictment for
treason.]
HEN8: I, 1.

wolvish toge, wolf in sheep's
clothing; hypocritical submis-
siveness or humility; toge or
toga was worn by upper-class
Romans.
COR: Coriolanus, II, 3, 122.

woman
She's beautiful, and therefore to
be woo'd;
She is a woman, therefore to be
won.
1H6: Suffolk, V, 3, 78. See also
TITUS: Demetrius, II, 1, 82.

A woman, that is like a German
clock,
Still a-repairing, ever out of
frame,
And never going aright, being a
watch,
But being watched that it may
still go right!
LLL: Berowne, III, 1, 192.

woman. See FRAILTY.

woman's mind
Win her with gifts, if she respect
not words,
Dumb jewels often in their silent
kind

More than quick words do move
a woman's mind.
2GENT: Valentine, III, 1, 89.

woman's reason
I have no other but a woman's
reason:
I think him so because I think
him so.
2GENT: Lucetta, I, 2, 23.

woman's war, an argument, a verbal battle.
RICH2: Mowbray, I, 1, 48.

woman-tired, henpecked, torn at
by a woman as by a bird of prey.
WINT: Leontes, II, 3, 74.

wombs
Good wombs have borne bad
sons.
TEMP: Miranda, I, 2, 120.

womby vaultages, hollow caverns
or caves.
HEN5: Exeter, II, 4, 124.

women
Under a compelling occasion
let women die. It were pity to
cast them away for nothing,
though, between them and a
great cause, they should be es-
teemed nothing.
A&C: Enobarbus, I, 2, 141.

. . . women are not
In their best fortunes strong; but
want will perjure
The ne'er-touched vestal.
A&C: Caesar, III, 12, 29. See
VESTAL.

. . . those that she makes fair
she scarce makes honest, and
those that she makes honest she
makes very ill-favouredly.
AYL: Celia, I, 2, 40. See HON-
EST.

. . . there's no motion
That tends to vice in man but I
affirm
It is the woman's part. Be it
lying, note it,
The woman's; flattering, hers;
deceiving, hers;
Lust and rank thoughts, hers,
hers; revenges, hers;
Ambitions, covetings, change of
prides, disdain,

Nice longing, slanders, mutability—
All faults name, nay that hell knows, why, hers
In part, or all—but rather all.
CYM: Posthumus, II, 5, 20.

. . . I'll write against them,
Detest them, curse them. Yet 'tis greater skill
In a true hate to pray they have their will:
The very devils cannot plague them better.
CYM: Posthumus, II, 5, 32.

. . . You are pictures out of doors,
Bells in your parlours, wildcats in your kitchens,
Saints in your injuries, devils being offended,
Players in your housewifery, and housewives in your beds.
OTH: Iago, II, 1, 110.

For women are as roses, whose fair flower,
Being once displayed, doth fall that very hour.
TWN: Duke, II, 4, 39.

women. See KINDNESS.

woo
We cannot fight for love, as men may do;
We should be woo'd, and were not made to woo.
MND: Helena, II, 1, 241.

Who wooed in haste and means to wed at leisure.
SHREW: Katherina, III, 2, 11.

wood (wode), mad, insane.
MND: Oberon, II, 1, 192.
2GENT: Launce, II, 3, 30.
1H6: Bastard, IV, 7, 35.

woodbine, honeysuckle; also climbing vines such as the Virginia creeper; bindweed.
MND: Oberon, II, 1, 251.
ADO: Ursula, III, 1, 30.

woodcock, fool; taken from fowl that was very easily trapped or caught.
LLL: Berowne, IV, 3, 84.
TWN: Fabian, II, 5, 92.
ADO: Claudio, V, 1, 518.

wooden O, circular theater; probably the CURTAIN THEATRE, a round frame structure.
HEN5: I, Prologue, 13.

Woodstock, Thomas of, late Duke of Gloucester; Gaunt's and York's murdered brother; uncle of Richard II, who was responsible for his murder.
RICH2: Gaunt, I, 2, 1.

Woodville, Lieutenant of the Tower; acting on orders from Cardinal Beaufort, he refuses admittance to Gloucester and his men. [Richard (d. 1469); created Baron Rivers (1448); eldest daughter, Elizabeth, married Edward IV (1464).]
1H6: I, 3. See RIVERS, Earl.

woolward, with woolen clothing worn next to the skin; without linen between wool and skin; worn as a penance; modern reference, hair shirt.
LLL: Armado, V, 2, 717.

woosel (ousel), blackbird; often referring to a brunette.
2H4: Silence, III, 2, 9.
MND: Bottom, III, 1, 128—merle of the thrush family.

woo't (wo't), wilt thou, wolt.
A&C: Antony, IV, 2, 7.

Worcester, Earl of, joins the rebellion of Northumberland and Hotspur; King offers to pardon him, but Worcester doesn't tell Hotspur; captured and killed. [Thomas Percy (c1343-1403); younger brother of Northumberland, uncle of Hotspur; helped Bolingbroke become Henry IV, but turned against him.]
1H4: I, 3.
RICH2: Bushy, II, 2, 58—Worcester disrupted the king's household by fleeing with his servants to join Bolingbroke.

word, promise; watchword, password.
HAM: Messenger, IV, 5, 104.
HAM: Hamlet, I, 5, 110.

word

How long a time lies in one little word!

RICH2: Bolingbroke, I, 3, 213.

. . . do set the word itself
Against the word.

RICH2: Richard, V, 5, 13.

word. See SUIT.

words

A man may break a word with you, sir, and words are but wind.

COFE: Dromio E., III, 1, 75.

My words fly up, my thoughts remain below.
Words without thoughts never to heaven go.

HAM: King, III, 3, 97.

Here are a few of the unpleasantest words
That ever blotted paper!

MERV: Bassanio, III, 2, 251.

Words to the heat of deeds too cold breath gives.

MACB: Macbeth, II, 1, 61.

But words are words. I never yet did hear
That the bruised heart was pieced through the ear.

OTH: Brabantio, I, 3, 218. See PIECE.

words. See MERE WORDS, TONGUES.

work, fortification, garrison.

OTH: Othello, III, 2, 3.

workmen

When workmen strive to do better than well,
They do confound their skill in covetousness;
And oftentimes excusing of a fault
Doth make the fault the worse by the excuse . . .

JOHN: Pembroke, IV, 2, 28.

world

. . . O God, God,
How weary, stale, flat, and unprofitable
Seems to me all the uses of this world!

HAM: Hamlet, I, 2, 132.

Why let the strucken deer go weep,

The hart ungalled play.
For some must watch while some must sleep,
Thus runs the world away.

HAM: Hamlet, III, 2, 282.

The world's a huge thing. It is a great price for a small vice.

OTH: Emilia, IV, 3, 70.

. . . O brave new world
That has such people in't!

TEMP: Miranda, V, 1, 183.

world. See OYSTER, STAGE, WORLD'S A STAGE.

world of man

Strives in his little world of man to outscorn
The to-and-fro-conflicting wind and rain.

LEAR: Gentleman, III, 1, 10.

world's a stage

All the world's a stage,
And all the men and women merely players.
They have their exits and their entrances,
And one man in his time plays many parts,
His acts being seven ages. At first the infant,
Mewling and puking in the nurse's arms.
Then the whining schoolboy, with his satchel
And shining morning face, creeping like snail
Unwillingly to school. And then the lover,
Sighing like furnace, with a woeful ballad
Made to his mistress' eyebrow. Then a soldier,
Full of strange oaths and bearded like the pard,
Jealous in honour, sudden and quick in quarrel,
Seeking the bubble reputation
Even in the cannon's mouth. And then the justice,
In fair round belly with good capon lined.
With eyes severe and beard of formal cut,
Full of wise saws and modern instances;

And so he plays his part. The sixth age shifts
Into the lean and slippered pantaloon,
With spectacles on nose and pouch on side,
His youthful hose, well saved, a world too wide
For his shrunk shank; and his big manly voice,
Turning again toward childish treble, pipes
And whistles in his sound. Last scene of all,
That ends this strange eventful history,
Is second childishness and mere oblivion,
Sans teeth, sans eyes, sans taste, sans everything.
    AYL: Jaques, II, 7, 139.

world's ransom, Christ who died to redeem the world.
    RICH2: Gaunt, II, 1, 56.

worm, snake, serpent.
    MND: Hermia, III, 2, 71.

wormwood, spitefulness, bitterness; a bitter herb used in making absinthe.
    HAM: Hamlet, III, 2, 191.
    LLL: Rosaline, V, 2, 856.

worser genius, evil or bad side of a man's nature; man was believed guided by both a good and an evil angel or spirit.
    TEMP: Ferdinand, IV, 1, 27.

wort, any plant or herb, especially a potherb; vegetable; sweet unfermented beer.
    MWW: Evans, I, 1, 123.
    LLL: Berowne, V, 2, 233.

worth
That what we have we prize not to the worth
While we enjoy it, but being lacked and lost,
Why, then we rack the value, then we find
The virtue that possession would not show us
While it was ours.
    ADO: Friar, IV, 1, 219. See RACK.

worthy, noble, superior, honorable.
    MND: Theseus, I, 1, 52.

wot, knows, has knowledge of.
    A&C: Cleopatra, I, V, 22.
    WINT: Hermione, III, 2, 77.
    HAM: Hamlet, II, 2, 435.

wound
He jests at scars that never felt a wound.
    R&J: Romeo, II, 2, 1.

wounded name
O good Horatio, what a wounded name
(Things standing thus unknown) shall live behind me.
If thou didst ever hold me in thy heart,
Absent thee from felicity awhile,
And in this harsh world draw thy breath in pain,
To tell my story.
    HAM: Hamlet, V, 2, 355.

wounds
Those wounds heal ill that men do give themselves.
    T&C: Patroclus, III, 3, 229.

wound the bark, sap a tree.
    RICH2: Gardener, III, 4, 58.

wrack, wreck, ruin; strive for, strain.
    MACB: Angus, I, 3, 114.
    RICH2: Ross, II, 1, 267—shipwreck.
    COR: Menenius, V, 1, 17.

wreak, vengeance, revenge.
    COR: Coriolanus, IV, 5, 90.
    TIMON: Apemantus, IV, 3, 229 —*wreakful,* vengeful.

wrest, twist the meaning of, misinterpret.
    ADO: Margaret, III, 4, 34.
    2H4: John, IV, 2, 58.

wrest, controlling or harmonizing influence; literally, tuning-key which tightens the pegs of a musical instrument (i.e. harp).
    T&C: Calchas, III, 3, 23.

wretchedness o'ercharged, unfortunate men trying to do more than they are able; burdened beyond capacity.
    MND: Hippolyta, V, 1, 85.

wrinch, rinse.
2NK: 1Queen, I, 1, 156.

wring, force, compel; wrench, wrest; writhe, suffer.
TEMP: Miranda, I, 2, 135.
3H6: Henry, III, 1, 16.
CYM: Belarius, III, 6, 79.

writ. See ERROR.

writhled, wrinkled, shriveled, wizened.
1H6: Countess, II, 3, 23.

wrong
But wrong not that wrong with a more contempt.
COFE: Adriana, II, 2, 174.

Know, Caesar doth not wrong, nor without cause
Will he be satisfied.
JC: Caesar, III, 1, 47.

wrying, swerving or deviating from the right path; going astray.
CYM: Posthumus, V, 1, 5.

Y

yare, ready, easily maneuvered, manageable; prompt, quick, brisk.
TEMP: Boatswain, I, 1, 6.
TwN: Toby, III, 4, 244.
A&C: Enobarbus, III, 7, 39.

Yaughan, Yohan, Johan, phonetic Danish for John, possibly an innkeeper near the GLOBE theater.
HAM: Clown, V, 1, 68.

yaw, nautical term for bad steering, which causes a boat to go off its course; zigzag; unsteady.
HAM: Hamlet, V, 2, 120.

ycliped, called, named.
LLL: Ferdinand, I, 1, 243. See CLEPE.

yearn (ern), grieve.
MWW: Quickly, III, 4, 45.
RICH2: Groom, V, 5, 76.
HEN5: King, IV, 3, 26.

yellowness, jealousy.
MWW: Nym, I, 3, 111.
HEN8: Prologue, 16 — yellow was also the color of fools.

yellow sands
Come unto these yellow sands,
And then take hands.
Curtsied when you have and kissed,
The wild waves whist,
Foot it featly here and there.
TEMP: Ariel, I, 2, 375. See WHIST.

yeoman, sheriff or bailiff's officer; keeper.
2H4: Host, II, 1, 4.
TwN: Malvolio, II, 5, 45.

yeoman's service, excellent or faithful service; farmers or small freeholders were famed as the most reliable and expert infantry soldiers and archers.
HAM: Hamlet, V, 2, 36.

yerk, jerk, jab, kick; thrust, stab.
HEN5: Herald, IV, 7, 84.
OTH: Iago, I, 2, 5.

yesty, frothy, foaming, superficial.
HAM: Hamlet, V, 2, 198.
WINT: Clown, III, 3, 95—*yeast* (yest).

yield, reward, repay.
A&C: Antony, IV, 2, 33.

yield the crow a pudding, proverbial expression meaning to die (usually on the gallows) and become a meal for the crows.
HEN5: Hostess, II, 1, 91.

yoke-devils. See TREASON.

Yonge, Bartholomew (c1555-c1612). English translator from the Spanish of MONTEMAYOR'S *Diana Enamorada* (pub., 1598), source of *The Two Gentlemen of Verona.*

Yorick, king's jester, a "fellow of infinite jest, of most excellent fancy."
HAM: Clown, V, 1, 198.

York, Archbishop of. See ROTHERHAM, SCROOP.

York, Duchess of, begs forgiveness of Bolingbroke (Henry IV) for the treason committed by Aumerle, her son. [Aumerle's mother died (1394); Joan Hol-

land, daughter of the Earl of Kent, was his stepmother, ten years his junior.]
RICH2: V, 2.]

York, Duchess of, mother of Edward IV, Clarence and Gloucester; opposes Richard as king. [Cicely Neville, daughter of the 1st Earl of Westmoreland; married Richard, 3rd Duke of York (1438).]
RICH3: II, 2.

York, Duke of, Edmund of Langley, good-intentioned but weak mediator; appointed Regent of England in Richard's absence; does not oppose Bolingbroke, preferring to remain "neuter"; reveals his son's plot to restore Richard to power to Bolingbroke (Henry IV). [(1341-1402), 5th son of Edward III; 1st Duke of York (1385); brother of Gaunt, father of Aumerle, uncle of Richard and Bolingbroke; his descendants were the Yorkists of the Wars of the Roses.]
RICH2: IV, 1.

York, Duke of, given command of the vanguard at Agincourt; killed. [Edward (c1373-1415), elder son of Edmund of Langley; created Earl of Rutland and Duke of Aumerle by Richard II; succeeded as the 2nd Duke of York (1402).]
HEN5: IV, 3.

York, Duke of, served in France (1H6); enemy of Somerset; condemns Joan of Arc; objects to the marriage of Henry to Margaret of Anjou (2H6); sent to Ireland as Regent; claims the throne; wins battle of St. Albans; makes peace (3H6) on promise that he will succeed Henry; captured and executed by Margaret and Lancastrians at Wakefield. [Richard Plantagenet (1411-60), only son of Richard, Earl of Cambridge, executed before Agincourt, and Anne Mortimer; grandson of Edmund of Langley; 3rd Duke of York; became

heir presumptive upon the death of Humphrey, Duke of Gloucester (1447); displaced by Prince Edward (1453); sons were Edward IV, George, Duke of Clarence and Richard III.]
1H6: II, 4; 2H6: I, 1; 3H6: I, 1.

York, Duke of, murdered in the Tower with his brother Edward by order of their uncle, Richard III. [Richard Plantagenet, 5th Duke of York (1472-83); second son of Edward IV.]
RICH3: II, 4.

York, Mayor of, allows Edward IV into the town.
3H6: IV, 7.

young. See OLD AGE.

young blood
As true we are as flesh and blood can be.
The sea will ebb and flow, heaven show his face;
Young blood doth not obey an old decree.
We cannot cross the cause why we were born;
Therefore of all hands must we be forsworn.
LLL: Berowne, IV, 3, 215.

young lady, boy who portrays female roles.
HAM: Hamlet, II, 2, 444.

young men's love
. . . Young men's love then lies
Not truly in their hearts, but in their eyes.
R&J: Friar, II, 3, 67.

younker, naïve youngster, novice, greenhorn, stripling.
1H4: Falstaff, III, 3, 92.
MERV: Gratiano, II, 6, 14.
3H6: Richard, II, 1, 24.

youth
My salad days,
When I was green in judgment, cold in blood.
A&C: Cleopatra, I, 5, 73.
In youth when I did love, did love,
Methought it was very sweet . . .
HAM: Clown, V, 1, 69—song,

badly garbled, was first printed in TOTTEL's *Miscellany* (1557), written by Lord Vaux and titled *"The aged louer renounceth love."*

. . . youth, the more it is wasted, the sooner it wears.

1H4: Falstaff, II, 4, 443.

You that are old consider not the capacities of us that are young. You do measure the heat of our livers with the bitterness of your galls; and we that are in the vaward of our youth, I must confess, are wags too.

2H4: Falstaff, I, 2, 195. See VAVARD.

Some say thy fault is youth, some wantonness;
Some say thy grace is youth and gentle sport.

SONNET: XCVI, 1.

Z

zany, minor clown, a clown's assistant; buffoon who imitates a professional fool.

TwN: Malvolio, I, 5, 96.
LLL: Berowne, V, 2, 464.

zounds, by God's wounds; a strong oath.

OTH: Iago, I, 1, 86. See 'SWOUNDS.

SHAKESPEARE'S LIFE AND THEATER

CRITICS AND SCHOLARS OF SHAKESPEARE

PEOPLE OF THE THEATER

MODERN PRODUCTIONS OF PLAYS

MUSIC

A SELECTED LIST OF RECORDINGS

AN INTRODUCTORY READING LIST

GENEALOGICAL CHARTS OF THE
HOUSES OF YORK AND LANCASTER

Shakespeare's Life and Theater

by Richard C. Harrier

We know more about William Shakespeare the dramatist (1564-1616) than we do about any other Elizabethan dramatist except Ben Jonson. What we know, however, is derived largely from legal records. During the 16th and 17th centuries the lives of artists were not thought important enough—either by themselves or their friends—to merit the preservation of personal documents. Further, the professions of actor and dramatist were particularly low on the social scale of the Elizabethan age. It should not surprise us that William Shakespeare wished to be known as "gentleman, of Stratford-upon-Avon." It is worth noting, however, that he won the right to that title and considerable wealth besides.

There is no doubt about the identity of the man who wrote the greatest plays in the English language. During the 17th century when anyone became curious about their author he went to Stratford-upon-Avon to ask around for anecdotes. This certainty as to Shakespeare's identity lasted all through the 18th century and into the 19th. Only in the middle of the 19th century did anyone get the strange idea that someone other than the man from Stratford had written the plays. Since then various people have been suggested as their author: Francis Bacon, Edward de Vere (17th Earl of Oxford), Christopher Marlowe (even after he was killed), Sir Walter Raleigh, Queen Elizabeth herself, or even Mary Queen of Scots. This list could be extended over a dozen names less familiar or completely unknown to the reader, including several alleged syndicates of writers. No arguments about the identity of Shakespeare need be taken seriously. An outline of what we know about him and his theater follows.

William Shakespeare the dramatist was baptized in Holy Trinity Church, Stratford-upon-Avon, on April 26, 1564. His exact birthdate is unknown, but the custom of baptizing children three days after birth would suggest April 23rd, which is also St. George's day, the patron saint of England. Shakespeare's father, John, was, during the dramatist's childhood at least, a prosperous glover and tanner who rose to the office of bailiff or mayor. His mother, Mary Arden, was from a very old landed family of Warwickshire. Shakespeare's background was therefore solid middle class. Although the school records of the Stratford school for that time have been lost, it is probable that as a child Shakespeare was educated in the town's grammar school. There he would have mastered more Latin than any American takes away with his B.A. degree. The schoolmaster of Stratford and his assistant were both well-paid graduates of Oxford. The school itself was no doubt one of the better schools of England. Aside from his natural genius Shakespeare would have had, then, some years of exacting literary training, including the study of Ovid, Cicero, Seneca, and the Latin pastorals of the popular Italian writer called Mantuan (Italian humanist, Baptista Speagnuoli, also known as Baptista Mantuanus).

The next group of facts we have about Shakespeare's life concern his marriage and the birth of his first child. He was married in 1582 to Anne Hathaway of the nearby village of Shottery, when he was 18 and she 26. Their first child, Susanna, was born in 1583, and like the twins to follow, also was christened in Holy Trinity Church. Very likely Shakespeare remained in Stratford until the birth of the twins, Hamnet and Judith, in 1585. These twins were no doubt named after the family friends Hamnet and Judith Sadler, bakers in the town. What happened in Shakespeare's life between 1585 and his first recorded presence in London remains obscure. According to one of the more plausible stories, he was a schoolmaster in the country. According to another he was a strolling actor. There is no reason why he couldn't have been both, but there is no positive evidence of either.

By 1592, however, Shakespeare was already a successful actor and dramatist in London, implying more than a year's activity there. In that year he was attacked by Robert Greene, a rival dramatist dying in poverty, as an "upstart crow" who had proved disloyal to those who had taught him to act and to write. It is difficult to make out exactly what Greene's accusation was; perhaps Greene was accusing Shakespeare of plagiarism. In any case, the attack itself is evidence of Shakespeare's success. And a defense of him which appeared a year later (in Henry Chettle's *Kind-Heart's Dream*) indicates that Shakespeare also had supporters from the social class above that of Greene and himself. By 1592 Shakespeare had probably written the three parts of *Henry VI*, *Titus Andronicus*, and *The Comedy of Errors*. No wonder he was the target of professional envy and the protégé of influential persons.

The years 1592 and 1593 were crucial in the history of Elizabethan drama. Largely due to a virulent attack of bubonic plague the theaters were closed during the latter half of 1592 and most of 1593. As a result many of the current theatrical troupes went bankrupt. There emerged from this chaos two dominant companies, the Lord Admiral's Men, with the great actor Edward Alleyn, and the Lord Chamberlain's Men, with two greater figures, the actor Richard Burbage and the actor-dramatist William Shakespeare. Shakespeare's career from this time on was inseparable from those of the men who made up the Lord Chamberlain's group. In 1603, when King James VI of Scotland became James I of England, largely the same group of men became the King's Men under a renewed charter. Shakespeare always wrote with particular actors in mind, as an actor himself and part-owner of a theatrical company.

During the enforced idleness of the theatrical closing in 1592-93, Shakespeare tried his hand at a more serious form of composition, the narrative poem. There was of course some leisure in which to write such poetry, but Shakespeare must also have had in mind presenting his talents to the public in a genre more likely to receive serious attention. As I have pointed out, plays were not at that time thought to be a serious form of literature. He therefore published two poems, *Venus and Adonis* (1593) and *The Rape of Lucrece* (1594), describing the former as "the first heire of my inuention." By that he meant that he was presenting to the world his first really serious effort at high literary style. Strange as it may seem to us, these poems were the only two works he ever published under his own name and saw through the press. The value he placed upon them is demonstrated by the fact that he dedicated both to Henry Wriothesley, third Earl of Southampton, who was then about 19 years old. The first dedication is modest and dignified in tone; the second more assured and expressive of feeling. For that reason Henry Wriothesley is one of the foremost candidates suggested as the Master W. H. named in the dedication of Shakespeare's sonnets (1609). In fact, however, we know nothing about Shakespeare's relations with Southampton beyond the two early dedications. Only surmises are possible. Two facts must be kept in mind, however, about the later dedication of the sonnet volume (1609). That dedication was signed not by Shakespeare but by the publisher of the book, Thomas Thorpe; and further, it is not likely that Shakespeare or his publisher would have insulted an earl in public and in print by addressing him as "Master."

When Shakespeare began writing his famous sonnets is a matter of dispute. One sonnet, number 107 in the original order of publication, is thought by some to refer to the Spanish Armada of 1588 ("the mortal moon"). That theory is more challenged than accepted, and with good reason. In any case, there is no evidence that the sonnets were printed in their order of composition, so we cannot date them as a sequence even if we find hints for dating any one or more of them. What seems most likely is that Shakespeare wrote them throughout the decade of the nineties and up to the date of their first publication as a group, 1609. When we read them in sequence, however, a story appears to emerge with several characters who have remained anonymous if they were indeed real: a dark lady, one or more handsome young men, and one or more rival poets.

From 1594 on Shakespeare's career was one of unparalleled success artistically and financially. His company was not only the public favorite but the one most often invited to perform at court. Aside from the rechartering of the company under the new King James in 1603, two major developments in his career may be briefly described. Up to 1598 the main theater used by the Lord Chamberlain's Men was the one called The Theatre, situated just north of the city walls outside Bishopsgate. With the impending expiration of their lease on the land occupied by The Theatre, the company planned in 1598 to move to a new site and build a new theater. This became the famous Globe, on the south side of the Thames in the popular area of entertainment called the Bankside. The timbers of The Theatre were actually carried off by the company to serve in the new structure, which opened in 1599. In this newly reorganized group Shakespeare held a ten percent ownership along with Augustine Phillips, Thomas Pope, John Heminges, and Will Kempe, the most popular comic actor of the time. The two Burbages, Cuthbert and Richard, each owned 25 percent shares.

The strongest competition Shakespeare's company encountered was not from their rivals of the Lord Admiral's Men but from the company of boy actors who leased the Blackfriars Theatre from 1596-1608. The Blackfriars was a property within the city walls which came under private leases after it was taken from the religious order that had possessed it up to the Reformation. The so-called "private" or "coterie" theater of the Blackfriars type was very different from the "popular" Shakespearean kind. The boy companies of Blackfriars performed indoors by artificial light. Its clientele was more select, or at least able to pay higher prices, and the whole effect of the indoor staging was more like what we now think of as "theater." In order to meet this competition, in 1608 the Burbages formed a new group to take over the Blackfriars as a theater to be used by their company. These new actor-entrepreneurs were Richard and Cuthbert Burbage, William Shakespeare, Thomas Evans, John Heminges, Henry Condell, and William Slye. From that date on we can imagine Shakespeare as writing for two quite different kinds of staging but still for actors whose talents he knew intimately.

The "popular" kind of theater represented by both The Theatre (built in 1587) and the Globe (1599) had several remarkable features. One was its hollow round or octagonal shape with the center space open to the skies. The time of performance was afternoon and comfort for many who stood in its central area depended on the weather. The stage itself was a large platform that projected out into the middle of the central standing area so that most of the time the actors were within easy hearing distance of the crowd at their feet. Around the platform-stage were galleries of varying privacy and comfort. The price of entry depended on where one wanted to be within the structure. Simple entry into the "pit" or standing area might cost only a penny, to go higher might cost as high as a shilling. This economic range is a very important fact, for in Shakespeare's audience there was a full spectrum of the Elizabethan social scale: vagrants and criminals, apprenticed young men and laborers, merchants and nobles. For the first and last time in the history of the secular English theater, there was assembled a truly national audience. One can see that the contrasting Blackfriars Theatre, with its higher-priced clientele, was inevitably much less representative of the nation as a whole.

The most puzzling aspect of Shakespeare's stage is still that part of the structure directly behind the stage-platform. There are various theories about its nature and origin. In general we can say that there was an elevated area or balcony of easy access to the platform on which scenes could be staged. Also, there was some sort of enclosed area which upon exposure ("discovery") could represent a scene within a house or palace. Recent theory has stressed the fact that both the elevated area and the "inner" staging area must have projected somewhat onto the platform in order to have the same visibility and audibility which the platform itself had. At present, however, the exact nature of these two areas and the whole rear structure or "tiring house wall" is in doubt. Shakespeare's stage was remarkably versatile, simple, and yet symbolic. Performance was continuous, scene upon scene without a break, and there were no "realistic" rules of time or place. One was supposed to concentrate upon the human context as the lines revealed it without wondering how the characters in the play got from one place to another. Anyone who studies Shakespeare's texts closely will see apparent impossibilities of physical and temporal space. These are irrelevant.

It is frequently observed that the whole structure of the universe as Shakespeare's audience understood it was symbolically represented in the stage structure. There was a heavens probably painted on the ceiling of "roof" of the rear portion of the platform (to which Hamlet refers) and a hell under the stage to which trapdoors gave access.

The several preceding centuries of religious drama in England along with the various forms of public pageantry had accustomed the people to recognize symbolic objects as constituting a "realm" of authority or a place for action. Thus a throne or a wall, a tree or a mound, was all Shakespeare needed to fix for his audience the sense of life which his lines suggested.

Shakespeare's success as an actor-sharer-dramatist led to the grant of a coat of arms in 1596, after which he styled himself as "gentleman, of Stratford-upon-Avon." When we realize that formal titles were the basis of society or at least the outward sign of its very nature, we need not be surprised that Shakespeare wished to confirm his position by a formal document. Meanwhile the money which he earned through his profession had gone into land and buildings in his place of birth. He acquired fields for leasing and a claim to the tithes—then actually rents—of certain fields near Stratford. His major purchase, however, was the rather imposing structure called New Place, a building of sufficient dignity to house Queen Henrietta Maria on her trip through Stratford some years after Shakespeare's death. As we can see, Shakespeare had carefully maintained and solidified his position in his home town during the years he worked in London. By 1612 we know he had retired there, for a lawsuit of that year brought him to London from his stated residence of Stratford.

This lawsuit—the Belott-Mountjoy suit—is almost the only non-theatrical evidence we have to document Shakespeare's life in London. What we learn from the testimony is that from about 1602 to at least 1604 Shakespeare lived with a family of French Huguenots near St. Olave's Church in northwest London. He became so trusted a friend of the family that he was asked to negotiate a marriage between Mary Mountjoy and one Stephen Belott. The details of the marriage settlement later came into dispute, thus occasioning Shakespeare's being called to testify. Again, however, we do not have any details about Shakespeare's life within the Mountjoy household. We only know that he must have been an intimate of the family.

Shakespeare had lived in retirement in Stratford for at least four years when he made his will in January, 1616. Then the marriage of his daughter Judith to Thomas Quiney, a vintner and tavern-keeper of the town, necessitated certain revisions. This revised will has been thoroughly studied for clues to Shakespeare's personal affections, but it is in fact a rather ordinary will for the times. Here are some of its provisions: to Judith his younger daughter he left his broad silver-gilt bowl and £300; to his only sister Mrs. Joan Hart he left the use of the old family house in Henley Street during her lifetime and £20; the three sons of Mrs. Hart got small sums; his granddaughter Elizabeth Hall received his plate; his godson William Walker received a small sum of gold; to the poor of Stratford he left £10; to his friend Thomas Combe he gave his sword; his closest friends in Stratford, Hamnet Sadler, Williams Reynolds, Anthony Nash and John Nash, received money to be used for memorial rings; the two overseers of his will, Thomas Russell and Francis Collins (also his real estate lawyer) received sums of money; to his wife Anne he left his "second best bed with the furniture"; and the bulk of his estate, including New Place and the financial investments, went to his eldest daughter Mrs. Susanna Hall.

The item which has caught many an eye is that singled out for his wife Anne. Very likely, however, the bed was a token of personal affection between them. Under the law of that day a widow would have received one third of her husband's estate without any specific provision in the will, so Anne was taken care of in any case by the mere fact of a will. Also, it was not the practice to list all of a man's personal property in a will; only certain items might be noted for particular gifts. Very likely, the "second best bed," like his sword and his broad gilt bowl, was something of sentimental value to be saved for his wife. The general aim of the will was to preserve as much of the wealth for his eldest daughter's line. Shakespeare's plan was not successful, however, for none of his grandchildren had children of their own.

The names of other people Shakespeare must have known, such as Richard Field the printer or John Combe, money-lender of Stratford, have been carefully researched. Even as mere names with the briefest of characters attached to them, they make up a rather well-documented picture of an enterprising middle-class for which a devotion to profitable business did not exclude a love of "brave translunary" things.

We owe an extraordinary debt to John Heminges and Henry Condell, two of those to whom Shakespeare left money for memorial rings. These two men were instrumental in the publication of 36 plays by Shakespeare in an imposing folio volume of 1623, the first collected text of his plays. Since Shakespeare himself had never troubled to put into print an authoritative text of his plays, and since there are no Shakespeare manuscripts extant (with the possible exception of one scene), one can understand the importance of this volume.

When the First Folio appeared Shakespeare had been dead seven years. He died on April 23rd, 1616, and was buried within the chancel of Holy Trinity Church, Stratford-upon-Avon, among other prominent citizens of the town. He is probably the author of the verses on the stone over his grave, a charm to prevent some future sexton from disturbing his bones. His monument, designed by Geraert Janssen, was erected before the appearance of the 1623 Folio. The only evidence of an actual likeness we have is the much changed monument figure itself and the engraving in front of the First Folio. None of the other suggested "portraits" of Shakespeare has any good authority. As the verses accompanying the First Folio engraving remind us, however, the true "figure" of Shakespeare lives within the pages of his book.

CRITICS AND SCHOLARS OF SHAKESPEARE

Adams, Joseph Quincy (1881-1946). American scholar; director of the Folger Shakespeare Library, Washington, D.C. (1931-46); author of *Shakespearean Playhouses* (1917), *A Life of William Shakespeare* (1923); general editor, *The New Variorum Shakespeare*.

Addison, Joseph (1672-1719). English essayist, poet, statesman; under-secretary of state (1706-08), member of Parliament (from 1708); wrote the opera *Rosamond* (1707) and the classical tragedy, *Cato* (1713); with Richard Steele, published the *Spectator* (1711-12); wrote for the *Tatler* (1709-11) and the *Guardian* (1713); secretary of state (1717-18); articles of Shakespearean criticism.

Alexander, Peter (1893-). Scottish scholar; professor at Glasgow University; author of *Shakespeare's Life and Art* (1939); *Shakespeare's Punctuation* (1945) and other works; editor of *Collins Tudor Shakespeare* (1951).

Archer, William (1856-1924). British critic and playwright; author of *The Old Drama and the New* (1923) which included Shakespearean criticism; best known as translator and popularizer of Ibsen in England.

Auden, Wystan Hugh (1907-). British-American poet, critic, lecturer, translator; educated at Oxford; to U.S. (1939); citizen (1946); winner of Pulitzer Prize

for *The Age of Anxiety* (1947), the second part of which, *The Seven Ages,* is a psychological interpretation of Jaques' speech in *As You Like It* (Act II, Scene 7); wrote *The Sea and the Mirror* (published with *For the Time Being,* 1944), closet drama based on *The Tempest;* author of *The Dyer's Hand* (1962), book of criticism containing several essays dealing with Shakespeare.

Baker, George Pierce (1866-1935). American professor of drama; at Harvard (1905-24); famous for his "47 Workshop" course in the drama; director of Yale Department of Drama (1925-33); *The Development of Shakespeare as a Dramatist* (1907), his most important book.

Baldwin, Thomas Whitfield (1890-). American scholar; professor of English, University of Illinois (from 1928); *Organization and Personnel of the Shakespearian Company* (1927), most important work; also wrote *William Shakspere's Small Latine and Lesse Greek* (2 vols., 1944) and *William Shakespeare's Five Act Structure* (1947).

Bartlett, John (1820-1905). American editor and publisher; best known for his *Familiar Quotations* (1855), also edited *The Complete Concordance to Shakespeare's Dramatic Works and Poems* (1894).

Beeching, Henry Charles (1859-1919). English scholar; Dean of Norwich (1911); edited *The Sonnets of Shakespeare* (1904), with important introduction and critical notes.

Bentley, Gerald Eades (1901-). American scholar at Princeton University; author of *Shakespeare and Jonson* (2 vols, 1945), *The Jacobean and Caroline Stage* (5 vols, 1941-56); *Shakespeare: A Biographical Handbook* (1961); important article, "Shakespeare and the Blackfriars" (*Shakespeare Survey* 1, 1948).

Bodenstedt, Friedrich Martin von (1819-92). German poet, author, scholar; professor at the University of Munich (1854-66); directed theater at Meiningen (1866-70); published his translation of *Shakespeare's Sonnets* (1862); with Hermann Kurz and Paul Heyse translated all the plays (9 vols, 1868-73).

Bowdler, Thomas (1754-1825). English editor; produced censored edition of the plays, *The Family Shakespeare* (pub., 1818).

Bowers, Fredson Thayer (1905-). American scholar; author of *On Editing Shakespeare* (1955) and *Textual and Literary Criticism* (1959), important contributions to the field.

Bradbrook, Muriel C. (1909-). British scholar; Mistress of Girton College, Cambridge; author of *Elizabethan Stage Conditions: a Study of Their Place in the Interpretation of Shakespeare's Plays* (1932); *Shakespeare and Elizabethan Poetry* (1952) and other works.

Bradley, Andrew Cecil (1851-1935). English lecturer, critic; professor of poetry at Oxford (1901-06); his *Shakspere, A Critical Study of His Mind and Art* (1875), outstanding work of period; *Shakespearean Tragedy* (1904) considered a brilliant

analysis of *Hamlet, Othello, Lear* and *Macbeth*.

Brandes, Georg Morris (Cohen) (1842-1927). Danish writer on esthetics and literature, critic; three-volume life of Shakespeare translated into English as *William Shakespeare, A Critical Study* (2 vols., 1898); contributed to the popularity of Shakespeare on the continent.

Brooke, C. F. Tucker (1883-1946). American scholar; professor at Yale University; author of *The Tudor Drama* (1911); *Shakespeare of Stratford* (1926), *Shakespeare's Sonnets* (1946); editor of *The Shakespeare Apocrypha* (1908) and with W. L. Cross of *The Yale Shakespeare* (40 vols., 1918-28).

Campbell, Lily Bess (1883-1967). American scholar; professor of English, University of California (1922); author of *Scenes and Machines on the English Stage during the Renaissance* (1923); *Shakespeare's Tragic Heroes: Slaves of Passion* (1930, 1952), *Shakespeare's Histories: Mirrors of Elizabethan Policy* (1947).

Campbell, Oscar James (1879-). American scholar; professor of English, Columbia University (from 1936); editor of several editions of the plays; *Shakespeare's Satire* (1943); co-author of *The Reader's Encyclopedia of Shakespeare* (1966).

Capell, Edward (1713-81). English scholar; seventh editor of Shakespeare; considered first of the great scholars; deputy-inspector of plays (1737); groom of the privy chamber (1745); bequeathed his priceless collection of Shakespeare Quartos to Trinity College, Cambridge, used for the *Cambridge Shakespeare* (1863-66); published edition of Shakespeare's work (10 vols., 1768); published commentary on nine of the plays (1774); *Notes and Various*

Readings, The School of Shakespeare (1779-83).

Chambers, Sir Edmund Kerchever (1866-1954). English scholar; official in the Education Department (1892-1926); author of standard works on Shakespeare and the stage: *The Medieval Stage* (2 vols., 1903); *The Elizabethan Stage* (4 vols., 1923); *William Shakespeare: A Study of Facts and Problems* (2 vols., 1930).

Chalmers, Alexander (1759-1834). Scottish editor, biographer; published *Glossary to Shakespeare* (1797); editor of the *General Biographical Dictionary* (1812-14).

Child, Harold Hannyngton (1869-1945). English drama critic for the *Observer* (1912-20); reviewer for the *Times* (40 years); contributed to *The Cambridge History of English Literature,* The New Cambridge Shakespeare, *A Companion to Shakespeare Studies* etc.

Chute, Marchette (1909-). American biographer and literary historian; best known for biographies: *Geoffrey Chaucer of England* (1946), *Shakespeare of London* (1949) and *Ben Jonson of Westminster* (1953); excellent portraits of the periods in which her subjects lived; also wrote *An Introduction to Shakespeare* (1951) and *Stories from Shakespeare* (1956).

Clark, William George (1821-78). English scholar, editor, poet; planned and co-edited the *Cambridge Shakespeare* (1863-66); co-editor, Globe Shakespeare (1864).

Clarke, Charles Cowden (1787-1877). English scholar and lecturer; with his wife, Mary Victoria Novello (1809-98), published edition of Shakespeare (1864-68); co-editor with his

wife of *The Shakespeare Key: Unlocking the Treasures of his Style* (1879); his lectures, *Shakespeare's Characters* (pub., 1863, 1864); his wife published the important *Complete Concordance to Shakespeare* (1845).

Clemen, Wolfgang H. (1909-). German scholar; professor, University of Munich (from 1946); important for his *Development of Shakespeare's Imagery* (1951); author of *English Tragedy before Shakespeare* (1961); *Shakespeare's Soliloquies* (1964) and other works.

Coleridge, Samuel Taylor (1772-1834). English poet and critic; leader of the Romantic school of Shakespearean criticism; important in his emphasis on Shakespeare's poetry as well as his estimate of him as a great dramatist; *Biographia Literaria* (pub., 1817) contains his best criticism; *Notes and Lectures upon Shakespeare* given 1808-19 (pub., 1849).

Collier, John Payne (1789-1883). English journalist, lawyer, critic; librarian to the Duke of Devonshire (1831); secretary of the royal commission on the British Museum (1847-50); published a number of books on Shakespeare (1835-50), including the *Memoirs of Edward Alleyn* (1841), the *Alleyn Papers* (1843) and *Diary of Philip Henslowe* (1845); founded the Shakespeare Society (with Halliwell-Phillipps, 1840); charges of forgery against him brought his work under suspicion.

Collins, John (1741-97). English scholar; vicar of Ledbury; *Notes and Various Readings of Shakespeare* (2 vols., 1781); *The School of Shakespeare;* defended Capell against Steevens.

Collins, John Churton (1848-1908). English essayist and critic; professor of English Literature, Birmingham University (1904-08); author of *Studies in Shakespeare* (1904), *Studies in Poetry and Criticism* (1905) and other works.

Cotgrave, Randle (d. c1634). English lexicographer; secretary to William Cecil, Lord Burghley; important for his *French-English Dictionary* (pub., 1611; 2nd edition, 1632), used by editors of Shakespeare's plays for its explanation of 17th-century words.

Craig, Hardin (1875-1968). American scholar; professor of English Literature, Stanford University (until 1942); University of Missouri (1949-60); author of *The Enchanted Glass: the Elizabethan Mind in Literature* (1936), *An Interpretation of Shakespeare* (1948) and other works; historical approach.

Craik, George Lillie (1798-1866). Scottish scholar; professor of History and English Literature, Queen's College, Belfast (1849); author of *The English of Shakespeare* (1856), early study of Shakespeare's versification; *English Prose* (5 vols., 1893-96); one of founders of first Shakespeare Society (1840).

Creizenach, Wilhelm (1851-1919). German literary historian, critic; professor at Cracow (1883-1913); author of many volumes on the history of the drama including one translated into English as *The English Drama in the Age of Shakespeare* (1916).

Croce, Benedetto (1866-1952). Italian philosopher, editor and literary critic; author of important studies of literary figures including Ariosto, Shakespeare, Corneille (1920); emphasis on the poetic personality, the character and development of his art rather than the biographical, objective, realistic approach; editor in chief of his monthly maga-

zine, *La Critica* (27 yrs); gained fame with the publication of his *Aesthetics as the Science of Expresion* (1902).

Delius, Nikolaus (1813-88). German Shakespearean scholar; professor at Bonn University (1855-80); important edition of Shakespeare (1854-61; 1882); pioneer in the study of the Elizabethan theater; wrote *Abhandlungen zu Shakspere* (essays on; 2 vols., 1888) and a *Shakspere Lexicon* (1852).

Dennis, John (1657-1734). Minor English critic, dramatist; author of *Three Letters on the Genius and Writings of Shakespeare* (1711), includes his best criticism; ridiculed by Pope in the *Dunciad*.

De Quincey, Thomas (1785-1859). English essayist; author of *On the Knocking at the Gate in Macbeth* (1823); best known for *Confessions of an English Opium-Eater* (1822); master of English prose and particularly of autobiographical writing.

Dickens, Charles (1812-70). English novelist; acted in Shakespeare's plays, including a performance as Justice Shallow in *The Merry Wives* before Queen Victoria; wrote articles on *King Lear, Much Ado About Nothing,* the characterizations of Hamlet and Iago, and others.

Dowden, Edward (1843-1913). Irish critic; professor of English Literature, Trinity College, Dublin (from 1867); author of *Shakespeare: A Critical Study of his Mind and Art* (1875); *Shakespeare Scenes and Characters* (1876); *Shakespeare Primer* (1877); *Introduction to Shakespeare* (1893); edited editions of the *Sonnets* and several of the plays.

Drake, Nathan (1766-1836). English physician; author of several important essays on Shakespeare; published *Shakespeare and his Times* (2 vols., 1817).

Dryden, John (1631-1700). Poet, dramatist, critic; important works of criticism include: *An essay of Dramatick Poesie* (1668), *Essay on the Dramatique Poetry of the Last Age* (1672), *Preface to Troilus and Cressida* (1679); adapted some of the plays; famed for verse satire, *Absalom and Achitophel* (1681); play, written in blank verse, *All for Love or, The World Well Lost,* produced at the Drury Lane (1677-78). (See Davenant.)

Eliot, Thomas Stearns (1888-1965). American born British poet, critic and playwright; British subject (1927); known for poetry including *The Waste Land* (1922), *Four Quartets* (1943); verse dramas, *Murder in the Cathedral* (1935), *The Cocktail Party* (1950); in his *Selected Essays* (1932) are well-known treatments of "Hamlet and His Problems" and "Othello."

Ellis-Fermor, Una (Mary) (1894-1958). British scholar; lecturer, University of London (1918-47); author of *The Jacobean Drama* (1936; 4th ed., 1958) which includes a discussion of Shakespeare's relationship to his contemporary dramatists; served on advisory board of *Shakespeare Survey;* general editor of The New Arden Shakespeare (1946).

Elze, (Friedrich) Karl (1821-89). German scholar, critic; professor of English literature and language at Halle University (from 1875); published critical studies in *Essays on Shakespeare* (Eng. trans., 1874), *Life of Shakespeare* and *Notes on Elizabethan Dramatists* (3 vols., 1880-84; Eng. trans., 1888).

Eschenburg, Johann Joachim (1743-1820). German scholar;

professor at the Carolinum at Brunswick; his prose versions of the plays (based on Wieland, 1775-82, 1798-1806) were the first complete translations of Shakespeare into German.

Farmer, Richard (1735-97). English scholar; Vice-Chancellor, Emmanuel College, Cambridge (1775); *Essay on the Learning of Shakespeare* (1767), important work; attempted to prove that Shakespeare's knowledge of foreign languages was not sufficient and his material must have come from translations.

Fergusson, Francis (1904-). American critic; best known for *The Idea of a Theatre* (1949) which includes analysis of *Hamlet;* and *The Human Image of Dramatic Literature* (1957), with discussion of *Macbeth* and the comedies; *Shakespeare: The Pattern in His Carpet* (1970).

Feuillerat, Albert Gabriel (1874-1952). French scholar; taught at Yale (1928-43); wrote series of articles on Shakespeare in France (*Shakespeare Jahrbuch,* 1910-12); edition of the minor poems for the Yale Shakespeare (1927); first volume of projected three-volume study of plays completed at his death, *The Composition of Shakespeare's Plays* (pub. posthumously, 1953).

Fleay, Frederick Gard (1831-1909). English scholar; as a leading member of the New Shakspere Society, he read his paper *On Metrical Tests as Applied to Dramatic Poetry* at their opening meeting (March, 1874); author of *A Chronicle History of the Life and Work of William Shakespeare* (1886), *Chronicle History of the London Stage, 1559-1642* (1890) and *Biographical Chronicle of the English Drama, 1559-1642* (2 vols., 1891).

French, George Russell (1803-81). English architect, scholar, author of *Shakespeareana Genealogica* (1869), a valuable source book for Shakespearean scholars.

Fripp, Edgar Innes (d. 1931). English scholar; valuable contribution was assembling documents under the title *Minutes and Accounts of the Corporation of Stratford-upon-Avon* (4 vols., 1921-29) which covered the period 1553-1620; author of *Shakespeare, Man and Artist* (2 vols., 1938), a standard work, and others.

Frye, Northrop (1912-). Canadian critic; author of *Anatomy of Criticism* (1957) and *A Natural Perspective: The Development of Shakespearean Comedy and Romance* (1965).

Furness, Horace Howard (1833-1912). American scholar; editor of the *New Variorum Shakespeare* (from 1871); with his wife, Helen Kate Furness (1837-83) compiled a *Concordance to the Poems of Shakespeare* (1874); work carried on by his son, H. H. Jr. (1865-1930).

Furnivall, Frederick James (1825-1910). English scholar, editor of the *New English Dictionary* (Oxford, 1861); founder of the Chaucer, Ballad, New Shakspere, Wyclif, Shelley and Browning societies; editor of over 100 works in English literature; supervised the production of facsimiles of Shakespearean quartos in 43 volumes.

Gervinus, Georg Gottfried (1805-71). German historian, critic; professor at Heidelberg (1835) and Gottingen (1836); published *Shakespeare* (4 vols., 1849-50, translated into English as *Shakespeare Commentaries,* 1863) and *Händel und Shakespeare* (1868).

Goethe, Johann Wolfgang von (1749-1832). German poet, dramatist, novelist, statesman; leading figure of the Sturm und Drang Romantic movement; a great admirer of Shakespeare, he wrote criticism of the plays and poetry; probably the most famous of all comments made on a Shakespearean character are those on Hamlet in Book V, Chapter IV of *Wilhelm Meisters Lehrjahre* or *Wilhelm Meister's Apprenticeship,* 1795/6); produced a version of *Romeo and Juliet,* while director of the Court theater at Weimar (1791-1813).

Gollancz, Sir Israel (1864-1930). English scholar; professor of English literature and language, King's College, London; fellow and secretary of the British Academy (from 1902); editor of the *Temple Shakespeare* (40 vols., 1894-96), wrote *The Book of Homage to Shakespeare* (1916); knighted (1919).

Granville-Barker, Harley. See entry under People of the Theater.

Greg, Sir Walter Wilson (1875-1959). English scholar; General Editor of the Malone Society (1907-39); associated with A. W. Pollard in work on Shakespeare's text; compiled and edited many important books on the period; knighted (1950).

Guizot, François Pierre Guillaume (1787-1874). French statesman, historian, writer; lectured at the Sorbonne (from 1812); minister of the interior (1830); prime minister (1840-48); wrote many works of history and *Sur la Vie et les Oeuvres de Shakespeare* (1821) and *Shakespeare et son Temps* (1852).

Gundolf, Friedrich (originally Gundelfinger) (1880-1931). German scholar, literary critic; professor at Heidelberg; author of *Shakespeare und der deutsche*

Geist (1911); translations of the plays (1908-14); *Shakespeare, Sein Wesen und sein Werk* (1928).

Halliwell-Phillipps, James Orchard (1820-89). English scholar; one of the founders of the first Shakespeare Society (1840); published his important *Life of Shakespeare* (1848); limited edition of *Shakespeare* (16 folio volumes, 1853-65) with critical notes; bought the theater at Stratford-on-Avon (1872), and was responsible for the purchase of New Place by the Stratford Corporation, and the establishment of the museum there.

Hanmer, Sir Thomas (1677-1746). Fourth editor of Shakespeare; Speaker of the House of Commons (1714); published edition of Shakespeare's works (six quarto vols., 1744).

Harbage, Alfred (1901-). American scholar; professor of English at Harvard University and the University of Pennsylvania; best known for *Shakespeare's Audience* (1941), *As They Liked It: An Essay on Shakespeare and Morality* (1947), *Shakespeare and the Rival Traditions* (1952), *Shakespeare: The Tragedies* (1964); general editor of the Pelican Shakespeare series.

Harris, Frank (James Thomas) (1856-1931). British-American writer; editor of the *London Evening News* (1882); *Fortnightly Review* (1888-93); gained control of the *Saturday Review* (1874-98); editor of *Vanity Fair* and *Pearson's,* New York (1916-23); author of *The Man Shakespeare and His Tragic Life-Story* (1909), *Shakespeare and His Love,* a play (1910), *The Women of Shakespeare* (1911) etc.

Harrison, George Bagshawe (1894-

). English scholar; Reader in English Literature, London University (1929-43); professor of English, Queen's University, Kingston, Ontario (1943); Professor Emeritus of English Literature, University of Michigan; author of *Elizabethan and Jacobean Journals* (1928-33; 1941-58); with A. Granville-Barker, edited *A Companion to Shakespeare Studies* (1934); author of *Shakespeare: The Man and His Stage* (1923), *The Genius of Shakespeare* (1927), *Shakespeare's Tragedies* (1951) and many other books; his edition of the *Complete Works* was published (1952); editor of Bodley Head Quartos and the Penguin Shakespeare.

Hazlitt, William (1778-1830). English critic, essayist; reviewer for the *Edinburgh Review* (c1808) and the *Examiner* (edited by the Hunts); important Shakespearean scholar-critic; author of *The Characters of Shakespear's Plays* (1817); one of the first to emphasize the poetry of the plays; *A View of the English Stage* (1818), *Dramatic Literature of the Age of Elizabeth* (1820); master of English prose, his work had a lasting influence on subsequent critics.

Hazlitt, William Carew (1834-1913). English barrister, author; grandson of above; edited *Shakespeare's Library* (6 vols., 1875), collection of the principal sources used by Shakespeare; author of *Shakespeare, the Man and the Work* (1902), and others.

Heine, Heinrich (1797-1856). German poet; settled in Paris (1830); author of *Shakespeares Mädchen und Frauen* (1839), a book of criticism.

Hotson, (John) Leslie (1897-). Professor of English, Elizabethan scholar; author of *The*

Death of Christopher Marlowe (1925), *The Commonwealth and Restoration Stage* (1928), *I, William Shakespeare* (1937), *The First Night of Twelfth Night* (1952); expert in literary detection.

Hubler, Edward (1902-65). American scholar; professor of English, Princeton University; author of valuable *The Sense of Shakespeare's Sonnets* (1952).

Hudson, Henry Norman (1814-86). American Shakespearean scholar, Episcopal clergyman; author of *Lectures on Shakespeare* (1848), *Shakespeare: his Life, Art, and Characters* (1872); edited *Shakespeare* (11 vols., 1851-56; 20 vols., 1880-81).

Hugo, Victor Marie (1802-85). French poet, novelist and dramatist; wrote *William Shakespeare* (1864) which, though ecstatic in its praise, and lacking any critical judgment, established Shakespeare's reputation in France; his son, François Victor (1828-73), published a prose translation of Shakespeare (1859-66), which won high praise from Swinburne.

Hunter, Joseph (1783-1861). English antiquary; published *New Illustrations of the Life, Studies, and Writings of Shakespeare, Supplementary to all the editions* (2 vols., 1845).

Ingleby, Clement Mansfield (1823-86). English scholar; author of *The Shakspere Fabrications* (1859) in which he exposed J. P. Collier's forgeries; also wrote *A Complete View of the Shakspere Controversy* (1861), *Shakespeare's Centuries of Prayse* (1874), *Shakespeare Hermeneutics* (1875), *Shakespeare, the Man and the Book* (2 vols., 1877, 1881); *Shakespeare's Bones* (1882).

Ireland, William Henry (1777-1835). English forger of Shakespeare manuscripts; son of Samuel Ireland, an engraver, antiquary and author; deceived his father into publishing *Miscellaneous Papers and Legal Instruments under the Hand and Seal of William Shakespeare* (1795-96); and *Vortigern and Rowena,* a tragedy supposedly written by Shakespeare, produced at Drury Lane by Sheridan; he also wrote *Henry II* and attempted to pass it off as a newly discovered Shakespearean history; finally confessed and vindicated his father; wrote *Confessions of William Henry Ireland* (1805).

Johnson, Samuel (Dr. Johnson, the Great Cham of Literature) (1709-84). English lexicographer, essayist and poet; *Miscellaneous Observations on the Tragedy of Macbeth* (1745), important essay; published an edition of *Shakespeare,* with notes (8 vols., 1765); critical and biographical *Lives of the Poets* (10 vols., 1779-81).

Jones, Ernest (1879-1958). Psychoanalyst and author of *Hamlet and Oedipus* (1949), a well-known study; his *Life and Work of Sigmund Freud* (3 vols., 1953-57) considered definitive.

Keats, John (1795-1821). English lyric poet; important comments on Shakespeare found in his letters and his personally annotated copy of Shakespeare's plays (7 vols., 1814).

Kittredge, George Lyman (1860-1941). American scholar; professor of English Literature at Harvard (1894-1936); expert on Chaucer, Beowulf and other early English literature; edited important edition of the plays (1936); his Shakespeare course at Harvard became a tradition and produced many famous Shakespearean scholars; also wrote *Chaucer and His Poetry* (1915), *Shakespeare* (1916), *Witchcraft in Old and New England* (1929), single volumes of the plays, with explanatory notes (pub., 1940-45), *Sixteen Plays* (1946), well annotated.

Knight, Charles (1791-1873). English publisher and author of *Popular History of England* (8 vols., 1856-62); edited the *Penny Magazine* (1832-45) and the *Penny Cyclopaedia* (1833-44); published *Pictorial Shakespeare* (8 vols., 1841); *Library Edition* (12 vols., 1842-44); member of the council of the first Shakespeare Society (1840).

Knight, George Wilson (1897-   ). Canadian critic, producer, scholar; professor of English at Trinity College, Toronto University (1931-40); author of *The Wheel of Fire* (1930), *Principles of Shakespearean Production* (1936) and other works.

Knights, Lionel Charles (1906-   ). British scholar, critic and author of *Shakespeare's Politics* (1957), *Some Shakespearean Themes* (1959) and *An Approach to Hamlet* (1960); well-known for essay, *How Many Children Had Lady Macbeth?* (1933) an attack on realistic analysis of Bradley and others.

Kott, Jan (1914-   ). Polish author of *Shakespeare Our Contemporary* (1964).

Kozintsev, Grigory. Russian author of *Shakespeare: Time and Conscience* (1966).

Kreyssig, Friedrich A. T. (1818-79). German scholar and critic; author of *Vorlesungen über Shakespeare* (lectures on; 3 vols., 1858-60), an important contribution.

Lamb, Charles (1775-1834). English essayist, critic; published *Tales founded on the Plays of Shakespeare* (1807), which

earned him success; *Specimens of English Dramatic Poets who lived about the time of Shakespeare* (1808); *On the Tragedies of Shakespeare, considered with reference to their fitness for Stage Representation* (1811), appeared first in Leigh Hunt's *The Reflector,* a quarterly periodical; known for his *Essays of Elia* (1823).

Lawrence, William Witherle (1876-1958). American scholar; author of *Shakespeare's Problem Comedies* (1931), forerunner of modern concern with Shakespeare's so-called problem plays.

Lee, Sir Sidney (1859-1926). English scholar and editor of the *Dictionary of National Biography;* his *Life of William Shakespeare* (1898) was the standard work on the subject for many years; also wrote *Stratford-on-Avon from the Earliest Times to the Death of Shakespeare* (1885), *Elizabethan Sonnets* (1904), *Shakespeare and the Modern Stage* (1906), *Shakespeare and the Italian Renaissance* (1915); knighted (1911).

Leech, Clifford (1909-   ). Canadian critic; professor of English at University of Toronto: author of *Shakespeare's Tragedies* (1950) and *Shakespeare: The Chronicles* (1962); general editor, *The Revels Plays.*

Legouis, Émile (1861-1937). French scholar; professor of English language and literature at the Sorbonne (1904-32); author of *Shakespeare* (1899) and *Histoire de la littérature anglaise* (with Louis Cazamian, 1925).

Lennox, Charlotte (Ramsay) (1720-1804). English author, actress; wrote *Shakespeare Illustrated; of the Novels and Histories on which the Plays are founded, Collected and Trans-*

lated (3 vols., 1753-54), first published collection of the sources of more than half the plays; author of *A Female Quixote; or the Adventures of Arabella* (2 vols., 1752) and a comedy, *The Sister* (1769).

Lessing, Gotthold Ephraim (1729-81). German dramatist and critic; author of *Hamburg-ishche Dramaturgie*, a series of articles associated with the establishment of the German National Theatre in Hamburg (1767-69), in which he urged German dramatists to follow Shakespeare's example rather than model their work after French neo-classical drama.

Lewis, (Percy) Wyndham (1882-1957). English writer and painter; leader of movement called vorticism; associated with Ezra Pound and Roger Fry in editing *Blast*, vorticist magazine (1914-15); paintings in many museums; author of novels, essays and *The Lion and the Fox: The Role of the Hero in the Plays of Shakespeare* (1927).

Lowell, James Russell (1819-91). American poet, essayist, diplomat; professor at Harvard (1857); first editor of the *Atlantic Monthly* (1857-62); lectured on the English dramatists at the Lowell Institute (1887); books of essays and criticism.

Ludwig, Otto (1813-65). German dramatist and novelist; introduced the *leit-motif* and the psychological novel into German literature; important critical studies include *Shakespeare Studien* (pub., 1871); best known for his novel *Zwischen Himmel und Erde* (Between Heaven and Earth, 1856).

Mackail, John William (1859-1945). English scholar; wrote on Greek and Latin literature; published *Approach to Shakespeare* (1930) and *Aspects of Shake-*speare (1933), selected lectures.

McKerrow, Ronald Brunlees (1872-1940). English scholar, bibliographer and publisher; professor of English, Tokyo (1897-1900; 1914-18); founder and editor, *Review of English Studies* (1925-40); author of *The Treatment of Shakespeare's Text by His Earlier Editors, 1709-1768* (1933); working on the *Oxford Shakespeare* at the time of his death; only volume published, *Prolegomena* (1939).

Madden, Dodgson Hamilton (1840-1928). Irish scholar; author of *The Diary of Master William Silence; a Study of Shakespeare and of Elizabethan Sport* (1897); *Shakespeare and His Fellows; an Attempt to decipher the Man and his Nature* (1916).

Malone, Edmund (Edmond) (1741-1812). Irish scholar and critic; in London, became a member of the literary circle or "Club"; wrote *Attempt to ascertain the Order in which the Plays of Shakespeare were written* (1778), included in Steevens' second edition of the plays; published 10-volume edition of Shakespeare (1790), following his quarrel with Steevens; denounced the Ireland forgeries; worked on a new edition of Shakespeare that was completed by James Boswell the younger (21 vols., pub., 1821), known as the *Third Variorum*.

Masefield, John (1878-1967). English poet, dramatist, novelist; Poet Laureate (from 1930); wrote *William Shakespeare* (1911), a book of criticism.

Matthew, (James) Brander (1852-1929). American scholar, critic, playwright; professor of English, Columbia University (from 1892); first to hold the post of professor of dramatic literature (1900-24); founded the The ater Museum there; author of many books including *Shakespeare as a Playwright* (1913).

Morgann, Maurice (1726-1802). British essayist; best known for *Essay on the Dramatic Character of Falstaff* (1777) anticipating Romantic criticism of Shakespeare.

Moulton, Richard Green (1849-1924). English critic, scholar, author; professor, University of Chicago (1892-1919); *Shakespeare as a Dramatic Artist: A Popular Illustration of Scientific Criticism* (1885), *The Moral System of Shakespeare* (1903), enlarged and reissued as *Shakespeare as a Dramatic Thinker* (1907).

Murry, John Middleton (1889-1957). English critic; editor of the *Athenaeum* (1919-21), the *Adelphi* (1923-30), *Peace News* (from 1940); author of *Keats and Shakespeare* (1925), *Shakespeare* (1936), *Countries of the Mind* (2 vols., 1922, 1931) which include his excellent Shakespearean criticism; husband of Katherine Mansfield.

Neilson, William Allan (1869-1946). American scholar; president of Smith College (1917-39); author of *The Facts About Shakespeare* (with A. H. Thorndike, 1913); *A History of English Literature* (1920); editor in chief of *Webster's New International Dictionary, Second Edition* (1934); editor of New Cambridge edition of Shakespeare's works (1906, revised edition, with Charles Hill, 1942).

Nichols, John (1745-1826). English printer and antiquary; important contributions include *Progresses and Public Processions of Queen Elizabeth* (3 vols., 1788-1877), *The Progresses, Processions, and Magnificent Festivities of King James the First* (4 vols., 1828).

Nicoll, (John Ramsay) Allardyce (1894-   ). English scholar; Professor Emeritus, English, University of Birmingham; taught history of the drama, Yale; founded Shakespeare Institute, Stratford (1951); editor of the *Annual Shakespeare Survey;* author of many books on the theater including *Dryden as an Adapter of Shakespeare* (1922) and *Studies in Shakespeare* (1927).

Oliphant, Ernest Henry Clark (b. 1862). Australian editor; author of *The Place of Shakespeare in Elizabethan Drama* (1914), *The Plays of Beaumont and Fletcher* (1927); president of the Melbourne Shakespeare Society.

Onions, Charles Talbut (1873-1965). English lexicographer, philologist; co-editor of the *Oxford English Dictionary* (1914-33); well-known for *A Shakespeare Glossary* (1911).

Orwell, George (Eric Arthur Blair) (1903-50). English author of *Animal Farm* (1945) and *Nineteen Eighty-Four* (1949); "Lear, Tolstoy and the Fool" (originally published 1947, appeared in *Collected Essays,* 1961), is answer to Tolstoy's attack on Shakespeare.

Pater, Walter Horatio (1839-94). English critic and essayist; fellow of Brasenose, Oxford (1864); known as a Renaissance scholar; author of *Appreciations, with an Essay on Style* (1889), containing important Shakespearean criticism.

Pollard, Alfred William (1859-1944). English bibliographer; author of *Shakespeare Folios and Quartos: A Study in the Bibliography of Shakespeare's Plays* (1909); *The Foundation of Shakespeare's Text* (1923); contributed the chapter on Shakespeare's text to the *Cam-*

bridge Companion to Shakespeare Studies (1934) etc., invaluable sources used by Shakespearean scholars.

Pope, Alexander (1688-1744). English poet, critic; second editor of Shakespeare (published his edition of the plays, 1725); translator of the *Iliad* and the *Odyssey;* wrote *An Essay on Criticism* (1711), *The Rape of the Lock* (1712) and *An Essay on Man* (1733-34).

Quiller-Couch, Sir Arthur Thomas (1863-1944). English scholar; professor of English Literature, Cambridge (from 1912); edited the Oxford Books of English Verse, English Prose etc.; *Adventures in Criticism* (1896); *Shakespeare's Workmanship* (pub., 1918), contains his most important Shakespearean criticism; joint-editor (with J. D. Wilson) of the New Cambridge edition of the *Works of Shakespeare.*

Raleigh, Sir Walter Alexander (1861-1922). English biographer, essayist; professor of English literature, Liverpool, Glasgow and Oxford (from 1904); his *Shakespeare* (1907) is considered an outstanding work; edited *Johnson on Shakespeare* (1908); knighted (1911).

Reed, Isaac (1742-1807). English editor, scholar; published *Biographia Dramatica* (2 vols., 1782), important reference work; edited Steevens' 10-volume edition of Shakespeare (1785) and the *First Variorum* (21 vols., 1803; reprinted, 1813).

Reynolds, George Fullmer (b. 1877). American scholar, professor of English Literature, University of Colorado (1919-45); author of *Some Principles of Elizabethan Staging* (1905), *The Staging of Elizabethan Plays* (1940), pioneer studies in Shakespeare's theater.

Richardson, William (1743-1814). British scholar; professor of Humanity, Glasgow University (1773-1814); published *A Philosophical Analysis and Illustration of some of Shakespeare's Remarkable Characters* (1774); followed by studies of *Lear, Richard III* and *Timon* (1784), and *Falstaff and the Female Characters* (1789).

Rollins, Hyder Edward (1889-1958). American scholar; succeeded Kittredge at Harvard (1939); edited major Elizabethan "poetical miscellanies," including *Tottel's Miscellany* (2 vols., 1928-29); edited variorum editions of *Shakespeare's Poems* (1938) and *Sonnets* (1944); general editor, Fourth Variorum (1947); edited standard edition of *The Letters of John Keats* (2 vols., 1958).

Rowe, Nicholas (1674-1718). English dramatist, critic, poet; first critical editor of Shakespeare with edition of the plays published in six octavo volumes (1709); second edition in nine volumes (1714); introduced the plays with a life of Shakespeare (first formal biography) for which he was indebted to Betterton; wrote *The Fair Penitent* (1703), *Ulysses* (1706), *The Tragedy of Jane Shore* (1714) and *The Tragedy of Lady Jane Grey* (1715), among other plays; appointed Poet Laureate (1715).

Rowse, Alfred Leslie (1903-). British historian; fellow of All Souls College, Oxford; outstanding authority on Elizabethan period; author of *William Shakespeare, A Biography* (1963), an edition of *Shakespeare's Sonnets* (1964) and *Christopher Marlowe, A Biography* (1964); claims Mr. W. H. of the sonnets was the Earl of Southampton; opinions controversial.

Rümelin, Gustav (1815-88). German scholar and statesman; published *Shakespeare Studies by a Realist* (1864), the first with that approach.

Saintsbury, George Edward Bateman (1845-1933). English critic, scholar; professor of Rhetoric and English Literature, Edinburgh (1895-1915); author of many works in the field of English literature containing some valuable criticism.

Schlegel, August Wilhelm von (1767-1845). German poet, critic; professor of literature and aesthetics at the University of Jena; lectured in Berlin, England and France; with his wife, translated Shakespeare into German (1797-1801), an important contribution to the German Romantic movement; interpreted Shakespeare in *On Dramatic Art and Literature* (pub., 1809-11); with his brother, Fredrich (1772-1829), founder of German Romanticism.

Schmidt, Alexander (1816-87). German scholar; *Shakespeare-Lexicon* (2 vols., 1874-75), most important contribution; definitions in English; edited several plays; articles on textual criticism.

Schücking, Levin Ludwig (1878-1964). German scholar; editor, *Character Problems in Shakespeare's Plays* (1919, trans., 1922); *Shakespeare and the Tragic Style of His Time* (1947); edited (with Walther Ebisch) *A Shakespeare Bibliography* (1931; Supplement, 1937), early 20th-century Shakespearean commentary.

Shaw, George Bernard (1856-1950). Irish-English dramatist, critic, novelist; wrote controversial, largely hostile, opinions of the plays, but praised Shakespeare's poetry; despised Shakespeare's tragic view of life but said "in manner and art nobody can write better than Shakespeare."

Simpson, Richard (1820-76). English scholar; published *An Introduction to the Philosophy of Shakespeare's Sonnets* (1868), *The School of Shakespeare, No. 1* (1872; complete 2 vols., 1878), with reprints of Elizabethan plays that Shakespeare might have had a part in writing.

Simrock, Karl (1802-76). German poet, translator, scholar; professor at Bonn (from 1850); translated some of Shakespeare's poems and dramas into German; wrote *Die Quellen des Shakespeare* (1831), collection of source material.

Sisson, Charles Jasper (1885-   ). British scholar; editor of the *Modern Language Review* (1926-57); author of *Lost Plays of Shakespeare's Age* (1936), *New Readings in Shakespeare* (2 vols., 1956), and *Shakespeare's Tragic Justice* (1961); edited one-volume edition of the *Complete Works* (1954).

Sitwell, Dame Edith (1887-1964). English poet; author of *A Poet's Notebook* (1943), which contained a section on Shakespeare, and *A Notebook on William Shakespeare* (1948); created a Dame of the British Empire (1954).

Skeat, Walter William (1835-1912). English philologist; published *Shakespeare's Plutarch* (1875); with A. L. Mayhew, a *Glossary of Tudor and Stuart Words* (1914); founder, English Dialect Society (1873); a founder of the Chaucer and New Shakspere societies; professor of Anglo-Saxon, Cambridge (1878-1912); published *Chaucer* (7 vols., 1894-7).

Smith, Logan Pearsall (1865-1946). American-English scholar; studied at Haverford, Harvard and Oxford; naturalized

British citizen (1913); author of a short volume *On Reading Shakespeare* (1933) and *Milton and His Modern Critics* (1940), arguing against pedantry of modern scholars.

Spencer, Hazelton (1893-1944). American scholar; professor of English at Johns Hopkins University (from 1937); author of *Shakespeare Improved: the Restoration Versions in Quarto and on the Stage* (1927); *The Art and Life of William Shakespeare* (1939).

Spencer, Theodore (1902-49). American critic; author of *Death and Elizabethan Tragedy* (1936) and *Shakespeare and the Nature of Man* (1942), discussion of the Elizabethan view of the universe.

Sprague, Arthur Colby (1895-   ). American scholar; author of *Shakespeare and the Audience* (1935), *Shakespeare and the Actors: The Stage Business* (1944), *Shakespearean Players and Performances* (1953) and *Shakespeare's Histories* (1964).

Spurgeon, Caroline (1869-1941). English scholar; professor of English, University of London (from 1913); author of *Shakespeare's Imagery and What It Tells Us* (1935), the classic book on the subject.

Steevens, George (1736-1800). English scholar; published *Twenty of the Plays of Shakespeare* (1766), reprints of the Quarto editions; with Dr. Johnson, published edition of *Shakespeare* (10 vols., 1773; reprinted, 1778, 1793); considered an incomparable Shakespearean scholar; rival of Malone.

Stoll, Elmer Edgar (1874-1959). American scholar; professor of English, University of Minnesota (1915-42); author of *Othello* (1915), *Hamlet* (1919), *Shakespeare Studies* (1927), *Art and Artifice in Shakespeare* (1933), *Shakespeare and Other Masters* (1940), *From Shakespeare to Joyce* (1944).

Stopes, Charlotte Carmichael (1841-1929). English scholar; defended Shakespeare in *Bacon-Shakespeare Question* (1888); author of *Shakespeare's Warwickshire Contemporaries* (1897), *Shakespeare's Family* (1901), *Burbage and Shakespeare's Stage* (1913) and *The Life of Henry, Third Earl of Southampton* (1922), identifying him as the friend of the *Sonnets,* and other works.

Strachey, (Giles) Lytton (1880-1932). English critic, biographer, essayist; member of the "Bloomsbury Group" of writers and artists; author of *Shakespeare's Final Period* (1906) and *Landmarks in French Literature* (1912), which compares the works of Racine and Shakespeare.

Swinburne, Algernon Charles (1837-1909). English poet, critic; primarily a lyric poet; author of *A Study of Shakespeare* (1880), *Shakespeare* (1909) and *Three Plays of Shakespeare* (1909); best known for criticism of *King Lear.*

Taine, Hippolyte Adolphe (1828-93). French historian, philosopher and critic; forerunner of French naturalism; his *Histoire de la littérature anglaise* (1856-65), which gained him an international reputation, contains important criticism of Shakespeare's work.

Tannenbaum, Samuel Aaron (1874-1948). Hungarian-American scholar; study of Elizabethan handwriting in *Problems in Shakspere's Penmanship* (1927); in *Shakspere Forgeries in the Revels Accounts* (1928) contended the manuscript a forgery; editor, Shakespeare Association

Bulletin (1934-47); donated his large Shakespeare library to the University of North Carolina.

Thorndike, Ashley Horace (1871-1933). American scholar; professor of English, Columbia University (from 1906); edited (with W. A. Neilson) the *Tudor Shakespeare* (39 vols., 1911-13); author of *Influence of Beaumont and Fletcher on Shakespeare* (1901), *The Facts About Shakespeare* (with Neilson, 1913); *Shakespeare's Theater* (1916) and *Shakespeare in America* (1927); first president of the Shakespeare Society of America.

Tieck, Johann Ludwig (1773-1853). German author; translated pre-Shakespearean dramas in *Alt-Englische Theater* (2 vols., 1811) and *Shakespeares Vorschule* (2 vols., 1823, 1829); completed von Schlegel's translations of the plays which became the standard German translation; essays and other critical writing.

Tillyard, Eustace M. W. (1889-1962). English scholar; Master of Jesus College, Cambridge (1945-59); author of *Shakespeare's Last Plays* (1938), *Shakespeare's History Plays* (1944) and *Shakespeare's Problem Plays* (1949).

Tolstoy, Count Lev (Leo) (1828-1910). Russian novelist; famed author of *War and Peace* (1865-69) and *Anna Karenina* (1875-77); essay, "Shakespeare and the Drama" (1906) attacked Shakespeare in detailed analysis of *King Lear*. See Orwell.

Traversi, Derek A. (1912-). English critic; author of *An Approach to Shakespeare* (1938); *Shakespeare: The Last Phase* (1954), *Shakespeare: from Richard II to Henry V* (1957), and *Shakespeare: The Roman Plays* (1963).

Trewin, John Courtenay (1908-

). English critic and author; literary and drama editor, the *Observer;* author of many books on the production of Shakespeare's plays, including *The Shakespeare Memorial Theatre* (1932), *The Stratford Festival* (1953) and *Shakespeare on the English Stage, 1900-1964* (1964).

Tyler, Thomas (1826-1902). English scholar; an original member of the New Shakspere Society; author of *The Philosophy of Hamlet* (1874); first to advance the theory that the Dark Lady of the *Sonnets* was Mary Fitton (1890).

Ulrici, Hermann (1806-84). German religious philosopher, scholar and critic; author of *Uber Shakespeares Dramatische Kunst* (1830), translated into English as *Shakespeare's Dramatic Art* (1846, third edition, 1876); influenced Furnivall and the New Shakspere Society.

Viëtor, Wilhelm (1850-1918). German philologist; wrote standard work, *Shakespeare's Pronunciation* (1906).

Vigny, Comte Alfred Victor de (1797-1863). French Romantic poet, dramatist and novelist; translated *Othello* (1839) and *Merchant of Venice* (retitled *Shylock*) into French verse.

Voltaire (François Arouet) (1694-1778). French writer; leading figure of the Age of Enlightenment; expressed his critical opinions of Shakespeare in his *Lettres philosophiques sur les anglais* (1734).

Voss, Johann Heinrich (1751-1826). German poet; translated Homer, Vergil, Horace; with sons Heinrich and Abraham, translated Shakespeare into German (pub., 1819-29).

Wallace, Charles William (1865-1932). American scholar; professor of English Dramatic Literature, University of Nebraska

(1912); extensive research (with his wife, 1907-16); discovered many important Shakespearean documents including the suit of *Belott v. Mountjoy;* author of *Globe Theatre Apparel* (1909), *Keysar v. Burbage and Others* (1910), *The Evolution of the English Drama up to Shakespeare* (1912).

Wendell, Barrett (1855-1921). American critic; professor at Harvard (from 1898); author of excellent work of criticism, *William Shakespeare: a Study in Elizabethan Literature* (1894).

White, Richard Grant (1821-85). American scholar; edited the *Works of William Shakespeare* (12 vols., 1857-66; reprinted as *Riverside Shakespeare,* 1883), best edition of his time; author of *Shakespeare's Scholar* (1854) and *Studies in Shakespeare* (1886).

Wieland, Christoph Martin (1733-1833). German poet; published prose translations of 22 of Shakespeare's plays (1762-66), the first in German; important influence in German literature.

Wilson, Frank Percy (1889-1963). English scholar; Merton Professor of English Literature, Oxford (1947-57), author of *The Plague in Shakespeare's London* (1927), *Shakespeare and the Diction of Common Life* (1941), *Marlowe and the Early Shakespeare* (1953) and important articles.

Wilson, John Dover (1881-   ). Outstanding English scholar; Regius Professor of Rhetoric and English Literature, University of Edinburgh (1936-45); co-editor (until 1944) with Quiller-Couch, of the New Cambridge Shakespeare (from 1921); author of *Life in Shakespeare's England* (1911), *The Essential Shakespeare* (1932), *What Happens in Hamlet* (1935), *The Fortunes of Falstaff* (1943) and *Shakespeare's Happy Comedies* (1962); in his *Introduction to the Sonnets of Shakespeare* (1964), he suggests William Herbert, third Earl of Pembroke, as the friend of the *Sonnets.*

Wright, Louis Booker (1899-   ). American director of the Folger Shakespeare Library, Washington, D.C. (from 1948); best known book, *Middle-Class Culture in Elizabethan England* (1935); co-editor with Virginia A. LaMar of the Folger paperback edition of the plays and *Life and Letters in Tudor and Stuart England* (1962); wrote *Shakespeare for Everyman* (1964).

Wright, Thomas (1810-77). English scholar; one of the founders of the Shakespeare Society (1840); edited *Queen Elizabeth and Her Times,* a series of original letters (1838); *Dictionary of Obsolete and Provincial English* (1857); with Halliwell-Phillips, revised edition of Nare's *Glossary of Shakespeare* (1859).

Wyndham, George (1863-1913). English author; essays and notes for *Shakespeare's Poems* (1868) outstanding; *Essays in Romantic Literature* (1919) contain those on Shakespeare.

PEOPLE OF THE THEATER

Members of the Shakespearean Contemporary Theater

ADMIRAL'S MEN

Name	Listed	Name	Listed
Alleyn, Edward	1585	Massey, Charles	1613
Bird (Borne), William	1597	Parr, William	1613
Brian, George	1585	Phillips, Augustine	1585
Cartwright, William	1613	Pope, Thomas	1585
Colbrand, Edward	1613	Price, Richard	1613
Donstone, James	1594	Rowley, Samuel	1613
Downton, Thomas	1594	Shank, John	1613
Grace, Frank	1613	Shaw, Robert	1597
Gunnell, Richard	1613	Singer, John	1594
Heminges, John	1585	Slater, Martin	1594
Jeffs, Humfrey	1613	Spencer, Gabriel	1597
Jones, Richard	1594	Stratford, William	1613
Juby, Edward	1594	Towne, Thomas	1594
Kempe, William	1585		

ACTORS OF THE CHAMBERLAIN'S-KING'S MEN (SHAKESPEARE'S COMPANY)

Name	Date of Joining	Name	Date of Joining
Armin, Robert	1599	Heminges, John	1594
Beeston, Christopher	c1598	Kempe, William	1594
Benfield, Robert	1614	Lowine, John	1603
Bryan, George	1594	Ostler, William	1608
Burbage, Richard	1594	Phillips, Augustine	1594
Condell, Henry	1594	Pope, Thomas	1594
Cooke, Alexander	1603	Rice, John	1620
Cowley, Richard	1594	Robinson, Richard	1611
Crosse, Samuel	1604	Sands, James	1605 (?)
Duke, John	1594 (?)	Shakespeare, William	1594
Ecclestone, William	1610	Shancke, John	1615
Field, Nathan	1616	Slye, William	1594
Fletcher, Lawrence	1603 (?)	Taylor, Joseph	1619
Gilburne, Samuel	1605	Tooley, Nicholas	1605
Goughe, Robert	1603	Underwood, John	1608

Important Contemporary Dramatists

Barnes, Barnabe, 1569-1609
Beaumont, Francis, 1584-1616
Chapman, George, c1560-1634
Chettle, Henry, c1560-c1607
Daborne, Richard, c1580-1628
Daniel, Samuel, 1563-1619
Day, John, c1574-c1640
Dekker, Thomas, c1572-1637
Drayton, Michael, 1563-1631
Fletcher, John, 1579-1625
Ford, John, 1586-c1639
Greene, Robert, 1558-92
Hathway, Richard, c1570-c1610
Haughton, William, c1575-1605
Heywood, Thomas, c1570-1641
Jonson, Ben, 1572-1637

Kyd, Thomas, 1558-94
Lodge, Thomas, c1557-1625
Lyly, John, c1554-1606
Marlowe, Christopher, 1564-93
Marston, John, c1575-1634
Massinger, Philip, 1583-1640
Middleton, Thomas, c1570-1627
Munday, Anthony, c1553-1633
Nashe, Thomas, 1567-c1601
Peele, George, c1557-96
Rowley, Samuel, c1570-c1630
Rowley, William, c1580-c1635
Tourneur, Cyril, c1575-1626
Webster, John, c1580-c1630
Wilson, Robert, c1550-c1605

Actors, Actresses, Directors and Producers

Abington, Frances Barton (1737-1815). English actress; associated with David Garrick at Drury Lane; played Shakespearean heroines and great ladies of comedy.

Adams, Maude (1872-1953). American actress; first appeared with E. H. Sothern's company (1888); worked with John Drew (1892-97); played Rosalind in *As You Like It* (1910), Portia in Otis Skinner's touring company production of *The Merchant of Venice* (1931) and Maria in *Twelfth Night* (1937) in summer theaters.

Aldridge, Ira Frederick (c1805-67). American Negro actor; protégé of Edmund Kean; debut as Othello at the Royalty Theatre, London (1826); acclaimed and honored in Europe (1853-56; 1858-67); played Othello, Aaron, Lear and Macbeth.

Allen, Viola (1869-1948). American actress; debut, New York (1882); gave series of Shakespearean revivals in New York (1904); played in *Twelfth Night, The Merchant of Venice, The Winter's Tale* and *Cymbeline*.

Alleyn, Edward (called Ned) (1566-1626). English actor; member of provincial company of Earl of Worcester (1583); joined Admiral's Men (c1590-97); married Joan Woodward, stepdaughter of Philip Henslowe; formed successful partnership with Henslowe in the management of the Rose and the Fortune theaters; considered a genius; performed works by Marlowe and Shakespeare.

Alleyn, John (c1551-96). English actor; elder brother of above; with provincial company of Lord Sheffield (1580), with Admiral's (1589-91).

Ames, Winthrop (1871-1937). American theatrical manager; managing director of the New Theatre and Booth Theatre, New York; produced *Antony and Cleopatra, Twelfth Night, The Merry Wives of Windsor, Will Shakespeare;* retired (1932).

Anderson, Dame Judith (1898-). Australian-American actress; first appearance in Sydney (1915); New York debut (1918); outstanding performances as Gertrude in Gielgud's *Hamlet* (1936), Lady Macbeth (1941), Medea (1947), played in *Hamlet* (1970); appeared in several TV productions of *Macbeth*.

Anderson, Mary Antoinette (1859-1940). American actress; debut as Juliet in *Romeo and Juliet*, Louisville, Kentucky (1875); in London (1883-89); played Rosalind in *As You Like It* at the opening of the Memorial Theatre, Stratford-on-Avon (1885); played Perdita in *The Winter's Tale* (doubling as Hermione; the first actress to do so); retired (1889); married and settled in England.

Anglin, Margaret (1876-1946). American actress; debut (1894); revived *As You Like It, The Taming of the Shrew* and *Twelfth Night* (1914); produced *As You Like It*, St. Louis (1916); last appearance (1943).

Armin, Robert (Robin) (d. 1615). English actor and playwright; joined Chamberlain's company (1599); excellent comedian; Shakespeare probably wrote the parts of Feste, Touchstone and the Fool in *Lear* for Armin; played Dogberry in *Much Ado*; with the King's Men (1603-1610); wrote *Nest of Ninnies* (1608); *Two Maids of Moreclack* (1609) etc.

Asche, Oscar (1871-1936). English actor, playwright, producer; debut (1893); managed the Adelphi, His Majesty's and Globe theaters; played Casca in *Julius Caesar* (1932), appeared in *The Merry Wives of Windsor* (1929).

Atkins, Robert (1886-   ). English actor and director; debut with Beerbohm Tree's company, London; joined Old Vic (1915); director (1920-25); produced *Henry V* at Stratford (1934); director there (1944-45).

Bancroft, Lady Marie Effie Wilton (1839-1921). English actress; debut in London (1856); with her husband, Sir Squire Bancroft (1841-1926), managed the old Prince of Wales' Theatre (1865-80) and the Haymarket Theatre (1880-85); appeared in *The Merchant of Venice* among others.

Barrault, Jean-Louis (1910-   ). French actor and director; worked with famous Comédie-Française; established own theatrical troupe, after World War II, with his wife, actress Madeleine Renaud; famous as Hamlet (first played, 1941); acted Hamlet again in André Gide's adaptation of the play (1946); successful performance in New York (1952).

Barrett, Lawrence (1838-91). American actor; leading performer in Boston Museum Theater (1858); served in Civil War; (with Lewis Baker) managed theater in New Orleans (1863-64); joint manager (with John McCullough) of the California Theater, San Francisco (1867-70); close associate of Edwin Booth; played with him in *Richard III;* played Shylock, Lear, Hamlet, Cassius and Othello; wrote biographies of theater personalities.

Barry, Ann (Street) (1734-1801). English actress; wife of Spranger Barry (see below); played Cordelia in *King Lear* at Crow Street Theatre, Dublin (1758); her portrayal of Desdemona in *Othello* was said to rival that of Mrs. Siddons; superb comedienne; retired (1798); buried in Westminster Abbey.

Barry, Elizabeth (1658-1713). Considered first great actress of English stage; not particularly successful until she joined Betterton as leading actress of his company (1680-1710); played Cordelia in Nahum Tate's rewritten *King Lear;* played Hamlet, Desdemona, Mrs. Page, Lady Macbeth etc.

Barry, Spranger (1719-77). Irish actor; debut (1744); first London appearance as Othello, his most famous role, Drury Lane (1746); successful as Macbeth, Romeo and Hamlet; performed at Covent Garden (1750); rival of Garrick; built and managed the Crow Street Theatre, Dublin; returned to the stage at Drury Lane, under Garrick (c1770); with his wife Ann (see above) moved to Covent Garden (1774).

Barrymore, Ethel (1879-1959). American actress; daughter of Maurice and Georgiana Drew Barrymore and sister of Lionel and John; starred under Charles Frohman's management (1900); played in *Hamlet* (1925) with Walter Hampden; opened the Ethel Barrymore Theater, New York (1928).

Barrymore, Georgiana Emma Drew (1856-93). American comedienne; daughter of John Drew, wife of Maurice, mother of Ethel, John and Lionel; appeared in Augustin Daly's company; played in *As You Like It*.

Barrymore, John Blythe (1882-1942). American actor; son of Maurice and Georgiana; debut (1903) in Chicago; won acclaim for portrayal of Richard III (1920); famed for his performance in *Hamlet* (1920); played same role at Haymarket Theatre in London (1925); in many films including *Romeo and Juliet* in which he played an exceptional Mercutio.

Barrymore, Lionel (1878-1954). American actor; best known for films and television performances; played Macbeth (1921).

Barrymore, Maurice (originally Herbert Blythe) (1847-1905). English actor; leading man with Helena Modjeska, Lily Langtry and Mrs. Minnie Maddern Fiske; debut (1872); husband of Georgiana, father of John, Ethel and Lionel.

Baylis, Lilian (1874-1937). Extremely successful English theater manager of the Old Vic; succeeded her aunt, Emma Cons, as manager of the Royal Victoria Hall and Coffee Tavern, which became known as the Old Vic; introduced opera and Shakespeare; took over the Sadler's Wells Theatre (1931) for ballet and opera, leaving Shakespearean drama at Old Vic.

Beeston, Christopher (?1570-1638). English comedian; listed with the Chamberlain's Men (1598); co-owner of the Cockpit Theatre (1616-17); son William (d. 1682) was also an actor.

Bellamy, George Anne (c1731-88). English actress; debut, Covent Garden (1742); played Juliet to Garrick's Romeo at Drury Lane (1750), in rival performance to that of Mrs. Cibber and Spranger Barry.

Benefield, Robert. English; a principal actor in Shakespeare's plays; member King's Men (1615); one of three who petitioned the Lord Chamberlain for the right to acquire shares in the Globe and Blackfriars (1635).

Benson, Sir Francis (Frank) Robert (1858-1939). English actor and theater manager; Paris in *Romeo and Juliet* under Irving at the Lyceum Theater (1882); formed his own Shakespearean touring company (1883); established Shakespeare Festival at Stratford, managed (from 1887); known for production of the history plays; portrayed Hamlet (1900); knighted (1916).

Benthall, Michael (1919-). English director; debut (1938); co-directed (with Tyrone Guthrie) *Hamlet* for Old Vic at New Theatre (1944); became director at Stratford (1947) with *The*

Merchant of Venice; directed *As You Like It* (New York, 1950); director of Old Vic (from 1953); directed production of *Macbeth* (Covent Garden, 1960).

Bergner, Elisabeth (1900-   ). Austrian actress; played Ophelia in *Hamlet* with Alexander Moissi; appeared in several Shakespearean productions at the Deutscher-Volkstheater under Max Reinhardt (c1925); appeared as Portia in *The Merchant of Venice* (1927); toured in *Romeo and Juliet* (1928); in London and New York (from 1933); played in the film version of *As You Like It* (1936).

Bernhardt, Sarah (originally Rosine Bernard) (1844-1923). French actress; played Cordelia in French version of *King Lear* (1872); first American tour (1880); played the leading role in *Hamlet* (1899).

Betterton, Thomas (c1635-1710). English actor, dramatist; joined Davenant's company at Lincoln's Inn Fields (1661); opened new playhouse there (1695); married Mary Saunderson (1662, see below); traveled to France at the command of Charles II and adapted French stage design to the British theater; praised by Pepys, Pope and others for his portrayal of Hamlet, Lear, Falstaff, Macbeth, Othello and King Henry VIII.

Betty, William Henry West (called the Young Roscius) (1791-1874). British actor; gained tremendous success in Dublin, Glasgow and Edinburgh; first appearance at Covent Garden (1804) drew huge crowds; most successful as Hamlet.

Booth, Barton (1681-1733). English actor; began his career in Ireland; acted with Betterton, succeeded him as great tragic actor of the period; at Drury Lane (after 1708); noted for portrayals of Lear, Othello, Coriolanus and Henry VIII; married actress, Hester Santlow, who appeared in many Shakespearean productions; buried in Westminster Abbey.

Booth, Edwin Thomas (1833-93). American actor, first to gain a European reputation; son of Junius Brutus Booth (below); debut with his father in *Richard III* (1849); manager of the Winter Garden Theatre, New York (1862-67); produced a number of Shakespeare's plays; built Booth Theatre in New York (1869); famous for portrayal of Hamlet; played most of the leading roles in original versions of the plays; founded the Players Club, New York (1888).

Booth, John Wilkes (1838-65). American actor; son of Junius Brutus, brother of Edwin; debut (1855); acclaimed as a Shakespearean actor, although he is remembered as the assassin of Abraham Lincoln.

Booth, Junius Brutus (1796-1852). English actor; first appearance at Covent Garden (1815); rival of Edmund Kean (although he played Iago to Kean's Othello); noted for portrayals of Richard III, Shylock and Iago; settled in the United States (1821) where he successfully popularized Shakespeare's plays; as manager of Adelphi Theater, Baltimore, introduced Charles Kean to American audiences; married Mary Anne Holmes; father of Edwin, John and Junius Brutus, Jr. (1821-83), all actors.

Bracegirdle, Anne (c.1673-1748). English actress; played with Thomas Betterton; known for performances as Desdemona, Juliet, Ophelia, Isabella, Cordelia and Portia.

Bridges-Adams, William (1889-

1965). English director; played Shakespearean repertory; directed Shakespeare Festival at Stratford (1919-34); founded and organized the New Shakespeare Company; toured Canada and U.S. with Stratford company; author of several books.

Brook, Peter (Stephen Paul) (1925-). English producer and co-director, Shakespeare Memorial Theatre (now Royal Shakespeare Theatre); produced *Romeo and Juliet* (1947), *Titus Andronicus* (1954), *The Tempest* (1956) and *King Lear* (1962) among others; composed music and designed sets for *Titus Andronicus* and *The Tempest;* directed *Hamlet* at Moscow Art Theatre (1955); produced unusual version of *A Midsummer Night's Dream,* New York (1971); television production of *King Lear* (1953).

Browne, Robert. English actor; with Alleyn in Worcester's company (1583); with John Bradstreet, Thomas Sackville and Richard Jones toured Europe (especially Germany) with a repertory of English plays (1592-93, c1594-99, 1601-07, 1618-20).

Bullock, Christopher (c1690-1724). English actor, playwright; played comedy roles; wrote adaptation of Induction to *The Taming of the Shrew (The Cobler of Preston)* produced in competition with Drury Lane company; wife, Jane Rogers (d. 1739) played Lady Macbeth, Cressida and other roles.

Burbage, Cuthbert (1566-1636). English theater manager; elder son of James (below); popular with the King's Men; owned a share in the Theatre, the Globe and Blackfriars.

Burbage (or Burbadge), James (c1530-97). English actor, theater manager; one of Leicester's Men; married Ellen, the sister of John Brayne, who gave Burbage the money to build "the Theatre" (the first in England) on property he owned; bought part of Blackfriars priory (1596) which he converted into a private theater; father of Cuthbert and Richard.

Burbage, Richard (c1567-1619). English actor and theater manager; one of the principal actors in Shakespeare's plays; younger son of James and brother of Cuthbert; rivaled Alleyn as outstanding actor of company; became leading player of Chamberlain's Men and of King's Men (after 1603); close friend of Shakespeare's; owned the largest share in the Globe and Blackfriars theaters.

Burt, Nicholas. English actor; member of Killigrew's company; played Othello (1660; mentioned by Pepys); also appeared as the Prince in a revival of *1 Henry IV*.

Burton, Richard (1925-). English actor; debut, Liverpool (1943); appeared as Hamlet with Old Vic, Edinburgh Festival (1953), for 210 performances in all; also appeared as Sir Toby Belch, Coriolanus, the Bastard *(King John),* Caliban, Iago and Othello; achieved great success in Gielgud's rehearsal-dress *Hamlet* produced in Canada and New York (1964); film and television star.

Campbell, Mrs. Patrick (maiden name, Beatrice Stella Tanner) (1865-1940). English actress; debut, Liverpool (1888); joined Ben Greet's company; appeared as Rosalind in *As You Like It,* Ophelia in *Hamlet,* Lady Macbeth and Juliet in *Romeo and Juliet;* first New York appearance (1902).

Cartwright, William (c1606-54). English actor; member of Admiral's Men (1613-1622), King's Revels company (1629-37); played Falstaff in *1 Henry IV* (mentioned in Pepys).

Cibber, Colley (1671-1757). English actor, dramatist, theater manager; member, Betterton's company (1690); minor roles, London Theatre Royal (1691); wrote *Love's Last Shift, or the Fool in Fashion* (1696), first play produced at Drury Lane Theatre; played Wolsey, Gloucester, Jaques, Iago, Shallow in versions of the plays popular at the time; adapted *Richard III* (1700; popular until 1821); wrote many plays, masques, etc.; co-manager of the Drury Lane (1711-32); much maligned Poet Laureate (1730).

Cibber, Susanna Maria (1714-66). English actress; wife of Theophilus (below) for a short time; began her career in opera (Haymarket, 1732); joined Garrick's company; played Constance (most popular role) in *King John,* Juliet, Cordelia, Desdemona, Lady Macbeth and Perdita in *The Winter's Tale.*

Cibber, Theophilus (1703-58). English actor and dramatist; son of Colley Cibber (above); produced his own version of *Henry VI,* parts 2 and 3 (1723), *Romeo and Juliet* (1744) and *Henry VIII;* played Pistol (most popular role) in *The Merry Wives* and *Henry V,* and Parolles in *All's Well.*

Clive, Catherine (Kitty Raftor) (1711-85). English comedienne; worked with Colley Cibber at Drury Lane (1728); played Portia in *The Merchant of Venice,* first play produced by Garrick as manager of Drury Lane (1747); Catherine in Garrick's *Catherine and Petruchio,* his version of *The Taming of the Shrew;* also appeared as Ophelia in *Romeo and Juliet,* Olivia in

Twelfth Night and Celia in *As You Like It;* retired (1769).

Coburn, Charles Douville (1877-1961). American actor; with his wife, Ivah (1882-1937), organized the Coburn Shakespearean Players (1906), which they maintained as a repertory company for many years; inaugurated the Mohawk Dramatic Festival, Schenectady, New York (1934); presented *The Merry Wives of Windsor;* popular in motion pictures.

Collier, Constance (1878-1955). English actress; debut as a fairy in *A Midsummer Night's Dream;* first London appearance (1893); with Sir Beerbohm Tree's company (1901-08), she acted in *Twelfth Night, Antony and Cleopatra* and *The Merchant of Venice;* played Gertrude to John Barrymore's Hamlet and Desdemona to Faversham's Iago in *Othello* (1914).

Colman, George (the Elder) (1732-94). English dramatist, theater manager; wrote the satirical farce, *The Jealous Wife* (1761), successfully produced by Garrick; as acting manager of Covent Garden (1767-74), produced versions of Shakespeare's plays and Oliver Goldsmith's comedies; bought the Haymarket Theatre (1777); turned over the management of the Haymarket (1789) to his son, George (1762-1836); wrote about 30 plays.

Condell (Cundell), Henry (d. 1627). English actor; one of the principal actors in Shakespeare's plays; joined the Chamberlain's (1594); with Heminges published the First Folio (1623) in memory of his close friend; one of the original housekeepers of the Blackfriars (1608); acquired shares in the Globe (1612).

Cooke, George Frederick (1756-1811). English actor; gained recognition for his portrayal of Othello in Dublin; first appeared at Covent Garden, London (1800), as Richard III; toured the United States (1810-11); played Falstaff, Shylock, Iago and Henry VIII; rival of Kemble; acted with Mrs. Siddons; died in New York.

Cornell, Katharine (1898-). American actress; debut, New York (1916); married Guthrie McClintic (1921), director, producer; appeared in *Will Shakespeare* (1923), *Romeo and Juliet* (1934) and *Antony and Cleopatra* (1947).

Cowl, Jane (1890-1950). American actress; debut (1903); appeared in *Romeo and Juliet* (1923), *Antony and Cleopatra* (1924) and *Twelfth Night* (1930).

Craig, Edward Gordon (1872-1966). English actor, producer, scenic and costume designer; son of Ellen Terry; acted in Sir Henry Irving's company; designed sets for Eleonora Duse, Florence (1906); founder of *The Mask* (1908), a theater arts journal; author of books on the theater; designed simple sets for Shakespearean productions; influenced Granville-Barker and others.

Cushman, Charlotte Saunders (1816-76). First outstanding American actress; best known for portrayal of Lady Macbeth; started in opera; performed in New Orleans, then went on tour with Macready; played Romeo at the Haymarket, London (1845), to her sister Susan's Juliet; played Wolsey and Queen Katherine in *Henry VIII;* considered a great tragic actress.

Daly, Augustin (John Augustin) (1838-99). American playwright and theater manager; opened Daly's Theater, New York (1879) and Daly's London

(1893); produced most of Shakespeare's comedies adapted to his own style; his production of *The Tempest* (1897) very successful; Ada Rehan, John Drew, Fanny Davenport and Otis Skinner were members of his company.

Dance, James (1722-74). English actor known best for his portrayal of Falstaff; wrote an adaptation of *Timon of Athens* (1768) and produced it in his own theater in Richmond.

Davenant, Sir William (1606-68). English dramatist, poet, theater manager; made Poet Laureate (1638); produced masques in association with Inigo Jones; wrote and produced his *Siege of Rhodes* (1656), the first English "opera," it marked the first appearance of a woman on the English stage; organized the Duke's company after the Restoration; with Betterton opened a theater in Lincoln's Inn Fields (1661); with John Dryden (1667) produced *The Tempest, or the Enchanted Island,* the most famous of his adaptations; buried in the Poet's Corner, Westminster Abbey; claimed by some to have been Shakespeare's illegitimate son.

Davenport, Edward Loomis (1815-77). American actor; appeared with Junius Brutus Booth and with Macready in London; scored greatest success as Brutus in *Julius Caesar.*

Davenport, Fanny Lily Sipsy (1850-98). American actress, daughter of above; debut (1858); acted under the management of Mrs. John Drew and Augustin Daly; successful in the roles of Ophelia in *Romeo and Juliet,* Rosalind in *As You Like It* and Mistress Ford in *The Merry Wives of Windsor.*

Drew, John (1827-62). Irish-American actor-manager; debut,

Bowery Theatre, New York (1846); gained popularity in Philadelphia (from 1852); with William Wheatley, managed the Arch Street Theatre, where he co-starred with his wife, Louisa (below).

Drew, John (1853-1927). American actor; eldest son of above; debut in Philadelphia (1873); with Daly's company in New York (from 1875); joined his brother-in-law, Maurice Barrymore, in barnstorming tour in Shakespearean roles; returned to Daly's (1879-93); played opposite Ada Rehan in *The Taming of the Shrew* and *As You Like It;* played 100 performances of *Twelfth Night* in London (1893).

Drew, Louisa Lane (1820-97). American actress-manager; wife of John (above); born in London, came to the United States (1827); debut with Junius Brutus Booth in *Richard III* in Philadelphia; assumed control of the Arch Street Theatre upon her husband's death; mother of three successful children: John, Sidney and Georgiana Drew Barrymore.

Du Maurier, Sir Gerald (1873-1934). English actor, producer; debut (1894); toured with Forbes-Robertson and Beerbohm Tree; played in *Hamlet* and other Shakespearean revivals.

Duse, Eleonora (also Eleanora) (1859-1924). Italian actress; played Juliet when 14 years of age; first real success (1878); appeared in the United States (1893); rivaled Bernhardt in London (acclaimed as superior by Shaw); associated with Gabriele D'Annunzio; appeared in eight performances at the Metropolitan Opera House, New York (1923).

Elliston, Robert William (1774-1831). English actor, manager; debut in *Richard III* at the Bath Theatre (1791); played leading Shakespearean roles; moved to London (1796); became a lessee of Drury Lane (1819) and one of the most successful theater managers of his day; last appearance as Falstaff (1826); best known for portrayals of Hamlet, Romeo and Hotspur.

Evans, Dame Edith (1888-   ). English actress; debut as Cressida, King's Hall, Covent Garden (1912); appeared as Gertrude in *Hamlet* (1914); toured with Ellen Terry in scenes from Shakespeare's plays (1918); became an accomplished Shakespearean actress at the Old Vic (from 1925); know for performances as Portia, Cleopatra, Beatrice, Rosalind and the nurse in *Romeo and Juliet;* created a Dame of the British Empire (1946).

Evans, Maurice (1901-   ). English actor-manager; debut, Festival Theatre, Cambridge (1926); in London (1927); joined Old Vic-Sadler's Wells company (1934), playing in six Shakespearean productions; toured the United States as Romeo to Katharine Cornell's Juliet (1935); produced and played title role in *Richard II* (1937); played unabridged *Hamlet,* New York (1938); appeared as Falstaff in *Henry IV* (1939), in *Twelfth Night* (1940) with Helen Hayes; produced and appeared in *Macbeth* (1941); became U.S. citizen (1941); appeared as Hamlet, Richard II, Prospero and Macbeth, and directed *Twelfth Night, The Taming of the Shrew* and *The Tempest* for television.

Faucit, Helena Saville (Lady Martin) (1817-98). English actress; debut at Covent Garden, London (1836); acted with Macready, whom she accompanied on a Paris tour (1844-45); best known for her portrayals of Portia, Desdemona and Juliet; her last appearance was as Beatrice in *Much Ado* at the opening of the Memorial Theatre, Stratford-on-Avon (1879).

Faversham, William (real name, William Jones) (1868-1940). American actor; born in London; debut (1887); arrived in New York (1888); joined Charles Frohman's Empire Theater Company (1893); played Romeo to Maude Adams' Juliet; starred as Antony in *Julius Caesar* (1912) and as Iago in *Othello* (1914).

Fechter, Charles Albert (1825-79). Started his very successful career as an actor in Paris; to London (1860) where he appeared as Hamlet, Othello and Iago; performed in the United States (after 1870); as manager of Lyceum Theater, New York, he was responsible for many stage innovations.

Fiske, Minnie Maddern (originally Mary Augusta Davey) (1865-1932). American actress; played Prince Arthur in production of *King John* at Booth Theatre, New York (1874); most famous for her performances in plays by Ibsen.

Foote, Samuel (1720-77). English actor and dramatist; first stage appearance as Othello (1744) was a failure; opened the Haymarket Theatre (1747) with *Diversions of the Morning* in which his exceptional talent for mimicry won him fame; granted a royal patent for the Haymarket by the Duke of York (c1766).

Forbes-Robertson, Jean (1905-). English actress; daughter of Sir Johnston (below); London debut (1925); appeared in *Twelfth Night, Romeo and Juliet* and other Shakespeare plays.

Forbes-Robertson, Sir Johnston (1853-1937). English actor; debut, Princess Theatre, London (1874); played Claudio in *Much Ado* and Buckingham in *Henry VIII* (with Irving and Terry), best known for his excellent portrayal of Hamlet; took over management of the Lyceum Theatre (1895) when he appeared as Romeo to Mrs. Patrick Campbell's Juliet; toured America several times in Shakespearean roles; knighted (1913).

Forrest, Edwin (1806-72). American actor; debut (1820); played Othello, New York (1826); gained fame in London (1836); successful until his performance as Macbeth was hissed in London (1845); probably best as Lear; rivalry with Macready believed to have caused Astor Place Riot (1849); last appearance, New York (1871).

Frohman, Charles (1860-1915). American manager in the U.S. and London (after 1897); organized the Charles Frohman Stock Company (1890); some of his stars included Maude Adams, Margaret Anglin, Ethel Barrymore, May Robson, Otis Skinner and others.

Frohman, Daniel (1851-1940). American manager; brother of above; first stock company included Henry Miller, William Faversham, Effie Shannon, Henrietta Crosman, May Robson and James K. Hackett; David Belasco worked as his stage manager.

Garrick, David (1717-79). English actor, manager, author; studied with Samuel Johnson (1736), accompanied him to London (1737); gained fame as Richard III, Goodman's Fields Theatre (1741); took over management of the Drury Lane Theatre (with Lacy, 1747-76); revolutionized acting techniques; produced 27 of Shakespeare's plays, rewriting some, presenting others in the original; developed stage lighting and effects; organized the Shakespeare Jubilee at Stratford (1769), failed; wrote or adapted almost 50 plays; died a very wealthy man; last actor to be buried in Westminster Abbey.

Gémier, Firmin (1866-1934). French actor, producer; director of the Odéon (1921-30); founder of the Shakespeare Society of France; brought his own company to New York for a three weeks' engagement (1924).

Gielgud, Sir (Arthur) John (1904-). Outstanding English actor; member of the famed Terry family; debut as the Herald in *Henry V* at the Old Vic (Nov., 1921); played Romeo (1924); considered the best Hamlet of his generation, he first appeared in the role (1930); again in Hamlet (London, 1934, New York, 1936, Elsinore, 1939); fine performance as Richard II (1938); returned to Old Vic in *King Lear* and *The Tempest* (1940); produced and appeared in many of Shakespeare's plays for the Sadler's Wells Company (from 1931); appeared in motion pictures as Cassius in *Julius Caesar* (1952) and as the Duke of Clarence in Olivier's *Richard III* (1955); presentation of speeches from Shakespeare, *The Ages of Man* (Dec., 1958-60), compiled by George Rylands, for stage, television and records; played Othello at Stratford (1961); directed Burton in *Hamlet* (New York, 1964); knighted (1953).

Granville-Barker, Harley (1877-1946). English playwright, actor, manager; debut (1891); appeared in Shakespeare with Ben Greet and William Poel, acted with Elizabethan Stage Society; performed opposite Mrs. Patrick Campbell; with J. E. Vedrenne, managed the Court Theatre (from 1904); guest lecturer at Yale (1940-41) and Harvard (1941-43); presented Shakespeare at the Savoy Theatre (1912 and 1914) in dynamic new productions that had an important influence on future presentations; wrote *Prefaces to Shakespeare* (5 series, 1927-47), provocative, stimulating essays on the plays and their production; collaborated with G. B. Harrison in editing *A Companion to Shakespeare Studies* (1934).

Green, John. English actor; toured Europe during the reign of James I in Germany with Robert Browne's company (1618); presented several of Shakespeare's plays in Germany with his own repertory company (1626).

Greet, Sir (Phillip Barling) Ben (1857-1936). British actor-manager; first London appearance in *Cymbeline* (1883); played with Mary Anderson, Beerbohm Tree and others; most important for open-air performances of Shakespeare's plays given by his repertory company in England and the United States; joined Lilian Baylis at the Old Vic (1914), making that theater famous for its Shakespearean productions; gave performances for the schoolchildren of London (from 1918); founder and manager of a training school for theater arts; knighted (1929).

Guinness, Sir Alec (1914-). English actor; debut in Shakespearean role as Osric and the Third Player in *Hamlet*, and small parts in *Romeo and Juliet* (1935); joined the Old Vic (1936/7); played Osric with Old Vic at Elsinore (1937); joined Gielgud's company in *Richard II* and *The Merchant of Venice;*

rejoined Old Vic to play Hamlet (1938); appeared in many Shakespearean roles for the company; produced *Twelfth Night* (1948) and played and directed *Hamlet* (1951); famous as a motion picture actor; knighted (1959).

Guthrie, Sir (William) Tyrone (1900-71). English director; directed Scottish National Players (1926-31); first London production (1931); directed at the Old Vic (1933/4, 1936), acted as administrator (1939-45); directed *The Taming of the Shrew* (Helsingfors, 1949, Stratford, Ontario, 1954); *Hamlet* (Dublin, 1950); *A Midsummer Night's Dream* (1952) and *Henry VIII* (1953) at Old Vic; *The Merchant of Venice* (Israel, 1959); other productions in Ontario, London and New York; founded Tyrone Guthrie Theater, Minneapolis (1963); knighted (1961).

Hackett, James Henry (1800-71). American actor; first native-born actor of considerable talent; first appearance in New York (1826); first American actor to appear on the English stage as a star; outstanding as Falstaff, which he played first in Philadelphia (1832).

Hackett, James K. (Keteltas) (1869-1926). American actor-manager; son of above; played leading Shakespearean roles under Augustin Daly (1892); joined Frohman (1895); played under his own management at Hackett's Theatre, New York; best known for performances as Othello (1914) and Macbeth (1916).

Hall, Peter (Reginald Frederick) (1930-   ). English director, manager; directed first London production (1955); *Love's Labour's Lost* (Stratford, 1956); founded International Playwrights' Theatre (1957); directed *Cymbeline, Twelfth Night, A Midsummer Night's Dream, The Two Gentlemen of Verona* and *Troilus and Cressida* (from 1957) at Shakespeare Memorial Theatre; appointed director of Royal Shakespeare Company (1960).

Hampden, Walter (Dougherty) (1879-1955). American actor; debut, London (1901); played in Shakespearean productions there (1901-04); debut in New York (1907); leased the Colonial Theatre, New York (1925) which he renamed Hampden's Theatre; staged revivals of the plays; played Romeo (1905), Macbeth (1918), Hamlet and Othello (1925), Shylock in *The Merchant of Venice* (1926) and many other Shakespearean roles; became president of the Players following the death of John Drew.

Hardwicke, Sir Cedric (1863-1964). English actor; first appeared at Old Vic (1913); directed at the Lyric (1928), appeared in all-star *Hamlet* (First Gravedigger); became famous as motion picture actor; played Sir Toby at Old Vic (1948); knighted (1934).

Hare, Sir John (1844-1921). English actor-manager; joint manager (with Kendal) of the St. James' Theatre (1879-88), where he was a leading actor; sole manager of the Garrick Theatre (1889); outstanding manager of the Globe (1897); successfully toured the United States; knighted (1907).

Harris, Henry (c1634-1704). English actor; with Davenant's Duke's company; most famous as Cardinal Wolsey, also played Horatio in *Hamlet* (1661), Romeo (1662) and other Shakespearean roles; joint manager (with Betterton) of the Dorset Garden Theatre (1671).

Hart, Charles (d. 1683). English actor; believed to have been the illegitimate child of William Hart (son of Joan, Shakespeare's sister); apprentice to Richard Robinson at the Blackfriars, playing primarily women's parts; fought on the royal side during the civil war; joined Killigrew's company at the Theatre Royal (1663-82); best known for performances as Brutus in *Julius Caesar* and for Othello; mentioned as Nell Gwyn's first lover, he trained her for the stage.

Harvey, Sir John Martin (also Martin-Harvey) (1863-1944). English actor; member of Irving's company (1882-96); took over management of Lyceum Theatre (1899); successful in Shakespearean productions (with his wife, Helena de Silva); knighted (1921).

Hayes, George (1888-). English actor; played Osric in Forbes-Robertson's *Hamlet* and Roderigo in *Othello* (1912); toured U.S. with Beerbohm Tree's company (1915/16); acted at the Old Vic (from 1923); played with New Shakespeare Company at Stratford (1928-30); played many Shakespearean roles; appeared in motion pictures (from 1935).

Hayes, Helen (Brown) (1900-). American actress; debut in Broadway musical comedy (1908); best known for performance as Victoria Regina (1935-39); played opposite Maurice Evans in *Twelfth Night* (1940); has appeared in films; married playwright Charles MacArthur (1928).

Helpmann, Robert (1909-). Australian actor, dancer, choreographer; London debut (1933) with Vic-Wells ballet; played Oberon (1937), Hamlet (1944), King John and Shylock (Strat-ford, 1948); directed *The Tempest* (1954), *As You Like It* (1955), *Romeo and Juliet* (1956) and *Antony and Cleopatra* (1956/7) for Old Vic; choreographer for theater and films.

Heminges, John (c1556-1630). English actor; associated with the Chamberlain's Men (from 1594); served as chief director and business manager; played in *Henry IV* and several other plays; principal shareholder in the Globe and Blackfriars; close friend of Shakespeare's (who mentions him in his will); with Condell, edited the First Folio (1623).

Henderson, John (1747-85). English actor; first appearance as Hamlet at Bath (1772); played under the name of Courtney, known as the "Bath Roscius"; played Shylock, under Colman, at the Haymarket Theatre (1777) and won wide acclaim; performed for Sheridan at Drury Lane; excelled in Shakespearean roles at Covent Garden (from 1778).

Henslowe, Philip (d. 1616). English manager; owner of the Boar's Head and other inns; bought property in Southwark, on the Bankside (1585); built the Rose Theatre there (1587); with Edward Alleyn, built the Fortune Theatre (1600); Master of the Game of Paris Garden (with Alleyn, 1604), which was a monopoly on the staging of bull- and bear-baiting contests.

Hepburn, Katherine (1909-). American actress; best known for her successful films, she has appeared as Rosalind in *As You Like It* (New York, 1950); toured with Old Vic company in Australia (1955) as Portia, Katharina and Isabella in *Measure for Measure;* played Portia, Beatrice, Viola and Cleopatra at the American Shakespeare Festival, Stratford, Connecticut (1957, 1960).

Hughes, Margaret (c1643-1719). English actress; played Desdemona in the King's company production of *Othello* at the Theatre Royal (c1660); first appearance of a professional actress on the London stage; retired to become the mistress of Prince Rupert; returned to the stage with the Duke's company (1676).

Hull, Thomas (1782-1808). English actor, dramatist; appeared in secondary roles in Shakespeare's plays at Covent Garden (1759-1808); wrote adaptations of *Timon of Athens* (1786) and *The Comedy of Errors* (1793).

Irving, Sir Henry (John Henry Brodribb) (1838-1905). English actor-producer; first appeared in Bulwer Lytton's *Richelieu* at the Sunderland Theatre (1856); after playing in Edinburgh and Manchester, returned to London (1859); his career was firmly established with his portrayals of Hamlet, Othello, Richard III and Macbeth, Princess Theatre (1872-78); took over the management of the Lyceum Theatre (1878-1902) where he appeared with Ellen Terry in *Hamlet, The Merchant of Venice* (1879), *Romeo and Juliet, King Lear, Coriolanus* (1901) and many others; his portrayal of Becket in Tennyson's play is considered his greatest role; toured the United States several times with his company; his two sons, Henry Brodribb (1870-1919) and Laurence Sidney (1871-1941) were both actors and writers; knighted (1895), the first actor to receive this honor; buried in Westminster Abbey.

Jackson, Sir Barry Vincent (1879-1961). English theater manager and playwright; founded the Birmingham Repertory Company (1913); Governor of the Old Vic and Sadler's Wells companies; manager of the Malvern Summer Festivals (1929-37); director, Shakespeare Memorial Theatre (1945-48).

Jones, Inigo (1573-1652). English architect and stage designer; famed for staging royal masques; introduced many stage innovations from Italy; best known for collaboration with Ben Jonson; stage and scenic technique influenced development of English stage in 17th century.

Jordan, Dorothea (Dorothy Bland) (1762-1816). Irish actress; debut as Phebe in *As You Like It,* Dublin (1777); best known as a comedienne; especially popular in the roles of Viola, Rosalind and Imogen at the Drury Lane (1785-1809); mistress of the Duke of Clarence (William IV, 1790-1811), by whom she had ten children; known by the name of Fitz-Clarence, they were ennobled.

Kean, Charles John (1811-68). English actor; son of Edmund Kean (below); made his own reputation with his portrayal of Hamlet at Drury Lane (1838); married the actress, Ellen Tree (1842); with her as his leading lady, appeared in many Shakespearean roles; led a successful company for many years; with Robert Keeley, leased the Princess Theatre (1850-59).

Kean, Edmund (1787-1833). English actor; abandoned by his mother, Anne Carey, the actress; played children's parts (c1790-95); ran away to sea; played with various companies (1801-14); debut as Shylock in *The Merchant of Venice* at the Drury Lane (1814) was a sensation; played Hamlet, Othello, Richard III and Lear; considered the outstanding actor of his day; appeared in New York (1820, 1825); his personal life was tragic; collapsed while playing Othello and died shortly after.

Kemble, Charles (1775-1854). English actor; son of Roger and Sarah Wood; brother of John Philip Kemble and Sarah Siddons; debut as Orlando in *As You Like It,* Sheffield; first London appearance as Malcolm to his brother's Macbeth (1794); succeeded his brother as joint proprietor of Covent Garden; played in many Shakespearean revivals; appeared as Hamlet in New York (1832); returned to the Haymarket, London (1835); best known for portrayal of Mercutio (from 1829).

Kemble, Fanny (Frances Anne) (1809-93). English-American actress; daughter of Charles; debut as Juliet at Covent Garden (1829); successful as Portia and Beatrice; went with her father to the United States (1832); married Pierce Butler (1834) and divorced him (1848); lived at Lenox, Mass.; gave her first successful Shakespearean readings at Willis' Rooms, Boston (1848-49); returned to the London stage (1851); author of several books including *Notes Upon Some of Shakespeare's Plays* (1882).

Kemble, John Philip (1757-1823). English actor; brother of Charles Kemble and Sarah Siddons; made his debut (1776) and played the York circuit; first appearance at Drury Lane (1783) as Hamlet; became manager of the theater (1788-1802); of Covent Garden (1803-08) and of New Covent Garden (from 1809); played opposite his sister in several Shakespearean productions; outstanding as Coriolanus, a favorite

role; wrote adaptations of the plays.

Kempe, William (Will Kemp) (d. c1603). English comedian; member of Leicester's company; toured the provinces with Strange's under Alleyn (1593); joined Chamberlain's company (1594); played Peter in *Romeo and Juliet,* Dogberry in *Much Ado;* an original shareholder in the Globe (1599); created a sensation by dancing from London to Norwich (1600); joined Earl of Worcester's Men (1602); possible that Shakespeare wrote the fools' parts in several plays for Kempe.

Killigrew, Thomas (1612-83). English dramatist; page to Charles I; went with Prince Charles to France; at the Restoration, with Davenant, received royal patent to build a theater and organize an acting company; formed the King's company; built famous Drury Lane Theatre (1663); became Master of the Revels (1673); most popular play, *The Parson's Wedding* (performed 1637, pub., 1664).

Komisarjevsky, Theodore (1882-1954). Russian born stage-designer and director; first to produce Chekov's plays in London; created controversy with productions of *Macbeth* (updated to World War I and using aluminum scenery) and *King Lear.*

Kynaston, Edward (c1645-1706). English actor; played women's parts in his youth; joined Killigrew's King's company (1660); portrayed Antony to Hart's Brutus in *Julius Caesar* (1672); joined Betterton in Lincoln's Inn Fields (1695).

Lacy, John (d. 1681). English actor and playwright; with Killigrew's company; noted as a comedian; wrote *Sir Hercules*

Buffoon, or the Poetical Squire (1684) and a version of *The Taming of the Shrew* called *Sauny the Scot.*

Langham, Michael (1919-). English director; directed in Coventry (1946-48), Birmingham (1948-50); first London play (1951); *Othello* for Old Vic in Berlin (1951), *The Merry Wives of Windsor* (in Dutch, The Hague, 1952); director and general manager Shakespeare Festival, Ontario, Canada (see listing); also has directed Shakespeare at Stratford, the Old Vic and in New York.

Laughton, Charles (1899-1962). British-American actor and director; played season at Old Vic-Sadler's Wells (1933) as Henry VIII, Angelo, Prospero and Macbeth; at Stratford (1959) portrayed King Lear and Bottom; successful as a director and as a motion picture star.

La Gallienne, Eva (1899-). American actress; born and educated in London; to the United States (1916); founded Civic Repertory Theatre, New York (1926); founded American Repertory Theater with Margaret Webster and Cheryl Crawford (1946); played Hamlet (1937) and several other Shakespearean roles.

Macklin, Charles (originally McLoughlin or M'Laughlin) (c1700-97). Irish-English actor, dramatist; gained fame with his portrayal of Shylock in *The Merchant of Venice* (1741) at Drury Lane; excelled as Iago and Touchstone; very successful until he was forced to retire (1789); wrote *Love à la Mode* (1759) and *The Man of the World* (1781), both popular comedies; first to give lectures on Shakespeare (1754); ran a coffee-house in Covent Garden and taught acting.

Macready, William Charles (1793-1873). English actor; debut as Romeo (1810) in Birmingham; first appeared in London at Covent Garden (1816); became manager of the theater (1837-39); produced *Coriolanus, King Lear* and *The Tempest* from the original texts; manager of Drury Lane (1841-43); performed in the United States; involved in the Astor Place Riot (see Forrest); known for performances as Lear, Henry IV, Macbeth, Iago and Cassius.

Mansfield, Richard (1857-1907). American actor; appeared in Gilbert and Sullivan operas; attained success with Irving at the Lyceum, London (1888); produced *Richard III* at the Globe (1889), first Shakespearean role; played Shylock (1893); staged elaborate *Henry V* (1900, New York); played Brutus in *Julius Caesar* (1902) and other roles.

Mantell, Robert Bruce (1854-1928). British-American actor; debut in England (1876); first appeared in the United States in support of Modjeska (1878); toured the United States, with his own company, playing Shakespeare.

Marlowe, Julia (originally Sarah Frances Frost) (1866-1950). American actress; debut, New York (1887); gained fame with E. H. Sothern (1904) whom she married (1911); particularly successful as Viola, Rosalind, Ophelia, Juliet and Beatrice.

Mathews, Charles James (1803-78). English actor, dramatist; with his wife, Madame Vestris, managed Covent Garden (1839); produced *Love's Labour's Lost, The Merry Wives* and *A Midsummer Night's Dream* (1840); wrote farces; played in comedies.

McCarthy, Lillah (1875-1960). English actress; appeared in the

Shakespearean productions of her first husband, Harley Granville-Barker, at the Savoy (1912-14); played Viola in *Twelfth Night*, Hermione in *The Winter's Tale* and Helena in *A Midsummer Night's Dream*.

McCullough, John Edward (1832-85). Irish-American actor; first appearance in Philadelphia (1857); played in the tragedies with Edwin Forrest and Edwin Booth; managed the California Theater; toured the country as Richard III, Othello, Lear and Iago.

Merivale, Philip (1880-1946). English actor; debut (1905); to America with Mrs. Patrick Campbell (1914); played in *The Merchant of Venice* (1922); acted in several of the plays including *Othello* and *Macbeth*.

Modjeska, Helena (Opid Modrzejewska) (1840-1909). Polish actress; to the United States (1876); first appearance at San Francisco (1877); gained fame as Camille, New York (1878); played Desdemona to Edwin Booth's Othello; performed in many Shakespearean roles including Beatrice, Rosalind, Juliet, Imogen, Ophelia and Lady Macbeth.

Moissi, Alexander (1880-1935). Italian actor; trained with Max Reinhardt; toured the United States (1927); most famous roles include Hamlet, Othello, Mark Antony, Shylock and Jaques.

Monck, Nugent (1877-1958). English manager; founded the Norwich Players (1911); opened the Maddermarket Theatre (1921), which had an Elizabethan stage; produced an influential series of Shakespearean plays; staged *Pericles* at Stratford-on-Avon (1947).

Neilson, (Lilian) Adelaide (originally Elizabeth Ann Brown, also known as Lizzie Bland) (1846-80). English actress; noted for performances as Juliet and Viola; first appeared in the United States (1872) at Niblo's Theater, New York; appeared under Daly's management (1877).

Neville, John (1925-). English actor and producer; played variety of Shakespearean roles with several companies; alternated with Richard Burton as Othello and Iago (Old Vic, 1955/6); toured the U.S. with Old Vic (1957/8); directed *Henry V* (1960, Old Vic). See recordings.

Nisbett, Louisa Cranstoun (c1812-58). English actress; played Rosalind, Portia and Lady Macbeth at Stratford; played Beatrice at the Haymarket (1830); in *Love's Labour's Lost,* and as Mrs. Ford in *The Merry Wives of Windsor* at Covent Garden (1835); excelled as comic actress.

Olivier, Sir Laurence Kerr (1907-). English actor and director; debut as Katharina in a performance of *The Taming of the Shrew* by a group of boys at Stratford-on-Avon (1922); alternated in the roles of Romeo and Mercutio in Gielgud's production (1935) of *Romeo and Juliet;* joined the Old Vic (1936); gained fame as Richard III (1944); played Hamlet, Henry V, Macbeth, Coriolanus and Iago; appeared as Romeo in a New York production (1940); co-director of the Old Vic Company (1944); played Hotspur and Lear (1945-46); knighted (1947); appeared in the title roles in many successful motion pictures including *Henry V* (1944), *Hamlet* (1948), *Richard III* (1956) and *Othello* (1965); director of Britain's National Theatre (since 1962). See Productions and Recordings.

O'Neill, Eliza (1791-1872). Irish actress; first appearance as the Duke of York in *Richard III* at Drogheda (1803); gained recognition as Juliet, Covent Garden (1814).

O'Neill, James (1849-1920). American actor; father of Eugene O'Neill; played with Edwin Booth and Adelaide Neilson; best known for his performance as Edmond Dantès in *The Count of Monte Cristo,* although he did play Hamlet and Othello.

Palmer, John (1744-98). English comedian; worked for Garrick; gained fame in Liverpool (1772); opened new theater there (1787) with *As You Like It,* playing Jaques; colorful personality; excellent as Sir Toby Belch, Touchstone, Jaques and Mercutio.

Payne, Ben Iden (b. 1881). English actor, director and producer; debut, London (1900); visiting professor of drama, Carnegie Institute (1919-34); produced and directed for Theatre Guild, New York and Goodman Repertory Theater, Chicago; director (succeeding Bridges-Adams) Shakespeare Memorial Theatre; produced *Antony and Cleopatra* (1935); returned to U.S. to teach (1942); directed *The Winter's Tale* for Theatre Guild, New York (1945); directed several summer Shakespeare festivals.

Phelps, Samuel (1804-78). English actor-manager; first successful appearance as Shylock in *The Merchant of Venice* at the Haymarket (1837); excelled as Lear and Macbeth; became theatrical manager of Sadler's Wells (1843-62) where he produced and acted in almost all of Shakespeare's plays, many of them virtually unknown to his audiences, restoring much of the original texts.

Planché, James Robinson (1796-1880). English dramatist, antiquary; wrote and designed sets for the Lyceum Theatre under Madame Vestris' management (1847); important as the author of *The History of British Costume* (1834), and for his archeological studies, which led to the authentic sets and costumes used in Shakespearean productions of the 19th century; designed Charles Kemble's revival of *King John* (1823), the Mathews production of *A Midsummer Night's Dream* (1840) and Benjamin Webster's revival of *The Taming of the Shrew* at the Haymarket.

Poel, (Pole) William (1852-1934). English actor-manager; pioneer of simplified staging of plays; produced the First Quarto version of *Hamlet* (1881) at St. George's Hall, London; manager of the Old Vic (1881-83); founded the Elizabethan Stage Society (1894); wrote *Shakespeare in the Theatre* (1913).

Porter, Eric Richard (1928-). English actor; at Stratford (1946); toured Britain and Canada with Sir Donald Wolfit's company; with Birmingham Repertory Company (1948-50); with Old Vic (1955) appearing as Henry IV, Banquo, Bolingbroke and others; at Stratford (1960) played Malvolio, Leontes and Duke of Milan; under contract Royal Shakespeare Company (1960-65); played Malvolio (1960), Bolingbroke (1964), Shylock (1965) and Lear (1968); popular on television (from 1945).

Power, Tyrone (1869-1931). American actor; debut, St. Augustine, Florida (1886); leading man in Daly's company (1890-96); appeared with Tree, Mrs. Fiske, Irving, Henrietta Crosman; played many Shakespearean roles.

Pritchard, Hannah (Vaughan) (1711-68). English actress; gained fame at the Haymarket under Cibber; with Garrick at Drury Lane (from 1747); excelled as Lady Macbeth and Queen Katherine in *Henry VIII.*

Quayle, Anthony (1913-). English actor, director and producer; played many Shakespearean roles in Old Vic productions of the 1930s; director Shakespeare Memorial Theatre, Stratford (1948-56); appeared in many of his own productions.

Quin, James (1693-1766). English actor; first appeared in London (1714) at Drury Lane; gained recognition as Falstaff (1720); rivaled Garrick in Shakespearean roles; played Lear, Othello, Richard III, Macbeth, Brutus, Coriolanus, among others; buried in Westminster Abbey.

Redgrave, Sir Michael (Scudamore) (1908-). English actor, director, theater manager and author; debut, Liverpool (1934); with Old Vic (1936) as Ferdinand in *Love's Labour's Lost,* Orlando in *As You Like It* and Laertes and Chorus in *Henry V;* played Bolingbroke in *Richard II* for Gielgud's company (1937); has played Hamlet, Macbeth and several other roles at Stratford and in various countries in the world; popular in films; knighted (1959); author of several books. See play listings and recordings.

Rehan, Ada (Crehan) (1860-1916). Irish-American actress; first appearance, Newark, New Jersey (1874); joined Daly's company (1879); played the leading role in Shakespeare's comedies; popular as Rosalind, Mistress Ford, Viola and in many other roles; performed in London (1884) and in Paris; outstanding as Katharina in *The Taming of the Shrew,* first played, New York (1887).

Reinhardt, Max (originally Goldmann) (1873-1943). German stage director and manager of the Neues Theater, Berlin (1903-20); staged outdoor production of *A Midsummer Night's Dream* at Covent Garden (1912); to Hollywood (1934); noted for elaborate, spectacular productions of *Macbeth, Julius Caesar, Hamlet* and *The Comedy of Errors.*

Reynolds, Frederick (1764-1841). English dramatist, producer of operatic versions of the comedies with music by Bishop, Mozart and Arne; wrote approximately 100 plays, the first was produced (1785).

Rich, John (1692-1761). English harlequin; famous for establishing English pantomime under the name of Lun (1716); opened the Covent Garden Theatre (Dec. 7, 1732) with production of *Hamlet;* produced *Measure for Measure* (1720) and *Much Ado* (1721); hired Garrick, Mrs. Cibber and Quin (1746); acted in productions of several of Shakespeare's plays but was best known for pantomime.

Richardson, Sir Ralph (1902-). English actor; played Lorenzo in *The Merchant of Venice* (1921); first London appearance at the Haymarket (1928); at Old Vic (from 1930); joint-director (1944); produced *Richard II* (1947); appeared in New York as Mercutio in *Romeo and Juliet* (1935); knighted (1947); has appeared in many motion pictures. See Recordings.

Ristori, Adelaide (1821-1905). Italian actress; ingénue in the company of the King of Sardinia (1837-55); married Marquis del Grillo; appeared with the Royal Sardinian Company in Paris (1855) with great success; rivaled Rachel; played Lady Macbeth (in Italian), London (1857); played the same role (in English) with Edwin Booth in New York (1885); considered the greatest of the tragediennes in the begininng of the century; often referred to as the Italian Mrs. Siddons; her analysis of the role of Lady Macbeth appeared in her *Memoirs* (pub., 1907).

Robinson, Mary (Darby, called Perdita) (1758-1800). English actress, poet, novelist; appeared with Garrick at Drury Lane as Juliet (1776); played Perdita in *The Winter's Tale* (1779) and attracted the attention of the Prince of Wales (George IV); became his mistress; after he deserted her, she left the stage and turned to writing under the name of Perdita.

Robson, Flora (1902-). English actress; first London appearance as Queen Margaret in *Will Shakespeare* (1921); played Shakespearean repertory with Ben Greet's company (1922-24); made American debut (1940).

Rossi, Ernesto (1827-96). Italian tragic actor; appeared as Hamlet at Drury Lane (1876) in Italian version he had performed in Rome; established an outstanding company; produced his own plays.

Ryan, Lacy (c1694-1760). English actor; performed at Lincoln's Inn Fields (1718-32) and at Covent Garden (1732-60); extremely versatile, he played many roles including Iago, Cassius, Macbeth, Hamlet, Richard III and Shylock.

Salvini, Tommaso (1829-1916). Italian tragedian; leading member of Adelaide Ristori's company (1847); fought in Italian War of Independence (1849); important roles included Othello, Hamlet, Lear, Macbeth and Coriolanus; visited England, Russia, Western Europe and the United States (5 times); played Othello (in Italian) to Booth's Iago (in English, 1886).

Saunderson, Mary (1647-1712). English actress; joined Davenant (1661); appeared with (and married) Betterton (1662); played Ophelia, Juliet, Lady Macbeth and other Shakespearean roles; one of the first successful actresses of the English theater.

Scofield, Paul (1922-). English actor; at Stratford (1946-48) appeared in many of the plays in leading roles; played Richard II with Gielgud (1952/3); toured as Hamlet (1955); played King Lear in Peter Brook's production (1962). See play listings and recordings.

Shaw, Glen Byam (1904-). English actor and director; appeared as Laertes (1934), Horatio (1939) and in other roles; directed Gielgud as Richard II (1935) and in *The Merchant of Venice* (1938); directed at Old Vic and co-director with Anthony Quayle of the Shakespeare Memorial Theatre (1952-56); continued as director with *Othello* (1956), *As You Like It* and *Julius Caesar* (1957), *Hamlet* and *Romeo and Juliet* (1958), and *King Lear* (1959 and 1960).

Sheridan, Thomas (1719-88). Irish actor and author; father of the dramatist Richard Brinsley Sheridan (1751-1816); debut, Richard III in Dublin; appeared as Hamlet at Drury Lane and Covent Garden (1744); became a leading actor; wrote and played the lead in *Coriolanus, or The Roman Matron,* an adaptation of Shakespeare's play (1754); author of the *General Dictionary of the English Language* (1780), edited Swift's works (in 17 volumes).

Siddons, Sarah (Kemble) (1755-1831). English actress; daughter of Roger Kemble, sister of John Philip and Charles; acted as a child; married William Siddons, an actor (1773); first London appearance (1775) as Portia in *The Merchant of Venice;* triumphed with Garrick at Drury Lane (1782); considered the greatest tragic actress of her time; hailed as Lady Macbeth, her most popular role (1785), and the Queen in her brother's production of *Henry VIII* (1788), her favorite part; also played Desdemona, Volumnia, Ophelia and Hermione; painted by Reynolds as "The Tragic Muse" (1783).

Skinner, Otis (1858-1942). American actor; debut, Philadelphia Museum (1877); played with Booth, Barrett and Daly's company (1880-90) in many Shakespearean roles; appeared as Romeo at the Globe (1890); co-starred wtih Ada Rehan playing Shylock in *The Merchant of Venice* and Petruchio in *The Taming of the Shrew* (1903); appeared as Falstaff in *Henry IV* (1926) and in *The Merry Wives* (1928); played Shylock on tour with Maude Adams (1931/2); author of four books.

Sothern, Edward Hugh (1859-1933). Anglo-American actor; son of Edward Askew Sothern (1826-81), an actor; London debut (1881); toured United States with John McCullough; leading man in Frohman's Lyceum company (1884-98); formed his own company (1899); first played Hamlet in New York (1900); first appearance with Julia Marlowe (whom he married in 1911) in *Romeo and Juliet* in Chicago (1904); many successful productions of Shakespeare including a season in New York at the Lyric Thea-

ter (1907); appeared in films and wrote several plays.

Sullivan, Barry (1821-91). Irish actor; first appeared in London as Hamlet (1852); known for performance as Richard III; played Benedick to Helen Faucit's Beatrice in *Much Ado,* first production of Shakespeare Memorial Theatre at Stratford (1879).

Swinley, Ion (1891-1937.) English actor; debut in *A Midsummer Night's Dream* (1911); appeared as Troilus at Stratford (1913); also played Hamlet, Romeo, Henry V and Prospero; considered a fine actor with a magnificent future at the time of his early death.

Tarlton, Richard (d. 1588). English clown and comic actor; member of the Queen's company (1583); the Queen's favorite clown; praised for his clever rhymes and impromptu jigs; ousted from court when he overstepped his role in attacks on Leicester and Raleigh; became an innkeeper; wrote *The Seven Deadly Sins;* believed to have been the inspiration for Yorick in *Hamlet.*

Tate, Nahum (1652-1715). Irish dramatist; to London (1673); collaborated with Dryden on second part of *Absalom and Achitophel* (1682); Poet Laureate (1692); best known for adaptations of Elizabethan plays, particularly Shakespeare's *Richard II* (1680), *Coriolanus* and *King Lear* (produced, 1681), distorted beyond belief, it nonetheless held the stage for 150 years.

Taylor, Joseph (1586-1652). English actor; joined the King's company (1619-42); successor of Richard Burbage in *Hamlet* and *Othello;* possibly the original Iago; his performance of

Hamlet remained as a model for many years.

Terry, Dame Alice Ellen (1847-1928). English actress; debut as Mamillius in Kean's production of *The Winter's Tale* (1856); played Katharina in Garrick's version of *The Taming of the Shrew* (1867); became Irving's leading lady at the Lyceum (1878) where she played Portia, Ophelia, Juliet, Desdemona and other roles in his Shakespearean revivals; visited the United States eight times; last performance was as the Nurse in *Romeo and Juliet* (1919); married three times; carried on well-known correspondence with G. B. Shaw.

Thorndike, Dame Sybil (1882-). English actress; debut with Ben Greet's company in *The Merry Wives,* Cambridge (1904); toured the United States in Shakespeare repertory (1903-07); joined Old Vic (1914-18); played Lady Macbeth, Rosalind, Portia and the less usual Gobbo in *The Merchant of Venice,* Ferdinand in *The Tempest* and Puck in *A Midsummer Night's Dream;* made Dame Commander of the British Empire (1931).

Tree, Ellen (1805-80). English actress; debut at Covent Garden in operatic version of *Twelfth Night* (1822/3); played Romeo to Fanny Kemble's Juliet (1832); on tour in United States (1836-39), played Rosalind, Portia and Beatrice; married Charles Kean (1842) and played in many roles opposite him; considered a fine actress.

Tree, Sir (Herbert Draper) Beer-bohm (1853-1917). English actor, theatrical manager, first appearance (1878), when he changed his name to Tree (from the German, bohm); manager of the Haymarket (1887-96); produced *The Merry Wives* (1889) playing Falstaff with his wife, Maud Holt, as Anne Page; played Hamlet to his wife's Ophelia (1892); produced a series of Shakespearean revivals at His Majesty's Theatre (1898-1912) including *Julius Caesar* (1898), *Henry VIII* (1910), *Macbeth* (1911) and *Othello* (1912); knighted (1909).

Vanbrugh, Violet Barnes (1867-1942). English actress; debut in London (1886); appeared as Anne Bullen in Tree's production of *Henry VIII* (1892) and as Queen Katherine in Tree's production (1910); married Arthur Bourchier, actor-manager (1894) and played Portia, Lady Macbeth and other roles in his productions; with her sister, Dame Irene (1872-1949), established an open-air theater in Regent Park and both played in *The Merry Wives of Windsor;* appeared in film, *Pygmalion* (1938).

Vestris, Elizabeth (Lucia Elizabeth Bartolozzi) (1797-1856). English actress, married Charles James Mathews (1838) and together they managed Covent Garden (from 1839); played in *Love's Labour's Lost, The Merry Wives* and *A Midsummer Night's Dream.*

Wallack, Lester (originally John Johnstone) (1820-88). American actor-manager; gathered many brilliant stars including Maurice Barrymore, E. A. Sothern, Rose and Charles Coghlan and John Gibbs Gilbert for his stock company; produced Shakespeare's plays during the 1860s.

Webster, Benjamin Nottingham (1797-1882). English dramatist, actor-manager; lessee of the Haymarket Theatre (1837-53); built new Adelphi Theatre; manager of the Princess and St. James' Theatres; produced *The*

Taming of the Shrew, Haymarket (1844), important because he staged the original text rather than Garrick's adaptation.

Webster, Benjamin (1864-1947). Grandson of above; appeared with Irving and toured the United States with Ellen Terry; gained success in the United States (1939); played Montague in Olivier and Leigh's *Romeo and Juliet;* husband of Dame May Whitty (1865-1948), popular on stage and in films.

Webster, Margaret (1905-). Daughter of above; debut (1917); successful as producer and director in United States and England; directed *Richard II* (1951), *Richard III* (1953), *The Merchant of Venice,* Stratford (1956); staged operas *Macbeth* (1957) and *The Taming of the Shrew* (1958), New York City Opera Company; staged Shakespearean productions at New York World's Fair (1939); author of *Shakespeare Without Tears* (1942). See La Gallienne.

Welles, (George) Orson (1915-). American actor, producer and director; debut in *Hamlet,* Dublin (1931); toured United States with Cornell as Mercutio in *Romeo and Juliet* (1933); director of the Negro People's Theatre (1936), directed *Macbeth;* director of Federal Theater Project, New York (1937); produced series of Shakespeare's plays for children's records; founded Mercury Theater (1937) which opened wtih modern-dress version of *Julius Caesar;* best known for portrayal as Othello (London, 1951) and King Lear (New York, 1956); famous for films *Citizen Kane* (1939) and *Macbeth* (1947).

Wilkinson, Tate (1739-1803). English actor and manager; known for imitations of well-known actors and actresses;

played Romeo, Hotspur, Lear, Hamlet and others at Portsmouth (1758); managed several theaters; produced own adaptation of *Hamlet* (1773).

Wilks, Robert (1665-1732). English actor; debut, as Othello, Dublin; played at Drury Lane; successful as Hamlet and Macduff; with Cibber and Thomas Doggett, sublet Drury Lane (1711-32).

Williams, (George) Emlyn (1905-). English actor, director, writer; debut, London (1927); with Old Vic as Angelo in *Measure for Measure* and Richard III (1937); at Stratford as Shylock, Angelo and Iago; directed plays and appeared in outstanding motion pictures (from 1932).

Williams, (Ernest George) Harcourt (1880-1957). British actor, producer; first London appearance in *Henry V* (1900); toured with Ellen Terry (1903); appeared as the Player King in Barrymore's *Hamlet* at the Haymarket (1925); producer at Old Vic (from 1929), involved in at least 50 productions; appeared in many Shakespearean roles; played Charles VI of France in Olivier's film, *Henry V* (1946); author of two books.

Woffington, (Margaret) Peg (c1714-60). Irish actress, debut as Ophelia, Dublin (1737); first London appearance at Covent Garden (1740); with Garrick at Drury Lane (from 1741); part of *ménage à trois* with Garrick and Macklin; played Lady Macbeth, Portia, Gertrude, Rosalind, Viola, Constance and other roles; an elegant and extremely successful woman.

Wolfit, Sir Donald (1902-68). English actor and manager; first London apearance as Biondello in *The Taming of the Shrew* (1924); joined Old Vic (1929/

30) and played Tybalt, Cassius, Touchstone, Macduff and Claudius; at Stratford (1936/7) appeared as Hamlet, Cassius and in other roles; formed his own Shakespeare company (1937) and toured as Hamlet, Macbeth, Shylock and Malvolio; first London season (1940); toured during World War II; presented *King Lear, The Merchant of Venice, Hamlet* and *Volpone* in New York (1947); with his company, he toured a good part of the world (1959 and 1960); knighted (1957).

Woodward, Henry (1714-77). English actor; played many comic characters in the Shakespeare productions at Drury Lane (1738-58); best known as Mercutio; joint-manager with Spranger Barry of the Crow Street Theatre, Dublin (1758-62).

Yates, Mary Ann (1728-87). English actress; first appeared with Garrick at Drury Lane (1753); played Rosalind, Portia, Viola and many other Shakespearean heroines; Cleopatra to Garrick's Antony (1759).

Yates, Richard (c1706-96). English actor; outstanding as a comedian, playing most of Shakespeare's clowns; original Grumio in Garrick's adaptation of *The Taming of the Shrew* (1754); First Gravedigger in *Hamlet* and Autolycus in *The Winter's Tale* were considered his best roles.

Young, Charles Mayne (1777-1856). English actor; played Hamlet, London (1807); appeared as Cassius to J. P. Kemble's Brutus in *Julius Caesar* (1812); leading tragic actor of the period; portrayed King John in Charles Kemble's revival (1823); final performance, as Hamlet, Covent Garden (1832).

Zeffirelli, G. Franco (Corsi) (1923-). Italian opera and stage producer and designer; has produced and designed operas and plays not only in Italy but in Great Britain and the United States (since 1949); produced *Romeo and Juliet* at the Old Vic (1960); opera, *Falstaff* at Covent Garden (1961); *Othello* at Stratford (1961); *Much Ado About Nothing,* National Theatre (1966); *The Taming of the Shrew* (film, 1965-66); new staging of opera, *Antony and Cleopatra,* Metropolitan Opera, New York (1966); *Romeo and Juliet* (1967).

MODERN PRODUCTIONS OF PLAYS

NEW YORK, 1900-1970

Antony and Cleopatra
1909   E. H. Sothern and Julia Marlowe opened the New Theatre

1924   Jane Cowl and Rollo Peters

1937   Conway Tearle and Tallulah Bankhead

1947   Katherine Cornell, Godfrey Tearle, Leonore Ulric and Kent Smith

1951   Laurence Olivier and Vivien Leigh

As You Like It
1902   Henrietta Crosman as Rosalind and Henry Woodruff as Orlando

1914   Margaret Anglin and Sydney Greenstreet

1923   Marjorie Rambeau and Ian Keith

1941   Helen Craig, Alfred Drake and Carol Stone

1947   Donald Wolfit and company

1950   Katherine Hepburn and William Prince

The Comedy of Errors
1938   Musical, *The Boys from Syracuse*, based on the play, starring Jimmy Savo and Eddie Albert

1964   Royal Shakespeare Company, Clifford Williams, director, with Paul Scofield, Alec McCowen and Irene Worth

Coriolanus
1954   Robert Ryan and Mildred Natwick

Cymbeline
1906   Viola Allen

1923   E. H. Sothern and Julia Marlowe

Hamlet
1900   E. H. Sothern's first appearance in New York, with Virginia Harned (his wife) as Ophelia

1904   E. H. Sothern and Julia Marlowe, Johnston Forbes-Robertson's first New York appearance, with Gertrude Elliott (wife) as Ophelia

1907   Ermete Novelli (Italian), first New York appearance

1912   John E. Kellard

1917   John Craig and Mary Young (his wife)

1922   John Barrymore, Rosalind Fuller, Blanche Yurka, Tyrone Power and Whitford Kane

1925   Walter Hampden and Ethel Barrymore
Basil Sidney and Adrienne Morrison

1936   John Gielgud, Judith Anderson and Lillian Gish
Leslie Howard

1938   Maurice Evans, Lili Darvas, Whitford Kane and Donald Randolph

1947   Donald Wolfit and company

1952   Barrault-Renaud Company (French), using translation by André Gide, with Jean-Louis

Barrault, Jean Desailly
and Simone Valère

1958   Old Vic (tour) with John
Neville, Barbara Jefford,
Margaret Courtenay and
Oliver Neville

1964   John Gielgud, director,
with Richard Burton,
Hume Cronyn, Eileen
Herlie and Alfred Drake

1967   *Rosencrantz and Guildenstern Are Dead* by
Tom Stoppard, based on
minor characters in the
play; leading roles played
by John Wood and Brian
Murray

1967   Old Vic company at New
York City Center with
Richard Pasco and
Barbara Leigh

Henry IV, Part I

1939   Maurice Evans, Laurence
Olivier, Margaret Leigh-
ton and Edmond O'Brien

1946   Old Vic with Laurence
Olivier, Margaret Leigh-
ton, Ralph Richardson
and Joyce Redman

1955   New York City Center
Company with Thayer
David, Michael Wagner,
Jerome Kilty and Peggy
Cass
Old Vic with Laurence
Harvey, Judi Dench and
Oliver Neville

Henry IV, Part II

1946   Old Vic wtih Laurence
Olivier, Margaret Leigh-
ton, Ralph Richardson
and Joyce Redman

Henry V

1912   Lewis Waller

Henry VIII

1916   Beerbohm Tree, Lyn
Hardin, Edith W. Matthi-
son

1946   American Repertory
Theater with Victor Jory

Julius Caesar

1902   Richard Mansfield played
Brutus

1912   William Faversham and

Ken Hunter

1937   Dennis King, Orson
Welles in modern dress
at the Mercury Theater

King John

1909   Robert B. Mantell

King Lear

1907   Ermete Novelli

1941   Erwin Piscator, director,
with Sam Jaffe as King
Lear, and Herbert
Berghof as the Fool

1947   Donald Wolfit and company

1956   Orson Welles, Viveca
Lindfors and Geraldine
Fitzgerald

1964   Peter Brook production
with Paul Scofield

Love's Labour's Lost

1953   Joseph Schildkraut,
Kevin McCarthy and
Meg Mundy

Macbeth

1900   Helena Modjeska, road
tour

1916   James K. Hackett and
Viola Allen

1921   Lionel Barrymore and
Julia Arthur

1924   Hackett and Clare Eames

1928   Lyn Harding and Florence Reed

1935   Philip Merivale and
Gladys Cooper

1941   Maurice Evans and Judith Anderson

1948   Flora Robson and
Michael Redgrave

1956   Old Vic (tour) with John
Neville, Claire Bloom
and Paul Rogers

1962   Old Vic with John Clem-
ents and Barbara Jefford

1967   *MacBird!* Off-Broadway
political satire by Bar-
bara Garson, based on
play, with Stacy Keach

Measure for Measure

1957   American Shakespeare
Company (Phoenix Thea-
ter) with Morris Carnov-
sky, Arnold Moss, Elias
Rabb and Nina Foch

1967   Old Vic at New York
        City Center

Merchant of Venice
1901   Nat C. Goodwin and
        Maxine Elliott
1903   Henry Irving and com-
        pany
1904   Robert Mantell
        Otis Skinner with Ada
        Rehan as Portia
1916   Sir Beerbohm Tree with
        Elsie Ferguson
1922   David Warfield and
        Mary Servass
1925   Walter Hampden
1930   Maurice Moscovitch
1931   Maude Adams and Otis
        Skinner on tour
1947   Donald Wolfit and com-
        pany
1953   Luther Adler, Margaret
        Phillips and Philip
        Bourneuf

The Merry Wives of Windsor
1916   James K. Hackett and
        Henrietta Crosman
1928   Mrs. Fiske, Otis Skinner
        and Henrietta Crosman

A Midsummer Night's Dream
1903   Nat C. Goodwin as Bot-
        tom
1927   Max Reinhardt's produc-
        tion with Lili Darvas and
        Vladimir Sokoloff
1954   Old Vic with Moira
        Shearer, Robert Help-
        mann and Stanley
        Holloway
1971   Peter Brook's unortho-
        dox production with
        Alan Howard and Sara
        Kestelman

Much Ado About Nothing
1900   Helena Modjeska on the
        road
1904   E. H. Sothern and Julia
        Marlowe with Jessie Mill-
        ward, Florence Rockwell,
        William Morris, Theo-
        dore Roberts and Wallace
        Eddinger
1912   Annie Russell and Old

English Repertory Com-
pany
1913   John Drew, Mary Boland
        and Laura Hope Crews
1952   Claire Luce, Melville
        Cooper and Anthony
        Eustrel
1959   John Gielgud, Margaret
        Leighton and Michael
        MacLiammoir

Othello
1904   Robert Mantell with
        Marie Booth Russell (his
        wife) as Desdemona
1907   Ermete Novelli
1914   William Faversham as
        Iago
1925   Walter Hampden
1935   Philip Merivale and
        Gladys Cooper
1937   Walter Huston and Brian
        Aherne
1943   Paul Robeson, José Fer-
        rer and Uta Hagen
1955   New York City Center
        Company with William
        Marshall, Jerome Kilty
        and Jan Farrand

Richard II
1937   Maurice Evans
1956   Old Vic (tour) with John
        Neville, Claire Bloom
        and Paul Rogers

Richard III
1904   Robert Mantell
1920   John Barrymore
1943   George Coulouris
1951   Maurice Evans and Kent
        Smith
1953   José Ferrer, Vincent
        Price, Florence Reed,
        Maureen Stapleton and
        Margaret Wycherly

Romeo and Juliet
1904   E. H. Sothern and Julia
        Marlowe
1922   Ethel Barrymore
1923   Jane Cowl and Rollo
        Peters
1933   Eva La Gallienne and
        Richard Waring
1934   Katharine Cornell, Basil
        Rathbone, Brian Aherne
        and Dame Edith Evans

1935   Maurice Evans, Ralph Richardson and Blanche Yurka
1940   Laurence Olivier and his wife, Vivien Leigh
1951   Olivia de Haviland, Douglas Watson and Evelyn Varden
1956   Old Vic (tour) with John Neville, Claire Bloom and Paul Rogers
1962   Old Vic with John Stride and Joanne Dunham

The Taming of the Shrew
1904   Ada Rehan
1921   E. H. Sothern and Julia Marlowe
1927   Basil Sydney and Mary Ellis in modern dress
1935   Alfred Lunt and Lynn Fontanne
1951   Claire Luce and Ralph Clanton
1952   *Kiss Me Kate,* musical by Cole Porter (1893-1964), based on play by Sam and Bella Spewack (1949), revived in 1956
1957   American Shakespeare Company (Phoenix Theater) with Nina Foch, Pernell Roberts and Morris Carnovsky

The Tempest
1916   Louis Calvert, Walter Hampden, Jane Grey and Marinoff (Ariel)
1945   Margaret Webster's production with Vera Zorina, Canada Lee and Arnold Moss

Troilus and Cressida
1956   Old Vic (tour) with John Neville, Claire Bloom and Paul Rogers

Twelfth Night
1904   Viola Allen
       Ben Greet's company with Edith Wynne Matthison as Viola and Ben Greet as Malvolio
1910   Annie Russell, Louis Calvert and Mathison Lang
1914   Phyllis Neilson-Terry
1921   E. H. Sothern and Julia Marlowe
1926   American Repertory Theater
1930   Jane Cowl and Leon Quartermaine
1940   Helen Hayes and Maurice Evans
1958   Old Vic (tour) with Jane Downs, Richard Wordsworth, Gerald Harper, John Humphrey and Barbara Jefford
1968   Rock musical, *Your Own Thing,* winner of NY Drama Critics' Circle award

The Two Gentlemen of Verona
1958   Eric House and Lloyd Bochner

The Winter's Tale
1946   Jessie Royce Landis, Florence Reed and Henry Daniell

Ages of Man, presentation based on George Ryland's *Shakespeare Anthology,* by John Gielgud
1958 and 1963

Will Shakespeare, a play by Clemence Dane (1888-1966)
1923   Katharine Cornell and Otto Kruger

NEW YORK SHAKESPEARE FESTIVAL, CENTRAL PARK, NEW YORK CITY

1957   Joseph Papp, producer. *The Two Gentlemen of Verona, Romeo and Juliet, Macbeth* and *Richard III*

1958   *As You Like It, Othello* and *Twelfth Night*

1959   *Julius Caesar*

1960   *Henry V, The Taming of*

the Shrew and *Measure for Measure*

1961 *Much Ado About Nothing, A Midsummer Night's Dream* and *Richard II*

1962 *The Merchant of Venice, The Tempest* and *King Lear*

1963 *Antony and Cleopatra, As You Like It* and *The Winter's Tale*

1964 *Hamlet* and *Othello*

1965 *Love's Labour's Lost,*

Coriolanus and *Troilus and Cressida*

1966 *All's Well that Ends Well, Measure for Measure* and *Richard III*

1967 *The Comedy of Errors, King John, Titus Andronicus* and *Hamlet*

1968 *Henry IV, Part I, Henry IV, Part II* and *Romeo and Juliet*

1969 *Twelfth Night, Henry VI, Part I and Part II* and *Richard III*

STRATFORD SHAKESPEARE FESTIVAL, STRATFORD, CONNECTICUT

1955 *Julius Caesar* with Raymond Massey, Christopher Plummer, Roddy McDowell and Hurd Hatfield
The Tempest with Raymond Massey, Roddy McDowell, Jack Palance and Joan Chandler

1956 *King John* with John Emery, Morris Carnovsky and Arnold Moss
Measure for Measure with Arnold Moss, Morris Carnovsky and Nina Foch
The Taming of the Shrew with Nina Foch and Pernell Roberts

1957 *The Merchant of Venice* with Katherine Hepburn and Morris Carnovsky
Much Ado About Nothing with Katherine Hepburn and Alfred Drake
Othello with Earl Hyman, Alfred Drake and Jacqueline Brooks

1958 *Hamlet* with Fritz Weaver, Inge Swenson, Geraldine Fitzgerald and Morris Carnovsky
A Midsummer Night's Dream with Jack Bittner, Morris Carnovsky, June

Havoc and Richard Waring
Romeo and Juliet with Inge Swenson and Richard Easton

1959 *The Merry Wives of Windsor* with Larry Gates, Nancy Wickwire and Nancy Marchand
The Winter's Tale with Richard Waring, John Colicos and Nancy Wickwire
All's Well that Ends Well with Aline MacMahon and Nancy Wickwire

1960 *The Tempest* with Morris Carnovsky and Earl Hyman
Twelfth Night with Katherine Hepburn and Clayton Corzatte
Antony and Cleopatra with Katherine Hepburn and Robert Ryan

1961 *Macbeth* with Pat Hingle and Jessica Tandy
As You Like It with Kim Hunter and Donald Harron
Troilus and Cressida

1962 "Shakespeare Revisited," readings by Helen Hayes

and Maurice Evans
Richard II with
Richard Basehart
Henry IV, Part I with
Eric Berry and Hal Hol-
brook

1963   *King Lear* with Morris
Carnovsky
The Comedy of Errors
and *Henry V*

1964   *Hamlet* with Lester Rawl-
ins, Philip Bosco and
Carmen Mathews
*Much Ado About Noth-
ing* with Philip Bosco and
Jacqueline Brookes
Richard III with Douglas
Watson and Margaret
Phillips

1965   *King Lear* with Morris
Carnovsky
Coriolanus with Philip
Bosco and Aline Mac-
Mahon
Romeo and Juliet with

Terrance Scammel, Maria
Tucci and Lillian Gish
The Taming of the Shrew
with Ruby Dee and Philip
Bosco

1966   *Julius Caesar* with Doug-
las Watson as Brutus
*Falstaff (Henry IV, Part
II)* with Jerome Kilty
Twelfth Night

1967   *The Merchant of Venice*
*A Midsummer Night's
Dream*
Macbeth

1968   *Richard II* with Donald
Madden
Love's Labour's Lost
As You Like It

1969   *Hamlet* with Morris
Carnovsky, Brian Bedford
and Kate Reid
Henry V with Leo Cariou
Much Ado About Nothing

1970   *Othello* with Moses Gunn
All's Well that Ends Well

STRATFORD FESTIVAL, STRATFORD, ONTARIO, CANADA

1953   *Richard III*, directed by
Tyrone Guthrie, with Alec
Guinness and Irene
Worth
All's Well that Ends Well

1954   *Measure for Measure*, directed by Cecil Clarke
The Taming of the Shrew,
directed by Tyrone
Guthrie

1955   *The Merchant of Venice*,
directed by Tyrone
Guthrie
Julius Caesar, directed by
Michael Langham

1956   *Henry V* and *The Merry
Wives of Windsor*, di-
rected by Michael Lang-
ham

1957   *Hamlet*, directed by
Michael Langham
Twelfth Night, directed
by Tyrone Guthrie with
Siobhan McKenna, Chris-
topher Plummer, Douglas

Campbell and Frances
Hyland in the casts of
both plays

1958   *Henry IV, Part I*, directed
by Michael Langham and
George McCowan with
Jason Robards, Jr. as
Hotspur
The Winter's Tale, di-
rected by Douglas
Campbell
*Much Ado About
Nothing*, directed by
Michael Langham with
Christopher Plummer and
Eileen Herlie in the casts
of both plays

1959   *Othello*, directed by Jean
Gascon and George
McCowan with Douglas
Campbell as Othello and
Douglas Rain as Iago
As You Like It, directed
by Peter Wood with Irene
Worth as Rosalind

1960   *King John,* directed by
Douglas Seale
*A Midsummer Night's
Dream,* directed by Douglas Campbell
Romeo and Juliet, directed
by Michael Langham with
Julie Harris as Juliet

1961   *Coriolanus,* directed by
Michael Langham with
Paul Scofield as
Coriolanus
Henry VIII, directed by
George McCowan with
Douglas Campbell as
Henry and Kate Reid as
the Queen
Love's Labour's Lost, directed by Michael Langham

1962   *Macbeth,* directed by
Peter Coe with Christopher Plummer and Kate
Reid
The Taming of the Shrew,
directed by Michael Langham
The Tempest, directed by
George McCowan with
John Colicos as Caliban

1963   *Troilus and Cressida,* directed by Michael Langham
The Comedy of Errors,
directed by Jean Gascon
Timon of Athens, directed
by Michael Langham

1964   *Richard II,* directed by
Stuart Burge with William
Hutt as Richard
King Lear, directed by
Michael Langham with
John Colicos as Lear

1965   *Henry IV, Part I,* directed
by Stuart Burge
Julius Caesar, directed by
Douglas Campbell
Falstaff, directed by
Stuart Burge

1966   *Henry V,* directed by
Michael Langham
Henry VI, directed by
John Hirsch
Twelfth Night, directed
by David William

1967   *Richard III,* directed by
John Hirsch with Alan
Bates and Zoe Caldwell
*The Merry Wives of
Windsor,* directed by
David William with Tony
van Bridge, Frances Hyland and Zoe Caldwell
Antony and Cleopatra,
directed by Michael Langham with Christopher
Plummer and Zoe Caldwell

1968   *Romeo and Juliet,* directed
by Douglas Campbell
*A Midsummer Night's
Dream,* directed by John
Hirsch

1969   *Hamlet,* directed by John
Hirsch
Measure for Measure,
directed by David Giles
with William Hutt

1970   *The Merchant of Venice,*
directed by Jean Gascon
with Donald Davis
Cymbeline, directed by
Jean Gascon

MUSIC

A Selected List of Composers of Music Based on the Works of Shakespeare

Ariosti, Attilio (1666-c1740). Italian opera composer; one of the first musical directors of the Royal Academy of Music, London; wrote *Cajo Marzio Coriolano* (1723) based on *Coriolanus*.

Arne, Thomas Augustine (1710-78). English composer; set "Under the greenwood tree," "Blow, blow thou winter wind" and "When daisies pied" for a production of *As You Like It* (1740); wrote incidental music for *Twelfth Night* (1741), *The Merchant of Venice* (1742) and *Romeo and Juliet* (1750); set "Where the bee sucks" for a revival of *The Tempest* (1746).

Bach, C.P.E. (1714-88). German composer; son of J. S. Bach; harpsichordist to Frederick the Great (1740); remarkable skill in improvisation; wrote overture to *Hamlet*.

Balakirev, Mili Alekseyevich (1837-1910). Russian composer; leader of the group of Russian nationalist composers known as the Kutchka (The Five); wrote incidental music for *King Lear* (1861-65).

Balfe, Michael William (1808-70). Irish composer of light operas; singer; first success *Siege of Rochelle,* produced at the Drury Lane (1835); best-known work, *The Bohemian Girl* (1843); composed *Falstaff* (1838) produced at His Majesty's Theatre.

Beethoven, Ludwig van (1770-1827). German master composer; wrote dramatic *Coriolan* overture (opus 62, 1807); piano sonata (opus 31, no. 2) possibly based on *The Tempest*.

Bellini, Vincenzo (1801-35). Italian composer of the opera *Montecchi E Capuletti* or *I Capuletti ed i Montecchi* (Montagues and Capulets) based on *Romeo and Juliet* (1830).

Bennet, Sir William Sterndale (1816-75). English composer and educator; conductor of the London Philharmonic orchestra (1856-66); Principal of the Royal Academy of Music (from 1866); wrote an overture to *The Merry Wives of Windsor;* knighted (1871); buried in Westminster Abbey.

Berlioz, (Louis) Hector (1803-69). French composer and conductor; composed a two-act opera comique, *Béatrice et Bénédict,* based on *Much Ado About Nothing* (1862); "dramatic fantasia with choruses" on *The Tempest* (1830); overture, *Le Roi Lear* (opus 4, 1831) based on *King Lear;* dramatic symphony with chorus, *Roméo et Juliette* (opus 7, 1838-39);

music based on *Hamlet* (opus 18, no. 3, 1848).

Bishop, Sir Henry Rowley (1786-1855). English composer and conductor; wrote the music for many of Frederick Reynolds' adaptations of Shakespeare's comedies; remembered for his setting of "Lo! here the gentle lark" (with flute obbligato) from *Venus and Adonis* (1853).

Blacher, Boris (1903-). German composer of *Romeo und Julia,* a dramatic or "scenic" oratorio based on Shakespeare's play, and a ballet based on *Hamlet* (1950).

Bliss, Arthur (1891-). English composer of incidental music to *The Tempest* (1921).

Bloch, Ernest (1880-1959). Swiss composer of the lyric drama *Macbeth,* performed in Paris (1910).

Blow, John (1649-1708). English composer of the masque *Venus and Adonis* (c1680-87); teacher of Purcell.

Brahms, Johannes (1833-97). Master German composer; composed "Come away, death" for female voices, two horns and harp (opus 17, no. 2) and five of Ophelia's songs from *Hamlet.*

Britten, (Edward) Benjamin (1913-). English composer of the chamber opera, *The Rape of Lucretia* (1946) and music for *A Midsummer Night's Dream,* which premiered at the Aldeburgh Festival (1960).

Carpenter, John Alden (1876-1951). American composer of orchestral suite based on "The Seven Ages of Man" from *As You Like It* (II, 7).

Carter, Elliott (1908-1955). American composer and critic; wrote incidental music and chorus for *Much Ado About Nothing* (1937).

Castelnuovo-Tedesco, Mario (1895-1968). Italian-American

composer of opera, *The Merchant of Venice* (1961) and seven overtures to the plays, including *The Taming of the Shrew* (1931), *Twelfth Night* (1933; first performed in Rome, 1935) and *King John* (1942); settings for 27 of the sonnets (using the original text), and the songs of the plays.

Chausson, Ernest (1855-99). French composer of *Chansons de Shakespeare,* opus 28 (1890-97).

Chelard, Hippolyte André Jean Baptiste (1789-1861). French composer of the opera *Macbeth* performed in Paris (1827), with libretto by Rouget de l'Isle.

Chignell, Robert (1882-1939). English composer of an opera based on *Romeo and Juliet.*

Clarke, James Hamilton Smee (1840-1912). English conductor and composer of incidental music to *Hamlet, King Lear* and *The Merchant of Venice.*

Colburn, George (1878-1921). American composer of symphonic setting for *Antony and Cleopatra* (1915).

Collingwood, Arthur (1887-). English composer and conductor, Sadler's Wells Opera (1931-47) where his opera, *Macbeth,* was presented (1934).

Copland, Aaron (1900-). American composer of music for Orson Welles' production of *Five Kings* (1939).

Dalayrac, Nicolas (1753-1809). French composer of the opera *Roméo et Juliette* (Opéra-Comique).

Debussy, Claude Achille (1862-1918). French composer of incidental music to *King Lear* (1904) and the prelude, *La Danse de Puck* (1910).

Delannoy, Marcel (1898-). French composer of the opera *Puck,* performed in Strasbourg (1949).

Delius, Frederick (1862-1934). English composer of German origin; composed *Romeo und Julia auf dem Dorfe (A Village Romeo and Juliet)* opera, performed in Berlin (1907).

Diamond, David (1915-). American composer of a concert suite for chamber orchestra, *Music for Romeo and Juliet* (1947), and a "symphonic portrait," *Timon of Athens* (1949).

Dittersdorf, Karl Ditters von (1739-99). Austrian composer of the opera, *The Merry Wives of Windsor* (1796).

Dukas, Paul (1865-1935). French composer of the overture, *King Lear* (1882).

Dupuis, Sylvain (1856-1931). Belgian composer of the symphonic poem, *Macbeth.*

Duvernoy, Victor Alphonse (1842-1907). French composer of the cantata, *La Tempête* (The Tempest).

Dvorak, Antonin (1841-1904). Czech composer of the overture *Othello,* opus 93 (1891-92).

Elgar, Sir Edward William (1857-1934). English composer of the symphonic study, *Falstaff,* opus 68 (1913).

Esposito, Michele (1855-1929). Italian composer of an overture to *Othello.*

Farwell, Arthur (1872-1952). American composer of the Shakespeare Tercentenary Masque, *Caliban* (1916), based on the character in *The Tempest.*

Fauré, Gabriel Urbain (1845-1924). French composer of *Shylock* (opus 57), performed at the Odéon, Paris (1889), based on the character in *The Merchant of Venice.*

Ferrari, Gustave (1872-1949). Swiss composer living in England (from 1901), wrote incidental music to *Hamlet* (1905).

Fibich, Zdenek (1850-1900). Bohemian composer of the symphonic poems, *Othello* (1873) and *The Tempest* (1880), and the opera, *The Tempest* (1894).

Filippi, Amedeo de (1900-). American composer of an opera in two acts, *Malvolio* (1937), based on the character in *Twelfth Night.*

Flotow, Friedrich von (1812-83). German composer of incidental music for *The Winter's Tale* (1859).

Förster, Joseph B. (1859-1951). Czech composer of suite *From Shakespeare* (1908-09).

Foss, Lukas (1922-). German-American composer of an orchestral suite from *The Tempest* (1942).

Foulds, John Herbert (1880-1939). English composer of incidental music for *Julius Caesar,* opus 39.

Frank, Ernst (1848-89). German composer of the opera *Der Stürm* (Hanover, 1887) based on *The Tempest.*

Frazzi, Vito (1888-). Italian composer of the opera *Re Lear* (King Lear) produced at the Florence May Festival (1939).

Gade, Niels Wilhelm (1817-90). Danish composer of *Hamlet,* an overture.

García Roblez, José (1838-1910). Spanish composer of the opera, *Julio César* (Julius Caesar).

Gatty, Nicholas Comyn (1874-1946). English composer of the operas *The Tempest* (London, 1920) and *Macbeth.*

German, Sir Edward (1862-1936). English composer and conductor at the Globe Theatre (1885-88) for which he wrote incidental music to *Richard III* (1889); also composed incidental music for *Henry VIII* (1892), *Romeo and Juliet* (1895), *As You Like It* (1896),

Much Ado About Nothing (1898); symphonic poem, *Hamlet* (1897); knighted (1928).

Giannini, Vittorio (1903-). American composer of the opera, *The Taming of the Shrew,* produced in Cincinnati (1953).

Gobatti, Stefano (1852-1913). Italian composer of the opera *Cordelia* (1881), based on the character in *King Lear.*

Godard, Benjamin Louis Paul (1849-95). French composer of incidental music for *Much Ado About Nothing* (1887).

Goetz, Hermann (1840-76). Prussian composer of the opera *Der Widerspenstigen Zähmung,* based on *The Taming of the Shrew,* produced at the Drury Lane, London (1878).

Gounod, Charles François (1818-93). French composer of the opera *Roméo et Juliette,* produced at the Théâtre-Lyrique, Paris (1867).

Hadley, Henry Kimball (1871-1937). American composer of an overture to *Othello.*

Hahn, Reynaldo (1875-1947). French composer of the opera *Le Marchand de Venise* (The Merchant of Venice) based on Shakespeare's play, produced at the Paris Opéra (1935).

Halévy, Jacques François (1799-1862). French composer of *La Tempesta* (The Tempest) written (with text by Eugène Scribe) especially for Her Majesty's Theatre, London (1850).

Handel, George Frederick (1685-1759). German composer; with Bach, the outstanding musician of his time; spent most of his life in London, composed 46 operas, 32 oratorios etc.; opera, *Guilio Cesare* (Julius Caesar), London (1724).

Hart, (Fritz) Bennicke (1874-1949). English composer; conductor of the Symphony Orchestra of Melbourne, Australia;

composed the opera *Malvolio,* based on the character in *Twelfth Night.*

Haydn, Franz Joseph (1732-1809). Austrian master composer; wrote incidental music for *Hamlet* and *King Lear;* set Viola's speech "She never told her love" from *Twelfth Night* (II, 4) as a canzonetta for voice and piano.

Holst, Gustav Theodore (1874-1934). English composer of the opera *At The Boar's Head,* based on *Henry IV,* produced at Manchester (April, 1925).

Honegger, Arthur (1892-1955). Swiss composer of an overture prelude and Ariel songs for *The Tempest* (1923).

Hornstein, Robert von (1833-90). German composer of incidental music for *As You Like It.*

Howells, Herbert (1892-). English composer of *Puck's Minuet* (1920) for small orchestra, inspired by the character in *A Midsummer Night's Dream.*

Humperdinck, Engelbert (1854-1921). German composer of incidental music to *The Merchant of Venice* (1905), *The Winter's Tale,* *The Tempest* (1906), *Twelfth Night* (1907) and *As You Like It* (1907).

Indy, Vincent d' (1851-1931). French composer of an overture to *Antony and Cleopatra* (1876).

Ireland, John (1879-1962). English composer of incidental music to *Julius Caesar* (1942) and song "When daffodils" from *The Winter's Tale* (IV, 3).

James, Dorothy (1901-). American composer (with Hamilton Forrest) of incidental music to *As You Like It* (1927).

Joachim, Joseph (1831-1907). German virtuoso violinist and composer; wrote overtures to

Hamlet (opus 4) and *Henry IV* (opus 7).

Johnson, Robert (c1585-1633). English lutenist; worked for Lord Hunsdon, a patron of Shakespeare's company (1595); one of the Musicians of the Lute to James I and Charles I (1604-33); wrote settings for the songs "Where the bee sucks" and "Full fathom five" from *The Tempest* (possibly, 1612-13); also set to music songs by Beaumont and Fletcher, Ben Jonson and Middleton.

Joncières, Victorien de (Félix Rossignol) (1839-1903). French composer of incidental music to *Hamlet*.

Jones, Robert (c1575-1615). English musician; wrote *First Book of Songs and Air* (1600), which includes "Farewell, dear heart" sung by Sir Toby and Feste in *Twelfth Night* (II, 3); converted his house in Blackfriars into a theater (1615).

Kaun, Hugo (1863-1932). German composer of *Sir John Falstaff*, opus 60, for orchestra, based on the character in *Henry IV* and *The Merry Wives of Windsor*.

Kelley, Edgar Stillman (1857-1944). American composer of incidental music to *Macbeth* for orchestra and chorus, opus 7.

Khachaturian, Aram (1903-). Armenian composer of music for *Macbeth*.

Koennecke, Fritz (d.1876). German-American composer of music for *The Tempest* (1917).

Korngold, Erich Wolfgang (1897-1957). German composer of music for *Much Ado About Nothing* (1919).

Lambert, Constant (1905-51). English composer of the music for the ballet *Romeo and Juliet*, commissioned by Diaghilev, performed at Monte Carlo (1926).

Lampe, John Frederick (1703-51). German bassoonist and composer; lived in Great Britain (from c1725); composed music for a version of Richard Leveridge's *Comic Masque* which included Pyramus and Thisbe scenes from *A Midsummer Night's Dream*, performed at Covent Garden (1745).

La Violette, Wesley (1894-). American composer; winner of the American Opera Society of Chicago's award for *Shylock* (1929), based on the character in *The Merchant of Venice*.

Leigh, Walter (1905-42). English composer of *Suite for A Midsummer Night's Dream* (1937).

Leveridge, Richard (c1670-1758). English singer and composer; wrote a short burlesque of Italian opera, *Comic Masque*, out of Pyramus and Thisbe scenes from *A Midsummer Night's Dream;* performed at Lincoln's Inn Fields (1716).

Levey, William Charles (1837-94). Irish composer of music to *Antony and Cleopatra*.

Linley, Thomas, Jr. (1756-92). English composer of incidental music for *The Tempest* (1775) and *An Ode on the Witches and Fairies of Shakspere* (1776).

Liszt, Franz (1811-86). Hungarian composer of the symphonic poem, *Hamlet* (1859).

Locke, Matthew (c1630-77). English composer of music for the Davenant Dryden adaptation of *The Tempest* (1667) and possibly for *Macbeth* (1672); incidental music for Shadwell's version of *The Tempest* (1673-74).

Loder, Edward James (1813-65). English composer of *Puck* (1848) based on the character in *A Midsummer Night's Dream*.

Lucas, Clarence (1866-1947). Canadian composer of overtures to *Othello, As You Like It* and *Macbeth*.

Luening, Otto (1900-). American composer; pioneer in the development of electronic music in America; wrote *King Lear Suite* for tape recorder alone (1956).

Lunssens, Martin (1871-1944). Belgian composer of the symphonic poems *Roméo et Juliette, Timon d'Athènes* and *Jules César,* based on the plays.

Macdowell, Edward Alexander (1861-1908). American composer of the symphonic poem, *Hamlet and Ophelia* (opus 22, 1885).

MacFarren, Sir George Alexander (1813-87). English composer of overtures to *The Merchant of Venice, Romeo and Juliet* and *Hamlet.*

MacKenzie, Sir Alexander Campbell (1847-1935). Scottish composer of incidental music to *Coriolanus* and an overture to *Twelfth Night* (1888).

Malipiero, Gian Francesco (1882-). Italian composer of the "music dramas" *Guilio Cesare* (1935), *Romeo e Giulietta* (1948-49) and *Antonio e Cleopatra* (1938).

Mancinelli, Luigi (1848-1921). Italian composer of the opera *Sogno di una notte d'estate* (A Midsummer Night's Dream).

Mannes, Leopold Damrosch (1899-). American composer of incidental music for children's performance of *The Tempest* (1930).

Marchetti, Filippo (1831-1902). Italian composer of a new version of *Romeo and Juliet* (1865).

Martin, Frank (1890-). Swiss composer of the opera *The Tempest* (1956), which had its premiere in Vienna.

Mendelssohn, Felix (Jakob Ludwig Felix Mendelssohn-Bartholdy) (1809-47). German composer of an overture to *A Midsummer Night's Dream* (1826) for Ludwig Tieck's production in Berlin; wrote incidental music to the same play (1843), at the request of King Frederick William IV of Prussia; conducted the work at Potsdam (Oct. 14) on the eve of the festival celebrating the King's birthday.

Milhaud, Darius (1892-). French composer of music for *Julius Caesar* (1936).

Miessner, W. Otto (1880-). American composer of incidental music for *As You Like It* and *The Tempest.*

Morley, Thomas (1557-1603). English musician and one of the greatest composers of Elizabethan songs for the lute and of madrigals; in *First Booke of Ayres* (1600) is a setting of "It was a lover and his lass" from *As You Like It;* in *First Booke of Consort Lessons* (1599) is music (without words) of "O mistress mine" from *Twelfth Night;* it is possible that Morley wrote the music first and Shakespeare wrote the words to fit his music.

Mortelmans, Lodewijk (1868-1952). Belgian composer of the cantata *Lady Macbeth* (1893), for which he won the Prix de Rome.

Murrill, Herbert Henry John (1909-52). English composer of incidental music to *Richard III.*

Napravnik, Eduard Franzevich (1839-1916). Czech composer of the opera *The Tempest* (1868).

Nicholl, Horace Wadham (1848-1922). English composer of symphonic poem, *Hamlet,* opus 14.

Nicolai, Carl Otto Ehrenfried

(1810-1849). German composer of the comic opera, *Die lustigen Weiber von Windsor* (The Merry Wives of Windsor), produced two months before his death at the Court Opera, Berlin; also set "It was a lover and his lass" from *As You Like It* (V, 3) (opus 16, no. 2).

Nilson, Einar (1881-   ). Swedish composer of incidental music for *As You Like It, Much Ado About Nothing* and *Henry IV*, produced at the Reinhardt Theater, Berlin.

Nordoff, Paul (1909-   ). American composer of incidental music to *Romeo and Juliet* (1935).

Orff, Carl (1895-   ). German composer; best known for *Carmina Burana* (1937); wrote six sets of incidental music to *A Midsummer Night's Dream* (1917-62).

Paine, John Knowles (1839-1906). American composer of the symphonic poem, *The Tempest,* and the overture, *As You Like It.*

Parry, Sir Charles Hubert H. (1848-1918). English composer of music to 20 songs and 5 of the sonnets of Shakespeare.

Pierson, Henry Hugo (1815-73). English-German composer; overtures to *Macbeth, As You Like It, Romeo and Juliet, Julius Caesar* and a *Funeral March for Hamlet* were among his compositions.

Pitt, Percy (1870-1932). English composer of incidental music to *Richard II.*

Pizzetti, Ildebrando (1880-1968). Italian composer of vocal and instrumental music for a performance of *As You Like It* in the Boboli Gardens, Florence (May, 1938).

Porter, Quincy (1897-1966). American composer of incidental music for *Antony and Cleopatra* (1935).

Prokofiev, Sergei (1891-1953). Russian composer of the ballet, *Romeo and Juliet,* opus 64 (1935); first performance, Moscow (Nov., 1936).

Purcell, Henry (1658-95). English composer of the opera, *Dido and Aeneas* (1680); an overture and masque for Shadwell's version of *Timon of Athens* (1678); music for Dryden's version of *The Tempest* (1690), and for his *The Fairy Queen* (based on *A Midsummer Night's Dream,* 1692); incidental music for Betterton's *Midsummer Night's Dream;* buried under the organ in Westminster Abbey.

Quilter, Roger (1877-1953). English composer of incidental music to *As You Like It* (1922) and settings of songs including a cycle, *To Julia.*

Radicati, Felice Alessandro (1778-1823). Italian composer of the opera, *Il Coriolano* (Coriolanus) produced in Amsterdam (1809).

Raff, Joseph Joachim (1822-82). German composer of overtures to *Romeo and Juliet, Othello, Macbeth* and *The Tempest.*

Reichardt, Johann Friedrich (1752-1814). German composer of the opera *Die Geisterinsel* based on *The Tempest.*

Rheinberger, Joseph Gabriel (1839-1901). German composer of an overture to *The Taming of the Shrew,* opus 18.

Rogers, Bernard (1893-1968). American composer of *Prelude to Hamlet* (1928).

Rossini, Gioacchino Antonio (1792-1868). Italian composer of the opera *Otello* (1816).

Roters, Ernst (1892-   ). German composer of music to *A Midsummer Night's Dream* and *Twelfth Night.*

Rubinstein, Anton (1829-94). Russian pianist and composer of overture to *Antony and Cleopatra* (opus 116).

Saint-Saëns, Camille (1835-1933). French composer of the opera *Henry VIII* (Paris, 1883), Covent Garden (1898).

Salsbury, Janet Mary (1881-   ). English composer of a song-cycle, *From Shakespeare's Garden.*

Salvayre, Gervais Bernard (called Gaston) (1847-1916). French composer of the opera *Richard III* (St. Petersburg, 1883).

Samuel, Harold (1879-1937). English pianist; composer of songs from *As You Like It.*

Sayn - Wittgenstein - Berleburg, Count Friedrich Ernst (1837-1915). German composer of the opera *Antonius und Kleopatra* (Antony and Cleopatra, 1883).

Scarlatti, (Giuseppe) Domenico (1685-1757). Italian composer; greatest writer of music for the harpsichord in Italy in his period; wrote an opera based on *Hamlet* (1715).

Schmitt, Florent (1870-1958). French composer of music for Gide's translation of *Antony and Cleopatra* (1920).

Schubert, Franz Peter (1797-1828). Austrian composer of the songs: "Come, thou monarch of the vine" (*Antony and Cleopatra,* II, 7), "Who is Sylvia?" (*The Two Gentlemen of Verona,* IV, 2, c1815) and "Hark, hark, the lark" (*Cymbeline,* II, 3, 1826).

Schumann, Robert (1810-56). German composer of an overture to *Julius Caesar* (F Minor, opus 128, 1851); a song, "When that I was and a little tiny boy" (*Twelfth Night*); and "Novelette" (opus 21, no. 3, for piano) which was believed written for the witches' dance in *Macbeth.*

Shostakovich, Dmitri (1906-   ). Russian composer of songs and incidental music for *Hamlet;*

Lady Macbeth of Mtsensk (produced, New York, 1935) based on novel by Leskov, not on Shakespeare's play, but with the bawdiness of the Elizabethan period.

Sibelius, Jean (1865-1957). Finnish composer of incidental music to *Twelfth Night* (1909) and *The Tempest* (for orchestra, opus 109, 1926).

Smetana, Bedvich (1824-84). Czech composer of a symphonic poem, *Richard III* (1858) and the first act of an opera, *Viola,* based on *Twelfth Night* (1884).

Smith (Schmidt), John Christopher (1712-95). English composer of the opera *The Fairies,* based on *A Midsummer Night's Dream* (1754) and music to Garrick's version of *The Tempest* (1756).

Smith, John Stafford (1750-1836). English organist and composer of music for the songs "Under the greenwood tree" (II, 5) and "What shall he have that killed the deer?" (IV, 2) from *As You Like It* (1792).

Smyth, Dame Ethel Mary (1858-1944). English composer of the overture, *Antony and Cleopatra* (1890).

Soloviev, Nikolai (1846-1916). Russian composer of the opera *Cordelia* (St. Petersburg, 1885) based on the character in *King Lear.*

Spohr, Ludwig (Louis) (1784-1859). German composer of an overture to *Macbeth,* B minor, (opus 75, 1825).

Stanford, Sir Charles Villiers (1852-1924). Irish composer of the opera *Much Ado About Nothing* (opus 76a, produced at Covent Garden, 1900).

Steibelt, Daniel (1765-1823). German composer of opera, *Romeo and Juliet,* produced in Paris (Sept., 1793).

Stephenson, Morton (1884-   ). English composer of incidental music for a *Shakespearean Masque.*

Strauss, Richard (1864-1949). German composer of a symphonic tone poem, *Macbeth,* opus 23 (1886); *Six Songs of Shakespeare and Goethe,* opus 67 (1919), Book I contains "Three Songs of Ophelia" from *Hamlet.*

Stravinsky, Igor (1882-1971). Russian composer of *3 Songs from William Shakespeare* for mezzo-soprano, flute, clarinet and viola (1954).

Sullivan, Arthur Seymour (1842-1900). English composer of incidental music to *The Tempest* (1862), *The Merchant of Venice, The Merry Wives of Windsor, Henry VIII* (1877), *Timon of Athens, Macbeth;* songs and duets.

Sutermeister, Heinrich (1910-   ). Swiss composer of the opera *Romeo und Julia* (Romeo and Juliet), produced in Dresden (1940).

Svendsen, Johan Severin (1840-1911). Norwegian composer of *Overture to Romeo and Juliet,* opus 18.

Taneiev, Alexander Sergeievich (1850-1918). Russian composer of a *Hamlet* overture, opus 31.

Taubert, Karl Gottfried Wilhelm (1811-91). German composer of the opera *Macbeth* (1857) and incidental music to *The Tempest* (1855).

Taylor, (Joseph) Deems (1885-1966). American composer of *Music for Will Shakespeare* for the theater.

Tchaikovsky, Peter Ilyich (1840-93). Russian composer of incidental music for *The Tempest* (opus 18, 1868), overture-fantasia, *Romeo and Juliet* (1869, final version, 1880); symphonic fantasy, *The Tempest*

(1873), fantasy overture, *Hamlet* (1885), incidental music for *Hamlet* (1891) and a duet for soprano and tenor, *Romeo and Juliet,* completed by Taneiev.

Tcherepnin, Nicolai (1873-1945). Russian composer of *Scene in the Witches' Cavern* from *Macbeth* (1901).

Theil, Fritz (b. 1886). German composer of *König Lear* (King Lear), tone-poem for orchestra.

Thomas, (Charles Louis) Ambroise (1811-96). French composer of *Le Songe d'une nuit d'été* (1850) superficially based on *A Midsummer Night's Dream;* opera, *Hamlet* (1868); music for the ballet, *La Tempête* (The Tempest, 1889).

Thomas, Robert Harold (1834-85). English composer of an overture to *As You Like It* (1864).

Thomé, Francis Lucien Joseph (1850-1909). French composer of incidental music to *Roméo et Juliette* (1890).

Thomson, Virgil (1896-   ). American composer of incidental music for *Hamlet* (1936).

Tiessen, Heinz (1887-   ). German composer of music for *Cymbeline, Hamlet* and *The Tempest.*

Toch, Ernst (1887-   ). Austrian composer of incidental music to *As You Like It* (1931).

Trapp, Max (1887-   ). German composer of music for *Timon of Athens.*

Unger, Gustav Hermann (1886-1958). German composer of music for *The Tempest.*

Vaccai, Nicola (1790-1848). Italian composer of *Giulietta e Romeo* (Romeo and Juliet, Milan, 1825).

Van der Stucken, Frank Valentin (1858-1929). American composer of incidental music to *The Tempest* (Breslau, 1862).

Van Westerhout, Niccolò (1862-98). Italian composer (Dutch parentage) of *Cimbelino* (Cymbeline, Rome, 1892).

Vaughan Williams, Ralph (1872-1958). English composer of *Sir John in Love* (1929) based on the character Falstaff in *The Merry Wives of Windsor; Serenade to Music,* cantata (based on Act V, *The Merchant of Venice*) for 16 voices with orchestra (1938).

Verdi, Giuseppe (1813-1901). Italian composer of the famous operas: *Macbetto* (Florence, 1847, revised, 1865), *Otello* (Milan, 1887), *Falstaff* (Milan, 1893), adapted by Arrigo Boito from *The Merry Wives of Windsor* and *Henry IV*.

Vierling, Georg (1820-1901). German composer of *Overture to The Tempest,* opus 6.

Volkmann, Friedrich Robert (1815-83). German composer of an overture to *Richard III,* opus 68.

Wagner, Richard (1813-83). German composer of *Das Liebesverbot* (Forbidden Love) based on *Measure for Measure,* produced Magdeburg (1836).

Walton, William Turner (1902-). English composer of music for the films *Henry V* (1944) and *Hamlet* (1947); *Prelude to Richard III* and *Shakespeare Suite* (1954).

Ward, Frank Edwin (1872-1953). American composer of *Shakespearean Moods,* opus 25.

Warlock, Peter (Heseltine) (1894-1930). English composer of *Saudades* (1918-28), including set of songs from Shakespeare; "Take, O take those lips away" from *Measure for Measure* best known.

Watson, Henry (1846-1911). English composer of incidental music to *Antony and Cleopatra* and *A Shakespearian Cantata.*

Weber, Carl Maria Friedrich Ernst von (1786-1826). German composer of lied for three women's voices and guitar, "Tell me where is fancy bred" for production of *The Merchant of Venice* (III, 2, Dresden, 1821); opera, *Oberon* (opus 9, based on *A Midsummer Night's Dream,* first performed, 1826).

Weingartner, Paul Felix (1863-1942). German composer of music for *The Tempest,* opus 65.

Weis, Karel (1862-1944). Czech composer of the opera, *Viola* (Prague, 1892; known later as *The Twins*) based on *Twelfth Night.*

Weismann, Julius (1879-1950). German composer of a new version of *A Midsummer Night's Dream,* commissioned by the Nazi government when Mendelssohn's work was not permitted.

Wellesz, Egon (1885-   ). Austrian composer of *Prosperos Beschwörungen,* a symphonic suite based on *The Tempest.*

Wetzler, Hermann Hans (1870-1943). German composer of incidental music to *As You Like It* (1917) opus 7.

Wickham, Florence (1882-1962). American composer of *Rosalynd* (Carmel, N.Y., 1938) based on *As You Like It.*

Wilson, John (1595-1674). English lutenist, Gentleman of the Chapel Royal, private musician to Charles I; wrote *Cheerful Ayres* (1660) which contains his setting of "Lawn as white as driven snow" from *The Winter's Tale.*

Winter, Peter von (1754-1825). German composer of the opera *Der Stürm* (1793) based on *The Tempest.*

Wolf, Hugo (1860-1903). German composer of a "Fairies' Song" (*Elfenlied*) for women's voices,

A Selected List of Recordings

Music

NOTE: Bold number indicates stereo.

Arne, Thomas. *Songs to Shakespeare's Plays,* Vienna Radio Orch. and Chor., West. **17075.**

Bergsma, William (1921-). *Carol on Twelfth Night* (1954), Lou. 545-10.

Beethoven, Ludwig van. *Coriolan overture:* Ansermet, Orch. Suisse Romande, Lon. **STS-15055;** Boult, London Phil. Prom. Orch., Van. **S-127;** Karajan, Berlin Phil., **DGG 139015;** Munch, Boston Sym., **VICS-6003;** Szell, Cleveland Orch., Col. **MS-6966,** among others.

Berlioz, Hector. *Béatrice et Bénédict,* Lon. Sym. Orch., and Chor., Oiseau-Lyre **S-256/7;** *Overture to Béatrice et Bénédict,* Boston Sym. Orch., Vic. **LSC-2438;** *Roméo et Juliette,* Op. 17 (complete), Elias, Tozzi with Munch, Boston Sym., New En-

gland Conservatory Chor., Vic. **LDS-6098;** Resnik, Monteux, London Sym. Orch. and Chor., West. **8127-2;** excerpts: Bernstein, New York Phil., Col. **MS-6170.**

Castelnuovo-Tedesco, Mario. *Overture to Much Ado About Nothing,* Lou. Orch., Lou. 545-4.

Diamond, David. Music for *Romeo and Juliet* (1947), Krenz, Polish Nat'l Orch., CRI **216;** *Timon of Athens: Portrait after Shakespeare* (1949), Lou. Orch., Lou. 605.

Dvorak, Antonin. *Othello Overture,* Op. 93, Kertész, London Sym., Lon. **6527;** Somogyl, Vienna St. Op. Orch., Mus. Guild, **S-833;** Talich, Czech. Phil., Artia **S-171.**

German, Edward (1862-1936). *Henry VIII: Dances* (1892), London "Pops" Orch., Mer.

427

50550, **90440;** Boston "Pops," Vic. LM-1803.

Goetz, Hermann. *The Taming of the Shrew,* Urania 221/3, **5221/3.**

Gounod, Charles. *Roméo et Juliette,* Freni, Corelli and Paris Op., Angel **S-3734;** (excerpts) **S-36731;** Carteri, Gayraud and Paris Op. Orch., Angel **S-36287.**

Handel, George F. *Julius Caesar,* Sills with Rudel, NYC Op., Vic **LSC-6182;** (excerpts) **LSC-3116;** Swarowsky, Orch. and Soloists, Vox **SVUX-52011;** Troyanos, Munich Bach Orch. & Cho. DDG 2711009; selections: Sutherland, Horne, Bonynge, New Sym., Lon. **25876;** Fischer-Dieskau, DGG **138637.**

Kabalevsky, Dmitri (1904-). *Romeo and Juliet* (Musical Sketches), Op. 55, State Radio Orch., Monitor 2078, **S-2078;** *Shakespeare Sonnets,* Monitor 2020.

Korngold, Erich. *Much Ado About Nothing,* Op. 11, Music Library 7017; Boston 411, **1012.**

Locke, Matthew. *Music of Matthew Locke,* Golden Age Singers, Puchito 11-64; West. 19082, **17082.**

Martin, Frank. *Tempest* (excerpts), Fischer-Dieskau, Berlin Phil., DGG 18871, **138871.**

Martirano, Salvatore (1927-). *0 0 0 0 that Shakespherian Rag* (1959), Princeton Choral Singers and Instr., CRI 164.

Mendelssohn, Felix. *Midsummer Night's Dream,* Op. 21 and 61, Ansermet, Orch. Suisse Romande Orch., Lon. **6186;** Golschmann, Vienna Op. Or. Van. **S-161;** Ormandy, Phil., Col. **MS-6628;** Leinsdorf, Boston Sym. Orch. & Cho. Vic. **LSC-2673,** and others.

Morley, Thomas. *Elizabethan Madrigals,* Deller Consort, Bach

5002; Greenberg, NY Pro Musica Antiqua, Count. **5520;** First Book of Ayres, DGG **ARC-3004.**

Nicolai, Otto. *The Merry Wives of Windsor,* Strienz, Ludwig, Rother, Urania **5214-3;** selections: Bernstein, N.Y. Phil., Col. **MS-7085;** DGG 136421; Angel **S-36149.**

Prokofiev, Sergei. *Romeo and Juliet,* Op. 64 (ballet), Bolshoi Th. Orch., Colos. 10209/10; *Romeo and Juliet,* Op. 75 (10 pieces from the ballet), Monitor, 2064; *Romeo and Juliet* (excerpts), Ansermet, Suisse Romande Orch. Lon. **6240;** Kurtz, Phil. Orch., Angel **S-36174** etc.

Purcell, Henry. *Songs from The Tempest,* Lon. Philomusica, Oiseau **60002.**

Shebalin, Vissarion (1902-63). *The Taming of the Shrew* (selection), Bolshoi Th., Ultraphone 123/6.

Smetana, Bedvich, *Richard III* (symphonic poem), Czech. Phil., Artia **117.**

Strauss, Richard, *Ophelia's Songs,* Op. 67, Bk. 1, Urania 7060, **57060.**

Stravinsky, Igor. *Three Shakespeare Songs,* Chamber Group, Col. ML-5107; **MS-7439.**

Tchaikovsky, Peter. *Hamlet, Fantasy Overture,* Op. 67a, Stokowski, N.Y. Stad. Sym., Evergreen **3011;** Maazel, Vienna Phil., Lon. **6463;** Boult, Lond. Phil., Somerset **S 11611;** *Romeo and Juliet,* Bernstein, N.Y. Phil., Col. **MS-6014;** Karajan, Berlin Phil., DGG **139029;** Mehta, L.A. Phil., Lon. **6670;** Munch, Boston Sym., Vic. **VICS-1197** and **LSC-2565,** and others.

Verdi, Giuseppe. *Falstaff,* Freni, Simionato, Elias, Merrill, Solti, Lon. **1395;** Ligabue, Sciutti, Resnik, Bernstein, Vienna Phil., Col. **M3S-750;** Schwarzkopf, Merriman, Gobbi, Karajan. Ang. **S-3552**; selections: Ligabue, Resnik, Downes, New Sym., Lon. **1154**; *Macbeth,* Nilsson, Prevedi, Taddei, Schippers, St. Cecilia Orch., Lon. **1380**; Rysanek, Warren, Leinsdorf, Met. Op., Vic. **VICS-6121**; selections: Angel **S-35763**, Lon. **25742**; *Otello,* Jones, McCracken, Fischer-Dieskau, Barbirolli, New Phil. Ambrosian Op. Cho., Angel **S-3742**; Rysanek, Vickers, Gobbi, Serafin, Rome Op. Vic. **LDS-6155**, (excerpts) **LSC-2844**; Tebaldi, Del Monaco, Protti, Karajan, Vienna Phil., Lon. **1324**; (excerpts) **25701**; *Otello: Ballet Music,* Act III, Kostelanetz, Col. **MS-7427**, Toscanini, Vic. **VICS-1321**; DGG **136211**; *Overtures and Preludes,* Dorati, Lon. Sym., Mercury **18053** and others.

Walton, William. *Henry V: Suite; Hamlet: Funeral March,* Angel **S-36198**; *Richard III: Prelude, Shakespeare Suite,* Angel, **S-36198**.

Weber, Carl Maria von. *Oberon* (selections) Bamberg Sym., Van. **C-10063**; overtures including *Oberon:* Ansermet, Orch. Suisse Romande Lon. **STS-15056**; Bernstein, N.Y. Phil., Col. **MS-6223**; Dorati, London Sym., Mer. **SR2-9134** and others.

Music of Shakespeare's Time, Nonesuch **73010**.

Elizabethan Consort of Viols/ Golden Age Singers—Shakespeare's Time, West. **17076**.

Shakespearean Songs, Vic. **VICS-1266**.

Songs From Shakespeare, Caed. **SRS-S-242**.

Plays

All's Well that Ends Well, Marlowe, Lon. **A-4370**, OSA-**1370**; Claire Bloom, Flora Robson, Caed. **S-212**.

Antony and Cleopatra, Anthony Quayle, Pamela Brown, Caed. **S-235**, TC-**1183**; Marlowe, Lon. A-4427, OSA-**1427**.

As You Like It, Marlowe, Lon. A-4336; Dublin Gate Th., Sp. Word A-4 (123/5); Vanessa Redgrave, Keith Michell, Caed. SRS-210, **SRS-210-S**; Sp. Arts **880** (abridged).

Comedy of Errors, The, Marlowe with George Rylands, Michael Bates, Lon. A-4252, OSA-**1252**; John Moffatt, Alec McCowen, Caed. SRS-205, **SRS-205-S**; Sp. Arts **888** (excerpts).

Coriolanus, Richard Burton, Jessica Tandy, Caed. **SRS-226**; Marlowe, Lon. A-4415; Dublin Gate Th., Sp. Word **A-17**.

Cymbeline, Boris Karloff, Claire Bloom, Pamela Brown, Caed. **SRS-236**; Marlowe, Lon. A-4425, OSA-**1416**; Folio Th. Players, Sp. Arts **899**.

Hamlet, Sir John Gielgud, Vic. LM-6007; Richard Burton, Col. **DOS-702**; Michael MacLiammoir, Dublin Gate Th., Sp. Arts **781**; Marlowe, Lon. A-4507, OSA-**1503**; Paul Scofield, Caed. SRS-232, **SRS-232-S**.

Hamlet and **Henry V** (excerpts), Laurence Olivier, Vic. LM-1924.

Henry IV, Part I, Marlowe, Lon. A-4421, OSA-**1409**; Sir Michael Redgrave, Pamela Brown, Dame Edith Evans, Anthony Quayle, Caed. SRS-217, **SRS-217-S**; Sp. Arts **815**.

Henry IV, Part II, Felix Aylmer, Pamela Brown, Dame Edith Evans, Anthony Quayle, Joyce Redman, Caed. SRS-218, **SRS-218-S**; Marlowe, Lon. A-4422, OSA-**1410**; Swan Theatre Players, Sp. Arts **816** (excerpts, Parts I & II).

Henry V, Marlowe, Con. A-4424, OSA-**1428**; Sir John Gielgud, Ian Holm, Caed. **SRS-219-S**;

Swan Th. Players (excerpts), Sp. Arts **817.**

Henry VI, Part I, Marlowe, Lon. A-4374, OSA-**1374; Part II,** Lon. A-4428, OSA-**1428; Part III,** Lon. A-4429, OSA-**1429.**

Henry VIII, Marlowe, Lon. A-4426, OSA-**1426;** Dame Sybil Thorndike, Sir Lewis Casson (excerpts), Sp. Arts **881.**

Julius Caesar, Marlowe, Lon. A-2334; Dublin Gate, Sp. Word **A-15;** Sir Ralph Richardson, Anthony Quayle, John Mills, Alan Bates, Caed. SRS-230, **SRS-230-S;** Michael MacLiammoir (excerpts), Sp. Arts **809.**

King John, Marlowe, Lon. A-4418, OSA-**1413;** Sir Donald Wolfit, Kenneth Haigh, Rosemary Harris, Caed. SRS-215, **SRS-215-S.**

King Lear, Marlowe, Lon. A-4423, OSA-**1414;** Dublin Gate, Sp. Word **A-9;** Paul Scofield, Pamela Brown, Ann Bell and Rachel Roberts, Caed. SRS-233, **SRS-233-S;** Dylan Thomas (reading selections), Caed. TC 1158; Sp. Arts **784.**

Love's Labour's Lost, Marlowe, Lon. A-4363, OSA-**1363.**

Macbeth, Marlowe, Lon. A-4343, OSA-**1316;** Anthony Quayle, Gwen Davies, Caed. SRS-231, **SRS-231-S;** (excerpts) TC 1167; Dublin Gate, Sp. Arts **782.**

Measure for Measure, Marlowe, Lon. A-4417, OSA-**1411;** Sir John Gielgud, Margaret Leighton, Caed. SRS-204, **SRS-204-S.**

Merchant of Venice, The, Marlowe, Lon. A-4416, OSA-**1412;** Michael MacLiammoir, Shelah Richards, Hilton Edwards, Dublin Gate (excerpts), Sp. Arts **810;** Dorothy Tutin, Hugh Griffith, Caed. SRS-209, **SRS-209-S.**

Merry Wives of Windsor, The, Marlowe, Lon. A-4372, OSA-**1372;** Anthony Quayle, Michael MacLiammoir, Joyce Redman, Caed. SRS-203, **SRS-203-S.**

Midsummer Night's Dream, A, Marlowe, Lon. A-4349, OSA-**1321;** Paul Scofield, Joy Parker, Caed. SRS-208, **SRS-208-S;** Eithne Dunne, Christopher Casson, Eve Watkinson (excerpts), Sp. Arts **882;** Dublin Gate, Sp. Word **A-5.**

Much Ado About Nothing, Marlowe, Lon. A-4362, OSA-**1362;** Maggie Smith, Robert Stephens, Albert Finney, National Theatre of Britain, Vic. VDM-104, **VDS-104;** Rex Harrison, Rachel Roberts, Caed. SRS-206, **SRS-206-S;** Dublin Gate, Sp. Word **A-6;** Eithne Dunne, Christopher Casson, Sp. Arts **883.**

Othello, Marlowe, George Rylands, Irene Worth, Lon. A-4414; Laurence Olivier, Frank Finlay, Maggie Smith, Joyce Redman, Derek Jacobi, Vic. VDM-100, **VDS-100,** (excerpts) **VDS-108;** Paul Robeson, José Ferrer, Uta Hagen, Col. SL-153; Dublin Gate, Sp. Arts **783;** Caed. SRS-225, **SRS-225-S;** Folk. **9618.**

Pericles, Marlowe, Lon. A-4377, OSA-**1377;** Paul Scofield, Judi Dench, Susan Engel, Felix Aylmer, Caed. **SRS-237-S.**

Richard II, Marlowe, George Rylands, Lon. A-4335; Sir John Gielgud, Caed. SRS-216, **SRS-216-S;** Folio Th. (excerpts), Sp. Arts **890.**

Richard III, Marlowe, Lon. A-4430, OSA-**1430;** Folio Th. (excerpts), Sp. Arts **891;** Laurence Olivier (film sound track) Vic. LM-6126; Robert Stephens, Peggy Ashcroft, Ian Holm, Cyril Cusack, Glenda Jackson, Nigel Davenport, Jeremy Brett, Caed. SRS-223, **SRS-223-S.**

Romeo and Juliet, Marlowe, Lon. A-4419, OSA-**1407;** Claire Bloom, Albert Finney, Dame Edith Evans, Caed. SRS-228, **SRS-228-S;** Kathleen Widdoes, Ion Berger, Folger Sh. Recordings 48950; Dublin Gate, Sp.

Words **A-16;** Swan Th. (excerpts), Sp. Arts **812;** Sir John Gielgud, Pamela Brown, Decca 9504; DGG 43003.

Taming of the Shrew, The, Marlowe, Lon. A-4367, OSA-**1367;** Margaret Leighton, Trevor Howard, Caed. SRS-211, **SRS-211-S;** Eve Watkinson, Christopher Casson, Sp. Arts **884;** Dublin Gate, Sp. Word A-7 (151/3); (excerpts) Folk. FL 9612.

Tempest, The, Marlowe, Lon. A-4346, OSA-**1318;** Sir Michael Redgrave, Hugh Griffith, Vanessa Redgrave, Anna Massey; Caed. SRS-201, **SRS-201-S;** Sp. Arts **886;** Dublin Gate, Sp. Word **A-10.**

Timon of Athens, Marlowe, Lon. A-4350, OSA-**1322.**

Titus Andronicus, Marlowe, Lon. A-4371, OSA-**1371;** Anthony Quayle, Maxine Audley, Colin Blakely, Caed. SRS-227, **SRS-227-S.**

Troilus and Cressida, Marlowe, Lon. A-4413; Jeremy Brett, Diane Cilento, Caed. SRS-234, **SRS-234-S;** Folio Th., Sp. Arts **892;** DGG 43003.

Twelfth Night, Marlowe, Lon. A-4354, OSA-**1326;** Siobhan McKenna, Paul Scofield, Robert Hardy, John Neville, Caed. SRS-213, **SRS-213-S;** Michael MacLiammoir, Sp. Word **A-3** (116 /8); Christopher Casson narrates and plays Feste in condensed version, Sp. Arts **887.**

Two Gentlemen of Verona, The, Marlowe, Lon. A-4344, OSA-**1315;** Caed. SRS-202, **SRS-202-S;** Folio Th. (excerpts), Sp. Arts **893.**

Winter's Tale, The, Marlowe, Lon. A-4420, OSA-**1408;** Sir John Gielgud, Peggy Ashcroft, Judith Scott, Alan Bates, SRS-214, **SRS-214-S;** Folio Th. (excerpts), Sp. Arts **894.**

Poems

Lover's Complaint, Marlowe, Lon. A-4344, OSA-**1315;** Claire Bloom (Max Adrian reads *Venus and Adonis* on reverse side), Caed. SRS-240, **SRS-240-S.**

Phoenix and Turtle, George Rylands, Marlowe, Lon. A-4346, OSA-**1318;** Anthony Quayle (readings), Sp. Arts **729.**

Rape of Lucrece, Marlowe, Tony Church, Peggy Ashcroft, Peter Holmes (readers), Lon. A-4251, OSA-**1251.**

Rape of Lucrece and Other Poems, Richard Burton, Dame Edith Evans, Sir Donald Wolfit read *Passionate Pilgrim, Phoenix & Turtle, Rape of Lucrece* and "Sonnets to Music," SRS-239, **SRS-239-S.**

Sonnets (complete), Marlowe, directed by George Rylands, Lon. A-4341; Sir John Gielgud, SRS-241, **SRS-241-S;** Anew McMaster, Sp. Word **SW1-154;** Ronald Colman, Audio Book, GL 607; Anthony Quayle, Sp. Arts **729;** *Sixteen Sonnets of William Shakespeare,* David Allen, Poetry Records PR-201.

Venus and Adonis, Marlowe, Lon. A-4250, OSA-**1250;** Max Adrian, Caed. SRS-240, **SRS-240-S.**

Special Recordings

The Life of William Shakespeare, Dr. Giles E. Dawson of Folger Shakespeare Library, Washington Tapes E-305.

Shakespeare's Ages of Man, Sir John Gielgud, Col. OL-5390; Vol. 2, *One Man in His Time,* Col. OL-5550.

Shakespeare/Soul of an Age, Sir Ralph Richardson narrates and Sir Michael Redgrave reads excerpts from the plays. Caed. TC-1170.

Homage to Shakespeare, Peggy Ashcroft, Dame Sybil Thorndike, Dame Edith Evans, Sir John Gielgud, Laurence Olivier, Paul Scofield, Lon. Argo NF-4, **ZNF-4.**

Homage to Shakespeare, Dame Edith Evans, Sir John Gielgud, Margaret Leighton, Col. OL-7020, **OS-2520.**

Scenes from the plays:
Scenes from the Comedies, Marlowe, Lon. A5787; *Scenes from the Histories,* Marlowe, Lon. A5788; *Scenes from the Tragedies,* Marlowe, Lon. A5786, A5789; Dublin's Abbey Theatre with Anew McMaster reading leading roles, Sp. Arts 766/67; Paul Rogers, Sp. Arts 723; Michael MacLiammoir and Hilton Edwards (soliloquies and scenes), Sp. Arts 836/7; *John Barrymore Reads Shakespeare,* Audio Rarities 2281.

Kings, Lovers and Philosophers: Shakespeare, Maurice Evans reads speeches, selected by Prof. Francis X. Connolly, Decca DL 9110.

Shakespeare at Stratford, Royal Shakespeare Company, excerpts by leading performers, Lon. A5770, **OSA-25770.**

Shakespeare's Cleopatra, Claire Luce, excerpts, Folk. FL-9845.

Love in Shakespeare, Martin Browne, Henzie Raeburn, Sp. Arts **901.**

Worlds of Shakespeare, The, adaptations by Marchette Chute and Ernestine Perry, performed by the School of Speech and Dramatic Art at Syracuse University, Syracuse Univ. Recordings (unnumbered).

Many Voices, Harcourt Brace & World (unnumbered) to accompany *Adventures in Reading: Romeo and Juliet Highlights* with Julie Harris as Juliet and Paul Stevens as Romeo. *Julius Caesar* with Hilton Edwards as Brutus and Michael MacLiammoir as Antony. *Macbeth* with Hilton Edwards as Macbeth, Nancy Manningham as Lady Macbeth, Michael MacLiammoir as Macduff and Christopher Casson as Banquo.

Songs from the Plays of Shakespeare: under the direction of Leslie Pearson, Caed. SRS-242, **SRS-242-S;** Christopher Casson with lute accompaniment, Sp. Word, **SW-159;** *Sounds and Sweet Airs,* Christopher Casson, Barbara McCaughey, Pamela Mant, Sp. Arts **900.**

Shakespeare: Great Actors, Gry. 900.

An Introductory Reading List

General Reference Works

Ebisch, Walter, and Levin L. Schücking. *A Shakespeare Bibliography*. Oxford, 1931. *Supplement 1930-1935*. Oxford, 1937.

Jaggard, William. *Shakespeare Bibliography*. Stratford-upon-Avon, 1911.

Smith, Gordon R. *A Classified Shakespeare Bibliography 1936-1958*. University Park, Pennsylvania, 1963.

See also the annual bibliographies published in *PMLA, Shakespeare Quarterly,* and *Studies in Philology*. Brief bibliographies for many of the plays will be found under the name of S. A. Tannenbaum.

Dictionaries and Language Guides

Abbot, E. A. *Shakespearian Grammar. London,* 1869.

Bartlett, John. *A New or Complete Concordance or Verbal Index . . . of Shakespeare*. New York, 1894.

Onions, C. T. *The Oxford Shakespeare Glossary,* Oxford, 1911-53.

Partridge, Eric. *Shakespeare's Bawdy*. New York, 1960.

Schmidt, Alexander. *Shakespeare-Lexicon*. 2 vols., Berlin, 1902.

Spevack, Marvin. *A Complete and Systematic Concordance to the Works of Shakespeare*. 6 vols., Hildesheim, 1968-70.

Biography

Adams, Joseph Q. *A Life of William Shakespeare*. Boston, 1923.

Alexander, Peter. *Shakespeare's Life and Art*. New York, 1961.

Bentley, Gerald E. *Shakespeare: A Biographical Handbook*. New Haven, 1961.

Chambers, E. K. *William Shakespeare, A Study of Facts and Problems*. 2 vols., Oxford, 1930.

Chute, Marchette. *Shakespeare of London*. New York, 1949.

Eccles, Mark. *Shakespeare in Warwickshire*. Madison, 1963.

Fripp, Edgar I. *Shakespeare, Man and Artist*. 2 vols., London, 1938.

Halliday, F. E. *The Life of Shakespeare*. London, 1961.

Hotson, Leslie. *I, William Shakespeare, Do Appoint Thomas Russell, Esquire. . . .* London, 1937.

―――. *Mr. W. H.* London, 1964.

Quennell, Peter. *Shakespeare: A Biography*. London, 1963.

Reese, M. M. *Shakespeare: His World and His Work*. New York, 1953.

Rowse, A. L. *William Shakespeare: A Biography*. New York, 1963.

―――. *Shakespeare's Southampton Patron of Virginia*. New York, 1965.

Schoenbaum, Samuel. *The Lives of Shakespeare*. London, 1970.

Smart, J. S. *Shakespeare: Truth and Tradition*. New edition with Preface by Peter Alexander. Oxford, 1966.

Wilson, J. D. *The Essential Shakespeare*. Cambridge, 1932.

Dramatical and Theatrical Background

Adams, J. C. *The Globe Playhouse.* Rev. ed. New York, 1961.

Adams, Joseph Q. *Shakespearean Playhouses.* Boston, 1917.

Armstrong, W. A. "Actors and Theatres," *Shakespeare Survey* 17. Cambridge, 1964. Pp. 191-204.

Baldwin, Thomas W. *The Organization and Personnel of the Shakespearean Company.* Princeton, 1927.

Beckerman, Bernard. *Shakespeare at the Globe 1599-1609.* New York, 1962.

Bentley, Gerald E. "Shakespeare and the Blackfriars Theatre," *Shakespeare Survey* 1. Cambridge, 1948. Pp. 38-50.

————. *Shakespeare and His Theatre.* Lincoln, 1964.

Bradbrook, M. C. *The Rise of the Common Player: A Study of Actor and Society in Shakespeare's England.* London, 1964.

Campbell, L. B. *Scenes and Machines on the English Stage during the Renaissance.* Cambridge, 1923.

Chambers, E. K. *The Elizabethan Stage.* 4 vols., Oxford, 1923.

Cowling, G. H. *Music on the Shakespearian Stage.* Cambrdge, 1913.

Craik, T. W. *The Tudor Interlude.* Leicester, 1958.

DeBanke, Cecile. *Shakespearean Stage Production: Then and Now.* New York, 1953.

Doran, Madeleine. *Endeavors of Art: A Study of Form in Elizabethan Drama.* Madison, 1954.

Foakes, R. A. "The Player's Passion: Some Notes on Elizabethan Psychology and Acting," *Essays and Studies Collected for the English Association,* 7 (1954), 62-77.

Gildersleeve, Virginia C. *Government Regulation of the Elizabethan Drama.* New York, 1908.

Greg, W. W. *Dramatic Documents from the Elizabethan Playhouses.* 2 vols., Oxford, 1931.

Harbage, Alfred. *Shakespeare's Audience.* New York, 1941

————. *Shakespeare and the Rival Traditions.* New York, 1952.

Harrison, G. B. *Elizabethan Plays and Players.* Ann Arbor, 1956.

Hillebrand, H. N. *The Child Actors.* Urbana, 1926.

Hodges, C. Walter. *The Globe Restored: A Study of the Elizabethan Theatre.* New York, 1954.

Hosley, Richard. "An Approach to the Elizabethan Stage," *Renaissance Drama,* 6 (1963), 71-8.

————. "The Origins of the Shakespearian Playhouse," *Shakespeare Quarterly,* 15 (1964), 29-39.

Hotson, Leslie. *Shakespeare's Wooden O.* London, 1959.

Joseph, B. I. *Elizabethan Acting.* Rev. ed. Oxford, 1964.

————. *The Tragic Actor.* London, 1959.

Kernodle, G. R. *From Art to Theatre: Form and Convention in the Renaissance.* Chicago, 1944.

Lawrence, W. J. *Pre-Restoration Stage Studies.* Cambridge, Mass., 1927.

————. *The Physical Conditions of the Elizabethan Public Playhouse.* Cambridge, Mass., 1927.

Linthicum, M. C. *Costume in the Drama of Shakespeare and his Contemporaries.* Oxford, 1936.

Murray, J. T. *English Dramatic Companies, 1558-1642.* Boston, 1910.

Nagler, A. M. *Shakespeare's Stage.* New Haven, 1958.

Nicoll, Allardyce. *Masques, Mimes and Miracles.* London, 1931.

—————. "Studies in the Elizabethan Stage Since 1900," *Shakespeare Survey* 1. Cambridge, 1948. Pp. 1-17.

Reynolds, G. F. *The Staging of Elizabethan Plays at the Red Bull Theater, 1605-1625.* New York, 1940.

Rosenberg, Marvin. "Elizabethan Actors: Men or Marionettes," *PMLA,* 69 (1954), 915-27.

Saunders, J. W. "Staging at the Globe, 1599-1613," *Shakespeare Quarterly,* 11 (1960), 401-25.

Seltzer, Daniel. "The Staging of the Last Plays," *The Later Shakespeare* (Stratford-on-Avon Studies No. 8). London, 1966. Pp. 127-66.

Sharpe, R. B. *The Real War of the Theatres.* Boston, 1935.

Shirley, F. A. *Shakespeare's Use of Off-Stage Sounds.* Lincoln, 1963.

Smith, Irwin. *Shakespeare's Blackfriars Playhouse, Its History and Design.* New York, 1964.

Southern, Richard. *The Medieval Theatre in the Round.* London, 1957.

Sprague, A. C. *The Doubling of Parts in Shakespeare's Plays.* London, 1966.

Steele, Mary S. *Plays and Masques at Court During the Reigns of Elizabeth, James, and Charles.* New Haven, 1926.

Thorndike, A. H. *Shakespeare's Theatre.* New York, 1916.

Wickham, Glynne. *Early English Stages, 1300-1660.* 2 vols., New York, 1959-63.

Shakespeare in the Theater, 1642-1968

Armstrong, W. A. "The Art of Shakespearean Production in the Twentieth Century," *Essays and Studies,* 15 (1962), 74-87.

Brown, J. R. "On the Acting of Shakespeare's Plays," *Quarterly Journal of Speech,* 39 (1953), 474-85.

—————. *Shakespeare's Plays in Performance.* New York, 1967.

Dean, Winton. "Shakespeare in the Opera House," *Shakespeare Survey* 18. Cambridge, 1965, Pp. 75-93.

Deelman, Christian. *The Great Shakespeare Jubilee.* New York, 1964.

Downer, A. S. *The Eminent Tragedian, William Charles Macready.* Cambridge, Mass., 1966.

England, M. W. *Garrick's Jubilee.* Columbus, 1964.

Glick, Claris. "William Poel: His Theories and Influence," *Shakespeare Quarterly,* 15 (1964), 15-25.

Harbage, Alfred. *A Theatre for Shakespeare.* Toronto, 1955.

Hogan, C. B. *Shakespeare in the Theatre, 1701-1800.* 2 vols., Oxford, 1952-57.

Joseph, B. L. *Acting Shakespeare.* New York, 1960.

Kitchin, Laurence. *Drama in the Sixties: Form and Interpretation.* London, 1966.

—————. "Shakespeare on the Screen," *Shakespeare Survey* 18. Cambridge, 1965. Pp. 70-74.

Knight, G. W. *Shakespearian Production, with Especial Reference to the Tragedies.* London, 1964.

Marder, Louis. *His Exits and his Entrances: The Story of Shakespeare's Reputation.* Philadelphia, 1963.

Odell, G. C. D. *Shakespeare from Betterton to Irving.* 2 vols. (reprinted). New York, 1966.

Poel, William. *Shakespeare in the Theatre.* London, 1913.

Shattuck, C. H. *The Shakespeare Promptbooks.* Urbana, 1965.

Spencer, Hazelton. *Shakespeare Improved: The Restoration Versions in Quarto and on the Stage.* Cambridge, Mass., 1927.

Sprague, A. C. *Shakespeare and the Actors: The Stage Business in His Plays (1660-1905).* Cambridge, Mass., 1944.

————. *Shakespearian Players and Performances.* Cambridge, Mass., 1953.

Stockholm, J. M. *Garrick's Folly.* London, 1964.

Trewin, J. C. *Shakespeare on the English Stage, 1900-1964.* London, 1964.

Watkins, Ronald. *On Producing Shakespeare.* New York, 1950.

Webster, Margaret. *Shakespeare Without Tears.* New York, 1942.

————. *Shakespeare Today.* London, 1957.

General Background

Baldwin, T. W. *William Shakspere's Small Latine and Lesse Greeke.* 2 vols., Urbana, 1944.

Byrne, M. St. Clare. *Elizabethan Life in Town and Country.* London, 1925-34.

Furnivall, F. J., ed. *William Harrison's Description of England in Shakespeare's Youth.* London, 1877-88.

Harrison, G. B., ed. *England in Shakespeare's Day.* London, 1928.

————. *A Jacobean Journal ... 1603-1606.* London, 1941.

————. *A Second Jacobean Journal ... 1607-1610.* Ann Arbor, 1958.

Judges, A. V. *The Elizabethan Underworld.* London, 1930.

Shakespeare's England. 2 vols., Oxford, 1916.

Spencer, Theodore. *Shakespeare and the Nature of Man.* New York, 1945.

Sugden, E. H. *A Topographical Dictionary to the Works of Shakespeare and His Fellow Dramatists.* Manchester, 1925.

Tillyard, E. M. W. *The Elizabethan World Picture.* London, 1943.

Wilson, F. P. *The Plague in Shakespeare's London.* Oxford, 1927.

————. *Elizabethan and Jacobean.* Oxford, 1945.

Wright, Louis B. *Middle-Class Culture in Elizabethan England.* Chapel Hill, 1935.

Critical Works and Collections

Alexander, Peter. *Shakespeare's Life and Art.* London, 1939.

————. *Hamlet, Father and Son.* Oxford, 1955.

————, ed. *Studies in Shakespeare: British Academy Lectures.* London, 1964.

Armstrong, Edward A. *Shakespeare's Imagination.* London, 1946.

Babcock, R. W. *The Genesis of Shakespeare Idolatry, 1776-1799.* Chapel Hill, 1931.

Barber, C. L. *Shakespeare's Festive Comedy.* Princeton, 1959.

Bentley, G. E. *Shakespeare and Jonson: Their Reputations in the Seventeenth Century Compared.* 2 vols., Chicago, 1945.

Bowers, Fredson T. *Elizabethan Revenge Tragedy 1587-1642.* Princeton, 1940.

Bradbrook, M. C. *Themes and Conventions of Elizabethan Tragedy.* Cambridge, 1935.

————. *Shakespeare and Elizabethan Poetry.* London, 1951.

Bradley, A. C. *Shakespearian Tragedy.* London, 1904.

————. *Oxford Lectures on Poetry.* London, 1909.

Brown, J. R. *Shakespeare and His Comedies.* London, 1957.

Burckhardt, Sigurd. *Shakespearean Meanings.* Princeton, 1968.

Campbell, Lily B. *Shakespeare's "Histories": Mirrors of Elizabethan Policy.* San Marino, California, 1947.

Campbell, O. J. *Shakespeare's Satire.* New York, 1943.

Chambers, E. K. *Shakespeare: A Survey.* London, 1925.

Charlton, H. B. *Shakespearian Comedy.* Cambridge, 1938.

————. *Shakespearian Tragedy.* Cambridge, 1948.

Clemen, Wolfgang. *The Development of Shakespeare's Imagery.* Cambridge, Mass., 1951.

Coleridge, S. T. *Shakespeare Criticism,* ed. T. M. Raysor. 2 vols., Cambridge, Mass., 1930.

Craig, Hardin. *An Interpretation of Shakespeare.* New York, 1948.

Dean, L. F., ed. *Shakespeare: Modern Essays in Criticism.* Rev. ed., New York, 1967.

Eastman, Arthur M. *A Short History of Shakespearean Criticism.* New York, 1968.

———— and Harrison, G. B. eds. *Shakespeare Critics from Johnson to Auden: A Medley of Judgments.* Ann Arbor, 1964.

Eliot, T. S. *Selected Essays.* New York, 1932.

————. *Essays on Elizabethan Drama.* New York, 1957.

Ellis-Fermor, Una. *Shakespeare the Dramatist,* ed. K. Muir. London, 1961.

Empson, William. *The Structure of Complex Words.* Norfolk, Conn., n.d.

Farnham, Willard. *The Medieval Heritage of Elizabethan Tragedy.* Berkeley, 1936.

————. *Shakespeare's Tragic Frontier.* Berkeley, 1950.

Fluchère, Henri. *Shakespeare and the Elizabethans.* New York, 1956.

Goddard, Harold C. *The Meaning of Shakespeare,* 2 vols., Chicago, 1951.

Gordon, George. *Shakespearian Comedy and Other Studies.* Oxford, 1944.

Granville-Barker, H. *Prefaces to Shakespeare.* 2 vols., Princeton, 1946/7.

Halliday, F. E. *Shakespeare and his Critics.* London, 1949.

Hazlitt, William. *Characters of Shakespeare's Plays.* London, 1817.

Heilman, R. B. *This Great Stage: Image and Structure in King Lear.* Baton Rouge, 1948.

Herford, C. H. *A Sketch of Recent Shakespearean Investigation, 1893-1923.* London, 1923.

Holloway, John. *The Story of the Night.* Cambridge, 1961.

Hubler, Edward. *The Sense of Shakespeare's Sonnets.* Princeton, 1952.

James, D. G. *The Dream of Learning.* Oxford, 1951.

Johnson, C. F. *Shakespeare and his Critics.* Boston, 1909.

Johnson, Samuel. *Johnson on Shakespeare,* ed. W. Raleigh. New York, 1960.

Kermode, Frank, ed. *Four Centuries of Shakespearean Criticism.* New York, 1965.

Kernan, Alvin B., ed. *Modern Shakespearean Criticism.* New York, 1970.

Knight, G. W. *The Wheel of Fire.* London, 1930.

————. *The Imperial Theme.* London, 1931.

Knights, L. C. *Explorations.* London, 1947.

————. *Some Shakespearian Themes*. London, 1959.

Leavis, F. R. *The Common Pursuit*. London, 1952.

Leech, Clifford. *Shakespeare's Tragedies*. London, 1950.

Lovett, David. *Shakespeare's Characters in Eighteenth-Century Criticism*. Baltimore, 1935.

Mahood, M. W. *Shakespeare's Wordplay*. London, 1957.

Monroe, John, ed. *The Shakespeare Allusion Book: A Collection of Allusions to Shakespeare from 1591 to 1700*. London, 1909.

Muir, Kenneth. "Fifty Years of Shakespearian Criticism, 1900-1950," *Shakespeare Survey* 4. Cambridge, 1951. Pp. 1-25.

Murry, John M. *Shakespeare*. New York, 1936.

Nicoll, Allardyce. *Shakespeare: An Introduction*. New York, 1952.

Palmer, J. L. *Political Chaarcters of Shakespeare*. London, 1945.

————. *Comic Characters of Shakespeare*. London, 1946.

Pascal, R. *Shakespeare in Germany, 1740-1815*. Cambridge, 1937.

Pettet, E. C. *Shakespeare and the Romance Tradition*. London, 1949.

Pillai, V. K. A. *Shakespeare Criticism from the Beginnings to 1765*. London, 1932.

Ralli, Augustus. *A History of Shakespeare Criticism*. 2 vols.. London, 1932.

Raysor, T. M., ed. *Coleridge's Shakespeare Criticism*. 2 vols., Cambridge, Mass., 1930.

Reese, M. M. *The Cease of Majesty*. London, 1961.

Ribner, Irving. *The English History Play in the Age of Shakespeare*. Princeton, 1957.

Ridler, Anne. *Shakespeare Criticism 1919-1935*. Oxford, 1936.

————. *Shakespeare Criticism 1935-1960*. Oxford, 1963.

Ridley, M. R. *Shakespeare's Plays: A Commentary*. New York, 1938.

Righter, Anne. *Shakespeare and the Idea of the Play*. Cambridge, 1962.

Robinson, H. S. *English Shakespearean Criticism in the Eighteenth Century*. New York, 1932.

Rosen, William. *Shakespeare and the Craft of Tragedy*. Cambridge, Mass., 1960.

Rylands, George. *Words and Poetry*. London, 1928.

Schücking, L. L. *The Baroque Character of the Elizabethan Tragic Hero*. Oxford, 1939.

Sewell, Arthur. *Character and Society in Shakespeare*. Oxford, 1951.

Sherbo, Arthur. "Johnson as Editor of Shakespeare: The Notes," in *Samuel Johnson: A Collection of Critical Essays,* ed. D. J. Greene. Englewood Cliffs, N.J., 1965.

Siegel, Paul N., ed. *His Infinite Variety: Major Shakespearean Criticism Since Johnson*. Philadelphia, 1964.

Smith, D. N. *Shakespeare Criticism: A Selection*. Oxford, 1916.

————, ed. *Eighteenth Century Essays on Shakespeare*. 2nd ed., Oxford, 1963.

Speaight, Robert. *Nature in Shakespearian Tragedy*. London, 1955.

Spivack, Bernard. *Shakespeare and the Allegory of Evil*. New York, 1958.

Spurgeon, Caroline F. E. *Shakespeare's Imagery and What It Tells Us*. London, 1935.

Stauffer, Donald. *Shakespeare's World of Images*. New York, 1949.

Stewart, J. I. M. *Character and Motive in Shakespeare*. New York, 1949.

Stirling, Brents. *Unity in Shakespearian Tragedy*. New York, 1956.

Stoll, E. E. *Shakespeare Studies*. New York, 1927.

—————. *Art and Artifice in Shakespeare*. Cambridge, 1933.

Tillyard, E. M. W. *Shakespeare's Last Plays*. London, 1938.

—————. *Shakespeare's History Plays*. New York, 1946.

—————. *Shakespeare's Problem Plays*. Toronto, 1949.

Traversi, D. A. *An Approach to Shakespeare*. 2nd ed., London, 1957.

Van Doren, Mark. *Shakespeare*. New York, 1939.

Walker, Roy. *The Time is Free*. London, 1949.

Watkins, W. B. C. *Shakespeare and Spenser*. Princeton, 1950.

Weisinger, Herbert. "The Study of Shakespearian Tragedy Since Bradley," *Shakespeare Quarterly*, VI (1955), 387-396.

Westfall, A. V. *American Shakespearean Criticism, 1607-1865*. New York, 1939.

Whitaker, Virgil K. *Shakespeare's Use of Learning: An Inquiry Into the Growth of His Mind and Art*. San Marino, Calif., 1953.

Wilson, F. P. *Marlowe and the Early Shakespeare*. Oxford, 1953.

Wilson, H. S. *On the Design of Shakespearian Tragedy*. Toronto, 1957.

Wilson, J. D. *What Happens in Hamlet*. Cambridge, 1935.

—————. *The Fortunes of Falstaff*. Cambridge, 1943.

Sources

Anders, H. R. D. *Shakespeare's Books*, Berlin, 1904.

Bullough, Geoffrey. *Narrative and Dramatic Sources of Shakespeare*. 6 vols., London, 1957- .

Collier, J. P., and Hazlitt, W. C., eds. *Shakespeare's Library*. 7 vols., London, 1875.

Gollancz, Israel, ed. *The Shakespeare Classics*. London, 1907-1926.

Lucas, F. L. *Seneca and Elizabethan Tragedy*. Cambridge, 1922.

MacCallum, A. W. *Shakespeare's Roman Plays and Their Background*. London, 1910.

Noble, Richmond. *Shakespeare's Biblical Knowledge and Use of the Book of Common Prayer*. London, 1935.

Phillips, James E. *The State in Shakespeare's Greek and Roman Plays*. New York, 1940.

Spencer, T. J. B., ed. *Shakespeare's Plutarch*. Harmondsworth, 1964.

Whitaker, Virgil K. *Shakespeare's Use of Learning*. San Marino, Calif., 1953.

Texts

The best one-volume texts of the plays are the editions of G. L. Kittredge (rev. by Irving Ribner, Waltham, Mass., 1971), W. A. Neilson and C. J. Hill, and Peter Alexander. Of the multi-volume editions the most useful is the *New Arden* series under the general editorship of Una Ellis-Fermor and H. F. Brooks, not yet completed. Interesting but uneven in quality is the *Cambridge* series edited by A. T. Quiller-Couch and J. D. Wilson. Many persons will enjoy browsing in the *New Variorum* Edition, begun in 1871 and still in progress, which will be in the reference room of any good large library.

For an accurate facsimile text of the first collected printing of the plays see Charlton Hinman, ed. *The Norton Facsimile: The First Folio of Shakespeare*. New York, 1968.

Genealogical Charts

showing

The English Royal Family and the Wars of the Roses

and

Henry V's Claim to the Throne of France

KEY TO SUPERSCRIPTIONS

1. *Richard II*
2. *1 Henry IV*
3. *2 Henry IV*
4. *Henry V*
5. *1 Henry VI*
6. *2 Henry VI*
7. *3 Henry VI*
8. *Richard III*
9. *Henry VIII*

---

b. = *born*
r. = *reigned*
d. = *died*
c. = *circa*

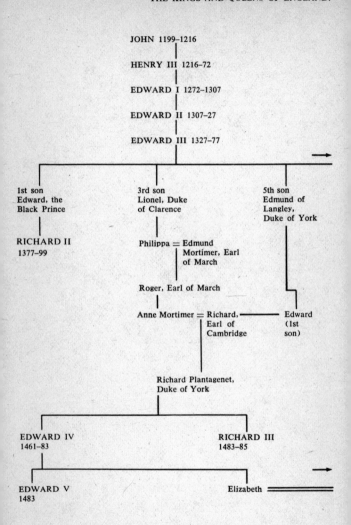

JOHN 1199–1216

HENRY III 1216–72

EDWARD I 1272–1307

EDWARD II 1307–27

EDWARD III 1327–77 ⟶

1st son	3rd son	5th son
Edward, the	Lionel, Duke	Edmund of
Black Prince	of Clarence	Langley, Duke of York

RICHARD II
1377–99

Philippa = Edmund Mortimer, Earl of March

Roger, Earl of March

Anne Mortimer = Richard, Earl of Cambridge ⟶ Edward (1st son)

Richard Plantagenet, Duke of York

EDWARD IV
1461–83   RICHARD III
                           1483–85   ⟶

EDWARD V
1483   Elizabeth ══════

---

* Please note that this chart is not a complete family tree.
  Its aim is to show how the royal family is connected.

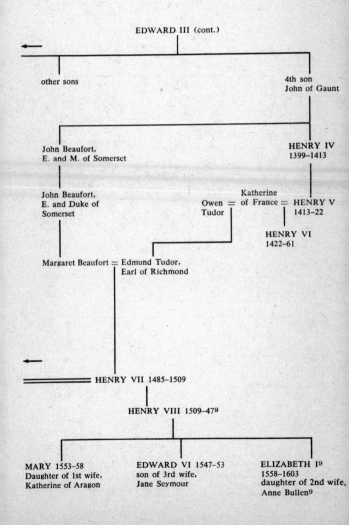

EDWARD III (cont.)

other sons

4th son
John of Gaunt

John Beaufort,
E. and M. of Somerset

HENRY IV
1399–1413

John Beaufort,
E. and Duke of
Somerset

Owen = Katherine = HENRY V
Tudor   of France   1413–22

HENRY VI
1422–61

Margaret Beaufort = Edmund Tudor,
Earl of Richmond

HENRY VII 1485–1509

HENRY VIII 1509–47[9]

MARY 1553–58
Daughter of 1st wife,
Katherine of Aragon

EDWARD VI 1547–53
son of 3rd wife,
Jane Seymour

ELIZABETH I[9]
1558–1603
daughter of 2nd wife,
Anne Bullen[9]

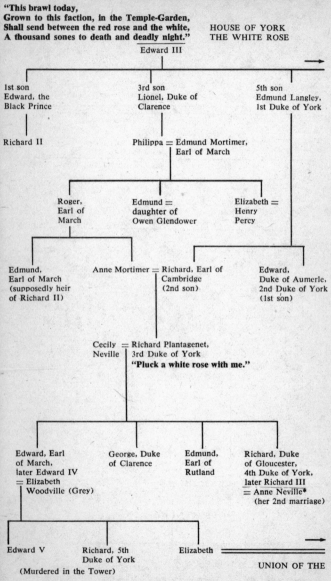

OUTLINE OF THE HOUSES OF YORK AND LANCASTER

"This brawl today,
Grown to this faction, in the Temple-Garden,
Shall send between the red rose and the white,
A thousand sones to death and deadly night."

HOUSE OF YORK
THE WHITE ROSE

Edward III

1st son
Edward, the
Black Prince

Richard II

3rd son
Lionel, Duke of
Clarence

Philippa = Edmund Mortimer,
Earl of March

5th son
Edmund Langley,
1st Duke of York

Roger,
Earl of
March

Edmund =
daughter of
Owen Glendower

Elizabeth =
Henry
Percy

Edmund,
Earl of March
(supposedly heir
of Richard II)

Anne Mortimer = Richard, Earl of
Cambridge
(2nd son)

Edward,
Duke of Aumerle,
2nd Duke of York
(1st son)

Cecily
Neville

= Richard Plantagenet,
3rd Duke of York
"Pluck a white rose with me."

Edward, Earl
of March,
later Edward IV
= Elizabeth
Woodville (Grey)

George, Duke
of Clarence

Edmund,
Earl of
Rutland

Richard, Duke
of Gloucester,
4th Duke of York,
later Richard III
= Anne Neville*
(her 2nd marriage)

Edward V

(Murdered in the Tower)

Richard, 5th
Duke of York

Elizabeth

UNION OF THE

* The same person

HOUSE OF LANCASTER
THE RED ROSE

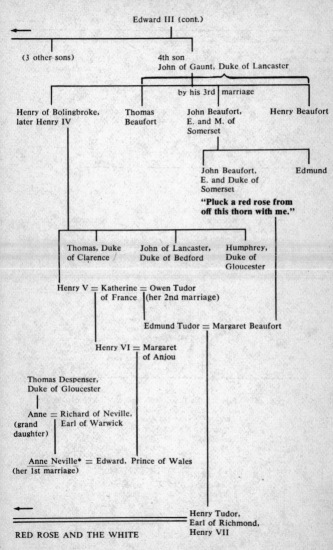

Edward III (cont.)

← (3 other sons)

4th son
John of Gaunt, Duke of Lancaster

by his 3rd marriage

Henry of Bolingbroke, later Henry IV

Thomas Beaufort

John Beaufort, E. and M. of Somerset

Henry Beaufort

John Beaufort, E. and Duke of Somerset

"Pluck a red rose from off this thorn with me."

Edmund

Thomas, Duke of Clarence

John of Lancaster, Duke of Bedford

Humphrey, Duke of Gloucester

Henry V = Katherine = Owen Tudor
of France (her 2nd marriage)

Edmund Tudor = Margaret Beaufort

Henry VI = Margaret of Anjou

Thomas Despenser, Duke of Gloucester

Anne = Richard of Neville, (grand Earl of Warwick daughter)

Anne Neville* = Edward, Prince of Wales
(her 1st marriage)

←

Henry Tudor, Earl of Richmond, Henry VII

RED ROSE AND THE WHITE

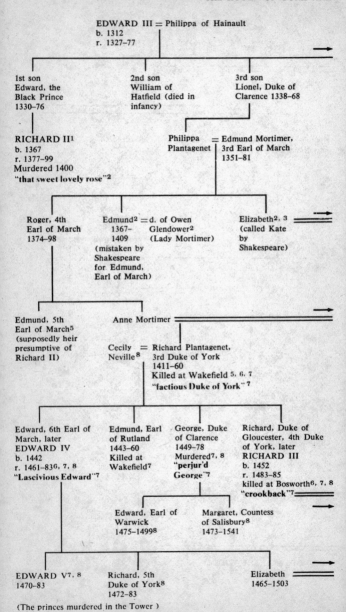

EDWARD III = Philippa of Hainault
b. 1312
r. 1327–77

1st son
Edward, the
Black Prince
1330–76

2nd son
William of
Hatfield (died in
infancy)

3rd son
Lionel, Duke of
Clarence 1338–68

RICHARD II[1]
b. 1367
r. 1377–99
Murdered 1400
"that sweet lovely rose"[2]

Philippa
Plantagenet = Edmund Mortimer,
3rd Earl of March
1351–81

Roger, 4th
Earl of March
1374–98

Edmund[2] = d. of Owen
1367–   Glendower[2]
1409   (Lady Mortimer)

(mistaken by
Shakespeare
for Edmund,
Earl of March)

Elizabeth[2, 3]
(called Kate
by
Shakespeare)

Edmund, 5th
Earl of March[5]
(supposedly heir
presumptive of
Richard II)

Anne Mortimer

Cecily = Richard Plantagenet,
Neville[8]   3rd Duke of York
1411–60
Killed at Wakefield[5, 6, 7]
"factious Duke of York"[7]

Edward, 6th Earl of
March, later
EDWARD IV
b. 1442
r. 1461–83[6, 7, 8]
"Lascivious Edward"[7]

Edmund, Earl
of Rutland
1443–60
Killed at
Wakefield[7]

George, Duke
of Clarence
1449–78
Murdered[7, 8]
"perjur'd
George"[7]

Richard, Duke of
Gloucester, 4th Duke
of York, later
RICHARD III
b. 1452
r. 1483–85
killed at Bosworth[6, 7, 8]
"crookback"[7]

Edward, Earl of
Warwick
1475–1499[8]

Margaret, Countess
of Salisbury[8]
1473–1541

EDWARD V[7, 8]
1470–83

Richard, 5th
Duke of York[8]
1472–83

Elizabeth
1465–1503

(The princes murdered in the Tower)

> "Edward's seven sons . . .
> Were as seven vials of his sacred blood."[1]

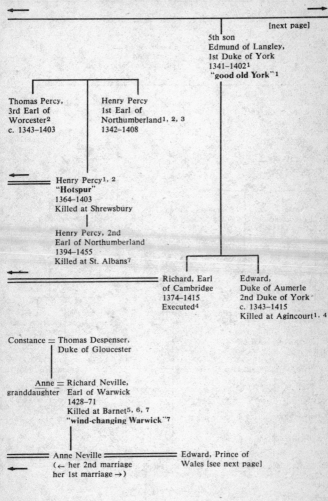

[next page]

5th son
Edmund of Langley,
1st Duke of York
1341–1402[1]
"good old York"[1]

Thomas Percy,
3rd Earl of
Worcester[2]
c. 1343–1403

Henry Percy
1st Earl of
Northumberland[1, 2, 3]
1342–1408

Henry Percy[1, 2]
"Hotspur"
1364–1403
Killed at Shrewsbury

Henry Percy, 2nd
Earl of Northumberland
1394–1455
Killed at St. Albans[7]

Richard, Earl
of Cambridge
1374–1415
Executed[4]

Edward,
Duke of Aumerle
2nd Duke of York
c. 1343–1415
Killed at Agincourt[1, 4]

Constance = Thomas Despenser,
Duke of Gloucester

Anne = Richard Neville,
granddaughter   Earl of Warwick
1428–71
Killed at Barnet[5, 6, 7]
"wind-changing Warwick"[7]

Anne Neville
(← her 2nd marriage
her 1st marriage →)

Edward, Prince of
Wales [see next page]

HENRY VII
[see next page]

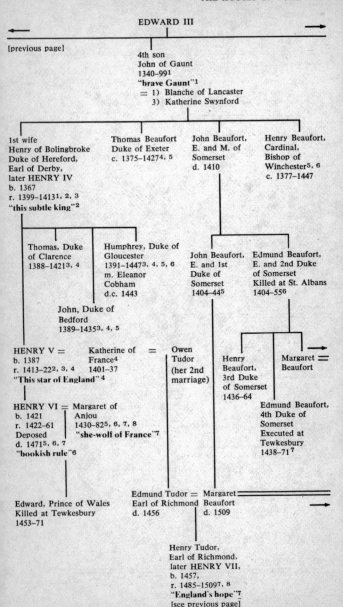

EDWARD III

[previous page]

4th son
John of Gaunt
1340-99[1]
"brave Gaunt"[1]
= 1) Blanche of Lancaster
3) Katherine Swynford

1st wife
Henry of Bolingbroke
Duke of Hereford,
Earl of Derby,
later HENRY IV
b. 1367
r. 1399-1413[1, 2, 3]
"this subtle king"[2]

Thomas Beaufort
Duke of Exeter
c. 1375-1427[4, 5]

John Beaufort,
E. and M. of
Somerset
d. 1410

Henry Beaufort,
Cardinal,
Bishop of
Winchester[5, 6]
c. 1377-1447

Thomas, Duke
of Clarence
1388-1421[3, 4]

Humphrey, Duke of
Gloucester
1391-1447[3, 4, 5, 6]
m. Eleanor
Cobham
d.c. 1443

John Beaufort,
E. and 1st
Duke of
Somerset
1404-44[5]

Edmund Beaufort,
E. and 2nd Duke
of Somerset
Killed at St. Albans
1404-55[6]

John, Duke of
Bedford
1389-1435[3, 4, 5]

HENRY V =
b. 1387
r. 1413-22[2, 3, 4]
"This star of England"[4]

Katherine of
France[4]
1401-37

= Owen
Tudor
(her 2nd
marriage)

Henry
Beaufort,
3rd Duke
of Somerset
1436-64

Margaret =
Beaufort

HENRY VI =
b. 1421
r. 1422-61
Deposed
d. 1471[5, 6, 7]
"bookish rule"[6]

Margaret of
Anjou
1430-82[5, 6, 7, 8]
"she-wolf of France"[7]

Edmund Beaufort,
4th Duke of
Somerset
Executed at
Tewkesbury
1438-71[7]

Edward, Prince of Wales
Killed at Tewkesbury
1453-71

Edmund Tudor =
Earl of Richmond
d. 1456

Margaret =
Beaufort
d. 1509

Henry Tudor,
Earl of Richmond,
later HENRY VII,
b. 1457,
r. 1485-1509[7, 8]
"England's hope"[7]
[see previous page]

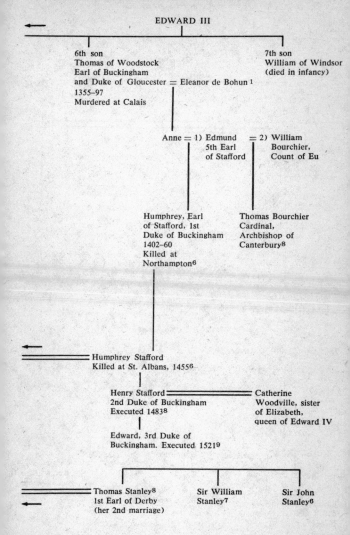

EDWARD III
←

6th son
Thomas of Woodstock
Earl of Buckingham
and Duke of Gloucester = Eleanor de Bohun [1]
1355–97
Murdered at Calais

7th son
William of Windsor
(died in infancy)

Anne = 1) Edmund
5th Earl
of Stafford
= 2) William
Bourchier,
Count of Eu

Humphrey, Earl
of Stafford, 1st
Duke of Buckingham
1402–60
Killed at
Northampton[6]

Thomas Bourchier
Cardinal,
Archbishop of
Canterbury[8]

←
Humphrey Stafford
Killed at St. Albans, 1455[6]

Henry Stafford
2nd Duke of Buckingham
Executed 1483[8]
= Catherine
Woodville, sister
of Elizabeth,
queen of Edward IV

Edward, 3rd Duke of
Buckingham. Executed 1521[9]

Thomas Stanley[8]
1st Earl of Derby
(her 2nd marriage)
←

Sir William
Stanley[7]

Sir John
Stanley[6]

CLAIM OF HENRY V TO THE
THRONE OF FRANCE

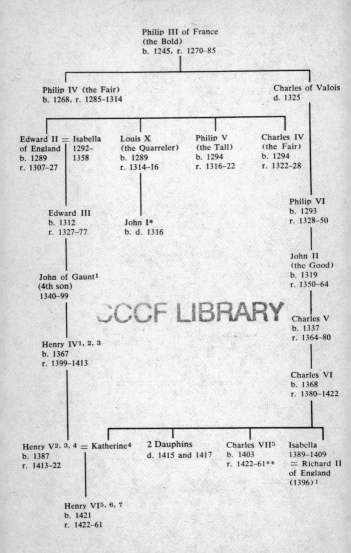

Philip III of France
(the Bold)
b. 1245, r. 1270–85

Philip IV (the Fair)
b. 1268, r. 1285–1314

Charles of Valois
d. 1325

Edward II = Isabella
of England   1292–
b. 1289   1358
r. 1307–27

Louis X
(the Quarreler)
b. 1289
r. 1314–16

Philip V
(the Tall)
b. 1294
r. 1316–22

Charles IV
(the Fair)
b. 1294
r. 1322–28

Philip VI
b. 1293
r. 1328–50

Edward III
b. 1312
r. 1327–77

John I*
b. d. 1316

John II
(the Good)
b. 1319
r. 1350–64

John of Gaunt[1]
(4th son)
1340–99

Charles V
b. 1337
r. 1364–80

Henry IV[1, 2, 3]
b. 1367
r. 1399–1413

Charles VI
b. 1368
r. 1380–1422

Henry V[2, 3, 4] = Katherine[4]
b. 1387
r. 1413–22

2 Dauphins
d. 1415 and 1417

Charles VII[5]
b. 1403
r. 1422–61**

Isabella
1389–1409
= Richard II
of England
(1396)[1]

Henry VI[5, 6, 7]
b. 1421
r. 1422–61

---

* Last of the direct line of the Capetians: neither Philip V nor Charles IV left a direct heir.

** Disinherited by the Treaty of Troyes (1420), but crowned by Joan of Arc in 1429.